The Russian Avant-Garde and Radical Modernism

An Introductory Reader

Cultural Syllabus

Series Editor:
Mark Lipovetsky (University of Colorado - Boulder)

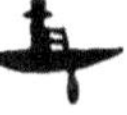

THE RUSSIAN AVANT-GARDE AND RADICAL MODERNISM

An Introductory Reader

Edited by Dennis G. IOFFE and Frederick H. WHITE

Boston 2012

Library of Congress Cataloging-in-Publication Data:
A bibliographic record for this title is available from the Library of Congress.

ISBN 978-1-936235-29-2 (hardback)
ISBN 978-1-936235-45-2 (paperback)
Book design by Adell Medovoy

Published by Academic Studies Press in 2012
28 Montfern Avenue
Brighton, MA 02135, USA
press@academicstudiespress.com
www.academicstudiespress.com

Contents

List of Illustrations

Note from the Editors

This Reader is a collection of the most salient texts about the Russian avant-garde and radical modernism. The previously published texts, for the most part, remain the way in which they originally appeared in print. Therefore, you will note seeming inconsistencies in the transliterations of names and possibly in titles of some works.

The transliteration systems employed in the volume vary between the (phonetically based) Library of Congress system of transliterating Russian Cyrillic and the International system (also called the scientific or the European system).

The editors of this volume decided not to standardize these transliterations as it might lead to further alterations, which would begin to impinge heavily upon the original text.

I

AN INTRODUCTION TO THE RUSSIAN AVANT-GARDE AND RADICAL MODERNISM

Introduction

Modernism, as a concept, may be understood as the totality of numerous aesthetic theories that began to take shape during the second half of the nineteenth century and achieved a measure of aesthetic coherence already before the First World War. Despite the absence of an all-encompassing manifesto, modernism demonstrated several consistent aesthetic principles and methods of creation that resulted in a fundamental revision of the universal values that had been previously culturally dominant. Post-Impressionism, Symbolism, Cubism, Imagism, Futurism, Dadaism, and Surrealism each represented an enthusiastic break with the positivist cultural heritage and humanistic beliefs of the nineteenth century. Although there existed within these movements intrinsic contradictions, expressed in manifestoes and declarations, there was one common artistic attitude, as a result of the unprecedented calamities of the era. All of these movements aimed to overthrow the basic aesthetics of classical Realism, which resulted in a radical opposition to these canons of realistic art that is now known as modernism.

This volume is intended for a student audience and aims at providing a general overview of the main currents that constituted the final stage of the modernist creative history—the Russian avant-garde described from a historical perspective. The collection features a number of original contributions commissioned specifically for the present volume along with some scholarly classics devoted to the relevant topics. The texts presented in this reader were selected with the aim of bringing the most suitable and accessible information on the issues in question. They reflect both a high caliber of scholarly rigor and professional substantiality along with an overall accessibility for students. Let us start with defining briefly the thematic issues that will be discussed in the following pages.

Constantly challenging the principles of artistic representation, modernism rejected traditional *realistic* art and literature by denying life-imitating techniques in favor of irrationalism and absurdity. To a certain degree, modernism was an aesthetic reaction to what was perceived as a chaotic modern world, following the unprecedented death and destruction caused by severe social cataclysms. Art seemed to present itself as a possible salvation from mankind's shattered reality that might create a new language, a new culture, a new actuality. Aesthetic movements of the time also exhibited radical elements such as the intense promotion of, or outright demand for, far-reaching social change and political reform.

One view of modernism suggests that it should be perceived as a "mega-period" that encompassed mutually hostile movements such as Symbolism and the avant-garde. In this case, modernism followed Realism as a reaction against rationalist aesthetics. There was a certain parallel overlap in France with Charles Baudelaire and later with Paul Verlaine and Rimbaud who in a certain sense "appeared before their age," thereby contributing to the early development of the modernist aesthetic even before it was formally conceived and defined. The central principles of modernist culture heralded a fundamental revision of most of the major philosophical doctrines that had dominated nineteenth-century culture and its aesthetics. Therefore, within Post-Impressionism, Symbolism, Cubism, Imagism, Futurism, Dadaism, and Surrealism there is a shared sense that the unprecedented chain of events of recent times had significantly altered mankind's universal values and humanistic beliefs.

The first phase of European modernism may be found in Symbolism and the experimental work of Stéphane Mallarmé. This movement had a far-reaching impact in the arts and the natural sciences, as well as in the intellectual lives of its adherents, which led to a significant re-perception of the modern world. One of Symbolism's principles was a new spiritualism and a quest for hidden realities. We might remember the famous Russian Symbolist motto: *a realibus ad realiora*—"from reality to a more-real hidden reality." This doctrine championed the search for unseen realities, reflecting dissatisfaction with the role that positivist philosophy had played within society in the nineteenth century. Darwinian evolution, which had greatly influenced culture and religion, was abandoned along with the rigorous empiricism of the new scientific establishment. Sensory faculties that had been used previously for exploring the empirical world were now directed toward the invisible spheres of human spirituality. As such, modernism began to challenge the traditional principles of mimetic representation, denying life-imitating techniques, instead proposing an irrationalism and alogism that depicted the *process of life* as a potential *problem*. This nexus of life/art/experiment suggested a potential relevance for a "Lebenskunst" (life-art) program that was followed by many modernist authors. Émile Zola, author of *The Experimental Novel* (1880), together with the post-realist school of Naturalism were very early examples of this new approach. Zola and other decadent figures depicted a reality that was constructed from the bitterly absurd, in which human individuality was frequently associated with *alienation*. This condition of alienation produced many distinctive works in which the main character finds him- or herself painfully isolated, almost speechless, in the presence of others. The works of Franz Kafka might be the best example of this tendency. In Russia, Symbolist literature and, especially, poetry were represented by such names as Valery Briusov, Dmitry Merezhkovsky, Vyacheslav Ivanov, Andrey Bely, Aleksandr Blok, Mikhail Kuzmin and Maximilian Voloshin. Two generations of Russian Symbolists were succeeded by several waves of cultural figures who exploited modernist fashions to create a distinctive Russian movement.

Following Symbolism, international Futurism together with Cubism, became the first truly radical phase of the Russian avant-garde and the modernist movement. International Futurism originated in Italy a few years before it appeared in Russia. The movement did much to re-define society's understanding of art and championed some of the more vivid traits of the new *technological age*, such as speed, dynamism, energy, mechanical strength, vitality, constant change, and, in some cases, vigorous physical activity. On 20 February 1909, the French newspaper *Le Figaro* published a manifesto written by the Italian poet and critic Filippo Tommaso Marinetti, thus giving birth to "International Futurism." Futurism enthusiastically celebrated the new technologies of *the machine* (the automobile in particular). Equally important was a brazen support for combat, in which physical violence would overcome the diseases of the weak—those destined to perish and eventually to fade away. Marinetti paid an important historical visit to Russia in the beginning of 1914. Although it was not well received, the Italian movement did indirectly influence the maturation of Russian Futurism, especially realized in two significant poets of the Russian avant-garde, the utopian Cubo-Futurists Velimir Khlebnikov and Vladimir Mayakovsky. Prior to Marinetti's visit, the Russian Futurists boldly acquired the name "Budetliane" (the Slavic etymological equivalent of "Futurists" playfully coined by Khlebnikov) and published their own manifesto in December 1912 entitled "A Slap in the Face of Public Taste," which was partially dependant on Italian Futurist proclamations.

The Russian Futurists explored a radical agenda in their public activities, attempting to shock the middle class into social and political change. They mocked and rejected the most sacred Russian cultural figures, such as Alexander Pushkin, Fedor Dostoyevsky, and Lev Tolstoy. Their attitude toward contemporary Russian Symbolist art and poetry was similarly militant and hostile. Both the Russian and the Italian Futurist poets rejected the conventionality of *logical* sentence structure and ordinary grammar with its transparent syntax. The Russian Futurists (some of whom later called themselves "Com-Futy"—Communists-futurists) intended to integrate into their innovative society new forms of art that would answer the demands of daily life within a revolutionary culture.

Constructivism was another important Russian avant-garde movement of the same period [the term Constructivism was first used in January 1921 in Moscow by the Stenberg brothers and Karel Ioganson]. This name, with its Latin root, was meant to signify technical, productive creation. This was a logical development of the recurrent modernist obligation to *construct* art, to reconcile art with a modernist lifestyle. Constructivism as an artistic and architectural movement was deeply influenced by European Cubism and, simultaneously, by Futurism. Its symbolic origins may be traced to the revolutionary abstract, geometrically inspired objects of Vladimir Tatlin produced in 1914, as well as the "Realistic Manifesto" published by Naum Gabo and his brother Antoine Pevsner in 1920. The passionate *futuristic* admiration for machines and technology, functionality, and modern industrial materials (plastic, steel, and glass) led Constructivist artists to be called *engineers of art*. Subsequently, the same metaphor was used when Soviet authors were designated as *engineers of human souls* (relevant for the "life-building" pathos of nascent Soviet culture). Important Constructivists included the photographer and designer Alexander Rodchenko and the painter El Lisitsky.

Equally as significant for the Russian avant-garde was Suprematism, one of the first to advocate formless and geometrical abstraction in painting. It was established ca. 1914 by the prominent Russian (of Polish descent) painter and art theoretician Kazimir Malevich. Malevich is well-known for his unique ideas of "economy" and "energy" developed within the radically new imagery of total "abstraction" unseen before, even in Vasily Kandinsky's "plain" objects. The Suprematist art of Malevich is now highly acclaimed in the West.

The Futurist, Suprematist and Constructivist preoccupation with *experimentation* and the profound reformulation of life, shaped by the power of art, was the common theme in all of these Russian cultural currents. As the old traditions collapsed, modernist groups tried to hasten their destruction so as to create novel systems of thinking, new languages and alternative ways to interact with society. Both in their own lives and in their art, modernists were outrageous and sensational because they were challenging the boundaries of *acceptable* cultural discourse.

This desire by modernists to challenge, to destroy and rebuild, was in some cases a reflection of the larger political and historical events of their times. Broadly speaking, Russian modernism can be situated in time from the 1890s to the 1930s, although some critics would argue that the movement (e.g. Baudelaire) began in the late 1850s. This period of over forty years was a period of intense social and political upheaval. In 1881, Russian terrorists assassinated Tsar Alexander II, which resulted in nearly twenty-five years of political stagnation. Russian society rebelled against what it perceived as the political excess of the *People's Will*, the terrorists who took responsibility for the regicide, becoming significantly more conservative for a time. This coincided with the abrupt end of Russia's golden age of literature with the silencing of Tolstoy and the deaths of both Dostoyevsky and Ivan Turgenev. As a consequence, the social and political direction of Russia was seemingly adrift and into this void stepped the Russian modernists.

With the accession of Nicholas II to the throne in 1894, liberals had hoped that the restrictions on press and political activities that had been enforced following the Tsar's assassination would be relaxed, but they were sorely disappointed. This only forced alternative political groups and their activities further underground. Even so, this was a period of rapid industrialization under the guidance of the Minister of Finance Sergei Witte. Russian industry, mining and oil production expanded significantly, yet wages and working conditions were still quite dismal for the lower class. At the same time, the Russian middle class was rapidly expanding. In the areas of manufacturing, commerce, banking and public transportation, Russia was beginning to resemble its European neighbors. As a result of a growing rate of literacy and greater access to education, many Russians soon took advantage of opportunities to study abroad, mostly in Germany, Switzerland and France.

Even so, the Russian *fin de siècle* was predominantly pessimistic and rife with an impending sense of apocalyptic doom. The Russian revolutionary movement heightened the natural tendency to see the end of a century in revelatory terms, in particular that human existence was fragile and near extinction. Whatever hope that some might have held for positive change with the coming of a new century was dashed with the failed Revolt of 1905, when peaceful protestors, mainly women and children, were slaughtered by the Tsar's cavalry. Although Nicholas was able to retain power for a time, the tsarist system was forever altered. A semi-constitutional monarchy with a parliament emerged after months of political protest, strikes and clashes with government forces. It was important for Russia that industrialization continue, as well as agrarian reform and modernization of the armed forces, yet political in-fighting hindered this much-needed process.

By 1914, Russian industrialization had created further important economic and social changes, while the agrarian reforms under Pyotr Stolypin produced a new class of independent farmers. Yet, numerous inequities and frictions still existed as the nobility carefully guarded their privileges and the clergy blocked all calls for religious reform. In August, Russia was still in the process of reforming its military, but entered the First World War. Initially, the war produced unity among the various political factions and a measure of patriotic resolve, but this soon dissolved as Russia's various military, governmental and financial problems became readily apparent. By March 1917, Russia was ripe for revolution and the government was toppled surprisingly quickly. A Provisional Government was eventually overthrown by a Bolshevik faction led by Vladimir Lenin in November of that same year.

This period of political instability was, in fact, the high point of the Russian avant-garde. In this vacuum of social and political instability, Russian modernists saw their opportunity to break the fetters of the old and to reformulate life anew. The major movements of this time included Constructivism, Cubo-Futurism, Rayonism, and Suprematism. Cubo-Futurism may be considered the dominant movement, which found adherents in poetry and the visual arts. Membership in one group, however, did not preclude participation in another of those listed above. During the years before and after the First World War, the major exponents of Cubo-Futurism included Alexander Archipenko, the brothers Burliuk, Aleksandra Ekster, Natalia Goncharova, Ivan Klyun, Mikhail Larionov, Lyubov' Popova, and Olga Rozanova.

Rayonism first appeared in 1911 as a radical movement of abstractionism. Its leading figures engaged in a polemic with the representatives of Western non-conformist art such as French Cubism on the one side and Italian Futurism on the other. The leading figures of Rayonism were Mikhail Larionov and Natalia Goncharova. As mentioned previously, Suprematism was established by Malevich, who was preoccupied with the idea that realistic art should be destroyed in order to establish a new artistic language of plain geometric forms. This new geometric vocabulary of crosses, squares and circles, combined with a sense of movement was meant to create a new artistic philosophy.

Constructivism, which appeared in 1921 with its major focus on art and architectural design, was intended to provide a blueprint for the new society that was to emerge after the World Revolution. Russian Constructivism exercised a very noticeable influence on artistic modernism, having a great theoretical and practical impact on such Western movements as the German Bauhaus and the Dutch De Stijl. Among the main members who were openly connected to the movement were Naum Gabo, El Lissitzky, Ivan Leonidov, Konstantin Melnikov, Antoine Pevsner, Lyubov Popova, Aleksandr Rodchenko, Vladimir Shukhov, Varvara Stepanova, Vladimir Tatlin and Alexander Vesnin.

After assuming power, the Bolsheviks sued for peace so as to withdraw from the war, but were soon after drawn into a bitter civil war that lasted for nearly four years. In an odd realization of many modernist positions, the Bolsheviks destroyed the old state, its political parties and economic systems. In its place, they established with revolutionary fervor a new socialist state. During this period, the Russian avant-garde played a very important role in both political and social agitation for radical change.

The transition to a completely new form of government was not an easy one and the Bolsheviks were able to maintain power only by use of force. As Lenin realized that a radical reformulation of the economy might not be possible immediately, he introduced the New Economic Policy (NEP), which lasted from 1921-1927. NEP was established to stimulate agricultural production for the urban market and eventually led to a limited consumer sector. The government maintained control over industry, transport and foreign trade, while individuals could buy and sell consumer goods to alleviate hoarding and forced requisitions of food items. This relaxation of what had been known as War Communism was also a period of particularly interesting aesthetic developments. The reality was that with so much concentration being paid by the government to military and economic issues, Russian modernists experienced a good degree of artistic freedom.

The death of Lenin in 1924 caused a great struggle for political power within the Bolshevik party. Four factions vied for control, but by 1928 Joseph Stalin emerged as the eventual winner. Stalin exploited the cult of Lenin during this struggle and positioned himself as the lawful *successor*, although this was not in fact the truth. Lenin, who had detested ceremony, was quickly made sacred by Stalin. Official decrees ordered monuments to Lenin throughout the country, Petrograd was renamed Leningrad, and the collected works of Lenin's writings were published. Lenin's body was quickly embalmed and a mausoleum was constructed on Red Square so that Lenin could remain on public display.

Moving away from Lenin's policy of collective leadership, Stalin secured total power over the party. Using a hagiographical cult of Lenin, Stalin created his own cult of personality. He destroyed the opposition of the peasantry and moved swiftly to forcibly collectivize agriculture. He also established the five-year-plans to rapidly increase industrialization and expand the working class. Even after Stalin had seemingly pacified all political opposition, he launched the Great Purge in 1936-1938, which eliminated the remaining old Bolsheviks.

For the Russian modernists, however, the establishment of Socialist Realism as state policy in 1932, most certainly had the greatest impact on their aesthetic production. Following the decree "On the Reconstruction of Literary and Art Organizations," many of the movements which had constituted the Russian avant-garde, such as Cubism, were viewed as *decadent bourgeois art*. The idea was that a proletarian civilization must produce its own culture. Many artists, such as Malevich, attempted to adhere to the new artistic principals of the state, but effectively, Russian radical modernism had come to an end. Russian modernists (the so-called *Second Russian Avant-garde*) continued to produce works of art into the 1960s, but this is what we might call *unofficial* art and often it was shared with only a select group of people. The final representative of what is known to be the "historical Russian avant-garde" was the OBERIU-group. It was constituted of *underground* writers and poets whose very existence was not widely known among Soviet citizens. None of the representatives of this "last Russian avant-garde" were officially allowed to publish their works. As such, some of the OBERIU members did not even attempt to distribute their works. Others sought alternative artistic outlets, like the main member of that group—Daniil Kharms, who was permitted to publish only his children's texts in the Soviet press.

* * *

This reader presents a collection of texts meant to further articulate what is meant by the Russian avant-garde and radical modernism. The volume is organized chronologically and thematically starting with Russian Futurism. We consider Russian Futurism to constitute one of the major pillars of the avant-garde in Russia. Our treatment excludes such preceding currents which, from a formal viewpoint of Russian modernism, were not integral to the avant-garde per se (primarily Symbolism).

For each section we have chosen several essays intended to be illustrative of a particular movement. For example, we have included one chapter from Vladimir Markov's classic work on Futurism that clearly articulates the various Futurist groups vying for aesthetic coherence in Russia at the beginning of the twentieth century. Separate essays are provided by Willem Weststeijn on Velimir Khlebnikov and Vladimir Mayakovsky, major poetic figures of the period. Elena Basner and Jane Sharp offer insightful articles on elements of Futurist visual art. Original texts of the avant-garde are translated and provided by John Bowlt. Finally, a conceptual argument is made by Boris Groys on how one might understand the lasting ramifications of the Russian avant-garde.

In the next major section, Suprematism and Constructivism are the main focus. A chapter from the classic work on Russian Constructivism by Christina Lodder is republished here. Evgeny Kovtun provides an essay on Kazimir Malevich and his art. Once again, these essays are supported with original documents that have been collected and translated by John Bowlt. The third section is concerned with the OBERIU circle with an essay by Evgeny Pavlov and selected poems translated by Eugene Ostashevsky and other translators of his cohort. The fourth section is concerned with Russian experimental performance and cinema.

Alexander Burry offers an introductory essay on the theater of Vsevolod Meyerhold, while Michael Klebanov explores Meyerhold's innovations in the context of subsequent theatrical movements. Frederick H. White furnishes a brief biography of Sergei Eisenstein and John MacKay examines the cinematography of Dziga Vertov. Finally, Dennis Ioffe offers an addendum to this collection in the form of a theoretical argument on the tradition of experimentation in Russian culture as a direct factor in the development of the Russian avant-garde.

In a collection such as this, it is difficult to represent every facet of a very dynamic period. The intention of the editors was to address representational figures and movements as an introduction to the concept of the Russian avant-garde and radical modernism, with the hope that this will lead to further advanced study. The scholars represented in this collection are some of the leading figures in their field and a search of their other works will provide a treasure trove of additional information on relevant subjects. We hope that this introductory reader will serve as a basis for further consideration of the Russian twentieth century cultural discourse that has had far-reaching influences in world culture.[1]

Dennis Ioffe
Frederick H. White

December 2011

1 We did not include separate entries on such artists as Vassily Kandinsky, Marc Chagall or Nathan Altman for two main reasons: 1) They do not correspond to any particular "current" in the Russian Avant-garde, being more individualistic figures. Our concentration here is on larger group movements; 2) Information on these figures is widely available in general introductory texts on twentieth-century art, thus making their inclusion here redundant. We also did not include such minor (though extremely valuable) artistic currents as the "Union of Youth," which was founded by Mikhail Matiushin and Voldemars Matvejs, or Ilia Zdanevich's group "41°" as separate entities, leaving them possibly for classroom discussions.

II

RUSSIAN FUTURISM AND THE RELATED CURRENTS

1. Hylaea[1]

Vladimir Markov

In November 1910,[2] Vasily Kamensky published a book entitled *Zemlyanka* ("The Mud Hut"). It is a romantic story with some autobiographical elements. Philip, a provincial turned fashionable writer now living in the capital, is a naively glamorized self-portrait of Kamensky down to the red shirt he wears, which Kamensky tried to use as a trademark. Philip's love affair with the beautiful Marina is on the rocks, and he is on the verge of committing suicide, but is distracted by the rising sun and the singing birds and decides to leave Marina for nine years to test her and his own love. He goes to live in the country, in a forest on the bank of a river, in a mud hut abandoned by some hunter, in the company of a peasant boy, a dog, and a thrush. Tortured thoughts of Marina are soon replaced by his communication with the vision of the fairytale-like Maika; but, finally, Philip meets a peasant girl, Mariika, with whom he finds paradisaic happiness through marriage.

The Mud Hut is an antiurbanistic work, and the first chapters are devoted to depicting the city as the reign of death. The protagonist abandons the tragic chaos of city life and returns to mother earth. In fact, for the author, the novel was an ambitious undertaking, something terribly significant, a kind of *Divine Comedy* with the hero going through the hell of city life, then cleansing himself in solitary communion with nature, and, at the end, entering the paradise of peasant life. The peasant, according to Kamensky, partakes of the "enormous mysteries of earth," which the author refuses to reveal to anyone. At the end of the novel, he does reveal, however, that he follows Leo Tolstoy. Tolstoy is mentioned by name and praised for his ability to write "in plain Russian so that one can understand him" while the rest of the Russian literati are dismissed as "Russian foreigners."

The best pages in *The Mud Hut* are those on which Kamensky describes nature. "Describes" is not the right word, because this lyric novel is an exuberant paean to nature, which it extols as the force making a wise child of a man. In all fairness, one should add, however, that though

Kamensky is certainly familiar with and fond of nature as it is found in his beloved Perm region, his observations concerning it are inaccurate: in his novel, for instance, buttercups, bluebells, and cornflowers grow at the same time. The lyric quality of the nature chapters is further intensified by the free verse poetry that often interrupts the emotional prose in which the work is written. Many of the *Mud Hut* poems were published earlier in *Sadok sudei*. Kamensky later attached much importance to the fact that he intermingled prose with poetry in his novel. He called *The Mud Hut* "a new kind of novel"[3] and was inclined to consider this intermingling a futurist device. Though some originality could be claimed in the employment of this device when seen within the context of Russian literature,[4] its use did not constitute futurism. Kamensky's later claim that he had achieved a *sdvig* ("dislocation, shift") through this intermingling of prose and poetry can hardly be recognized, because poetry does not actually interrupt prose in his work, thus producing a dissonant effect, but rather enhances the lyricism that fills the prose throughout the novel. Otherwise, the mixture of monologue and third-person narrative, the frequent exclamations, and the fragmentary composition of the work add further to the impressionistic effect. Actually, Kamensky's originality is somewhat diminished by the fact that Guro used the same device in a less obtrusive and more subtle way. Kamensky appears as a pupil of Guro also in the frequent use of one-word sentences and in his admonitions to preserve the child in oneself. He also borrows from E. Nizen (the scene with children playing in a city-garden has much in common with her "Children's Paradise") and from Khlebnikov (some poems are obviously patterned on the latter's "Zoo"; reproducing birdcalls comes from Khlebnikov, too).

As a whole, to put it mildly, *The Mud Hut* is hardly a masterpiece. It needs much cutting, its diction is often banal, and it shows that Kamensky's taste was always his weak point. When Philip is in distress after Marina has left him, and the homeless dogs in the streets come and sniff with sympathy at his tears dropping to the sidewalk, it is too much. The childish exuberance of the hero's communion with nature can also be too much, as when he, overcome by the child awakening in him, jumps fully clothed into the river from a steep bank, holding the burning tree trunk pulled out of a bonfire. Nevertheless, the novel occupies an important place in this history because (1) it is another example of the impressionist beginnings of Russian futurism; (2) it is the first major work published by a leading futurist; and (3) it is the first extensive presentation of Kamensky's favorite subject, nature in Russia, especially that aspect of it associated with hunting and fishing. It is also interesting that while Kamensky is here an impressionist in technique, this work could be labeled primitivist in ideology because of his preaching a return to nature; and primitivism was to be the next preoccupation of the Russian futurists. Kamensky wrote *The Mud Hut* surrounded by the best comforts of civilized life, having just married a very wealthy woman (who, unfortunately, was soon to go bankrupt). This wife (the first of many for Kamensky) did not like the novel. When clippings of negative reviews began to arrive, Kamensky's authority in the family dropped drastically, and he left literature in disillusionment. To regain his self-respect, he decided to enter aviation, another dangerous occupation and one that was then in its infancy in Russia. After training in Europe, he bought an airplane in France and soon became a famous pioneer pilot in Russia, until his airplane crashed in Poland before a festive audience during one of his demonstration flights. Kamensky survived, but gave up aviation, and, having purchased a farm near Perm, went there to practice what he had preached before in *The Mud Hut*. Until 1913 he was outside literature; and if it had not been for David Burliuk, he might never have reentered it.

David Burliuk, in the meantime, was as active as ever. He studied art in Moscow.[5] He participated not only in Kulbin's "Triangle" exhibition, but also in another St. Petersburg modernist artists' exhibition, the "Union of Youth," both at the beginning of 1910. In the summer, he went to spend his vacation with his family in the south of Russia, and he took along two guests, Velimir Khlebnikov and the artist Mikhail Larionov. That winter Burliuk participated in the first exhibition of the most important group of the Russian artistic avant-garde, "Bubnovyi valet" ("Jack of Diamonds"). He did not neglect his friend, Vasily Kamensky, for he disturbed the latter's rural solitude with boisterous letters, inviting him to come back at once and rejoin the movement. Soon, Burliuk made perhaps the greatest discovery in the history of futurism. While studying at the Academy of Painting, Sculpture, and Architecture in Moscow, in September, 1911, he met another student, a poorly dressed young giant, unkempt and unwashed, with penetrating eyes and a deep bass voice—Vladimir Mayakovsky. About a year after this meeting, Mayakovsky read Burliuk a short poem. "You're a genius," declared Burliuk, and he began to introduce him to people as a genius of Russian poetry. At about the same time, Alexei Kruchenykh, Burliuk's acquaintance of several years who was to become one of the most colorful figures of Russian futurism, joined the movement.

In December, 1911, when David Burliuk, on his way to his father's place to spend his Christmas vacation, stopped in Kiev, a fellow artist, Alexandra Exter,[6] introduced him to Benedict Constantinovich Livshits (1887-1939), a twenty-four-year-old student of law and son of a wealthy merchant. Livshits was the last addition to Russian futurism. The group soon became very exclusive and accepted no new members, though they did ally themselves on occasion with other groups and individuals. Burliuk evidently saw in Livshits, a well-read young man and an admirer of Corbiere and Rimbaud, the potential theoretician of the group. Livshits had been at that time a contributor to *Apollon* and the author of one book of verse, *Fleita Marsiya* ("The Flute of Marsyas"), published in 1911 and reviewed rather favorably by the influential Bryusov. More than twenty years after this meeting, Livshits wrote a book of memoirs, *Polutoraglazyi strelets* ("The One-and-a-half-eyed Archer"), which, though it covered a span of only three years, still remains not only the best source on the history of Russian futurism, but also one of the best among Russian memoirs, deserving translation into other languages. In late 1911, however, Livshits, a constant searcher, considered his first book a thing of the past and was looking for new ways in poetry. Symbolism, in his opinion, had led the poetic word into a blind alley. The new ways seemed to be opening up for him in modern painting, whose discoveries needed only translation into the verbal medium. With the zeal of a recent convert, Livshits wanted a complete break with the past, and he saw a duplicity in Vladimir Burliuk's painting still-lifes in the Dutch manner at school while experimenting with cubism at home. But the healthy and energetic Burliuks looked like valuable cofighters for the new aesthetics because they had strong fists, both literally and metaphorically; thus, Livshits so readily followed David Burliuk after the latter's unexpected invitation to spend the vacation with him at Chernyanka.

Chernyanka was a place in the area of the former Tavrida (Taurida) Government not far from the city of Kherson and the Black Sea coast, and from there the Burliuks' father managed the huge estate belonging to Count Mordvinov. The senior David Burliuk lived there in patriarchal simplicity and abundance, surrounded by a big family (three sons and three daughters) and enormous expanses of the steppes on which uncountable herds of sheep and pigs were grazing. For Livshits, there was something Homeric in this way of life. Prehistory looked at him not only from the meandering ornamental patterns on the houses and from the Scythian arrows found in numerous mounds, but also from the simplicity of their eating, hunting, and courtship habits. In short, it was the Hylaea ("Gileya" in Russian),[7] the name used by the ancient Greeks for this area, mentioned four times by Herodotus, and familiar to all these future futurists from their school lessons in classical history as the setting of some of the deeds of Hercules. "Hylaea, the ancient Hylaea, trod upon by our feet, took the meaning of a symbol and had to become a banner." To Livshits, it meant a new and fresh vision of the world, so indispensable for the new art they were going to create, and it was full of "animalistic power." "The world lies before you, wherever your eye can reach, in utter nakedness. . . . Grab it, tear it, bite into it, crumple it, recreate it—it belongs to you, all of it," he wrote.[8]

The brothers Burliuk were very busy during that vacation. They had just discovered Picasso and cubism, and were trying to assimilate the discovery in time for the next "Jack of Diamonds" exhibition, which was to take place in Moscow in a month. But all the methods they used—multiple perspective, flatness of portrayal, dislocation of planes, unusual coloring, even throwing the freshly painted canvas into the mud and, after this, painting it over again to make the surface "less quiet"—served, for Livshits, a single purpose, that of "the renovated vision of the world."[9] Livshits' failure at painting did not prevent his applying to poetry the methods he learned from the painters. He called his prose work "Lyudi v peizazhe" ("People in a Landscape") "100 percent cubism transferred to the area of organized speech."[10] In addition to technical problems, some ideological contours began to take shape for Livshits at that early time, the shape of Hylaean nationalism: atavistic layers, "diluvial" rhythms, flooded by the blinding light of prehistory, moving toward the West, and, ahead of all these, the wildly galloping Scythian warrior, the one-and-a-half-eyed archer. Livshits was deeply shaken by his acquaintance with Khlebnikov's manuscripts, left by the poet in Chernyanka after his sojourn there a year before, because of his own ideological outlook and because in them he found that amorphous, antediluvial verbal mass. But, of course, Livshits exaggerated in his newly acquired Hylaean enthusiasm, and he underestimated the strong rationalistic element in the work of Khlebnikov, who was an engineer of the word, too.

Thus the three brothers Burliuk and Benedict Livshits founded the group "Hylaea." The name was used for more than two years before they began to call themselves futurists. It went without saying that Khlebnikov was one of them. Shortly thereafter, Mayakovsky and Kruchenykh were to join the group. Livshits did not care very much for the name "Hylaea," which, he thought, sounded too "languorous" and was the result of their "being stuffed with high school classical reminiscences and yielding to the temptation of the mythology that surrounded them"[11] at Chernyanka. He would have preferred the meaningless, but strong and energetic-sounding, word, *chukuryuk*, invented by Vladimir Burliuk for one of his pictures.

The Burliuks were going to Moscow to impress their colleagues with the newly found cubism; but, poetically speaking, Hylaea did not mean cubism at all (cubism began to be felt in Russian futurist poetry later), but primitivism. Russian primitivism was broad in its extent and complex in its sources. It included not only painting and poetry, but music as well (the best example is Stravinsky's *Rite of Spring*). Its beginnings were, in one sense, connected with the symbolists' wide interest in Slavic mythology, as well as with the theme of the human beast in the Russian prose of the period (Leonid Andreyev, Artsybashev). In a more specific sense, however, Russian primitivism began in December, 1909, with the third exhibition of the Golden Fleece, which boasted not only examples of the fauvist line and the abstract use of color, but also specimens of folk art, such as lace, popular lithographs (*lubok*), icons, and even ornamented cookies. Soon after that, Kulbin wrote about "the art of children and prehistoric men"[12] in the same context with manifestations of beauty in nature (flowers, crystals). Even the conservative *Apollon* showed interest in children's drawings (the article by Bakst in no. 3, 1909).

The three outstanding figures of primitivism in Russian art are David Burliuk, Natalya Goncharova, and Mikhail Larionov. Burliuk's primitivistic art (unfortunately, still little studied and insufficiently appreciated) is of complex origin, being not only an outgrowth of his interest in ancient Scythian sculpture (*kamennye baby* of the southern Russian steppes, which more than once appear in Khlebnikov's poetry) and in contemporary signboards (Burliuk had a large collection of such signboards), but also based on his study of Polynesian and old Mexican art.

Goncharova was strongly influenced by icons, *lubok*, and folk ornament; and Larionov added infantilist features to his primitivism (as did Khlebnikov), which contained elements of parody (also to be found in Khlebnikov) and eroticism (and in this Larionov resembles Kruchenykh). This primitivistic art was created in close personal cooperation as Larionov and Goncharova were husband and wife, and Burliuk was their close friend from 1907 until 1911. Larionov was probably the artist whose work had the greatest influence on the primitivistic poetry of the Russian futurists, especially on that of Khlebnikov and Kruchenykh. There is much truth in Camilla Gray's words that the futurist poets took from Larionov "the use of 'irreverent-irrelevant' associations, the imitation of children's art, and the adaptation of folk-art imagery and motifs."[13] As mentioned above, both Larionov and Khlebnikov were Burliuk's guests at Chernyanka in the summer of 1910, and it is a great pity that we do not know any details of this sojourn, which might have been the real prologue to Hylaea. At any rate, in some of Khlebnikov's poetry, one can find imitation of such specific devices of painting as *protekayushchaya raskraska* ("color extending beyond the outline").

There were three main areas that attracted Russian futurist poets in their efforts to create primitivism. Childhood was one of them, and here primitivist futurism overlaps with its own impressionist stage, for example, when the inner processes in a child's life drew Guro's attention. Guro also preached (as did Kamensky) the preservation of the childlike in man. Now, in the Hylaean period, Khlebnikov used infantilism as an artistic method, and later he tried to build some of his poems on a child's vocabulary. Both Khlebnikov and Kruchenykh were interested in poetry and prose written by children and made efforts to publish it. Kamensky collected children's drawings. Another area that interested these futurist writers of primitivistic poetry was prehistory. Khlebnikov placed the action of some of his longer poems in an imaginary "Slavic Stone Age," and some of his short poetic sketches may remind the reader of drawings on cave walls. Finally, both Khlebnikov and Kruchenykh were preoccupied with certain kinds of Russian folklore. It is, however, not the "respectable" imitation of, or use of motifs from, folk epics, lyrical songs, and fairy tales which is so widespread in Russian literature. It is, instead, an interest in the naive and "illiterate" imitation and distortion of literature, especially of romantic poetry, in numerous songs, ballads, and poems which seldom attracted the attention of scholars, who to this day tend to dismiss them as having no artistic merit.

The greatest achievements of Russian poetic primitivism are, undoubtedly, some of the longer poems by Khlebnikov. In 1911 he wrote "The Forest Maiden" and "I and E"; in 1912 appeared *A Game in Hell* (which he wrote with Kruchenykh), "The End of Atlantis," "A Vila and a Wood Goblin," and "A Shaman and Venus." After the Revolution, Khlebnikov was to continue his primitivism in "The Sylvan Sadness" and, partly, in *Ladomir*, "Poet," and "Razin's Boat."[14] The combination of naiveté and of a special kind of freshness with technical clumsiness, which is characteristic of any primitivist art, is achieved by Khlebnikov through the use of a system of artistic devices in which absurdity of situation or imagery in one poem may be followed by naive and unaccountable omissions or anticipations of events in another one, as well as by deliberate inarticulateness in relating these events. All this is presented against a highly involved lexical and metrical background, where many kinds of irregularities are used in a virtuoso way. After Khlebnikov, only the Soviet poet Nikolai Zabolotsky (1903-1958) was able to reproduce primitivistic absurdity with such consummate skill.

The Hylaea group made its appearance only at the end of 1912 with *A Slap in the Face of Public Taste*; but for many months before its publication, leading futurists actively participated in discussions of modern art, which accompanied the exhibitions sponsored by the main groups of avant-garde painters. These discussions, often resulting in public scandals, created the atmosphere in which literary futurism was to thrive for many years. In order to understand this situation, a very short survey of Russian Avant-garde art is needed, though it may repeat a few facts previously mentioned.

On December 20, 1907, a group of artists, most of whom were destined to play important roles in the history of Russian Avant-garde art, opened an exhibition in Moscow under the name "Stephanos." In addition to the artists from the Blue Rose, an impressionist group that tended toward lyric mysticism, the following exhibited their work in it: David and Vladimir Burliuk, as well as their sister Lyudmila, Larionov, Goncharova, Lentulov, Yakulov, Sapunov, and Sudeikin. After a split, the Burliuks and Lentulov organized in St. Petersburg, in 1908, another exhibition under the tautological name of "Venok Stephanos" ("The Wreath Stephanos"), whereas Larionov remained in alliance with the Blue Rose and was instrumental in organizing, under the auspices of the magazine Golden Fleece and its millionaire founder and sponsor N. Ryabushinsky, two consecutive exhibitions, in 1908 and 1909, in which paintings by Cezanne, Van Gogh, Gauguin, Matisse, Rouault, and Braque were shown. In November, 1908, David Burliuk and Alexandra Exter were responsible for the exhibition in Kiev, "Zveno" ("Link"), which had little success.

In 1909, David Burliuk allied his Wreath Stephanos to Kulbin's impressionist Triangle, which resulted the following year in a joint exhibition in St. Petersburg under the latter name. Incidentally, it was during this exhibition that *The Studio of Impressionists* appeared (as planned) and *Sadok sudei* was prepared. A year before, in 1908, Kulbin, also in St. Petersburg, organized "The Exhibition of Modern Art," which some sources also call "The Impressionists" (and which included, among others, some paintings by a blind artist). A much more profound influence, however, was exercised by the exhibitions in Odessa, Kiev, and St. Petersburg of the "Salon" of V. Izdebsky, which opened in October, 1909, and, together with the works of Larionov, Lentulov, Matyushin, Exter, and children's drawings, showed paintings by Braque, Matisse, and other famous European postimpressionists. It was this exhibition that made so deep and lasting an impression on the young Kievan poet, Benedict Livshits.[15] A little later, some Russian avant-garde Artists (including David and Vladimir Burliuk, Larionov, and Goncharova) showed their work abroad at the exhibitions of "Der blaue Reiter" and "Der Sturm."

It was during this complex and rich period that Russian painting assimilated and went beyond Western impressionism, and, on the basis of European postimpressionist trends in the arts, the original Russian contribution began to take shape. It is mostly connected with the activities of the *Bubnovyi valet* ("Jack of Diamonds"), a small group that soon became an influential organization, dominating Russian artistic life for several years. Its first exhibition took place in December, 1910, in Moscow, and included the works of Larionov, Goncharova, the Burliuks, Exter, Kandinsky, A. Lentulov, Konchalovsky, Ilya Mashkov, Robert Falk, and Tatlin. By the time the Hylaea group was organized, the members of Jack of Diamonds were getting ready for their second exhibition, which opened in Moscow on January 25, 1912.

In addition to the exhibition, it was decided to have lectures with discussions about modern art. Such a thing had been done before in St. Petersburg by another avant-garde group, the Union of Youth. Despite the participation of David Burliuk, this earlier lecture-discussion had passed without incident and was conducted on an almost academic note; however, at the first and historic debate of Jack of Diamonds, which took place in Moscow on February 12 in the over-filled auditorium of the Polytechnical Museum, Burliuk shocked the audience. In his lecture about cubism, he declared that the subject of painting did not matter and that Raphael and Velazquez were philistines and photographers. The audience was entertained much more, however, by Goncharova, who appeared on the stage with an unscheduled attack on Jack of Diamonds and an announcement about the coming exhibition of a new avant-garde group under the name of Oslinyi khvost ("Donkey's Tail"). The evening ended in an uproar.

There was no disturbance during the second Jack of Diamonds debate, held two weeks later without representatives of Donkey's Tail. This time Burliuk spoke on "Evolution of Beauty and Art." He insisted that the life-span of any truth in the arts is twenty-five years and, therefore, that any concept of beauty is relative and temporary. Art for Burliuk was not a copy of life, but its distortion, and he posited three artistic principles, which he called disharmony, dissymmetry, and disconstruction. The interesting fact is that Burliuk, during this lecture, mentioned Italian futurism for the first time publicly. Though at that time he knew next to nothing about Italian futurism, having not even seen a single reproduction of paintings by Italian futurists, he accused it of sacrificing the principles of the arts in favor of literature. Donkey's Tail, on the other hand, was in favor of Italian futurism, though in the work of Goncharova, Malevich, and others it never developed into an artistic *Weltanschauung*, remaining just an episode.

Donkey's Tail began to take shape before the open break of its members with members of the Jack of Diamonds group in January, 1912, for Larionov's idea to organize the group goes back to the beginning of 1911. The group, which included also Malevich, Tatlin, Von Wiesen, Ledentu, and Marc Chagall, took issue with Jack of Diamonds' "conservatism" and predilection for theorizing, insisting that subject matter was of great importance in painting and stressing its own ties with Russian primitive folk art, as well as with Oriental art. Members of the group were also against Burliuk's fighting the past and did not see anything new in cubism (cubism could be found in Russian dolls and in ancient Scythian sculptures, they said). There was also much that was personal in this break between the essentially similar founders of Russian primitivism, Goncharova and Larionov on the one side, and David Burliuk on the other. Their friendship had come to an end by 1913, and was never renewed.

In comparison with the tension and militancy displayed in artistic circles during this time, peace and tolerance were characteristic of the literary activities of the future futurists (a clumsy, but practically unavoidable expression). At the beginning of 1912 Benedict Livshits continued to contribute to *Apollon*, Nikolai Burliuk had plans to enter the Guild of Poets, which was the cradle of Russian Acmeism, and both saw in such actions no conflict with their membership in Hylaea. Preparations for new action were under way, even though during the rest of 1912 Hylaean activities in literature seemed to be in the doldrums, with Livshits having to join the army for one year, David Burliuk traveling in Europe in the summer, and Kamensky enjoying nature at his farm in the distant Urals. There was, however, some activity. Nikolai Burliuk was entrusted by his brother, David, with editorial duties, and he collected material for future joint publications quietly and efficiently. He found a common language with the demanding Livshits, who was less and less satisfied with David because of the latter's tendency to compromise and his utter unconcern with theoretical consistency.

Upon his return from Europe, David Burliuk found time to help Khlebnikov publish his first work in an individual edition—the pamphlet *Uchitel i uchenik* ("A Teacher and a Pupil"), published in Kherson with Burliuk's money. In this booklet, Khlebnikov uses dialogue as a vehicle for theorizing on the problem of "internal declension," and criticizes leading Russian symbolist writers for being preoccupied with death and violence while being far from the roots of Russian folk poetry. It was also the first presentation of Khlebnikov's attempts to find the mathematical foundations of history, which enabled him to make a strangely correct prediction about a collapse of "some empire" in 1917. No matter what one thinks about the scientific value of Khlebnikov's formulas, this preoccupation makes him practically the only real "futurist" among his friends, who rather deserve the name of "presentists."

David Burliuk had plans to publish a book, financed by Jack of Diamonds, in which both the artists and the Hylaean poets would participate. The book was in preparation throughout 1912, but did not materialize because Jack of Diamonds did not like the fact that Khlebnikov and Kruchenykh began publication of several books with illustrations by their archenemies, Goncharova and Larionov, as well as by other artists from the Donkey's Tail group. This disagreement led the Hylaeans to break with Jack of Diamonds and search for other publishers. These publishers were finally found by David Burliuk in George Kuzmin, a pilot, and Sergei Dolinsky, a composer; and *A Slap in the Face of Public Taste* was the result.

Before *A Slap in the Face of Public Taste* was published, there appeared three little books by Kruchenykh (two of them written in collaboration with Khlebnikov): *Igra v adu* ("A Game in Hell"), *Starinnaya lyubov* ("Old-Time Love"), and *Mirskontsa* ("Worldbackwards"). Alexei Eliseyevich Kruchenykh, born in 1886 to a peasant family near Kherson, was a high school art teacher when he met the Burliuks in 1907. He helped David Burliuk organize some of his exhibitions and exhibited impressionist canvases himself. Soon he moved to Moscow and, having abandoned painting for literature, became one of the most controversial of Russian futurists and probably the most radical innovator among them. He called himself "the wildest one."[16] These three books by Kruchenykh aimed at a creation of primitivistic poetry, but in some of them he went much further than that in his technique. No less important was the outward appearance of these books: they were illustrated by some of the most radical artists of the day (mostly by Goncharova and Larionov), and the texts were either written by hand and then mimeographed, or printed as if by hand in stamped letters of unequal size. All kinds of misprints or errors, as well as deletions or corrections, abounded in them. It was obviously meant to be a complete break with the tradition of symbolist deluxe editions. The illustrations were either primitivist in the manner of folk art, or imitative of children's drawings, but some of them could be termed nonobjective.

Igra v adu ("A Game in Hell") appeared in August, 1912, with sixteen illustrations by Goncharova, and was printed by hand in characters resembling Old Church Slavonic letters. This long poem about a card game going on between devils and sinners in hell was begun by Kruchenykh in the style of a folk lithograph (*lubok*), as he himself admitted.[17] Then Khlebnikov added his own stanzas and lines, with the result that the text became even more disorganized. Both Khlebnikov and Kruchenykh added to, and changed parts of, the poem after it was published. In the resulting new form, the poem was published again at the end of 1913, in a new edition, illustrated this time by Olga Rozanova and Kazimir Malevich.

Simultaneously with *A Game in Hell* (or perhaps even prior to it), there appeared another primitivist book, this time authored by Kruchenykh alone, under the title *Starinnaya lyubov* ("Old-Time Love"). Most of its illustrations, by Larionov, were in the style we now would probably call abstract expressionist. The poems were printed by hand with deliberate misprints and omissions of commas and periods, but exclamation marks were used. There were seven poems altogether, written in different manners. The first one, for instance, may be slightly parodic of the love poetry written by provincials. To the clichés and melancholy languor of nineteenth-century romantic poetry are sometimes added stylistic dissonances or nonaesthetic details (e.g., pus, vomit). Two poems form a cycle entitled "Natasha's Letters to Herzen," and are straightforward imitations of the romantic poetry of the past without any persiflage.[18] Later, in 1913, Kruchenykh added to this book a few poems and stanzas by Khlebnikov and himself, illustrating it himself in collaboration with Rozanova and Kulbin, who drew Kruchenykh's portrait for this edition. Kruchenykh also provided dedications to two poems previously not dedicated to anyone and published the entire book under the new title, *Bukh lesinnyi* ("A Forestly Rapid"). This habit of reprinting old writings in new contexts and under new titles was to become Kruchenykh's favorite method. In the same year there appeared a book whose title was a combination of both old ones, *Old-Time Love-A Forestly Rapid*. This version was built around the old material, again with addition of some new poems by both Khlebnikov and Kruchenykh.[19]

Much more experimental was the third of the three books, *Mirskontsa* ("Worldbackwards"), published by Kruchenykh in 1912 and illustrated by Larionov, Goncharova, Tatlin, and I. Rogovin in a semiabstract or primitivist manner. Outside, a polyfoil green leaf is pasted on each side of the book's yellow cover, and inside, the texts are printed only on odd pages, some in handwriting, others as if individual rubber stamps of various sizes had been used for each letter. Lapses and errors reign supreme in this book, with wrong word transfers, incorrect spelling, spaces of varying length between words, capital letters inside words, and repetitions of some texts (sometimes printed upside down). Many but not all of the letters in one poem by Khlebnikov are printed in mirror image form. Khlebnikov is represented in the book by a haphazard selection of poems, excerpts from longer works, and impromptu material. Kruchenykh's work, to which most of the book is devoted, reveals new qualities. In addition to the rather solemn introductory poem written in traditional iambic tetrameter, there are verses that imitate the spoken idiom and are full of crude energy in their short, uneven lines. In their content, they are mostly strings of images without much connection (in one poem, such an image string is motivated by a dream). Most interesting in the book are the attempts to write a new kind of prose. For instance, there are twenty pages of text printed without punctuation, with sentences overlapping and blending, under the title "A Voyage across the Whole World," which does describe some kind of travel despite the inclusion of much irrelevant material and seems to be an exercise in automatic writing.

These three books were followed by three more by Kruchenykh at the very beginning of 1913, also published by Kuzmin and Dolinsky. *Poluzhivoi* ("Half Alive") is another book of primitivist verse, illustrated by Larionov. This poem is rather obscure and in it predominate images of war and violence, culminating in the picture of a vampire sucking the blood of dead and wounded warriors on a battlefield. Analysis of the diction and metrics of the poem reveals a conscious imitation of the primitivistic style of Khlebnikov even to the smallest detail—and Khlebnikov actually "retouched" this book as he did the next one and others that followed. Another book, *Pustynniki* ("Hermits"), contains two long poems, the second being "Pustynnica" ("A Hermit Woman"). It begins as an imitation of *dukhovnye stikhi* ("religious folk poetry") about life in a hermitage, but develops into an almost surrealistic succession of images, which depict not only the life of the holy men, but their conscious and suppressed desires. The main theme is usually quite clear, but it is in the development and in the details that Kruchenykh resorts to absurdity and alogism. A closer scrutiny of "A Hermit Woman" is imperative in any study of Russian primitivism because this poem points, in some passages, as far into the future as the poetry of Nikolai Zabolotsky, written in the 1920's. Kruchenykh's familiar tendency to shock his audience manifests itself here in the emphasis he places on erotic scenes, as well as in the pictures he paints of holy men and women as anything but holy, which, in 1913, seemed blasphemous. Both eroticism and blasphemy are shown in excellent illustrations by Goncharova, in which she reflects the strong influence of Russian icon painting. *Pomada* ("Pomade"), published in January, 1913, is a very small book, containing less than a dozen poems, three of them, with tricky compound rhymes, written, as Kruchenykh notes on the last page, together with E. Lunev.[20] Pomade was illustrated by Larionov not only in a primitivistic style (as, for example, the drawing on the cover which shows a diminutive barber suspended in the air and rubbing pomade into the hair of a big head underneath), but in his new, "rayonist" manner.

The book's value in reference to the history of futurism lies mainly in the fact that it opens with three tiny poems written, as the author says in a very short introduction, "in my own language differing from the others: its words do not have a definite meaning." In short, here Kruchenykh introduced what later was to become known as *zaum*, the so-called *transrational language*, of which he would become one of the main practicians and theoreticians. Later the first of these three poems became particularly familiar to many because the author announced in a subsequent booklet that it was more Russian than all the poetry of Pushkin. After this announcement dozens of critics began to quote it or refer to it, often distorting it. The poem begins with energetic monosyllabics, some of which slightly resemble Russian or Ukrainian words, followed by a three-syllable word of shaggy appearance. The next word looks like a fragment of some word, and the two final lines are occupied with syllables and just plain letters, respectively, the poem ending on a queer, non-Russian sounding syllable:

dyr bul shchyl
ubeshshchur
skum
vy so bu
r l èz[21]

Thus, in his first publishing ventures, Kruchenykh added his own note to Russian primitivism; created, mainly with the artists Goncharova and Larionov, the classic form of a futurist publication; and inaugurated the most extreme of all futurist achievements, *zaum*. Credit is overdue to this fascinating writer, who never in his life achieved anything but cheap notoriety. Even his own colleagues tended to dismiss him as the man who "brought to absurdity some of our extreme tenets by his flippant extremism."[22]

When *Half Alive*, *Hermits*, and *Pomade* appeared, the most famous joint publication of the Hylaean poets, *A Slap in the Face of Public Taste*, had already been published. After the Jack of Diamonds refused to finance this publication, Burliuk found backers in Kuzmin and Dolinsky, guaranteeing them the gratitude of posterity for their part in his publishing venture. *A Slap* was printed on gray and brown wrapping paper, and the cover was of coarse sackcloth, later described by reviewers as being the color of "a fainted louse."[23] Otherwise, there was nothing shocking about the book, the texts being printed in large, clear print, with no illustrations accompanying them. Strangely enough, there was no mention of Hylaea anywhere in the book. The opening piece, also entitled "A Slap in the Face of Public Taste," was the first and most famous manifesto of the group. It was signed by only four of the seven contributors, and one of the signatories, Khlebnikov, did not participate in its writing. Livshits and Nikolai Burliuk were not in Moscow, so their signatures were not there. Livshits makes it clear that he would not have signed it anyway, and his refusal was based on grounds other than that, as a soldier, he could not afford at that time to take part in controversial enterprises. Even Livshits was unable to determine (as set forth in his memoirs) who was the actual author of the manifesto, but he recognized in it one of his own phrases used in a conversation with Mayakovsky. "A Slap" was probably written by David Burliuk, Kruchenykh, and Mayakovsky[24] together in November or December, 1912, in the Romanovka Hotel in Moscow, where they spent their evenings. The recently married Burliuk lived there with his wife, a student of music, because there one could practice voice or instruments from 9 a.m. to 11 p.m. (and so the hotel was full of students from the Conservatory). Here is the complete text of the manifesto:

> To the readers of our New First Unexpected:
>
> Only *we are the face of our Time*. The horn of time trumpets through us in the art of the word.
> The past is crowded. The Academy and Pushkin are more incomprehensible than hieroglyphics.
> Throw Pushkin, Dostoyevsky, Tolstoy, et al, et al, over-

board from the Ship of Modernity.

He who does not forget his first love will not recognize his last.

But who is so gullible as to direct his last love toward the perfumed lechery of a Balmont? Does it reflect the virile soul of today?

Who is so cowardly as to be afraid to strip the warrior Bryusov of the paper armor he wears over his black tuxedo? Is the dawn of an undiscovered beauty seen there?

Wash your hands, you who touched the filthy slime of the books written by all those innumerable Leonid Andreyevs.

All those Maxim Gorkys, Kuprins, Bloks, Sologubs, Remizovs, Averchenkos, Chernyis, Kuzmins, Bunins, etc., etc. need only a dacha on a river. Tailors are rewarded by destiny in this way.

We look at their nothingness from the heights of skyscrapers! . . .

We decree that the poets' *rights* be honored:

1) to enlarge vocabulary in its scope with arbitrary and derivative words (creation of new words).
2) to feel an insurmountable hatred for the language existing before them.
3) to push aside in horror from our proud brow the wreath of dirt-cheap fame, which you have fashioned from bathhouse venik's ["swishes"].
4) to stand on the solid block of the word "we" amid the sea of boos and indignation.

And if for the time being even our lines are still marked with dirty stigmas of your "common sense" and "good taste," there tremble on them for the first time the summer lightnings of the New-Coming Beauty of the Self-sufficient (self-centered) Word.

Moscow, 1912, December
D. Burliuk, Alexander Kruchenykh[25]
V. Mayakovsky, Victor Khlebnikov

As a polemical work, the manifesto was effective. The attacks on the popular writers of the day drew the attention of literary circles and of the press, though it does not seem that any of the victims felt offended. The appeal to discard the classics created an even greater sensation, and it has never been forgotten. Both points were purely tactical and did not express the real ideas of the writers. Most of them were far from actually rejecting Pushkin, and they were on good terms with some of the attacked contemporaries. And when in 1915 Maxim Gorky publicly endorsed some of the leading futurists, the attitude shown by them was that of almost servile gratitude rather than of "pushing aside with horror." Strictly speaking, only Kruchenykh, in the overwhelming majority of his subsequent works, lived up to the declaration of "hatred for the language existing before them," as well as to the professed rejection of common sense and good taste. On the other hand, the promise to stand on the solid block of the word "we" (if one is to understand it as the intention to stick together as fellow futurists) has been, on the whole, kept even during times of adversity. As far as the positive program of the manifesto is concerned, it is vague and insufficient, betraying the fact that the writers were unsure of their purpose. Creation of new words was not enough for aesthetic foundations of a movement; moreover, only Khlebnikov actually practiced it to some extent (not to speak of Igor Severyanin who was not a Hylaean). The mention of the "self-centered word" (which also could be translated as "autotelic") was unfortunately only a mention.

The rest of *A Slap* was a letdown in the sense that it contained no "skyscrapers," some of the works being as passé as they could be, as far as subject matter was concerned. But, unlike *Sadok sudei*, the quality of the material presented was consistently good. The book begins with, and gives the largest amount of space to, Khlebnikov. Eight of his short poems are printed (under a wrong heading), and most of them are veritable gems, especially the semiabstract "Bobeobi," perfect in its sound painting. Among more sizable works, one should single out "Devii bog" ("The Maidens' God"), a dramatic work set in pagan Russia. In this play, which is marked by anachronisms, different levels of action are mixed. Then there are "I and E," Khlebnikov's primitivistic masterpiece, and "Pamyatnik" ("The Monument"), perhaps artistically the most successful expression of his nationalism. "Pesn miryazya" ("The Song of the

Peacer") should be mentioned, too, as Khlebnikov's most typical piece of neologistic prose.

Benedict Livshits is represented in *A Slap* by six poems printed in his second collection of verse, *Volchye solntse* ("The Sun of the Wolves"). They are full of allusions, exquisite artificiality, and restrained beauty, some of them resembling Rimbaud's works. After reading Khlebnikov, one cannot help noticing Livshits' non-Russian sound (this was also one of the characteristic features of much Russian Symbolist poetry). The most arresting piece by Livshits is his "People in Landscape," whose title was taken by the poet from one of Leger's paintings. Consisting of three short chapters written in prose, its aim is "a cubist shaping of the verbal mass,"[26] and it represents an attempt to create a much more sophisticated futurist prose than that exemplified by Kruchenykh's *Worldbackwards*. Typical of Livshits are the lack of predicates, unusual use of adverbs and prepositions, and words placed together in an alogical way.

Nikolai Burliuk showed himself in *A Slap* exclusively as a prose writer. There is a pleasant strangeness (as well as some influence of Khlebnikov and Guro) in his three pieces, but they are neither cubistic nor primitivistic, but rather impressionistic. In "Smert legkomyslennogo molodogo cheloveka" ("Death of a Frivolous Young Man"), the hero takes poison and dies; but, after crossing Lethe with Charon, he finds that Hades has been abolished. "Tishina Ellady" ("The Stillness of Hellas") a piece of lyric prose describing the Black Sea region (i.e., Hylaea). Autobiographical elements can be seen in the description of a childhood on a country estate in "Solnechnyi dom" ("A Sunny House") which develops into a fantasy about the mysterious forces that conquer one room of the house after another. David Burliuk's several poems united under the title "Sadovnik" ("The-gardener") show a firmer hand and the same old inability to make his points clearly.

Vasily Kandinsky's participation in *A Slap* adds special interest to this book although the futurists themselves later described it as an accident.[27] His four little sketches in prose are the Russian originals of some of his writings published in Munich in German under the title *Klänge*. They are written in an impressionistic manner and show Kandinsky, at that time, at least, a better prose writer than Nikolai Burliuk, even if Livshits called the latter's prose in *A Slap* "delightful."

Kruchenykh made his debut as a member of the group with an interesting primitivist poem, written in a kind of trochee which later gives way to rhymed prose, with a suggestion of a plot involving an officer and the redheaded Polya. The poem is printed without punctuation or capital letters, and contains words incorrectly stressed (glázami) which is one of Kruchenykh's trademarks. At the end there is the author's note to the effect that the events in the poem are not related in their chronological sequence, but in the order 3-1-2. Another debut proved later to be of the greatest historical importance because the name of the poet was Vladimir Mayakovsky. His two short poems, "Noch" ("Night") and "Utro" ("Morning"), with their colorful urbanism and anthropomorphism, are a strange and dissonant note in this rather peaceful book, for Mayakovsky's thunderous voice can already be heard in them. Their dynamism reminds one of Italian futurism, rather than, to quote Khlebnikov, the "pure Slavic element in its golden, linden tree quality."[28]

A Slap concludes with four essays. The first two, wrongly attributed to Nikolai Burliuk, are actually by David. "Kubizm," written in a deliberately disorganized fashion, with capital letters in the wrong places, contains both long-winded, impressionistic passages, which remind one of the worst excesses of symbolist criticism, and excellent professional observations. Painting, says Burliuk, has become an art only in the twentieth century, because it is now an aim in itself. Earlier painting knew only line and color; the new painting has discovered surface and texture. Cezanne is declared the father of cubism, and cubism is defined as "understanding of everything we see only as a series of certain cuts through various flat surfaces." He also speaks of "free drawing" and sees the best examples of it in children's drawings, as well as in Kandinsky and Larionov; in poetry, its equivalent is free verse, the best example of which Burliuk finds in Khlebnikov. In both articles, Burliuk uses generously the terms *sdvig* ("shift, dislocation") and *faktura* ("texture"), which were to become also the favorite words of futurist literary criticism. The second article, "Faktura," is written in fanciful, lyric prose which alternates with dry and specific outlines. In content it ranges from attacks on traditional art criticism (with the artist and art historian Alexander Benois serving as Burliuk's usual whipping boy) to a highly detailed classification of picture surfaces, and subtle observations about the textures of paintings by Monet, Cezanne, and some Russian contemporaries. Khlebnikov's "Obrazchik slovonovshestv v yazyke" ("A Sample of Neologisms") demonstrates the first premise of the manifesto. *A Slap* concludes with Khlebnikov's earlier prediction of the fall of an empire in

1917. This prediction had so impressed Burliuk that he placed it at the end of the book in the form of a simple list of names and dates.[29]

(Perhaps to confound future bibliographers, the Hylaeans, in February, 1913, published in Moscow a leaflet also entitled *A Slap in the Face of Public Taste*. It echoes the main tenets of the miscellany manifesto, but, on the whole, differs widely from its famous predecessor. In the leaflet the authors castigate the leaders of Russian literature for not having recognized Khlebnikov as a genius in 1908 (sic), after the publication of *Sadok sudei*. They attack the leading journalists of the day, who mistook the Hylaeans for "decadents," and describe the group around Khlebnikov as people who are united in their rejection of the word as a means and their glorification of the self-sufficient word, though each goes his own artistic or literary way. Instead of signatures, the leaflet, which also contained some poetry by Mayakovsky, ends with a photograph of Mayakovsky, Khlebnikov, David and Nikolai Burliuk, and both publishers of the Hylaeans, Kuzmin and Dolinsky.)

Simultaneously with *A Slap*, Burliuk started collecting material for another joint publication to be printed in St. Petersburg by Guro and Matyushin. To emphasize continuity in the development of the movement, it was decided to call the book *Sadok sudei II*, but the name of the group, as in the first *Sadok sudei*, was not identified, because Guro was against using the word "Hylaea." With her northern background (Finland and St. Petersburg), she was not impressed by the classical connotations of that southern Russian area. The book appeared in February, 1913, with a cover only slightly reminiscent of the wallpaper on which the first volume had been printed. It was illustrated not only by Guro and Matyushin themselves and by Vladimir and David Burliuk, but also by Larionov and Goncharova who, despite their break with the group, participated in a Hylaean venture, but for the last tune. Myasoyedov and Gei, two minor participants in the first *Sadok sudei*, were not among the contributors this time; and particularly conspicuous was the absence of one of the group's "stars," Vasily Kamensky, who, still bitter about the failure of his first novel, *The Mud Hut*, was nursing his wounds in the seclusion of his farm.

The most important single piece in *Sadok sudei II* is its untitled manifesto which opens the book, as in *A Slap*. Although it never received as much publicity as the latter, it is in a way more interesting because it tries, for the first time, to provide the movement with a specific and detailed constructive program. Yet, it lacks the unity and thrust of the manifesto that opened *A Slap*. On the whole, it is also too diffuse, being an eclectic combination of the favorite ideas of individual group members, rather than an attempt to set forth basic tenets common to them all. It is also confusing, not only because of the clumsy use of scholastic terminology, which in 1913 was rudimentary, but also because of the wrong claims and contradictory statements that characterize it. At the beginning of the manifesto, which, surprisingly, does not contain any attacks on literary enemies, there is the rather highhanded declaration that all the principles outlined there had been fully expressed in the first *Sadok sudei*, which the authors must have known to be false because the first *Sadok sudei* was a very shy and inept attempt to create a "new art." The formative stage is said to be past, and what was born in 1908 (sic) is now open to development by "those who have no new tasks." Thus the manifesto's authors strike the pose of adults far ahead of the children who come behind and are still busy repeating the discoveries of their predecessors, though they never make clear what new tasks lay ahead. From the rest of the manifesto, which enumerates in detail the achievements of the group, it becomes clear that theory is once again marching ahead of practice. One obscure statement in the introductory part deserves special attention. It speaks rather inarticulately about "having given a start" (*vydvinuv*) to the "formerly notorious" (*ranee preslovutykh*) and wealthy futurists. The reference is to the St. Petersburg group of ego-futurists, who at exactly this time clearly turned to verbal experimentation and thus became rivals of the Hylaeans. It is amusing to see that someone else is called "futurist" by people who were themselves to become (for everyone else) *the* Russian futurists. The "new principles of creation," which occupy the rest of the manifesto, are enumerated and discussed briefly below.

1. "We have ceased to look at word formation and word pronunciation according to grammar rules, beginning to see in letters only the determinants of speech. We have shaken syntax loose." The author of these words was Khlebnikov. Despite some confusing parts (e.g., mixing pronunciation and grammar) and questionable terminology ("letters"), which may make modern linguists wince, this is a reasonably accurate statement of what Khlebnikov himself tried to or did accomplish; Livshits, who made his own effort to "shake syntax loose" in *A Slap*, was in complete agreement.

2. "We have begun *to attach meaning to words according to their graphic and phonic characteristics*" seemed like a good program for any consistent futurism.

3. "The role of prefixes and suffixes has become clear to us" is another statement that Khlebnikov could have made about himself.

4. "In the name of the freedom of personal chance [*svoboda lichnogo sluchaya*], we reject orthography." This principle was fully demonstrated by Kruchenykh in his mimeographed publications.

5. "We characterize nouns not only by adjectives (as was chiefly done before us), but also by other parts of speech, as well as by individual letters and numbers:

a) considering corrections [*pomarki*] and the vignettes of creative expectation inseparable parts of a work,

b) deeming that the handwriting is an ingredient [*sostavlyayushchaya*] of a poetic impulse,

c) therefore, we have printed in Moscow 'self-written' books (of autographs)." This lengthy paragraph obviously refers to Kruchenykh's publications.[30]

6. "We have abolished punctuation, which for the first time brings the role of the verbal mass consciously to the fore." Livshits liked this one, and it is certainly a fascinating explanation of what the Hylaeans actually did, but they were never consistent in such efforts, nor was the whole idea so new.

7. "We think of vowels as space and time (the character of direction); consonants are color, sound, smell." Only a few years later David Burliuk expressed the same ideas in a poem. Khlebnikov's experiments with consonants were contained in "Bobeobi," printed in *A Slap*.

8. "We have smashed rhythms. Khlebnikov brought the poetic cadence [*razmer*] of the living conversational word. We have ceased to look for meters in textbooks; every new turn of movement gives birth to a new and free rhythm for a poet." Khlebnikov did introduce conversational rhythms, but so did his symbolist teacher, Mikhail Kuzmin. Besides, Khlebnikov's main efforts were concentrated on something else, namely, on mixing identifiable meters in adjacent lines or within a line. Only after the Revolution did he begin to practice free verse consistently. The Mayakovsky revolution in Russian metrics also was to come later. Burliuk could never really break with the "textbook meters"; Livshits never even tried.

9. "The front rhyme (David Burliuk), the middle and reversed rhymes (Mayakovsky) have been worked out by us." "Worked out" is a cautious term, and the authors probably were afraid of claiming the invention of these kinds of rhyme because many of them were used before by the symbolists.

10. "The poet's justification is in the richness of his vocabulary." This statement refers not only to Khlebnikov's neologisms, but to the futurists' general tendency to introduce regional and unusual words in their writings.

11. "We consider the word a creator of myth; the word, when dying, gives birth to a myth and vice versa." This point, hardly original, was proposed by Nikolai Burliuk, who was seconded by Livshits. Livshits realized that the statement smacked of Potebnya's philological theories, but thought it necessary "to tie a scholarly theory, directed toward the sources of human existence, to the artistic practice of today."[31]

12. "We are obsessed with new themes: futility, meaninglessness, and the mystery of a power-hungry mediocrity were glorified by us." This point by Kruchenykh was particularly resented by Livshits.

13. "We despise fame; we experience feelings that did not exist before us." Though Livshits attributes this point to Kruchenykh, it is actually a repetition of what was said before in the manifesto, *A Slap*. The document ends with the words, "We are new people of new life"; and there follow the signatures of D. Burliuk, Guro, N. Burliuk, Mayakovsky, Nizen, Khlebnikov, Livshits, and Kruchenykh.

Though Livshits signed the manifesto, he did not like its confusion and heterogeneity, for which he blamed David Burliuk. But it was inevitable, for each of the members was already beginning to acquire his own poetic technique, whose details might not have been shared by the rest. For this reason, the Hylaeans dropped all aesthetic subtleties in the next joint manifesto (in *Roaring Parnassus*) and concentrated on offending the rest of contemporary literature, a familiar method used with great success in *A Slap*.

Other than the manifesto, there was little that was new in *Sadok sudei II*. Livshits, disillusioned by the manifesto, gave for the book only a few poems, which were written soon after his first book of verse and which he himself considered "academic." Khlebnikov, as usual, was the main attraction with his two longer poems, both written in a primitivistic manner. "The End of Atlantis" was somber and restrained, almost classical in its texture, whereas "A Shaman and Venus" was built on absurdity and travesty. There was also a delightful exercise in infantilistic romanticism in "Maria Vetsera," a poem about the famous Mayerling tragedy; "Krymskoe" ("Crimean"), a free verse poem written as an exercise in intricate rhymes, mostly homonymic; a few exercises in neologism, similar to the laughter poem, and a short poem-palindrome, Khlebnikov's first attempt to appropriate the technique he would perfect in 1920 to produce his 408-line palindromic masterpiece, "Razin." The short essay, "O brodnikakh" ("On Roamers"), which followed was a historical sketch about ancient Slavs containing some etymological ideas. Contrary to the identification in the book, it was not by David Burliuk, but also by Khlebnikov. The old-fashioned diction, melody, and metrics of the fourteen poems, however, indicate they are indisputably the work of David Burliuk; but this time Burliuk tried very hard to appear as radical and experimental in other aspects of his verse as possible. In "Opus 29" (Burliuk continued here, as elsewhere, the count of his poems in this way, beginning with the first *Sadok sudei*, for instance, he not only uses the sound "s" in abundance, but tells the reader about it in a footnote. He also introduced the device of printing a few words in a poem in a larger print size, explaining this in another footnote as "leading words" (*leitslova*). But such devices were only a later touching-up of poems written mostly between 1908 and 1910, which explains why some of them are clearly impressionistic (e.g., "Opus 29" and "Opus 33"). Two later poems, however, show Burliuk's experiment of stringing words in an alogical manner,[32] similar to what Kruchenykh did a few pages later and, in a much subtler way, to what Livshits tried in his "People in a Landscape." Here, as an example, is Burliuk's "Opus 38," written in 1912:

Temnyi zloba golovatyi
Sero glazoe pila
Utomlennyi rodila
Zvezd zhelatelnoe laty

As to Nikolai Burliuk, he continued here to develop further his impressionistic manner in the two prose miniatures, "Sbezhavshie muzy" ("The Muses Who Fled"), about the Muses who vanished from a picture, and his first real artistic achievement, "Polunochnyi ogon" ("Midnight Fire"). In this story the protagonist arrives home and finds a letter with an oak leaf enclosed. During the night he is awakened by a noise in the shower and discovers there a young stranger with closed eyes. Fire approaches the youth and, through water, devours him, while he is transformed into an oak leaf. Less original and still very much in the symbolist tradition are several poems by Nikolai Burliuk, but they are appealing in their quiet modesty. Nikolai Burliuk was probably the only group member who entered neither the area of primitivism nor that of verbal experimentation, but stuck to his impressionism. On the other hand, Kruchenykh seems in *Sadok sudei II* to have adopted completely the new, abstract or semiabstract manner. His poems, printed under the general title "Myatezh v snegu" ("Rebellion in Snow") and subtitled "Words with Someone Else's Bellies," begin with four and a half lines of words, invented, distorted, or, sometimes, taken from the existing Russian lexicon, all printed without punctuation (except a comma after the first word).[33] The next poem is vertical in that nearly every word occupies a separate line, there being almost no logical connection between them. In one poem, several lines end in capital vowel letters which are not parts of words. Much of *Sadok sudei II*'s space is given to Guro's prose which, after her death, was to become part of her *The Baby Camels of the Sky*. Her sister, E. Nizen, is represented by one prose work, "Pyatna" ("Spots"), built on a stream-of-consciousness technique. A curious finale to the book are the two poems written by a thirteen-year-old girl, Militsa, from the Ukraine. Khlebnikov virtually forced the editors to print these and even withdrew one of his own poems to give space to the girl. These examples of authentic primitivism must have appealed to him, but even dearer to his nationalistic heart must have been the beginning of the first of the poems:

> I want to die,
> And in Russian soil
> They will bury me.
> I'll never study French,
> I won't look into a German book.

In March, 1913, the Hylaeans again appeared in print as a group, scarcely giving their reading audience time for a breather. This time they appeared as an autonomous section of the group of the St. Petersburg avant-garde known as the Union of Youth.[34] Formed at the beginning of 1910, this group had held its first exhibition in March of that year. Sponsored by a wealthy patron of the arts, L. Zheverzheyev, the group had a less pronounced artistic profile than either Donkey's Tail or Jack of Diamonds. Nor could it boast the same consistency of achievement. Among the Union of Youth, only Olga Rozanova and Pavel Filonov could be considered first-rate artists. Nevertheless, they fought for the ideals of the "new art," however vaguely understood. They popularized the recent trends of art in Western Europe and tried to go beyond European borders and discover new areas in Oriental and African art. David Burliuk was in touch with them from the very beginning, participating in their exhibitions and public lectures. The alliance that he engineered between the Union of Youth and his Hylaea lasted until December, 1913, soon after which the Union of Youth dissolved.

In 1912, the Union of Youth began to publish a magazine, *Soyuz molodezhi* ("Union of Youth"), which printed not only articles on art, but also translations of Chinese poetry. In its second issue, two manifestos of the Italian futurist artists were printed. The Hylaeans found a place in the publication's third issue, and their mention on the title page marked the first time they publicly called themselves "Hylaea." The preface to this third issue announced the creation of an autonomous section, "Hylaea," within the Union of Youth and stated that the time had come for a union of artists and poets in general. The poetry of the Hylaeans was referred to as that of the most essential and perceptive poets. There was also an enumeration of rather vague points uniting the two organizations: (1) the definition of the philosophically beautiful; (2) the establishment of a difference between the creator and the cospectator [*soglyadatai*]; and (3) the fight against automatism and temporality [*mekhanistichnost i vremennost*]. These first three points were followed by three points "which unite as well as separate": (1) the extension of the evaluation of the beautiful beyond the limits of consciousness (the principle of relativity); (2) the acceptance of the theory of knowledge as a criterion; and (3) the unity of the so-called material.

The third issue of *Union of Youth* was divided into two parts, and the first part was devoted to essays on the arts. Among these, the following are of interest: Avgust Ballyer's polemics with *Apollon* entitled "Apollon budnichnyi i Apollon chernyavyi" ("The Everyday Apollo and the Negritudinous Apollo"); "Osnovy novogo tvorchestva" ("The Foundations of the New Art") by O. Rozanova; and M. V. Matyushin's synopsis of *Du cubisme* by Gleizes and Metzinger intermingled with long quotations from Peter Ouspensky's *Tertium Organum*. Two Hylaeans also contributed essays. Nikolai Burliuk wrote the essay "Vladimir Davidovich Burliuk," in which he mentions his brother's name only once—in the last paragraph—devoting the rest of his work to a discussion of Vladimir's aesthetics. Khlebnikov is represented here by a shortened version of his *Teacher and Pupil*, published earlier in book form, and by another dialogue, "Razgovor dvukh osob" ("A Conversation between Two Personages"), which attacks Immanuel Kant and tries to demonstrate the relationships between word and number. The second part of the magazine contains the verse of the Hylaean poets. David Burliuk is represented by two poems; his brother Nikolai, by six, most of which are among his best (see especially "Πάντα ρέι" and "Babochki v kolodtse" ["Butterflies in a Well"]); and Livshits, by three. Among Kruchenykh's four poems, two deserve attention. "Tyanut konei" ("Horses Are Pulled") is essentially a typographical poem with most letters being uppercase; there are some curious anticipations of e.e. cummings' devices as, for example, in printing the word *zazhatyi* ("clamped") as *zAZHAtyi*. The second poem, which describes the pleasure of lying on the ground next to a pig, was to become a favorite source of quotations for critics of futurism. Guro printed only one short, impressionistic sketch, "Shchebet vesennikh" ("Chirping of Springtime [creatures]"), and Khlebnikov is represented as a poet by his magnificent tour de force, "Voina smert" ("The War, the Death"), his only long poem built on neologisms.

Also in March, 1913, Kuzmin and Dolinsky published another futurist miscellany, *Trebnik troikh* ("The Missal of the Three"). The title is a triumph of alliteration over meaning, because there are four participants in this book, even if one does not count its illustrators, Vladimir and Nadezhda Burliuk and V. Tatlin. These four are Khlebnikov, Mayakovsky, and David and Nikolai Burliuk, with Mayakovsky and David Burliuk contributing illustrations as well as poems. The appearance of the book is rather conservative with the title printed on a white label pasted on the gray cover and each poem printed on a separate page in clear print. There are portraits of Khlebnikov, Mayakovsky, and all Burliuks, including Vladimir. *The Missal of the Three* differs from all previous futurist joint publications in that it contains neither articles nor prose. Its aim is to present pure poetic achievement, and in this it succeeds. In previous publications, Khlebnikov was usually represented by his longer works; here for the first time he could be seen as a master of the miniature fragment, and there are twenty-five of these in *The Missal*. Later, scholarly editors had difficulties in deciding which of these were finished products and which were just sketches for future works, and they accused the first publisher, David Burliuk, and one another of confusing these two categories. In the Soviet five-volume edition of Khlebnikov's works, some of the best poems were, therefore, relegated to the back of a volume. It is true that Burliuk, to put it mildly, was not very scholarly when he published Khlebnikov at this or any other time. Nevertheless, the selection in *The Missal* is very good, and the majority of the poems are gems, so that one suspects that, for once, Burliuk acted with the author's consent. Furthermore, scholars have always maintained that it is hard to draw a line between Khlebnikov's finished and unfinished works; and more than once the author himself incorporated an earlier, finished poem into a later, longer and more complex work. Most of Khlebnikov's poems in *The Missal* are built on, or contain, neologisms, and many are perfect in what can be paradoxically described as their transparent obscurity. Even some of the mere enumerations of neologisms printed one under another are successful poems. Especially ingenious is a list of the names of dramatis personae from some imaginary Russian tragedy (which could have been written by Sumarokov, for example): Negava, Sluzhava, Belynya, Bystrets, Umnets, Vlad, Sladyka. Here the names express the qualities or positions of the characters in a true eighteenth-century manner, and one even begins to distinguish the vague outline of the plot behind them.

As to Mayakovsky, his urbanist cubism was never better presented than in *The Missal*. Later he made changes in some of these poems, but not all of them were improvements. For instance, his well-known "Iz ulitsy v ulitsu" ("From One Street to Another"), as printed here,[35] reads like a succession of five shorter poems, and I think some readers would prefer it in this form. It is also interesting to note that in this early version of the poem, which later received the title "Vyveskam" ("To the Signboards"), there is a first example of compound rhyme, which later became Mayakovsky's trademark (*parche ven: kharcheven*).

The most fascinating thing about *The Missal* is that the poetry of Nikolai and David Burliuk which it contains is practically on the same level as that of their colleagues. Nikolai Burliuk shows in his fifteen poems (some of them reprints) that he has grown into a mature minor poet with varied artistic devices, which only maliciously could be described as eclecticism. To look in his work for the familiar "futurist" features, such as loud tone, coarse imagery, and radical verbal experiment, would lead to disappointment. Often he reminds one of Khlebnikov, especially in his short, four-line sketches, but he does not use neologisms. He may mix archaisms and poeticisms with "low" diction (*K lanitam klonitsya koryavyi palets*), but he never stresses this device. In fact, he sometimes seems an Acmeist with occasional eccentricities; and one is almost tempted to call him an Acmeist among futurists who would prefer to appear as a futurist among Acmeists. Actually, though, he belongs to no party, and it is no accident that in one of these poems he mentions the "soul of a dissenter" (*dusha inovertsa*). He is a quiet and independent soul who goes his own way. It is easy to imagine the following little poem in the hands of another futurist (or a postrevolutionary imagist): it would be defiant and involved. Nikolai Burliuk makes it almost classical:

Nad stepyu krysh
I stadom trub
Plyvet luny
Sozhzhennyi trup

(Over the steppe of roofs
And the herd of stacks
There floats
the burnt cadaver of the moon)

It is also necessary to note the beginning of the futurists' shift toward the Orient in his first poem, which ends with the words:

Vo mne ariitsa golos smolk
Ya vizhu minarety Kryma

(The Aryan's voice is silent in me.
I see the minarets of Crimea)

Much more amazing is the selection that David Burliuk printed in *The Missal*. Nothing in his previous publications (or his later ones, for that matter) prepares us for the consistently high quality displayed in this book. David Burliuk is often a provincial who can hardly camouflage his old-fashioned poetic culture with superdaring "innovations," who drowns in the banal while trying to be original; an artist who clumsily applies the devices of his painting to verse without noticing that this transferal does not save the situation; a versifier who thinks that a cerebral rhyme he has just invented or a shocking image suffices to make his poem avant-garde. But in *The Missal* Burliuk, for once, succeeds both rhythmically and stylistically. There is an energetic stubbornness in many of his poems here, but even the autumnal ones are full of convincing strangeness. There is not a single superfluous word in his slightly primitivistic "Zakat malyar shirokoi kistyu"; the four-line "Veshchatel' tainogo soyuza" is worthy of a Khlebnikov; and his little poem about "that flea of the swamps, the frog," is excellent. None of the strain often noted in Burliuk's work is present in his exercise in rhymed beginnings of lines or in other rhyming tours de force. Only four of the sixteen poems fall short of this surprising level of poetic achievement.

If in *A Slap* the Russian futurists suddenly and violently attacked the present and the past of Russian literature, if in *Sadok sudei II* they made a claim at being the possessors of a new aesthetics and in Union of Youth they demonstrated that they had allies in Russian art, in *The Missal* they showed they could create first-rate poetry of consistently high quality.

Endnotes

1 This text was originally published as the second chapter of Markov, *Russian Futurism*, 29-60.

2 The year 1911 is printed on the cover of the book. "Predates" were widespread at the time, so that a book very often actually appeared during the last months of the year preceding the one indicated on its cover. Publishers followed this practice to make a book look new longer.

3 Kamensky, *Put' èntuziasta*, p. 124.

4 Such mixing of prose and poetry was not very original, however, because even in Russian literature one can find precedents such as Karolina Pavlova's *Dvojnaja žizn'* (1848) and other examples. In western European literature it was, of course, a time-honored tradition with well-known examples extending from *Aucassin et Nicolette* and *La Vita Nuova* to *Heinrich von Ofterdingen*.

5 This study, coming as it did after Burliuk's participation in so many modern art exhibits, was a necessary bow to academic art in order to obtain a diploma, without which

making money through painting would have been difficult, if not impossible.

6 Aleksandra Aleksandrovna Èkster, Léger's pupil, frequently lived abroad, and her art evolved from impressionism to cubism. She took an active part in Russian avant-garde painting. After the Revolution, she was connected with the Kamernyi Theater in Moscow.

7 The suggestion of V. Pjast (*Vstreči*, p. 246) that Gileja derives from gil' ("nonsense") belongs itself to the category of gil'.

8 PS, pp. 29, 43, 26. [Livšic, *Polutoraglazyi strelec*]

9 Ibid., p. 40.

10 Livšic, *Gileja* (New York, 1931), p. 8.

11 PS, p. 57. [Livšic, *Polutoraglazyi strelec*]

12 Kulbin, "Svobodnoe iskusstvo kak osnova žizni", *Studija impressionistov*, 1910, p. 9.

13 Camilla Gray, *The Great Experiment: Russian Art, 1863-1922* (London: Thames and Hudson, 1962), p. 94.

14 A detailed analysis (and the Russian titles of the enumerated works) may be found in my *The Longer Poems of Velimir Khlebnikov*.

15 At the end of 1910 and the beginning of 1911, Izdebskij organized his second "Salon," which this time exhibited only the Russian avant-garde in Odessa and Nikolaev. Like the first "Salon," this exhibit brought financial losses to the organizer.

16 [Kručenyx], *15 let russkogo futurizma*, p. 57.

17 Ibid., 24.

18 S. Tret'jakov sees, however, in *Starinnaja ljubov'* "a pulling-up of the genteel album poetry's skirt" (*Buka russkoj literatury*, p. 5).

19 This edition, which boasted a new cover by Larionov, abandoned the "handwriting" method of the preceding versions and used typographical print of various shapes and sizes.

20 Lunev seems to have been Kručenyx's pseudonym for some of his collaborations with Khlebnikov, but he also used it later for work written by himself alone. In some instances this name is also found under the poems written by Khlebnikov alone. At any rate, the situation is complex. N. Khardziev considers all three Lunev poems to be Khlebnikov's (NP, p. 405), but Kruchenykh reprinted one of them under his own name in the later *Tè-li-lè*. [Xlebnikov, *Neizdannye proizvedenija*, 405]

21 Later, in *Sdvigologija*, p. 35, Kruchenykh saw a "menace" in the final line of the poem. In *Zaumnyi jazyk* i *Seifullinoj* . . . (p. 28), he described the poem as a "hollow and heavy series of sounds, having a Tartar tinge." Burliuk later (in *Kitovras*, no. 2, p. 4) distorted the first line into *dyrbulščol* and deciphered this line as *dyroj budet lico sčastlivyx oluxov*.

22 PS, p. 133. [Livšic, *Polutoraglazyi strelec*]

23 See PŽRF, p. 106. [*Futuristy*]

24 Kručenyx describes (in *Zverinec* [Moscow, 1930], pp. 13-14) some circumstances of the creation of the manifesto: "We wrote it for a long time, argued over every phrase, every word, and every letter." Kručenyx claims to be the author of the famous "throwing Puškin etc." phrase, but says that Majakovskij changed the original *brosit'* to *sbrosit'*. Otherwise, Majakovskij said, it could mean that the classics were on the ship by themselves, whereas *sbrosit'* would imply taking them to the ship by force and throwing them from it. Kručenyx contradicts some sources (Livšic) and claims that Xlebnikov was the author of some sentences (e.g., the one about the block of the word we and, strangely enough, the one containing the skyscrapers). Xlebnikov did not want to sign the manifesto if the offensive mention of his admired mentor, Kuzmin, was not re-

moved. A promise to him to do so was not fulfilled.

25 Kručenyx at first used Aleksandr as a part of his pen name (under the manifesto in *Poščečina*, and also in *Troe*), then dropped it and used his real first name, Aleksej, or the initial A. Occasionally he put Aleksandr in parentheses, after Aleksej (as in his *Deklaracija slova kak takovogo*).

26 PS, p. 50. [Livšic, *Polutoraglazyi strelec*]

27 Ibid., p. 128. I have been told that Kandinskij, in a letter to a newspaper, later protested against his inclusion in the book and called the whole thing "hooliganism."

28 SP, II, 7. [*Sobranie proizvedenij Velimira Xlebnikova*, volume II]

29 The reaction of the daily press to *Poščečina* was predictably either derisive or indignant. Reputable journals, however, decided not to react to the "hooliganism." Thus there was no review in *Apollon*, and *RM* [*Russkaja Mysl'*] waited until March, 1913 (i.e., fifteen months), before it decided to discuss the manifesto and the book. It is interesting that France spoke about *Poščečina* not much later, when *Mercure de France* ([Nov.—Dec, 1913], p. 202) was puzzled by the desire of some Russian poets to "biffer Pouchkine, sour le prétexte, assez inintelligent du rest, qu'on le trouve hieroglyphique et incomprehensible."

30 It may be appropriate here to mention that as early as 1910 Kul'bin exhibited samples of the handwriting of famous Russian writers and singers (for example, Chaliapin), and this part of the exhibit attracted larger crowds than the paintings.

31 PS, p. 139. [Livšic, *Polutoraglazyi strelec*]

32 In *Kitovras*, no. 2, p. 7, Burljuk calls such a method *mozaika nesoglasovannostej*.

33 Sergej Tret'jakov (*Buka russkoj literatury*, p. 5) was later to describe enthusiastically the initial words of the sequence (*sarča kroča*) as containing *parča* ("brocade"), *saryn'* ("gang"), *ryčat'* ("to roar"), and *krov'* ("blood"), "thrown together like a bold pattern in one carpet-like stroke."

34 About this alliance (as well as about the production of Majakovskij's tragedy, described in chap. 4), see the memoirs of L. Zeverzeev in *Majakovskomu: Sbornik vospominanij i statej* (Leningrad, 1940). Zeverzeev gives April as the month for the appearance of the third issue of the magazine.

35 It was printed earlier in the leaflet *Poščečina obščestvennomu vkusu*.

1a. Velimir Khlebnikov—A "Timid" Futurist[1]

Willem G. Weststeijn

Just like Marinetti's Italian Futurism, Russian Futurism was a "loud" movement, that is to say, the members of the movement tried to attract as much attention as possible by writing provocative manifestoes and organising meetings at which they deliberately shocked the public with their scandalous behaviour. Whereas Marinetti sang the praises of the new technology: fast cars and even airplanes, the Russian Futurists attacked the entire artistic tradition and everything that smacked of conventionality.

The Russian Futurist poets—Russian Futurism was predominantly a literary movement—were particularly opposed to their direct predecessors, the Symbolists. They loathed the aestheticism of Symbolist poetry, which aimed at beautiful, poetical words and sound harmony. The Futurists were anti-aesthetic. One of their slogans was that one had to write "as a truck in a drawing room". Instead of harmonious sound effects they preferred a cacophony of sounds and emphasized the poetic value of the complex Russian consonants such as the sh (ш), the ch (ч) and the shch (щ), which were taboo for the Symbolists. They also introduced into their poetry a new vocabulary: words from everyday language, vulgarisms and, particularly, neologisms: entirely new, non-existent words.

One of the first Futurist manifestoes was *A Slap in the Face of Public Taste* (Poshchochina obshchestvennomu vkusu), published in 1912.

> *We* alone are the *face* of *our* Time. Through us the horn of time blows in the art of the word.
>
> The past is too tight. The Academy and Pushkin are less intelligible than hieroglyphics.
>
> Throw Pushkin, Dostoyevsky, Tolstoy, *etc., etc.* overboard from the Ship of Modernity.
>
> (...)
>
> Wash your hands, which have touched the filthy slime

> of the books written by those countless Leonid Andreevs.
>
> All those Maxim Gorkys, Kuprins, Bloks, Sollogubs, Remizovs, Averchenkos, Chornys, Kuzmins, Bunins, etc. need only a dacha on the river. Such is the reward that fate gives to tailors.
>
> From the heights of skyscrapers we gaze at their insignificance!...
>
> We *order* that the poets' *rights* be revered:
>
> 1. To enlarge the *scope* of the poet's vocabulary with arbitrary and derivative words (Word-novelty).
>
> 2. To feel an insurmountable hatred for the language existing before their time.[2]

More even than by their manifestoes, the Futurists became notorious for the poetry evenings they organised and at which they read their works dressed up in vividly-colored jackets and with painted faces. With his impressive figure and stentorian voice that easily shouted down the most tumultuous public, Vladimir Mayakovsky was generally the heart and soul of these happenings, avidly supported by Aleksey Kruchenykh with his clownish acts. The latter wrote many of the Futurists' manifestoes and became the main theoretician of the movement.

There was, however, one Futurist who did not stand out at all in this turbulent atmosphere and tried to stay away from all of the upheaval and noisy public performances. This was the most original of them: Velimir Khlebnikov. Khlebnikov's timidity and often clumsy behaviour (when he recited from his own work, which seldom happened, he usually said after a few lines: "and so forth" and stopped reading) made him unsuitable to play the role of a "real" Futurist. That he, nevertheless, remained a member of the movement, is not due to himself, but to his fellow-Futurists, who considered him the greatest talent of their group and did not want to lose him for all the world. When Marinetti in 1914 visited Russia and rather condescendingly expressed his opinions on contemporary Russian art and literature, the Russian Futurists praised Khlebnikov and compared his role with that of Pushkin in the first half of the nineteenth and of Lomonosov in the eighteenth century. Mayakovsky wrote about Khlebnikov in an obituary after his death in 1922:

> Khlebnikov's fame as a poet is immeasurably less than his significance.
>
> Out of hundred people who have read him, fifty simply called him a hack, forty read them for pleasure, but were amazed that they did not find any satisfaction from it, and only ten (...) knew and loved this Columbus of new poetic continents, which are now peopled and cultivated by us.
>
> Khlebnikov is not a poet for consumers. You cannot read him. Khlebnikov is a poet for producers.[3]

Who was this poet, who was considered by some as a genius, the greatest Russian poet of the twentieth century, and by others as an unreadable idiot, whose work cannot be taken seriously?

Khlebnikov was born in 1885 in a village near the Southern Russian city of Astrakhan, where the river Volga flows out into the Caspian Sea. The poet always attached great importance to his birthplace, as it lay in a region in which East and West, the Asian and Slavic peoples met each other; Khlebnikov's interest in Asia and the Far East has left many traces in his work.

Khlebnikov descended from a typically Russian pre-Revolutionary intelligentsia milieu. His father was a teacher and an enthusiastic conservationist, one of the founders of a nature reserve near Astrakhan. He was a great ornithologist and a follower of Darwin and Tolstoy. His father's influence is clearly noticeable in Khlebnikov's preference for the natural sciences and his excellent knowledge of flora and fauna, in particular bird life. One of the interesting aspects of his poetical language is the creation in it of a special bird language, in which all kinds of bird songs and bird sounds are imitated. Khlebnikov's mother had studied history; she was a good narrator and stimulated the poet's early awakened interest in the past of the Slavic peoples.

When Khlebnikov was twelve years old the family moved to Kazan, like Astrakhan—a partially Asian city on the Volga. He became an excellent pupil at a grammar school, apparently thanks to his prodigious memory. His main interests were mathematics and Russian language and literature; moreover he showed artistic talent. After grammar school, Khlebnikov enrolled at the university as a student in the faculty of natural sciences. He read quite a lot, scientific but also philosophical and literary works, in particular the Symbolist poets. He started to write himself and sent some of his texts to Maksim Gorky, who commented on them.

Khlebnikov continued to write poetry when he moved to St. Petersburg in 1908. In St. Petersburg he also signed up at the university, studied biology, Sanskrit and Slavic languages and literatures, but never took a final examination. In 2011 he was removed from the university's register because he had not paid his tuition fees. He could not care less, as he had made his way in literary circles and was not interested at all in a university career.

Soon after his arrival in St. Petersburg Khlebnikov became a visitor of the so-called "Academy of Poetry", a weekly literary soirée in the house of the symbolist poet Vyacheslav Ivanov. Here, someone started calling him Velimir instead of Viktor (his real name) and Khlebnikov maintained this mythological-sounding pseudonymous first name for the rest of his life. Ivanov, one of the leading figures in the literature of that time, recognized the young poet's talent. Despite his support, Khlebnikov did not succeed in publishing his poems in the famous Symbolist literary journal *Apollon*, as its editor-in-chief did not appreciate them. After this refusal Khlebnikov definitely broke up with the Symbolists.

In the meantime, Khlebnikov had made contact with an entirely different group of poets. Already in 1908 Khlebnikov had shown his manuscripts to the poet Vasily Kamensky and he had chosen some of Khlebnikov's poems to be published in his journal *Spring* (Vesna). This publication gradually led to more contacts between Khlebnikov and all kinds of modernist poets and painters who had nothing to do with the literary establishment.

In the beginning of 1910 a number of these young poets and artists planned to make a joint illustrated publication. The book appeared under the title "A Trap for Judges" (Sadok sudei) and is generally considered as the beginning of Futurism in Russia. Apart from Khlebnikov and Kamensky, contributors to the book were the poet Elena Guro and the brothers Burlyuk, who, like many Futurists, were poets as well as professional painters.

"A Trap for Judges" was printed on wallpaper in a limited edition. In order to attract the attention of the literary world, the book was distributed among the guests of Ivanov's literary soirée: someone entered

Ivanov's cloakroom and simply put the books into the pockets of the coats that were hanging there. The book caused quite a stir for its striking appearance, its modernist illustrations and, not in the least, the "poems", poetic experiments that were quite different from the "usual" Symbolist poem.

One of the most striking experiments in the first year in which the Futurists manifested themselves as a group was Khlebnikov's famous "Incantation by Laughter" (Zaklyatie smechom), a poem that is built with words, both existing and new ones, that contain the root *laugh* (smekh):

Hlaha! Uthlofan, lauflings!
Hlaha! Ufhlofan, lauflings!
Who lawghen with lafe, who hlaehen lewchly,
Hlaha! Ufhlofan hlouly!
Hlaha! Hloufish lauflings lafe uf beloght lauchalorum!
Hlaha! Loufenish lauflings lafe, hlohan utlaufly!
Lawfen, lawfen,
Hloh, hlouh, hlou! Luifekin, luifekin,
Hlofeningum, hlofeningum.
Hlaha! Uthlofan, lauflings!
Hlaha! Ufhlofan, lauflings![4]

"A Trap for Judges" and other joint publications did not contain a manifesto, a general declaration of the new group in which the new ideas were enunciated. These manifestoes came only two years later, in 1912. At that time, the group around Kamensky and Khlebnikov had been supplemented by the enormously active Mayakovsky and Kruchenykh. They now called themselves Cubo-Futurists and by their actions and public appearances attracted much attention.

Khlebnikov was not a noisy bourgeois-shocking Futurist, but his contribution to Futurist *poetry* is of paramount importance. One of the starting-points of Russian Futurism was its emphasis on the word, the word as such, as the material with which the poet is working. Contrary to the Symbolists, who used words to describe some higher reality or a philosophical idea, the Futurists considered language itself as the source of poetry. Just as the abstract painters were not interested any more in imitating reality, but restricted themselves to their bare materials, color and line, the Futurist poets concentrated on *their* material: the word, letters and sounds from which the word is created. Hence, we find many experiments with words and sounds in Futurist poetry. The Futurists developed even a new language, which consisted of sounds and non-existing words. They called it *zaum* (literally "behind reason"), a language one cannot understand rationally, but only intuitively.

The unrivalled master of experimental poetical language was Khlebnikov. In the poetical word he discovered all kinds of new possibilities, by which he not only had a great influence on his fellow Futurists, but also on later generations of poets. His experiments with words and sounds are intriguing and surprising, as he succeeded in making real poetry with the aid of these experiments. Even his most experimental works have a poetic and aesthetic power, which cannot be said of all of the Futurist experimental poetry. An important reason for this is that Khlebnikov did not carry out his experiments merely for the sake of experiment, but because he was always looking for new meaning in language. In the words, in their structure, and in the relationship between words, he continuously discovered new, never before recognized, meaning. It makes his work difficult, but at the same time semantically rich and suggestive.

One of Khlebnikov's favorite devices was to create new words by connecting a word stem with new prefixes and suffixes. An example is the poem "Incantation by Laughter," in which a number of words are brought together that are derived from the stem "laugh." In the "covering" of these word stems Khlebnikov was very creative. He drafted for instance a large number of words for the world of aviation, which was a developing area of specialty in the beginning of the twentieth century and required many new words. All Khlebnikov's suggestions were built with the stem "fly" (let). For his neologisms Khlebnikov preferred Slavic word stems, not out of some kind of purism, but because he thought that the Slavic stems had much more "basic" meaning than foreign words. For that reason he called his own group of poets not Futurists (in Russian "futuristy"), but "Budetlyane" (containing the Russian future tense of "to be").

In Khlebnikov's poetry we also find many instances of poetic etymology: the suggestion that words that resemble each other in sound might be traced back to the same word stem and, therefore, have more or less similar meanings. One of Khlebnikov's examples—several times occurring in his work—is the combination of words with the stem "liud" (people) and "liub" (love). Khlebnikov suggested in poems that these words are semantically related. He expressed his visionary views on the future of mankind: at present still divided, one nation fighting the other, but forming one great brotherhood in the future.

Related to poetic etymology is the palindrome: a word or a sentence that can be read from left to right, but also vice versa. Using palindromes is usually only a bit of a trick, but Khlebnikov succeeded in making real poetry out of it. His tour de force is a long poem, *Razin*, that completely consists of palindromes. The figure of Razin, the famous Cossack free spirit, plays an important role in Khlebnikov's work. The poet often compared himself with him. Moreover, Razin contains Ra, the name of the Egyptian god of the sun, another character that frequently occurs in his work. Interestingly, the palindrome of Razin, "nizar" is the Russian name for someone who lives at the lower reaches of the Volga. Khlebnikov made a lot of all such correlations of sound and meaning.

That his experiments with poetical language were a very serious affair for him is demonstrated by the following story. It is taken from a book by the poet Benedikt Lifshits, who has written interesting memoirs about the Futurists and was a personal friend of Khlebnikov's.

> On the evening of "Lenten magic" I introduced him to a student of the theatre studio, Lelia Skalon. She captivated him immediately. He asked me repeatedly to help him meet her, but, for reasons which I don't recall, I didn't manage to fulfil his wish
>
> One morning he came to see me on Guliarnaia Street and declared that he had made up his mind to secure a meeting, but that he didn't know how to do it. I replied that the only way was to invite Lelia Skalon and her friend Lilia Iliashenko (who performed the role of *The Stranger*) to the Stray Dog;[5] but that for this, of course, a certain sum of money was necessary for supper and wine, money which neither he nor I had.
>
> Since he continued to insist and wouldn't take no for an answer, I suggested that he take my mackintosh and top hat to the pawnbroker and get a loan for them. He returned an hour later, completely dejected. They had of-

fered so little for the things that he hadn't thought it necessary to leave them in pawn.

We were gloomy and silent, trying to find a way out of the impasse.

Suddenly, Velimir's face lit up:

"Perhaps we could get some money from Gumilyov?"[6]

"Gumilyov? Why him?"

"Because he's not in pecuniary circumstances and he's our enemy."

"It's awkward to turn to someone who hasn't shaken hands since our manifesto."

"Never mind! First I'll tell him everything I think about his poetry and then I'll request money. He'll give it. I'll go to Tsarskoe right now, and you invite Lelia and Lilia to the Dog for tonight."

He disappeared, after putting on my ill-starred top hat for greater solemnity.

He returned towards evening apparently pleased with the outcome of his journey. Only Akhmatova who was present during the conversation with Gumilyov could say whether Khlebnikov carried out his intention to the full or not, but anyway he brought the money.

At the Stray Dog we took a table in the middle of the hall. Velimir couldn't take his eyes off the pretty student seated opposite him, and only now and then did he move his lips noiselessly. It fell to my lot to entertain the two friends which certainly didn't fit in with my plans because I had invited the girls only on Khlebnikov's insistence. Apart from that it was time to think about supper, but Velimir was still not taking steps in that direction.

I managed to whisper a few words to him. He rushed off to the bar. A minute later a mountain of sandwiches towered on the table and screened our opposite numbers from us. Khlebnikov had bought up all the sandwiches at the bar, but he hadn't had the sense to save any money for fruit and tea, much less for wine.

Growing bolder behind his screen, he at last decided to open his mouth. The facile mechanics of entertaining

> small talk was double-dutch to him. Faithful unto himself and understanding his mission quite differently, he spoke a monologue in which all the words were of the same root. In this "root-wording" he eulogized the object of his love, sounding rather like this:
>
> O skal
> Oskal
> Skal on
> Skalon.
>
> He didn't get to the end of his word-creative hymn because both girls burst out laughing. In their view Khlebnikov was a half-sane eccentric.
>
> Scarcely touching the refreshments—for the sake of which Velimir had gone out to Tsarskoe Selo and had wrangled with Gumilyov over the fates of Russian literature, Iliashenko and Skalon beat a hasty retreat from the Dog not even wishing to use us as escorts.
>
> I tucked into the sandwiches and looked at Khlebnikov frowning despondently in the corner. He was inconsolable and probably still did not understand the reason for his defeat.[7]

An interesting aspect of Khlebnikov's experiments with poetical language is that he connected sounds with fixed meanings. Particularly relevant for him was the first sound of a word, as according to him the first sound for the greater part determines the meaning of a word. He expounded on these ideas in one of his best known theoretical treatises, *Our Fundamentals* (Nasha osnova, 1920).

> Beyond-sense language (*zaum*) is based on two premises:
> 1. The initial consonant of a simple word governs all the rest—it commands the remaining letters.
> 2. Words that begin with an identical consonant share some identical meaning; it is as if they were drawn from various directions to a single point in the mind.
>
> Let us take the words *chasha* [cup] and *choboty* [a kind

> of boot]: the sound *ch* governs both words. If we make a list of words that begin with *ch—chulock* [stocking], *choboty* [a kind of boot], *chereviki* [high-heeled boots for women], *chuviak* [slipper], *chuni* [rope shoes: dial.], *chupaki* [felt boots], *chekhol* [underdress] and *chasha* [cup], *chara* [magic spell], *chan* [vat], *chelnok* [barque], *cherep* [skull], *chakhotka* [consumption], *chuchelo* [stuffed animal], then we observe that all these words coalesce at the point of the following image: whether we speak of a stocking [*chulok*] or a cup [*chasha*], in both instances the volume of one body [foot or water] fills up the emptiness of another body which serves as its surface. Whence magic spell [*chara*] as an enchanted casing or envelope that holds motionless the will of the thing enchanted—like water as far as the magic spell is concerned; whence also *chaiat'* [to expect], that is, to be a cup for water that is yet to come. Thus *ch* is not merely a sound, *ch* is a name, an indivisible unit of language.[8]

In an analogical way Khlebnikov determined the meaning of all the consonants. He was convinced that the alphabet of sounds or letters corresponded to an alphabet of the mind, a set of abstract notions that could be considered as universal categories. Having determined all the "basic meanings" it would be possible, he thought, to create a universal language, a language of the future that would unite mankind that was understandable for everybody.

Typical for Khlebnikov is that he wanted to create a language of the future by going back to the past: the basic meanings as they must have come into being in the protolanguage and since have left their traces in all the languages. Contrary to some other Futurists, he was not only focused on the future, but was highly interested in the past, in particular the distant past, the mythic history of the Slavic peoples. Khlebnikov's world is surprisingly extensive and comprehensive. Apart from visions of the future and half practical, half impossible projects for the future he incorporated Slavic and other mythologies into his poetry and also dealt with contemporary themes, such as the Second World War and the Revolution.

In the old Slavic world, the Russian empire of Kiev and the still earlier heathen periods of the Slavic peoples, Khlebnikov saw a way out of the problems and calamities of modern times. In one of his first longer poems, *Malusha's granddaughter* (Vnuchka Malushi, 1909), he placed in opposition old Russia, which had hardly been Christianized and was still full of heathen elements, to contemporary St. Petersburg. According to Khlebnikov, modern times lack what existed formerly: a direct relationship with nature and the surrounding world. For primitive man the objects in the world around him were charged with profound meaning. During the course of time, this understanding of the world has disappeared and Khlebnikov considered it his task as a poet to recreate the direct relation between man and his surroundings. With this in mind, he created new myths. We find such a modern myth, for example, in his long poem *The Crane* (Zhuravl', 1910), in which is given a grotesque, apocalyptic image of St. Petersburg. The dead objects of the city: factory chimneys, houses, bridges, become alive. Together they rise in revolt and contribute to the forming of an enormous bird, a crane, to which people are sacrificed. The symbolic implications are clear: the hoisting crane-bird denotes on the one hand destructive industry and technology, on the other nature, which regains its power and control of mankind.

Much of Khlebnikov's prerevolutionary work is about the distant past. This does not mean that he lived outside of his own time. On the contrary; the most important historical events that took place during his life have found a clear echo in his poetry, even if they are often mixed up with events from other periods and other nations. A profound impression on him was made by the Russian-Japanese war of 1904-1905, which was waged rather clumsily by the Russians. In Khlebnikov's poetry this war is described as an antithesis between the Slavic and the Eastern elements. He often invokes the martial Kievan princes from the beginning of the Russian empire, to whom even the mighty Byzantium succumbed.

When the First World War broke out Khlebnikov abandoned his belligerent tone, substituting it for a pacifistic attitude. He contributed to a number of antimilitaristic Futurist collections, which, however, did not mean that the Russian authorities left him alone. In 1916 he was drafted into the military and became a soldier in a reserve battalion. Used to his freedom and, moreover, being highly impractical—Khlebnikov did not have a fixed abode and led a wandering life, carrying along his manuscripts in a pillowcase—the disciplined life in the army was unbearable for him. "I am a dervish, a Yogi, a Martian, anything you want, but I am *not* a private in a reserve infantry regiment,"[9] he wrote in a letter to one of his friends. With great difficulty he succeeded in being admitted to a mental hospital, but when a committee declared him "normal," he was again assigned to an army unit.

This horrible experience of life as a soldier—the military discipline entirely destroyed his personal rhythm—once and for all changed Khlebnikov's ideas about war. Whereas formerly he associated war with courage and bravery, he now only connected it with death and destruction. War is a disaster that threatens mankind. In one of his poems, *War in a Mousetrap* (Voina v myshelovke, 1919), a compilation of a number of shorter poems he wrote in the years 1915-1917, war becomes a mythological being, a goddess of death, relentless in her lust for human lives. Mankind reverts to a state of savage barbarism; the war devours entire generations and brings doom and destruction.

> "Hey!" the wolf cries out in blood,
> "I eat the meat of strong young men!"
> and a mother says: "My sons are gone."
> But we are your elders! *We* decide.
>
> Anyway, young men are cheaper nowadays,
> no? Dirt-cheap, slop-cheap, coal-chute cheap!
> Pale apparition, scything our man crop,
> sinews all sunburnt, be proud of your work!
>
> "Young men dying, young men dead,"
> the city wails along its streets,
> wails like the barrow-boy hawking his birds—
> new feathers for all your cups![10]

Apart from the theme of war there occurs in *War in a Mousetrap* another theme: that of the revolution. Khlebnikov greeted the revolution, if only because it freed him from his disastrous military service. In his characteristic manner, he described the revolution not as a mere contemporary political and historical event, but as a universal transformation of the entire world, a world revolution with mythical dimensions.

When freedom comes, she comes naked
and fills our hearts with flowers.
We march in time to her music
and talk to the sky like a lover.

We are Freedom's fighters, we bang our fists
on our harsh, uncompromising armor:
"Now let the people rule themselves,
everywhere and forever!"[11]

Whereas this passage is a direct reaction to the Russian revolution of 1917, in other, later poems Khlebnikov develops his vision of the revolution and the future of mankind. We see this, for example, in the longer poem *Lightland* (Ladomir, 1920), one of his most accomplished works. In this poem the revolution is described as a purifying thunderstorm, an inevitable punishment for the exploiters of the people. However, Khlebnikov does not stop at the description of the present and the past. More important than the demolition of the old world is that at last the revolution has liberated mankind and enables it, armed with scientific knowledge, to become the creator of history, the organizer and master of the universe. In *Lightland* Khlebnikov paints a compelling picture of the future of mankind. In his description he shows a rock-solid belief in the development of technology, but at the same time connects this progress with old legends about animate nature. Only when the scientific principle develops in living nature, the "lad mira", the harmony of the world will be realized, so that even death will be vanquished.

Thinking about the fate of the world, its past and future, and the possibility to steer the world in the right direction, Khlebnikov developed some highly original ideas about time and history. Already early in his life he became convinced that important historical events did not occur randomly, but that there existed some underlying pattern. He spent a lot of time and energy to detect this pattern and believed that the distance in time between certain historical events, such as campaigns and naval battles, was subject to mathematical rules. One of his grandiose projects was to discover "the laws of time" and he made an immense number of calculations to succeed in this utopian, but mathematically implemented idea. The core of these calculations can be found in his *The Tables of Destiny* (Doski sud'by, 1922), which was published shortly before his death.

After the revolution Khlebnikov resumed his wandering life. In the thick of the civil war he lived some time in great poverty in Kharkov, twice suffered from typhus and several times fell into the hands of the Reds and the Whites, who in turn captured the city and immediately arrested the suspicious-looking Khlebnikov, who, of course, did not have any papers to identify himself. At the end of 1920 Khlebnikov succeeded in reaching Baku, where he joined the Red Army as a propagandist. The army was preparing for a campaign in Persia in order to start the revolution there and in the wake of the army Khlebnikov traveled to Persia. The months he was there were some of the happiest of his life. He became totally absorbed in the colorful Eastern world and wrote a number of his best poems, among which was the longer poem *The Gul-Mullahs's Trumpet* (Truba Gul' Mully, 1921-22). In his poems about Asia, his favorite idea about the unity of mankind is often expressed. All nations, religions and teachings are equal, as they are in all pages of the "one, the only book" of humanity.

> I have seen the black Vedas,
> the Koran and the Gospels
> and the book of the Mongols
> on their silken boards—
> all made of dust, of earth's ashes
> of the sweet-smelling dung
> that Kalmyk women use each morning for fuel—
> I have seen them go to the fire,
> lie down in a heap and vanish
> white as widows in clouds of smoke
> in order to hasten the coming
> of the One, the Only Book
> whose pages are enormous oceans
> flickering like the wings of a blue butterfly,
> and the silk thread marking the place
> where the reader rests his gaze
> is all the great rivers in a dark-blue flood:

Volga, where they sing the Razin songs at nighttime,
yellow Nile, where they worship the sun,
Yangtze-Kiang, oozing with people,
and mighty Mississippi, where the Yankees strut
in star-spangled trousers, yes, in pants
all covered with stars.
and Ganges, whose dark people are trees of the mind,
and Danube, white people in white shirts
whose whiteness is reflected in the water,
and Zambezi, whose people are blacker than boots,
and stormy Ob, where they hack out their idol
and turn him to face the wall
whenever they eat forbidden fat,
and the Thames which is boring, boring.

Race of Humanity, you are readers of the Book
whose cover bears the creator's signature,
the sky-blue letters of my name![12]

Back from Persia, Khlebnikov lived for some time in the Caucasian spa of Pyatigorsk, where he worked as a night porter and was treated for chronic undernourishment. At one point, he went to Moscow, in vain looking for a publisher of his work. In the summer of 1922, he decided to go home to Astrakhan, but weakened and ill he died on the road in a small village.

Endnotes

1 For studies in English on Khlebnikov see: Cooke, *Velimir Khlebnikov*; Lonnqvist, *Xlebnikov and Carnival*; Markov, *The Longer Poems of Velimir Khlebnikov*; Vroon, *Velimir Khlebnikov's Shorter Poems*; Weststeijn, *Velimir Chlebnikov and the Development of Poetical Language in Russian Symbolism and Futurism*.

2 Quoted from Lawton, *Russian Futurism through Its Manifestoes*, 51-52.

3 Mayakovsky, *Polnoe sobranie sochinenii*. T. 12, 23.

4 *Collected Works of Velimir Khlebnikov*. Vol. III, 30.

5 The famous favorite pub of the Futurists and other contemporary avant-garde groups.

6 Nikolaj Gumilyov (1885-1921), the leader of the Acmeists, another post-Symbolist group of poets. He was married to Anna Akhmatova, also an Acmeist poet. Suspected

of antirevolutionary activities, he was shot by the Communists in 1921.

7 Lifshits, *The One and a Half-Eyed Archer,* 228-29.

8 *Collected Works of Velimir Khlebnikov.* Vol. I, 384.

9 Ibidem. p. 108. The letter was directed to Nikolai Kulbin, a patron of the Russian Futurists, but also an army doctor, attached to the staff of the Russian army.

10 *Collected Works of Velimir Khlebnikov.* Vol. II, 311.

11 Ibidem. p. 316.

12 *Collected Works of Velimir Khlebnikov.* Vol. III, 77.

1b. Mayakovsky as Literary Critic[1]

Willem G. Weststeijn

The Russian futurist poet Vladimir Mayakovsky (1893-1930) is well-known for his rebellious attitude: he hated bourgeois society and was an ardent supporter of the revolution. In his poetry he created a complex image of himself: that of a rebel, but at the same time of someone who is "unimpeachably tender" and, like Christ, is ready to sacrifice himself for mankind. Still another image appears from his literary criticism and literary activities. He was an excellent editor (LEF and New LEF), had a keen sense for what is really worthwhile in literature (Chekhov, Khlebnikov) and was an able craftsman with clear ideas about how poetry should be written. His most elaborate piece of literary criticism, *How Are Verses Made?* (Kak delat' stikhi?, 1926), which includes a description of the way in which he wrote his poem "To Sergey Esenin," can be considered his credo.

Literary authors are, generally, not much concerned with the work of their contemporary fellow writers. That is to say, they read it, undoubtedly form an opinion about it, but do not express this opinion in the form of critical articles. There are, of course, exceptions (Thomas Mann, D.H. Lawrence, John Updike), but as a rule writers and poets stick to their own creative work and leave the writing of literary criticism to professional critics and reviewers.

Mayakovsky can be considered, to a lesser degree, in this group. He has one extensive critical article to his name, *How Are Verses Made?*, some pieces on the occasion of the death of authors and a number of shorter and longer declarations, statements, lectures and—stenographed—addresses and speeches at literary meetings, conferences and public appearances.[2] This does not make Mayakovsky a real literary critic, but is certainly enough to study him as such and to assess what he has accomplished in the field of literary criticism.

Russian Futurism appeared on the literary scene in the beginning of the second decade of the twentieth century. The movement consisted of several groups: the Cubo-Futurists, at first known as the Hylaeans, the

Ego-Futurists, the Centrifuge and the Mezzanine of Poetry. The Cubo-Futurists, most of whom were artists as well as poets, hence their name, were undoubtedly the best known. Apart from Mayakovsky members of the group were David Burlyuk, Vasily Kamensky, Velimir Khlebnikov and Alexei Kruchenykh. The latter two laid the foundation of the so-called "zaumnyi jazyk" (transrational language), one of the most important and productive "discoveries" of Russian twentieth century poetry. Just as the painters of the time were not interested any longer in depicting reality, but tended to abstract art, an "independent" structure of color and line, the poets did not consider the word in its referential function, but, primarily, as a constellation of letters and sounds without any definite referential meaning.

This emphasis on "the word as such" (slovo kak takovoe) was already apparent in Khlebnikov's early poetry (from 1908), but was publicly announced only in the Cubo-Futurists' first manifesto, *A Slap in the Face of Public Taste* (Poshchechina obshchestvennomu vkusu, 1912). In this manifesto the Futurists declared themselves as fierce opponents of the cultural establishment and of the entire literature of the past.

> To the readers of our New First Unexpected.
>
> We alone are the face of our Time.
> Through us the horn of time
> blows in the art of the word.[3]

The Futurists did not restrict themselves to rude and aggressive statements on paper, but took their aesthetic revolution out on the street. As Vladimir Markov has pointed out, in 1913, the *annus mirabilis* of Russian Futurism, the Cubo-Futurists became notorious for their public poetry readings, which often ended in a scandal. The Futurists deliberately insulted their public and offended the audience by their provocative behavior as well as with their lectures and poetry. Mayakovsky, a born actor with a stentorian voice, was the central figure of these happenings. To advertise the poetry readings he paraded along the streets in a yellow blouse with a wooden spoon in the buttonhole and with a painted face. This guaranteed success. Tickets were generally sold out before the recitals started.

Despite their professed hatred for the literature of the past (particularly the work of their immediate predecessors, the refined symbolists) and their *épater le bourgeois* attitude, the Futurists took their poetry very seriously and devoted themselves with heart and soul to their literary profession. The outwardly rebellious Mayakovsky ("No, we don't need your poor old songs, capable only of making a man feel sentimental... The man of the future should be hard, brave, daring, the master of life and not its slave")[4] proved to be a fine and versatile lyric poet with an excellent ear for original sound effects. Moreover, in his early poetry there was no trace of his publicly announced "hard, brave, daring master of life." Among the Futurists he was the most personal of poets, combining a loathing for philistinism and smugness with a real concern for humanity, a full awareness of his vocation as a poet and eternal doubts about his ability to realize this vocation.

Mayakovsky's dual personality,[5] of which he was perfectly aware himself,[6] is clearly apparent in his early lyrics and particularly in his first longer poems, *Vladimir Mayakovsky: A Tragedy* (Vladimir Mayakovsky—Tragedia, 1913) and *A Cloud in Pants* (Oblako v shtanakh, 1915). The Cloud consists of four parts, each of which has a different theme: love, art, revolution and God. In the introduction to this unequivocally autobiographical poem Mayakovsky gives a double image of himself:

If you like
I'll rage and roar on raw meat
—and then, like the sky, changing my hue—
if you like
I'll be unimpeachably tender,
not a man, but a cloud in pants.[7]

In the poem the lyric "I" rages and roars indeed, but is tender as well and, typically for Mayakovsky's early work, compares himself with Christ, who is ready to sacrifice himself for mankind, even if it does not accept him.

I am wherever pain is—anywhere;
on each drop of the tear stream
I have crucified myself
[...]
And there wasn't a one

who
didn't shout
"Crucify him!
Crucify him!"[8]

Mayakovsky, the compassionate rebel and extraordinarily talented poet, had a keen eye for what was really worthwhile in literature. He hated humbug and people who followed the latest fashion, but did not take the slogans of the *Slap*, to throw all the past literature overboard from the Ship of Modernity, too seriously. Mayakovsky's hatred of philistinism and bourgeois smugness, combined with his excellent literary taste, is clearly apparent from an article he wrote in 1914, "Two Chekhovs" (Dva Chekhova), to commemorate the tenth anniversary of the death of the great Russian storyteller and playwright. The two Chekhovs of the title are, in the first place, the Chekhov as he is read and admired by the general public, i.e. the bourgeois reader, in the second place the Chekhov as he has to be read according to Mayakovsky. In his article Mayakovsky scoffs at all those readers who think of Chekhov as "the poet of twilight," "the defender of the insulted and injured," "the humorist" or someone "who loves mankind as a woman or only a mother loves." For Mayakovsky, Chekhov is, first and foremost, a writer, someone who renewed the Word and introduced into literature an entirely new layer of language: the coarse and vulgar language of businessmen and shopkeepers, of "trading Russia."

Chekhov put an end to the aristocratic language of aristocratic writ ers such as Tolstoy and Turgenev, who only wrote about life at the country estates and he ridiculed the "chords" and "silver distances" of the symbolist poets who "sucked art out their fingers." "Chekhov's language is concise and laconic as "good day," simple as "give me a glass of tea." In this terseness and simplicity Mayakovsky sees the basis of the language of the future, which cries for austerity. As a master of the word Mayakovsky carries out the real tasks of art.

> The figure of Chekhov so familiar to the average citizen as a grumbler, as society's advocate for the ridiculous man, the figure of him as the 'singer of the twilight' now fades, revealing the outline of another Chekhov—a strong, cheerful word-smith.[9]

Although Mayakovsky in his article on the two Chekhovs attacked the symbolist poets—as he used to do whenever he had a chance—he made an exception for the greatest among them, Alexander Blok. Just as in Chekhov's case, he realized that Blok was an extremely gifted poet, belonging, it is true, to his immediate and for that reason especially hated predecessors—Blok was only thirteen years older than Mayakovsky—but someone he could not help but admire. When Blok died in 1921 Mayakovsky wrote a short obituary.

> The creative writings of Alexander Blok are an entire poetic era, the era of the recent past. A wonderful master-symbolist, Blok had an enormous influence on the whole of contemporary poetry. There are some who, to this day, cannot break free of his enchanting verse—they take a phrase of Blok's and expand it into whole pages, building all their poetic wealth on it. Others have outgrown the romanticism of his early period, have declared poetic war on it and, after getting the fragments of symbolism out of their system, are digging the foundations of new rhythms, laying the bricks of new images and fastening their lines together with new rhymes: they are putting in heroic efforts to create the poetry of the future. But Blok is remembered by the former and the latter with equal love.[10]

Less surprising, but equally perspicuous was Mayakovsky's judgment of his fellow Futurist Velimir Khlebnikov. Shortly after Khlebnikov's death in 1922[11] Mayakovsky wrote a commemorative article in the literary journal *Red Virgin Soil* (Krasnaya Nov'), in which he highly praised Khlebnikov, calling him "the Columbus of the new poetic continents which have now been populated and are being developed by us".[12] Of the Futurist poets Mayakovsky was by far the most popular one, conquering the public with his brilliant readings and performances. The shy Khlebnikov was, in this respect, his very antipode. Khlebnikov did not like the public performances at all and usually backed out of them. As Mayakovsky remembers: "When reading aloud, he often stopped in mid-word and commented: 'Well, anyway, et cetera.'"[13] However, Khlebnikov had other qualifications and Mayakovsky was well aware of them. More than the other Futurists and more even than Mayakovsky himself, Khlebnikov was the real innovator of Russian poetic language. Whereas Mayakovsky was a master of rhyme and introduced many "words from the street" into his poetry, Khlebnikov discovered the rich possibilities of language, in particular the semantic potential of the elements of language: sounds, letters and, in line with these, neologisms. For him the word was not in the first place a means to denote reality: objects, feelings or thoughts but an independent force, an independent entity, in which "hidden wisdom" may be discovered and which itself is "organizing the material of feelings and thoughts."[14]

Among his fellow Futurists Khlebnikov was considered a genius, in Mayakovsky's words "not a poet for consumers, but for producers"[15] and in any case the poet who most consistently, in his articles as well as in his poetical works, advanced the new vision of poetic language.

> To retain a proper literary sense of perspective, I consider it my duty to publish in black and white on my own behalf and, I have no doubt, on behalf of my friends, the poets Aseyev, Burlyuk, Kruchenykh, Kamensky and Pasternak, that we considered and still do consider him one of our poetry teachers and the most magnificent and most honourable knight in our poetic struggle.[16]

Contrary to Khlebnikov, who first and foremost was concerned with the revolution in poetic language, Mayakovsky was a "real" revolutionary, in the sense that he wanted to change society and dedicated himself and his poetic talent to this cause. He was an active supporter of the revolution and the Bolshevik government as he sincerely believed that the revolution would clear the way for the new, wished for, bourgeois-less society and wrote a lot of agitprop poetry, that culminated in verses on propaganda posters,[17]and long, epic poems such as *150,000,000* (1919) and *Vladimir Ilich Lenin* (1924). As a member of the Futurist avant-garde, Mayakovsky was convinced that Futurist art should become the new art of the new proletarian state. He was the moving spirit behind LEF (Left Front of Art), a group of revolutionary artists, poets and critics, who considered themselves the founders of communist culture and aimed at the complete integration of life and art. The journal of the group, LEF, that existed from 1923-1925 was edited by Mayakovsky.[18]

LEF was fiercely polemical. It had to struggle with rival organizations of proletarian artists and writers, who often had conventional artistic tastes and neither liked nor understood Futurist experimental art. LEF also felt compelled to attack the byt, "everyday life", which soon after the revolution threatened to become petrified by the new hierarchy of party bosses with their, seemingly indestructible, petty-bourgeois mentality. Mayakovsky's hatred for the new philistinism and general narrow-mindedness was not less than his aversion to the same elements in pre-revolutionary Russian society. His "eternal" struggle for sincerity and authenticity in art as well as in byt is expressed most clearly in his longest and most substantial critical text *How are Verses Made?* The direct reason to write this article was to react once more to the death of the poet Sergey Esenin, who had hanged himself at the end of 1925 in a hotel in Leningrad. Esenin, an extremely popular poet in Russia and in the West well-known for his love-affair with Isodora Duncan, was thirty years old at the time of his suicide and left behind a farewell poem, written in his own blood and ending with the lines: "In this life it's nothing new to die, / But to live, of course, isn't newer."

Mayakovsky's first reaction to Esenin's death was the poem "To Sergey Esenin." He wrote this to counteract the pessimistic feeling expressed by Esenin's farewell poem and by the act of suicide itself, but there was, undoubtedly, more to it. Mayakovsky was intrigued by Esenin's suicide (five years later he also killed himself) and was, moreover, jealous of Esenin's popularity. Esenin's melodious and singable lyrics proved to be more appealing to the public than Mayakovsky's revolutionary verse. As Mayakovsky considered it his task to challenge the general feelings of pessimism evoked by Esenin's death, his poem on Esenin lacks the elegiac tone that is characteristic for commemorative poems. Mayakovsky's poem strikes the reader even by the absence of sympathy with a fellow poet who chose such a hard fate for himself. One of the reasons for Mayakovsky to write *How are Verses Made?* was to explain this seemingly cold attitude and lack of sympathy. Eventually, his text went further than that and became a general statement about his own making of verse and about the way it should be done in general. Mayakovsky, a professional and very successful reciter of poetry, has always been very attentive to the problems and possibilities of poetic technique.[19] He had very clear ideas of how to renew poetry, not only regarding content, but also regarding form. He was convinced that the new times needed a new kind of literature and that the old forms had to be abolished. Being, perhaps suitable for their own times, they had outlived themselves and could not express the essence of the new age. This was certainly not clear to everybody.

> In different literary debates, in conversations with young workers from various workshops of the word (Rapp, Tapp, Papp, etc.),[20] in reprisals against critics, I have often been obliged, if not to smash to pieces, at least to discredit the old poetics. Of course we didn't interfere with old poetry that was in itself quite blameless. It drew our wrath only if avid protectors of the old hid from new art behind the backside of monuments. . . . Our chief and enduring hatred falls on sentimental-critical Philistinism. On those who see all the greatness of the poetry of the past in the fact that they too have loved as Onegin loved Tatyana (elective affinities!) or in the fact that even they can understand these poets (they studied them at school), and iambuses caress their ears too.[21]

Mayakovsky did not believe in the general high-flown ideas about writing poetry ("the only method of production is the inspired throwing back of the head while one waits for the heavenly soul of poetry to descend on one's bald patch in the form of a dove, a peacock or an ostrich"[22]—nor in the possibility to write real poetry according to the poetry handbooks with their rules of metre, rhyme and harmony. These books should not be called "how to write" but "how they used to write." The new age in particular demands an entirely new and different kind of poetry.

> The Revolution, for instance, has thrown up on to the streets the unpolished speech of the masses, the slang of the suburbs has flowed along the downtown boulevards; the enfeebled sub-language of the intelligentsia, with its emasculated words "ideal", "principles of justice", "the transcendental visage of Christ and Antichrist"—all these expressions, pronounced in little whispers in res-

> taurants, have been trampled underfoot. There is a new linguistic element. How can one make it poetic? The old rules about "love and dove," "moon and June," and alexandrines are no use. How can we introduce the spoken language into poetry, and extract poetry from this spoken language? . . . It's hopeless to shove the bursting thunder of the Revolution into a four-stress amphibrach, devised for its gentle sound![23]

In his *How are Verses Made?* Mayakovsky contends that he does not know of iambuses and trochees and that when snatches of these metres are found in his poetry it is because you come across them everywhere in language. Just like a game of chess, a poetical work has only a few general rules about how to begin. After a few moves everything becomes new and unexpected. The essential rules for beginning a poem are, according to Mayakovsky, a problem in society that can only be tackled by a work of poetry—the theme, and an awareness of the desires of one's class—a target, aim or standpoint. Further, as material, words; then tools of production and equipment for the enterprise, from pen and paper to an umbrella for writing in the rain, a room large enough to pace up and down while at work and a bicycle for going to the publishers. Last, but not least, word-processing techniques, which can only be acquired after years of daily toil and which are extremely personal: rhymes, images, alliteration, headings, pathos, etc. Accordingly, Mayakovsky adds, a good poetic work will be one that has been written to the social command of the Comintern, with the victory of the proletariat as its target. It has a new vocabulary, comprehensible to all, is written on a desk as recommended by the Scientific Organization of Labour and delivered to the publisher by the latest and most modern means of transport, the aeroplane.

Despite this caricaturing and exaggerated description of the poetic "rules" Mayakovsky is absolutely serious about the task of the poet and about the intensity of poetic writing: taking up the greater part of the day (from ten to eighteen hours) it results in a daily production of eight to ten lines. In short, writing poetry is one of the hardest and most laborious jobs there is. To illustrate this Mayakovsky describes in the second part of *How are Verses Made?* how he wrote "To Sergey Esenin," in his own opinion one of the most effective of his latest poems. When

Mayakovsky met Esenin for the first time in an apartment in Leningrad he was not really impressed by his decorative outfit: a peasant shirt and bast shoes, making him look like something out of a comedy and certainly not the real peasant he pretended to be. His countrified verses too were not to the taste of the Futurist Mayakovsky. Later on Esenin broke free from his idealized rusticism and developed in the direction of VAPP, the All-Russian Association of Proletarian Writers, being "rather envious of any poet who had become organically one with the Revolution and the proletariat." In Mayakovsky's opinion this was at the root of Esenin's self-dissatisfaction and heavy drinking. When after Esenin's suicide his powerful last lines were published his death became a literary fact: it was important to counteract these pessimistic lines as they were already taking effect.

Such poetry had to be fought with poetry, but what to write and how? Theme and aim being established: Esenin's death and the wish to make his last lines uninteresting, to neutralize its effects and "to replace the facile beauty of death by another beauty, since toiling mankind needs all its strength to sustain the Revolution it has begun."[24] Mayakovsky extensively describes his problems in finding the right tone and right words for the first few lines. He warns for expressions of endearment as were found in "piffle" poems by Esenin's friends and, in general, for being too intimate with the theme or subject described: "Any description of contemporary events by those taking part in the struggles of the day will always be incomplete, even incorrect, or at any rate one-sided."[25] Distance is obligatory, contrasts often work well (take a horribly crowded bus if you want to write about the tenderness of love) and take your time: even hasty agitational poems call for highly intensive work. Mayakovsky intermingles his "rules" with a description of the creative process. Fundamental to all poetry, its basic force and basic energy, is rhythm. It comes to Mayakovsky when he walks through the city.

> I walk along, waving my arms and mumbling almost wordlessly, now shortening my steps so as not to interrupt my mumbling, now mumbling more rapidly in time with my steps. So the rhythm is trimmed and takes shape—and rhythm is the basis of any poetic work, resounding through the whole thing. Gradually individual words begin to ease themselves free of this dull roar.

> Several words just jump away and never come back, others hold on, wriggle and squirm a dozen times over, until you can't imagine how any word will ever stay in its place (this sensation, developing with experience, is called talent). More often than not the most important word emerges first: the word that most completely conveys the meaning of the poem, or the word that underlies the rhyme. The other words come forward and take up dependent positions in relation to the most important word. When the fundamentals are already there, one has a sudden sensation that the rhythm is strained: there's some little syllable or sound missing. You begin to shape all the words anew, and the work drives you to distraction. It's like having a tooth crowned. A hundred times (or so it seems) the dentist tries a crown on the tooth, and it's the wrong size; but at last, after a hundred attempts, he presses one down, and it fits. The analogy is all the more apposite in my case, because when at last the crown fits, I (quite literally) have tears in my eyes, from pain and relief.[26]

In the poem "To Sergey Esenin" there was at first only rhythm. Then, gradually, the words took shape. It took quite a long time before Mayakovsky was satisfied with the first lines. In the very first line, for instance, it was extremely difficult to find the right words for the middle part of the line after the beginning and the end had been determined.

> You went off ra ra ra to a world above

Mayakovsky tried a number of variants that would harmonize with the rhythm:

> You went off, Seryozha, to a world above ...
> You went off forever to a world above ...
> You went off, Esenin, to a world above ...

However, he discarded them all. "Seryozha" would be false, as he was not on such intimate terms with Esenin; "forever" is redundant: there is no return ticket to death; "Esenin" is too serious as it would suggest that Mayakovsky believed in life after death, it turns the poem into a kind of funeral ode instead of one with an aim. The final solution: "You went off, they say, to a world above" was satisfactory for Mayakovsky because of its objectiveness: "neither dancing at a funeral, nor, on the other hand, yielding to the professional mourners".[27]

Mayakovsky continues with a discussion of, apart from rhythm, a number of other indispensable elements of a poem, in particular rhyme,[28] images, alliteration and, closely connected with matters of technique, tone. He warns for affectation and exaggeration ("You must always remember that a policy of economy in art is the most important principle of every product of aesthetic value")[29] and underlines the relativity of all rules about writing poetry. It is not possible, Mayakovsky states, to proffer ready-made formulas for poetry since the essence of poetic activity, the basis of poetic composition is not the simple application of rules, but the ability to invent different technical devices, different ways of technically polishing words. *How are Verses Made?* is not meant for the poetaster, but for him who knows that poetry is one of the most difficult things to produce, but despite all obstacles wishes to be a poet.

Mayakovsky ends his article with a number of general conclusions in which he once more emphasizes that poetry is production, very complex and difficult, but production. As such it needs an aim, the best materials, an excellent technique and regular hard work. However, these "universal rules" are openly endorsed only by the LEF poets.

> We, the poets of the Left Front, never claim that we alone possess the secrets of poetical creativity. But we are the only ones who want to lay these secrets open, the only ones who don't want to surround the creative process with a catchpenny religio-artistic aura of sanctity.[30]

Mayakovsky has often been accused of devoting his great talent to the revolution instead of to poetry. In his own view it was not a question of either-or, but of both-and. He never yielded to the temptation to write "easy" revolutionary verse, but, on the other hand, could not leave the revolution and the desired new society out of his poetry. This led to a serious predicament as he felt himself neither understood nor accepted by the proletarian masses. A few weeks before he shot himself he stated his problem quite clearly in an address to a Komsomol club at an evening dedicated to twenty years of his poetic activity.

> I've not spent my whole life working hard so as to make pretty pieces and caress the human ear; the upshot has always been that I've somehow caused everybody a lot of unpleasantness. My main work is cussing and deriding what seems wrong to me and must be fought. And twenty years of my literary work have been mainly, to put it bluntly, neither more nor less than literary snout-bashing, not in the exact sense of the word, but in the best!—that is, every minute I've had to defend various revolutionary literary positions, fight on their behalf and fight the inertia that can be met in our thirteen year-old Republic.[31]

At his death Mayakovsky left a suicide note with the words: "As they say, 'The incident is closed.' The love boat has smashed against convention". Usually the words "smashed love boat" are considered to be referring to his ill-fated romance with Tatyana Yakovleva,[32] which was doomed by byt. However, byt had also doomed his love for the new classless society for which he had fought during his entire career as a poet.[33] Mayakovsky could not conquer the byt, but the byt also could not conquer Mayakovsky. He would rather die than change his opinion about the extremely difficult art of writing poetry.

Endnotes

1 A version of this essay was originally published in: *Avant-Garde Critical Studies, Avant-Garde and Criticism*. Edited by Klaus Beekman and Jan de Vries, Rodopi, Amsterdam, 2007, 139-155.

2 All of Mayakovsky's writings have been published in the thirteen volume edition of his complete collected works (Moscow 1955-1961). This edition appeared because Stalin had declared Mayakovsky "the best and most talented poet of our Soviet epoch", which made it possible to study him in detail. To the phrase "Mayakovsky was and remains the best and most talented poet of our Soviet epoch", which was apparently suggested to Stalin by the formalist critic Osip Brik, who had complained to him about the neglect

of Mayakovsky, Stalin added: "Indifference to his memory and his works is a crime" (See Brown 1973: 370). Accordingly, it became more or less compulsory to read, study, and publish Mayakovsky's work. Of all the great avant-garde poets of the Silver Age of Russian poetry, Mayakovsky was the only one to be officially accepted by the Soviet state. Boris Pasternak and Anna Akhmatova were not allowed to publish after 1930, Nikolay Gumilyov was executed as an anti-communist conspirator, Osip Mandelshtam perished in a camp, and Marina Tsvetayeva emigrated, went back to Russia and hanged herself after her husband had been shot and her daughter arrested. Velimir Khlebnikov, Mayakovsky's fellow futurist, had died in 1922. The works of all these poets were suppressed during Soviet times. Complete editions of their works appeared in Russia only after the collapse of the Soviet Union.

3 Translation in Lawton *Russian Futurism through its Manifestoes*, 51-52.

4 From a speech Mayakovsky made in Kishinyov. See Kamensky, *Zhizn s Mayakovskim*, 103.

5 See, for instance, Jakobson, *Smert' Vladimira Mayakovskogo* and Brown, *Mayakovsky: A Poet in the Revolution*, especially chapters four and five.

6 In 1915 Mayakovsky wrote an article, "About the Various Mayakovskys" (O raznykh Mayakovskykh), in which he described himself as an insolent person and a cynic, but, by quoting from his own poetry, showed an entirely different side of his personality.

7 Mayakovsky, *Polnoe sobranie sochinenii I-XIII*, vol. I: 175. I quote the literal translation from Brown, *Mayakovsky: A Poet in the Revolution*, 116.

8 Ibid, 184-85; 122-23.

9 Ibid, 301. My translation.

10 *Polnoe sobranie sochinenii I-XIII.* I quote the translation in Mayakovsky 1987: 166.

11 Khlebnikov died at the age of 37, just like Pushkin. When Mayakovsky killed himself he was of the same age.

12 Mayakovsky, *Polnoe sobranie sochinenii I-XIII.*

13 Ibid.

14 Ibid., 168.

15 Ibid., 167.

16 Ibid., 170-71.

17 From 1919-1921 Mayakovsky produced, on commission for the Russian Telegraph Agency (ROSTA), more than 600 revolutionary posters with cartoon-like drawings and verse slogans. Many of the posters or "windows" as they were called were displayed in shop-windows, so that the public did not see the empty shops (after the revolution and during the civil war the economy was in a disastrous state) and at the same time were urged to support the revolution.

18 LEF was revived as Novyi LEF in 1927, again under the editorship of Mayakovsky. Its last number appeared in 1928.

19 See, for instance, the article "Mayakovsky on the Quality of Verse" (Mayakovsky o kachestve stikha) in Khardzhiev and Trenin, *Poeticheskaya kultura Mayakovskogo.* Many statements have been made about the important role of the audience as "co-participant" of Mayakovsky's creative work. The best study in this respect is Vinokur, *Mayakovsky novator jazyka.* Kozhinov, "Mayakovsky and Russian Classical Literature," quotes him as follows: "The first and most common stylistic feature of Mayakovsky's diction is that it is wholly permeated by the element of the spoken and, moreover, the predominantly loud spoken word. . . . A form of speech in which, as it were, direct contact with the listener is expressed is Mayakovsky's most usual method, whether he is stating a personal and intimate theme or whether he is formulating some universally significant

proposition . . . It is interesting to compare, for instance, the objectively affirmative tone of Pushkin's Monument and the inevitable address to the listener . . . with which Mayakovsky's own Monument begins" and adds: "It would, of course, be wrong to think that there had been no form of lyrical address before Mayakovsky's poetry, and especially Nekrasov's. It is only with Mayakovsky, however, that the address to the reader becomes a dominant feature of the style, and only with Mayakovsky does this address seem to demand an immediate reaction, a vocal response, urge and action" (84).

20 There were several associations of proletarian writers: RAPP, the Russian association, MAPP, the Moscow association, VAPP, the All-Russian association.

21 Mayakovsky, *How are Verses Made?*

22 Ibid., 12.

23 Ibid., 15.

24 Ibid., 32.

25 Ibid., 33.

26 Ibid., 36-37.

27 Ibid., 40.

28 ". . . without rhyme . . . poetry falls to pieces. Rhyme sends you back to the previous line, reminds you of it, and helps all the lines that compose one thought to hold together." Ibid., 42.

29 Ibid., 52.

30 Ibid., 58.

31 Mayakovsky, *Selected Works in three Volumes. Vol. 3: Plays. Articles. Essays*, 255.

32 Tatyana Yakovleva was an emigrée whom Mayakovsky had met in Paris in 1928. She seems to have been a kind of femme fatale and Mayakovsky fell totally in love with her. He tried to persuade her to follow him to Russia and marry him. She refused to do so and married instead a French diplomat.

33 A few months before his death Mayakovsky left LEF and became a member of RAPP, the leaders of which he had attacked for a long time because they preferred Tolstoyan realism to Futurist experimental art. This desperate attempt to find a home among the proletarian writers failed. RAPP accorded him a cold reception and tried to re-educate him in the spirit of proletarian ideology. "Some people recalled that on the eve of his suicide, already cut off from friends and collaborators of long standing, he was in a state of defenseless misery as a result of his sessions with the talentless dogmatists and petty literary tyrants whose organization he had joined." *Mayakovsky: A Poet in the Revolution*, 367.

2. Russian Art of the Avant-Garde[1] (Translated Texts)

John E. Bowlt

Content and Form, 1910 — VASILII KANDINSKY

Born Moscow, 1866; died Neuilly-sur-Seine. 1944. 1890: arrived in Munich; 1896: with Alexei von Jawlensky et al. founded the Neue Künstlerveremigung (New Artists' Association); began Improvisations; 1909-10: Munich correspondent for *Apollon*; 1910: contributed to the first "Knave of Diamonds" exhibition; 1910 onwards: began to explore an abstract mode of painting; 1911-12: exhibitions of *Der Blaue Reiter* [The Blue Rider]; 1914-21: back in Russia; 1920: participated in the organization of Inkhuk; 1921: participated in the organization of the Russian Academy of Artistic Sciences; 1921: emigrated; 1922-33: taught at the Bauhaus.

The text of this piece, "Soderzhanie i forma", is from the catalogue for the second "Salon" exhibition, organized by Vladimir Izdebsky in Odessa in 1910. Apart from the list of exhibitors and this text, the catalogue included articles by Izdebsky, Nikolai Kulbin, a certain "Dr. Phil. A. Grinbaum, Odessa" (perhaps the philosopher Anton Grinbaum), a discourse on "Harmony in Painting and Music" by Henri Rovel, a long poem by Leonid Grossman (later to achieve fame as a literary critic), and Kandinsky's translation of Arnold Schoenberg's "Parallels in Octaves and Fifths." With such a synthetic composition and, moreover, with a cover designed, after a Kandinsky woodcut, this catalogue might well have formed the prototype for *Der Blaue Reiter* almanac itself. Although most contemporary trends in Russian painting were represented at the exhibition—from neoprimitivism (David and Vladimir Burliuk; Mikhail Larionov, Vladimir Tatlin, etc.) to symbolism (Petr Utkin), from the St. Petersburg Impressionists (Kulbin) to the World of Art (Mstislav Dobuzhinsky), the Munich artists (Jawlensky, Kandinsky, Gabriele Munter, Marianne von Werefkin) constituted an impressive and compact group. Indeed, the German contribution both to the exhibition and to the catalogue was indicative of Izdebsky's own interest in Kandinsky (he intended, for example, to publish a monograph on him in 1911) and, generally, in the Neue Künstlerveremigung.

Kandinsky's text shares certain affinities with his article "Kuda idet 'novoe' iskusstvo" (Whither the 'New' Art), which was published a few weeks later (also in Odessa) and in which he went so far as to assert that "any kind of content is unartistic and hostile to art. . . . Painting as such, i.e., as 'pure painting' affects the soul by means of its primordial resources: by paint (color), by form, i.e., the distribution of planes and lines, their interrelation (movement)..." Of course, both this article and the text below constituted previews of Kandinsky's *On the Spiritual in Art*, which was given as a lecture by Kulbin on Kandinsky's behalf at the All-Russian Congress of Artists in St. Petersburg on December 29 and 31, 1911. The present text reflects both Kandinsky's highly subjective interpretation of art and his quest for artistic synthesism, attitudes that were identifiable with a number of Russian artists and critics at this time, not least Kulbin, Aleksandr Skryabin, and of course, the symbolists. Kandinsky's attempts to chart the "artist's emotional vibration" and to think in comparative terms is still evident in his programs for the Moscow Inkhuk and for the Russian Academy of Artistic Sciences.

* * *

A work of art consists of two elements:
the inner and
the outer.

The inner element, taken separately, is the emotion of the artist's soul, which (like the material musical tone of one instrument that compels the corresponding tone of another to covibrate) evokes a corresponding emotional vibration in the other person, the perceptor.

While the soul is bound to the body, it can perceive a vibration usually only by means of feeling—which acts as a bridge from the nonmaterial to the material (the artist) and from the material to the nonmaterial (the spectator).

Emotion—feeling—work of art—feeling—Emotion.

As a means of expression, therefore, the artist's emotional vibration must find a material form capable of being perceived. This material form is the second element, i.e., the outer element of a work of art.

A work of art is, of necessity, an indissolubly and inevitably *cohesive* combination of inner and outer elements, i.e., *content and form*.

"Fortuitous" forms scattered throughout the world evoke their own inherent vibrations. This family is so numerous and diverse that the effect of "fortuitous" (e.g., natural) forms appears to us to be also fortuitous and indefinite.

In art, form is invariably determined by content. And only that form is the right one which serves as the corresponding expression and materialization of its content. Any accessory considerations, among them the primary one—namely, the correspondence of form to so-called nature, i.e., outer nature—are insubstantial and pernicious, because they distract attention from the single task of art: the embodiment of its content. *Form is the material expression of abstract content.* Hence the quality of an artistic work can be appreciated *in toto* only by its author: content demands immediate embodiment, and the author alone is permitted to see whether the form that he has found corresponds to the content, and if so, to what extent. The greater or lesser degree of this embodiment or correspondence is the measure of "beauty." *That work is beautiful whose form corresponds entirely to its inner content* (which is, as it were, an unattainable ideal). In this way the form of a work is determined essentially by its inner necessity.

The principle of inner necessity is the one invariable law of art in its essence.

Every art possesses one form that is peculiar to it and bestowed on it alone. This form, forever changing, gives rise to the individual forms of individual works. Hence, whether or not the same emotions are involved, every art will clothe them in its own peculiar form. In this way each art produces its own work, and therefore, it is impossible to replace the work of one art by another. Hence there arises both the possibility of, and the need for, the appearance of *a monumental art*: we can already sense its growth, and its color will be woven tomorrow.

This monumental art represents the unification of all the arts in a single work—in which (1) each art will be the coauthor of this work while remaining within the confines of its own form; (2) each art will be advanced or withdrawn according to the principle of direct or reverse contact.

Thus the principle of a work's construction will remain the one that is the single basis of creation in each individual art.

The great epoch of Spirituality is beginning, and even yesterday, during the apparent climax of materialism, it had already emerged in its embryonic state; it will provide, and is providing, the soil on which this monumental work must mature. A grand transvaluation of values is now taking place as if one of the greatest battles between spirit and matter were about to begin. The unnecessary is being rejected. The necessary is being studied in all its aspects. This is also taking place in one of the greatest spheres of the spirit—in everlasting and eternal art.

The means of expression of every art have been prescribed and bestowed on it from time immemorial and, essentially, cannot change; but just as the spirit is being "refined" continuously, divesting itself of the soul's materiality, so, correspondingly and partially beforehand, the means of art must be "refined" also, inflexibly and irrepressibly.

Therefore (1) every art is eternal and invariable, and (2) every art changes in its forms. It must guide the spiritual evolution by adapting its forms for greater refinement and lead the way prophetically. Its inner content is invariable. Its outer forms are variable. Therefore, *both the variability and the invariability of art constitute its law.*

These means, fundamental and invariable, are for

music—sound and time
literature—word and time
architecture—line and volume
sculpture—volume and space
painting—color and space

In painting, color functions in the shape of paint. Space functions in the shape of the form confining it ("painterly" form) or in the shape of line. These two elements—*paint and line—constitute the essential, eternal, invariable language of painting.*

Every color, taken in isolation, in uniform conditions of perception, arouses the same invariable emotional vibration. But a color, in fact, cannot be isolated, and therefore its absolute inner sound always varies in different circumstances. Chief among these are: (1) the proximity of another color tone, (2) the space (and form) occupied by the given tone.

The task of pure painting or painterly form follows the first stipulation. *Painting is the combination of colored tones determined by inner necessity.*

The combination is infinitely fine and refined, infinitely complex and complicated.

The task of drawing or drawn form follows from the second stipulation. *Drawing is the combination of linear planes determined by inner necessity.* Its refinement and complexity are infinite.

The first task is, in fact, indissolubly linked to the second and represents, generally speaking, the primary task in a composition of painting and drawing; it is a task that is now destined to advance with unprecedented force, and its threshold is the so-called new painting. It is self-evident that this innovation is not a qualitative one (fundamentally) but a quantitative one. This composition has been the invariable law of any art of any period, beginning with the primitive art of the "savages." The imminent Epoch of the Great Spirituality is emerging before our very eyes, and it is precisely now that this kind of composition must act as a most eminent prophet, a prophet who is already leading the pure in heart and who will be leading the whole world.

This composition will be built on those same bases already familiar to us in their embryonic state, those bases that will now, however, develop into the simplicity and complexity of musical "counterpoint." This counterpoint (for which we do not have a word yet) will be discovered further along the path of the Great Tomorrow by that same ever-faithful guide—Feeling. Once found and crystallized, it will give expression to the Epoch of the Great Spirituality. But however great or small its individual parts, they all *rest on one great foundation*—the PRINCIPLE OF INNER NECESSITY.

Preface to Catalogue of One-Man Exhibition, 1913 — NATALYA GONCHAROVA

Born near Tula, 1881; died Paris, 1962. 1898-1902; studied at the Moscow Institute of Painting, Sculpture, and Architecture, attending sculpture classes under Paolo Trubetskoi; thereafter turned to painting; 1910: one-man exhibition at the Society of Free Aesthetics in Moscow resulting in a scandal—works called pornographic [see Mikhail Larionov: "Gazetnye kritiki v roli politsii nravov" (Newspaper Critics in the Role of Morality Police) in *Zolotoe runo,* Moscow, no. 11/12,

1909(=1910), pp. 97-98]; ca. 1913 illustrated futurist booklets; 1910-15: contributed to the "Knave of Diamonds," "Donkey's Tail," "Target," "No. 4," "Exhibition of Painting; 1915," and other exhibitions; 1914: went to Paris with Larionov; after outbreak of war, returned to Moscow briefly; 1915: joined Sergei Diaghilev in Lausanne; 1917: settled in Paris with Larionov.

The translation is of the preface to the catalogue of Goncharova's second one-woman exhibition in Moscow, pp. 1-4, which displayed 768 works covering the period 1900-1913 and ran from August until October 1913; at the beginning of 1914 it opened in St. Petersburg, but on a smaller scale. This Moscow exhibition did not create the scandal associated with the 1910 show, although Goncharova's religious subjects were criticized as they had been at the "Donkey's Tail." The catalogue saw two editions.

* * *

In appearing with a separate exhibition, I wish to display my artistic development and work throughout the last thirteen years. I fathomed the art of painting myself, step by step, without learning it in any art school (I studied sculpture for three years at the Moscow Institute of Painting, Sculpture, and Architecture and left when I received the small medal). At the beginning of my development I learned most of all from my French contemporaries. They stimulated my awareness and I realized the great significance and value of the art of my country—and through it the great value of the art of the East. Hitherto I have studied all that the West could give me, but in fact, my country has created everything that derives from the West. Now I shake the dust from my feet and leave the West, considering its vulgarizing significance trivial and insignificant—my path is toward the source of all arts, the East. The art of my country is incomparably more profound and important than anything that I know in the West (I have true art in mind, not that which is harbored by our established schools and societies). I am opening up the East again, and I am certain that many will follow me along this path. We have learned much from Western artists, but from where do they draw their inspiration, if not from the East? We have not learned the most important thing: not to make stupid imitations and not to seek our individuality, but to create, in the main, works of art and to realize that the source on which the West draws is the East and us. May my example and my words be a good lesson for those who can understand its real meaning.

I am convinced that modern Russian art is developing so rapidly and has reached such heights that within the near future it will be playing a leading role in international life. Contemporary Western ideas (mainly of France; it is not worth talking of the others) can no longer be of any use to us. And the time is not far off when the West will be learning openly from us.

If we examine art from the artistic monuments we have at our disposal without bearing time in mind, then I see it in this order:

The Stone Age and the caveman's art are the dawn of art. China, India, and Egypt with all their ups and downs in art have, generally speaking, always had a high art and strong artistic tradition. Arts proceeding from this root are nevertheless independent: that of the Aztecs, Negroes, Australian and Asiatic islands—the Sunda (Borneo), Japan, etc. These, generally speaking, represent the rise and flowering of art.

Greece, beginning with the Cretan period (a transitional state), with its archaic character and all its flowering, Italy right up to the age of Gothic represent decadence. Gothic is a transitional state. Our age is a flowering of art in a new form—a painterly form. And in this second flowering it is again the East that has played a leading role. At the present time Moscow is the most important center of painting.

I shake off the dust of the West, and I consider all those people ridiculous and backward who still imitate Western models in the hope of becoming pure painters and who fear literariness more than death. Similarly, I find those people ridiculous who advocate individuality and who assume there is some value in their "I" even when it is extremely limited. Untalented individuality is as useless as bad imitation, let alone the old-fashionedness of such an argument.

I express my deep gratitude to Western painters for all they have taught me.

After carefully modifying everything that could be done along these lines and after earning the honor of being placed alongside contemporary Western artists—in the West itself —I now prefer to investigate a new path.

And the objectives that I am carrying out and that I intend to carry out are the following:

To set myself no confines or limitations in the sense of artistic achievements

To attempt to introduce a durable legality and a precise definition of what is attained—for myself and for others.

To fight against the debased and decomposing doctrine of individualism, which is now in a period of agony.

To draw my artistic inspiration from my country and from the East, so close to us.

To put into practice M. F. Larionov's theory of rayonism which I have elaborated (painting based only on painterly laws).

To reduce my individual moments of inspiration to a common, objective, painterly form.

In the age of the flowering of individualism, I destroy this holy of holies and refuge of the hidebound as being inappropriate to our contemporary and future way of life.

For art, individual perception can play an auxiliary role—but for mankind, it can play none at all.

If I clash with society, this occurs only because the latter fails to understand the bases of art and not because of my individual peculiarities, which nobody is obliged to understand.

To apprehend the world around us in all its brilliance and diversity and to bear in mind both its inner and outer content.

To fear in painting neither literature, nor illustration, nor any other bugbears of contemporaneity; certain modern artists wish to create a painterly interest absent in their work by rejecting them. To endeavor, on the contrary, to express them vividly and positively by painterly means.

I turn away from the West because for me personally it has dried up and because my sympathies lie with the East.

The West has shown me one thing: everything it has is from the East.[2]

I consider of profound interest that which is now called philistine vulgarity, because it is untouched by the art of blockheads—their thoughts are directed exclusively to the heights only because they cannot attain them; and also because philistine vulgarity is predominant nowadays—contemporaneity is characterized by this. But there is no need to fear it; it is quite able to be an object of artistic concern.

Artist vulgarity is much worse because it is inevitable: it is like the percentage of crime in the world, uniform at all times and in all arts. My last word is a stone thrown at artistic vulgarity—ever aspiring to occupy the place of an achievement of genius.

P.S.:

My aspiration toward the East is not my last development—I mean only to broaden my outlook; countries that value artistic traditions can help me in this.

For me the East means the creation of new forms, an extending and deepening of the problems of color.

This will help me to express contemporaneity—its living beauty—better and more vividly.

I aspire toward nationality and the East, not to narrow the problems of art but, on the contrary, to make it all-embracing and universal.

If I extol the art of my country, then it is because I think that it fully deserves this and should occupy a more honorable place than it has done hitherto.

Cubism (Surface-Plane), 1912 — DAVID BURLIUK

Born Kharkov, 1882; died Long Island, New York, 1967. 1898-1904: studied at various institutions in Kazan, Munich, Paris; 1907: settled in Moscow; soon befriended by most members of the emergent avant-garde; 1911: entered the Moscow Institute if Painting, Sculpture, and Architecture, but was expelled in 1913; ca. 1913: illustrated futurist booklets; 1910-1915: contributed to the "Triangle," "Knave of Diamonds," "Union of Youth," "Exhibition of Painting 1915," and other exhibitions; 1915: moved to the Urals; 1918-1922: via Siberia, Japan, and Canada, arrived in the United States; active as painter and critic until his death.

The text of this piece, "Kubizm," is from the anthology of poems, prose pieces, and articles, "Poshchechina obshchestvennomu vkusu" (A Slap in the Face of Public Taste) (Moscow, December 1912). The collection is prefaced by the famous declaration of the same name signed by David Burliuk, Velimir Khlebnikov, Aleksei Kruchenykh, and Vladimir Mayakovsky and dated December 1912. The volume also contained a second essay by David Burliuk on texture, verse by Khlebnikov and Benedikt Livshits, and four prose sketches by Vasilii Kandinsky. Both the essay on cubism and the one on texture were signed by N. Burliuk, although, it is obvious that both were written by David and not by Nikolai (David's youngest brother and a poet of some merit). David Burliuk was deeply interested in the question of cubism and delivered several lectures on the subject: on February 12, 1912 he gave a talk "On Cubism and Other Directions in Painting" at a debate organized by the Knave of Diamonds in Moscow, and on the twenty-fourth of the same month, again under the auspices of the Knave of Diamonds, he spoke on the same title under the title "The Evolution of the Concept of Beauty in Painting"; on November 20, 1912, he spoke on "What Is Cubism?" at a debate organized by the Union of Youth in St. Petersburg, which occasioned a scornful response by Alexandre Benois which, in turn, occasioned a reply by Olga Rozanova. Burliuk's references to the Knave of Diamonds members Vladimir Burliuk, Alexandra Exter, Kandinsky, Petr Konchalovsky, and Ilya Mashkov, all of whom had contributed to the first and second "Knave of Diamonds" exhibitions (and Mikhail Larionov and Nikolai Kulbin, who had been at the first and second exhibitions, respectively), would indicate that the text is an elaboration of the Knave of Diamonds lecture; moreover, the Knave of Diamonds debate had been chaired by Konchalovsky, and it had witnessed a heated confrontation between the Knave of Diamonds group as such and Donkey's Tail artists. As usual with David Burliuk's literary endeavors of this time, the style is clumsy and does not make for clarity; in addition, the text is interspersed somewhat arbitrarily with capital letters.

* * *

Painting is colored space.
Point, line, and surface are elements
of spatial forms.
the order in which they are placed arises
from their genetic connection.
the simplest element of space is the point.
its consequence is line.
the consequence of line is surface.

all spatial forms are reduced to these three
elements.
the direct consequence of line is plane.

It would perhaps not be a paradox to say that painting became art only in the twentieth century.

Only in the twentieth century have we begun to have painting as art—before there used to be the art of painting, but there was no painting Art. This kind of painting (up to the twentieth century) is called conventionally—from a certain sense of compassion toward the endless sums spent on museums—Old Painting, as distinct from *New* Painting.

These definitions in themselves show that everyone, even the most Ignorant and those with no interest in the Spiritual, perceives the eternal gulf that has arisen between the painting of yesterday and the painting of today. An eternal gulf. Yesterday we did not have art.

Today we do have art. Yesterday it was the means, today it has become the end. Painting has begun to pursue only Painterly objectives. It has begun to live for itself. The fat bourgeois have shifted their shameful attention from the artist, and now this magician and sorcerer has the chance of escaping to the transcendental secrets of his art.

Joyous solitude. But woe unto him who scorns the pure springs of the highest revelations of our day. Woe unto them who reject their eyes, for the Artists of today are the prophetic eyes of mankind. Woe unto them who trust in their own abilities—which do not excel those of reverend moles! . . . Darkness has descended upon their souls!

Having become an end in itself, painting has found within itself endless horizons and aspirations. And before the astounded eyes of the casual spectators roaring with laughter at contemporary exhibitions (but already with caution and respect), Painting has developed such a large number of different trends that their enumeration alone would now be enough for a big article.

It can be said with confidence that the confines of This art of Free Painting have been expanded during the first decade of the twentieth century, as had never been imagined during all the years of its previous existence!

Amid these trends of the New Painting the one that Shocks the spectator's eye most is the Direction defined by the word *Cubism*.

The theoretical foundation of which I want to concentrate on now—thereby Placing the erroneous judgment of the contemporary "admirer" of art on a firm, more or less correct footing.

In analyzing the art of former painters, e.g., Holbein and Rembrandt, we can infer the following tenets. These two artistic temperaments comprehend Nature: the first chiefly as line.

The second as a certain complex of chiaroscuro. If for the first, color is something merely, but with difficulty, to be abolished traditionally by the help of drawing (contour)—then for the second, drawing (contour) and line are an unpleasant feature of the art of his time. If Rembrandt takes up the needle, his hand hastens to build a whole forest of lines so that "the shortest distance between two points" would vanish in this smokelike patch of etching. The first is primarily a draftsman. Rembrandt is a painter.

Rembrandt is a *colorist*, an impressionist, Rembrandt senses *plane* and colors. But of course, both are the Blind Instruments of objects—both comprehend art as a means and not as an aim in itself—and they do not express the main bases of the Modern New Painting (as we see in our best modern artists).

The component elements into which the essential nature of painting can be broken down are:

I. line
II. surface
(for its mathematical conception see epigraph)
III. color
IV. texture (the character of surface)

To a certain extent Elements I and III were properties, peculiarities of old painting as well. But I and IV arc those fabulous realms that only our twentieth century has discovered and whose painterly significance Nature has revealed to us. Previously painting only Saw, now it Feels. Previously it depicted an object in two dimensions, now wider possibilities have been disclosed....[3] I am not talking about what the near future will bring us (this has already been discovered by such artists as *P. P. Konchalovsky*) a Sense of *Visual ponderability*—A Sense of color Smell. A sense of *duration of the colored moment* . . . (I. I. Mashkov).

I shall avoid the fascinating task of outlining the plan of this inspired march along the path of secrets now revealed. Instead, I shall return to my subject.

In order to understand Painting, the art of the New Painting, it is essential to take the same standpoint vis-a-vis Nature as the artist takes. One must feel ashamed of the fatuous adolescent's elementary view of Nature—an extremely literary, narrative standpoint. One must remember that Nature, for the Artist and for painting, is Exclusively an object of visual Sensation. Indeed, a visual sensation refined and broadened immeasurably (compared with the past) by the associative capacity of the human spirit, but one that avoids ideas of the coarse, irrelevant kind. Painting now operates within a sphere of Painterly Ideas and Painterly Conceptions that is accessible only to it; they ensue and arise from those Elements of visual Nature that can be defined by the four points mentioned above.

The man deprived of a Painterly understanding of Nature will, when looking at Cezanne's landscape *The House*, understand it purely narratively; (1) "house" (2) mountains (3) trees (4) sky. Whereas for the artist, there existed I linear construction II surface construction (not fully realized) and III color orchestration. For the artist, there were certain lines going up and down, right and left, but there wasn't a house or trees . . . there were areas of certain color strength, of certain character. And that's all.

Painting of the past, too, seemed at times to be not far from conceiving Nature as Line (of a certain character and of a certain intensity) and colors (Nature as a number of colored areas—this applies Only to the Impressionists at the end of the nineteenth century). But it never made up its mind to analyze visual Nature from the viewpoint of the essence of its surface. The conception of what we see as merely a number of certain definite sections of different surface Planes arose only in the twentieth century under the general name of Cubism. Like everything else, Cubism has its history. Briefly, we can indicate the sources of this remarkable movement.

I. If the Greeks and Holbein were, as it were, the first to whom *line* (in itself) was accessible.

II. If Chiaroscuro (as color), texture, and surface appeared fleetingly to Rembrandt.

III. then Cezanne is the first who can be credited with the conjecture that Nature can be observed as a Plane, as a surface (surface construction). If line, Chiaroscuro, and coloration were well known in the past, then Plane and surface were discovered only by the new painting. Just as the whole immeasurable significance of Texture in painting has only now been realized.

In passing on to a more detailed examination of examples of a surface analysis of Nature in the pictures of modern artists, and in passing on to certain constructions of a theoretical type that ensue from this view of Nature—as plane and surface—I would like to answer the question that should now be examined at the beginning of any article devoted to the Theory of the New Painting: "Tell me, what is the significance of establishing definite names for Definite Painterly Canons, of establishing the dimensions of all you call the Establishment of Painterly Counterpoint? Indeed, the pictures of modern artists don't become any better or more valuable because of this. . . ." And people like to add: "Oh, how I dislike talking about Painting" or "I like this art."

A few years ago artists wouldn't have forgiven themselves if they'd talked about the aims, tasks, and essence of Painting. Times have changed. Nowadays not to be a theoretician of painting means to reject an understanding of it. This art's center of gravity has been transferred. Formerly the spectator used to be the idle witness of a street event, but now he as it were, presses close to the lenses of a Superior Visual Analysis of the Visible Essence surrounding us. Nobody calls Lomonosov a crank for allowing poetic meter in the Russian language. Nobody is surprised at the "useless" work of the scientist who attempts in a certain way to strictly classify the phenomena of a certain type of organic or inorganic Nature. So how come you want me—me, for whom the cause of the New painting is higher than anything—as I stroll around museums and exhibitions looking at countless collections of Painting, not to attempt to assess the specimens of this pretty, pretty art by any means other than the child's categorization of pictures; Genre, portrait, landscape, animals, etc., etc., as Mr. Benois does? Indeed in such painting, photographic portraits should be relegated to the section with the heading "unknown artist." No, it's high time it was realized that the classification, the only one possible, of works of painting must be according to those elements that, as our investigation will show, have engendered painting and given it Life.

It has been known for a long time that what is important is not the what, but the how, i.e., which principles, which objectives, guided the artist's creation of this or that work! It is essential to establish on the basis of which canon it (the work) arose! It is essential to reveal its painterly nature! It must be indicated what the aim in Nature was that the artist of the given picture was So attracted by. And the analysts of painterly phenomena will then be a Scientific criticism of the subject. And the spectator will no longer be the confused enemy of the new art—this unhappy spectator who has only just broken out of the torture chamber of our newspapers' and magazines' cheap, presumptuous, and idiotic criticism, a criticism that believes that its duty is not to learn from the artist but to teach him. Without even studying art. Many critics seriously believe that they can teach the artist What he must do and how he must do it! ... I myself have personally encountered such blockheaded diehards.

Line is the result of the intersection of 2 planes...

One plane can intersect another on a straight line or on a curve (surface).

Hence follow: I *Cubism* proper—and II *Rondism.*

The first is an analysis of Nature from the point of view of planes intersecting on straight lines, the second operates with surfaces of a ball-like character.

> Disharmony is the opposite of harmony,
> dissymmetry is the opposite of symmetry,
> deconstruction is the opposite of construction,
> a canon can be constructive,
> a canon can be deconstructive,
> construction can be shifted or displaced
> *The canon of displaced construction.*

The existence in Nature of visual poetry—ancient, dilapidated towers and walls—points to the essential, tangible, and forceful supremacy of this kind of beauty.

> Displacement can be linear.
> Displacement can be planar.
> Displacement can be in one particular place or it can be general.

Displacement can be coloristic—(a purely mechanical conception).

The canon of the Academy advocated: symmetry of proportion, fluency, or their equivalent harmony.

The New painting has indicated the existence of a second, parallel canon that does not destroy the first one—the canon of displaced construction.

1) disharmony (not fluency)
2) disproportion
4) coloristic dissonance
3) deconstruction

All these concepts follow from the examination of works of the New painting. Point 3) I placed out of sequence, and it has already been examined above. Both Cubism and Rondism can be based on all these four basic concepts of the Canon of Displaced Construction.

But Cubism and Rondism can also live and develop in the soil of the Academic Canon. . .

Note. In the past there was also a counterbalance to the Academic Canon living on (fluency) harmony, proportion, symmetry: all barbaric Folk arts were based partly on the existence of this second canon (of displaced Construction*).

A definitive examination of our relation to these arts as raw material for the modern artist's creative soul would take us out of our depth.

**Note to above note*. In contrast to the Academic Canon which sees drawing as a definite dimension, we can now establish the canon of Free drawing. (The fascination of children's drawings lies precisely in the full exposition in such works of this principle.) The pictures and drawings of V.V. Kandinsky. The drawings of V. Burliuk.

The portraits of P. P. Konchalovsky and I. Mashkov, the *Soldier* Pictures of M. Larionov, are the best examples of Free drawing... (as also are the latest works of N. Kul'bin).

In poetry the apology is vers libre—the sole and finest; representative of which in modern poetry is Viktor Khlebnikov.

Note II. The examination of the wide field of (painting's) concepts does not fall into the scope of this article:

Line
Color orchestration
which ought to be the subject
of separate investigations.

Cubism, 1912 — NATALYA GONCHAROVA

The text of this piece, "Kubizm," is part of an impromptu speech given by Goncharova at the Knave of Diamonds debate on February 12, 1912. Benedikt Livshits mentions that Goncharova composed a letter on the basis of this speech and sent it the day after the debate to various newspaper offices in Moscow, but it was not published until the French translation. Eli Eganbyuri (Ilya Zdarievich) in his book on Goncharova and Mikhail Larionov quotes a very similar text and states that its source is a letter by Goncharova, obviously the unpublished one to which Livshits refers. Goncharova spoke at the debate in answer to David Burliuk's presentation on cubism; Larionov also spoke but was booed down. The tone of the speech reflects the rift that had occurred between Larionov/Goncharova and Burliuk/Knave of Diamonds and that had resulted in Larionov's establishment of the Donkey's Tail in late 1911. Two sources put the date of the debate at February 12, 1911; although more reliable evidence points to 1912. The actual letter by Goncharova is preserved in the manuscript section of the Lenin Library, Moscow.

***

Cubism is a positive phenomenon, but it is not altogether a new one. The Scythian stone images, the painted wooden dolls sold at fairs are those same cubist works. True, they are sculpture and not painting, but in France, too, the home of cubism, it was the monuments of Gothic sculpture that served as the point of departure for this movement. For a long time I have been working in the manner of cubism, but I condemn without hesitation the position of the Knave of Diamonds, which has replaced creative activity with theorizing. The creative genius of art has never outstripped practice with theory and has built theory on the basis of earlier works. If religious art and art exalting the state had always been the most majestic, the most perfect manifestation of man's creative activity, then this can be explained by the fact that such art had never been guilty of theoreticalness. The artist well knew *what* he was depicting, and *why* he was depicting it. Thanks to this, his idea was clear and definite, and it remained only to find a form for it as clear and as definite. Contrary to Burliuk, I maintain that at all times it has mattered and will matter what the artist depicts, although at the same time it is extremely important *how* he embodies his conception.

Why We Paint Ourselves: A Futurist Manifesto, 1913 — ILYA ZDANEVICH and MIKHAIL LARIONOV

Larionov—Born Tiraspol, 1881; died Paris, 1964. 1898: entered the Moscow Institute of Painting, Sculpture, and Architecture; 1906: went to Paris at Sergei Diaghilev's invitation for the Salon d'Automne. 1910: mainly responsible for establishment of the Knave of Diamonds, which he soon rejected: early 1910s: 15 contributed to the "Donkey's Tail," "Target," "Exhibition of Painting. 1915." and other exhibitions; ca. 1913: illustrated futurist booklets; 1914: went to Paris to work for Diaghilev at the outbreak of the war was forced to return to Moscow; 1915: wounded on the East Prussian front and hospitalized in Moscow; 1915: left to Moscow to join Diaghilev in Lausanne; 1918: settled in Paris with Natalya Goncharova.

Zdanevich—Born Tiflis, 1894; died Paris, 1975. Brother of the artist and critic Kirill; 1911: entered the Law School of the University of St. Petersburg; 1912; with Kirill and Mikhail Le-Dantiyu discovered the primitive artist Niko Pirosmanishvili; 1913: under the pseudonym of Eli Eganbyuri (the result of reading the Russian handwritten form of Ilya Zdanevich as Roman characters) published a book on Goncharova and Larionov; 1914: met Marinetti in Moscow; 1917-1918: with Kirill, Aleksei Kruchenykh, and Igor Terentev organized the futurist group 41° in Tills; 1921: settled in Paris.

The text of this piece, "Pochemu my raskrashivaemsya" appeared in the magazine *Argus* (St. Petersburg), Christmas number, 1913. The text is similar in places to the Italian futurist manifestoes *La pittura futurista* and *Gli espositori al pubblico*, both of which had appeared in Russian translation in *Soyuz molodezhi* [Union of Youth] (St. Petersburg), The original text in Argus contains photo portraits of Goncharova, Larionov, Mikhail Le-Dantiyu and Ilya Zdanevich with their faces decorated with futurist and rayonist designs, a practice that they and others (including David Burliuk) engaged in during some of their public appearances , in 1912 and 1913. Several of these photographs had been reproduced already in connection with a court case involving Le-Dantiyu (see the journal *Zhizn' i sud* [Life and Court] [St. Petersburg], May 9, 1913). *Argus* was by no means an avant-garde publication, and this piece was included evidently to satisfy the curiosity of its middle-class readers.

* * *

To the frenzied city of arc lamps, to the streets bespattered with bodies, to the houses huddled together, we have brought our painted faces; we're off and the track awaits the runners.

Creators, we have not come to destroy construction, but to glorify and to affirm it. The painting of our faces is neither an absurd piece of fiction, nor a relapse—it is indissolubly linked to the character of our life and of our trade.

The dawn's hymn to man, like a bugler before the battle, calls to victories over the earth, hiding itself beneath the wheel until the hour of vengeance; the slumbering weapons have awoken, and spit on the enemies.

The new life requires a new community and a new way of propagation.

Our self-painting is the first speech to have found unknown truths. And the conflagrations caused by it show that the menials of the earth have not lost hope of saving the old nests, have gathered all forces to the defense of the gates, have crowded together knowing that with the first goal scored we are the victors.

The course of art and a love of life have been our guides. Faithfulness to our trade inspires us, the fighters. The steadfastness of the few presents forces that cannot be overcome.

We have joined art to life. After the long isolation of artists, we have loudly summoned life and life has invaded art, it is time for art to invade life. The painting of our faces is the beginning of the invasion. That is why our hearts are beating so.

We do not aspire to a single form of aesthetics. Art is not only a monarch, but also a newsman and a decorator. We value both print and news. The synthesis of decoration and illustration is the basis of our self-painting. We decorate life and preach—that's why we paint ourselves.

Self-painting is one of the new valuables that belong to the people as they all do in our day and age. The old ones were incoherent and squashed flat by money. Gold was valued as an ornament and became expensive. We throw down gold and precious stones from their pedestal and declare them valueless. Beware, you who collect them and horde them—you will soon be beggars.

It began in '05. Mikhail Larionov painted a nude standing against a background of a carpet and extended the design onto her. But there was no proclamation. Now Parisians are doing the same by painting the legs of their dancing girls, and ladies powder themselves with brown powder and like Egyptians elongate their eyes. But that's old age. We, however, join contemplation with action and fling ourselves into the crowd.

To the frenzied city of arc lamps, to the streets bespattered with bodies, to the houses huddled together, we have not brought the past: unexpected flowers have bloomed in the hothouse and they excite us.

City dwellers have for a long time been varnishing their nails using eye shadow, rouging their lips, cheeks, hair—but all they are doing is to imitate the earth.

We, creators, have nothing to do with the earth; our lines and colors appeared with us. If we were given the plumage of parrots, we would pluck out their feathers to use as brushes and crayons.

If we were given immortal beauty, we would daub over it and kill it—we who know no half measures.

Tattooing doesn't interest us. People tattoo themselves once and for always. We paint ourselves for an hour, and a change of experience calls for a change of painting, just as picture devours picture, when on the other side of a car windshield shop windows flash by running into each other: that's our faces. Tattooing is beautiful but it says little—only about one's tribe and exploits. Our painting is the newsman.

Facial expressions don't interest us. That's because people have grown accustomed to understanding them, too timid and ugly as they are. Our faces are like the screech of the trolley warning the hurrying passers-by, like the drunken sounds of the great tango. Mimicry is expressive but colorless. Our painting is the decorator.

Mutiny against the earth and transformation of faces into a projector of experiences.

The telescope discerned constellations lost in space, painting will tell of lost ideas.

We paint ourselves because a clean face is offensive, because we want to herald the unknown, to rearrange life, and to bear man's multiple soul to the upper reaches of reality.

Rayonists and Futurists. A Manifesto, 1913 — MIKHAIL LARIONOV and NATALYA GONCHAROVA

The text of this piece, "Luchisty i budushchniki. Manifest," appeared in the miscellany *Oslinyi khvost i Mishen* (*Donkey's Tail* and *Target*] (Moscow, July 1913). The declarations are similar to those advanced in the catalogue of the "Target" exhibition held in Moscow in March 1913, and the concluding paragraphs are virtually the same as those of Larionov's "Rayonist Painting." Although the theory of rayonist painting was known already, the "Target" acted as the formal demonstration of its practical achievements. Because of the various allusions to the Knave of Diamonds, "A Slap in the Face of Public Taste," and David Burliuk, this manifesto acts as a polemical response to Larionov's rivals. The use of the Russian neologism *budushchniki*, and not the European borrowing *futuristy*, betrays Larionov's current rejection of the West and his orientation toward Russian and Eastern cultural traditions. In addition to Larionov and Goncharova, the signers of the manifesto were Timofei Bogomazov (a sergeant-major and amateur painter whom Larionov had befriended during his military service—no relative of the artist Aleksandr Bogomazov) and the artists Morits Fabri, Ivan Larionov (brother of Mikhail), Mikhail Le-Dantiyu, Vyacheslav Levkievsky, Vladimir Obolensky, Sergei Romanovich, Aleksandr Shevchenko, and Kirill Zdanevich (brother of Iliya). All except Fabri and Obolensky took part in the "Target" exhibition, and *Oslinyi khvost* i *Mishen'* carried reproductions of some of their exhibits.

* * *

We, Rayonists and Futurists, do not wish to speak about new or old art, and even less about modern Western art.

We leave the old art to die and leave the "new" art to do battle with If; and incidentally, apart from a battle and a very easy one, the "new" art cannot advance anything of its own. It is useful to put manure on barren ground, but this dirty work does not interest us.

People shout about enemies closing in on them, but in fact, these enemies are, in any case, their closest friends. Their argument with old art long since departed is nothing but a resurrection of the dead, a boring, decadent love of paltriness and a stupid desire to march at the head of contemporary, philistine interests.

We are not declaring any war, for where can we find an opponent our equal?

The future is behind us.

All the same we will crush in our advance all those who undermine us and all those who stand aside.

We don't need popularization—our art will, in any case, take its full place in life—that's a matter of time.

We don't need debates and lectures, and if we sometimes organize them, then that's by way of a gesture to public impatience.

While the artistic throne is empty, and narrow-mindedness, deprived of its privileges, is running around calling for battle with departed ghosts, we push it out of the way, sit up on the throne, and reign until a regal deputy comes and replaces us.

We, artists of art's future paths, stretch out our hand to the futurists, in spite of all their mistakes, but express our utmost scorn for the so-called egofuturists and neofuturists, talentless, banal people, the same as the members of the *Knave of Diamonds, Slap in the Face of Public Taste,* and *Union of Youth* groups.

We let sleeping dogs lie, we don't bring fools to their senses, we call trivial people trivial to their faces, and we are ever ready to defend our interests actively.

We despise and brand as artistic lackeys all those who move against a background of old or new art and go about their trivial business. Simple, un-corrupted people are closer to us than this artistic husk that clings to modern art, like flies to honey.

To our way of thinking, mediocrity that proclaims new ideas of art is as unnecessary and vulgar as if it were proclaiming old ideas.

This is a sharp stab in the heart for all who cling to so-called modern art, making their names in speeches against renowned little old men—despite the fact that between them and the latter there is essentially not much difference. These are true brothers in spirit—the wretched rags of contemporaneity, for who needs the peaceful renovating enterprises of those people who make a hubbub about modern art, who haven't advanced a single thesis of their own, and who express long-familiar artistic truths in their own words!

We've had enough Knaves of Diamonds whose miserable art is screened by this title, enough slaps in the face given by the hand of a baby suffering from wretched old age, enough unions of old and young? We don't need to square vulgar accounts with public taste—let those indulge in this who on paper give a slap in the face, but who, in fact, stretch out their hands for alms.

We've had enough of this manure; now we need to sow.

We have no modesty—we declare this bluntly and frankly—we consider ourselves to be the creators of modern art.

We have our own artistic honor, which we are prepared to defend to the last with all the means at our disposal. We laugh at the words "old art" and "new art"—that's nonsense invented by idle philistines.

We spare no strength to make the sacred tree of art grow to great heights, and what does it matter to us that little parasites swarm in its shadow—let them, they know of the tree's existence from its shadow.

Art for life and even more—life for art!

We exclaim: the whole brilliant style of modern times—our trousers, jackets, shoes, trolleys, cars, airplanes, railways, grandiose steamships—is fascinating, is a great epoch, one that has known no equal in the entire history of the world.

We reject individuality as having no meaning for the examination of a work of art. One has to appeal only to a work of art, and one can examine it only by proceeding from the laws according to which it was created.

The tenets we advance are as follows:

Long live the beautiful East! We are joining forces with contemporary'Eastern artists to work together.

Long live nationality! We march hand in hand with our ordinary house painters.

Long live the style of Rayonist painting that we created—free from concrete forms, existing and developing according to painterly laws!

We declare that there has never been such a thing as a copy and recommend painting from pictures painted before the present day. We maintain that art cannot be examined from the point of view of time.

We acknowledge all styles as suitable for the expression of our art,
4 styles existing both yesterday and today—for example, cubism, futurism, orphism, and their synthesis, rayonism, for which the art of the past, like life, is an object of observation.

We are against the West, which is vulgarizing our forms and Eastern forms, and which is bringing down the level of everything.

We demand a knowledge of painterly craftsmanship.

More than anything else, we value intensity of feeling and its great sense of uplifting.

We believe that the whole world can be expressed fully in painterly forms:

Life, poetry, music, philosophy.

We aspire to the glorification of our art and work for its sake and for the sake of our future creations.

We wish to leave deep footprints behind us, and this is an honorablewish.

We advance our works and principles to the fore; we ceaselessly change them and put them into practice.

We are against art societies, for they lead to stagnation.

We do not demand public attention and ask that it should not be demanded from us.

The style of rayonist painting that we advance signifies spatial forms arising from the intersection of the reflected rays of various objects, forms chosen by the artist's will.

The ray is depicted provisionally on the surface by a colored line.

That which is valuable for the lover of painting finds its maximum expression in a rayonist picture. The objects that we see in life play no role here, but that which is the essence of painting itself can be shown here best of all—the combination of color, its saturation, the relation of colored misses, depth, texture; anyone who is interested in painting can give his full attention to all these things.

The picture appears to be slippery; it imparts a sensation of the extratemporal, of the spatial. In it arises the sensation of what could be called the fourth dimension, because its length, breadth, and density of the layer of paint are the only signs of the outside world—all the sensations that arise from the picture are of a different order; in this way painting becomes equal to music while remaining itself. At this juncture a kind of painting emerges that can be mastered by following precisely the laws of color and its transference onto the canvas. Hence the creation of new forms whose meaning and expressiveness depend exclusively on the degree of intensity of tone and the position that it occupies in relation to other tones.

Hence the natural downfall of all existing styles and forms in all the art of the past—since they, like life, are merely objects for better perception and pictorial construction.

With this begins the true liberation of painting and its life in accordance only with its own laws, a self-sufficient painting, with its own forms, color, and timbre.

Rayonist Painting, 1913 — MIKHAIL LARIONOV

The text of this piece, "Luchistskaya zhivopis," appeared in the miscellany *Oslinyi khvost* i *Mishen'* [*Donkey's Tail* and *Target*] (Moscow, July 1913) and was signed and dated Moscow, June 1912. Larionov seems to have formulated rayonism in 1912, not before; no rayonist works, for example, figured at his one-man exhibition at the Society of Free Aesthetics in Moscow in December 1911, Goncharova was the first to use the term *rayonism*, although Larionov's interest in science (manifested particularly while he was at high school) had obviously stimulated his peculiarly refractive conception of art. While rayonism had apparent cross-references with Franz Marc, the Italian futurists, and later, with Lyonel Feininger, the upsurge of interest in photography and cinematography in Russia at this time provided an undoubted stimulus to Larionov's concern with light and dynamics. It is of interest to note that in 1912/1913 the Moscow photographer A. Trapani invented the photographic technique of "ray gun" (*luchistyi gummi)*—a version of the gum-arabic process—which enabled the photographer to create the illusion of a radial, fragmented texture. Larionov himself exhibited several "photographic studies" at the "Donkey's tail" in 1912, and his famous picture *Glass* (1912-1913) at the Guggenheim Museum demonstrates an obvious interest in optics. Of possible relevance to Larionov's derivation of rayonism was the peculiarly "broken" texture that Mikhail Vrubel favored in so many of his works in the 1890s and 1900s—a technique admired by a number of young Russian artists. Moreover, Vrubel's theory of visual reality came very close to Larionov's formulation, as the following statement by Vrubel would indicate: The contours with which artists normally delineate the confines of a form in actual fact do not exist—they are merely an optical illusion that occurs from the interaction of rays falling onto the object and reflected from its surface at different angles. In fact, at this point you get a 'complimentary colour'—complementary to the basic, local color." Goncharova shared Larionov's interest in radiation and emanation and at her one-man exhibition in 1913 presented several works based on the "Theory of transparency" formulated by her fellow artist Ivan Firsov.

* * *

Painting is self-sufficient;
it has its own forms, color and timbre.
Rayonism is concerned with
spatial forms that can
arise from the intersection
of the reflected rays of different objects,
forms chosen by the artist's will.

* * *

How they are provided for upon the earth, (appearing at intervals).

How dear and dreadful they are to the earth.

How they inure to themselves as much as to any—what a paradox appears their age,

How people respond to them, yet know them not.

> How there is something relentless in their fate all times,
> How all times mischoose the objects of their adulation and reward,
> And how the same inexorable price must still be paid for the same great purchase.
>
> —Walt Whitman

> I hear it was charged against me that I sought to destroy institutions,
> But really I am neither for nor against institutions,
> (What indeed have I in common with them? or what with the destruction of them?).
>
> —Walt Whitman

Throughout what we call time various styles have emerged. A temporal displacement of these styles would in no way have changed the artistic value and significance of what was produced during their hegemony. We have inherited Egyptian, Assyrian, Greek, Cretan, Byzantine, Romanesque, Gothic, Japanese, Chinese, Indian styles, etc. There is a great deal of such classification in art history, and in fact, there are infinitely more styles, not to mention that style that is peculiar to each work outside the general style of the time.

Style is that manner, that device by which a work of art has been created, and if we were to examine all art objects throughout the world, then it would transpire that they had all been created by some artistic device or other; not a single work of art exists without this.

This applies not only to what we call art objects, but also to everything that exists in a given age. People examine and perceive everything from the point of view of the style of their age. But what is called art is examined from the point of view of the *perception of artistic truths*; although these truths pass through the style of their age, they are quite independent of it. The fact that people perceive nature and their environment through the style of their age is best seen in the comparison of various styles and various ages. Let us take a Chinese picture, a picture from the time of Watteau, and an impressionist picture—a gulf lies between them, they examine nature from completely different points of view, but nevertheless the people who witnessed their creation understood them, just as the artists themselves did, and did not doubt for a moment that this was the same life and nature that surrounded them (at this juncture I am not concerned with connoisseurs of art as such). And often the artist Utamaro, whose age coincided with that of Watteau, is spumed by those who reject the age of Watteau, but who cannot surmount the difference of style between Japan and our eighteenth century. There are ages that are completely rejected, and even those who are interested in art ignore them. These are eras that are very remote, for example, the Stone Age. There are styles that are in the same position because of a considerable difference between the cultures of the people who created them and those who have to respond to them (Negro, Australasian, Aztec, Kolushes, etc.) despite the fact that whole nations have apprehended and embodied life only in that way, age after age.

Any style, the moment it appears, especially if it is given immediate, vivid expression, is always as incomprehensible as the style of a remote age.

A new style is always first created in art, since all previous styles and life are refracted through it.

Works of art are not examined from the point of view of time and are essentially different because of the form in which they are perceived and in which they were created. There is no such thing as a copy in our current sense of the word, but there is such a thing as a work of art with the same departure point-served either by another work of art or by nature.

In examining our contemporary art we see that about forty of fifty years ago in the heyday of impressionism, a movement began to appear in art that advocated the colored surface. Gradually this movement took hold of people working in the sphere of art, and after a while there appealed the theory of displaced colored surface and movement of surface. A parallel trend arose of constructing according to the curve of the circle—rondism. The displacement of surfaces and construction according to the curve made for more constructiveness within the confines of the picture's surface. The doctrine of surface painting gives rise naturally to the doctrine of figural construction because the figure is in the surface's movement. Cubism teaches one to expose the third dimension by means of form (but not aerial and linear perspective together with form) and to transfer forms onto the canvas the moment they are created. Of all techniques, chiaroscuro, in the main, is adopted by cubism. For the most part this trend has decorative characteristics, although all cubists are engaged in easel painting—but this is caused by modern society's lack of demand for purely decorative painting. A movement parallel to cubism is spherism.

Cubism manifests itself in almost all existing forms—classical, academic (Metzinger), romantic (Le Fauconnier, Braque), realist (Gleizes, Léger, Goncharova)—and in forms of an abstract kind (Picasso). Under the influence of futurism on the cubists, there appeared a transitory cubism of futurist character (Delaunay, Levy, the latest works of Picasso, Le Fauconnier).

Futurism was first promoted by the Italians: this doctrine aspires to make reforms not merely in the sphere of painting—it is concerned also with all kinds of art.

In painting, futurism promotes mainly the doctrine of movement—dynamism.

Painting in its very essence is static—hence dynamics as a style. The Futurist unfurls the picture—he places the artist in the center of the picture; he examines the object from different points of view; he advocates the translucency of objects, the painting of what the artist knows, not what he sees, the transference of the sum total of impressions onto the canvas and the transference of many aspects of one and the same object; he introduces narrative and literature.

Futurism introduces a refreshing stream into modern art—which to a certain extent is linked to useless traditions—but for modern Italy it really serves as a very good lesson. If the futurists had had the genuine painterly traditions that the French have, then their doctrine would not have become part of French painting, as it now has.

Of the movements engendered by this trend and dominant at present, the following are in the forefront: postcubism, which is concerned with the synthesis of forms as opposed to the analytical decomposition of forms; neofuturism, which has resolved completely to reject the picture as a surface covered with paint, replacing it by a screen—on which the static, essentially colored surface is replaced by a light-colored, moving one; and orphism, which advocates the musicality of objects—heralded by the artist Apollinaire.

Neofuturism introduces painting to the problems posed by glass and, in addition, natural dynamics; this deprives painting of its symbolic origin and it emerges as a new kind of art.

Orphism is concerned with painting based on this musical sonority of colors, on color orchestration; it is inclined toward a literal correspondence of musical to light waves, which stimulate color sensation—and it constructs painting literally according to musical laws. In fact, painting must be constructed according to its own laws—just as music is constructed according to its own musical laws; the laws germane only to painting are:

Colored line and texture.

Any picture consists of a colored surface and texture (the state of this colored surface is its timbre) and of the sensation that arises from these two things.

Nobody would begin to assert that the art connoisseur turns his primary attention to the objects depicted in a picture—he is interested in how these objects are depicted, which colors are put on the canvas, and how they are put on. Therefore, he is interested in the one artist and appreciates him, and not another, despite the fact that both paint the same objects. But the majority of dilettanti would think it very strange if objects as such were to disappear completely from a picture. Although all that they appreciate would still remain—color, the painted surface, the structure of painted masses, texture.

They would think it strange simply because we are accustomed to seeing what is of most value in painting in the context of objects.

In actual fact, all those painterly tasks that we realize with the help of objects we cannot perceive even with the help of tangible, real objects. Our impressions of an object are of a purely visual kind—despite the fact that we desire to re-create an object in its most complete reality and according to its essential qualities. The aspiration toward the most complete reality has compelled one of the most astonishing artists of our time, Picasso, and others with him, to employ types of technique that mutate concrete life, create surfaces of wood, stone, sand, etc., and change visual sensations into tactile ones. Picasso, with the aim of understanding an object concretely, stuck wallpaper, newspaper clippings onto a picture, painted with sand, ground glass; made a plaster relief—modeled objects out of papier-maché and then painted them (some of his "violins" are painted in this manner).

The painter can be expected to possess complete mastery of all existing types of technique (tradition plays a very important role in this) and to work according to the laws of painting, turning to extrinsic life only as a stimulant.

Chinese artists are allowed to take examinations only after they have learned to master the brush so well that brushstrokes in Indian ink on two transparent sheets of paper of the same size coincide when one sheet is placed on the other. From this it is obvious just how subtly the eye and hand must be developed.

The first to reduce a story to painterly form were the Hindus and Persians—their miniatures were reflected in the work of Henri Rousseau, the first in modern Europe to introduce a story into painterly form.

There are reasons to suppose that the whole world, in its concrete and spiritual totality, can be re-created in painterly form.

Furthermore, the qualities peculiar to painting alone are what we value in painting.

Now, it is necessary to find the point at which having concrete life as a stimulant—painting would remain itself while its adopted forms would be transformed and its outlook broadened; hence, like music, which takes sound from concrete life and uses it according to musical laws, painting would use color according to painterly laws.

In accordance with purely painterly laws, rayonism is concerned with introducing painting into the sphere of those problems peculiar to painting itself.

Our eye is an imperfect apparatus; we think that our sight is mainly responsible for transmitting concrete life to our cerebral centers, but in fact, it arrives there in its correct form not thanks to our sight, but thanks to other senses. A child sees objects for the first time upside down, and subsequently this defect of sight is corrected by the other senses. However much he desires to, an adult cannot see an object upside down.

Hence it is evident to what degree our inner conviction is important with regard to things existing in the outside world. If with regard to certain things, we know that they must be as they are because science reveals this to us, we do remain certain that this is as it should be and not otherwise despite the fact that we cannot apprehend this directly by our senses.

In purely official terms, rayonism proceeds from the following tenets:

Luminosity owes its existence to reflected light (between objects in space this forms a kind of colored dust).

The doctrine of luminosity.

Radioactive rays. Ultraviolet rays. Reflectivity.

We do not sense the object with our eye, as it is depicted conventionally in pictures and as a result of following this or that device; in fact, we do not sense the object as such. We perceive a sum of rays proceeding from a source of light; these are reflected from the object and enter our field of vision.

Consequently, if we wish to paint literally what we see, then we must paint the sum of rays reflected from the object. But in order to receive the total sum of rays from the desired object, we must select them deliberately because together with the rays of the object being perceived, there also fall into our range of vision reflected reflex rays belonging to other nearby objects. Now, if we wish to depict an object exactly as we see it, then we must depict also these reflex rays belonging to other objects—and then we will depict literally what we see. I painted my first works of a purely realistic kind in this way. In other words, this is the most complete reality of an object—not as we know it, but as we see it. In all his works Paul Cezanne was inclined toward this; that is why various objects in his pictures appear displaced and look asquint. This arose partly from the fact that he painted literally what he saw. But one can see an object as flat only with one eye, and Cezanne painted as every man sees—with two eyes, i.e., the object slightly from the right and slightly from the left.

At the same time, Cezanne possessed such keenness of sight that he could not help noticing the reflex rubbing, as it were, of a small part of one object against the reflected rays of another. Hence there occurred not the exposure of the object itself, but as it were, its displacement onto a different side and a partial truncation of one of the object's sides—which provided his pictures with a realistic construction.

Picasso inherited this tradition from Cézanne, developed it, and thanks to Negro and Aztec art, turned to monumental art; finally, he grasped how to build a picture out of the essential elements of an object so as to ensure a greater sense of construction in the picture.

Now, if we concern ourselves not with the objects themselves but with the sums of rays from them, we can build a picture in the following way:

The sum of rays from object A intersects the sum of rays from object B; in the space between them a certain form appears, and this is isolated by the artist's will. This can be employed in relation to several objects, e.g., the form constructed from a pair of scissors, a nose, and a bottle, etc. The picture's coloration depends on the pressure intensity of dominant colors and their reciprocal combinations.

The high point of color tension, density, and depth must be clearly shown.

A picture painted in a cubist manner and a futurist picture provide a different kind of form (a rayonist one) when they radiate in space.

Perception, not of the object itself, but of the sum of rays from it, is, by its very nature, much closer to the symbolic surface of the picture than is the object itself. This is almost the same as the mirage that appears in the scorching air of the desert and depicts distant towns, lakes, and oases in the sky (in concrete instances). Rayonism erases the barriers that exist between the picture's surface and nature.

A ray is depicted provisionally on the surface by a colored line.

What has most value for every lover of painting is revealed in its most complete form in a rayonist picture—the objects that we see in life play no role here (except for realistic rayonism, in which the object serves as a point of departure); that which is the essence of painting itself can best be revealed here—the combination of colors, their saturation, the interrelation of colored masses, depth, texture; whoever is interested in painting can concentrate on all these things to the full.

The picture appears to be slippery; it imparts a sensation of the extratemporal, of the spatial. In it arises the sensation of what could be called the fourth dimension, because its length, breadth, and density of the layer of paint are the only signs of the outside world all the sensations that arise from the picture are of a different order; in this way painting becomes equal to music while remaining itself. At this juncture a kind of painting emerges that can be mastered by following precisely the laws of color and its transference onto the canvas. Hence the creation of new forms whose significance and expressiveness depend exclusively on the degree of intensity of tone and the position that this occupies in relation to other tones. Hence the natural downfall of all existing styles and forms in all the art of the past—for they, like life, are merely objects for the rayonist perception and pictorial construction.

With this begins the true liberation of painting and its own life according to its own rules.

The next stage in the development of rayonism is pneumorayonism, or concentrated rayonism; this is concerned with joining elements together into general masses between spatial forms present in a more sectional, rayonist background.

Pictorial Rayonism, 1914 — MIKHAIL LARIONOV

The text of this piece, "Le Rayonisme Pictural," appeared in French in *Montjoie!* (Paris), no. 4/5/6, April/May/June, 1914. This was Larionov's first contribution to the French press and was printed just as the "Exposition de Natalie Gontcharowa et Michel Larionow" opened at the Galerie Paul Guillaume, Paris, at which rayonist works by both Goncharova and Larionov were presented. In places the text is similar to that of Larionov's "Rayonist Painting"; however, the occasional repetitions have been retained in order to preserve the original format of this, the first elucidation of rayonism to be published in the West.

* * *

Every form exists objectively in space by reason of the rays from the other forms that surround it; it is individualized by these rays, and they alone determine its existence.

Nevertheless, between those forms that our eye objectivizes, there exists a real and undeniable intersection of rays proceeding from various forms. These intersections constitute new intangible forms that the painter's eye can see. Where the rays from different objects meet, new immaterial objects are created in space. Rayonism is the painting of these intangible forms, of these *infinite* products with which the whole of space is filled.

Rayonism is the painting of the collisions and couplings of rays *between* objects, the dramatic representation of the struggle between the plastic emanations radiating from all things around us; rayonism is the painting of space revealed not by the contours of objects, not even by their formal coloring, but by the ceaseless and intense drama of the rays that constitute the unity of all things.

Rayonism might appear to be a form of spiritualist painting, even mystical, but it is, on the contrary, essentially plastic. The painter sees new forms created between tangible forms by their own radiation, and these are the only ones that he places on the canvas. Hence he attains the pinnacle of painting for painting's sake inspired by these real forms, although he would neither know how to, nor wish to, represent or even evoke them by their linear existence.

Pictorial studies devoted to a formal representation by no matter what kind of geometrical line—straight, curved circular still regard painting, in my opinion, as a means of representing forms. Rayonism wishes to regard painting as an end in itself and no longer as a means of expression.

Rayonism gives primary importance only to color. To this end, rayonism has come naturally to examine the problem of color depth.

The sensation a color can arouse, the emotion it can express is greater or lesser in proportion as its depth on the plane surface increase or decreases. Obviously, a blue spread evenly over the canvas vibrates with less intensity than the same blue put on more thickly. Hitherto this law has been applicable only to music, but it is incontestable also with regard to painting: *colors have a timbre* that changes according to the quality of their vibrations, i.e., of their density and loudness. In this way, painting becomes as free as music and becomes self-sufficient outside of imagery.

In his investigations the rayonist painter is concerned with variety of density, i.e., the depth of color that he is using, as much as with the composition formed by the rays from intervibrant objects.

So we are dealing with painting that is dedicated to the domination of color, to the study of the resonances deriving from the pure orchestration of its timbres.

Polychromy is not essential. For example, in a canvas painted in one color, a street would be represented by one flat, very brilliant and lacquered surface between houses depicted in relief with their projections and indentations; above would be a very smooth sky. These different masses would be combined by the intersections of the rays that they would reflect and would produce a supremely realistic impression—and just as dynamic—of how the street appeared in reality.

This example is actually rather clumsy and serves only to elucidate the question of color timbre, since in a rayonist canvas a street, a harvest scene, a sky exist only through the relationships between their intervibrations.

In rayonist painting the intrinsic life and continuum of the colored masses form a synthesis-image in the mind of the spectator, one that goes beyond time and space. One glimpses the famous fourth dimension since the length, breadth, and density of the superposition of the painted colors are the only signs of the visible world; and all the other sensations, created by images, are of another order—that superreal order that man must always seek, yet never find, so that he would approach paths of representation more subtle and more spiritualized.

We believe that rayonism marks a new stage in this development.

From Cubism and Futurism to Suprematism: The New Painterly Realism, 1915 — KAZIMIR MALEVICH

Born near Kiev, 1879; died Leningrad, 1935. 1903 onwards: studied in Moscow; ca. 1910: influenced by neoprimitivism; 1913: took part in a futurist conference in Uusikirkko, Finland; designed decor for the Aleksei Kruchenykh-Mikhail Matyushin opera *Victory over the Sun*, produced in December in St. Petersburg; illustrated futurist booklets; 1914: met Filippo Marinetti on the latter's arrival in Russia; 1915-16: first showing of suprematist works at "0.10"; 1911-17: contributed to the "Union of Youth," "Donkey's Tail," "Target," "Tramway V," "Shop," "Knave of Diamonds," and other exhibitions; 1918: active on various levels within Narkompros; 1919-22: at the Vitebsk Art School, where he replaced Marc Chagall as head; organized Unovis [Uniya novogo iskusstva/Utverditeli novogo iskusstva - Union of the New Art/ Affirmers of the New Art]; 1920 to late 1920s: worked on his experimental constructions the so-called *arkhitektony* and *planity*; 1922: joined IKhK; 1927: visited Warsaw and Berlin with a one-man exhibition; contact with the Bauhaus; late 1920s: returned to a more representational kind of painting.

The translation is of Malevich's *Ot kubizma i futurizma k suprematizmu. Novyi zhivopisnyi realizm* (Moscow, 1916). This text, written in its original form in 1915, saw three editions: the first appeared in December 1915 in Petrograd under the title Ot kubizma ⊠ suprematizmu. Novyi zhivopisnyi realizm (From Cubism to Suprematism. The New Painterly Realism) and coincided with the exhibition "0.10"; the second followed in January 1916, also in Petrograd; the third, from which this translation is made, was published in November 1916, but in Moscow, and is signed and dated 1915. The first eight paragraphs of the text are similar to

Malevich's statement issued at "0.10". The style is typical of Malevich's writings, and the grammatical eccentricities and somewhat arbitrary italicizing create occasional ambiguities. Certain ideas and expressions used in the text recall the writings of Nikolai Kulbin, Vladimir Markov, and Olga Rozanova, which Malevich undoubtedly knew.

* * *

Only when the conscious habit of seeing nature's little nooks, Madonnas, and Venuses in pictures disappears *will we witness a purely painterly work of art.*

I have transformed myself *in the zero of form* and have fished myself out of the *rubbishy slough of academic art.*

I have destroyed the ring of the horizon and got out of the circle of objects, the horizon ring that has imprisoned the artist and the forms of nature

This accursed ring, by continually revealing novelty after novelty, leads the artist away from the *aim of destruction.*

And only *cowardly consciousness* and insolvency of creative power in an artist yield to this deception and establish *their art on the forms of nature*, afraid of losing the foundation on which the *savage and the academy* have based their art.

To produce favorite objects and little nooks of nature is just like a thief being enraptured by his shackled legs.

Only dull and impotent artists veil their work with *sincerity*. Art requires *truth*, not *sincerity*.

Objects have vanished like smoke; to attain the new artistic culture, art advances toward creation as an end in itself and toward domination over the forms of nature.

The Art of the Savage and Its Principles

The savage was the first to establish the principle of naturalism: in drawing a dot and five little sticks, he attempted to transmit his own image.

This first attempt laid the basis for the conscious imitation of nature's forms.

Hence arose the aim of approaching the face of nature as closely as possible.

And all the artist's efforts were directed toward the transmission of her creative forms.

The first inscription of the savage's primitive depiction gave birth to collective art, or the art of repetition.

Collective, because the real man with his subtle range of feelings, psychology, and anatomy had not been discovered.

The savage saw neither his outward image nor his inward state.

His consciousness could see only the outline of a man, a beast, etc.

And as his consciousness developed, so the outline of his depiction of nature grew more involved.

The more his consciousness embraced nature, the more involved his work became, and the more his experience and skid increased.

His consciousness developed in only one direction, toward nature's creation and not toward new forms of art.

Therefore his primitive depictions cannot be considered creative work.

The distortion of reality in his depictions is the result of weak technique.

Both technique and consciousness were only at the beginning of their development.

And his pictures must not be considered art.

Because unskillfulness is not art.

He merely pointed the way to art.

Consequently, his original outline was a framework on which the generations hung new discovery after new discovery made in nature.

And the outline became more and more involved and achieved its flowering in antiquity and the Renaissance.

The masters of these two epochs depicted man in his complete form, both outward and inward.

Man was assembled, and his inward state was expressed.

But despite their enormous skill, they did not, however, perfect the savage's idea:

The reflection of nature on canvas, as in a mirror.

And it is a mistake to suppose that their age was the most brilliant flowering of art and that the younger generation should at all costs aspire toward this ideal.

This idea is false.

It diverts young forces from the contemporary current of life and thereby deforms them.

Their bodies fly in airplanes, but they cover art and life with the old robes of Neros and Titians.

Hence they are unable to observe the new beauty of our modern life. Because they live by the beauty of past ages.

That is why the realists, impressionists, cubism, futurism, and suprematism were not understood.

The latter artists cast aside the robes of the past, came out into modern life, and found new beauty.

And I say:

That no torture chambers of the academies will withstand the days to come.

Forms move and are born, and we are forever making new discoveries.

And what we discover must not be concealed.

And it is absurd to force our age into the old forms of a bygone age.

The hollow of the past cannot contain the gigantic constructions and movement of our life.

As in our life of technology:

We cannot use the ships in which the Saracens sailed, and so in art we should seek forms that correspond to modern life.

The technological side of our age advances further and further ahead, but people try to push art further and further back.

This is why all those people who follow their age are superior, greater, and worthier.

And the realism of the nineteenth century is much greater than the ideal forms found in the aesthetic experience of the ages of the Renaissance and Greece.

The masters of Rome and Greece, after they had attained a knowledge of human anatomy and produced a depiction that was to a certain extent realistic:

Were overrun by aesthetic taste, and their realism was pomaded and powdered with the taste of aestheticism.

Hence their perfect line and nice colors.

Aesthetic taste diverted them from the realism of the earth, and they reached the impasse of idealism.

Their painting is a means of decorating a picture.

Their knowledge was taken away from nature into closed studios, where pictures were manufactured for many centuries.

That is why their art stopped short.

They closed the doors behind them, thereby destroying their contact with nature.

And that moment when they were gripped by the idealization of form should be considered the collapse of real art.

Because art should not advance toward abbreviation or simplification, but toward complexity.

The Venus de Milo is a graphic example of decline. It is not a real woman, but a parody.

Angelo's David is a deformation:

His head and torso are modeled, as it were, from two incongruent forms.

A fantastic head and a real torso.

All the masters of the Renaissance achieved great results in anatomy.

But they did not achieve veracity in their impression of the body.

Their painting does not transmit the body, and their landscapes do not transmit living light, despite the fact that bluish veins can be seen in the bodies of their people.

The art of naturalism is the savage's idea, the aspiration to transmit what is seen, but not to create a new form.

His creative will was in an embryonic state, but his impressions were more developed, which was the reason for his reproduction of reality.

Similarly it should not be assumed that his gift of creative will was developed in the classical painters.

Because we see in their pictures only repetitions of the real forms of life in settings richer than those of their ancestor, the savage.

Similarly their composition should not be considered creation, for in most cases the arrangement of figures depends on the subject: a king's procession, a court, etc.

The king and the judge already determine the places on the canvas for the persons of secondary importance.

Furthermore, the composition rests on the purely aesthetic basis of nice-ness of arrangement.

Hence arranging furniture in a room is still not a creative process.

In repeating or tracing the forms of nature, we have nurtured our consciousness with a false conception of art.

The work of the primitives was taken for creation.

The classics also.

If you put the same glass down twenty times, that's also creation.

Art, as the ability to transmit what we see onto a canvas, was considered creation.

Is placing a samovar on a table also really creation?

I think quite differently.

The transmission of real objects onto a canvas is the art of skillful reproduction, that's all.

And between the art of creating and the art of repeating there is a great difference.

To create means to live, forever creating newer and newer things.

And however much we arrange furniture about rooms, we will not extend or create a new form for them.

And however many moonlit landscapes the artist paints, however many grazing cows and pretty sunsets, they will remain the same dear little cows and sunsets. Only in a much worse form.

And in fact, whether an artist is a genius or not is determined by the number of cows he paints.

The artist can be a creator only when the forms in his picture have nothing in common with nature.

For art is the ability to create a construction that derives not from the interrelation of form and color and not on the basis of aesthetic taste in a construction's compositional beauty, but on the basis of weight, speed, and direction of movement.

Forms must be given life and the right to individual existence.

Nature is a living picture, and we can admire her. We are the living heart of nature. We are the most valuable construction in this gigantic living picture.

We are her living brain, which magnifies her life.

To reiterate her is theft, and he who reiterates her is a thief, a nonentity who cannot give, but who likes to take things and claim them as his own. (Counterfeiters.)

An artist is under a vow to be a free creator, but not a free robber.

An artist is given talent in order that he may present to life his share of creation and swell the current of life, so versatile.

Only in absolute creation will he acquire his right.

And this is possible when we free all art of philistine ideas and subject matter and teach our consciousness to see everything in nature not as real objects and forms, but as material, as masses from which forms must be made that have nothing in common with nature.

Then the habit of seeing Madonnas and Venuses in pictures, with fat, flirtatious cupids, will disappear.

Color and texture are of the greatest value in painterly creation—they are the essence of painting; but this essence has always been killed by the subject.

And if the masters of the Renaissance had discovered painterly surface, it would have been much nobler and more valuable than any Madonna or Giaconda.

And any hewn pentagon or hexagon would have been a greater work of sculpture than the Venus de Milo or David.

The principle of the savage is to aim to create art that repeats the real forms of nature.

In intending to transmit the living form, they transmitted its corpse in the picture.

The living was turned into a motionless, dead state.

Everything was taken alive and pinned quivering to the canvas, just as insects are pinned in a collection.

But that was the time of Babel in terms of art.

They should have created, but they repeated; they should have deprived forms of content and meaning, but they enriched them with this burden.

They should have dumped this burden, but they tied it around the neck of creative will.

The art of painting, the word, sculpture, was a kind of camel, loaded with all the trash of odalisques, Salomes, princes, and princesses.

Painting was the tie on the gentleman's starched shirt and the pink corset drawing in the stomach.

Painting was the aesthetic side of the object.

But it was never an independent end in itself.

Artists were officials making an inventory of nature's property, amateur collectors of zoology, botany, and archaeology.

Nearer our time, young artists devoted themselves to pornography and turned painting into lascivious trash.

There were no attempts at purely painterly tasks as such, without any appurtenances of real life.

There was no realism of painterly form as an end in itself, and there was no creation.

The realist academists are the savage's last descendants.

They are the ones who go about in the worn-out robes of the past.

And again, as before, some have cast aside these greasy robes.

And given the academy rag-and-bone man a slap in the face with their proclamation of futurism.

They began in a mighty movement to hammer at the consciousness as if at nails in a stone wall.

To pull you out of the catacombs into the speed of contemporaneity.

I assure you that whoever has not trodden the path of futurism as the exponent of modern life is condemned to crawl forever among the ancient tombs and feed on the leftovers of bygone ages.

Futurism opened up the "new" in modern life: the beauty of speed.

And through speed we move more swiftly.

And we, who only yesterday were futurists, have reached new forms through speed, new relationships with nature and objects.

We have reached suprematism, abandoning futurism as a loophole through which those lagging behind will pass.

We have abandoned futurism, and we, bravest of the brave, have spat on the altar of its art.

But can cowards spit on their idol—
As we did yesterday!!!

I tell you, you will not see the new beauty and the truth until you venture to spit.

Before us, all arts were old blouses, which are changed just like your silk petticoats.

After throwing them away, you acquire new ones.

Why do you not put on your grandmothers' dresses, when you thrill to the pictures of their powdered portraits?

This all confirms that your body is living in the modern age while your soul is clothed in your grandmother's old bodice.

This is why you find the Somovs, Kustodievs, and various such rag merchants so pleasant.

And I hate these secondhand-clothes dealers.
Yesterday we, our heads proudly raised, defended futurism—
Now with pride we spit on it.
And I say that what we spat upon will be accepted.
You, too, spit on the old dresses and clothe art in something new.

We rejected futurism not because it was outdated, and its end had come. No. The beauty of speed that it discovered is eternal, and the new will still be revealed to many.

Since we run to our goal through the speed of futurism, our thought moves more swiftly, and whoever lives in futurism is nearer to this aim and further from the past.

And your lack of understanding is quite natural. Can a man who always goes about in a cabriolet really understand the experiences and impressions of one who travels in an express or flies through the air?

The academy is a moldy vault in which art is being tin collated.

Gigantic wars, great inventions, conquest of the air, speed of travel, telephones, telegraphs, dreadnoughts are the realm of electricity.

But our young artists paint Neros and half-naked Roman warriors.

Honor to the futurists who forbade the painting of female hams, the painting of portraits and guitars in the moonlight.

They made a huge step forward: they abandoned meat and glorified the machine.

But meat and the machine are the muscles of life.

Both are the bodies that give life movement.

It is here that two worlds have come together.

The world of meat and the world of iron.

Both forms are the mediums of utilitarian reason.

But the artist's relationship to the forms of life's objects requires elucidation.

Until now the artist always followed the object.

Thus the new futurism follows the machine of today's dynamism.

These two kinds of art are the old and the new futurism: they are behind the running forms.

And the question arises: will this aim in the art of painting respond to its existence?

No!

Because in following the form of airplanes or motorcars, we shall always be anticipating the new cast-off forms of technological life, . . .

And second:

In following the form of things, we cannot arrive at painting as an end in itself, at spontaneous creation.

Painting will remain the means of transmitting this or that condition of life's forms.

But the futurists forbade the painting of nudity not in the name of the liberation of painting and the word, so that they would become ends in themselves.

But because of the changes in the technological side of life.

The new life of iron and the machine, the roar of motorcars, the brilliance of electric lights, the growling of propellers, have awakened the soul, which was suffocating in the catacombs of old reason and has emerged at the intersection of the paths of heaven and earth.

If all artists were to see the crossroads of these heavenly paths, if they were to comprehend these monstrous runways and intersections of our bodies with the clouds in the heavens, then they would not paint chrysanthemums.

The dynamics of movement has suggested advocating the dynamics of painterly plasticity.

But the efforts of the futurists to produce purely painterly plasticity as such were not crowned with success.

They could not settle accounts with objectism, which would have made their task easier.

When they had driven reason halfway from the field of the picture, from the old calloused habit of seeing everything naturally, they managed to make a picture of the new life, of new things, but that is all.

In the transmission of movement, the cohesiveness of things *disappeared* as their flashing parts hid themselves among other running bodies.

And in constructing the parts of the running objects, they tried to transmit only the impression of movement.

But in order to transmit the movement of modern life, one must operate with its forms.

Which made it more complicated for the art of painting to reach its goal.

But however it was done, consciously or unconsciously, for the sake of movement or for the sake of transmitting an impression, the cohesion of things was violated.

And in this breakup and violation of cohesion lay the latent meaning that had been concealed by the naturalistic purpose.

Underlying this destruction lay primarily not the transmission of the movement of objects, but their destruction for the sake of pure painterly essence, i.e., toward attainment of nonobjective creation.

The rapid interchange of objects struck the new naturalists—the futurists—and they began to seek means of transmitting it.

Hence the construction of the futurist pictures that you have seen arose from the discovery of points on a plane where the placing of real objects during their explosion or confrontation would impart a sense of time at a maximum speed.

These points can be discovered independently of the physical law of natural perspective.

Thus we see in futurist pictures the appearance of clouds, horses, wheels, and various other objects in places not corresponding to nature.

The state of the object has become more important than its essence and meaning.

We see an extraordinary picture.

A new order of objects makes reason shudder.

The mob howled and spat, critics rushed at the artist like dogs from a gateway.

(Shame on them.)

The futurists displayed enormous strength of will in destroying the habit of the old mind, in flaying the hardened skin of academism and spitting in the face of the old common sense.

After rejecting reason, the futurists proclaimed intuition as the subconscious.

But they created their pictures not out of the subconscious forms of intuition, but used the forms of utilitarian reason.

Consequently, only the discovery of the difference between the two lives of the old and the new art will fall to the lot of intuitive feeling.

We do not see the subconscious in the actual construction of the picture.

Rather do we see the conscious calculation of construction.

In a futurist picture there is a mass of objects. They are scattered about the surface in an order unnatural to life.

The conglomeration of objects is acquired not through intuitive sense, but through a purely visual impression, while the building, the construction, of the picture is done with the intention of achieving an impression.

And the sense of the subconscious falls away.

Consequently, we have nothing purely intuitive in the picture.

Beauty, too, if it is encountered, proceeds from aesthetic taste.

The intuitive, I think, should manifest itself when forms are unconscious and have no response.

I consider that the intuitive in art had to be understood as the aim of our sense of search for objects. And it followed a purely conscious path, blazing its decisive trail through the artist.

(Its form is like two types of consciousness fighting between themselves.)

But the consciousness, accustomed to the training of utilitarian reason, could not agree with the sense that led to the destruction of objectism.

The artist did not understand this aim and, submitting to this sense, betrayed reason and distorted form.

The art of utilitarian reason has a definite purpose.

But intuitive creation does not have a utilitarian purpose. Hitherto we have had no such manifestation of intuition in art.

All pictures in art follow the creative forms of a utilitarian order. All the naturalists' pictures have the same form as in nature.

Intuitive form should arise out of nothing.

Just as reason, creating things for everyday life, extracts them from nothing and perfects them.

Thus the forms of utilitarian reason are superior to any depictions in pictures.

They are superior because they are alive and have proceeded from material that has been given a new form for the new life.

Here is the Divine ordering crystals to assume another form of existence.

Here is a miracle...

There should be a miracle in the creation of art, as well.

But the realists, in transferring living things onto the canvas, deprive their life of movement.

And our academies teach dead, not living, painting.

Hitherto intuitive feeling has been directed to drag newer and newer tomb into our world from some kind of bottomless void.

But there has been no proof of this in art, and there should be.

And I feel that it does already exist in a real form and quite consciously.

The artist should know what, and why, things happen in his pictures.

Previously he lived in some sort of mood. He waited for; the moonrise and twilight, put green shades on his lamps, and all this tuned him up like a violin.

But if you asked him why the face on his canvas was crooked, or green, he could not give an exact answer.

"I want it like that, I like it like that..."

Ultimately, this desire was ascribed to creative will.

Consequently, the intuitive feeling did not speak clearly. And thereafter its state became not only subconscious, but completely unconscious.

These concepts were all mixed together in pictures. The picture was half-real, half-distorted.

Being a painter, I ought to say why people's faces are painted green and red in pictures.

Painting is paint and color; it lies within our organism. Its outbursts are great and demanding.

My nervous system is colored by them.

My brain burns with their color.

But color was oppressed by common sense, was enslaved by it. And the spirit of color weakened and died out.

But when it conquered common sense, then its colors flowed onto the repellent form of real things.

The colors matured, but their form did not mature in the consciousness.

This is why faces and bodies were red, green, and blue.

But this was the herald leading to the creation of painterly forms as ends in themselves.

Now it is essential to shape the body and lend it a living form in real life.

And this will happen when forms emerge from painterly masses; that is, they will arise just as utilitarian forms arose.

Such forms will not be repetitions of living things in life, but will themselves be a living thing.

A painted surface is a real, living form.

Intuitive feeling is now passing to consciousness; no longer is it subconscious.

Even, rather, vice versa—it always was conscious, but the artist just could not understand its demands.

The forms of suprematism, the new painterly realism, already testify to the construction of forms out of nothing, discovered by intuitive reason.

The cubist attempt to distort real form and its breakup of objects were aimed at giving the creative will the independent life of its created forms.

Painting in Futurism

If we take any point in a futurist picture, we shall find either something that is coming or going, or a confined space.

But we shall not find an independent, individual painterly surface.

Here the painting is nothing but the outer garment of things.

And each form of the object was painterly insofar as its form was necessary to its existence, and not vice versa.

The futurists advocate the dynamics of painterly plasticity as the most important aspect of a painting.

But in failing to destroy objectivism, they achieve only the dynamics of things.

Therefore futurist paintings and all those of past artists can be reduced from twenty colors to one, without sacrificing their impression.

Repin's picture of Ivan the Terrible could be deprived of color, and it will still give us the same impressions of horror as it does in color.

The subject will always kill color, and we will not notice it.

Whereas faces painted green and red kill the subject to a certain extent, and the color is more noticeable. And color is what a painter lives by, so it is the most important thing.

And here I have arrived at pure color forms.

And suprematism is the purely painterly art of color whose independence cannot be reduced to a single color.

The galloping of a horse can be transmitted with a single tone of pencil.

But it is impossible to transmit the movement of red, green, or blue masses with a single pencil.

Painters should abandon subject matter and objects if they wish to be pure painters.

The demand to achieve the dynamics of painterly plasticity point to the impulse of painterly masses to emerge from the object and arrive at color as an end in itself, at the domination of purely painterly forms as ends in themselves over content and things, at nonobjective suprematism—at the new painterly realism, at absolute creation.

Futurism approaches the dynamism of painting through the academism of form.

And both endeavors essentially aspire to suprematism in painting.

If we examine the art of cubism, the question arises what energy in objects incited the intuitive feeling to activity; we shall see that painterly energy was of secondary importance.

The object itself, as well as its essence, purpose, sense, or the fullness of its representation (as the cubists thought), was also unnecessary.

Hitherto it has seemed that the beauty of objects is preserved when they are transmitted whole onto the picture, and moreover, that their essence is evident in the coarseness or simplification of line.

But it transpired that one more situation was found in objects—which reveals a new beauty to us.

Namely: intuitive feeling discovered in objects the energy of dissonance, a dissonance obtained from the confrontation of two contrasting forms.

Objects contain a mass of temporal moments. Their forms are diverse, and consequently, the ways in which they are painted are diverse.

All these temporal aspects of things and their anatomy (the rings of a tree) have become more important than their essence and meaning.

And these new situations were adopted by the cubists as a means of constructing pictures.

Moreover, these means were constructed so that the unexpected confrontation of two forms would produce a dissonance of maximum force and tension.

And the scale of each form is arbitrary.

Which justifies the appearance of parts of real objects in places that do not correspond to nature.

In achieving this new beauty, or simply energy, we have freed ourselves from the impression of the object's wholeness.

The millstone around the neck of painting is beginning to crack.

An object painted according to the principle of cubism can be considered finished when its dissonances are exhausted.

Nevertheless, repetitive forms should be omitted by the artist since they are mere reiterations.

But if the artist finds little tension in the picture, he is free to take them from another object.

Consequently, in cubism the principle of transmitting objects does not arise.

A picture is made, but the object is not transmitted.

Hence this conclusion:

Over the past millennia, the artist has striven to approach the depiction of an object as closely as possible, to transmit its essence and meaning; then in our era of cubism, the artist destroyed objects together with their meaning, essence, and purpose.

A new picture has arisen from their fragments.

Objects have vanished like smoke, for the sake of the new culture of art.

Cubism, futurism, and the Wanderers differ in their aims, but are almost equal in a painterly sense.

Cubism builds its pictures from the forms of lines and from a variety of painterly textures, and in this case, words and letters are introduced as a confrontation of various forms in the picture.

Its graphic meaning is important. It is all for the sake of achieving dissonance.

And this proves that the aim of painting is the one least touched upon.

Because the construction of such forms is based more on actual superimposition than on coloring, which can be obtained simply by black and white paint or by drawing.

To sum up:

Any painted surface turned into a convex painterly relief is an artificial, colored sculpture, and any relief turned into surface is painting.

The proof of intuitive creation in the art of painting was false, for distortion is the result of the inner struggle of intuition in the form of the real.

Intuition is a new reason, consciously creating forms.

But the artist, enslaved by utilitarian reason, wages an unconscious struggle, now submitting to an object, now distorting it.

Gauguin, fleeing from culture to the savages, and discovering more freedom in the primitives than in academism, found himself subject to intuitive reason.

He sought something simple, distorted, coarse.

This was the searching of his creative will.

At all costs not to paint as the eye of his common sense saw.

He found colors but did not find form, and he did not find it because common sense showed him the absurdity of painting anything except nature.

And so he hung his great creative force on the bony skeleton of a man, where it shriveled up.

Many warriors and bearers of great talent have hung it up like washing on a fence.

And all this was done out of love for nature's little nooks.

And let the authorities not hinder us from warning our generation against the clothes stands that they have become so fond of and that keep them so warm.

The efforts of the art authorities to direct art along the path of common sense annulled creation.

And with the most talented people, real form is distortion.

Distortion was driven by the most talented to the point of disappearance but it did not go outside the bounds of zero.

But I have transformed myself in the zero of form and through zero have reached creation, that is, suprematism, the new painterly realism nonobjective creation.

Suprematism is the beginning of a new culture: the savage is conquered like the ape, betrayed.

The square is not a subconscious form. It is the creation of intuitive reason.

The face of the new art.

The square is a living, regal infant.

The first step of pure creation in art. Before it there were naive distortions and copies of nature.

Our world of art has become new, nonobjective, pure.

Everything has disappeared; a mass of material is left from which a new form will be built.

In the art of suprematism, forms will live, like all living forms of nature

These forms announce that man has attained his equilibrium; he has left the level of single reason and reached one of double reason.

(Utilitarian reason and intuitive reason.)

The new painterly realism is a painterly one precisely because it has no realism of mountains, sky, water...

Hitherto there has been a realism of objects, but not of painterly, colored units, which are constructed so that they depend neither on form, nor on color, nor on their position vis-a-vis each other.

Each form is free and individual.

Each form is a world.

Any painterly surface is more alive than any face from which a pair of eyes and a smile protrude.

A face painted in a picture gives a pitiful parody of life, and this allusion is merely a reminder of the living.

But a surface lives; it has been born. A coffin reminds us of the dead; a picture, of the living.

This is why it is strange to look at a red or black painted surface.

This is why people snigger and spit at the exhibitions of new trends.

Art and its new aim have always been a spittoon.

But cats get used to one place, and it is difficult to house-train them to a new one.

For such people, art is quite unnecessary, as long as their grandmothers and favorite little nooks of lilac groves are painted.

Everything runs from the past to the future, but everything should live in the present, for in the future the apple trees will shed their blossoms.

Tomorrow will wipe away the vestige of the present, and you are too late for the current of life.

The mire of the past, like a millstone, will drag you into the slough.

This is why I hate those who supply you with monuments to the dead.

The academy and the critics are this millstone round your neck. The old realism is the movement that seeks to transmit living nature.

They carry on just as in the times of the Grand Inquisition.

Their aim is ridiculous because they want at all costs to force what they take from nature to live on the canvas.

At the same time as everything is breathing and running, their frozen poses are in pictures.

And this torture is worse than breaking on the wheel.

Sculptured statues, inspired, hence living, have stopped dead, posed as running.

Isn't this torture?

Enclosing the soul in marble and then mocking the living.

But you are proud of an artist who knows how to torture.

You put birds in a cage for pleasure as well.

And for the sake of knowledge, you keep animals in zoological-gardens.

I am happy to have broken out of that inquisition torture chamber, academism.

I have arrived at the surface and can arrive at the dimension of the living body.

But I shall use the dimension from which I shall create the new.

I have released all the birds from the eternal cage and flung open the gates to the animals in the zoological-gardens.

May they tear to bits and devour the leftovers of your art.

And may the freed bear bathe his body amid the flows of the frozen north and not languish in the aquarium of distilled water in the academic-garden.

You go into raptures over a picture's composition, but in fact, composition is the death sentence for a figure condemned by the artist to an eternal pose.

Your rapture is the confirmation of this sentence.

The group of suprematists—*K. Malevich, I. Puni, M. Menkov, I. Klyun, K. Boguslavskaya, and Rozanova—has waged the struggle for the liberation of objects from the obligations of art.*

And appeals to the academy to renounce the inquisition of nature.

Idealism and the demands of aesthetic sense are the instruments of torture.

The idealization of the human form is the mortification of the many lines of living muscle.

Aestheticism is the garbage of intuitive feeling.

You all wish to see pieces of living nature on the hooks of your walls.

Just as Nero admired the torn bodies of people and animals from the zoological-garden.

I say to all: Abandon love, abandon aestheticism, abandon the baggage of wisdom, for in the new culture, your wisdom is ridiculous and insignificant.

I have untied the knots of wisdom and liberated the consciousness of color!

Hurry up and shed the hardened skin of centuries, so that you can catch up with us more easily.

I have overcome the impossible and made guild with no breath.

You are caught in the nets of the horizon, like fish!

We, suprematists, throw open the way to you.

Hurry!

For tomorrow you will not recognize us.

Suprematism in World Reconstruction, 1920 — EL LISSITZKY

Real name Lazar M. Lisitsky. Born near Smolensk, 1890; died Moscow, 1941. 1909-1914: at the Technische Hochschule in Darmstadt; also traveled in France and Italy; 1914: returned to Russia; 1918-1919: member of IZO Narkmpros; professor at the Vitebsk Art School; close contact with Kazimir Malevich; 1920: member of Inkhuk; 1921: traveled to Germany; 1922: in Berlin, edited *Veshch/Gegenstand/Objet* (Object) with Ilya Ehrenburg; 1925: returned to Moscow; taught interior design at Vkhutemas.

The text of this piece is from a typescript in the Lissitzky archives and, apart from the notes, is reproduced from Sophie Lissitzky-Küppers, *El Lissitzky* (London and Greenwich, Conn., 1968). Despite its title, this essay acts as a retrospective commentary on Malevich's original formulation of suprematism and advances a far wider concept with its emphasis on such ideas as visual economy and the universal application of suprematism (ideas also developed by Malevich in his ⊠ *novykh sistemakh v iskusstve* (On New Systems in Art) (Vitebsk, 1919); Both for Lissitzky and for Malevich, but more so for the former, the architectural discipline presented itself as an obvious vehicle for the transference of basic suprematist schemes into life itself. In this respect, Lissitzky's so-called Prouns (*proekty ustanovleniia novogo*—projects for the establishment of the new), which he designed between 1919 and 1924 were of vital significance since they served as intermediate points between two- and three- dimensional forms or, as Lissitzky himself said, "as a station on the way to constructing a new form".

In a wider context, the spatial graphics of Petr Miturich, the linear paintings of Aleksandr Vesnin, and the mono- and duochromatic paintings of Aleksandr Rodchenko, all done about 1919, symbolized the general endeavor to project art into life, to give painting a constructive dimension. More obviously, the suprematist constructions—the so-called *arkhitektony* and *planity*—modeled as early as 1920 by Malevich and the *unovisovtsy* (members of the Unovis group organized by Malevich in Vitebsk) also supported this trend, thereby proving Ilya a Ehrenburg's assertion that the "aim of the new art is to fuse with life". Lissitzky's description of the radio transmitting tower as the "centre of collective effort" is therefore in keeping with this process and anticipates the emergence of constructivism and the emphasis on industrial design a few months later. In this context, Lissitzky's references to the "plumbline of economy" and the "counterrelief" remind us of Naum Gaho and Vladimir Tallin, respectively, and of course, reflect the general concern with veshch [the object as such] on the one hand, and the contrary call for its utilitarian justitification on the other, manifested in Inkhuk in the course of 1920.

* * *

at present we are living through an unusual period in time a new cosmic creation has become reality in the world a creativity within ourselves which pervades our consciousness.

for us SUPREMATISM did not signify the recognition of an absolute form which was part of an already-completed universal system, on the contrary here stood revealed for the first time in all its purity the clear sign and plan for a definite new world never before experienced a world which issues forth from our inner being and which is only now in the first stages of its formation. for this reason the square of suprematism became a beacon.

in this way the artist became the foundation on which progress in the reconstruction of life could advance beyond the frontiers of the all-seeing eye and the all-hearing ear. thus a picture was no longer an anecdote nor a lyric poem nor a lecture on morality nor a feast for the eye but a sign and symbol of this new conception of the world which comes from within us. many revolutions were needed in order to free the artist from his obligations as a moralist as a story-teller or as a court jester, so that he could follow unhindered his creative bent and tread the road that leads to construction.

the pace of life has increased in the last few decades just as the speed of the motor bicycle has been exceeded main times over by the aeroplane.

after art passed through a whole series of intermediate stages it reached cubism where for the first time the creative urge to construct instinctively overcame conscious resolve. from this point the picture started to gain stature as a new world of reality and in this way the foundation stone for a new representation of the shapes and forms of the material world was laid, it proved to be essential to clear the site for the new building, this idea was a forerunner of futurism which exposed the relentless nature of its motivating power.

revolutions had started undercover, every thing grew more complicated, painting economical in its creative output was still very complicated and uneconomical in its expression, cubism and futurism seized upon the purity of form treatment and colour and built a complicated and extensive system with them combining them without any regard for harmony,

the rebuilding of life cast aside the old concept of nations classes patriotisms and imperialism which had been completely discredited.

the rebuilding of the town threw into utter confusion both its isolated elements—houses streets squares bridges—and its new systems which cut across the old ones—underground metro underground monorail electricity transmitted under the ground and above the ground, this all developed on top of a new powerhouse whose pumps sucked in the whole of creation.

technology which in its achievements took the most direct route from the complexity of the train to the simplicity of the aeroplane from the basic primitiveness of the steam boiler to the economy of the dynamo from the chaotic hubbub of the telegraphic network to the uniformity of radio was diverted by the war from the path of construction and forced on to the paths of death and destruction.

into this chaos came suprematism extolling the square as the very source of all creative expression, and then came communism and extolled work as the true source of man's heartbeat.

and amid the thunderous roar of a world in collision we, ON THE LAST STAGE OF THE PATH TO SUPREMATISM BLASTED ASIDE THE OLD WORK OF ART LIKE A BEING OF FLESH AND BLOOD AND TURNED IT INTO A WORLD FLOATING IN SPACE. WE CARRIED BOTH PICTURE AND VIEWER OUT BEYOND THE CONFINES OF THIS SPHERE AND IN ORDER TO COMPREHEND IT FULLY THE VIEWER MUST CIRCLE LIKE A PLANET ROUND THE PICTUIRE WHICH REMAINS IMMOBILE IN THE CENTRE.

the empty phrase "art for art's sake" had already been wiped out and in suprematism we have wiped out the phrase "painting for painting's sake" and have ventured far beyond the frontiers of painting.

first of all the artist painted the natural scene which surrounded him. then this was obscured by towns roads canals and all the products of man for this reason the artist began to paint artificial nature—but involuntarily he referred in his works to the method for depicting this new nature. suprematism itself has followed the true oath which defines the creative process consequently, our picture has become a creative symbol and the realization of this will be our task in life.

when we have absorbed the total wealth of experience of painting when we have left behind the uninhibited curves of cubism when we have grasped the aim and system of suprematism—then we shall give a new face to this globe. we shall reshape it so thoroughly that the sun will no longer recognize its satellite. in architecture we are on the way to a complete new concept, after the archaic horizontals the classical spheres and the gothic verticals of building styles which preceded our own we are now entering upon a fourth stage as we achieve economy and spatial diagonals.

we left to the old world the idea of the individual house individual barracks individual castle individual church, we have set ourselves the task of creating the town, the centre of collective effort is the radio transmitting mast which sends out bursts of creative energy into the world. by means of it we are able to throw off the shackles that bind us to the earth and rise above it. therein lies the answer to all questions concerning movement

this dynamic architecture provides us with the new theatre of life and because we are capable of grasping the idea of a whole town at any moment with any plan the task of architecture—the rhythmic arrangement of space and time—is perfectly and simply fulfilled for the new town will not be as chaotically laid out as the modern towns of north and south America but clearly and logically like a beehive, the new element of treatment which we have brought to the fore in our painting will be applied to the whole of this still-to-be-built world and will transform the roughness of concrete the smoothness of metal and the reflection of glass into the outer membrane of the new life, the new light will give us new color and the memory of the solar spectrum will be preserved only in old manuals on physics.

this is the way in which the artist has set about the construction of the world—an activity which affects every human being and carries work beyond the frontiers of comprehension, we see how its creative path took it by way of cubism to pure construction but there was still no outlet to be found here, when the cubist had pressed forward and reached the very limits of his canvas his old materials—the colors on his palette—proved to be too pale and he put into his picture cement and concrete and home-made iron constructions, not content with that he started to build a model of the structure he had depicted on canvas and then it was only a short step to transform the abstract cubistic still-life into a contre-relief which was complete in itself.

the short step then required to complete the stride consists in recognition of the fact that a contre-relief is an architectonic structure, but the slightest deviation from the plumbline of economy leads into a blind alley, the same fate must also overtake the architecture of cubist contre-relief. cubism was the product of a world which already existed around us and contre-relief is its mechanical offspring, it does however have a relative that took the straight path of economy which led to a real life of its own. the reference is to the narrow technical discoveries for example the submarine the aeroplane the motors and dynamos of every kind of motive power in each part of a battle-ship, contre-relief is instinctively aware of their legitimate origin their economy of form and their realism of treatment.

by taking these elements FROM THEM for itself it wants to become equally entitled to take its place alongside them as a new creation, it seeks to demonstrate its modernity by surrounding itself with all the devices of modern life although this is really nothing other than a decoration of its own self but with intestines stomach heart and nerves on the outside.

in this fragment of TECHNICAL INVENTIVENESS we can see the construction of these pattern systems in the artist's materials, there is iron and steel copper tin and nickel glass and guttapercha straight and curved areas and volumes of every description and color nuance, it is being made by several master-craftsmen who well know the work of their colleagues but not the beauty of their materials, this complicated structure taken as a whole represents a UNIFIED organism, is it not therefore for that very reason "artistic"?

there is one element to which special importance attaches—scale, the scale gives life to relationships in space, it is that which determines whether every organism remains whole or is destroyed—it holds all the parts together, the index for the growth of modern man is the ability to see and appreciate the relative scales of everything that has been made, it is right that this perceptivity shall pass judgment on man's concept of space on the way he reacts in time, cubism demonstrated in its constructions its modernity in relation to scale. but in painting and contre-relief we have in front of us an absolute scale which is this—forms in their natural size in the ratio 1:1. if however we wish to transform the contre-relief into an architectural structure and therefore enlarge it by one hundred times, then the scale ceases to be absolute and becomes relative in the ratio of 1:100. then we get the American statue of liberty in whose head there is room for four men and from whose hand the light streams out.

seven years ago suprematism raised aloft its black square but no one sighted it for at that time a telescope for this new planet had not yet been invented, the mighty force of its movement however caused a succession of artists to focus on it and many more were influenced by it. yet neither the former nor the latter possessed sufficient inner substance to be held fast by its attractive power and to formulate a complete world system from the new movement, they loosed their hold and plunged like meteorites into irrelevancy extinguishing themselves in its chaos, but the second much-improved phase is already following and the planet will soon stand fully revealed.

those of us who have stepped out beyond the confines of the picture take ruler and compasses—following the precept of economy—in our hands, for the frayed point of the paintbrush is at variance with our concept of clarity and if necessary we shall take machines in our hands as well because in expressing our creative ability paintbrush and ruler and compasses and machine are only extensions of the finger which points the way.

this path into the future has nothing in common either with mathematics and scientific studies or with raptures over sunset and moonlight—or indeed with the decline of the subject with its plague-ridden aura of indo individualism—rather is it the path leading from creative intuition to the increased growth of foodstuffs for which neither paintbrush nor ruler neither compasses nor machine were required.

we must take note of the fact that the artist nowadays is occupied with painting flags posters pots and pans textiles and things like that, what is referred to as "artistic work" has on the vast majority of occasions nothing whatever to do with creative effort: and the term "artistic work" is used in order to demonstrate the "sacredness" of the work which the artist does at his easel, the conception of "artistic work" presupposes a distinction between useful and useless work and as there are only a few artists buyers can be found even for their useless products.

the artist's work lies beyond the boundaries of the useful and the useless. it is the revolutionary path along which the whole of creation is striding forward and along which man must also bend his steps, "artistic work" is but an obstacle on this path and in consequence a counter-revolutionary concept, the private property aspect of creativity must be destroyed all are creators and there is no reason of any sort for this division into artists and nonartists.

by this reckoning the artist ceases to be a man who is not producing useful things and must not strive to attain his title to creative activity by painting posters in the prescribed form and color on which any attempt to pass judgment shows a GROSS LACK OF FEELING, such work now belongs to the duty of the artist as a citizen of the community who is clearing the field of its old rubbish in preparation for the new life.

therefore THE IDEA OF "ARTISTIC WORK" MUST BE ABOLISHED AS A COUNTER-REVOLUTIONARY CONCEPT OF WHAT IS CREATIVE and work must be accepted as one of the functions of the living human organism in the same way as the beating of the heart or the activity of the nerve centers so that it will be afforded the same protection.

it is only the creative movement towards the liberation of man that makes him the being who holds the whole world within himself, only a creative work which fills the whole world with its energy can join us together by means of its energy components to form a collective unity like a circuit of electric current.

the first forges of the creator of the omniscient omnipotent omnific constructor of the new world must be the workshops of our art schools, when the artist leaves them he will set to work as a master-builder as a teacher of the new alphabet and as a promoter of a world which indeed already exists in man but which man has not yet been able to perceive.

and if communism which set human labor on the throne and suprematism which raised aloft the square pennant of creativity now march forward together then in the further stages of development it is communism which will have to remain behind because suprematism—which embraces the totality of life's phenomena—will attract everyone away from the domination of work and from the domination of the intoxicated senses, it will liberate all those engaged in creative activity and make the world into a true model of perfection, this is the model we await from kasimir malevich.

AFTER THE OLD TESTAMENT THERE CAME THE NEW—AFTER THE NEW THE COMMUNIST—AND AFTER THE COMMUNIST THERE FOLLOWS FINALLY THE TESTAMENT OF SUPREMATISM.

Program Declaration, 1919 — KOMFUT

Komfut (an abbreviation of Communists and futurists) was organized formally in Petrograd in January 1919 as an act of opposition to the Italian futurists, who were associating themselves increasingly with Fascism. According to the code of the organization, would-be members had to belong to the Bolshevik Party and had to master the principles of the "cultural Communist ideology" elucidated at the society's own school. Prominent members of Komfut were Boris Kushner (chairman), Osip Brik (head of the cultural ideology school), Natan Altman, Vladimir Mayakovsky, and David Shterenberg. Komfut prepared for publication several brochures including "The Culture of Communism," "Futurism and Communism," "Inspiration," and "Beauty," but none, apparently, was published.

The text of this piece, "Programmnaya deklaratsiya," is from *Iskusstvo kommuny* [Art of the Commune] (Petrograd), no. 8, January 26, 1919. A second Komfut statement giving details of proposed lectures and publications was issued in *Iskusstvo kommuny*, no. 9, February 2, 1919. The destructive, even anarchical intentions of Komfut, while supported just after 1917 by many of the leftist artists, including Kazimir Malevich, were not, of course, shared by Lenin or Anatolii Lunacharsky, who believed, for the most part, that the pre-Revolutionary cultural heritage should be preserved. In its rejection of bourgeois art, Komfut was close to Proletkult, although the latter's totally proletarian policy excluded the idea of any ultimate ideological consolidation of the two groups. Altman's, Kushner's, and Nikolai Punin's articles of 1918-1919 can, in many cases, be viewed as Komfut statements.

* * *

A Communist regime demands a Communist consciousness. All forms of life, morality, philosophy, and art must be re-created according to communist principles. Without this, the subsequent development of the Communist Revolution is impossible.

In their activities the cultural-educational organs of the Soviet government show a complete misunderstanding of the revolutionary task entrusted to them. The social-democratic ideology so hastily knocked together is incapable of resisting the century-old experience of the bourgeois ideologists, who, in their own interests, are exploiting the proletarian cultural-educational organs.

Under the guise of immutable truths, the masses are being presented with the pseudo teachings of the gentry.

Under the guise of universal truth—the morality of the exploiters.

Under the guise of the eternal laws of beauty—the depraved taste of the oppressors.

It is essential to start creating our own Communist ideology. It is essential to wage merciless war against all the false ideologies of the bourgeois past.

It is essential to subordinate the Soviet cultural-educational organs to the guidance of a new cultural Communist ideology—an ideology that is only now being formulated.

It is essential—in all cultural fields, as well as in art—to reject emphatically all the democratic illusions that pervade the vestiges and prejudices of the bourgeoisie.

It is essential to summon the masses to creative activity.

Endnotes

1 These selections were originally published in Bowlt (ed), *Russian Art of the Avant-Garde*.

2 The impressionists from the Japanese. The synthetists, Gauguin from India spoiled by its early renaissance. From the islands of Tahiti he apprehended nothing, apart from a tangible type of woman. Matisse—Chinese painting. The cubists—Negroes (Madagascar), Aztecs. As for the past—certain historians are sadly mistaken in deducing a Romanesque influence, even a German influence, on our icons. This is so only in isolated cases; generally speaking, what is the Romanesque style but the last stage of Byzantine development? Romanesque style is based on Grecianized, Eastern, Georgian, and Armenian models. If Eastern influence reached us in a roundabout way, then this does not prove anything—its path was from the East, and the West, as now, served merely as an intermediate point. Suffice it to consider Arabian and Indian depictions to establish the genesis of our icons and of the art that has hitherto existed among the common people.

3 The Painting of Aleksandra Exter—hitherto little noticed by the Russian critics—provides interesting attempts at widening the usual methods of depiction. The questions she raises with such conviction how to solve color orchestration, how to achieve the sense of plane—and her unceasing protest against redundant forms, place her among the most interesting of modern artists.

3. The Phenomenon of David Burliuk in the History of the Russian Avant-Garde Movement[1]

Elena Basner[2]

Translated from the Russian by Kenneth MacInnes

"...Blind in one eye, artist of strapping health."

If, in the history of the Russian avant-garde, we were to try to select a figure who imbibed its whole energy, concentrating around himself the most active and vigorous of its forces and giving them a definite direction, then such a figure would very likely be David Burliuk.

And although Mikhail Larionov's remarkable talent proved far more valuable in regenerating painting and Velimir Khlebnikov's brilliant observations stimulated twentieth century literature far more than the sum total of Burliuk's offerings in art and poetry ever did, it was Burliuk who went down in the history of modern art as "The Father of Russian Futurism." Such was the name given to him by his friends and which he himself often used.

It was David Burliuk—with his inordinate "Homeric" love of life, his eternally passionate, impetuous even, enthusiasm for people and ideas and his ability to quickly win these same people over to his own ideas and give vigorous breadth to them—who for contemporaries and their offspring alike personified a "Futurist of Futurists". Everything contributed to that image: his truly oratorical ardour and all his scandalous outbursts at lectures, bringing faint-hearted listeners to the verge of passing out (there was such a case); his unforgettable appearance—glass eye, monocle which he claimed belonged to Marshal Davout of the Napoleonic army, his corpulent woman's figure, trademark baggy clothes (add to that a top hat)—which he further exploited with his great actor's talent; and of course his surname, which gave journalists wide scope for fantasy.

Poet, orator, painter, theorist and publisher all rolled into one, he was both a fanatical Kulturträger and an exceptionally talented person. He was a personality—and this is the most important thing of all.

In his 1913 article on the middle Burliuk brother (the artist Vladimir), the youngest Burliuk brother, the poet Nikolai, wrote the following: "Modern art <...> teaches us to love not just the artist's pictures, but also the artist himself <...> Hence I apologise here and now if it becomes necessary to define the creation by its creator"[3]. And when speaking of David Burliuk the artist we too first and foremost define the creation by its creator.

* * *

The image of David Burliuk is so vividly and convincingly presented in Benedikt Livshits' memoirs "The One-And-A-Half-Eyed Archer" and Velimir Khlebnikov's poem "Burliuk" that we have decided to let these two wonderful portraits of Burliuk, left to us by his friends and fellow-thinkers, form the basis of this article.

* * *

> The brothers and sisters, robust in their laughter, giants
> all,
> With their brittle skin,
> Loose like sacks of flour.

The warm and friendly Burliuk family, in which David was the eldest of six children, was the first debt he owed for his exceptional character, his artistic temperament that often went over the top and for his voracious love of life. Without understanding this it is difficult to understand the nature of his gift for painting and poetry, as well as to understand the simple human charm with which he was over-flowing.

"The bonds of a remarkable love united all members of the family. The clan principle bared itself on a philological basis. Driven by the planetary winds to this corner of the earth, to the one-storey house swept by the steppe winds, the Burliuks anxiously pressed close to one another, as if trying to preserve the last piece of human warmth on earth."[4]

Apart from this very descriptive artistic image of the Burliuk family, Benedikt Livshits also depicts its every member in turn: "The Burliuk family consisted of eight people: the parents, three sons and three daughters. The father, David Fyedorovich, manager of the Chernaya

Dolina estate, was of peasant origin. A self-taught person with much practical experience as an agricultural bailiff, he had published a series of pamphlets on agricultural science. His wife, Liudmila Josifovna, possessed some talent for painting and the children undoubtedly inherited this gift from their mother."[5]

Not only the eldest son, David, but two of the others also went on to become artists: the middle son Vladimir and one of the sisters Liudmila, who married the sculptor V. Kuznetsov in 1911. They often exhibited their works together, providing the critics with further ammunition for gibes. "When you go into the exhibition," Igor Grabar wrote in 1908, "you get the impression that, apart from Burliuk, there is no one else there and yet there seems to be a lot of them: ten, maybe, twenty Burliuks. It then turns out that there are three of them and that one of them paints in squares and figures, another in commas and the third with a mop. A close scrutiny reveals that the one who paints with the mop is a woman and the one possessing the greatest talent. Yet the other two are also without a doubt talented and full of the same innocuous short-lived fervour. Just so long as you don't over-burlook."[6] This verdict may have been witty, but it was short-sighted, for the "innocuous fervour" or "burlooking" did not just fade away with the passage of time, but actually acquired a fighting strength.

One of his most authoritative contemporaries, M. V. Matiushin, believed that Vladimir Burliuk, "as an artist...was much better than his elder brother."[7] Nevertheless, however much you appraise the subdivision of roles and the arrangement of creative forces within the Burliuk family, David Burliuk's standing as the "firstborn" was all the same recognised unconditionally.

It is completely obvious that it was in the family circle, which he could always rely on to be his attentive listeners, well-disposed viewers and, most important of all, devoted adherents of his ideas, that Burliuk could first of all feel himself to be a leader who stimulated the creative energy of those surrounding him, the role foreordained to him in the history of Russian art.

* * *

Wide brush in hand, you trotted
And disconcerted the streets of Munich

With your red calico shirt
Scaring them all with your red cheeks.
Nicknamed by your Teacher of painting
"The ungovernable mare
from the Black Earth of Russia."

David Burliuk's first steps along the road of life are perhaps only conspicuous for the constant moves from town to town—from Kharkov to Sumy, then to Tambov, Tver, Kazan and Odessa (he attended art school in the last two towns), as their father sought work. His childhood years, spent in the Ukraine, left a deep impression in his memory—so much so that later, in his memoirs, he would affirm that "...in me the Ukraine has her most loyal son. My colours are deeply nationalist. 'Fiery-yellow', green-yellow-red and blue tones crash down like the Niagara Falls from my brush."[8] In Kharkov in 1892 he made friends with the landscape artist K.K. Pervukhin who, as he himself put it, "infected" him with painting for life.

Burliuk recalls that he first saw the Tretyakov Gallery in 1897 and that these years, right up to 1904, passed for him "under the star of Shishkin, Kuindzhi and Repin, with a bit of Serov."[9] And if we remember that around this time the young Kazimir Malevich became acquainted with the artist N.K. Pimonenko and "was agape at all that he saw in his studio"[10] and who, like Burliuk, confessed his love of Shishkin and Repin, then we have a starting point for measuring and, hence, a logical structure for evaluating the development of the views on classical art of its two bitterest enemies. Such an evolution, from worship to negation, is of course far from being an isolated example and was not incidental, though typical when taken in the light of growing revolutionary murmurings.

It is futile to search in Burliuk's life in his early years for some sort of exceptionality which might have indicated the future rebel. A love of drawing from his very childhood which led him even to forget about all other games and amusements, his first successes and the praise of his lecturers can all be found in the biography of almost any artist. And like many painters of his generation, including both those who went on to world fame and those who simply passed away into obscurity, he fastened on to European art culture, spending about a year in Munich before moving on to Paris, to study with Fernand Cormon.

The works of his Munich and Parisian periods are unavailable for study, though it seems likely that the fledgling artist was most attracted to the standard neo-Impressionism, "interpreted, though, highly radically and subjectively,"[11] as he later wrote. Burliuk also recalled the appraisal of Anton Azhbe, in whose school he studied for several months in 1904: "Azhbe was delighted with me, showing my work to all the pupils and calling me a 'wonderful wild steppe horse'."[12]

There would seem to be no need to speak about the assiduousness and regularity he showed in his painting lessons. Yet the time Burliuk spent in two of the leading European centres of modern art provided him with the most important thing of all—the possibility to appraise the modern artistic process and to define his own direction in it (even if in the most general of forms). The Russo-Japanese War hastened his return to Russia where, as he put it, he "continued to work madly."[13] "This time in my painting is marked by a despairing realism", Burliuk admitted, "Every shoot, every twig, every blade of grass—everything is depicted in detail. As regards colour, I try to accommodate it in such a way that at a distance it agrees completely with life."[14]

The Russian Museum owns Burliuk's very earliest works (from those which remain to this day), which feature just those distinguishable features which he referred to as a "despairing realism." These are "Landscape with a flower-bed," dated 1906, and "Boat on the shore," which are indeed painted with no small share of raw, naive diligence. But one ought also to note that in this work we can already see the main quality of Burliuk's paintings—his love of texture, albeit still expressed rather timidly.

And yet a landscape such as this could have sprung from the brush of any one of the students of Anton Azhbe (Burliuk's art teacher in Munich)—even those not accorded the noble comparison with a "wild steppe horse"—or any of the second-class painters at the "Union of Russian Artists." And, to all intents and purposes, his ideological outlook at this time differed little from the views of any of the similarly-aged young artists who had only just begun searching for new paths in art.

Something had to happen in his life to lift him to a completely different frame of mind and to accelerate his transformation into that David Burliuk whose name would resound in the press—for some as a symbol of unacknowledged innovativeness, and for others as a symbol of nihilism. And this was indeed what happened, although the process which followed relates not so much to his painting as to his other creative activities.

* * *

You, you buxom giant, your laughter rang out through-
out the whole of Russia,
A branch of the Dnepr estuary holding you tightly in its
fist.
Defender of the people's rights in the art of Titans,
You took Russia's soul out onto wide sea shores.

What actually happened was a series of events which launched David Burliuk as a leader of the rapidly-growing avant-garde movement. It would be difficult to say with certainty which of them was the most decisive—either his acquaintance with Mikhail Larionov in 1907 in Moscow, which rapidly grew into a friendship (incidentally, it was very much in keeping with both of their characters to suddenly fall for a person to the complete exclusion of everything else) but which several years later turned into a similarly vehement enmity, or his association in Kiev with Alexandra Ekster, with whom the Burliuk brothers organised the "Link" exhibition in November 1908. Here they brought together an impressive array of the forces of innovation, in the face of the aforementioned Mikhail Larionov, Natalia Goncharova, Aristarkh Lentulov and Alexander Bogomazov. It was at this exhibition that Burliuk distributed the leaflet "The Voice of an Impressionist—In Defence Of Painting," in which no one escaped—not Repin, Makovsky, Aivazovsky, the "Diagilevites", nor backward, unenlightened tastes.

Not that this was the first time that the Burliuk brothers had appeared in the role of exposers of philistinism. That had occured that spring, at the opening of the "Modern Tendencies In Art" exhibition in St. Petersburg, organised by Nikolai Ivanovich Kulbin, well-known "mad doctor" and active exponent of new directions in art. And it is essential to include this meeting with Kulbin amongst the events which played a role in Burliuk's growth as an artist.

At the exhibition's opening Burliuk met Vasily Kamensky and, through him, Velimir (then still Viktor Vladimirovich) Khlebnikov, who had come to Petersburg to continue studying mathematics at the university. And when Kamensky brought the Burliuks to the home of the artist and musician Mikhail Matiushin and his wife, Elena Guro, poetess and artist, here we already have the nucleus of the first unification of the Russian Futurists.

One should note that even Matiushin, himself an initiator of new undertakings of Petersburg youth, emphasised the organisational impulse that Burliuk carried within him: "David Burliuk, with spectacular and unmistakable flair, rallied round him forces which could aid the development of the new movement in art". Matiushin also highly rated the paintings of both brothers: "Their paintings were brave and original. These works can be considered the start of Cubo-Futurism. They were simple in form, yet of considerable volume, though at the same time they didn't completely depart from Impressionism (in colour)."[15]

As far as Burliuk himself was concerned, Elena Genrikhovna Guro's personality had an enormous influence on him. Matiushin recalled: "Our new friends the Burliuk brothers, who had the reputations of being mischief-makers and 'hooligans', not afraid of anything and without exception, became reflective and concentrated in the presence of Elena Guro. Guro hated any aesthetic pretentiousness whatsoever and an artistic intensity of such force emanated from her that the Burliuks were immediately filled with deep respect for her."[16] There is little doubt that Guro's scope of creativity, encompassing painting, drawing, prose and poetry, was valuable for Burliuk namely for that naturally acquired synthesis which he himself sought in his activities.

And so a new literary-artistic circle was formed in February 1910 in Matiushin and Guro's house on Litseiskaya Street. A little later the group would adopt the name "Hylea," based on the Ancient Greek name for the Scythian lands at the mouth of the Dnepr which centuries later became the Burliuks' homeland. The name says a lot. It is an indication of the antiquity of their sources, an underlining of their unique Eurasian character (an outlook akin to Blok's). And, of course, in the very name itself we have not so much a scandalous, as a romantic note: "You took Russia's soul out onto wide sea shores..."

When speaking of the most significant events in Burliuk's life right at the start of the 1910s, one must not overlook what was possibly the brightest and most important page in his biography—his friendship with Mayakovsky, which became for them both (and this is important to underline) a source of creative energy and revolutionary zeal. Burliuk's name was long associated in Russian research matter mainly with the name of the "best and most talented poet of the era" (indeed, there was no denying Mayakovsky's lines in his autobiography "I Myself" where he refers to Burliuk as his "real teacher"), which is the reason behind the exhaustive studies of this period of Burliuk's life.

They first met at the start of September 1911 at the Moscow School of Painting, Sculpture and Architecture, from which both would be expelled in February 1914, then becoming inseparable at exhibitions, in the publication of Futurist collections and in public appearances. "Burliuk and Mayakovsky are developing a bubbling reputation in Moscow, not missing a single chance to talk about themselves, participating in all debates either as speakers or as antagonists, trying to wedge their names into any event on the Moscow literary and artistic circuit."[17]

Their Kulturträger activities even spread beyond the boundaries of the capital. At the end of 1913, with Kamensky, they began their famous tour of Russian towns, reading lectures on modern art and their own poetry, entering into fierce debates (sometimes not only verbal) with members of the public and wreaking a trail of a scandal.

* * *

> The antagonist was held in the spell of your will,
> suddenly drawn towards the abyss' black confusion.
>
> What force was it that crippled
> Your unrecognized might
> And boldly affirmed
> The words: "Burliuk and a mean knife
> In the heart of wretched art"?
> On "Ivan the Terrible" a seam—
> Though later hastily patched up—
> Was by Balashov ripped clean.

The first half of the 1910s became for David Burliuk a time of intense public activities. He took part in almost every debate devoted to modern painting and poetry. His tireless propagation of modem art—and not just in Moscow and in Petersburg, but in provisional towns too—was truly amazing. "I deeply believe, to the point of fanaticism, in my civilising mission in art" Burliuk wrote in 1917.[18] His famous speeches—referred to at length in memoirs—at debates held by the "Jack of Diamonds" society (which Burliuk, incidentally, had done much to create) have gone down in the history of Russian avant-garde. In February 1912 the Polytechnical Museum in Moscow was the scene for "an historic debate, which," as Livshits wrote, "set us off on our further public appearances, sparked off the feud between the "Jack of Diamonds" and "The Donkey's Tail" and lent an aura of scandal to the still relatively unknown names of the champions of modern art."[19]

The reason for the "quarrel between the 'tails' and the 'jacks'", which gave inexhaustable material to the composers of satirical newspaper articles, was Burliuk's speech, followed by Natalia Goncharova's infamous appearance, expressing her protest. For amongst the pictures shown by Burliuk as examples of the art of the "Jack of Diamonds" were two of her own works. As she declared that she belonged to the "Donkey's Tail" group, the reaction from the rest of the hall was of course indescribable.

Yet what is of interest for us here is not so much the picture that this episode paints of Goncharova's character, nor even the conflict in itself, once again confirming the fact that the left-wing of Russian art was far from being as united in its battle against its predecessors and its opponents on the right as we might be led to believe. Much more important for us are the positions in Burliuk's speech, for he would vary those same themes in his many future appearances.

When relating the circumstances of the debate, Benedikt Livshits first of all contrasts the oratorial methods of Kulbin, who appeared first with the speech "Free Art As The Basis of Life", with those of Burliuk: "Kulbin would outline general schemes and put forward vague formulae for the development of art . . . Burliuk immediately breathed new life into Kulbin's vacant constructions, declaring that the essence of what an artist is depicting should be completely indifferent for the viewer. The only thing of interest to him ought to be the technique or manner of reproducing an object on a plane. Coming down on Benois, who reviewed pictures according to their subjects, he said that into the basis of the purely academic history of painting—not even begun by anyone yet—there would enter a new method: successions of artistic principles, independent of subject, which to our day is identified with the picture's contents."[20]

That same thought was repeated even more sharply and angrily in the pamphlet published by Burliuk a year later "The Clamouring 'Benoises' And New Russian National Art": ". . .what you say about content, about spirituality, about ideological content (like the subject: wrapped up in philosophical terms) is the highest crime before true art."[21]

Let us note that it was this point of Burliuk's, shared in those years by the majority of young artists attached to the "Jack of Diamonds" and the Petersburg "Union of Youth," that Goncharova attacked, declaring: ". . .I affirm, in contrary to what was said at the debate and what was and always will matter, that what to depict will be as equally important as how to depict."[22] However, as Livshits continues, "that statement, paradoxical for its time, could never hope to rouse the drowsy audience and scatter its sleepy indifference to the four winds. What they needed was a good knock on the head. Which is exactly what Burliuk did. He rolled up his sleeves and set about desecrating their idols."[23]

This "desecration of idols"—moreover idols of both long past and more recent times—which constituted the most expressive and vivid side of Burliuk's appearances, judging by the newspaper reports, would seem natural in chronological terms. For the nihilistic spirit tends to prevail over any positive programme when one is on the eve of revolutionary transformations.

There is probably no need to relate his attacks on all the great names, beginning with Raphael and ending with Repin, at any great length. The same goes for an attempt to analyze the flow of abuse from newspaper critics which poured down on Burliuk and his associates and which covered the whole spectrum of emotions—from outraged indignation to light-hearted mockery. Anyway, Burliuk himself in 1914 published excerpts from those damning newspaper reviews under the title "The Pillory Of Russian Critique" in the "First Journal Of The Russian Futurists."

Worthy of mention, however, is the scandal with Repin, which took place after the incident with the picture "Ivan the Terrible and his son Ivan," cut to pieces in January 1913 by the madman A Balashov (this episode is immortalised by Khlebnikov in his poem). Journalists rushed to accuse the Futurists of vandalism. At the debate given over to this incident, as Burliuk's wife later recalled, after the first speech by Maximilian Voloshin, Repin called out from his seat in indignation: "Yes . . .the new . . . Burliuks are to blame for the crime."[24] Burliuk for his part chose a tried and tested means of defence, accusing Repin's picture of naturalism—and not without basis. As far as the form of his "anti-Repinist" utterances are concerned, they did not so much shock as downright scandalise the audience. Such statements as "Serov and Repin are just pieces of water-melon peel floating about in a slop-tub" which Burliuk threw at the hall, naturally made a continuation of his own speech impossible.[25]

But it is interesting, in order that we might have a more complete picture, to cite an episode relating to Burliuk's visit to Repin in Kuokkala, which he later described in his memoirs. He depicts this visit, which took place in February 1915, in the most idyllic of tones, even with a touch of sentimentality: "Semi-filial feelings of a thankful pupil once again enter my soul, even if I have strayed far from my teacher's tenets."[26] Any mention of filial feelings was unimaginable in Burliuk's "infuriated speeches" (Mayakovsky's words) of 1913!

His feud with Alexander Benois had a perhaps more obvious base, which he himself admitted: "When the venerable I. Repin curses all that is new, we respect his animosity. But what a storm of aversion and disgust A. Benois' two-faced tactics evoke."[27] Burliuk saw Benois' "two-faced tactics" as his "flirtation" with the young "left-wing" artists. Back in 1909 Benois had spoken positively—albeit slightly condescendingly—of Burliuk's exhibitional activities (and to this relatively interesting reference we shall return). Then in February 1910 in an article published in the "Rech" [Speech] newspaper he had called those young artists who had taken part in the "Union of Russian Artists" exhibition "tactless" and "mad" hooligans, provoking angry censure from Burliuk.

Burliuk's letter to Benois is part of the Russian Museum's archives and is on show at this exhibition. It is written with passion, as if in one deep breath. Noting the unfair treatment of members of the younger generation by he who he had always regarded as a defender of the new in Russian art, Burliuk recounts the difficulties encountered by young artists, against whom everyone—the organizers of exhibitions who did not wish to give them space and the police—was ranked, while "The public, who do not provide us with either orders or buyers, is also against us", ". . .you don't beat a man when he's down," Burliuk finishes his letter, "and so I beg you, Alexander Nikolaevich, only don't lay too much store by it! . . You are siding with the majority—even of the general public! Yours is the satisfaction of success. Whereas mine, perhaps, is the sickly grimace of the cornered man."[28]

Benois did not accord the letter a reply, although in a second article concerning the Union's exhibition ("Rech", March 5th 1910) he did mention that he had received a "fiery and even rather touching letter" from one of the representatives of the "left-wing" of Russian art.

Such were the relations between the leader of the young avant-garde movement and one of the ideological chiefs of the older generation. Yet at the same time, Benois' articles and Burliuk's letters to him and his pamphlets later on contain a theme of much more significance than the mutual reproaches of representatives of not just two different cultures, but two different stages in history (the cause of the conflict in the first place). And it is worth stopping here to deal with that theme separately.

* * *

Russia, the vast continent,
Amplified the voice of the West,
As if carrying a monster's roar
A thousand times louder.

This theme is the question of the influence of the West on the new Russian art. It was a question that different people resolved for themselves in completely different ways (Larionov and Burliuk for example), but on which the majority of newspaper and journal writers were completely unanimous. The main reproaches made of members of the younger generation by Benois and other art critics were concentrated around one main postulate: that Russian innovators were just trying to imitate the West. We can find either open or veiled comparisons of Western and Russian innovators—obviously not finding in favour of the latter—in almost every article on modern Russian art written at that time.

"Our young artists, in the vast majority of cases, are completely incapable of understanding and valuing the significance of the complex evolution through which the paintings of the French school have passed over the previous decades. . . They hear third-hand all 'the latest words' from Paris and rip into the avant-garde with all the recklessness of the Russian temperament."[29]

It cannot be denied that Livshits' description of the Burliuk brothers poring over a reproduction of one of Picasso's latest works, fresh from Paris, "like conspirators over captured plans of an enemy fortress"[30] could serve to illustrate these words. But even this example does not give one the right to reduce the question of the exceedingly complicated genesis of Russian avant-garde solely to the influence of the French school, as it might have often seemed to contemporaries.

What is more, Burliuk himself (unlike Larionov) never denied the enormous influence brought to bear on him by the masters of the new French school. And even three years later, when the national self-consciousness of the "left-wing" artists had strengthened and Larionov would proclaim: "We are against the West, which debases both ours and eastern forms, leveling everything,"[31] Burliuk, answering the attacks of critics whom he saw as the embodiment of his "clamouring Benoises", stressed that "young Russian art has stood on its feet", learning "from the West and from the great national art of our motherland."[32] He and Larionov were always as one in their love of Russian national art, but unlike Larionov Burliuk also remained loyal to the French masters, whom he revered all his life as his teachers. (At times his glorification even went a little too far, like when he wrote in his memoirs that "the art of Cezanne, Gauguin and Van Gogh was the precursor of the proletariat's victory over Tsarism and capitalism in Russia.")[33]

It must be stressed that Burliuk always defended modern Russian national art's right to an independent existence. The only truth in art, according to Burliuk, "is whether or not it is searching for new paths". He was mostly referring to the most complete and original form of self-expression (he loved this word)—whether it be in a manifesto or on a canvas—which depended not so much on the nature of its starting point, as on the creative will and personality of the artist.

* * *

Mountains of mighty canvases stood on the walls.
In circles, in corners, in rings,
Shilling with a black raven's coal-blue beak.
Solemnly and darkly hung the crimson and green canvases,
Others in mounds, like black sheep, fretting,
Their rugged surface, uneven—
Small pieces of iron and glass sparkle in them.
The brush deposited a painting of clotted blood
In hills of coloured pock-marks.

For another artist (Larionov perhaps), all that has been mentioned above—the exhibition activities, the initiative taken in order to rally like-minded people and do battle with ideological opponents or simply with competitors and the appearances in print and at public debates—might have been no more than an entertaining, but purely superficial, topic. But when dealing with David Burliuk we ought to first recognize that it was this that made up the essential side of his art. And that, getting to the heart of the matter, Burliuk the innovator, Burliuk the battler with the art of the past and pitiless underminer of foundations, existed mainly in his manifestoes and pamphlets and the numerous Futurist publications. Painting reflected only one side of his nature—his temperament—but not his innovatory character. Indeed, his contemporaries had already noted the much more sedate nature of his paintings, when compared with his outer bombast.[34]

Burliuk's works displayed, above all, that same enthusiasm that won over both his fellow-thinkers and the often skeptical viewers and that same immense energy that was a feature of all his actions. His trademark unrestrained "inner" vigour broke out into his paintings, independent of his own theoretical constructions. Somewhat later, when the days of the bitterest debates had passed, he would write: "Understanding various tendencies in modern painting, such as style, I believe everyone's art, including my own, free to follow those paths along which it is led by theme and 'star time'. When I paint real life, I am sincere."[35]

When he succeeded in doing so, when more sincere, his natural feeling for colour prevailed over the rational, the (what's more) momentary and the superficial, picked up purely for want of yet another exhibition scandal. And his canvases acquired a true and earnest pictorial character. As Alexandre Benois himself noted: "His pictures possess a certain depth and compactness. They are full of great feeling for nature and portray with originality the august despondency of the steppe expanse."[36]

Forever at the epicenter of the battle for modern art, Burliuk himself proclaimed in his famous "A Slap In The Face of Public Taste": "In our time not to be a theorist of painting means to refuse to understand it."[37] And, indeed, almost every single Russian avant-garde artist recognised the importance of theoretical tasks, among them Mikhail Larionov and Alexander Shevchenko, Olga Rozanova and Mikhail Le Dantu, Alexander Bogomazov and Alexander Grischenko, not to mention Matiushin,

Malevich, Kandinsky and Filonov. And much of their art could serve as a good example of how theoretical work was naturally counterbalanced by practical work and how these two fields constantly interacted and mutually enriched one another.

It is difficult to say the same regarding Burliuk. His theoretical standpoints were often rather confused (not that he was the only one) and led an independent existence, hardly appearing in his paintings. His attempts both at lectures and in articles to formulate such concepts as "Cubism" or "Futurism" remained just that. For example, he wrote that "CUBISM is nature with an altered view, reworked according to a definite planal system. And FUTURISM is the free representation of life—nature taken at the moment of its creative movement. As a Futurist I am a representative of symbolic Futurism."[38]

Still less convincing though nonetheless interesting is Nikolai Burliuk's attempt to "substantiate" the term "Cubism": "Explaining the tasks and achievements of Russian "Cubism" schematically, I will first of all explain why I choose this name and in what sense. It is to be valued for its conspicuousness and—say what you like—its purity (you can't call Mayakovsky a Cubist), i.e. it's the name that we have for everything that is incomprehensible and unexplained."[39]

For all the futility of such a "formulation"—as we can see today and as people maybe even saw in those days—it still incorporates a popular notion. For the term "Cubism"—and to an even greater extent "Futurism"—were indeed at that time labels, often employed randomly to all that broke free of existing canons. It is no accident that Livshits, who avoided using the term "Futurism" and pointedly named his fellow-thinkers "Hylites," wrote in one of his articles about the history of "a movement which by an unhappy misunderstanding adopted the totally unbased name of Futurism."[40]

All this bears witness to just how unclear the terminology was in those years (as indeed it remains so to this day). And, returning specifically to Burliuk's work, it is worth bearing this in mind and thus not attempt to artificially "drag" his canvases towards any definite conception. He himself tried to do this far too persistently, only his personality was too natural and incapable of analysis. Nonetheless, one can cite the example of a really fruitful combination of theory and practice in his art. This is his relationship with texture. As a matter of fact, in all his canvases, with the exception of several specifically-designed works, he treated the single question that really worried him: texture, the state of a pictorial surface. One of the most talented of his articles, published in the collection "A Slap In The Face of Public Taste," is devoted to problems of texture.

Burliuk's description of his sense for the surface of a canvas can be placed on an equal footing as a work of poetry: "We now want to cross surfaces of coloured frozen lava, fused in the vermillion, red-black and sky cobalt of coloured lava, preserving the picture of a titanic race, a maelstrom of enthusiasm and inspiration, forever in the furrows of its brow. Could it perhaps be the sea, its waves raised to the heavens with the white foam of a grey old man's iron blows, with pearly patches from black to light-green, suddenly freezing to a halt, strengthening the picture of rebellion and willfulness. Of surges and creative daring."[41]

He then offers his own classification of texture, dividing the plane of a picture into "even" and "uneven," going on to present the whole spectrum of "divisions" for each of the groups. So an even surface may be "brightly shining, shining, dimly shining-flickering." The nature of the shine can also be differentiated into "1) metallic shine 2) glass shine 3) fatty shine 4) mother-of-pearl shine 5) silky shine."

But even more expressively characterized by him is the "uneven surface," which comes "splintery, hooked, sallow (dull and dusty), shell-like."[42]

All this does of course contain more than a hint of an attempt to shock with a touch of that pseudo-scientific terminology, like the Latin beloved of Moliere's heroes, used by the Burliuk brothers when thinking up names for their pictures (wonderfully described by Benedikt Livshits). But what is much more important is that here we can observe a measure of wit and at the same time a lively and highly sensual feel for the material. And the latter represents the most expressive and strongest feature of Burliuk's canvases.

By varying different styles of painting—from delicately layered paintings, when the brush only slightly "wears through" the canvas, which retains its natural ruggedness ("Houses in the steppe," 1908), to deep protuberances with raised grooves, likening the pictorial motif to the life one ("Field" and "Morning. Wind")—Burliuk seems to be using his canvases to illustrate his own ideas: "Earlier a painting only saw, now it Feels" and "The development of Free Modern Painting will no doubt entail the further development of Texture," wrote Burliuk, "and m(ay) b(e) the time when It alone will serve as the end for many pictures is not far off."[43]

While on the subject of his paintings of the 1910s, it is also worth picking out those works which feature a blatant audacity. Burliuk would seem to be asserting his innovativeness in them. Benedikt Livshits describes one of them, "Bridge," which currently belongs to the Russian Museum: ". . .a black man in a high top hat has stepped out after a mare, which is examining its hindquarters in astonishment. This is too naturalistic, but a quarter of an hour passes and the spirally whirling space smashes at right angles; the mirror smoothness of the water sparkles over the head of the man in the top hat; a little steamship skims across it, its mast penetrating the surface of the earth and like some fleshy snake of smoke tries to stretch out to the pedestrian. One more fracture of space and the sailing ship, like those that children make out of paper, will rip the tent of Jacob our forefather."[44]

"Bridge" or "Landscape from four points of view" (as is written in French on the back of the canvas), with the scandalous inscription "the picture's bottom," was shown in 1912 at the "Jack of Diamonds" exhibition under the title: "Synthetic landscape: elements of sky and moments of decomposition of planes, introduced into the representation from four points of view." This is one of those same quasi-scientific titles which, as Livshits testified, the Burliuks thought up "splitting their sides with laughter." They hit the mark, however, and provoked the furious indignation of Benois.[45]

This picture relates specifically to the programmistic works of Burliuk, which Matiushin—to whom the picture actually belonged before going to the Russian Museum—considered "the start of Cubo-Futurism" (although the conventionality of this term regarding Burliuk's works has already been mentioned). It is no accident that many years later Burliuk would do a small repetition of it and then employ that same approach—depiction from four points of view—in several of his American pictures, particularly in "Landscape with carriage and mill."

Burliuk's "Portrait of Vasily Kamensky" (1917), his friend of many years, comrade in the battle for "left-wing" art and one of the leading representatives of the new Russian poetry, represented another one of his original pictorial manifestoes. And just as three years earlier Malevich had painted his "Completed portrait of Kliun," with its blasphemous transformation of an icon-like representation into a Cubist-Futuristic composition, so too did Burliuk create his own style of "icon," even if not so conclusively and keeping within the boundaries of a wholly realistic resemblance, yet at the same time clearly not without the influence of Malevich. The inscription on the halo reads as follows: "King of the poets song-warrior Futurist Vasily Vasilyevich Kamensky 1917 Republic of Russia."

The portrait of Kamensky was unveiled in December 1917 at the last "Jack of Diamonds" exhibition. Before the exhibition closed, Burliuk, Kamensky and Malevich read speeches on the theme "Graffiti and Pornography". The epoch continued and at the same time changed. A new period in Russia's history and culture, as well as in the history of the avant-garde movement, had dawned.

* * *

A strange shattering of pictorial worlds
Was the forerunner of freedom and our liberation from chains.
And so you trod, art,
Towards the great song of silence.

In the summer of 1915 Burliuk and his family had moved to Bashkiria, where they settled in the village of Iglino, close to Ufa. But right up to the terrible year of 1918 he was still to be seen in Moscow. Together with Mayakovsky and Kamensky they made up, in the words of the latter, "an inseparable triumvirate," continuing to take active part in all appearances of Futurists, tinted by a revolutionary zeal from February 1917 onwards.

It would seem that Burliuk was as indefatigable as ever. He was one of the organizers of the famous "Poets' Café" on Nastasinsky Lane and an habitué of other places—the "Pittoresque" and "Domino" cafes—where both former and future poetic and artistic notables gathered. And just as in days gone by, he was still capable of the most audacious and shocking escapades. One of his contemporaries recalled how "David Burliuk, clambering up the staircase, nailed one of his pictures to the wall of the building on the corner of Kuznetsky Most and Nyeglinnaya. For two years it loomed up in front of everyone."[46] But here we are already dealing with a myth about an artist.

He also continued to publish, releasing in March 1918 "The Futurists' Gazette" (although the newspaper's first edition was also to be its last) in which he published his "Manifesto Of The Flying Federation Of Futurists." His "Manifesto" called for a "Third Revolution—a Revolution of the Spirit" and demanded the separation of art from the state and the introduction of "universal art education." Hence it was written with the most frenzied revolutionary ardour.

Burliuk remained the same propagandist of modern art and poetry. Moving further and further east as the civil war spread, he, according to his own words, "read his way round every town in Siberia. He promoted Vladimir Mayakovsky and Vasya (Kamensky) across the taiga and down the mines."[47]

And yet, although the former enthusiasm remained, something went out of his life never to return. The times had changed forever and the Omsk of 1919, where he held his exhibitions and lectures, inflaming the audience with his passionate calls to do battle with the old art, was a world away from the Moscow of 1913. And Burliuk's speeches could hardly cause his listeners, witnesses during the years of civil war to convulsions much more terrible and irreversible than the destruction of the classical canons of painting, to faint anymore.

His era passed away, as did his youth. Yet Burliuk was destined to live out a long life, far from Russia—in Japan and then in the United States. And in spite of everything he still continued to assert his right to his art, to work actively and to shock. And he succeeded in doing so. He even retained enough of the former Burliuk to begin his autobiography with the words: "Great people are usually compared to high mountains; they rise up above the monotony of life and can be seen far away in time."[48] But it was already another life and another time.

Endnotes

1 This article was originally published in *Russian Futurism and David Burliuk, "The Father of Russian Futurism"* (editor-in-chief Yevgenia Petrova; translation from the Russian, Kenneth MacInnes). St. Petersburg, Palace Editions, 2000.

2 I would like to thank Alexandr E. Parnis for his kind attention to my work and for his corrections.

3 Burliuk, "Vladimir Davidovich Burliuk. Ego tvorchestvo," 35.

4 Livshits, *Polutoraglazyi strelets*, 325.

5 Ibid., 323.
6 Grabar', "Soiuz" and "Venok," 355-56.
7 Khardzhiev, *K istorii russkogo avangarda,* 140-41.
8 Burliuk, *Fragmenty iz vospominanii futurista,* 141.
9 Ibid., 116.
10 Khardzhiev, *K istorii russkogo avangarda,* 113.
11 Burliuk, *Fragmenty iz vospominanii futurista,* 121.
12 Ibid., 115.
13 Ibid., 121.
14 Ibid., 116.
15 Khardzhiev, *K istorii russkogo avangarda,* 140.
16 Ibid., 141.
17 Livshits, *Polutoraslazyi strelets,* 420.
18 *Katalog vystavki kartin Davida Burliuka,* 4.
19 Livshits, *Polutoraslazyi strelets,* 364.
20 Ibid., 361.
21 Burliuk and Burliuk, *Galdiashchie "benua" i novoe russkoe nazional'noe isskustvo,* 12.
22 A letter by Goncharova, published in "*Protiv techenia,*" no. 3, 16 March (1912): 4.
23 Livshits, *Polutoraslazyi strelets,* 361.
24 Burliuk, *Fragmenty iz vospominanii futurista,* 282.
25 Livshits, *Polutoraglazyi strelets,* 443, 663 f. 18.
26 Burliuk, *Fragmenty iz vospominanii futurista,* 83.
27 Burliuk and Burliuk, *Galdiashchie "benua" i novoe russkoe nazional'noe isskustvo,* 16.
28 OR GRM (State Russian Museum) f. 137, ed. khr. 766, ob. l. 2.
29 Makovskii, "Khudozhestvennye itogi," 29-30.
30 Livshits, *Polutoraglazyi strelets,* 320.
31 See Zdanevich, *Oslinyi khvost i mishen',* 13.
32 Burliuk and Burliuk, *Galdiashchie "benua" i novoe russkoe nazional'noe isskustvo,* 12.
33 Burliuk, *Fragmenty iz vospominanii futurista,* 136.
34 See for example the review of the critic Iv. Lazarevskii, "I tut zhe neistovyi Burliuk."
35 *Katalog vystavki kartin Davida Burliuka,* 6.
36 Khardzhiev, *K istorii russkogo avangarda,* 79. Originally in *Rech',* 22 March (1909).
37 Burliuk, et al, *Poshchechina Obshchestvennomu Vkusu,* 99.
38 *Katalog vystavki kartin Davida Burliuka,* 5.
39 Burliuk, "Vladimir Davidovich Burliuk. Ego tvorchestvo," 35.
40 Livshits, *Polutoraglazyi strelets,* 633 f. 58.
41 Burliuk, et al, *Poshchechina Obshchestvennomu Vkusu,* 99.
42 Ibid, 105.
43 Ibid., 97, 108.
44 Livshits, *Polutoraglazyi strelets,* 326-27.
45 Burliuk and Burliuk, *Galdiashchie "benua" i novoe russkoe national'noe isskustvo,* 11.
46 Luchishkin, *Ia ochen' liubliu zhizn',* 49. See also Evseeva, *David Burliuk,* 31.
47 Evseeva, *David Burliuk,* 32.
48 Burliuk, *Biografiia i stikhi,* 39.

4. The Revolutionary Art of Natalia Goncharova and Mikhail Larionov[1]

Jane A. Sharp

On 30 September 1913, Natalia Goncharova's mammoth one-person exhibition opened in Moscow with over eight hundred works on display, accompanied by a catalogue that proclaimed a shift in her orientation from West to East. The exhibition of such a body of work was a major coup for any artist in 1913—but especially for a woman representing Moscow's most radical avant-garde faction. Goncharova could count on most viewers to react with surprise. All parties, critics, and the public understood that although she might declare West European modernism "outlived," the exhibition proved beyond all doubt that she spoke as one of its key exponents. In presenting her work to the public on such a massive scale, Goncharova and her colleagues gained a rare opportunity to neutralize—even reverse—the critical prejudice that cast Russian art as a failed mimesis of Western (French) modernism. No longer exclusively focused on participating in the Parisian art world, they addressed their audiences from a newly empowered cultural sphere, more Eastern than Western. Written in the spring of 1913 in the wake of two exhibitions, the *Donkey's Tail* and *Target*, which she dominated, Goncharova's catalogue *Preface* claims that Russia's cultural plurality makes its art truly avant-garde: a challenge from Europe's eastern periphery to its center. These professions of cultural identity, and the practices that underpin them, defined Russian modernism at a pivotal moment—between the revolution of 1905 and the First World War.

Goncharova's tremendous output and conspicuous status as Mikhail Larionov's colleague and consort (it was he who principally promoted her work) put her on the modernist map before 1913. In Moscow and St. Petersburg her practices seemed to gain significance and sophistication in inverse proportion to her adherence to the imperatives of modernist art history established in the West. The promotion of Goncharova's turn to the East, of *neoprimitivism* and *vsechestvo* as historical movements, countered the image of the European master artist, author of a singular style, with a complex feminine creative persona who openly appropriates and seeks to perpetuate plural traditions. Goncharova's elusiveness as author, and particularly her celebration of the East, cast doubt on the homogeneity of modernist discourse at a critical moment in its Russian formation.[2]

She has been represented as an "amazon of the avant-garde" any number of times, but today we appreciate her contribution to Russian modernism still less than viewers of her retrospective did in 1913.[3] A pioneer of abstract painting, rayism (*luchizm*) was only one, and perhaps not the most important, of her identities. In gaining visibility, Goncharova represented avant-garde difference along two axes: those of gender and of cultural voice. As the focus of "new" Eastern-oriented, Muscovite painting (and conspicuously female), she became a lightning rod for critics, reviled in obvious analogy to the antichrist—as antiartist (*anti-khudozhnik*).[4] In 1914, her art and its reception dominated critical review in the Russian art world but would be eclipsed by war and overwhelmed by Malevich's invention of suprematism within the course of a year. The self-conscious mediation of traditions East and West that she presented to Russian viewers, whatever their cultural inclination, finally was rendered irrelevant—or at least seriously compromised—by her emigration to France. Having appropriated individual Western and period styles with particular purpose, she herself became transformed into something other than the preeminent artist provocatrice; "after Russia" she became, almost by default, the purveyor of Russian *orientalia* for Sergei Diagilev's *Saisons Russes*.[5]

By 1913, Goncharova strongly opposed the emerging narrative of originality and individual style as "the hidebound of holies" in contemporary art criticism. In the texts she produced that year, she sought to distance herself from artists whose work seemed to presage or confirm a modernist canon—the *Jack of Diamonds* painters (also based in Moscow). Yet with her disengagement from this group, Goncharova was perceived as epitomizing the aspirations (and deficiencies) of "new Russian painting." Such staged disagreements within avant-garde groupings polarized the urban art world and challenged the authority of its institutions with plural and sometimes contradictory versions of its own recent history. This tension lies at the heart of Goncharova's early success and is a condition of Russian avant-garde praxis that cannot be explained through any single methodological paradigm.

Following Goncharova's cues, we are advised to suspend our belief in the particular master narrative for modernism writers had established for new painting in Paris. The turns in her career are both stunning and confusing—and, I believe, crucial for understanding developments in Russian art before and after the revolutions of 1917. Her career forever reminds us that the faith we have (as early twenty-first-century viewers) in the trajectory of modernist painting was by no means secure in the Moscow of 1913. This is a difficult leap, for Goncharova does not supply us with the usual reinforcement. Like her Muscovite colleagues, Goncharova adopted not one but several models of creative practice within a short period of time (1910-1914). Some paintings signal her commitment to recent Western European art as a venture parallel to her own; she quotes the individual styles of major modernists and therefore seems to validate their work as an historical precedent. But the same images also derive from a practice and theory of copying that perpetuated the Byzantine tradition in Russia. Fauvist, cubist, and futurist, Goncharova's work draws even more deliberately from the icon and broadsheet and their means of production. She worked from an historical perspective that was also self-consciously regional, concerned with locally relevant, if still disputed, cultural values. Ironically (and predictably), her emulation of diverse models created expectations for conformity to the development of a singular style, the laborious work toward "mastery" exemplified in the painting techniques of Paul Cézanne, Henri Matisse, and, increasingly, Pablo Picasso. Contemporary critics had difficulty identifying Goncharova's "essential I" (as one critic phrased the problem) because her individual mark was not easily added to theirs—it was also distinctly part of another cultural tradition.

Goncharova drew on the Byzantine and Orthodox icon and broadsheet not as artifacts to be salvaged but as diverse realizations of artistic practice that continued into the present. The logic of Goncharova's oeuvre is revealed through her involvement with these media. Traditions based on the material identity of origin and copy gave another kind of historical legitimacy to the contemporary artist's assimilation of models from both East and West. If modernist paintings could be imagined as both original works and copies, as a function of their means of production, the value critics assigned to originality could be historicized, accepted as an idea or construct, and demystified as an essential condition of creativity. Goncharova did not participate in a history of modernism, or primitivism transcendent, a display of individual genius bracketed off from the contingencies of production. Appropriation in her oeuvre paradoxically imparts a sense of the artist engaged fully in re-presenting her connection to the concerns of her immediate social and aesthetic milieu. Conceived in a symbiosis between past and present, East and West, Goncharova's eclecticism so disrupted viewing habits as to require censorship, precisely when she began to enter art history through critical journalism and commercial gallery and museum presentations. In this respect, she clearly contributes to the history of modernist art as European and avant-garde; her purpose must be distinguished from that motivating the non-Western models she emulated: icons, broadsheets, and the like.

Goncharova's shifts in style and the pro-Asian rhetoric of her texts both responded to and aimed at reshaping European views of Russian difference (and French universality). By representing contemporary culture as syncretic, integrating traditions high and low, East and West, of the icon, broadsheet, and European easel painting, she positioned herself on the other side of a discourse on national identity and formal mastery that had long marginalized the Russian artist. At critical moments in her career, Goncharova managed her identity by recognizing and activating existing stereotypes, including that of Russia as oriental and the decorative as feminine. It is this strategy for reclaiming agency—and not the artist's signature style—that runs "like a red thread" throughout her work and gives narrative coherence to the multiple cultural forms present in her paintings and texts.[6]

The avant-garde's "turn to the East" can be interpreted through much of the literature on Russian orientalism, first, as a legacy of state interests in empire building that sought to dominate and assimilate a "backward," "barbaric" Asian and Caucasian periphery. Although neither Goncharova nor Larionov supported the enterprise itself, much of their writing reproduces a familiar network of cultural associations and stereotypes that we may identify as orientalist. Yet the Russian avant-garde artist's ambition to counter West European hegemony in the visual arts reveals a pattern of assimilation and disavowal that is not easily accommodated by the discursive concerns of Edward Said.[7] In studying Asia, artists, writers, and ethnographers may express their love of Eastern culture (*vostokofil'stvo*) or claim to follow its example (*vostoknichestvo*), both of which imply a devotion, even subordination, to the East that exceeds orientalist discourse in the West. These last terms extend (through their suffixes) the historical opposition in Russia of Slavophile to Westernizer to include Russia within Asia.[8] *Vostokofil'stvo* was the term coined by the critic Iakov Tugendkhol'd in 1913, however, to recognize the inadequacy of this binary conception of Russian history and culture specifically as regards Goncharova's turn to the East and her representation of the Russian peasantry.[9]

Modernism

To acknowledge the dialogue between East and West as a central feature of Russian modernism, and Goncharova's role as catalyst, is to begin where Peter Wollen concluded his study of orientalism in the art of the *Ballets Russes* over a decade ago.[10] Early-twentieth-century Russian art historical polemics quickly focused on Goncharova's shifts in style and cultural priorities. Her course drew questions of gender, the value of the decorative, and cultural identity, into crucial debates over modernist art. At a time when prominent artists and critics advocated the formal autonomy of art as an index of originality, Goncharova among others was committed to translating form through ornament and recasting ornament as high art. Traditions of design in the decorative arts, where ornament migrates from one medium (textile) to another (wood carving), influenced Russian modernist claims to originality. These practices produced a view of art history that differed significantly from the tenets of early-twentieth-century modernism in its foundational texts, from those by Clive Bell to those by Alfred Barr, Clement Greenberg, and Michael Fried.

Russian artists valued new French modernist painters (impressionists, postimpressionists, fauves, and cubists) for their mastery of form—in a culture that demanded moral and political accountability of its artists. It is true, as many critics of new Russian painting complained, that the Muscovites' understanding of West European modernism was somewhat superficial. Not familiar with the public reception and social context for modernist art in Western Europe, they apparently took seriously the declarations of formal purity that were delivered by some European artists and contemporary Russian art critics. By contrast, in a native context the Muscovite artists' understanding of visual form was charged with the real consequences of working in conditions of political upheaval through years of revolution and reaction. These included various forms of censorship and the physical suppression of speech through police intervention in the exhibition space. As artists organized outside of official channels to present new work they polarized public discourse on the social role of the artist. Questions of national identity, of the values attributed to "new Russian painting," arose repeatedly in the critical literature, each writer linking cultural preferences to the ambitions of a particular social class but often to different ends. In light of the priority Western modernist art history has ceded to Greenberg's "specialization of the medium,"[11] it cannot be overstated that in Russia, affirmations of the autonomy of form meant different things to different groups and always had a polemical purpose. Moscow, though westward looking, was not Paris; the economic, political, and social conditions for making and viewing art differed in crucial ways.

Goncharova's art and its reception suggest that representations of the Parisian center, the "West," are as fraught with ambiguity as is orientalism's object, the "East." Painting in the style of Cézanne and the icon, Goncharova exposes the values of modernist autonomy as just that—assumptions that have obtained historical currency but do not exhaust the connections that obtain between images, audiences, and institutions. It was not until 1913 that the occasional critic would recognize mastery in either Goncharova's or Picasso's art, and at this time they were seen as equals.[12] In the same year, Goncharova and Larionov argued that if Picasso had turned to Africa, and Matisse to the Orient, to revolutionize art in Western Europe, it was now time for artists in the East (with Russia as the avant-garde) to reclaim modernism as a radically syncretic—not eurocentric—project. Two events, one local, the other cataclysmic and international, altered Russian artists' perceptions of their place in the East/West continuum and thus the power dynamic among avant-garde groups. Goncharova and Larionov's departure to Paris was followed by Tatlin's and Malevich's successes in their Moscow and St. Petersburg exhibitions of 1914 and 1915 respectively. In the same year, 1914, Russia joined with Europe to fight a war over imperial hegemony. These new conditions made primitivism and orientalism as a strategy of national *self*-definition and empowerment among Russian artists obsolete.

Chronology

As an avant-garde movement, neoprimitivism is associated with the generation that came of age in Moscow in the first two decades of the twentieth century and included as its principal exponents Goncharova, Larionov, Aleksandr Shevchenko, Mikhail Le Dantiu, and Il'ia Zdanevich (the latter two were based in St. Petersburg). Correspondence by several other participants in these exhibitions is important as well for their detailed discussions of theories and practices of copying—a central preoccupation of this group. Maurice Fabbri, Evgenii Saigadochnyi, and Le Dantiu have been considered secondary figures as painters, in part because they looked to Goncharova and Larionov for guidance in their art practices and institutional politics. But their writings, together with Goncharova's recently recovered diaries, provide important insight into the ways avant-garde painters approached their creative work.

In the spring of 1913, neoprimitivism was formulated to signify the Eastern focus of the "Donkey's Tail" and "Target" exhibitions; the term was introduced in Aleksandr Shevchenko's publication by that title.[13] Not conceived as a style, but as a polemical discourse, neoprimitivism was constituted through publications and lectures to rout rival avant-garde groups with which Larionov and Goncharova had established temporary allegiances, beginning with the World of Art and ending with the Jack of Diamonds and Union of Youth, and their collective opposition: long-established art organizations, such as the Society of Itinerant Painters and the Union of Russian Painters. Within the same year, *vsechestvo* was theorized and presented by Zdanevich in lectures on Goncharova's oeuvre in November 1913 and again in April 1914. It was further developed as a theory in the writings of Le Dantiu, a member of the Union of Youth group who remained connected, however ambivalently, to the Muscovites and authored the essay "Painting of the Everythingists."[14]

The exhibitions and debates that promoted new national cultural agendas during the first two decades of the twentieth century took place in Moscow but with the following caveats. The Muscovite Donkey's Tail group first exhibited their work and received their first public reviews in St. Petersburg as an extension of the Union of Youth group in December 1911. In a reciprocal fashion, the Moscow debut of the Donkey's Tail group the following spring (1912) contained a separate section (on the second floor of the Moscow Art School's exhibition space) of work by

Union of Youth group artists.[15] Throughout the period of 1910-1913, Moscow artists from both Donkey's Tail and Jack of Diamonds participated in a number of Union of Youth exhibitions, including those that traveled to other provincial capitals.[16] In a sense, neo-primitivism emerged through a practical alliance—that turned to rivalry—between groups in each city. Allegiances within groups and across city cultures constantly shifted, forged as they were out of a common interest in self-defense against hostile critics.[17]

In 1913 arguments among artists over tactics, and the degree to which each group accepted Western models, led to a split along the same divide; Larionov's Target exhibition and debate finally separated this group from both the Union of Youth in St. Petersburg and the Jack of Diamonds (based principally in Moscow). In his public lectures, Zdanevich presented *vsechestvo*, the movement that rejected current art historiographical preoccupations with period and individual styles, as essentially Muscovite, through contrasts with the stultified culture of St. Petersburg. Certainly the tenor of the debates held in Moscow became far more strident, and resulted in more extreme public responses, than those held in St. Petersburg (whether organized by the Jack of Diamonds or the Union of Youth).

Outside of Russia, Natalia Goncharova is known more for her stage designs for Diagilev's *Saisons Russes* than for her art as a painter. Yet before her 1915 emigration to Paris, Goncharova's paintings, no less than Larionov's aggressive promotion of her, defined avant-garde practice in Russia. Her colossal retrospective exhibitions held in Moscow and St. Petersburg in 1913 and 1914 respectively were the first accorded a "new" artist by an independent gallery.[18] In prerevolutionary Russia, where icon painting and the decorative arts were living professional practices, her secular (modernist) reworking of religious imagery was considered both transgressive and flawed. A "westernizing" modernist, she has not been accepted as an exponent of the Western canon since.[19] Her paintings and statements are frequently considered too transparent and culturally specific to Russia to figure universally as avant-garde. She alternately accommodated the Western tradition and undermined its key feature: the progressive master narrative of a singular, individual language or style. Goncharova's paintings directed her viewers to both Western and Eastern sources, which made it difficult for audiences to locate what was unique to Russian culture in her oeuvre. Her multiplicity disrupted stable ethnic, cultural, or civic categories of difference. Frequent epithets, "decorative" and "eclectic," describe both feminine and avant-garde difference in her work. Far from gaining acceptance as a decorative artist and woman painter (as did her compatriot Sonia Delaunay), she was the only artist to be censored with any regularity. Censorship, or "the arrest" of paintings, resulted in her trial for pornography (1910), and the imposition of a ban on her religious images by the Spiritual Censorship Committee of the Holy Synod (1914). Goncharova became the bearer of a transgressive national imagery for much of her audience; she replaced the image of woman as a vehicle for official projections of national unity with a different model of female creative agency that made her a magnet for denunciations in the press—and the most visible member of the Donkey's Tail group.

Exposed: Natalia Goncharova's One-Day Exhibition and the Trial of 1910

The avant-garde's agenda for new Russian painting developed through a series of public exchanges among artists, their critics, and their audiences. A series of extensively reported events in 1910 linked Goncharova with the group expelled from the Moscow School in January. The public debut of the Jack of Diamonds set the tone and pattern; it was framed by the arrest of several of Goncharova's paintings after her 24 March 1910, one-day exhibition and her trial for pornography on 22 December 1910, in which members of the group served as witnesses (for the defense). Goncharova's marginal role as a woman artist was both confirmed and contradicted as a function of the reception of new art in Moscow in reviews of the first Jack of Diamonds exhibition. When the Jack of Diamonds exhibition opened to a scandalized public reception on 10 December, the daily papers posted headings such as "The Diamonds Lady goes to Court," which quickly identified Goncharova as a central figure in both contexts.[20]

The critical and official reaction to Goncharova's exhibition demonstrates the extreme consequences of public review in 1910. Muscovite factions and their sponsors formally aired their internal disagreements in front of audiences and the media beginning with the debates organized by the Jack of Diamonds in February 1912. The artistic debate made conflict among groups and between artist and critic immediately accessible to a public who now paid to participate. A predictable sequence of events, from public review and press criticism to police interference and court proceedings, linked the social role played by avant-garde artists with their cultural interests. At issue in the press was the legitimacy of this generation as representatives of a new national school, their mimicry of Western models, and, increasingly, the relevance of popular art, mass-produced and handcrafted, to high-art audiences. Much of the discussion addressed, if only implicitly in critical response to avant-garde work, the gendered identity and marginal status of the new, left-wing (*krainiaia levaia*) artist.

It was unusual, given the limited number of spaces and sponsors for new art, for an artist to receive the kind of prominence Goncharova did in 1910, and later in 1913 and 1914, in the form of a one-person exhibition. The privilege of intellectual and commercial promotion that they represented clearly identified Goncharova as the leading figure among the new generation of Muscovite artists. Independent artists continued to rely primarily on the sponsorship of entrepreneurial art journals (*The World of Art* and *Golden Fleece*) and/or the resources of individual members (Nikolai Kul'bin for Impressionists and Triangle, etc. and David Burliuk for the Wreath and Wreath *Stefanos*).

The sequence of events that led to the civil trial for Goncharova and her exhibition's organizers was so frequently repeated that it can be said to constitute a trend radicalizing the reception of avant-garde art. Her exhibition crystallized an extreme situation in which the artist and members of the press acted reciprocally, each anticipating the other's response through to the court proceedings. According to several accounts, Goncharova exhibited twenty to twenty-two paintings on the evening of 24 March 1910, in a closed session for members of the Society of Free Aesthetics in Moscow, which she and Larionov attended.[21] Seeking to prove the subversive character of these meetings, a member of the press managed to infiltrate the event and published an inflammatory article denouncing Goncharova's paintings the next day in the *Voice of Moscow*, a daily Moscow (Octobrist party or center-right) newspaper. The author, later identified as (Vladimir?) Giliarovskii, declared her "Nudes" "so completely decadent in their manner of depiction and so indecent that the secret anatomical divisions of the Gasner museum seem mild compared to these images of disturbing perversity." Among the pictures named, several nudes and those of a (masculine) "God" were reported to have "surpassed the pornography of secret postcards." The self-selected audience, which would seem to eliminate any problematic reactions to the work, is cited in the article as sufficient proof of deviancy in itself: "among the aesthetes! That is how they name their closed meetings. Only their own people can attend (*svoi liudi*), just like at the secret meetings of the 'brotherhood.'"[22]

The writer leaves no doubt that Goncharova's gender was the primary reason for his critical diatribe: "It is most disturbing that the painter is a woman, who under the influence of half-sick, overblown decadent types, has stepped beyond the boundary of morally correct behavior."[23] This notice was followed the next day in the same paper by a poetic caricature of the meeting, entitled "Our Aesthetes," which likewise connected the Society's decadent literary reputation with Goncharova's paintings:

> Literary blabbermouths, Half-witted poetics,
> Uncensored and impetuous Prophets of aesthetics,
> Symbolist-declaimers, Decadent artists,
> Though in art they may be reformers,
> They are bootmakers in creativity;...
> They wail as if through brass trumpets,
> And at their uncensored ravings
> Only the poor walls blush
> In the literary circle ...
> While innovative women artists,
> (Let's give the poor things an epigraph!)
> Having forgotten their needles and scissors,
> Exhibit pornography,
> Or brazenly,
> Following; their bold confreres;
> The decadent meetings/
> They console with their speeches...
> Here are speeches on nudity
> And immodest creations ...
> And the bold ladies are delighted,
> Predominantly the redhaired ones![24]

The article and poem achieved the desired results: on the following day, the police confiscated Goncharova's nudes and began an official investigation into the activities of the Society. Abused by the press, Larionov and Goncharova quickly used the press to their advantage. He published a defense of Goncharova in the last issue of the *Golden Fleece* to clarify the sequence of events and protest the official seizure of the pictures.[25] Due principally to the fact that the meeting had been closed to the public, Goncharova and the rest were acquitted.[26] Because the charge was obviously a fabrication, Larionov and others argued that the trial demonstrated the limits of freedom of expression in the arts.

The devolution of authority from Academy to gallery and press did not immediately obviate the need for official control over the arts. The incident occurred during a time when censorship policies were being revised, and this no doubt prompted Larionov and others to ascribe great importance to its outcome.[27] Many individuals had been successfully prosecuted for publishing political material. Goncharova's trial, however, was unique as a case for pornography in high art.[28] Larionov observed that it would redefine government censorship policies for art independently produced and exhibited and encourage police intervention in the exhibition space. The trial was called to justify the seizure of specific works of art, setting a precedent through which the local censors, police, and courts might act as the *de facto* censors of independent exhibitions.

Goncharova's exhibition was received in the context of the expansion of women's participation in the public sphere. In December 1908, the First All-Russian Women's Congress had taken place, the result of an effort to create a unified women's movement in the Russian empire, and had spawned a series of newspaper interviews with women participants and observers.[29] Further prominence had been given to "the woman question" by the radical political activity and well-publicized sexual views of Aleksandra Kollontai during the first decade of the twentieth century. As Kollontai's most important work, *Social Bases of the Woman Question*, was published in 1909 in St. Petersburg,[30] it is likely, if not inevitable, that a conservative critic would have associated the views of such a prominent advocate of sexual freedom and socialist politics with any transgression of accepted feminine social behavior. But probably more important was the coincidence of Goncharova's exhibition with the publication of Anastasiia Verbitskaia's erotic *Keys of Happiness* (*Kliuchi schast'ia*), narrated by Russia's first sexually liberated heroine.[31] As Laura Engelstein has observed, the extensive public debate provoked by the novel was predicated on a reversal of gender roles enacted by the writer/artist herself. As author, Verbitskaia succeeded in persuading her readers that women were no longer "the object of tragedies centered on men, but had become the subjects of their own, independent tragedies."[32] Similarly, as a painter in the public sphere, Goncharova could no longer be perceived by her audiences as naturally feminine (objectified), but rather as a subject in her own right, an artist/producer possessing a gaze. The fact that she did not disguise her cohabitation with Larionov would have only heightened her visibility as a sexualized subject.[33] Goncharova's presentation of the nude in the context of a liberal salon gathering was a further demonstration of the degradation of high literature and art into the realm of "boulevard pornography," as it was currently being discussed in the pages of the press and in elite journals—precisely because the author was female.

Given this reception context, it is significant that Goncharova's only recorded reaction to the arrest of her pictures and trial reveals no self-consciousness regarding the relevance of her gender (or lifestyle) to critical perceptions of her work. On the contrary, she identified herself and her work with the mainstream vanguard assault on the Academy:

> As regards my manner [says the artist] it should never be described as impressionistic as has been done in the papers. After all, impressionism is the transmission of the first, often unclear, indistinct impression. I, however, like the newest [noveishie] French painters (Le Fauconnier, Braque, Picasso) attempt to attain concrete form, a sculptural clarity, and simplified line, the depth and the brilliance of colors.[34]

Goncharova's response to the accusations launched against her in the press was published within a week of the confiscation of her paintings as part of the sympathetic press interview cited above. The anonymous interviewer reports that Goncharova did not consider her nudes provocative; she is quoted as being "stunned by the unexpected reactions to her work." Her own statement conspicuously does not address the charge of moral indecency. Instead she disavows her interest in impressionism and claims for the first time an alliance with Georges Braque and Picasso. Thus the issue of gender that apparently motivated Giliarovskii's accusation of pornography is sublimated and transposed to a discussion of style in new West European painting.

Goncharova's problems arose with her increasing visibility as a woman who painted subjects associated with masculine creative identities, especially the nude life study. Such choices contradicted behavior expected for a woman, and occurred at a time when feminine stereotypes were being established, challenged, and endlessly analyzed. The Russian translation in 1909 of Otto Weininger's 1903 text *Geschlecht und Charakter*, together with the numerous publications by Praskov'ia Tarnovskaia, which had provided Cesare Lombroso with much of his material on female crime, created a discursive context in which any expression of female subjectivity could be construed as criminal deviancy. Lombroso's text equates feminine genius in the arts with the sexualized female subject; both are represented as a perversion of nature. Like any female affirming her own agency, the woman artist is seen posturing as masculine.[35] Lombroso's paradigm was fully assimilated by Goncharova's critics, who perceived her as the inverted image of femininity. Like the female poet (*poetessa*), the woman artist (*zhenshchina-khudozhnitsa*) was an artist with a sex—neither naturally female nor invisibly male.

But beyond this gendered distinction in reception, Goncharova's critics perceived an even greater threat in her images—to the extent that they resembled mass-produced erotic postcards. Both in function and form, the resemblances invoked by her critics are contrived. Although her torso figure might depict a specific model (like the photograph) and her frontal pose can be found in explicit images, it is also common to academic studio practice. Moreover, such similarities are challenged by the absence in Goncharova's work of any of the paraphernalia one comes to expect from both the erotic or pornographic nude and the elite production of academic painters, particularly that of Henryk Semiradskii.[36] Indeed, the differences in Goncharova's iconography (precisely her omission of props, costume, and decor) exposed the scopophilic objectives shared by the mass-produced carte and the academic nude and pointed to censorable similarities between the two genres of nude imagery. Unlike the academic nude, Goncharova's nudes are not new glosses on "ideal" beauty; they are portraits of individuals who can be traced to a particular context for the production of avant-garde art. The resemblance between one of Goncharova's models (the torso figure) and a model used frequently by Valentin Serov and Il'ia Mashkov allows us to assemble a portrait of a particular individual. When considered in the context of studio production, together with nude life studies by Mashkov, Larionov, and Serov, they mark the integration of the female painter into the domain of the life study class, newly initiated by Serov at the Moscow School, and these avant-garde artists in their own studio.[37] In this way, too, Goncharova's paintings represented a challenge to the Tret'iakov museum nude that exceeded any possible resemblance to mass-produced cards. They bared the devices of censorship through which individual members of the press would manipulate their privileged access to public discourse so as to deprive another, in this case a woman artist, of the same.

These connections were, predictably, not debated at the time of Goncharova's trial. Instead, the unconventional structural and iconographical features of Goncharova's images made them appear both excessive and inadequate. Critical silence on the relationship between values ascribed to women's art and the construction of gender more broadly ensured that the genre of the nude would remain the natural domain of the male artist. Goncharova's most subtle critics, however, preferred to analyze features of her work as both "masculine" and "feminine", because she did not conform to their expectations for a woman artist.

Thus it was Goncharova—as a woman artist—who first faced the limits encountered by other radical artists at various points in their careers. Over the course of the year 1910, a major and long-lived independent society was formed in response to a similar politics of exclusion from official institutions and accusations of moral deviancy. As students of the Moscow School of Painting, Sculpture and Architecture, new artists were charged with inadequate mastery of Western traditions and of lacking formal rigor—judgments that earlier had applied primarily to women's art. With the naming of this society, Jack of Diamonds, the Muscovites simultaneously marked and protested their disenfranchisement (their expulsion). But Larionov's long-term goal was to counter negative press criticism that neutralized differences between factions and made all the youth seem an indistinguishable, boorish mass. In the case of the Jack, signage gave the faction unique prominence and advanced difference as a means of self-definition. The categories of exclusion that defined the group were, however, those of mass theatrical, urban street, and even criminal culture. They embraced the political prisoner, the buffoon, and the "soldier-clown (*soldat-gaer*)."[38] And the prior values that pejoratively singled-out the woman artist extended to the vanguard project in surprising ways.

Following Goncharova's trial, considerations of address determined both the content and sequence of Larionov's exhibitions from the Jack of Diamonds through the No. 4 in 1914. His choice of names was premeditated provocation of a particular kind. In each instance exhibition titles initiated a complex dialogue between audience and artist. Thus, to confront the Jack of Diamonds was to deal with the "ace of diamonds"—to imagine real social and political enfranchisement. This was the *épatage*, the "slap in the face": a public forced to consider what high art typically concealed; the limits of franchise and its consequences. Just as political opposition and social transgressions (such as prostitution on Moscow's main thoroughfares) were made invisible by various punitive and repressive measures in the Pyotr Stolypin era, so, too, some critics and viewers sought to remove avant-garde (*peredovoi*) new art from view. Reactions to both the first Jack of Diamonds and the Donkey's Tail exhibitions actually realized the strategy anticipated by the artist. Before either exhibition opened, in reaction to newspaper announcements of the title alone, public responses of outrage and calls for censorship were recorded in the press.[39]

The Jack of Diamonds: Marking the Artist

When the Jack of Diamonds was formed in 1910 by former Moscow School artists and their colleagues they were perceived as a collec tive whose radicalism derived from their mimicry of new West European art. The art critic Sergei Glagol' refined his criticism of the third Golden Fleece exhibition in his review of the first Jack of Diamonds exhibition where he noted the influence of Gauguin and Vincent van Gogh on the young Russians. In fact, he restated his earlier opinion of student work by asserting that, whereas audiences "did not believe in Larionov and Mashkov, [Gauguin's and van Gogh's] painting is sincere and not deliberate."[40] Glagol' missed the Russian shift in focus; the impact of Cezanne and Matisse was more pronounced in the Jack of Diamonds exhibition, and this new focus of emulation was encouraged by contemporary evaluations of their work.[41] Just as Glagol' had celebrated the primitivism of Gauguin's art in 1909, in early 1910 Iakov Tugendkhol'd praised Cezanne and Matisse for their "decorative" and "monumental" art. Tugendkhol'd's reviews of these artists' work occupy an equally prominent place in the literature both in terms of the views he expressed and their place of publication. Like Glagol', Konstantin Makovskii, and Aleksandr Benois, he was a contributing art critic to a major periodical, *Apollon*. Published in St. Petersburg (1909-17), *Apollon* succeeded *The World of Art*, *The Scales* (or Balance), and *Golden Fleece* as the most important art/literary journal in Russia (Makovskii was its editor).

In distinct contrast to the World of Art group, who invoked the aristocratic, eighteenth-century European enlightenment as their cultural model, the Jack of Diamonds entered into the common culture by invoking or exploiting genres of visual imagery long associated with urban mass culture. Their imagery and formal appropriations were locked into a system of promotion that included mass literature, the solicitation of critical review in the daily press, and, eventually, the public artistic debate. The meanings that viewers/readers associated with the name derived from a long tradition in popular Russian and French culture that connected the politically suspect "Jack of Diamonds" with the roguish and amorous "Jack of Hearts"; it encompassed the history of French playing cards, Molière's plays, and popular "boulevard" novelettes.[42] In Russia as in France, the "Jack of Hearts" symbolized the lover and, more generally, as Gleb Pospelov argues, "galant motifs in life as in the theater." Russia inherited as well the association of the "Jack of Diamonds" with "rogues, swindlers, men not worthy of respect." Pospelov argues that the tremendous popularity in Russia of Ponson du Terrail's *The Club of Jack of Hearts* (translated from French into Russian in the 1860s) in particular had the effect of confusing the associations of the "knave" with certain forms of criminal behavior, including the political.[43] Because the meanings of the term were so transparent to viewers of the exhibition, one can only infer that Larionov sought to invoke the associations that arose between criminal status and the vanguard artist's position at the margins of the urban art world. To what extent he was motivated by radical political commitments is open to question. However, not all the artists in the group approved of the name, and once it was accepted it soon acquired connotations of "youthful vitality."[44]

While he was on leave from the army, Larionov painted numerous scenes of soldiers bathing and drinking and their female companions (probably prostitutes, as sometimes they were inscribed with the word *kurva* [whore]) as nude "Venuses" (*Venery*) that parody European representations of the odalisque and courtesan.[45] This cycle redefined provincial genre painting by drawing from a variety of popular visual art forms, including urban graffiti and the signboard (and thematically, the broadsheet). The Venus series was exhibited first in the Donkey's Tail exhibition. But considered together with his other scenes of army and provincial life, some of which were painted in the barracks, we may conclude that soldiers, too, probably constituted part of his intended audience. His Venus, then, disrupts viewing habits in two ways: the outlining and monochrome ground suggest an amateur hand, echoing the graffiti Larionov is known to have admired, and it may well have been directed at an audience that produced such images. As he later stated, when in 1910 he first displayed his soldier cycle, the paintings would have been seen and appreciated for completely different reasons by the common soldier and elite high art clientele.

If Larionov's work represented the provocative and oppositional aims of the Jack of Diamonds group, Goncharova's contributions to the same exhibition epitomized a dialogical construction of national identity, European and Other, in vanguard painting. According to Aristarkh Lentulov, Larionov was less concerned to promote his own work than he was to advance Goncharova's career in this exhibition. He gave her priority in the space allocation for the show. In the first Jack of Diamonds exhibition she included a number of works of religious subject matter that evidently referred to the icon, fresco, and *lubok* and were simply entitled *Religious Compositions*. In addition, her diptych *Spring (in the City)* and *Spring (in the Country)* (Vesna [gorod], Vesna [derevnia]) reveal her interest in the work of a number of Western European painters, primarily Cézanne, Matisse, and Picasso. Paintings such as *Wrestlers* (Bortsy), completed a year or two before.

For most, the Jack of Diamonds exhibition marked the beginning of a new level of intensity in the confrontation between artist and public. Although the artists did not publish a manifesto, the sign posted at the entrance to the exhibition was perceived as the group's logo, identifying the artist as hooligan and criminal. At the same time, however, the artists' program derived from a European modernist tradition that celebrated the work of art as an authentic expression of the artist's idiosyncratic life experience and temperament. Larionov's commitment to this view of the artist, and his desire to maintain a confrontational dynamic in his public address, led him to break with his colleagues. Turning to the East was not yet part of the promotional agenda.

The Donkey's Tail, Debates, and the Turn to the East

In December 1911, Larionov formally announced the dissolution of the Jack of Diamonds and its split into two mutually hostile camps. Larionov explained that by refusing to register as a society, he intended to deprive the press and public of "name recognition." His counter strategy was to propose a succession of exhibitions that would permanently frustrate a public seeking continuity in style and group aesthetics. He asserts that "with us there will be nothing that refers to the past. Not a single stroke will be in any way habitual [privichnoi]." For this reason, he announces that not only will the group not register with the city administration but also each exhibition will bear a different name; the first would be the Donkey's Tail (Oslinyi khvost) and the second was already planned as the Target (Mishen').[46]

In organizing the rival Donkey's Tail, Larionov sought to reinforce the public dialogue that had been generated through his first exhibition, the Jack of Diamonds, and further develop the role of the socially engaged artist. His goal was to create new conditions for the public reception of his art, something that he believed could be achieved only by displacing the authority of art critics and government institutions. Both were negatively predisposed to Larionov and contemporary art. Instead of soliciting major critics for reviews, as he had done earlier, Larionov sought to provide more direct public access to his work through press interviews, debates, and the publication of manifestos. The significance of Larionov's program has never been fully recognized, as scholars have focused more on his formal innovations (rayonism) than on his rhetorical ones. Yet the latter feature of the shift from Jack of Diamonds to Donkey's Tail proved to be at least as important as Larionov's actual stylistic progression. It was also crucial to Malevich's promotion of suprematism.

One critic asserted that Larionov was not concerned with the public at all; he "is only for himself."[47] The logical extension of this contradictory dynamic was the theatrical forum of the debate. Here, more than in any other type of cultural performance, Larionov and other artists expanded their public visibility while adopting an antagonistic posture in actual encounters with members of their audience. Larionov's analysis of the formation and fragmentation of the Jack of Diamonds group is prophetic for the prewar period as a whole and coincides with the observations many of his critics made regarding the instability of vanguard alliances and aesthetics. Thus, if his justifications for his strategy are sometimes dissembling, they are always rhetorically sensible.

If disagreement over public strategy can be identified as the reason for the Moscow schism, then the criticisms of Western influences that first united these artists as an oppositional force soon defined each faction's counter-agenda. In an interview with the press just two weeks after the announcement of the rift between the two groups, Larionov appended an evaluation of Russian "national" traditions in the visual arts to a lengthy critique of the formation of the Jack of Diamonds Society. Within a few months, Goncharova and Larionov together with a number of their colleagues began to articulate their differences with the Jack of Diamonds by opposing East to West, native "origins" to European "derivative" styles. They did so in reaction to the accusations of westernization and epigonism that had dominated the reception of new Muscovite painting in the press. But the privileged place the Jack of Diamonds gave French painting in their exhibition irked Larionov even more. The second Jack of Diamonds exhibition, which opened on 25 January 1912 (preceding the Donkey's Tail opening by just under two months), contained a much more extensive inventory of contemporary French painting than the first; it included works by Albert Gleizes, André Derain, Robert Delaunay, Othon Friesze, and Fernand Léger, as well as drawings by Matisse and Picasso (Le Fauconnier sent his study for *L'Abondance*). The Die Brücke artists, as well as those associated with Der Blaue Reiter that same year were also well represented.

In rethinking what might constitute a new national school of Russian painting, Larionov and Goncharova essentially took up the same weapon that had been used against the vanguard as a unified group before the schism. Larionov, Goncharova, and their supporters argued that the Jack of Diamonds artists were poor "copyists" of Cézanne, Matisse, and Gauguin. By February 1912, they presented their revised program to the press, one that would shape all future exhibitions, and their rhetoric of public address. Proposing for the first time to integrate popular art into their exhibition, the plan was summarized as follows: "'Oslinyi Khvost' derives exclusively from Russian traditions and does not invite even a single foreign artist. Out of respect for ancient national art, the organizers of the exhibition propose to devote a large section to popular prints, and P. P. Shibanov, who owns a well-known antique shop has promised to obtain a large collection of broadsheets beginning with the epoch of Peter the Great and ending with works of contemporary popular art."[48]

The expression of group differences became newsworthy in the autumn of 1911, but especially so following a series of public debates, the first of which was organized by the Jack of Diamonds (Petr Konchalovskii presided as chair). This debate, "On Contemporary Art," took place on 12 February 1912, in the large auditorium of the Polytechnical Museum in Moscow. The debacle that closed it was unprecedented. According to one press summary the event was so popular that the hall, which seated 1,000, was packed, all tickets sold out.[49] The evening began with Nikolai Kul'bin's lecture on "Free Art," which he delivered as a string of aphorisms, such as "academicism—decadence, decay, putrefaction" and "romanticism—flowering, fruit—new art, new styles, free creation." Although Vassily Kandinsky was one of the scheduled speakers, he did not appear; Kul'bin reread the lecture he had delivered at the Congress of Artists on Kandinsky's behalf. David Burliuk presented the Jack of Diamonds position and began his lecture on "the methods of the history of art" by cursing Benois as he quoted from the critic's books and reviews. In parodistic response to criticism of the Russian artist's lack of technical ability, Burliuk advocated rewriting the history of art as a "succession of artistic principles independent of what is depicted" and even proposed replacing the term work of art (*khudozhestvennoe proizvedenie*) with "object made by human hands" (*delo ruk chelovecheskikh*). This derived from a series of contrasts and comparisons of "works of art" juxtaposing Raphael (as a bad example) with (positive) examples of Egyptian and Assyrian art and paintings by French artists (Monet, Cézanne, Matisse, and Picasso) together with work by members of the Jack of Diamonds. The same reviewer explained that all these images were projected in succession "without distinctions, in one group" as a means of eliciting analogies between the "primitive" and the "modern."

Following this presentation, the real debate (*preniia*) began with Voloshin refining or contradicting Burliuk's assertions and a brief statement by a member of the Jack of Diamonds group. Not invited to speak as a lecturer, Goncharova nevertheless stole the show by announcing, as she prepared to refute several of Kul'bin's assertions regarding her art, that she was no longer part of the Jack of Diamonds group but would exhibit with the Donkey's Tail. She protested the use of her paintings such as *Spring in the City* to illustrate points made about the aims of the Jack of Diamonds group and their theoretical exposition of cubism (slides of her work were shown by both Kul'bin and Burliuk). According to all accounts, the audience broke into laughter but fell silent when she challenged them to view the upcoming Donkey's Tail exhibition.[50]

Goncharova's impromptu remarks were followed by Larionov's accusations that the Jack of Diamonds "copied the French." When he called them "my epigones," he was booed and sent down from the stage. Reports of the incident follow carefully the audience's reactions to each speaker and indicate that, although impatient with Burliuk, they found Larionov intolerable, as whistles, feet stomping, and shouts of "get out" accompanied his presentation. The debate was considered such a success that it was repeated in March, but to less effect, as it was dominated this time by Voloshin and attended by the police.[51]

Goncharova was so concerned to define her differences from the agenda presented at this debate that she sent a written summary of her reply to local Moscow newspapers. The statement records her first public attempt to define her relationship to European modernism, which she asserts is informed by her assimilation of national traditions in the visual arts, comprising Scythian stone statuettes, and various popular art forms. Her diary entry expresses a view of French modernism that was found in many press accounts. The Jack of Diamonds exhibition itself, she writes, was "boring, boring," whereas the French, "are not bad at all, with marvelous technique, only broken up into crystals. The varieties of Cubism give me little joy. The Russian imitators, of the likes of Ekster and Lentulov are beneath any criticism."[52]

The Donkey's Tail exhibition, which opened on 11 March 1912, was their first public appearance as the "extreme left" (*krainie levye*). The group had appeared earlier as part of the Union of Youth exhibition in St. Petersburg, where they were already identified as a group even further to the "left" of the Jack of Diamonds.[53] All the reviews suggest that the group had generated sufficient expectations among the gallery-going public before the opening to recreate the sensation caused by the first Jack of Diamonds exhibition.

This exhibition constituted a break equal to if not more significant than the first Jack of Diamonds exhibition.[54] As points of entry into avant-garde networks for Malevich and Vladimir Tatlin, this is probably true. Malevich contributed his series of provincial town scenes, painted in gouache on paper, including the Courbet-inspired *Burial of a Peasant*, now lost. The Donkey's Tail exhibition just preceded the artist's shift from gouache to oil painting. The predominance of peasant themes in work he presented at this exhibition has led scholars to emphasize the impact of Goncharova's peasant cycles on his, especially during the years 1910-1912. These works, very much like Goncharova's, draw on popular traditions (broadsheet and icon) while referring to specific models within the European.

This was the exhibition that first united Larionov, Goncharova, Malevich, and Tatlin—although they would dramatically end their association by the close of the year (1912), at least in part owing to Larionov's monopolization of the group's present and future projects. Because the Donkey's Tail exhibition was organized through Larionov's initiative, both he and Goncharova were able to control the selection and hanging of works for the first time since 1904-1905 and to overwhelm by sheer force of number. Both artists exhibited the most work they had ever hung together in a public space: Goncharova had approximately fifty-four works on view and Larionov, fifty-nine, as opposed to Malevich's twenty-four and Tatlin's twenty-six paintings and twenty-three set designs. Goncharova's work was the first a viewer encountered upon entering the space.[55] Among her prominent rural images, *Peasants Gathering Apples* and *Round Dance* are recognizable sources for Malevich. Although these paintings were created in 1910-1911, they demonstrate her commitment to models both European and Russian. They suggest Cézanne's facture but in figural types characteristic of the broadsheet; for example, the subject of the "Circle Dance" (*khorovod*) was a popular theme in this medium. In 1912 her presentation of primitivism was even more deliberately eclectic. The Donkey's Tail exhibition included her various *Artistic Possibilities on the Image of the Peacock* (in "Chinese," "Futurist," "Egyptian," "Cubist," and "Russian embroidery" styles).[56] Goncharova also subtitled a work "in the Venetian style" (*Woman with a Basket on her Head*). *The Smoker*, which is described in the catalogue as having been painted in the "style of tray painting," also referred viewers to Cézanne's painting by the same title.[57]

Several critics of Goncharova's contributions to this exhibition count on the audience's pejorative view of feminine practice in the visual arts in their condemnation of new Russian art. Goncharova, the most prominent woman artist in the show, was eclectic, lacked "mastery," and, conversely, excelled at the decorative arts. Earlier, critics had remarked on Goncharova's dialogue with Russian decorative arts, but because the work exhibited in the Donkey's Tail exhibition embraced a diverse range of popular traditions, her approach seemed too transparent. In a review of the Union of Youth exhibition that launched the Donkey's Tail group, a critic for the liberal newspaper *Protiv techeniia* takes Goncharova's primitivism as a case study for the entire show. Their collective effort is diminished by eclecticism and excessive quotation. Decoration degenerates to formlessness: "The most significant phase in their development is their turn to antiquity. I noted this even last year. Now the work of a few artists carries a more self-conscious character, a more individualistic one in the sense of intentional copying, which has its unquestionable raison d'être. In this respect, one must single out N. Goncharova. Her genre paintings of haycutters, women with rakes, peasants picking apples with their crude straight lines, and twisted faces are positively disgusting. Every line, every spot here speaks of an intention to be ugly, and in very bad taste. One cannot believe, positively, that the artist herself is capable of seeing in these exercises even the shadow of some kind of expression of an idea."[58]

The critic's debt to Western concepts of originality and his expectation that a coherent style might emerge organically from a shared sense of national ethos are poignantly apparent in his reading of Goncharova's pictorial priorities. But he turns this critique into one of the strongest positive statements regarding her primitivism. She has "lovingly studied the images of primitive popular art . . . which may not please the eye, but she doesn't pretend to end up in the Salon. But if you look closely at her work, you will feel that the genuine primitive emanates from it. This is not a copy, not simple imitation, nor even a paraphrase of the broadsheet. This work is painted by a person who knows how to enter the spirit of the past, who has acquired a primitive point of view." The debate over definitions of originality preoccupied critics and vanguard artists as they sought to formulate criteria for a new national school of painting. Assimilation and adaptation of various master styles disrupted the historical legitimization of a school or trend, and nowhere are the two more interconnected than in reviews of Goncharova's work.

Goncharova is singled out here for two lapses; she appropriates what the Itinerants had established as a national iconography (the image of the peasant) and the forms of popular expression associated with that world. Her project remobilizes a tradition of rural handcraft that had found its place decades before in ethnographic exhibitions and more recently in kustar shops. As she draws wood-carving, lace embroidery, and icon painting into the gallery, she provides a different productive context for these objects—where authenticity might imperil originality. Further, for the avant-garde artist, the future of peasant cottage industry is no longer to be determined by the bureaucracy of the Ministry of Agriculture and State Domains. Instead, newly aligned with radical contemporary art, it will participate fully in reshaping the public sphere. Some critics understood this process ideally as a shift in the artisan's status, from one of objectified welfare (the state acts on the peasants' behalf) to agency (peasant artifacts alter the priorities of high art). The commentary described above registers this shift as a threat through emotionally keyed phases: "distortions" and "disgust." These phrases keep at bay the expanding reach of mass culture and resist its incursions into the realm of high art currently underway.

It is equally clear in the review cited above that Goncharova's critic conflated her gendered presence as author with that of her peasant subject matter, a problem similar to the one presented by her nude life studies. In a discourse on identity generated within the Academy by men, where the image of woman projects national values, Goncharova intervenes as an artist/producer of national values in her own right. Her paintings transgress social boundaries because she cannot redefine the terms of the discourse, she may only embody them. Thus, the critic concludes that her approach may be perceived as authentic only to the extent that she enacts or realizes the primitive qualities proper to her sources. It is significant that only the occasional critic attempted to discuss Goncharova's work (or that by the other participants in the exhibition) as deriving from specific traditions, so concerned were most to note the appearance (or lack thereof) of a clearly defined style. In the press, the artists were perceived as a "group" more as a result of their public profile than their common interests or appropriations. Voloshin again proves a telling commentator. He observes that Goncharova's references to different styles in the "Peacock" series are "literary" and cede too much to the public. His review concludes that this concern to elucidate sources actually undermines the radical tenor of the Donkey's Tail artists' challenge both to the artistic establishment and to the public.[59]

Voloshin's point, that the artists are concerned primarily with "address" over substance or style, is confirmed by another critic. An anonymous reviewer for *Rech'*, "The Foreigner" ("Chuzhoi"), agrees that rhetoric replaces a true shift in direction. However, by contrast, he argues that the artist's work is perceived by the public as "radical." Transposing issues of style to a discussion of the public reception of the exhibition, he reminds viewers that Larionov, who once produced paintings "that can be admired by all," now achieves the effect of a "disgusting caper, a ridicule of nature and man, an apologia of ugliness. . . . it's exactly like an eternally drawn-out horrible nightmare." Again, it is the dynamic of public address implied by paintings of hairdresser interiors, soldiers' odalisques, in the match of subject and style, that impresses the reviewer: "If Larionov is not sincere, then is not he—and those who run after him—gripped by a grimacing, clownish, young militant passion, a desire to demonstrate his fearlessness, and to laugh at those who pass judgment and rank his paintings? And closer to the truth, isn't this an attempt to get even, to boldly shock them?"[60]

Although the critic acknowledges Larionov's militancy, he denies that his central aim, to disrupt viewing habits, can ever be achieved. He claims that unlike viewers at the first Jack of Diamonds exhibition, those at the Donkey's Tail were not particularly shocked. Larionov has "wasted his time," because the strategy "no longer works, the audience is not angry, nor disturbed, but sorry for him." The review then charts the process of habituation Larionov sought to estrange; the critic finds that within a quarter of an hour, "The 'Donkey's Tail' no longer disturbs the audience; it bores them." It is significant that the reviewer attributes this reaction to the presence of so many "scholars," that is, professional art critics and historians, at the opening of the exhibition. Although they rejected Larionov's aims, critics overwhelmed the packed opening. The dynamic was reciprocal, as "Chuzhoi" observed: no matter how much the artists profess to detest the "public at large," they were popular with them: "Truthfully, the opening of the 'Donkey's Tail' exhibition was a success, that is, it had a large public. There were as many in the hall as there were at the stately openings of 'The World of Art' and 'The Union'."

Both reviews, for all their divergences, point to the same effect of the Donkey's Tail exhibition. Although it may well have been a turning point in Malevich's stylistic development, it was not identified at the time as marking a coherent stylistic impulse. Rather, the exhibition intensified the sense of reciprocity between the artist and public that made the vanguard artist appear increasingly "leftist" and "militant," on the one hand, and increasingly "popular" with an audience, on the other. The exhibition was also important in that it continued criticism of "Russian derivativeness" vis-à-vis the French. Both Voloshin and "Chuzhoi" questioned the artists' sincerity, just as Glagol' and Benois had done (Glagol' in 1909, Benois as late as 1912), comparing the Russians unfavorably with the French. "Chuzhoi" wrote that the specialists gathered at the opening "denied [Larionov] even his independence, they saw here simply bad imitations, mostly of Rousseau." A few lines below he observed that if "Larionov is imitating the French, then others are imitating him."[61]

Critics thus continued to distinguish the creative potential of the French school from the "stillborn" acrobatics and empty rhetoric of the Russians. In 1912, the forum of the debate allowed artists to respond directly to their critics and viewers with new definitions of national traditions. Within a year these debates would be reproduced as historical argument and theory. After the 1911 schism between the Jack of Diamonds and Donkey's Tail, artists devised a more ambitious strategy to counter the negative influence of critical press reviews on the public reception of their art. They published their own texts that continued the polemics of the debates while revising art history. Burliuk's text of 1913, *The "Defamers of Benois" and New National Russian Art*, reframes the Jack of Diamond's dispute by elaborating his theories of form and including an analysis of audience receptivity. Aleksandr Shevchenko's *Principles of Cubism and Other Contemporary Trends in Painting of All Eras and Peoples*, as well as his manifesto *Neoprimitivism* (both published in 1913), address critical prejudice, first, by reevaluating the function of the copy, and second, by arguing that Western painting, particularly French cubism, has formal affinities with the "primitive" and with contemporary (avant-garde) Russian art. In *Principles of Cubism,* Shevchenko allies the eclectic assimilation of form and traditions embraced by the Russians with Picasso's collages. He cites ancient Russian art forms, such as the revêtment of the icon, as an Eastern example of the same appropriative, additive process. Other features are considered in their plural manifestations, such as the decorative-symbolic use of color in painted representations of Astarta and the perspectival distortions of Egyptian reliefs.[62] In *Neoprimitivism* Shevchenko takes great pain to describe the qualities of Cézanne's work that the Russians seek to assimilate and promote. Here he singles out specific formal devices, such as the use of line and adjoining planes of color (passage), and considers them in various contexts, especially broadsheets. In summary, he rebuts the criticism of Benois, Glagol', and Makovskii by identifying the Russian turn to the East with the French artists' rejection of the Academy.

In perhaps what was to become his first of many public appearances, Il'ia Zdanevich in 1912 represented the Donkey's Tail position on the break between the Academy and new art by citing Benois' criticism in detail. In a speech for the Petersburg Artistic Association (*Khudozhestvenno-artisticheskaia Assosiatsiia*) he refers his audience to the dates and numbers of each article from which he quotes. Zdanevich's speech, reported in the press, rejects the critic's charge that new art alienates viewers and argues that the Donkey's Tail group was poised to reverse the trend. "The present moment is not a revival but a great decline. The cubists exist only in order that a few may get a laugh, and so that a few maecenases may buy their work. Contemporary art does not respond to the spirit of our age. Art must be connected to life, otherwise it is superfluous. That art should be for only a few is a lie. It is time to reject 'intimacy,' the formula of 'art for art's sake.' We must go out on the streets. Art must be applied."[63]

Zdanevich's lecture is the first clear indication of the use to which native, popular art forms would be put in Donkey's Tail group exhibitions, and why it would be necessary to link these art forms with the East. The popular arts were reconceived at this point as a continuous indigenous cultural tradition that arose prior to Russia's Europeanization. Avant-garde artists whose work was exhibited and received outside of academic institutions could align their aims with this tradition and thereby bridge the gap between European elite and Russian popular culture. Goncharova's response to Kul'bin's lecture (12 February 1912) on "Free Art" was yet another appeal for public interaction, and it closely resembles Zdanevich's. Her letter to the press documents not only her objections to Kul'bin's theorizing; it also expounds her view of West European modernist art in relation to Russia's indigenous traditions. Her letter clarifies her interest in having readers acknowledge her prior experience with cubist form and her appreciation of national schools in Europe, particularly Italy and France. But it also documents her belief that access to her ideas will result in greater public comprehension and acceptance of new art and indigenous popular traditions—knowledge of one enhances access to the other. Her optimism was shared by other avant-garde artists, who followed through with a stream of publications, debates, and exhibitions.

Beginning with the Donkey's Tail exhibition, Goncharova, Larionov, and their colleagues advanced the view that popular traditions and the arts of the East should be the focus of new Russian painting. Acknowledging this dimension of Russia's cultural legacy would provide the link between high art and the experiences of daily life—between elite artist and mass culture—to project a more socially inclusive national identity. Their role as collectors and interpreters of broadsheets, signboards, wood-carvings, and icons afforded them new insights into indigenous traditions. They also claimed that the work they produced would achieve this union.

The schism within the Jack of Diamonds collective was the source of all future "radical" positions and actions undertaken by the vanguard. Larionov's insistence on his leadership of the Muscovites led to Malevich's and Tatlin's break with him in 1912 and the final separation of the Donkey's Tail group from both the Union of Youth and Jack of Diamonds in early 1913. Although the Donkey's Tail exhibition may well represent the "flowering" of primitivism, not all artists supported unequivocally the group's direction and leadership. Extensive correspondence related to the exhibition, in addition to the variety of work exhibited, testifies to their disagreements and their different approaches to questions of style. Feuds among members also surface in the text *Donkey's Tail and Target* (*Oslinyi khvost i Mishen'*), which Larionov undertook to publish in the spring of 1913. As the pseudonymous author of the lead article, Larionov here criticizes a number of the exhibition's participants while isolating himself and Goncharova for praise.[64] This atmosphere of division dominated Russian vanguard culture from February 1912 through 1915, when Malevich launched his public promotion of suprematism as a new national (and universal) style of painting, in competition with Tatlin.[65]

Endnotes

1 This text is drawn from Jane A. Sharp, *Russian Modernism between East and West: Natal'ia Goncharova and the Moscow Avant-Garde*. Cambridge University Press, 2006, Introduction and Chapters 1, 2, 3.

2 I take as the most coherent presentation of high modernism (based on the writings of Clement Greenberg), the account given by the collective authors of the series *Modern Art: Practices and Debates* (New Haven, 1993), which they distinguish from the broader cultural and social conditions of modernity in Europe; see Sharp, "Review Essay," 502-506. See also Clark, *Farewell to an Idea*, 2-13; 137-8.

3 Bowlt and Drutt, *Amazons of the Avant-Garde*. Although doing a great service to the field by grouping together a number of the great women artists, the curators' selection implied a similarity of priorities, social, cultural, formal that neutralized Goncharova's contribution in particular. Her art was represented in something of its diversity, but without the necessary context to give this diversity meaning.

4 Songaillo, *O Vystavke kartin Natalii Goncharovoi*, 4-5.

5 Tsvetaeva, "Natal'ia Goncharova: Zhizn' i tvorchestvo". This longer version of her manuscript was republished in Russian by Ariane Efron, with notes and introduction by D. V. Sarabianov. See Tsvetaeva, "Natal'ia Goncharova," 1967, 141-162. All citations refer to this last publication. Recognizing precisely these effects of emigration, Tsvetaeva appropriately divided Goncharova's life into two halves: "Rossiia i posle Rossii," ("Russia and after Russia").

6 Tugendkhol'd, "Vystavka kartin Natalii Goncharovoi," 72. The phrase, not the argument, is Tugendkhol'd's.

7 Edward Said, *Orientalism*.

8 Tugendkhol'd used the term *vostokofil'stvo* (love of the East) to designate an orientation that is more extreme than Slavophilism in Goncharova's work; similarly, *vostoknichestvo* (going or turning to the East) depends on the sense imparted by *narodnichestvo* (going to the "people"). Its primary sense is similar to that of the first term; both oppose *zapadnichestvo* (the condition of following or turning to the West). This pairing devolves from the respective roots: *Vostok* = East; *Zapad* = West. Tugendkhol'd, "Sovremennoe iskusstvo i narodnost'," 155.

9 Ibid. Tugendkhol'd writes that an "abyss" separates the populism of the nineteenth-century Itinerants from Goncharova's *vostokofil'stvo*.

10 Wollen, "Fashion/Orientalism/the Body," 29.

11 Greenberg, "Towards a Newer Laocoön," 296-310.

12 The first major articles on Picasso published in Russian were Berdiaev, "Picasso," 57-8 and 161-2; Chulkov, "Demony sovremennosti," 64-75. On the reception of Picasso's work following the revolution see Doronchenkov, "Picasso in Russia at the Turn of the 1920s," 69-80.

13 Shevchenko, *Neo-primitivizm*.

14 Two versions of Mikhail Le Dantiu's *Zhivopis' Vsekov* have been documented; neither appear to have been published when written, in the spring of 1914. One text was published in Russian by John Bowlt (from Ilia Zdanevich's Paris archive): "Zhivopis' Veskov," 183-202. A second and slightly different manuscript, "Zhivopis' Veskov" is in RGALI, 792/1/1.

15 *Vystavka kartin gruppy khudozhnikov "Oslinyi khvost,"* (Moscow, 1912). In a review entitled "Moskovskie otkliki" (signed "Chuzhoi"), the Union of Youth artists are

criticized as "peterburgskie larionovtsy." Chuzhoi, "Moskovskie otkliki, Oslinyi khvost." 2. After this alliance broke up in 1913, Larionov polemically asserted that the St. Petersburg Union of Youth exhibitions "reflected the influence of a movement begun in Moscow," "Oslinyi khvost i Mishen", 79. Although Varsonofii Parkin is the acknowledged author, he remains an unknown figure. Because of the text's polemical purpose and language, I am inclined to agree with Elena Basner that Larionov is the real author of the essay.

16 *Soiuz molodezhi. Katalog vystavki* (St. Petersburg, 1910, 1911, 1911-1912). All catalogues identify the location of participants, the catalogue *Oslinyi khvost* gives their addresses. A review of the St. Petersburg exhibition which opened on 26 December 1911, represents the Donkey's Tail artists as the "Moscow group of the exhibition," Rostislavov, "Vystavka Soiuza molodezhi," 3. A. Rostislavov describes the Moscow contingent of this exhibition as representing the "newest aspirations." "Vystavka Soiuza molodezhi," 3.

17 Jeremy Howard has argued that the St. Petersburg Union of Youth group remained more committed to expanding their audience and circle of members by traveling exhibitions to other cities than either Moscow group: *The Union of Youth*, 58-9 and 156-60. By the end of 1913 Larionov had isolated himself from rival groups and, in 1914, as a result of his opportunity to exhibit in Paris, focused his attention on expanding the Russian presence there.

18 Her Moscow retrospective contained over eight hundred works (in the catalogue an error in numbering sequence accounts for the lesser number of 769 works listed) and was held at Klavdiia Ivanovna Mikhailova's Art Salon on Bolshaia Dmitrovka from September 30 to November 5, 1913. A smaller retrospective was held at Nadezhda Evseevna Dobychina's Art Bureau on the Moika Canal in St. Petersburg from March 15 to April 20, 1914.

19 After emigration, Larionov and Goncharova were rarely recognized as major avant-gardists in modernist art historiography (particularly as compared to their one-time colleagues Malevich and Tatlin), owing equally to the biases of modernist discourse itself and to a frustrating lack of access to images and archives. Prior to publication of my book *Russian Modernism between East and West*, only one monograph had been devoted to Goncharova, and it was published in French: Chamot, *Goncharova.*, which was followed by her descriptive catalogue of a limited number of Goncharova's paintings, *Goncharova: Stage Designs and Paintings*. A few have attempted to write her into that history: Linda Nochlin and Ann Sutherland Harris recognized her status as major modernist woman artist in their exhibition, "Women Artists 1550-1950," The Los Angeles County Museum of Art (New York, 1976). More recently M. N. Yablonskaya devoted a chapter to the artist confirming her prominence as one of Russia's pioneering modernist "amazons," Yablonskaya, "Natalya Goncharova," 52-81. John Bowlt's exhibition "Amazons of the Russian Avant-Garde" (Royal Academy of Arts, London, 1999) underscored Goncharova's formal innovations as a pioneer of neoprimitivism, cubofuturism, and rayism.

20 Anonymous, "Bubnovaia dama pod sudom," 4.

21 Anonymous, "Moskovskaia khronika," 3, and Anonymous, "Bubnovaia dama pod sudom," 4.

22 The presentation of her work is compared to ritual group-sex (sval'nyi grekh). [Giliarovskii] "Brattsy-estety," 4. Long fragments of this article are quoted in Briusov, *Dnevniki*, 191-2, and in Larionov, "Gazetnye kritiki v rolii politsii navrov," 97-8.

23 [Giliarovskii] "Brattsy-estety," 4.
24 "Nashi estety" was published by the poet-caricaturist "Weg." Extracts were quoted in Briusov, *Dnevniki*, 191-2.
25 Larionov, "Gazetnye kritiki v roli politsii nravov," 97-8.
26 Of the accused only Goncharova, Igumnov, and Troianovskii actually appeared at court. Anonymous, "Moskovskaia Khronika," 3. Konstantin Krakht was a sculptor and set designer with whom Goncharova had studied privately in Moscow in 1909. It was in his studio that she produced her first set designs for *Svad'ba Zobeidy* in that vear: Mochul'skii, *Teatral'naia entsiklopediia*, 66-7. Goncharova and Krakht maintained a friendship during these years, documented by letters in the manuscript division of the Russian National Library, Moscow.
27 Censorship laws had been relaxed by decree on 24 November 1905 and now required that the government engage in immediate legal action following the confiscation of materials. Yet, during the period of conservative reaction that followed (accelerated by the ministry of Petr Stolypin from 1907 until his assassination in 1911), constant abuses and reversals of this decree undermined the rights and provisions it was designed to guarantee. Temporary rulings issued as early as 18 March and 26 April 1906 reversed the November decree as it applied to drawings and prints. By the end of 1913 it was widely feared that the enactment of new censorship laws would return literature and the arts to practices of the pre-revolutionary period. The large number of articles in newspapers describing trials, executions, confiscation of printing materials and publications, subsumed under the generic title "Repressions" (Repressii), gave this aspect of public life particular prominence during the prewar years. See, for example, *Rech': Ezhegodnik* (St. Petersburg, 1912 and 1914), for lists of newspapers fined and arrests of editors.
28 The artist I. I. Bilibin was placed under "administrative arrest" in January 1906 for publishing a caricature of Nicholas II, "Osei (Equus Asinus) v 1/20 natural'noi velichiny," in the third number of *Zhupel'*, "Chronology," Bilibin, *Stati, pis'ma, vospominanie o khudozhnike*, 20. Vladimir Maiakovskii, a member of the RSDRP from 1908, was arrested on three occasions and served prison terms in 1908 and 1909-1910 for operating an illegal press. Maiakovskii, "Ia Sam," 16-18, 423-4.
29 A complete account of the proceedings was published: *Trudy 1Ogo s'ezda pri zhenskom obshchestve v S-Peterburge, 10-16 dekabria, 1908ogo goda*, (1909).
30 For more on Kollontai, see Stites, *The Women's Liberation Movement in Russia*, 423-6.
31 The first volume of Verbitskaia's series was published that spring; it was discussed at the literary-artistic circle just three days before Goncharova's exhibition, "Zhenshchina o zhenshchine," 5. For a study of Verbitskaia's persona and the largely female audience for her work see Holmgren, "Gendering the Icon: Marketing Women Writers in Fin-de-Siècle Russia," 321-46; Engelstein, *The Keys to Happiness*, 396-420; and Brooks, *When Russia Learned to Read*, 153-60.
32 Kollontai, "Novaia zhenshchina," 153-4, 185 (original emphasis), as quoted by Engelstein, *The Keys to Happiness*, 399.
33 Although it was widely known that Goncharova was not married to Larionov while they were living together in Moscow, she is referred to frequently in the press as his wife. Documents from the archives of the Moscow School of Painting, Sculpture and Architecture indicate that Larionov maintained a separate apartment at least at the beginning of his studies there (Pokrovka, Vvedenskii pereulok, dom Shcheglova, no. 14, apt. 3): RGALI, 680/2/1517, Personal File, M. F. Larionov, registration form. In

March 1912, in the catalogue *Vystavka gruppy khudozhnikov "Oslinyi khvost,"* Larionov's address is listed as apt. 10 in the Goncharov house on Trekhprudnyi pereulok. They shared a studio in her father's house until their departure for France in April 1914.

34 Anonymous, "Beseda s N. S. Goncharovoi," 3.

35 The critic's view of Goncharova's moral bearing clearly derived from a tradition that encompasses both Darwin and the physiopsychologist Cesare Lombroso. Lombroso argued that women were by nature incapable of genius and that those rare women who developed their intellects did so "at the expense of their sex." Lombroso, *E. G. Ferrero*, 161-3, 179-80. See also Engelstein on Tarnovskaia, *Keys to Happiness*, 133-52.

36 Beatrice Farwell and Gerald Needham suggest that in composition and often in detail, the pornographic image, and the whole history of the libertine print and photograph, was grounded in the subjects and compositional motifs of high art. Farwell, *Manet and the Nude*, 134, 147-155, 231-232; Needham, "Manet, 'Olympia,' and Pornographic Photography," 80-89, esp. 81: "The mixture in 'Olympia' of an exotic odalisque setting with the very real, unexotic woman is typical of the photographs, which often sought a veneer of respectability by borrowing trappings from the nude paintings that proliferated in the Salon." The symbiosis between the two was further reinforced by the production, at least in France, of a genre of nude photo specifically for artists' use and sold only within the walls of the Ecole des Beaux Arts. McCauley points out that the line drawn between this "legally allowable photo" and the pornographic carte was not all that clear, as it "depended on the definition of a 'natural pose' and was often violated, resulting in series of arrests and rejections by the depot legal censors": McCauley, *A. A. E. Disderi and the Carte de Visite Portrait Photograph*, 106-9. The presence in early-twentieth-century Russia of French (and German) postcards suggests that international borders presented no obstacle to the marketing of pornographic material in Russia. A review in *Russkoe slovo*, for example, cites the sale of pornographic cards on Teatral'naia ploshchad' (facing the Bolshoi Theater) in Moscow, observed by a French citizen who sent a newspaper article on the subject to the head of the Moscow City Duma: Guchkov, "Inostranets o Moskovskoi pornografii," 5.

37 Repin was the first to introduce the live nude model into academic studio practice at the St. Petersburg Academy; Serov led the way in Moscow with this and other innovations in studio practices. See Valkenier, *Ilya Repin and the World of Russian Art*, 134-36.

38 Pospelov, "O 'valetakh' bubnovykh i valetakh chernykh," 127-42.

39 Pospelov in "O 'valetakh' bubnovykh" cites numerous examples of these reactions; of particular relevance is Maksimilian Voloshin's commentary: "Even before its opening, the Jack of Diamonds through name alone aroused the unanimous indignation of Moscow art critics. They observed that the exhibition opening had been delayed for so long because the mayor has placed a ban on it . . .," Voloshin, "Bubnovyi valet," 11.

40 Glagol', "Bubnovyi valet," 5.

41 Among the most detailed reviews of Matisse's work in terms of sources (gothic art, stained glass, etc.), is a review by B. Skanskii (pseudonym for Viktor Petrovich Iving), "Anri Matiss."

42 This summary is drawn from Pospelov, "O 'valetakh' bubnovykh i valetakh chervonnykh," 132-3; it differs little from his account in his book, *Bubnovyi valet*, 99-102.

43 Pospelov, Bubnovyi valet, 100-1.

44 Glagol', "Bubnovyi valet," 5. The critic asks "Why 'jack of diamonds'? They say the 'diamond' is an emblem of happiness, joy, and that the 'jack' represents youth, and perhaps the 'jack of diamonds' therefore signifies youthful happiness."

45 This particular painting is inscribed "Sonia/kurva" on the recto; the verso is inscribed in Larionov's hand "La belle du sol-dats/Mischel Larionoff/500 roubles," with his Moscow address (Trekhprudnyi pereulok) in both Russian (cyrillic) and French. Based on an archival photograph, Elena Basner has identified the work as *Markitantka Sonia*, first shown at the Donkey's Tail exhibition. The photo is inscribed (artist's hand) with both this title and *Soldatskaia devushka*, as well as the exhibition title: Basner, "Metamorfy 'chuzhogo siuzheta' v zhivopisi M. F. Larionova i N. S. Goncharovoi," 56.

46 The summary that follows is drawn from an article by "Cherri," entitled "Ssora 'Khvostov' s 'Valetami'" (Rift between the 'Tails' and the 'Knaves'), 5.

47 Mukhortov, "Progressivnyi paralich," 5. Here the critic refers to Larionov's manner of painting, linking his "vision" with his posturing: "It is unfortunate that he [Larionov] has such a particular way of seeing. He doesn't stop for anything, only so that he can say whatever he wants. He is not for the public. He is for the few, perhaps even only for himself."

48 Anonymous,"O. Kh."

49 Lopatin-Shuiskii summarized the lectures that evening in a newspaper article, "Moskva: Khudozhestvennyi disput," 3. My discussion is based primarily on this account. See also Livshits later summary (1933), *The One and a Half-Eyed Archer*, 81-4. The most complete Russian citations of press reports are given by Krusanov, *Russkii avantgard*, 50-60.

50 Livshits summarized the dispute in *Polutoraglazyi strelets*, 68-73.

51 "Referent," "Bubnovyi valet—khudozhestvennyi disput", 4.

52 Natal'ia Goncharova, Diary fragment, Vinogradov Archive, Moscow.

53 "The more established group of contemporary realists of the left camp has become frightened of the extremism of 'O. Kh.', and has decided to remain content with their achievements. They will organize their own exhibition using the name that has already gained them popularity, 'Jack of Diamonds.' The exhibitors will include Mashkov, Lentulov, Konchalovskii, and Fal'k." Announcement, "Bubnovyi valet," *Golos Moskvy*, no. 295 (23 December 1911).

54 Malevich's debt to Goncharova was recognized in the first comprehensive publications on the Russian avant-garde (in English), such as Camilla Gray's *The Great Experiment: Russian Art, 1862-1922*. See also Andersen, *Moderne Russisk Kunst*, 24-5.

55 Parkin (Larionov), "Oslinyi khvost i Mishen'," 54-5.

56 Eli Eganbiuri (I. Zdanevich), *Natalia Goncharova. Mikhail Larionov*, XI. Correspondence between Larionov and Zdanevich confirms his authorship of the book under a pseudonym: Archives of the State Russian Museum, Fond 177/88, pp. 11-13.

57 Ivan Morozov acquired Cézanne's painting in 1910: see Barskaia, *French Painting in the Hermitage from the mid-18th to the 20th Century.*

58 Lopatin-Shuiskii, "Vystavka 'Sojuz Molodezhi'," 2.

59 Voloshin, "Oslinyi khvost." 105-6. Reprinted in Voloshin, *Liki tvorchestva*, 287-9.

60 Chuzhoi, "Moskovskie otkliki, Oslinyi khvost," 2.

61 Ibid.

62 Shevchenko, *Printsipy kubizma*, 17-18.

63 E. Pskovitinov reported speech in a summary of the lectures by Nikolai Kul'bin and Il'ia Zdanevich (Zagdevich in text). Pskovitinov, E., "Oslinyi khvost," 4-5.

64 Parkin (Larionov), "Oslinyi khvost i Mishen'"; for criticism of the Jack of Diamonds see 53-54.

65 An evening of lectures by Malevich and Ivan Puni was organized after the opening of

the "0.10" exhibition, "Publichnaia nauchnaia populamaia lektsiia Suprematistov," followed by Ksenia Boguslavskaia's poetry reading. The event took place in the Concert Hall of the Tenishev School (where the previous Union of Youth debates had been held) on 12 January 1916.

III

RUSSIAN SUPREMATISM AND CONSTRUCTIVISM

1. Kazimir Malevich: His Creative Path[1]

Evgenii Kovtun (1928-1996)

Translated from the Russian by John E. Bowlt

The renewal of art in France dating from the rise of Impressionism extended over several decades, while in Russia this process was consolidated within a span of just ten to fifteen years. Malevich's artistic development displays the same concentrated process. From the very beginning, his art showed distinctive, personal traits: a striking transmission of primal energy, a striving towards a preordained goal, and a veritable obsession with the art of painting. Remembering his youth, Malevich wrote to one of his students: "I worked as a draftsman... as soon as I got off work, I would run to my paints and start on a study straightaway. You grab your stuff and rush off to sketch. This feeling for art can attain huge, unbelievable proportions. It can make a man explode."[2]

Transrational Realism

From the early 1910s onwards, Malevich's work served as an "experimental polygon" in which he tested and sharpened his new found mastery of the art of painting. His quest involved various trends in art, but although Malevich flirted with Cubism and Futurism, his greatest achievements at this time were made in the cycle of paintings he called "Alogism" or "Transrational Realism." *Cow and Violin, Aviator, Englishman in Moscow, Portrait of Ivan Kliun*—these works manifest a new method in the spatial organization of the painting, something unknown to the French Cubists. In using "Alogism," Malevich tried to go beyond the boundaries of "common sense" the condition that establishes relationships between surface phenomena. Endeavouring to find a deeper understanding of the world through intuition, Russian painting—through Malevich's experiments—attempted to master intuition as a creative method. This same aspiration inspired the work of poets such as Velimir Khlebnikov, Alexei Kruchenykh, Elena Guro, and others. What was closed to common reason would now become accessible through intuition, allowing the deliberate extraction of ideas from the unconscious.[3] Malevich's *Cow and Violin* is the earliest "manifesto" of "Alogism." On the back of the canvas Malevich wrote: "Alogical comparison of the two forms—violin and cow—as an element in the struggle against logic, natural order, and philistine meaning and prejudice. K. Malevich." Absurd from the view of common sense, the combination of a cow and violin proclaims the general interconnection of phenomena in the world. Intuition reveals distant connections within the world, connections which logic interprets as absurd. This same position was maintained by Khlebnikov, who wrote: "There exist certain quantities through the transformation of which the blue color of a cornflower (I mean pure sensation), is changing continuously and passing through spheres of rupture unknown to us, turns into the sound of a cuckoo bird calling or that of a child crying—and it becomes it."[4] To recognize any isolated event as part of a universal system, to see and incarnate the invisible revealed through "spiritual sight"—this is the essence of the Post-Cubist research in Russian painting, and the most intense expression of this movement is found in Malevich's work. For him "transrational" did not mean madness—its logic was of a higher order. In 1913 Malevich wrote Matiushin: "We come to the rejection of reason, but this has been possible only because a *different* form of reason has arisen within us. When compared with what we are repudiating, one could call it transrational. It has its own law and construction and also meaning, and only in the light of this knowledge will our work be based on a totally new, transrational precept."[5]

A painting executed according to the system of Transrational Realism which manifests a new relationship, with the environment. It still has a sense of "above" and "below," but is now deprived of weight. Its plastic structures are, as it were, suspended within universal space. This "absence of gravity" as a structure-organizational principle finds vivid expression in *Aviator* where the figure seems to rise or soar in weightlessness.

Victory over the Sun

The idea of Futurist performance arose after the merging of the Union of Youth artists and the Hylaea literary group in March 1913 (the members of Hylaea were Khlebnikov, Guro, Kruchenykh, Vasilii Kamensky, David and Nikolai Burliuk, and Benedikt Livshits).[6] The First All-Russian Congress of Futurists was held during the summer of 1913 at Matiushin's dacha in Uusikirkko (on the Karelian Isthmus). Malevich and Kruchenykh both attended this gathering. The participants issued a manifesto announcing the establishment of a Futurist theater and impending performances and it was here at the dacha that work began on the opera *Victory over the Sun*.[7] Kruchenykh wrote the libretto, Matiushin the music, and Malevich sketched the costume designs. They were united by a mutual understanding: "Kruchenykh, Malevich, and I worked together. And each one of us used his particular theoretical approach to enhance and elucidate the others' work. The opera grew out of our collective efforts—via words, music, and the artist's spatial image."[8] Produced on 3 and 5 December 1913 in St. Petersburg's Luna Park, the opera combined the endeavours of the poets Khlebnikov and Kruchenykh, the composer Matiushin, and the artist Malevich.[9]

Khlebnikov wrote the prologue to *Victory over the Sun*, but it was declaimed by Kruchenykh who also played the roles of the Reciter and the Enemy who fight among themselves—"an end to future wars" is how Matiushin defined the sense of this image. Overturning the conventional notion of theatre, this unusual opera provoked outrage among the audience, which divided into two factions—an indignant crowd, and a small circle of cheering spectators. The curtain was not drawn apart but ripped in half. Brilliantly lit by the glare of a spotlight, the characters appeared on stage before the stunned spectators. The "future strongmen" were especially impressive. Matiushin recalled: "In the first act, in order to create the colossal size of the two strongmen, [Malevich] built shoulders level with their mouths, the head was constructed of cardboard like a helmet—thereby creating the impression of two enormous human figures."[10]

Malevich's designs for this production provided crucial groundwork for the development of Suprematism. Most of them followed the tenets of Cubism, leaning towards the non-objective, and Suprematist restructuring was particularly evident in the backdrop designs. In Act V, the drama unfolds against the background of an entirely "Suprematist" square depicted in black and white. At this time Malevich himself was not aware of the importance of these changes in his creative work, but his subsequent realization is evident in a letter he wrote to Matiushin—before the projected second staging of *Victory over the Sun* in 1915: "I'll be very grateful if you yourself would position my curtain design for the act in which the victory is won. . . This drawing will have great significance for painting; what had been done unconsciously, is now bearing extraordinary fruit."[11] It was precisely in his designs for *Victory over the Sun* that Malevich took the definitive step towards Suprematism.

The Exhibition of the "Last Futurists"

For some time the new direction in Russian painting remained untitled. Until the fall of 1915 no one besides Matiushin knew what was going on in Malevich's studio, but by mid-1915, after producing no less than 30 non-objective canvases, Malevich finally named his new trend Suprematism. In 1915, as Moscow artists prepared for the last Cubo-Futurist exhibition, Malevich prepared to show and affirm his new art. Ivan Kliun and Mikhail Menkov, the first artists to adopt the ideas of Suprematism, exhibited their work together with Malevich's. However, the other participants refused to enter Malevich's work as "Suprematist" in the catalogue. Malevich was forced to concede to his fellow artists, although he had already prepared a brochure about Suprematism which he distributed at the opening of the exhibition. In addition he hung up a sign alongside his paintings reading "Suprematism of Painting, K. Malevich."[12] The "Last Futurist Exhibition of Paintings 0.10 (Zero Ten)" opened on 17 December 1915 at Nadezhda Dobychina's Art Bureau on the Field of Mars in Petrograd. No one pondered over the strange numerical ending to the exhibition's name: evidently it was regarded simply as one more Futurist whim.

Critics noted that the title of the exhibition was "arithmetically incorrect," and, in actual fact, "0.10" (i.e. "one tenth") did not correspond to the explanation in parentheses—"zero, ten." However, Malevich's correspondence provides some insight into the idea behind the title. On 29 March, 1915 he wrote: "We are undertaking the publication of a journal and are beginning to discuss the whys and wherefores. In view of the fact that we are preparing to reduce everything to nothing, we have decided to call the journal Zero. Later on we too will go beyond zero."[13] The idea of reducing all figurative forms to nothing and step beyond zero—to the non-objective—came from Malevich. In the brochure circulated at the exhibition Malevich announced his complete break with figurative forms: "I have transformed myself in the zero of forms and have gone beyond 0-1."[14] The nine remaining participants in the exhibition also strove "to go beyond 0." Hence the parenthetic message—"zero–ten." This explanation is corroborated by Ivan Puni's letter to Malevich dated June, 1915: "We have to paint a great deal right now. The premises are too big, and if all 10 of us paint 25 pictures each, then even so, that will still be hardly enough."[15] Malevich showed forty-nine canvases at the exhibition, including the famous *Black Square*—the visual manifesto of Suprematism. For decades critics have been perturbed by this square. Loathe to admit that after the Suprematist period Malevich also painted a large number of figurative paintings, critics relate all of his creative work back to the square rather than to his final work. However, these figurative paintings exerted a considerable influence on post-Revolutionary Russian art.

The exhibition encountered a barrage of "heavy artillery" from the critics. Alexandre Benois led the attack. He, in particular, was enraged by the *Black Square*, "the 'icon' that the Futurists propose as a replacement for Madonnas and shameless Venuses. *Black Square on a White Background*—is not just a joke, not a simple challenge, not a small chance episode which happened to take place on the Field of Mars. It is an act of self-affirmation—of the principle of vile desolation. Through its aloofness, arrogance, and desecration of all that is beloved and cherished, it flaunts its desire to lead everything to *destruction*."[16] Malevich was unable to respond to Benois' criticism through a newspaper, so he sent his rebuff directly to the critic with the intention of publishing his letter as a separate brochure. However, his mobilization prevented publication.

Suprematism

But while receding ever further from the portrayal of visible reality, Malevich never completely lost touch with nature, and he persisted in defining his creative methods by titles such as "Cubo-Futurist Realism" and "Transrational Realism." Even the Suprematist manifesto bore the subtitle, "New Painterly Realism." The "naturalism" of Malevich's Suprematist canvases was simply expressed on a different level—that of the interplanetary cosmos.

Malevich's non-objective paintings immediately attracted the attention of Khlebnikov who followed his fellow artist's progress with great interest. According to Vladimir Tatlin's correspondence with Nikolai Khardzhiev, Khlebnikov attended the "0-10" exhibition in December

1915. The following spring, most likely in March, he visited Malevich's Moscow studio in order to get a closer look at the non-objective drawings. In an unpublished letter, Malevich wrote to Matiushin: "Khlebnikov came to see me. He took away several drawings in order to study the ratio between their various dimensions—and came up with the numbers 317 and, apparently, 365. Apparently, he has established the laws for various causes with these very same numbers." Further on Malevich added: "The numbers that Khlebnikov has discovered suggest that something powerful lies within 'Supremus'; an inherent law governs this sphere, perhaps the very same law that has guided world creativity. Through me passes that same force, that same mutual harmony of creative laws that governs everything. Whatever existed heretofore just wasn't the real thing."[17] Khlebnikov's interest in Malevich's new work focused on the concept of "planetary autonomy" in which each art work was a kind of "little universe" subordinate to specific numerical expression. According to Khlebnikov, the category of time is at the very foundation of the universe. The poet decided to "calculate" Malevich's plastic worlds in order to show that these worlds were subordinate to the same concept, and he did this in 1919 in his theoretical draft, *The Head of the Universe, Time in Space*, which resulted from an analysis of "shaded drawings," or in other words, of Malevich's sketches. Khlebnikov wrote about the unity of the macro- and micro-worlds. This unity results from the category of time located at the foundation of both worlds. Comparing the earth's surface with that of a red blood cell, "Man—Citizen of the Milky Way," Khlebnikov wrote: "An agreement has been drawn up between the citizen of the heavens and the citizen of the body. It reads: the surface area of the earthen star divided by the surface area of a blood cell equals 365 to the tenth power (365^{10})—the two worlds exist in perfect harmony, and it is man's right to be first on earth." He then added: "The dead Milky Way and the living one, here, have signed the agreement as two citizens with equal rights before the law." From this position Khlebnikov "calculated" Malevich's designs and came up with the same fundamental number, 365, about which Malevich had written 3 years before. According to the poet, this number represented the 'shaded year.' Khlebnikov's text presents two theses, concluding with the results of his analysis of Malevich's designs: "In several of Malevich's shaded drawings, among his favored black planes and spheres, I have discovered that the ratio between the area of the largest shaded square and that of the smallest black circle is 365. Thus, within these collections of planes there is the shaded year and the shaded day. In the sphere of painting, I have seen anew that time is governed by space. Within this artist's consciousness, the colors white and black now wage a battle with themselves and, now completely disappearing, yield to a pure dimension."[18] Within these few lines lies the key to understanding Malevich's non-objective art. Just as an all-consuming concern with time is evident throughout Khlebnikov's work, so Malevich's vivid appreciation of space permeates his thinking and determines his artistic relationship to the world. During the summer of 1917 he even pronounced himself "president of space."[19] Moving away from the previously understood role of space in art, Malevich noted that in Futurism and Cubism "only space is the exclusive object of elaboration while form connected to objectness did not even provide the imagination with a sense of universal space. Space is confined to the space which separates things from each other on earth."[20]

In Malevich's Suprematist paintings space is both the model and the analogue of cosmic space. His painting feels "cramped" on earth and "strains towards the heavens." He wrote: "my new painting does not appertain solely to the earth. . . And at the same time, in man, in his consciousness, there is a yearning towards space, a pressing 'alienation from earth.'"[21] In cosmic space, planets move in unity, and, believing that pictorial space resembles cosmic space, Malevich constructed a corresponding interrelationship of figures within his art so that "weight would be distributed throughout systems of weightlessness."[22] In developing his ideas about space in art, Malevich was the first Russian artist to arrive at analogous futurological conclusions. In 1913 he was already dreaming about a time "when large cities and studios of contemporary artists will be held up by zeppelins."[23] In 1920 he published a brochure in which he substantiated the possibility of interplanetary flight with satellites orbiting earth and intermediary satellite space stations—allowing man to master the cosmos.[24] One of these "futurological" projects the artist called Future "Planity" (Houses) for Earth Dwellers (People). From the very first, Suprematism exerted an enormous influence on the work of many artists both in Russia and then abroad. Among Malevich's followers were the artists Olga Rozanova, Kliun, Puni, Nadezhda Udal'tsova, Varvara Stepanova, Liubov Popova, and Alexander Rodchenko. Suprematism was a sign of the times. After 1920 the movement extended beyond the limits of studio painting. As early as 1915, at the exhibition of the "Last Futurists," Kliun, Malevich's disciple, showed several volumetrical Suprematist constructions—the first examples of the *arkhitektony* on which Malevich would start to work in the 1920s. The spatial ideas in Malevich's paintings would become "objectivised" through these *arkhitektony*—Suprematist structures would enter the domain of real volume. Malevich's *arkhitektony* became the prototypes for contemporary architecture. During the 1920s, Malevich and his students Nikolai Suetin and Ilia Chashnik also devoted time to porcelain production, textiles, printing, and various other forms of the applied arts.

The Revolutionary Years: Unovis

Malevich's creative work and his social activities reached new heights during the Revolutionary years. He directed the Art Department of the Moscow Soviet and was a member of the IZONKP Collegium, a senior artist at the Moscow Svomas, and a professor at the restructured Academy of Art. He also printed programmatic articles in the newspaper *Iskusstvo kommuny* [Art of the Commune] and in the journal *Izobrazitelnoe iskusstvo* [Visual Art]. At the same time, Malevich continued to work creatively. He made the designs for Vladimir Maiakovsky's *Mystery-Bouffe* that premiered in Petrograd in the fall of 1918 and had his first one-man exhibition in Moscow the following year.

In November, 1919 Malevich arrived in Vitebsk in order to teach at an art school there. As fate would have it, within a short time this sleepy provincial town turned into a hotbed of artistic life. In December 1918 Marc Chagall, who had organized the art school, wrote: "The city of Vitebsk has begun to stir. In this provincial 'hole' of almost a hundred thousand inhabitants—today, in the days of October—it's being shaken up by a tremendous amount of revolutionary art."[25] With Malevich's arrival, life at the Vitebsk school suddenly started in full swing. He not only knew how to talk, but was able to show and explain things with pencil and brush in hand. His indomitable energy, his belief in the validity of his own ideas which had opened new artistic horizons—within a short time these qualities helped Malevich establish a collective of artists who came to play a major role in the development of Soviet art. During his stay in Vitebsk, the artist Lev Yudin made a typical entry in his diary: "How strong K.S. is—while we are all whining and complaining about expenses and it really seems as if the world has come to an end. K.S. turns up and immediately you fall into a different atmosphere. He's a true leader."[26]

In January, 1920 the group called Posnovis (Followers of the New Art) was founded at the school, opening its first exhibition on 6 February 1920. Then, on February 14, the group Unovis (Affirmers of the New Art) was founded at a meeting of artists in which Malevich participated. Unovis sought to renew the world of art completely according to the tenets of Suprematism and to transform the utilitarian-material aspect of life through new forms. After its establishment in Vitebsk, Unovis started up other groups in Moscow, Petrograd, Smolensk, Samara, Saratov, Perm, Odessa, and other cities. Under the leadership of Malevich, the nucleus of Unovis was composed of the artists Vera Ermolaeva, El Lissitzky, Nina Kogan, Chashnik, Suetin, and Lazar Khidekel.

Unovis brought a new alacrity and dynamic energy to the Vitebsk art scene. The town suddenly experienced an artistic explosion, something especially noticeable during the Revolutionary celebrations. On those days, Vitebsk was adorned in a remarkable manner which must have been quite incomprehensible to the town residents. The artist Sofia Dymshitz-Tolstaia recalled: "I arrived in Vitebsk after the October celebrations, but the town still glittered with Malevich's decorations—circles, squares, dots, lines of various colors, and Chagallian people flying through the air. I felt as if I'd stumbled into a bewitched city. At the time everything was possible, everything was fantastic, and the inhabitants of Vitebsk all seemed to have turned into Suprematists.[27]

Unovis presented a series of theatrical productions in Vitebsk: the Kruchenykh-Matiushin opera, *Victory over the Sun*, designed by Ermolaeva, the prologue from Maiakovsky's *Mystery-Bouffe*; and Maiakovsky's *War and Peace*. Unovis also organized and participated in many exhibitions, and several of them took place in Vitebsk. Twice—in 1920 and 1921—Malevich's students showed their work at the Cezanne Club under the auspices of the Moscow Vkhutemas. The 1922 Russian art exhibition in Berlin also displayed the work of Malevich, Ermolaeva, Lissitsky, and a group of students from the Vitebsk school.

Malevich's sojourn in Vitebsk was extraordinarily productive for him, especially in terms of theoretical work. His research attained such a point of intensity that in December 1920, putting aside paint and canvas, he announced: "I will describe in writing all that I see in regard to the infinite expanse of man's skull."[28] The meetings organized by Unovis and devoted to experimental drawing—always involving the analysis of students' work—held special importance for the development of the analysis of plastic forms. The following is an excerpt from the minutes of one such meeting, dated 22 March 1920:

"Zuperman (showing one of his paintings): For me the violin did not exist as a subject. I constructed a particular, straight plane and demonstrated depth. The entire construction should be reduced to the energy of the painterly masses, to painting in its purest aspect, without objects."

Malevich: At this point in the development of his work, Zuperman is following a painterly approach—he doesn't need any subjects; the forms of the object were simply painterly masses which have been reproduced in a completely arbitrary construction. We must view the object as a purely painterly manifestation of substance. Before us stands an organized body—the separate elements become one within the structure of the body. Similarly, the artist brings together various elements in order to create a unified whole—and this ability constitutes his genius. If in the old days an artist's work portrayed things and various episodic adventures, the painting now becomes its *own justification* for creative forms.[29]

Ginkhuk: The Theory of the Additional Element

The Vitebsk 'renaissance' proved to be short-lived. In 1922 Malevich, along with a large group of his students, moved to Petrograd. Once there they began to work at the State Institute of Artistic Culture (Ginkhuk).

A number of artists, acutely aware of the significant developments in Russian art, had conceived the idea of a research center dedicated to the elaboration of new problems in art. Pavel Filonov described the proposed plan as the "transferral of the center of gravity in art to Russia."[30] The new artistic trends required a theoretical basis; traditional criticism proved inadequate for the interpretation of the problems raised by new art; and the rift between the public and artists had widened. Artists had no choice but to take up theoretical work themselves. The State Institute of Artistic Culture was founded in 1919, as is noted in the catalogue *The First Regular Exhibition of the Chief Administration for Science within Narkompros* (Moscow, 1925). However, before the ideas espoused by the Institute could find full expression, it had to pass through an "incubation period." Everything began with the foundation of the Museum of Artistic Culture (MKhK), and the following are certain documentary highlights in the development of Ginkhuk.

On 5 December 1918 the Commission for the Organization of MKhK held a meeting—the participants were Natan Altman, Alexei Karev, and Alexander Matveev. On 11 February 1919 a Museum Conference took place in the Winter Palace, ratifying the organization of MKhK. MKhK was then given space in the Miatlev Mansion on St. Isaac's Square, and Altman was appointed chief organizer. On 3 April 1921 the MKhK Painting Department was opened to the public showing works from the most contemporary artistic trends. Later on, departments devoted to drawing, icons, and industrial art were also opened. Thus MKhK became the first museum in the world dedicated to the latest trends. At a Museum Conference in Petrograd, on 9 June 1923, Filonov gave a paper in which—as a member of the "group of leftist artists"—he proposed that MKhK be changed into an "Institute for the Research of the Culture of Contemporary Art." On 15 August, Malevich was elected director of MKhK, and on 1 October, research divisions opened under its auspices. In October, 1924 MKhK became the State Institute of Artistic Culture (Ginkhuk). Malevich was elected director with Punin as deputy. In addition to these two artists, the Institute's Council was composed of Tatlin, Matiushin and Mansurov. On 17 March 1925, the People's Commissariat ratified Inkhuk's status as a state institution. Ginkhuk became a large center for theoretical research in art with its various departments headed by Malevich, Tatlin, Matiushin, Mansurov, and Punin. The Ginkhuk artists sought an art whose spatial structures would develop according to the principle of natural form, i.e. an art based on a primary, essential foundation. They felt that in its form and construction art should derive from the natural experience. Organics versus mechanics and "machine" civilization—that is how we might define the spirit of the research conducted at Ginkhuk.

Overturning the accepted logic that dictated using a right angle as the basis for construction, the Constructivist Tatlin designed his Monument to the Third International using an inclined construction and a spiral. Exhibited in Paris, in 1925, the model for Tatlin's Tower was actually made at Ginkhuk. Establishing his method of "Analytical Art," Filonov tried to make the painting "grow" and structure itself in the way a living organism develops. As early as 1912, in his unpublished article "Canon and Law," Filonov denounced the impasse that Cubo-Futurism had reached "thanks to its mechanistic and geometric bases."[31] Matiushin's work was based on a careful examination of the laws of nature which led him to evolve his theory of "extended viewing." At the Institute he was the most brilliant exponent of the question of an organic artistic culture, even naming his department the Department of Organic Culture. Finally, in the Experimental Department, Mansurov also worked on the problems of "organics," examining the influence of natural structures on artistic form. The most important department at Ginkhuk was the Department of Formal Theory headed by Malevich. Its staff consisted of research assistants, graduate students, and student interns, and many famous Leningrad artists spent time there, including Chashnik, Khidekel, Valentin Kurdov, Anna Leporskaia, Konstantin Rozhdestvensky, Vladimir Sterligov, Suetin, and Yurii Vasnetsov. The Department had two colour and form laboratories directed by Ermolaeva and Yudin. Malevich's collective of research assistants began an intense study of the five major systems of the new art: Impressionism, Cezannism, Futurism, Cubism, and Suprematism. In elaborating his theory of the supplementary element in art, Malevich relied substantially on these findings. Kazimir Malevich was not only a gifted artist, but also a researcher, seeking to understand both the causes for new forms in the world and art, and the logic of their evolution. Intense theoretical effort followed the appearance of the Black Square, for Malevich did not think of Suprematism as an isolated phenomenon, but as a decisive step in the global development of artistic culture. In 1913-1916 Malevich found ready support for his enthusiastic researches in theory thanks to a very fortunate circumstance: he found an interlocutor in the person of Matiushin, a man deeply involved in the study of the new, as yet unnamed, movement in art, who became the editor and publisher of the first Suprematist manifesto. In their correspondence we can find the embryo of the ideas that would result in the creation of the theory of the supplementary element.

In order to study artistic development, to see it not as a chance occurrence, but as a logical progression from one plastic form to another, one should believe at the very least that its progression is governed by indisputable and concrete laws, even if they remain unknown. From the very first, this was the position that Malevich maintained.

In May 1916, in a letter to Alexandre Benois, Malevich defended

Suprematism: "And I am happy that the face of my Black Square cannot fuse with any other artist or any other time. Right? I have not heeded my predecessors, and I don't resemble them. And I am a step—not. Do you or don't you like it—art doesn't ask you that, just as it didn't ask you when it created the stars in the sky."[32]

The evolution of plastic forms is not arbitrary and has its own inner logic just as Malevich thought. Indeed, there is a consistent and inevitable "world line" in the movement of art. Not only is the strict regularity of this evolution evident in the past, but the vector of its movement into the future can also be determined. This vector is neither invented nor constructed, but is formed through the study of each phenomenon that helps the development to "come forth." In this lies the peculiar spirit of Malevich's research—manifest both in his early documentary studies and in the theory of the supplementary element that he evolved at Ginkhuk. It is difficult to determine exactly when the idea of the supplementary element came to Malevich, although he claimed that he was already thinking about it when he arrived in Vitebsk. Once there he encountered a group of young people obsessed by art and involved in a program which ran counter to all of the various new trends in art. Malevich recalled: "Before me there arose the possibility of conducting various experiments to research the effect of additional elements on the painterly perceptions of the nervous system in real people."[33]

With the establishment of Ginkhuk, elaboration of the theory of the supplementary element became the major task of Malevich's department. Malevich understood the "supplementary element" to be a new structural principle arising in the process of artistic evolution. The introduction of this new principle into a fully developed painterly-plastic system tunes this system to a different pitch. During structural analysis, supplementary elements were found in numerous examples of the new art: the "fibrous graph line" of Cezanne, the "crescent line" of Cubism, the "straight line" of Suprematism, and these "supplementary elements" were determined for each system both in color and form. For example, the introduction of the Cubist crescent graph into a Cezannesque structure can reorganize the resulting picture into the scheme of a Cubist painting. Malevich made considerable use of the theory of the supplementary element in his teaching. He would present a novice with "still-life recipes" (incorporating the plastic elements of this or that artistic system) in order to determine the artistic inclinations of the student. After making a "diagnosis," Malevich would then guide the novice's work in such a way as to encourage the development of individual, artistically original elements. During one of the discussions concerning Kurdov's work, Malevich said: "We should look for all the elements in Kurdov's work and improve them, but not so as to turn you into a Cubist, Suprematist, etc. . . We must try to preserve the unknown element [peculiar to the individuality of the artist—E.K.] and allow it to develop in the future, while getting rid of borrowed elements." This analysis occurred during one of Malevich's visits to the studios. Kurdov has preserved a remarkable document—notes taken during three such visits (the above quotes are taken from these notes).

Malevich's theory of the supplementary element was an original experiment in the structural analysis of a work of art. The results of this analysis revealed the effective elements or "signs" that determine the artistic "organism" of a work within each artistic trend. The value of this "sign system" lay in its ability to explain the development of plastic forms and reveal the "mechanism" whereby from one form grew into the next.

The proofs of Malevich's article "An Introduction to the theory of the Supplementary Element in Art" date from 1925.[34] Banned by the Chief Science Administrator to which Ginkhuk was subordinate, the article was composed but never published, and, from the mid-1920's onwards, Ginkhuk came under continuous attack. With its high standards of creative work, Ginkhuk was a thorn in the side of AKhRR (the Association of Artists of Revolutionary Russia) which was then gaining in political force. Talented young people aspiring to commune with genuine art-AKhRR now deflected them from the ranks of Ginkhuk. For Ginkhuk, 1926 proved fatal. The next exhibition of the institute's research and creative work opened in June of that year, featuring the work of Malevich and his followers, the Matiushin group, and Mansurov's experimental works. Mansurov put up two manifestoes, one of which declared: "At this time, the artist's peculiar position compels him to oppose, with every means at his disposal, those ideas that have no concrete or even simple, logical basis in their application to art, i.e. the ideas of the administrators, politicians, and businessmen whose philosophy has now filled every possible position convenient for their discourse with the people. The predominant political philosophy has resulted in the physical extinction of the artist just as it has the total destruction of the art school."[35]

The critic G. Seryi attended the exhibition, presenting himself to Malevich as an ideologist from AKhRR and publishing his review. "A State Supported Monastery," in the newspaper, *Leningradskaya pravda* [Leningrad Pravda] on 10 June, 1926: "A monastery with several crazy residents has taken refuge under the disguise of a state institution. Making a travesty of our Soviet educational organs, these people, perhaps unconsciously, are openly spreading the counter-revolutionary word." This was one of the first articles in which an analysis of works of art, i.e. art criticism, descended to the level of ideology or, more exactly, political denunciation. This kind of publicistic genre was to be used extensively later on. After the *Leningradskaya pravda* article, investigations and commissions began to scrutinize the work in Ginkhuk. Composed of serious scholars, they confirmed the scientific merit of the research conducted at Ginkhuk. But the wheel was already turning and its direction could not be reversed. On June 16, at a general meeting of the Institute's research assistants, Malevich expressed regret that "perhaps it will not be possible to continue these meetings. Tomorrow, thanks to Seryi's article in *Leningradskaya pravda*, there will be a commission that may well put an end to all of Ginkhuk's cultural activities—activities which could be so beneficial to the study of art and the explanation of its nature."[36] In the fall of 1926, in spite of the defence it received from the academic world, Ginkhuk was liquidated.

The Berlin Exhibition

Malevich had long standing connections with German art. As early as the 1912 Munich exhibition organized by the *Blaue Reiter* association, Malevich showed his canvas the *Head of a Peasant*. In 1922 a large Soviet exhibition opened in Berlin organized by IZO NKP at which Malevich showed five paintings—four Suprematist works, including *White on White*, and the 1911 Futurist canvas *The Knife Grinder. The Flashing Principle*. A meeting with German artists during the Vitebsk period also took place. According to Unovis (put out by the Vitebsk Committee for Artistic Creativity) for 20 November 1920, "a cargo of Unovis materials has been sent off to Germany." Unfortunately, hitherto we have not been able to establish of what exactly this "cargo" consisted. Malevich's Berlin exhibition had a fairly long prehistory. By early 1925, motivated by an invitation from Germany, the Ginkhuk Academic Council had already decided to organize an exhibition of the Institute's work abroad. On 16 March 1925 Malevich sent a letter to the Leningrad Department of the Chief Science Administration mentioning among other things that: "The reason for this exhibition is the considerable interest displayed both by the Western press and by people visiting from abroad who have found the Institute's work to be of primary importance. This is confirmed by the fact that private entrepreneurs such as the Kestner-Gesellschaft in Hannover are also interested in organizing a similar kind of exhibition."[37] While the official letters went backwards and forwards the entire Institute prepared for the exhibition, for it was intended that the departments under Malevich, Mansurov, Matiushin, and Tatlin would all take part, Malevich was preparing to acquaint the West with the theory he had developed about the supplementary element in painting, and his assistants drew up diagrams and graphics to illustrate the tenets of this theory. However, the idea of an exhibition abroad did not meet with the sympathy of the Chief Science Administration.

In a second letter that he sent to the Chief Science Administration, Malevich, no longer hoping to secure the exhibition, asked for a research trip abroad for himself, Punin, Suetin, and Boris Ender, and if this would prove to be to be unfeasible, he wrote, "then request your cooperation in receiving visas and a mandate to help me make the journey to France via Warsaw and Germany by foot. I expect to start out on 15 May, reaching Paris by 1 October, and intend returning by train on 1 December."[38] Not until September 1926 did Malevich receive permission to make a trip at his own expense. Leaving for Berlin in 1927, Malevich took with him: 1) paintings, 2) drawings and gouaches, 3) arkhitektony, 4) explanatory theoretical tables, 5) several theoretical manuscripts and 6) a number of Matiushin's theoretical tables. On the way to Germany Malevich stopped off in Warsaw, where he had a small exhibition at the Hotel Polonia. Malevich reported back to Matiushin: "On the 20th I'm opening an exhibition in Warsaw. The exhibition is tiny, just 30 canvases."[39] The Polish avant-garde received Malevich warmly and the exhibition was a success. On 25 March Malevich gave a talk to the Polish artists about Ginkhuk's theoretical research. The note sent to Matiushin attests to the very positive impression that the Warsaw meetings had on Malevich: "My dear Misha, I showed them your tables as I did my own. Both promoted strong interest. Ah, there is a wonderful attitude here. Praise pours down like rain. But they've brought me back to the right path and when I return in May, I'll tell you about everything: in detail. Give my greetings to all of yours. Twenty-five banquets and that's it."[40]

In March Malevich arrived in Berlin, remaining there until 5 June. His one-man exhibition—part of the "Grosse Berliner Kunstausstellung" was open from 7 May to 30 September. After visiting the exhibition, Anatolii Lunacharsky wrote: "Within his own genre, Malevich has attained significant results and great skill. I don't know whether canvases like these will be painted after he's gone, but I am sure that his method—which, for example, the late Popova used could well have a rich future as a decorative method."[41] In June 1927, Malevich left Berlin before the close of his exhibition.

After Suprematism

The last period of Malevich's extraordinary creative activity began soon after his return from Berlin. During a four to five year span, he created more than a hundred paintings and a multitude of drawings. Almost all of these pieces were part of the "Second Peasant Cycle," a kind of painting that had not been included in Malevich's pre-Revolutionary exhibitions. Such works are not in Amsterdam and they were not at the exhibitions of the 1920s. So how and when is it possible to date the first of these works? In 1929 the Tretiakov Gallery opened a one-man exhibition of Malevich's work consisting of sixty works. A booklet containing an article by Alexander Fedorov-Davydov was published, but there was no catalog.[42] In the list of the paintings which we have now located,[43] several titles allow us to infer that this exhibition did include a number of canvases from the late peasant cycle. However, these paintings were first recorded publicly in the catalogue of the exhibition "Artists of the RSFSR over the last XV Years" held in the Russian Museum in 1932 which included *Colored Composition. Three Figures*, *Sportsmen*, *Red House*, and other canvases. The emergence of similar characters and resolutions in the work of Malevich's followers also attests to the later appearance of these *White Faces*, for it is only after the 1932 exhibition that we see them in the paintings of Ermolaeva, Eduard Krimmer, Leporskaia, Sterligov, and Suetin.

This was the last exhibition at which Malevich showed his canvases, and for many decades thereafter they were absent from museum displays. Malevich's later works manifest his unique creative evolution.

During the 1910s he came to non-objectivity, to the *Black Square* which was the negation of the art of painting in the traditional sense. To return to objective forms of art might have seemed impossible Indeed, we would be hard put to find another artist in the 20th century who managed to return to figurative painting after non-objectivity—not only to return, but also to create works of brilliance. Malevich's later works testify to a new flowering of the artist's painting talent.

As early as 1919 Viktor Shklovsky predicted this return to objectivity: "I don't think that painting will remain non-objective forever. Artists did not strive toward the fourth dimension in order to remain in two dimensions. . . Suprematists have done in art what chemists have done in medicine. They have isolated the active element of their medium."[44] Yes, Malevich returned to figurative painting. But it was enriched by the achievements of Suprematism, something that we can see in the very different sense of colour and form—pure, severe, penetrating, laconic. The faces and figures of the peasants against the background of the colored fields connect with Ancient Russian art, although certainly with less immediacy and proximity than in the pre-Revolutionary "peasant heads." Malevich strove consciously toward a distinctive acuity of image thanks to his economy of plastic means and visual understatement. He told Yudin: "Non-objective objects and half-figures such as my peasants have the greatest significance for our time. They have the sharpest effect."[45]

Peasant images extend throughout all of Malevich's work. From 1908 to 1912 there are the paintings of work in the fields and the peasant heads close in their severe devoutness to the Russian icon. Even at the beginning of the Suprematist period the artist tried to maintain a connection with these images. For example—in the catalogue of the 1915 exhibition the famous *Red Square* was called *Painterly Realism of a Peasant Women in Two Dimensions*. Recalling his early years in his autobiography, Malevich kept emphasizing his interest in the peasant way of life and folk art: "The life of peasants has had a powerful hold on me."[46] His enthusiasm was the manifestation of an anti-urbanist which he retained throughout his life. It was amidst the boundless Ukrainian fields where Malevich spent his youth that the colored impulses of his future canvases were born: "Peasants, young and old, worked on the plantations, and I, the future artist, feasted my eyes on the fields and the 'colored' workers, who hoed or planted the beetroot. Platoons of girls in colourful clothes advanced side by side across the entire field."[47]

Malevich's second cycle of peasants of 1928-32 differs significantly from the first. Characteristics of everyday life are now missing, there are no reaper-women or mowers, and in all the paintings the peasants are seen against the background of the colored fields. They are always depicted *on face* and any of the pictures in this cycle elicits the impression of the solemnity, monumentality, and significance of what is occurring, even though there's nothing very special in the subject-matter. *Peasant Woman (with a Black Face)* and the other characters in the peasant cycle seem to have become an organic component of Malevich's "Suprematist universe" which hitherto had remained uninhabited. Created after Suprematism, many pieces in this cycle such as *Girls in the Field* and *Sportsmen* preserve the same "cosmic" impression that Malevich's non-objective works had also expressed so sharply.

Malevich's last paintings—their depth and inner complexity, their plastic perfection—are now one of the most vivid and original phenomena of twentieth century painting. Malevich died more than 40 years ago, but his artistic ideas have maintained their value, and interest in his creative work continues to grow throughout the world. The passage of time has left no doubt that Malevich belongs to that select group of artists whose creative endeavour can change the artistic physiognomy of an entire epoch.

Endnotes

1 Another version of this article was originally published as: "Kazimir Malevich: His Creative Path," in *Kazimir Malevich 1878- 1935*, ed. Wim A. L. Beeren and Joop M. Joosten (Amsterdam: Stedelijk Museum, 1988) 159-170.

2 L. Yudin, diary, entry for 27 October 1934. Family archive, Leningrad.

3 Matiushin, "O vystavke poslednikn futuristov," 18.

4 Khlebnikov, *Neizdannye proizvedeniia*, 320.

5 Malevich, letter to Matiushin (June, 1913) in the Manuscript Section, TZGALI f. 25, d. 9, 1.8.

6 Mikhail Matiushin and Elena Guro were responsible for the idea of establishing the Union of Youth (1910-14). Its members included Pavel Filonov, Waldemars Matvejs (Vladimir Markov), Olga Rozanova, losif Shkolnik et al., and on 3 January, 1913 the Muscovites David Burliuk, Kazimir Malevich, and Vladimir Tatlin were also elected to the association. Natalia Goncharova and Mikhail Larionov were regular contributors to the Union's exhibitions.

7 M. Matiushin, A. Kruchenykh, K. Malevich, "Pervyi Vserossiiskii sezd baiachei budushchego (poetov-futuristov). Zasedaniia 18 i 19 iulia 1913 goda v Uusikirkko (Finliandiia)," in *Za sem' dnei*, Moscow, 15 August (1913).
8 Matiushin, *Tvorcheskii put' khudozhnika*, in the Manuscript Section, Pushkin House: Institute of Russian Literature (IRLI), f. 656.
9 Khlebnikov wrote the Prologue for the Opera.
10 Matiushin, *Tvorcheskii put' khudozhnika*.
11 Malevich, Letter to Matiushin (27 May 1915), in *Ezhegodnik Rukopisnogo otdela Pushkinskogo doma na 1974 god*, 185-86.
12 See Alexander Rostislavov's note in *Apollon*, p. 1916, No. 1, 37.
13 Malevich, Letter to Matiushin (29 May 1915) in *Ezhegodnik*, 186.
14 Malevich, *Otkubizmaksuprematizmu*, 14.
15 The ten participants were: Kseniia Boguslavskaia, Ivan Kliun, Kazimir Malevich, Mikhail Menkov, Vera Pestel, Liubov Popva, Ivan Puni, Olga Rozanova, Vladimir Tatlin, and Nadezhda Udaltsova. They were joined by Natan Altman, Mariia Vasilieva, Vasilii Kamensky and A. M. Kirillova. Quote from the Manuscript Section, IRLI, L, f. 172, d 871.
16 Benois, "Posledniaia futuristskaia vystavka."
17 Malevich, Letter to Matiushin (4 April 1916) in the Manuscript Section, IRLI, f. 656.
18 V. Khlebnikov, *Golova vselennoi, vremia v prostranstve*, 1919, in the Central State Archive of Literature and Art (TsGALI), f. 665, op. 1, d. 32.
19 Malevich, Letter to Matiushin (10 January 1917) in *Ezhegodnik*, 182.
20 Ibid., 192.
21 Ibid.
22 Malevich, "Bog ne skinut" in *Otkubizma k suprematizmu* 15.
23 Malevich, Letter to Matiushin (9 May 1913) in the Manuscript Section, TG, f. 25, d. 9, 1.2.
24 Malevich, *Suprematism*.
25 Chagall, *Iskusstvo kommuny*.
26 L. Yudin, Diary, entry for 12 November 1922. Family archive, Leningrad.
27 S. Dymshitz-Tolstaia, Vospominaniia in the Manuscript Section, RM, f. 100, d. 249, 1.67.
28 Malevich, *Suprematism*, 4.
29 UNOVIS-Protocols in the Manuscript Section, RM, f. 55, d. 1, 11.7-8.
30 Filonov, *Intimnaia masterskaia zhivopistsev i risovalshchikov "Sdelannie kartiny."*
31 Manuscript Section, IRLI, f. 656.
32 Malevich, Letter to A. Benois (May 1915) in the Manuscript Section, RM, f. 137, d. 1186.
33 Malevich, *Vvedenie v teoriiu pribavochnogo elementa v zhivopisi*, 1925 (galley proofs). Private archive, Leningrad/Malevich Archives, Stedelijk Museum Amsterdam. See also Andersen, *The world as Non-Objectivity*, 173.
34 An expanded version was published by the Bauhaus as a separate book, i.e. Malevich, *Diegegenstandlose*.
35 P. Mansurov, *Vmesto opisaniia rabot*, 1926 in LGAOR (Leningradskij Gosudarstvennyj arhiv Oktjabr'skoj revoljucii) t. 4340, op. 1, d. 66, 1.12.
36 Malevich, Paper presented at an interdisciplinary meeting of Ginkhuk personnel. Meeting was convoked to critique and discuss the works of all departments. Stenograph (16 June, 1926) in LGAOR, f. 2555, op. 1, d. 1018,1.160.
37 LGAOR, f. 2555, op. 1, d. 805, 1. 34.
38 LGAOR, f. 4340, op. 1,d. 66,1.207.
39 Manuscript Section, TG, f. 25, d. 9, 1. 23.
40 Ibid., 1 24.

41 Lunacharsky, "Russkie khoduzhniki v Berline."
42 *Vystavka proizvedenii K.S. Malevicha*, Moscow, TG, 1929.
43 Manuscript Section, TG, f. 811, d. 286, 1. 31.
44 Shklovsky, V. "Prostranstvo v iskusstve i suprematisty."
45 L. Yudin, Diary, entry for 21 September 1934. Family archive, Leningrad.
46 Malevich, "Glavy iz avtobiografii khudozhnika," 107.
47 Ibid., 103.

2. Constructivism and Productivism in the 1920s[1]

Christina Lodder

"All forms of everyday life, morals, philosophy, and art must be recreated on communist principles. Without this the further development of the communist revolution is not possible."[2]

Boris Kushner's comment of early 1919 expresses the strong identification that artists were beginning to make, in the first years after the October Revolution, between their own activity and the social and political aims of the new state. His words epitomize the artists' aspiration to use their art in the service of the Revolution, a desire that underpinned the formulation of Productivist theory and Constructivist practice during this period. In this essay, I should like to look at some of the ways in which this theory and practice developed in the following decade, in response both to external pressures and internal debates.

A practical and ideological emphasis on industrial technology is inherent in Lenin's famous remark of 1920 "Communism equals Soviet Power plus the electrification of Russia." Indeed, the idea of uniting art and industrial manufacture appeared soon after the October Revolution. David Shterenberg, the head of the Department of Fine Arts of the Commissariat of Enlightenment (Otdel izobrazitelnykh iskusstv pri Narodnom komissariate po prosveshcheniu, IZO, Narkompros) asserted that as soon as it was established in 1918 the department was committed to "art's penetration" into production.[3] As another writer observed, "the theory of production art was developed in 1918-19 and formulated in the pages of the newspaper *Art of the Commune* (Iskusstvo kommuny)."[4] The paper was published by IZO in Petrograd between 7 December 1918 and 13 April 1919. Its contributors included theorists and critics like Osip Brik, Nikolai Punin and Boris Kushner, artists such as Natan Altman and the poet Vladimir Mayakovskii. As the official organ of IZO, the journal expounded a whole range of ideas that were being discussed by avant-garde artists at the time, including such fundamental issues as the nature of proletarian art, the role of art in a socialist society, and whether art itself was not an essentially bourgeois phenomenon. It is not surprising that the journal was eclectic and never formulated a coherent program. Nevertheless, many of the ideas that were later developed by the Constructivists were first articulated within its pages. As Nikolai Chuzhak later pointed out, "It was a time of happy attacks on the most inviolable 'cultural values' . . . all the most important words used later were employed in *Art of the Commune* . . . but half were issued by accident."[5]

In the first number, Mayakovskii issued his famous poem, "Order to the Army of Art," which exhorted artists to go out into the urban environment, proclaiming "the streets are our brushes; the squares are our palettes."[6] Brik went further in bringing art into closer contact with everyday life. He declared, "Do not distort, but create . . . art is like any other means of production . . . not ideas, but a real object is the aim of all true creativity".[7] As soon as Brik defined art as a category of work, or rather of industrial work, he opened up the way for the concept of production art. He declared that the existing division between art and production was "a survival of bourgeois structures". Punin tried to distinguish between this new relationship between art and industry and the already established category of applied art. He stated, "It is not a matter of decoration, but of the creation of new artistic objects. Art for the proletariat is not a scared temple for lazy contemplation, but work, a factory, producing completely artistic objects."[8]

Some of these ideas were developed at greater length in a small collection of essays entitled *Art in Production*, written in November 1920 and published the following year by the Art and Production subsection of IZO Narkompros.[9] According to the editorial, "The problem of art in production in the light of the new culture is, for us, one of the basic problems of liberated work, linked in the closest way to the problem of the transformation of production culture on the one hand, and with the problem of the transformation of everyday life on the other."[10]

The booklet was not at all unified in the solutions that it offered, which suggests that in the winter of 1920-21 a clearly formulated theory of production art had not as yet emerged. Indeed, the phrase "artistic production" (khudozhestvennoe proizvodstvo) seems to have been used almost as much as the term "production art" (proizvodstvennoe iskusstvo). At this point, the two terms seem to have been employed almost interchangeably; both were used to denote the rather imprecise and general involvement of art in the manufacturing industries. In his own article, Shterenberg emphasized the role that art could play in improving the quality of factory-made items, and highlighted the importance that Narkompros and the government placed on this aspect in their official policies, which were geared to promoting the coming together of art and industry.[11] Yet, his praise of revolutionary ceramics as a paradigm of the potentials of what he called "artistic production" (khudozhestvennoe proizvodstvo) suggested that his idea of production art differed very little from the old concept of applied art. Brik's contribution was far more visionary. Clearly influenced by the recent publication of fragments of Karl Marx's *The German Ideology*, with its liberating vision of the future, communist society, Brik foresaw the eventual destruction of the existing divisions between work and art. He argued therefore that the aim had to be a "conscious and creative attitude towards the production process" which would result in "not a beautifully decorated object, but a consciously made object." To achieve this, he stressed that "the worker must become a conscious and active participant in the creative process of the creation of the object," and the artist must be persuaded to "put all his creative powers into industry."[12]

Further debate was galvanized by Vladimir Tatlin's *Model for a Monument to the Third International*, which was exhibited in Moscow in December 1920. This important event was accompanied by Tatlin's statement of intent, which challenged the avant-garde to expand their sphere of activities beyond the studio.[13] Subsequently, in March 1921, a group of artists called the Working Group of Constructivists was set up within Inkhuk (Institut khudozhvennoi kultury—The Institute of Artistic Culture) in Moscow.[14] The group consisted of seven members in all: the three founders Aleksandr Rodchenko, Varvara Stepanova, and Aleksei Gan, as well as Georgii and Vladimir Stenberg, Konstantin Medunetskii and Karl Ioganson.[15] The seven defined and embraced a new synthesis between art and industry. As their program made clear, their intention was to relegate their purely artistic explorations to the role of "laboratory work," and to extend their experiments of manipulating three-dimensional forms in a purely abstract way into the real environment by participating in the industrial production of useful objects. They called the new type of activity that they envisaged "intellectual production," proclaiming that their ideological foundation was "scientific communism, built on the theory of historical materialism" and that they intended to attain "the communistic expression of material structures" by organizing their material in accordance with the three principles of *tektonika* or tectonics (the social and politically appropriate use of industrial material), construction (the organization of this material for a given purpose), and *faktura* (the conscious handling and manipulation of it).[16]

Their formal concerns were epitomized by the works shown at the *Second Spring Exhibition of the Society of Young Artists* (Obshchestvo molodykh khudozhnikov—Obmokhu), which opened in Moscow in May 1921.[17] The majority of works exhibited were constructed in space using materials like glass and metal as well as more traditional wood. The works by the Stenberg brothers comprised open-work, skeletal constructions, containing strong references to the materials, forms and articulations of existing engineering structures such as bridges and cranes. This is very evident in Vladimir Stenberg's *Construction for a Spatial Structure No. 6* of 1920-21, which is built up of small metallic elements, some of which seem like miniaturized versions of I and T beams. Alongside these, Rodchenko exhibited a series of hanging constructions, made from wood painted silver: an ellipse, a square, a circle, a triangle, and a hexagon. They shared a common method of construction. Concentric geometrical shapes were cut out from a single plane of plywood. These shapes were then arranged within each other and rotated from a two dimensional plane into a three dimensional form, suspended in space with wire. The emphasis on basic materials and simple, economical methods of construction were seen by certain theorists, for example Boris Arvatov, to parallel and therefore to be highly compatible with industrial processes.[18] He argued that an artist who had no knowledge of working with materials was "utterly meaningless in a factory."[19]

Quite rapidly, interest in Constructivist ideas began to extend beyond the confines of the initial group. By the end of 1921, Lyubov Popova and Aleksandr Vesnin had also adopted a Constructivist position, while artists like Anton Lavinskii and Gustav Klucis became aligned after coming into contact with Constructivist ideas at the Vkhutemas (Vysshie Gosudarstvennye khudozhestvenno-tekhnicheskie masterskie—the Higher State Artistic and Technical Workshops), which were set up at the end of 1920 to train "highly qualified master artists for industry."[20] Of particular importance were the Basic Course and the Wood and Metal Working Faculty of the Vkhutemas, the latter directed by Rodchenko. Here, the new generation of artists was being trained to be "engineer-constructors" or "artist-constructors" who would fuse a complete grasp of artistic skills with a specialized knowledge of technology. At the same time, it was in these faculties that a design methodology was being developed by Rodchenko, Lavinskii and others. Yet within the Vkhutemas the Constructivists were always in a minority. As the avant-garde and pro-Constructivist magazine *Lef: Left Front of the Arts* (Levyi front iskusstv) reported in 1923, "The position of the Constructivists is extraordinarily complicated. On the one hand, they have to fight the purists [easel painters] to defend the productivist line. On the other, they have to put pressure on the applied artists in an attempt to revolutionize their artistic consciousnesses."[21]

Perhaps it is not surprising therefore to find that the practical implementation of Constructivist ideas seems to have been relatively slow. The circumstances outside the school were hardly propitious. Industry had been decimated following almost seven years of conflict, and those enterprises that had survived were not sufficiently progressive to accommodate the new type of designer. When Tatlin approached the New Lessner Factory in Petrograd, with the aim of becoming involved in designing products for mass manufacture, he was directed to the technical drawing department.[22] The government encouraged and promoted production art in general, but had far more traditional aesthetic attitudes than the Constructivists. Narkompros was reorganized in 1921, and most of the avant-garde employees, including all the Constructivists, lost their jobs. By 1922 Gan was complaining of the open and covert campaign being waged by the State and the Party against the avant-garde.[23] In this situation, there were several different strategies that the artists could adopt. Gan, for instance, devoted considerable energy to advertising and propagandizing Constructivist ideas through his brochure *Constructivism* of 1922 and through numerous articles. Others tended to publicize the Constructivist approach by working in areas where the idea of artists' participation had already been established, such as in the theatre (the Stenberg brothers), and in typographical and poster design (Rodchenko). As one artist complained in 1923, the two chief areas of practical activity for the dedicated Constructivist were designing advertising posters or constructing models.[24] For these reasons, in the first years after 1921, Constructivist products tended to be experimental or exploratory in nature, rather than being fully utilitarian and practical in solutions to specific tasks.

Some of the earliest Constructivist designs were prototypes for temporary agitational stands or small, portable and sometimes collapsible kiosks. Among the former are Gustav Klucis' designs of 1922 for a series of "radio-orators," "radio-tribunes" and "cinema-photo stands" with three-dimensional and dynamic slogans. These were to be placed on the streets of Moscow during the celebrations of the Fourth Congress of the Comintern and the fifth anniversary of the October Revolution.[25] The stands were devised to perform specific agitational functions: displaying photographic material and posters, or giving a spatial and audiovisual presence to revolutionary slogans. Some performed only one function as a loudspeaker or "radio-orator" while others were conceived to execute several different tasks simultaneously, e.g. *Propaganda Stand, Screen and Loudspeaker Platform*. Using a language clearly derived from the kind of stands utilized by the Stenberg brothers for their sculptures at the Obmokhu exhibition of 1921, Klucis reduced the construction of his various propaganda items to their essential elements, clearly revealing the structure of each stand, and providing stability through a multiplicity of vertical, diagonal and horizontal supports. Although material scarcities may have encouraged this method of construction, in many of the stands the geometry of the straight lines and their interactions seem to have provided a design impetus in their own right. All the stands appear to have been made from wood, canvas and cables and were painted red, black and white. In conjunction with this, Klucis developed a kind of modular system, not far removed from the principle inspiring the modular wooden constructions of Rodchenko, which explored the variety of structural frameworks that could be devised using essentially similar elements. In *Screen-Tribune-Kiosk*, the openwork frame supports the tribune, the screen, and the book display unit at the bottom. The tribune sits on top of an open-work, box-like structure, which is strengthened by a central pillar and at the top, bottom and two sides by the crossed struts and on the remaining two sides by the larger vertical supports which hold the screen. The screen here surely also has a double function, acting not only as film screen, but also as a visual device to frame the speaker and perhaps even offer him a measure of protection during inclement weather conditions. The box device elevates the speaker, but also gives the tribune a sense of weightlessness. The central inner pillar is also utilized to support the book stand. In *Propaganda Stand, Screen and Loudspeaker Platform*, Klucis has incorporated a bookstand, loudspeaker, screen and an expanding structure at the bottom right, which might be for the display of posters. The compression of several functions into a small compact unit, along with economy of space, manufacture and materials and other features that Klucis devised became established components of Constructivist design.

A natural extension of the stand was the kiosk. Amongst the earliest was Gan's folding street sales stand (skladnoi stanok) of c. 1922-23 for Mosselprom (Moskovskii trest po pererabotke selskokhazaistvennoi produktsii—Moscow Association of Enterprises Processing Agricultural and Industrial Products). This was a small folding structure, apparently made from wood, which could be carried to its destination and then quickly erected in the street or any open public space. After use, it could easily be re-folded and carried away. It contained a tray (on collapsible legs) with a removable glass lid for displaying small items of merchandise such as stationery supplies or cigarettes. Gan also designed a larger structure for the sale of books and journals in c. 1923. This was not a portable piece as such, although it could be moved. It consisted of two cuboid structures of different sizes, which opened out to form a large area of shelving for displaying books and magazines. This prototype clearly went into production at some point and, with certain modifications, was manufactured from wood for use inside public buildings, like the entrance halls of Moscow University and of the stations on the Moscow Metro, where some examples are still in use. When shut, the prominent lettering advertised the role of the kiosk and with the colored panels provided elements of decoration.

Working along similar lines, in 1924 Lavinskii produced a more permanent structure for Gosizdat (the State Publishing House). This design was to be erected on the streets, and at least one kiosk was built on Revolution Square in Moscow. The essential structure elaborated the basic cube and consisted essentially of a truncated, four-sided pyramid, with the corners cut away, which had been inverted over a cuboid base. All four sides were used for display. The windows and service hatch were covered by flaps, which could then hang down when the kiosk was open in a way that repeated the shape of the top. This arrangement meant that items could be left on display indefinitely in the windows. The exciting articulation of the roof angles necessitated an effective drainage system. The design was attractive, compact, economic to manufacture, and easy to use. With its innovative design and practicality, this kiosk represented an enormous advance over the almost classically inspired model that Lavinskii had produced for the All Union Agricultural Exhibition of 1923.

A similarly adventurous approach to geometry characterized Gan's design for a rural kiosk of c. 1924. Primarily intended for the sale of books, it was also conceived to serve as a focal point for the social activities of the village. In an attempt to convey, in the structure of the kiosk, the important ideological role that it was to play in the life of the community, Gan turned his design into a piece of permanent propaganda and made it literally look like a flag ship. The nautical imagery was utilized in the prow-like arrangement of the facade and the rigging, with structures echoing the crows nest, and the funnels being attached to the top of the building. Although these features make the *Rural Kiosk* visually arresting and architecturally exciting, their maritime emphasis seems somewhat inappropriate for the rural settings of the vast land-locked areas of Russia. In other respects, the design displays an admirable pragmatism. The steep inclines of the walls and roofs, for instance, were justified on climatic grounds: it was intended to channel the snow and rain in such a way as to keep the entrance clear. Despite this, the whole design has a decidedly more rhetorical feel than Gan's more temporary structures such as the folding sales stand and his book kiosk, and, of course, there is no evidence whatsoever that it was ever actually built.

Whatever their success, such items were only limited realizations of Constructivist ideas. One area of creative endeavor in which it seemed possible to realize a synthesis of "the new way of life" with a total visual environment was the theatre: "In the theatre, Constructivism . . . united constructive furnishings (the decor, the props and the costumes)—designed to show, if not the objects themselves, at least their models—with constructive gestures, movements and pantomime (the biomechanics of Vsevolod Meierkhold)—the actors organized according to rhythms."[26] If the actor was transformed into a kind of robot, the stage was transmuted into a machine. The first Constructivist stage set was Popova's design for Meierkhold's production of Crommelynck's farce *The Magnificent Cuckold*, which opened on 15 April 1922. The mill of the action became a multi-leveled, skeletal apparatus of platforms, revolving doors, ladders, scaffolding and wheels, which rotated at differing speeds at particularly intense moments during the play. The traditional costumes were replaced by overalls or production clothing (*prozodezhda*), working clothes, the form of which was determined by the function to be performed. In this instance, they were designed to facilitate the actors' movements on the stage. Popova stressed that in her design overall she had been concerned "to translate the task from the aesthetic plane onto the Productivist plane."[27] A similar approach determined Vesnin's set for the Kamerny Theatre's production of Chesterton's *The Man who was Thursday* of 1923, which was enacted on a far more complex construction, incorporating elements derived from engineering and industrial structures as well as more specific urban elements of scaffolding, stairs, and a lift.[28] Stepanova's set for Meierkhold's production of Sukhovo-Kobylin's *The Death of Tarelkin*, which opened in November 1922, was less architectural. She devised a series of separate apparatuses, each built using thin planks of wood of standard thickness, painted white. Although their functions tended to be playful within the theatrical context, the principles inspiring their production could be applied more widely and directed to the design of objects of greater utility in everyday life, such as chairs and tables. Nevertheless, there were severe limitations on the extent to which the theatre could function as an experimental laboratory for design in the wider environment. Perhaps recognizing this fact, for *The Earth in Turmoil* in 1923, Popova devised a set based on a gantry crane and simply employed a plethora of props, which all consisted of objects that had in fact been mass produced.

During this early period, the only area in which the Constructivists established a working relationship with any specific industrial enterprise for the design of everyday objects for mass manufacture was in the field of textile design.[29] Popova and Stepanova accepted the invitation issued in 1923 by the First State Textile Print Factory for artists to work there. Once employed, they began to wage a battle "against naturalistic design in favor of the geometricization of form,"[30] producing numerous designs based on the manipulation of one or more geometric forms and usually one or two colors. Undoubtedly, the venture was a success because the artist had an established role within the industry. It was an area of "applied art", which was far more bound up with traditional ideas of ornament and embellishment than with re-organizing the material environment in a fundamental way. Even so, Popova and Stepanova effected some changes in the patterns of the fabrics produced, and asserted the importance of such elements within the wider environment. In writing about this new area of Constructivist activity, Brik explained the opinion, which Popova and Stepanova undoubtedly shared, that "a cotton print is as much a product of artistic culture as a painting."[31]

Given the constraints and frustrations, it is not surprising that the Constructivist movement began to fragment. It is difficult to date this precisely, but it had certainly occurred by mid 1922, when Gan published his book *Constructivism*, in which he referred quite explicitly to The First Working Group of Constructivists.[32] It seems probable that he was distancing himself, Rodchenko and Stepanova from the Stenberg brothers and Medunetskii who had exhibited as the Constructivists in January 1922.[33] By adding the epithet "First," Gan was asserting the priority of himself, Rodchenko and Stepanova in developing the term and the concept. In an article of 1922 he explicitly stated that they were the founders of the group, thus by implication relegating other users of the Constructivist label, such as the Stenbergs and Medunetskii, to a secondary status.[34] The rift between the two factions is confirmed by the fact that in 1924 the catalogue for the *First Discussional Exhibition of Active Revolutionary Art Groups* listed the Constructivists as the Stenberg brothers and Medunetskii and placed them in a group, which was distinct from Gan and his entourage.[35] But by this time, the cohesion of the movement had fractured even further. Gan, Rodchenko and Stepanova no longer presented a united front. The First Group of Constructivists was now listed under Gan's leadership alone and its membership was given as comprising Grigorii Miller, Aleksandra Mirolyubova, L. Sanina, N[ikolai?] G. Smirnov, Galina and Ol'ga Chichagova.[36] By 1925 Viktor Shestakov was included.[37] This faction asserted quite categorically its independence from "all other groups calling themselves Constructivists" such as "the Constructivists from the Kamerny theatre" (presumably the Stenbergs, Medunetskii and Vesnin), "the Constructivists of Meierkhold's theatre" (Popova and Stepanova), and "the Constructivists of *LEF*" (Rodchenko, Stepanova, Lavinskii, Popova, and Vesnin).[38]

Clearly the largest grouping outside of Gan and his entourage were the Constructivists associated with *LEF*.[39] The magazine had been founded in 1923 and among its other activities it promoted the work of the Constructivists, using the weapons of "example, agitation and propaganda."[40] The magazine published Constructivist projects and numerous articles about them. Boris Arvatov was perhaps the first theorist to distinguish between Productivists and Constructivists. For him, the Productivists were primarily theoreticians, whereas the Constructivists were artists, who were actually attempting to implement a practical link with industry.[41]

The validity of Productivist theory and the effectiveness of Constructivist practice were brought into question and subjected to close and critical scrutiny on 16 January 1925 at LEF's first conference. The presidium of the meeting included practicing Constructivists like Lavinskii, Gan, Rodchenko, and Shestakov, as well as writers and critics like Mayakovskii, Brik and Chuzhak.[42] Over 150 attended. At this and at a further meeting in July that year, it was agreed that there was a crisis and certain fundamental issues were raised.[43]

Some of the severest criticisms were voiced by Nikolai Chuzhak, who considered it essential to eradicate the remaining influence of the vulgar simplifications and excesses of the early Productivist theoreticians (1918-1920), particularly their intransigent opposition to art itself. Although he did not name these Productivists he was presumably referring to Gan and his fellow contributors to *LEF*, Brik and Arvatov.[44] Chuzhak was equally negative about the practice of the Constructivists and asserted that "Rodchenko's group is worried about 'style' and textiles, which Brik idolizes. The Constructivists comprising Gan and company have made 'production' a fetish, almost an aim in itself."[45] The remedy for this, as Chuzhak saw it, was for the Constructivists to engage in more concrete, practical activity, and undertake projects that were tied into the real, rather than the hypothetical needs of society.[46]

Pertsov was equally brutal and frank in his assessment of the problems confronting the Constructivists, and identified some of the weaknesses in the theoretical principles of the Productivists. He argued that the notions of "the artist as the organizer of production" and the "rejection of fine art" were fallacious concepts, based on a total misunderstanding of communist ideas.[47] He also criticized the Constructivists' current output, which he considered amounted to little more than a new kind of "applied art." He suggested that the greatest contribution that the artist could make to industry lay precisely in his "technical ignorance and the fact that he is not tied down to earth by so called 'technical possibilities,' and that he can easily imagine a general technical idea, industrial form, project and combination."[48] Pertsov suggested a new slogan: "Artist! Remember—your Constructive idea can fertilize industry."[49]

To some extent the crisis was due not so much to internal disagreements, the inadequacy of Productivist theory or the shortcomings of Constructivist practice, as to external pressures.[50] The market forces, which Chuzhak had mentioned, were powerful influences, acting against the production of Constructivist designs by industrial enterprises. Evidence suggests that manufacturers were far from eager to embrace the Constructivists' rather austere and perhaps unduly utilitarian products. Even in the textile industry, which had initially welcomed geometric patterns, there seems to have been a change of heart. By July 1925 Stepanova had reported that fabric designs were being accepted for mass production only if they contained naturalistic imagery: "Drawings reminiscent of the town and industry, for example straight lines, and circles are not being made now, they are accepting only drawings recalling the countryside: streams and flowers."[51] The social and political situation was also not advantageous. Gan highlighted the fundamental problem of taste under the conditions of the New Economic Policy, explaining that those responsible for selecting merchandise to be sold in the shops were reluctant to invest in Constructivist designs. He also emphasized the increasing role that negative criticism, supported by official dislike of the avant-garde, was playing in closing doors against the Constructivist designer.

Gan claimed that these critics tended to support the traditional categories of artistic activity and the aesthetic position of realism. Gradually, as official policies hardened and began to have an impact, and social and political values came to be more firmly linked to academic values in painting, Constructivists became more vulnerable. Pletnev observed: "It is no accident that right-wing art has driven LEF into a corner . . . LEF has lost its socialist orientation, and where can you go without a foundation."[52]

It is against this background of neglect by the market and attack by the critics that one of the most important manifestations of Constructivist design during the 1920s must be viewed—the Workers' Club, which was designed by Rodchenko and made for the *Exposition Internationale des Arts Decoratifs et Industriels Modernes*, held in Paris in 1925. It perhaps underlines the gulf between Constructivist aspiration and reality that the only completely Constructivist environment ever made was produced for an international exhibition, not in communist Russia but in capitalist France. For an occasion that was regarded as a publicity promotion exercise, the government was able to direct valuable resources towards the realization of Constructivist principles. Although Constructivism was neglected at home and derided by officialdom, the government nevertheless realized the enormous propaganda value of such artistic innovation abroad. As one Soviet reviewer pointed out, "our section at the Paris Exhibition constituted an undoubted cultural victory for the USSR."[53]

The ideological significance of the workers' clubs was immense. They were regarded as crucibles for creating the new society, centers for the diffusion of culture, and even places where the new proletarian culture would be created by the people themselves.[54] The cultural programs that were undertaken by the clubs ranged from basic literacy to more advanced courses in artistic and literary creativity. The clubs were also intended to combat the old way of life and to eradicate habits associated with the former social and political system. The club had a social role in replacing the old social center of the church in the life of the community, a political role in inculcating the new social and political values of collective life and communism, and a cultural role in educating the workers, helping them to acquire and appreciate existing "bourgeois" culture and helping them to liberate their own creative potential so that they could develop their own culture.

The ideological importance of the Workers' Club is indicated in Rodchenko's design by the prominence given to Lenin. Rodchenko includes a Lenin Corner. This practice had become common after the leader's death in 1924 and represented an adaptation to socialist purposes of the traditional Red Corner where the icons had hung in pre-revolutionary Russian Orthodox homes.[55] In Paris, this consisted of a large poster-sized picture of Lenin, complemented by the famous poster by Adolf Strakhov, issued shortly after the great Bolshevik died in 1924 to celebrate his revolutionary vision. At the top of one wall, Lenin's name is spelt out in large letters. It is interesting to note that this skeletal lettering is built up from standard squares and triangular divisions, and therefore acts as a programmatic statement of Rodchenko's method of standardization and economy, which he had employed in the Club's overall design. Indeed, all of the designs for items within the Club consisted of strictly rectilinear combinations of Euclidean geometric forms.

The furniture was painted in four colors, white, red, grey and black, either alone or in combination, to reinforce the ideological significance of the forms themselves. These colors, particularly red and black, had come to symbolize the Revolution during the Civil War.

Rodchenko's approach entailed devising furniture for "simplicity of use, standardization, and the necessity of being able to expand or contract the numbers of its parts."[56] This was achieved by making some items collapsible, so that they could be removed and stored when not in use. Into this category come the folding tribune, screen, display board and bench. Moreover, dynamism was an intrinsic element of the conception, from the revolving hexagonal display components of the show case, lit from below, to the chess table with its rotating chess board, and pieces of furniture like the tribune complex, which were compact in storage, but folded out for use.[57]

The pragmatism of Rodchenko's approach was also underlined by the fact that he used wood. It was undoubtedly the most economic material at that time in Russia. It was cheap and plentiful, whereas steel was expensive, difficult to process, and in very short supply. Moreover, Russian industry already possessed considerable expertise in the mass production of wooden furniture. The choice of wood was therefore a highly sensible decision, based on the state of the Russian economy and the nature of the country's natural resources. Yet the choice of wood hardly seems compatible with the Constructivist commitment to technology, which was stressed in the program of the Working Group of Constructivists, and which Rodchenko underlined further in the original model, which bore the slogan "technology improves life: the newest inventions." He was also at pains to reduce the impact that the nature of wood as a material would have on the look of his designs. He painted the wood so that the texture of its surface was completely smooth and free from any characteristics that would give it a rural or organic resonance. Perhaps the ultimate irony was that for reasons of convenience, the furniture was actually made in Paris.

The components of Rodchenko's design were intended to cater to every aspect of club life, and so included chairs, reading tables, cabinets for exhibiting books and journals, storage space for current literature, display windows for posters, maps and newspapers and a Lenin corner.[58] The most prominent element was the reading table. In place of the traditional flat surface, the top consisted of a flat central piece abutted by two sloping sides. The sloping sides supported books and journals easily for reading, while allowing the top to be used for temporarily storing books not in current use. This arrangement is more economic in the space it occupies than a flat reading table would be. At the base, two triangular wedges ran along the length of the table, providing support for the readers' feet, structurally strengthening the upright supports at either end, but also playing a formal role in reiterating the slope of the reading section of the table.

This rethinking of basic items pervaded the whole scheme. It is also clearly seen in the chairs. These comprised three uprights (two thinner rods at the front and a wider plank behind) which are attached together at three levels: at the top by the open semi-circular form, at the seat level by the flat semicircular plane of wood and at the bottom with three standardized wooden elements. Throughout the design, the forms of the structural units are derived from the three basic geometrical forms: the circle, rectangle and triangle, in the manner of Rodchenko's earlier hanging constructions and unit constructions, but these forms are combined in a new way to provide a sturdy easily constructed chair.

Amongst the most ingenious devices was the apparatus that compressed into a box for storage, but, when required, could be folded out to incorporate a film screen, a tribune for political and educational speakers, a bench and a display board. This answered the need for strict economy in materials, and mode of production, but it was also space saving. Rodchenko employed telescopically extending parts and ball and socket jointing to achieve this transformation.[59] Once again the design relates to the earlier phase of "laboratory work." The principle of construction, incorporating the collapsible strut, has affinities with the kinds of folding and rigid constructions made by Ioganson and displayed at the Obmokhu exhibition of May 1921. Some of these changed their spatial parameters when the string was pulled, returning to the original configuration when the string was pulled again. Rodchenko's design can also be seen as a development from the principle of the skeletal structural framework, which had been utilized by Gustav Klucis in his designs for a *Screen-Tribune-Kiosk* and for a *Propaganda Stand, Screen and Loudspeaker Platform* of 1922. There are particular similarities between Rodchenko's and Klucis' book display units. Both artists exploited telescoping devices and the same set of bold colors. Rodchenko was also harnessing elements from Stepanova's theatrical devices of 1923, which had been constructed from rods. In devising the various elements for the Workers' Club, therefore, Rodchenko was working within an established language of design.

Rodchenko's Workers' Club as a prototype, worked out in every detail according to utilitarian and aesthetic demands, stands as one of the great achievements of Constructivism. It is a design that combines an authentic functionalism with a powerful programmatic statement about the kind of art and environment that Constructivism might create in the new Communist world. It demonstrates precisely how the Constructivists applied the principles of tectonics, *faktura* and construction to the solution of a specific design task. In devising the Workers' Club, Rodchenko took into account the ideological requirements of Communism, and the industrial processes involved in manufacturing the various items. He also chose his material in line with those two factors and in response to the given function of each piece of furniture. For the Constructivists, tectonics embraced both the physical and ideological function of the object. They believed that geometry and standardization embodied the impersonality and rationality of the collective and were vital ingredients in their technological vision of the Communist future. Hence, construction entailed reducing each object to its essential geometric components and discarding all extraneous details, while *faktura* resulted in the wood being treated in a way that minimizes its associations with nature and maximizes its affinities with the machine. Along with Tatlin's Tower, the Workers' Club represents one of the canonical creations of the Constructivist aesthetic. Sadly, it remained an isolated realization of Constructivist potential.

Whatever the actual quality of their designs, in their statements, the Constructivists tended to assert the exclusive importance of the "utilitarian" at the expense of the symbolic and ideological purpose of form and design. Their stridency should be seen as a particular response to a specific situation. In order to combat the "old aestheticism," the Constructivists adopted a crusading and somewhat intransigent tone, demanding "an end to art". In trying to formulate a new relationship between art and reality, they had to clear the path of previous approaches, which included the whole range of applied art from the World of Art's theatrical designs onwards. In asserting their close link with industry, the Constructivists were expressing the need for artists to take contemporary technology and its practical manifestations in industry into account in their work. Ultimately, the Constructivists were idealists, wedded to a belief in the possibility of fusing the aesthetic, the political, the social, the technological and the industrial into a new unity.

Laudable as such aspirations were, the undeniable fact was that they were operating in a very un-ideal environment. They had given their allegiance to the Revolution, which had compromised with capitalism in 1921 with the New Economic Policy. The result was that they were working in a mixed economy for a society that did not yet exist. They embraced industry, but this was at lower ebb than it had been in 1913. While they were committed to abstract formal values and a new language for the new society, the government increasingly supported academic painting and realism.

Moreover, during the New Economic Policy, the taste of the new entrepreneurial class with money was for more ornate, traditionally conceived furniture, and the austere designs of the Constructivists seemed to exert little charm. Likewise, the Constructivists had no success with the working class or its leaders, who were equally dismissive of strict utility, and dreamt of more luxurious artifacts. It was perhaps as a response to obvious consumer demand that later Constructivist designs display a more conventional approach towards the articulation of furniture. Rodchenko's sets for the play *Inga* epitomize this development, indicating a subtle change in both his stylistic language and in his approach to the whole problem of interior design. The play concerned the new communist woman and the environment in which she lived. Just as 1925 had allowed him to demonstrate how Constructivism could create the ideal Workers' Club, so *Inga* gave Rodchenko the opportunity to demonstrate another hypothetical new interior, as well as the enormous potential of rationally designed items, some of which could fold away. Yet in place of his innovative, geometric and skeletal designs of 1925, Rodchenko modified his basic elements to more curvilinear planes, demonstrating their adaptability and potential universality using one set of easily constructed elements and creating items that could easily be modified to represent the internal furnishings of a club, an apartment, a bedroom and an office. In a published statement he expressed his disillusionment with items of furniture that performed a dual function. He had obviously come to realize that "It is not possible for a table transformed into a bed to perform its straightforward duties."[60]

Ultimately, however, the solutions are less formally exciting than his earlier work. The wardrobe, for instance, is compact, and possesses some ingenious storage features, but these are arranged within a structure, which, although devoid of ornamentation, and entirely geometric, represents a simplification of existing wardrobe types, rather than embodying any new structural concepts. It is not reduced to an essential skeletal structure, and the method of construction is not revealed on the exterior. The integral, material plane has replaced the wooden rod. The same can be said of the 1929 showcase, which, in contrast to the display units of 1925, comprises four segments of circles arranged around a central square and built up of wooden planes. Rodchenko's designs possess some innovative qualities, but these are clothed in more traditional outward forms. A critic unsympathetic to Constructivism could perhaps justifiably deride them as "old wine in new bottles",[61] but for those engaged in the arduous task of trying to develop and promote new furniture design, Rodchenko's solutions were viewed in a more positive light. They were "constructed in an interesting fashion" and their use on the stage had "great educational significance." The sympathetic critic hoped that these prototypes might eventually go into mass production.[62]

My account of their design endeavors might suggest that the late 1920s were years of unremitting gloom for the Constructivists. This is not so. They did achieve some notable successes, particularly in the field of photomontage. Even in 1925, Pertsov had regarded this as an isolated area of positive achievement.[63] Yet not all critics found such developments desirable. Chuzhak, for one, could not see its potential and regarded it less as a desirable end in itself than as an interim, rather transitory development.[64] Such an analysis of its potential may have been responsible for the Constructivists' initial decision to become involved in such areas. But typographical, poster and exhibition design also had the important advantages at the time of representing small-scale, well-defined design tasks which fitted into traditional artistic categories. Moreover, the Party's stated aesthetic preferences were for realism, and government bodies, such as the Trades Unions and the Red Army, actively patronized artists who supplied realistic paintings. The photograph provided a way of using images without resorting to conventional realism. At the same time, the photograph was the product of a mechanical process: it could be mechanically reproduced and it thus complemented the Constructivists' commitment to technology. The ability of photomontage to present a concrete image, which linked the everyday life of the viewer with the political and social precepts of the Communist Party, made it a valuable propaganda weapon. Klucis' photomontages employed the diagonal and asymmetrical compositional principles that he had developed in his earlier paintings and constructions. Posters such as *We Will Repay the Coal Debt to the Country* (1930) create an impact through the unusual viewpoint of the figures and the rhythm created by the ascending parallels of their diagonally advancing legs, which endow them with the coherence, power and dynamism of a collective machine. The simplicity, monumentality and documentary nature of such images makes them most persuasive. A similar approach is displayed in Lissitzky's work for his exhibition layouts such as *Pressa* (Cologne 1928) which rely on the impression created by combining integral images within a monumental format. The use of the medium, however, exerted its own pressure, and the illustrative image eventually came to dominate the formal principles with which it was manipulated, a process encouraged by the more stringent demands of the Party in the early 1930s.

Yet while conditions were fostering this pragmatism, certain Constructivists like Tatlin and Petr Miturich were revealing a heightened idealism as they concentrated on developing an alternative technology. These artists sought to return to an intensive investigation of nature and to the fundamental principles of growth and movement in organic form. Their studies led both of them to evolve new forms of transport. Miturich developed the concept of "wave-like motion" based on the principle that the curved line conserves more energy than the straight line. He demonstrated this with an apparatus, which consisted of two three-meter paths; one of these possessed three level stretches, with inclined planes between them (like three large, descending steps); and the other comprised three downward, curved swoops. Setting off two metal balls simultaneously, the ball on the curved path completed the course, while the other was only two-thirds of the way along its trajectory.[65] Convinced that wave-like motion was therefore faster, Miturich used this principle as the basis for the design of a series of vehicles, the *Volnoviks* and the *Letun* or flying machine. Working separately, though in a similar direction, Tatlin developed a flying machine, the *Letatlin* or Air Bicycle. He rejected the solutions of contemporary aviation and science, and is reported to have said: "The engineers make hard forms.

They are evil. With angles. They are easily broken. The world is soft and round."[66] His studies of baby birds, like wild cranes, their physical structure and its adaptation to the problem of flight provided the basis for the mechanics and the form of the *Letatlin*. Like Leonardo and his design for a flying machine, Tatlin and Miturich studied nature in order to re-create it. They both used nature to give man wings and emancipate man from the restrictions of nature, to liberate him from gravity. From the reconstruction of man's physical environment, Tatlin and Miturich had attempted to move beyond this to the reconstruction of man's physical capabilities. From designing a liberating environment, they designed objects to liberate human beings from the laws of gravity. This is perhaps the ultimate idealism, and it epitomizes the visionary impulse which runs through the entire Constructivist episode in Russian art.

Endnotes

1 A version of this article was first published in the catalogue of Andrews and Kalinovska, 99-116.
2 Kushner, "Kommunisty-futuristy," 3.
3 Shterenberg, "Pora ponyat'," 5.
4 Pertsov, *Za novoe iskusstvo*, 56.
5 Chuzhak, "Pod znakom zhiznestroeniya," 27.
6 Mayakovskii, "Prikaz po armii iskusstva," 1.
7 Brik, "Drenazh iskusstvu," 1.
8 Osip Brik, "Primechanie redaktsii," 2 and Nikolai Punin cited by Chuzhak, "Pod znakom zhiznestroeniya," 27.
9 Although it was published in 1921, the editor's introduction is dated November 1920. See *Iskusstvo v proizvodstve*, 4. The Art and Production Sub-section of Izo was set up in August 1918. (See *Iskusstvo v proizvodstve*, 36).
10 "Ot redaktsii," *Iskusstvo v proizvodstve*, 3.
11 Shterenberg, "Pora ponyat'," 5-6.
12 Brik, "V poryadke dnya," 6-7.
13 Tatlin, et al, "Nasha predstoy-i rabota," 11.
14 See "Programma uchebnoi podgruppy konstruktivistov Inkhuka." For details concerning Inkhuk, see Lodder, *Russian Constructivism*, 78 ff. and Khan-Magomedov, *Rodchenko*. The name of the group has been given variously as The Working Group of Constructivists and The First Working Group of Constructivists. Archival material gives the name of "The Working Group of Constructivists," but the first public pronouncement about the group to appear in the press in August 1922 in the Moscow magazine *Ermitazh* (no. 13, 3-4) used both names. The introduction entitled "Konstruktivisty" gave the group its full title declaring that "On 13 December 1920 the First Working Group of Con-

structivists was formed." It cited Rodchenko, Stepanova and Gan as the founders and stated, "Directing their attention to the future culture of communism and proceeding from present specific conditions, they worked out a program and production plan and started to enlist collaborators." This introduction was followed by "The First Program of the Working Group of Constructivists." The presence of both names in this publication, suggests that they were used concurrently and inter-changeably. It may well be that the shorter form was a short-hand version of the fuller name and that both names were used in this way from the very beginning.

Alternatively, the affixing of "First" to their title may have been a later development, possibly of 1922. In the introduction Gan mentions that "Constructivism has become fashionable". The "First" may, therefore, simply have been adopted to distinguish his group from any other groups or artists using the name. It may have been prompted, for example, by the exhibition of the Stenberg Brothers and Medunetskii at the Cafe Poetov which took place in January 1922 and for which the catalogue used the title *Konstruktivisty*. Although the Stenbergs were members of the group at the time of their exhibition, there may have been subsequent fundamental disagreements, as yet not documented. The tensions between Medunetskii and Stepanova were clearly manifest in the debate that followed Stepanova's paper "On Constructivism" on 22 December 1921, when Medunetskii said "Stepanova should keep drawing tadpoles" (See "Transcript of the Discussion of Comrade Stepanova's paper 'On Constructivism'." December 22, 1921 in Andrews and Kalinovska 1990, 74). This may have resulted in a split even before the January 1922 exhibition and the *Ermitazh* publication of August 1922.

Certainly, the longer title is encountered in subsequent publications. For instance, "Konstruktivisty" in *LEF*, no. 1, 1923, 251-2. This article announced preparations for the group's exhibition, and listed the items by Rodchenko that comprised "socially interpreted artistic work." Gan's book *Constructivism* dated 1922 also refers to "The First Working Group of Constructivists." It is clear that at this time Gan, Rodchenko and Stepanova are still united, as we know from the *Ermitazh* publication. When Gan eventually split with Rodchenko and Stepanova (probably sometime in 1923) Gan took the name with him and gave it to his own group.

15 Documentation published by Khan-Magomedov 1986 makes the development of the group much clearer. According to "The Report No. 1. The Assembly for the Organization of the Working Group of Constructivists of Inkhuk" held on 18 March 1921, Gan was president of the group. In the following meeting (28 March 1921) Gan was asked to write a publicity statement for the group.

16 "Programma uchebnoi pod-gruppy."

17 This exhibition used to be known as the Third Obmokhu exhibition.

18 Arvatov, "Proletariat i levoe iskusstvo," 10.

19 Ibid. Of course, Arvatov has his own axe to grind here, and it should be pointed out that "the works are unstable, caught mid-way between different categories, rather than markers on an unproblematic track towards 'art in production'" (Fer, "Metaphor and Modernity," 14).

20 *Izvestiya VTsIK*, 25 December 1920.

21 "Razval Vkhutemasa," 28.

22 Nevertheless, Arvatov and Tatlin were reported to have set up a "production laboratory" at the New Lessner Factory in Petrograd ("Institut khudozhestvennoi kul'tury," *Sovetskoe iskusstvo*, no. 2/3, 1923, 88).

23 Gan, *Konstruktivism*, 15.

24 Neznamov, "Proz-raboty A. Lavinskogo," 77.

25 One was erected outside the hotel on Tverskoi Boulevard in Moscow in which the delegates were staying (Oginskaya 1981, 26). Fourteen of these designs were exhibited in Riga in 1970. See *Katalog vystavki proizvedenii Gustava Klutsisa* . One was made in 1925 for the exhibition accompanying the Fifth Congress of the Comintern (Ibid., no. 26, 44). Apparently, Klutsis was active in organizing this exhibition (Eght, "Khudozhnik G. Klutsis," 8).

26 Chuzhak, "Pod znakom zhiznestroeniya," 32.

27 Popova, "Vstuplenie k diskussii Inkhuka o 'Velikodushnom rogonostse'."

28 Vesnin's project was cramped by the proscenium arch. In its full glory it clearly alludes to mines, factory chimneys, as well as industrial and urban complexes.

29 This, of course, excludes the type of poster and typographical work being undertaken by Rodchenko, Lavinskii and Gan for State enterprises and for publishers.

30 Varvara Stepanova, "O polozhenii i zadachakh khudozhnika-konstruktivista v sittsenabivnoi promyshlennosti v svyazi s rabotami na sittsenabivnoi fabrike" in Minutes of Inkhuk's meeting on 5 January 1924. For details concerning the date when Stepanova and Popova entered the factory see Lodder, *Russian Constructivism*, 291-92, n. 6.

31 Brik, "Ot kartiny k sittsu," 34.

32 Gan, *Konstruktivism*, 5.

33 *Konstruktivisty. K. K. Medunetskii, V. A. Stenberg, G. A. Stenberg.*

34 "Front khudozhestvennogo truda. Materialy k Vserossiiskii konferentsii levykh v iskusstve. Konstruktivisty. Pervaya programma rabochei gruppy konstruktivistov", *Ermitazh*, (Moscow), no. 13, 1922, 3-4.

35 "1-ya diskussionnaya vystavka ob'edinenii aktivnogo revolutsionnogo iskusstva 1924g." in Matsa 1933, 314.

36 Ibid. The catalogue contained information relating to the activities of the group and a statement of its theoretical position which, of course, closely echoed the precepts of Gan's *Konstrnktivizm*. The members of the group seem to have mainly been students from the Vkhutemas. The group was apparently organized into different sections, dealing respectively with furniture and equipment needed in everyday life (Gan, Miller and Sanina), children's books (the Chichagova sisters and Smirnov), special clothing (Mirolyubova, Sanina and Miller), and typographical production (Gan and Miller). Their exhibits at the show included designs for typographical layouts, items of everyday use including furniture and equipment, industrial clothing (production clothing), specialized clothing, and children's books (ibid., 316-17).

37 Pertsov, *Za novoe iskusstvo*, 56. Writing in 1925, Pertsov clearly differentiated between the group led by Gan and the other Constructivists. He called Gan's group "The First Working Group of Constructivists" and listed its members.

38 "1ya diskussionnaya vystavka" in Matsa, *Sovetskoe iskusstvo za 15 let*, 314.

39 Ultimately, the antagonism between these two major groupings became such that in an article of 1928 Gan rewrote the history of Constructivism completely, and pre-dated the split between the "Constructivists" and the artists whom he now referred to as "the productivists of LEF" to 1920! See Gan, "Chto takoe konstruktivism?" 79-81.

40 *LEF*, No. 2, 1923, 9.

41 Arvatov, "Oveshchestvelennaya utopiya," 61.

42 "Pervoe soveshchnie rabotnikov *Lefa*" in Pertsov, *Za novoe iskusstvo*, 135.

43 The discussions and conclusions of the January and July meetings were published in Pertsov 1925.

44 Arvatov was unable to attend the conference because he was ill. Brik participated and so did Gan.
45 Pertsov, *Za novoe iskusstvo*, 136.
46 Ibid., 137.
47 Ibid., 79.
48 Ibid., 76.
49 Ibid.
50 The disagreements between different members were far more wide reaching and numerous than the specific elements of the debate that I have chosen to highlight here.
51 Ibid., 143.
52 Ibid., 145.
53 Tugendkhol'd, "SSSR na parizhskoi vystavke," 932.
54 See Kopp, *Constructivist Architecture in the USSR*, 112.
55 In this way the Bolsheviks had learnt from the practice of the Christian church, which had itself taken over rituals and locations from from paganism, adapted them, and thus supplanted the previous religion effectively.
56 Varst, "Rabochii klyub," 36.
57 Lavrentiev, "Experimental Furniture Design in the 1920s," 151-2.
58 "Rodchenko v Parizhe."
59 Lavrentiev, "Experimental Furniture Design in the 1920s," 151.
60 A. Rodchenko "Diskussii o novoi odezhde i mebeli—zadacha oformleniya" in Glebov, *Inga*, 12.
61 Berezark, "Veshch' na stene," 10.
62 Lukhmanov, "Bez slov," 4.
63 Pertsov, *Za novoe iskusstvo*, 79.
64 Nikolai Chuzhak, "Ot illyuzii k materii (po povody 'Revizii Lefa')" in Pertsov, *Za novoe iskusstvo*, 113-4.
65 Although the apparatus seems to be very convincing, it is based on unscientific principles. In his unpublished note "The Miturich idea of *volnovoe dvizhenie* (wavelike motion)," George Gerstein explained that "The principle in no way depends on wave-like motion, although it does involve a descent and possibly much later a rise of the moving object . . . the usual explanation of such things is in terms of potential and kinetic energy. The tracks start at the same height, therefore both balls have the same amount of initial potential energy and no kinetic energy. Total energy, i.e., the sum of potential and kinetic energy of each ball, is always constant. The lower a ball gets on its trajectory, the less potential energy and hence the more kinetic energy (and hence velocity) it will have." Miturich's apparatus works because the curved path goes lower than the straight path, and the ball that travels along it will go faster than along the straight path.
66 Begicheva, "Vospominaniya o Tatline," 18.

3. The Birth of Socialist Realism from the Spirit of the Russian Avant-Garde[1]

Boris Groys

I

Students of Soviet culture have recently devoted increasing attention to the period of transition from the avant-garde of the 1920s to Socialist Realism of the 1930s and 1940s.[2] Earlier, this transition did not seem problematic. It was usually regarded as the result of the crushing of "true, contemporary revolutionary art of the Russian avant-garde" by Stalin's conservative and despotic regime and the propagation of a "backward art" in the spirit of nineteenth century realism. According to prevailing opinion, the shift also reflected the low cultural levels of the broad Soviet masses and Party leadership. But as this period is studied more closely, such a purely sociological explanation of the transition is no longer satisfactory.

There is an essential difference in the approach to the represented subject, rightly stressed by Soviet criticism, between nineteenth-century realism, customarily called "critical realism" in Soviet art history, and the art of Socialist Realism. Unlike the former, Socialist Realism has a positive relation to its subject. Its aim is to "celebrate Socialist reality," instead of keeping it at arm's length and treating it objectively and "realistically." This difference has also been noted by Paul Sjeklocha and Igor Mead:

> To us "Westerners" this realism implies a dispassionate analytical stance which is assumed by the artist without sentiment. If emotion enters into realism, it is generally of a critical nature intended to instruct by way of bad example rather than a good. . . . In short, although such realism is essentially didactic, it is also essentially negative. Visionary artists have not been found among the realists. However, the Soviet State requires that its artists combine realism and visionary art.[3]

Socialist Realism shows the exemplary and the normative, which are worthy of emulation. Yet it cannot be considered a new version of classicism, although we may indeed find classical elements in Socialist Realist artistic compositions. Antiquity and the Renaissance were highly praised by Soviet critics, but the art of Socialistic Realism is without the direct antique stylization so characteristic, for example, of the art of Nazi Germany, which is in many other respects quite similar to Socialist Realism. Unlike typical West European neoclassicist art, Socialist Realism judges the reality created in the Soviet Union to be the highest achievement of the entire course of human history and does not, therefore, oppose the antique ideal to the present as a "positive alternative" or a "utopia already once realized."[4] Socialist Realism is just one of the ways in which world art in the 1930s and 1940s reverted to the figurative style after the period of relative dominance of avant-garde trends—this process embraces such countries as France (neoclassicism), the Netherlands and Belgium (different forms of magical realism), and the United States (regional painting) as well as those countries where various forms of totalitarianism became established. At the same time, the stylistic differences between Socialist Realism and other, parallel artistic movements are obvious on even the most superficial examination.

All this indicates that the Socialist Realism of the Stalin period represents an original artistic trend with its own specific stylistic features, which cannot simply be identified with other artistic principles and forms familiar from the history of art. Therefore it also becomes impossible to speak of the simple "propagation" of Socialist Realism: before something can be propagated, it must already exist. Although, like any other artistic trend, Socialist Realism belongs to its time and place, it cannot be regarded in a purely sociological and reductionist light, but should, first and foremost, be subjected to normal aesthetic analysis with the object of describing its distinctive features.

This task is not, of course, possible within the framework of the present essay. My aim, rather, is to distinguish in the most general terms between Socialist Realism and a number of other artistic phenomena with which it may be confused. By artistic means that are similar to those in conventional nineteenth-century realistic painting—above all the work of the Russian Wanderers (Peredvizhniki)—Socialist Realism seeks to express a completely different ideological content in radically changed social and historical conditions. This naturally leads to a fundamental disruption of the form of traditional realistic painting itself. Thus, difference of form proves to be bound up with a definite purpose in regard to content; to ignore this change may result in an inadequate interpretation of formal difference, as has often happened in the past.

A similar situation occurs in relation to the art of the Russian avant-garde. It is often regarded in an aestheticized, purely formal, stylistic light,[5] although such a view is opposed to the objectives of the Russian avant-garde, which sought to overcome the traditional contemplative attitude toward art. While today, the works of the Russian avant-garde hang in museums and are sold in galleries like any other works of art, one should not forget that Russian avant-garde artists strove to destroy the museum, to wipe it out as a social institution, ensuring the idea of art as the "individual" or "hand-made" production by an artist of objects of aesthetic contemplation which are then consumed by the spectator. As they understood it, the artists of the Russian avant-garde were producing not objects of aesthetic consumption but projects or models for a total restructuring of the world on new principles, to be implemented by collective actions and social practice in which the difference between consumer and producer, artist and spectator, work of art and object of utility, and so on, disappeared. The fact that these avant-garde projects are hung in present-day museums as traditional works of art, where they are viewed in the traditional light, signals the ultimate defeat of the avant-garde, not its success. The Russian avant-garde lost its historical position: in fact, the true spirit of the Russian avant-garde was more aptly reflected by its place in the locked storerooms of Soviet museums, to which it was consigned as a consequence of its historical defeat, but from which it continued to exercise an influence on the victorious rulers as a hidden menace.

As the modern museum experiences a period of general expansion, it increasingly includes the utilitarian: museums of technology, aeronautics, contemporary utensils, and the like are constantly opening. In the past, icons, which to a great extent constituted a reference point for adherents of the Russian avant-garde, became part of museum collections; they, too, were not regarded as "works of art" by their creators or by their "consumers." Today, however, neither in Russia nor in the West is Socialist Realist art represented faithfully in museums. In Russia it vanished from the eyes of the public during the period of the "thaw," while in the West it was never seriously regarded as art. The position of Socialist Realism "outside art" is, in itself, sufficiently convincing testimony to its inner identification with the avant-garde era, when the desire to go beyond the bounds of the museum became the motivating force of artistic experiment. Like the art of the avant-garde, the art of Socialist Realism wanted to transcend the traditional "artist-spectator-aesthetic object" relationship and become the direct motivating force of social development. The collectivist project of Socialist Realism was expressed in the rejection of the artist's individual manner, of the direct perception of nature, of the quest for "expressiveness" and "picturesqueness"—rejection, in general, of all that is characteristic of traditional realistic art and, in particular, of the art of the Wanderers. As a result, Socialist Realism is often judged to be traditional realism of "low quality," and it is forgotten that Socialist Realism, far from seeking such artistic quality, strove, on the contrary, to overcome it wherever it reared its head. Socialist Realist pictures were regarded as at once works of art and utilitarian objects—instruments of Socialist education of the working people—and as a result could not but be standardized in accordance with their utilitarian function.

In this elimination of boundaries between "high" and "utilitarian" art Socialist Realism is the heir not so much of traditional art as of the Russian avant-garde: Socialist Realism may be said to be the continuation of the avant-garde's strategy by different means. This change of means is not, of course, fortuitous and will be singled out for special examination later. But it cannot be regarded merely as something imposed from outside, artificially halting the development of the avant-garde, which otherwise would have continued in the spirit of Kazimir Malevich or Alexander Rodchenko. It has already been noted that by the end of the 1920s the artists of the Russian avant-garde had begun to return to representation. While Malevich had adopted a new interpretation of traditional painting, Rodchenko, El Lissitzky, Gustaf Klutsis, and others increasingly devoted themselves to photomontage. In the framework of the avant-garde aesthetic, their activity signified a turn toward figurativeness while preserving the original avant-garde project.

This project, which consisted in moving from portraying life toward artistic shaping of life, is also the motivating force of Socialist Realism. The Russian avant-garde adopted from the West a new relationship, developed within the framework of cubism, to the work of art as a construct and made it the basis of a project for the complete reconstruction of reality on new principles. In this the work of art itself underwent fundamental changes—the Russian avant-garde displayed its constructive nature with unprecedented radicalism—which subsequently enabled the secondary aestheticization of its achievements and their interpretation exclusively in terms of the search for a new artistic form. In the 1970s a number of Soviet artists engaged in aestheticizing the achievements of Socialist Realism within the framework of the Sots Art[6] movement, making possible a new approach to Socialist Realism as a purely aesthetic phenomenon, just as the approach of pop art to commercial art stimulated its study as art.

These mechanisms of secondary aestheticization cannot be examined in this essay, but they point indirectly to the mechanisms of primary utilitarianization implemented by the Russian avant-garde and Socialist Realism and, in part, the commercial art of advertising. Behind the external, purely formal distinction between Socialist Realism and the Russian avant-garde (a distinction made relative by the photomontage period and by the art of such groupings in the 1920s as the Society of Easel Painters [OST]), the unity of their fundamental artistic aim—to build a new world by the organizational and technical methods of "socialist construction," in which the artistic, "creative," and utilitarian coincide, in place of "God's world," which the artist was able only to portray—should, therefore, be revealed. While seeming initially to be realistic, the art of "Socialist Realism" is, in fact, not realistic, since it is not mimetic. Its object is to project the new, the future, that which should be, and it is for this reason that socialist art is not simply a regression to the mimesis of the nineteenth century but belongs wholly to the twentieth century. The central issue of Socialist Realism remains, incidentally, why and how the transition from planning in the spirit of the avant-garde to planning in the spirit of realism took place. This transition was connected both with the immanent problems of avant-garde art and with the overall process of Soviet ideological evolution in the 1920s and 1930s.

II

Art as "life-building" (*zhiznestroitel'stvo*) is a tradition that, in Russia, can be traced back at least to the philosopher Vladimir Solov'ev, who conceived of the practice of art as theurgy,[7] a conception later borrowed by the Russian Symbolists. However, the decisive step toward interpreting art as transformation rather than representation was taken by Malevich in his works and writings. For Solov'ev and the Symbolists, the precondition of theurgy was the revelation by the artist of the concealed ideal order of the cosmos (*sofiinost'*) and of society (*sobornost'*); however, Malevich's *Black Square* marked the recognition of nothingness or absolute chaos lying at the basis of all things. For Malevich the black square meant the beginning of a new age in the history of man and the cosmos, in which all given forms of cosmic, social, psychological or other reality had revealed their illusoriness.

Malevich possessed a contemplative and mystical nature and on more than one occasion rejected technical progress and social organization as artificial attempts to impose definite goals on life after the traditional aims of Christianity had been discredited. At the same time Malevich concluded from his discovery that a new restructuring of the world with the object of restoring lost harmony and a kind of "aesthetic justification of the world" was necessary.[8] Malevich conceived his "arkhitektony" or "planity" as projects for such restructuring; his suprematist compositions were at one and the same time direct contemplations of cosmic internal energies and projects for a new organization of the cosmos. It was no coincidence that, during the controversy with AKhRR (Association of Artists of Revolutionary Russia), Malevich took as his standpoint the position of "life creation,"[9] demonstrating the fundamental unity of the avant garde's intentions despite the wide variety of its views and its internal quarrels and conflicts, from which one must detach oneself when giving an overall exposition of avant-garde attitudes. Despite the fact that such detachment leads inevitably to simplification, it does not result in fundamental distortion of the aims of the avant-garde: in their polemics with opponents in other camps, artists and theoreticians themselves reveal the high degree of similarity of their attitudes.

The logical conclusion from Malevich's concept of suprematism as the "last art" was drawn by, among others, the constructivists Vladimir Tatlin and Rodchenko, who called for the total rejection of easel painting in favor of designing the new reality directly. This rejection undoubtedly arose from the inherent logic of avant-garde artistic development and may be observed to a greater or lesser extent in the West: for example, in the activities of the Bauhaus, which, it may be noted, did not come into being without Russian influence; in the Dutch group De Stijl; and others. However, the radicalism of the constructivist position can be explained only by the specific hopes aroused in artists by the October Revolution and its call for the total reconstruction of the country according to a single plan. If, for Marx, philosophy had to move from explaining the world to changing it, this Marxist slogan only confirmed for the artists of the Russian avant-garde their goal of relinquishing portrayal of the world in favor of its creative transformation.

These parallels between Marxist and avant-garde attitudes show that the artist with his "life building" project was competing with a power that also had as its goal the total reconstruction of reality, though on economic and political, rather than aesthetic, principles. The project to transform the entire country—and ultimately the entire world—into a single work of art according to a single artistic design through the efforts of a collective united by common artistic conceptions, which inspired the Russian avant-garde during the first postrevolutionary years, meant the subordination of art, politics, the economy, and technology to the single will of the artist: that is, in the final analysis to the will of one Artist, since a total project of this kind cannot result from the sum of many individual efforts. Marx himself, in an observation constantly quoted in Soviet philosophy and art history, wrote that the worst architect was better than the best busy bee, since the former had in his head a unified plan of construction.

In a certain sense the avant-garde position marks a return to the ancient unity of art and technique (*tekhne*), in which Socrates also included the activity of the legislator. The rejection by the avant-garde of the tradition of artistic autonomy in the modern age and the "bourgeois" relationship between "artist and spectator," understood as "producer and consumer," led in effect to the artist's demand for total political power in order to realize his project. The concept of this new political authority as an ideal instrument for implementing his artistic aims was especially characteristic of the early pronouncements of Russian avant-garde artists and theoreticians.

Thus, Alexei Gan, one of the theorists of Russian Constructivism, wrote:

> We should not reflect, depict and interpret reality but should build practically and express the planned objec-

> tives of the newly active working class, the proletariat, . . . the master of color and line, the combiner of spatial and volumetric solids and the organizer of mass action—must all become Constructivists in the general business of the building and movement of the many millioned human mass.[10]

Statements of this kind, which occur constantly in the polemical writings of the Russian constructivists, could be multiplied. At the same time, the constructivists themselves were by no means blind to the contradictions and illusions of their own program. Ivan Puni, for example, noted that, in essence, the artist has nothing to do with manufacture, since engineers and workers have their own criteria for this.[11] However, the logic of the avant-garde's development began to overstep these sober reflections. While Rodchenko, Tatlin, and others were at first in the forefront of those struggling for the new reality, they themselves gradually came to be accused of giving priority to purely artistic design over the demands of production and the direct formation of reality. The evolution of the avant-garde from Malevich to constructivism and, later, to LEF proceeds by way of increasingly radical demands for the rejection of traditional artistic individualism and the adoption of new social tasks.[12] In itself this evolution refutes the idea that artists were only at first victims of an illusion of omnipotence which they were obliged gradually to abandon. Quite the contrary: if it is supposed that the artist's move toward forming reality is the result of illusion, it must be acknowledged that this illusion by no means weakened but burgeoned with time.

Thus, it may be observed, both in the internal polemics of members of the avant-garde and in their confrontations with other artistic groupings, that the number of direct political accusations grew constantly. As artistic decisions were recognized more and more to be political decisions—for increasingly, they were perceived as defining the country's future—the fierceness of the controversy and the realization that positions which had formerly seemed similar were now incompatible also grew. The quest for collective creation inevitably led to a struggle for absolute leadership. The productionist position of LEF and its subsequent aspiration to equate art, technology, and politics, uniting these three contemporary modes of forming reality in a single total project, represent the extreme point of development of the avant-garde and its internal intentions. In the course of this development the avant-garde itself rejected its earlier manifestations as individualistic, aestheticist, and bourgeois. Thus, later criticism in this spirit by the theoreticians of Socialist Realism did not represent anything fundamentally new: in essence, such criticism only repeated the accusations formulated in the process of the development of the avant-garde itself. These accusations had become an integral part of the rhetoric of the avant-garde by the time of its liquidation at the end of the 1920s—coincidentally, the time when the avant-garde had achieved the peak of its theoretical, if not its purely artistic, development.

The artists of the avant-garde are commonly accused of neglecting the human factor in their plans for reconstructing the world: indeed the majority of the Russian population then held utterly different aesthetic ideas. In essence, the avant-garde intended to make use of the political and the administrative power offered it by the Revolution to impose on the overwhelming majority of the population aesthetic and organizational norms developed by an insignificant minority of artists. This objective certainly cannot be termed democratic. However, it should not be ignored that the members of the avant-garde themselves were hardly aware of the totalitarian character of their endeavor.

The artists of the avant-garde shared the Marxist belief that public taste is formed by the environment. They were "historical materialists" in the sense that they thought it possible, by reconstructing the world in which man lives, wholly to rebuild his inner mechanisms of perception and judgment. Malevich considered that, at the sight of his black square, "the sword will fall from the hero's hands and the prayer die on the lips of the saint."[13] It was not fortuitous, therefore, that an alliance formed within the framework of LEF between the avant-garde and "vulgar sociologists" of the Boris Arvatov type: both were inspired by a belief in the direct magical effect on human consciousness of changes in the conditions of man's "material existence." The artistic engineers of the avant-garde disregarded man because they considered him to be a part or element of social or technical systems or, at best, of a universal cosmic life: for a member of the avant-garde to be an "engineer of the world" also automatically meant being an "engineer of human souls."

The avant-garde artist was above all a materialist. He strove to work directly with the material "basis" in the belief that the "superstructure" would react automatically. This avant-garde "historical materialism" was also connected with its purely "aesthetic materialism." The latter consisted in the maximum revelation of "the materiality of material," "the materiality of the art work itself," concealed from the spectator in traditional painting, which used material in a purely utilitarian way to convey a definite content.[14] Such "aesthetic materialism," which gave an important fillip to the future formal development of art and is an important achievement of the Russian avant-garde, presupposes, however, a contemplative, anti-utilitarian understanding of materialism which was repudiated by the avant-garde in the context of LEF's productivism. Moreover, as already noted, a shift took place within the avant-garde toward the complete, extra-aesthetic "utilitarianism" of the project; that is, the purely aesthetic, nonutilitarian contemplative dimension of the avant-garde, which enabled its secondary aestheticization, was recognized by the avant-garde as a relic of traditional artistic attitudes that were ripe for rebuttal. In practice, the art of the avant-garde during its LEF period assumed an increasingly propagandist character that was not creative in the sense of productivism. Avant-garde artists, lacking direct access to the "basis," turned increasingly to propagandizing "Socialist construction" implemented by the political leadership on a "scientific foundation." The principal occupation of the avant-garde became the creation of posters, stage and exhibition design, and so on—in other words, work exclusively in the sphere of the "superstructure." In this respect the observation by the theorists of AKhRR, that the activities of LEF, for all its revolutionary phraseology and emphasis on its proletarian attitude toward art, differed little in essence from capitalist commercial advertising and borrowed many of its devices,[15] is justified. For AKhRR the utilitarian orientation of LEF had no specific Socialist content. It amounted to a shift on the part of the artist from cottage to mass production dictated by the general change in the technical level of manufacture in both West and East, not by the goals of "Communist upbringing of the workers."

III

There is a widespread opinion among scholars that the transition to Socialist Realism marked the victory of AKhRR in the struggle against avant-garde trends. It is common to see the genealogy of Socialist Realism exclusively in the turn toward representationalism taken by

AKhRR as early as the 1920s (just as, in literature, it is usual to interpret the establishment of Socialist Realism as the victory of the Russian Association of Proletarian Writers [RAPP]). This point of view is based first on the external similarity between the realistic style of AKhRR and Socialist Realist style and on the fact that many artists moved from AKhRR to key positions in the new unified artistic associations of the era of Socialist Realism. The official criticism of both AKhRR and RAPP during the period preceding the proclamation of Socialist Realism is usually overlooked. As a rule it is judged to be merely a tactical move by the authorities with the object of pacifying artists from other groupings and integrating them in unified "creative unions."

However, criticism of this kind has been persistently repeated in Soviet historical writing over several decades, which alone renders untenable the view that it represented no more than a temporary tactical move. Comparison with avant-garde criticism, that is, criticism by LEF of AKhRK, reveals both a similarity and a difference, prompting a revision of some established ideas.

The turn toward realism in Russian postrevolutionary art is placed at different times. It is dated by some as early as the formation of AKhRR in 1922, while others place it in 1924-25. At the same time, critics belonging to the avant-garde camp and those who were already laying the foundations of the theory of Socialist Realism displayed a noticeable coincidence in assessing the reasons for this turn and the reasons for its significance. Their common view was that rebirth of representational easel painting was connected with the New Economic Policy (NEP) and the emergence of a new stratum of art consumers with definite artistic tastes. Critics holding avant-garde views cited artistic reaction as corresponding to economic and political reaction. The landscapes, portraits, and genre scenes with which AKhRR and so many other groups of the time, such as the Society of Easel Painters (OST) and "Bytie" ("Being"), supplied the market aroused a similar response. These paintings were regarded as symptoms of the same process, although AKhRR was welcomed for its mass approach and its "progressive" character, while OST was praised for a higher level of professionalism. A. Fedorov-Davydov, for example, who became a leading critic and art historian during the Stalin period, noted as early as 1925 the general turn by both Soviet and West European art towards realism, singling out neoclassicism in France and Italy and expressionism in Germany. He observed that neoclassicism, although "close to the proletariat in its striving for organization, order and discipline," could not serve as a basis for proletarian art because of its quality of stylization while expressionism saw things in too gloomy a light, and concluded that the attention to detail of neoclassicism should be combined with the passion of expressionism—advice which, in a slightly amended form, would be heeded in the Stalin period. Turning to Soviet experience, Fedorov-Daydov wrote:

> In order to understand and evaluate AKhRR, we must understand what kind of realists they are. We shall scarcely be mistaken if we say that they understand realism in the sense of naturalistic, figurative—in essence, genre—realism. It is in this, disregarding the question of talent, that, perhaps, the reason lies for their inability genuinely to reflect the revolution. Enthusiasm and the heroic cannot be conveyed by the passive methods of naturalism.[16]

The same judgment was passed by Ia. A. Tugendkhol'd, who sympathized with AKhRR's turn toward realism. Writing of the current AKhRR's exhibition, he referred to the "naturalism of AKhRR painting" and concluded: "They were large illustrations in color, but not what AKhRR expected, not the painting genuinely needed by us in the sense of 'heroic realism'—which was found in Vasilii Surikov and, in part, in I'lia Repin and Sergei Ivanov."[17] The arguments heard later during the era of Socialist Realism may easily be recognized here. One further quotation, from Alfred Kurella, who also played an important role in preparing the ground for Socialist Realism, underlines this point. In an article characteristically entitled "Artistic Reaction Behind the Mask of Heroic Realism" ("Khudozhestvennaia reaktsiia pod maskoi geroicheskogo realizma"), Kurella wrote of the necessity for "organizing the ideology of the masses by the specific means of representational art,"[18] failing to find what he wanted in AKhRR, he accused it of naturalism.

These accusations of naturalism, which constituted the initial reaction not only of avant-garde critics but also of the future theoreticians of Socialist Realism and opponents of avant-garde art, were later repeated officially during the campaign against AKhRR in the late 1920s and early 1930s, which preceded the formation of Socialist Realism. It was at this time that AKhRR was accused of fellow-traveling ideology, lack of involvement in the achievements of the Revolution and Socialist construction, and refusal to participate directly in Socialist construction as its "vanguard," as well as of "disparaging criticism" and "Communist arrogance." These accusations are also rehearsed in contemporary Soviet historical writings. E. I. Sevost'ianov, longtime head of Iskusstvo publishing house, provides a characteristic view of the 1930s artistic situation in a special article devoted to this problem. The author quotes sympathetically the observations of critics of the 1930s concerning the "imitative Wanderer approach of AKhRR" and the necessity for criticism to struggle simultaneously against "formalist tricks" and "passive naturalism."[19] Similar quotations exist in many other Soviet publications, reminding us that a struggle against groupings of the likes of RAPP and RAPKh (Russian Association of Proletarian Artists, which had emerged from AKhRR)—by that time the avant-garde had been effectively eliminated—preceded the appearance of Socialist Realism.

In recalling the actual context of the period, we should note that it coincided with the liquidation of NEP—that is, of the milieu in which, according to the general view, the art of groupings like AKhRR had developed. The transition to the 1930s and the Five-Year Plans meant the implementation of measures that had been proposed in their time by the left ("plundering the peasantry," accelerated industrialization, and so forth), although by other methods and in a different historical context. Amid conditions of intensifying centralization, the program of "building Socialism in one country" and the "growing enthusiasm of the masses," Vladimir Mavakovsky was proclaimed the greatest poet of the age and the Leninist slogan "it is necessary to dream" was quoted with increasing frequency in the press. In these new circumstances Socialist Realism put into effect practically all the fundamental watchwords of the avant-garde: it united the artists and gave them a single purpose, erased the dividing line between high and utilitarian art and between political content and purely artistic decisions, created a single and easily recognizable style, liberated the artist from the service of the consumer and his individual tastes and from the requirement to be original, became part of the common cause of the people, and set itself not to reflect reality but to project a new and better reality.

In this respect Socialist Realism was undoubtedly a revival of the ideals of the avant-garde after a definite period in which individualized artistic production with its purely reflective, mimetic character had dominated. Most importantly, a break with tradition was made in the very role and function of the artist in society. Socialist Realist painting, like the work of the avant-garde, is above all a political decision concerning how the future should look, and is judged by purely political criteria. The Socialist Realist artist renounces his role as an observer detached from real life and becomes a part of the working collective on equal terms with all its other parts. However, all the obvious similarity in the way the avant-garde and Socialist Realism conceptualize the role of art does not provide an answer to a key question: why is there so little external, purely visual similarity between the avant-garde and Socialist Realism?

IV

Apart from the inherent laws of artistic development whereby, after a period of time, art changes its course and begins to move in a new direction, the reason for the changed character of the visual material with which the avant-garde had worked lay primarily in the changed position of the artist in Soviet society as it evolved. Avant-garde art was a reductionist art that adhered to the principle of newness—it was advancing from Malevich's black square as the sign of absolute zero and absolute rejection of the world as it is. The art of the 1930s was confronted by a "new reality," whose authors were political leaders, not the artistic avant-garde. If avant-garde artists had striven to work directly with the "basis," utilizing political power in a purely instrumental way, clearly by the 1930s work with the basis could be implemented only by the political authorities, which did not brook competition.

A similar situation developed in philosophy. While Marxist philosophy had proclaimed the primacy of practice over theoretical cognition, this primacy was understood initially to denote the gaining by the philosopher of political power with the aim of changing the world instead of knowing it. But as early as the late 1920s and the beginning of the 1930s the primacy of social practice could only be understood as the primacy of decisions by the political leadership over their theoretical interpretation, leading to the ultimate liquidation of the philosophical schools that had earlier emerged.[20] Similarly, artists, nurtured on the principle of the primacy of transformation over representation, could not but recognize, following their own logic, the dominance of the political leadership in the strictly aesthetic sphere as well. The artists left this sphere in order to subordinate political reality to themselves, but in so doing they destroyed the autonomy of the artist and the work of art, thus subordinating the artist himself to political reality "at the second move." Having made social practice the sole criterion of truth and beauty, Soviet philosophers and artists inevitably found themselves obliged to recognize political leaders as better philosophers and artists than themselves, thus renouncing the traditional right of primacy.

In these circumstances the question of the artist's role in society and the objective significance of his activity at a point where both the representation and transformation of reality had escaped his control naturally arose again. LEF had already marked out this new role, which consisted in agitation and propaganda for the decisions of the political leadership. The emergence of this role signaled too a significant shift in the consciousness of artists and of Soviet ideologists as a whole.

The theoreticians of the avant-garde proceeded from the conviction that modification of the "basis" would lead almost automatically to change in the "superstructure" and that, in consequence, purely "material" work with the basis was sufficient to achieve a changed view of the world, a changed aesthetic perception. In the late 1920s and early 1930s this widespread opinion was judged to be "vulgar sociologism" and sharply criticized. The sum of ideological, aesthetic, and other conceptions, the superstructure was proclaimed to be relatively independent and situated in a "dialectical," rather than a one sided causal, relationship with the basis: defining the superstructure, the basis is "strengthened" as well as "weakened" by it. This new emphasis on the superstructure, brought about in the first instance by the disillusionment with the prospects for world revolution in the developed Western countries (as a result of the "unreadiness" of the proletariat), made art a definite, partially autonomous area of activity. Art, together with philosophy, literature, history, and other "superstructural" forms of activity, was given the task, if not of defining the overall face of the new reality, then, at any rate, of promoting its formation in a particular sphere: specifically, by forming the consciousness of Soviet citizens, who in their turn stood in a dual, dialectical relationship to this reality as both its creators and its "products."

Of the many examples that illustrate this development, we may cite a few of the later pronouncements by Soviet art theorists. They do not differ in essence from the principles worked out in the 1930s, though they are more elaborate. In a 1952 article by N. Dmitrieva entitled "The Aesthetic Category of the Beautiful" ("Esteticheskaia kategoriia prekrasnogo"), the author describes such Stalinist projects as canals, hydroelectric stations, irrigation programs, and industrial installations: "This is the formation of being according to the laws of beauty," writes Dmitrieva.[21] According to her, the beautiful is the "harmoniously organized structure of life, where everything is mutually coordinated and every element forms a necessary link in the system of the whole."[22] In essence, therefore, the beautiful coincides for the author with "systematic practical activity" and does not reside in art alone as a specific form of activity. The beautiful is, in the first instance, reality itself, life itself, if it is beautifully organized, but "the beautiful in art nevertheless does not fully coincide with the beautiful in life,"[23] since art fixes the attention on "the typical features of beauty" of each given period; "typical" here means not the "statistical mean" but the common aesthetic ideal of the age, that is, the artistic norm for the formation of reality itself. The beautiful in art, reflecting the "typically beautiful in life," thus may play a formative role in relation to reality.

G. Nedoshivin takes a similar position in his article "On the Relationship of Art to Reality" ("Ob otnoshenii iskusstva k deistvitel'nosti"), emphasizing the educative role of art as being "inseparable from its cognitive role."[24] Art, like science, simultaneously cognizes and forms life, doing this, however, not theoretically but in typical images. The typical is again oriented toward practical social goals, toward the future and the "dream." Many similar observations could be cited. All, in essence, are interpretations of Stalin's renowned directive to writers to "write the truth."

To write or "depict" the truth meant for Soviet criticism of that time to show the objectives toward which social practice in reality strove, not to impose objectives upon society from outside, as formalism tried to do, or to observe the movement of society toward these objectives as this really happened, which "uninspired naturalism" did. However, such a purpose presupposes that social practice develops not spontaneously but with the object of realizing certain definite ideals in the mind of the "architect" of this process, who is distinguished from "the very best bee." Naturally, the political leadership, namely Stalin, was seen in the role of architect.

It was, indeed, to Stalin that the avant-garde role of creator of "the beautiful in life itself," that is, the task of "transforming" rather than "representing" life, passed during the 1930s. The political leadership responded to the demand by philosophy and art for political power in order to realize in practice their plans for reconstructing the world by appropriating philosophical and aesthetic projects to itself. Stalin, as the artist of reality, could transform it in accordance with a unified plan, and by the logic of the avant-garde itself, could demand that others standardize their style and direct their individual efforts toward harmony with the style of life Stalin envisioned. The demand to "paint life" has meaning only when that life becomes a work of art. The avant-garde had previously rejected this demand, since, according to the formula "God is dead," it no longer perceived the world as the work of God's art. The avant-garde artist laid claim to the vacant place of the total creator, but in fact this place had been filled by political authority. Stalin became the only artist, the Malevich, so to speak, of the Stalin period, liquidating the avant-garde as a competitor in accordance with the logic of the struggle—a logic which was not foreign to avant-garde artists either, who willingly resorted to administrative intrigues.

Socialist Realism, despite its collectivist ideals, strove for a single, unified style, as did suprematism, for example, or the analytical art of Filonov. It should not be forgotten that the stylistic variety of the avant-garde was associated with the constant rifts and struggles among leading artists, a situation reminiscent in this respect of the struggle during the early stages of evolution of the Communist Party. Within each faction, however, discipline and the striving for standardization prevailed, making, for example, the faithful disciples of Malevich almost indistinguishable. Such standardization inevitably resulted from the ideology of the avant-garde, which apparently scorned the individualism of a "unique artistic manner" and stressed adherence to the "objective laws of composition." The new world could not be built on a polystylistic basis, and the cult of the personality of the single, unique artist creator was, therefore, deeply rooted in avant-garde theory and practice. Of course, individual variations were always possible within the framework of a school, but these were as a rule explained by the necessity for broadening the sphere of reality that was embraced, that is, in terms of the individual nature of the specific task and not that of the artist.

A similar situation confronts the student of the art of the Stalin period. Contemporary artists were in essence "followers of Stalin" (by analogy with "followers of Malevich"), who all worked in the "Stalinist style," but with variations depending on whether their task was to portray the great future, celebrate the workers in the factory or in the field, struggle against the imperialist inciters of war, or depict the building of socialism in a particular national republic. In all these situations style underwent definite changes, while at the same time the general trend was toward the elimination of these subject-related differences. Thus, artists, particularly during Stalin's last period, described in detail and with pride how they had succeeded in freeing themselves from all tokens of individual style and even of the "nontypical" characteristic of the represented subject.[25]

The criticism of the Stalin period constantly demanded that artists bring their vision closer to the "normal" vision of "normal" Soviet people, the creators of the new life. In the last years of Stalin's rule the "team method" of manufacturing pictures, directed at overcoming completely the individuality of a particular painter, was widely practiced. Thus, the Soviet artist of the Stalin period did not occupy the position of a realistic reflector of the new reality—this was precisely the position that had been condemned in the case of AKhRR. The artist of Socialist Realism reflected not reality itself but the ultimate goal of its reconstruction: he was at once passive and active in that he varied and developed Stalin's thinking about it.

The difference between Socialist Realism and the avant-garde consists not in their relationship to art and its goals but in the area of application of this new relationship: while the avant-garde—at any rate in its pre-LEF period—directed itself toward forming actual material reality. Socialist Realism set itself above all the goal of forming the psychology of the new Soviet person. The writer, following Stalin's well-known definition, is "an engineer of human souls." This formulation points both to continuity with the avant-garde (the writer as engineer) and to a departure from it, since a new area of application is provided for the avant-garde principle of engineering design after responsibility for projecting reality itself has been assumed by others. At the same time this role proved to be more an honorary one, since the initial slogan of the Five-Year Plan, "technology decides everything," was soon replaced by another—"the cadres decide everything."

However, the problem of projecting the New Man presents the artist with tasks other than those of projecting material reality. In the absence of what might now be called "genetic engineering," the artist is inevitably tied to unchanged human appearance—from which also emerges the necessity of turning again to traditional painting. This represents not only the statement of achieved successes but also an acknowledgment of certain limits. It is in this sense that Socialist Realism is "realistic": realism here is equated with *realpolitik*, which is opposed to the utopianism of the avant-garde. The task of educating the New Man proved much more difficult than had been initially supposed.

The transition from the avant-garde to Socialist Realism was thus dictated by the logic of development of the avant-garde idea of projecting a new reality, not by concessions to the tastes of the mass consumer, as has often been claimed. There is no doubt that the avant-garde was foreign to the ordinary spectator. It is equally beyond doubt that the return to easel painting during the NEP was influenced by the new mass demand for art. However, the centralization of Soviet art from the beginning of the 1930s made it totally independent of consumer tastes, an independence on which, we may note, the theoreticians of LEF had insisted from the very outset. The art of Socialist Realism does not give ordinary spectators the opportunity to identify with it, since it is opposed to them as an educative institution. With the passing of time the Union of Soviet Artists gained great economic power and relative economic independence, even from official institutions and their tastes, since the union itself determined purchasing policy. No link existed at any level between the ordinary consumer and the union, and the art of Socialist Realism interested the ordinary Soviet person as little as did the art of the avant-garde. In the absence of economic criteria or sociological surveys, the unprecedented success during the post-Stalin era of an artist like Ilia Glazunov provides an indirect indication of the spectator's real tastes. Other examples may also be cited, which indicate that the mass spectator in the Soviet Union, while inclined toward realistic painting, was by no means oriented toward Socialist Realist painting.

At all events, in fulfilling its basic mission of projecting the New Man, Socialist Realism was limited from the outset, as has been stated, by the unchanging quality of the human countenance and the necessity to take this into account. LEF, too, was obliged to reckon with this constant factor when, at the end of the 1920s, the artists of the Russian avant-garde began to use the human face and figure in their propaganda montages. However, for the art of Socialist Realism representation of the human being occupied a central place; indeed, all other purposes were subsumed by it. As the theoreticians of Socialist Realism recognized from the beginning, this circumstance restricted compositional opportunities and expressive means of painting. The subject of representation became the expression of the human face and the pose of the human body, testifying to the person's inner spiritual state.

Practically all art criticism of the Stalin period devoted itself to endless analyses of the poses and facial expressions portrayed in Soviet pictures in relation to the psychological content they were supposed to convey. The methods and criteria of such analyses, as well as relevant examples, cannot be examined here in greater detail. It is sufficient to state that with time artists and critics jointly elaborated a distinctive and complex code for external appearance, behavior, and emotional reaction characteristic of the "true Soviet man." This code embraced the most varied spheres of life. Highly ritualized and semanticized, it enables any person brought up in Stalinist culture to judge from a single glance at a picture the hierarchical relationships between the figures, the ideological intentions of the artist, the moral character of the figures, and so on. This canon was elaborated over many years prior to Stalin's death, when it began to disintegrate gradually. Painters and critics painfully worked out a new canon under the presupposition that reliance on classical models of the past was impossible. Their main goal was to define which poses and facial expressions should be considered "flabby," "decadent," and bourgeois or, conversely, energetic, but energetic in the Soviet, not the Western, especially the American, style, that is, with a genuine understanding of the prospects for historical progress. They determined which pose could be considered inspired but not exalted, calmly brave but not static, and so on. Today, Socialist Realism is perceived as somewhat colorless by comparison with the classics. But in making such a comparison it should not be forgotten that Socialist Realism lacked the opportunity for prolonged, consistent, and unbroken development that was enjoyed by the classics. If we recall that its entire evolution occupied no more than a quarter of a century, we must acknowledge that, by the end of Stalin's rule, Socialist Realism had achieved a very high degree of internal unity and codification.

Tugendkhol'd set out quite clearly at the very inception of this process the reasons for the turn by Soviet art from the basis to the superstructure. In his essay "The Painting of a Revolutionary Decade" ("Zhivopis' revoliutsionnogo desiatiletiia"), which is still insufficiently "dialectical" from the standpoint of later Soviet art history but is as a result quite clearly written, he argues against the notion of the left that its practice was based on a materialist view of the world. Tugendkhol'd quotes Punin in this connection, who wrote: "Being defines consciousness, consciousness does not define being. Form = being. Form-being defines consciousness, that is, content. . . . Our art is the art of form, because we are proletarian artists, artists of a Communist culture."[26] Tugendkhol'd expresses the following objection:

> For Punin [form] is the command given by the age, at once Russian and Western, proletarian and bourgeois. In other words, this form is set by the objective conditions of the age, which are identical for all. Punin did not understand that, since the form of the age is obligatory to all, the difference between proletarian and nonproletarian art consists not in form but in the idea of utilizing it . . . it is in the fact, too, that [in our country] the master of the locomotives and machines is the proletariat itself that the difference between our industrialism and Western industrialism lies; this is our content.[27]

Thus, Tugendkhol'd directly links the appearance of man in art to the discovery of the relative independence of the superstructure from the level of production. Man and his organizing attitude toward technology are at the very heart of the definition of the new social system, which is thereby given a psychological foundation. In art the concentration on the figure of Stalin as the creator of the new life par excellence represents the extreme expression of this new "cult of personality."

Tugendkhol'd also notes that the decisive move toward the portrayal of man was connected with the death of Lenin, when "everyone felt that something had been allowed to pass away."[28] In the future the image of Lenin and, later, Stalin would stand at the center of Soviet art as the image of the ideal, the exemplar. The numerous portraits of Lenin and Stalin, which may seem monotonous to the contemporary observer, were not monotonous to the artists and critics of that period: each was intended to "reveal a side of their multi-faceted personality" (recalling Christ's iconography, which defines different, dogmatically inculcated means of presenting the personality of Christ in its various aspects). These portraits posed a definite risk to the artist, since they represented not only an attempt at an external likeness but also a specific interpretation of the personality of the leaders that had no less ideological and political significance than a verbal or literary interpretation. Characteristically, when the critics failed to find this type of clear-cut interpretation in the portrait and when the interpretation was seen as "unoriginal," it was invariably condemned as a failure.

By the end of Stalin's rule Socialist Realist art had begun to move increasingly toward the creation of an integral, monumental appearance of Soviet cities and, ultimately, a unified appearance of the entire country. Plans were drawn up for the complete reconstruction of Moscow in accordance with a single artistic concept, and painting was being increasingly integrated with architecture while, conversely, buildings of a functional character—factories, underground stations, hydroelectric stations, and so forth—began to take on the character of works of art. Portraits of Lenin and Stalin as well as other leaders, not to mention the "typical workers and peasants," over time became increasingly depersonalized and depsychologized. The basic canon was already so formalized and ritualized that it was now possible to construct a unified reality from elements created in preceding years.

This new monumental style bore little external resemblance to the avant-garde, yet in many respects it realized the latter's aims: total aestheticization of reality and the rejection of individualized easel painting and sculpture that lacked a monumental purpose. The importance of museums began, correspondingly, to decline: an exhibition of gifts to Stalin was mounted in the Pushkin Museum of West European Art in Moscow.

Neither may this style be considered a simple restoration of the classical. It is true, of course, that the Academy of Arts was reorganized at this time and the struggle against the "undervaluation of the old Russian Academy of Arts" began at its very first sessions. At the same time the "Chistiakov system," named after the teacher of many of the Wanderers,[29] began to be propagated. The campaign sought to demonstrate that the Wanderer artists descended directly from the Russian classical school, whereas earlier interpretations had focused on their break with the academic tradition. A new approach to justifying the necessity of "a solicitous attitude toward the cultural heritage" also dates from this time. While, previously, this necessity had been based on the theory that each class creates progressive art during the period of its rise and reactionary art during the period of its decline and that Soviet art should, therefore, imitate the art of periods of progressive development, such as, for example, the art of antiquity, of the Renaissance, and of nineteenth-century Russian realism (the avant-garde was regarded here as the art of decline and decadence), now this theory, too, deriving from the very first declarations of the Party leadership in the area of cultural policy,[30] was accused of representing "vulgar sociologism." The new, far more radical justification advanced was that, in essence, all "the genuinely good art of the past" expressed the interests not of a definite class—even if progressive—but of an entire people and thus, given the total victory and the "flourishing"[31] of the people, could be fearlessly imitated.

Despite all these obvious references to the past, the art of the Stalin period is not classical in the same sense as, for example, the art of the Renaissance or the art of the French Revolution. Antiquity was still ultimately rated an age of slave owning, and the hero of Soviet books on the period was, above all, Spartacus. The same is true of all other historical epochs: all were regarded as no more than preparatory stages on the road toward the contemporary Soviet age and never as independent models or exemplars. In the profoundest sense Socialist Realism remained the heir of the avant-garde to the end. Like the avant-garde, it regarded the present age as the highest point of history and the future as the embodiment of the aspirations of the present. Any stylization was, therefore, foreign to it, and, for all the monumentality of their poses, Lenin was represented without any feeling of clumsiness in jacket and cap and Stalin in semi-military jacket and boots.

This teleological perception of history led inevitably to an instrumentalization of the artistic devices of the past and to what, seen from the outside, was taken as eclecticism but was in fact not eclecticism. The art of previous ages was not regarded by Soviet ideology as a totality that should not be arbitrarily dismembered. In accordance with the Leninist theory of two cultures in one, each historical period was regarded as a battleground between progressive and reactionary forces, in which the progressive forces ultimately aimed at the victory of Socialism in the USSR (even if the clash took place in the remote past), while the reactionary forces strove to block this. Such an understanding of history naturally led to quotation from the past of everything progressive and rejection of everything reactionary. Viewed externally, this approach seems to result in extreme eclecticism, since it violates the unity of style of each era, but in the consciousness of Soviet ideology, it possessed the true unity of everything progressive, popular and eternal, and rejected everything ephemeral and transitory associated with the class structure of society. Ideas of the progressive or reactionary quality of a given phenomenon have naturally changed with time, and what is or is not subject to quotation has changed correspondingly. Thus, in the art of Socialist Realism quotation and "eclecticism" have a semantic and ideological, rather than an aesthetic, character. The experienced Soviet spectator can always readily decipher such an "eclectic composition" which, in fact, possesses a unified ideological significance. However, this also means that Socialist Realism should not be conceived of as a purely aesthetic return to the past, contrasting with the "contemporary style" of the avant-garde.

The real difference between the avant-garde and Socialist Realism consists, as has already been stated, in moving the center of gravity from work on the basis (the technical and material organization of society) to work on the superstructure (engineering the New Man). The shift from basis to superstructure was necessary because work on the former became the exclusive prerogative of Stalin and the Party. If, thereby, Socialist Realism finally crushed the avant-garde—to regard the avant-garde as a purely aesthetic phenomenon, which contradicts the spirit of the avant-garde itself—at the same time it continued, developed, and, in a certain sense, even implemented its program. Socialist Realism overcame the reductionism of the avant-garde and the traditional contemplative standpoint associated with this reductionism (which led to the success of the Russian avant-garde in the "bourgeois" West) and instrumentalized the entire mass of culture of the past with the object of building a new reality as *Gesamtkunstwerk*. The practice of Socialist Realism is based not on a kind of primordial artistic contemplation, like Malevich's *Black Square*, but on the sum total of ideological demands, which in principle make it possible freely to manipulate any visual material (this ability, it may be noted, enabled the preservation of the principles of Socialist Realism even after Stalin's death, although, visually, Soviet art also underwent definite changes).[32]

By the same token Socialist Realism took the principle, proclaimed by the avant-garde, of rejecting aesthetics to its extreme. Socialist Realism, free of any concrete aesthetic program—despite the apparent strictness of the Socialist Realist canon, it could be changed instantly in response to political or ideological necessity—is indeed that "non-art" the avant-garde wanted to become. Socialist Realism is usually defined as art "Socialist in content and national in form," but this also signifies "avant-garde in content and eclectic in form," since "national" denotes everything "popular" and "progressive" throughout the entire history of the nation. Avant-garde purity of style is, in fact, the result of the still unconquered attitude of the artist toward what he produces as an "original work", corresponding to the "unique individuality" of the artist. In this sense the eclectic may be regarded as the faithful expression in art of a truly collectivist principle.

The collectivism of Socialist Realism does not, of course, mean anything like democracy. At the center of Socialist Realism is the figure of the leader, who is simultaneously its principal creator (since he is the creator of Socialist reality itself, which serves as the model for art) and its main subject. It is in this sense that Stalin is also a *Gesamtkunstwerk*. As leader, Stalin has no definite style—he appears in different ways in his various personas as general, philosopher and theoretician, seer, loving father, and so on. The different aspects of Stalin's "multifaceted personality," usually incompatible in an ordinary person, seem eclectic in turn, violating standard notions of the original, self-contained human personality: thus, Stalin—as a figure in the Stalin myth—unites in himself the individual and the collective, taking on superhuman features which the artist of the avant-garde, although he too strives to replace the divine project with his own, nevertheless lacks.

If, at first glance, the transition from the original style of the avant-garde to the eclecticism of Socialist Realism appears to be a step backwards, this is only because the judgment is made from a purely aesthetic standpoint based on the unity of what may be called the "world museum." But Socialist Realism sought to become the world museum itself, absorbing everything progressive and worthy of preservation and rejecting everything reactionary. The eclecticism and historicism of Socialist Realism should, therefore, be seen not as a rejection of the spirit of the avant-garde but as its radicalization: that is, as an attempt ultimately to identify pure and utilitarian art, the individual and the collective, the portrayal of life and its transformation, and so on, at the center of which stands the artist-demiurge as the ideal of the New Man in the new reality. To repeat: overcoming the concrete, historically determined aesthetic of the avant-garde meant not the defeat of the avant-garde project but its continuation and completion insofar as this project itself consisted in rejecting an aestheticized, contemplative attitude toward art and the quest for an individual style.

Endnotes

1 A version of this essay was published in Bowlt and Matich, *Laboratory of Dreams*, 198-217.
2 Günther, "Verordneter oder gewachsener Kanon?"
3 Sjeklocha and Mead, *Unofficial Art in the Soviet Union*, 35.
4 Gethmann-Siefert, "Das klassiche als das Utopische."
5 Lodder links this aestheticization of the Russian avant-garde in the West with the Berlin exhibition of 1922. Lodder, *Russian Constructivism*, 227-30.
6 Tupitsyn, *Sots-art*. This source is the catalogue of an exhibition of works by an unofficial Russian art movement of the 1970s and 1980s, which played with the icons of the Stalinist era. See also Groys, *The Total Art of Stalinism*, 75ff.
7 Solov'ev, *Sobranie sochinenii*, 6: 90.
8 Malevich, "God Is Not Cast Down."
9 Gassner and Gillen, "K. Malevich on AKhRR."
10 Gan, as quoted in Lodder, *Russian Constructivism*, 98-99.
11 Lodder, *Russian Constructivism*, 77.
12 Arvatov, "Über die Reorganisation der Kunstfakultaten an den VChUTEMAS."
13 Malevich, *Suprematismus*, 57.
14 Gassner, *Alexander Rodschenko*, 50-51.
15 Gassner and Gillen, *Zwischen Revolutionskunst*, 286-87.
16 Fedorov-Davydov, "Vopros o novom realizme v sviazi s zapadno-evropeiskimi techeniiami v iskusstve."
17 Tugendkhol'd, "Zhivopis' revoliutsionnogo desiatiletiia," 34.
18 Gassner and Gillen, *Zwischen Revolutionskunst*, 288.
19 Sevost'ianov, *Esteticheskaia priroda sovetskogo izobrazitel'nogo iskusstva*, 206.
20 Iakhot, *Podavlenie filosofii v SSSR (20-30gody)*.
21 Dmitrieva, "Esteticheskaia kategoriia prekrasnogo," 78.
22 Ibid.
23 Ibid., 79.
24 Nedoshivin, "Otnoshenie iskusstva k deistviternosti," 80-90.
25 Neprintsev, "Kak ia rabotal nad kartinoi Otdykh posle boia," 17-20.

26 Punin, as quoted in Tugendkhol'd, "Zhivopis' revoliutsionnogo desiatiletiia," 24.
27 Ibid., 24-25.
28 Ibid., 31.
29 Gerasimov, "Zadachi khudozhestvennogo obrazovaniia," 62.
30 Bogdanov, "The Proletarian and the Art," 177.
31 Stambok, "O nekotorykh metodologicheskikh voprosakh iskusstvoznaniia."
32 This was evident in, for example, the "Aspekte sowjetischer Kunst der Gegenwart," exhibition at the Museum Ludwig (Cologne, 1981).

4. Russian Art of the Avant-Garde[1]

(Translated Texts)

John E. Bowlt

The Paths of Proletarian Creation, 1920 — ALEKSANDR BOGDANOV

Aleksandr Bogdanov: Pseudonym of Aleksandr Aleksandrovich Malinovsky. Born Grodno Province, 1873; died Moscow, 1928. 1896: joined the Social-Democratic Party; 1899: graduated from the medical faculty of Kharkov University; 1903: joined the Bolsheviks; 1905: took an active part in the in the first Revolution; 1907: arrested and exiled to Western Europe; 1909: with Anatolii Lunacharsky organized the Bolshevik training school on Capri; 1914-1918: internationalist; 1917 on: played a major role in the organization and propagation of Proletkult; member of the Central committee of the All-Russian Proletkult and coeditor of *Proletarskaya kultura* [Proletarian Culture]; maintained close contact with Proletkult in Germany, where several of his pamphlets were published; 1929: became less active in politics and returned to medicine; 1926: appointed director of the Institute of Blood Transfusion, Moscow; 1928: died there while conducting an experiment on himself.

The text of this piece, "Puti proletarskogo tvorchestva," is from *Proletarskaya kul'tura* [Proletarian Culture] (Moscow), no. 15/16, 1920. This text demonstrates Bogdanov's ability to argue in terms both of art and of science and testifies to Proletkult's fundamental aspiration to conceive art as an industrial, organized process. The text also reveals Bogdanov's specific professional interest in neurology and psychology. He wrote several similar essays.

* * *

1. *Creation*, whether technological, socioeconomic, political, domestic, scientific, or artistic, represents a kind of labor and, like labor, is composed of organizational (or disorganizational) human endeavors. It is

exactly the same as labor, the product of which is not the repetition of a ready-made stereotype, but is something "new." There is not and cannot be a strict delineation between creation and ordinary labor; not only are there all the points of interchange, but often it is even impossible to say with certainty which of the two designations is the more applicable.

Human labor has always relied on collective experience and has made collective use of perfected means of production; in this sense human labor has always been collective; this was so even in those cases where its aims and outer, immediate form were narrowly individual (i.e., when such labor was done by one person and as an end in itself). This, then is creation.

Creation is the highest, most complex form of labor. Hence its methods derive from the methods of labor.

The old world was aware neither of this social nature germane to labor and creation, nor of their methodological connection. If dressed, up creation in mystical fetishism.

2. All methods of labor, including creation, remain within the same framework. Its first stage is the combined effort and its second the selection of results—the removal of the unsuitable and the preservation of suitable. In "physical" labor, material objects are combined; in "spiritual" labor, images are combined. But as the latest developments in psychophysiology show us, the nature of the efforts that combine and select are the same—neuromuscular.

Creation combines materials in a new way, not according to a stereotype, and this leads to a more complicated, more intensive selection. The combination and selection of images take place far more easily and quickly than those of material objects. Hence creation takes place very often in the form of "spiritual" labor—but by no means exclusively. Almost all "fortuitous" and "unnoticeable" discoveries have been made through a selection of material combinations, and not through a preliminary combination and selection of images.

3. The methods of proletarian creation are founded on the methods of proletarian labor, i.e., the type of work that is characteristic for the workers in modern heavy industry.

The characteristics of this type are: (1) the unification of elements in "physical" and "spiritual" labor; (2) the transparent, unconcealed, and unmasked collectivism of its actual form. The former depends on the scientific character of modern technology, in particular on the transference of mechanical effort to the machine: the worker is turning increasingly into a "master" of iron slaves, while his own labor is changing more and more into "spiritual" endeavor—concentration, calculation, control, and initiative; accordingly, the role of muscular tension is decreasing.

The second characteristic depends on the concentration of working force in mass collaboration and on the association between specialized types of labor within mechanical production, an association that is transferring more and more direct physical, specialist's work to machines. The objective and subjective uniformity of labor is increasing and is overcoming the divisions between workers; thanks to this uniformity the practical compatibility of labor is becoming the basis for comradely, i.e., consciously collective, relationships between them. These relationships and what they entail—mutual understanding, mutual sympathy, and an aspiration to work together—are extending beyond the confines of the factory, of the professions, and of production to the working class on a national and, subsequently, a universal scale. For the first time the collectivism of man's struggle with nature is being thought of as a conscious process.

4. In this way, methods of proletarian labor are developing toward monism and collectivism. Naturally, this tendency contains the methods of proletarian creation.

5. These aspects have already managed to express themselves clearly in the methods peculiar to those areas in which the proletariat has been most creative—in the economic and political struggle and in scientific thought. In the first two areas, this was expressed in the complete unity of structure in the organizations that the proletariat created—party, professional, and cooperative organizations: one type, one principle—comradeship, i.e., conscious collectivism; this was expressed also in the development of their programs, which in all these organizations tended toward one ideal, namely, a socialist one. In science and philosophy Marxism emerged as the embodiment of monism of method and of a consciously collectivist tendency. Subsequent development on the basis of these same methods must work out a universal organizational science, uniting monistically the whole of man's organizational experience in his social labor and struggle.

6. The proletariat's domestic creation, inasmuch as it derives from the framework of the economic and political struggle, has progressed intensely and, moreover, in the same direction. This is proved by the

development of the proletarian family from the authoritarian structure of the peasant or bourgeois family to comradely relationships and the universally established form of courtesy—"comrade." Insofar as this creation will advance consciously, it is quite obvious that its methods will be assimilated on the same principles; this will be creation by a harmonically cohesive, consciously collective way of life.

7. With regard to artistic creation, the old culture is characterized by its indeterminate and unconscious methods ("inspiration," etc.) and by the alienation of these methods from those of labor activity and other creative areas. Although the proletarian is taking only his first steps in this field, his general, distinctive tendencies can be traced clearly. Monism is expressed in his aspiration to fuse art and working life, to make art a weapon for the active and aesthetic transformation of his entire life. Collectivism, initially an elemental process and then an increasingly conscious one, is making its mark on the content of works of art and even on the artistic form through which life is perceived. Collectivism illuminates the depiction not only of human life, but also of the life of nature: nature as a field of collective labor, its interconnections and harmonies as the embryos and prototypes of organized collectivism.

8. The technical methods of the old art have developed in isolation from the methods of other spheres of life; the techniques of proletarian art must seek consciously to utilize the materials of all those methods. For example, photography, stereography, cinematography, spectral colors, phonography, etc., must find their own places as mediums within the system of artistic techniques. From the principle of methodological monism it follows that there can be no methods of practical work or science that cannot find a direct or indirect application in art, and vice versa.

9. Conscious collectivism transforms the whole meaning of the artist's work and gives it new stimuli. The old artist sees the revelation of his individuality in his work; the new artist will understand and feel that within his work and through his work he is creating a grand totality—collectivism.

For the old artist, originality is the expression of the independent value of his "I," the means of his own exaltation; for the new artist, originality denotes a profound and broad comprehension of the collective experience and is the expression of his own active participation in the creation and development of the collective's life. The old artist can aspire half-consciously toward truth in life—or deviate from it; the new artist must realize that truth, objectivity support the collective in its labor and struggle. The old artist need or need not value artistic clarity; for the new artist, this means nothing less than collective accessibility, and this contains the vital meaning of the artist's endeavor.

10. The conscious realization of collectivism will deepen the mutual understanding of people and their emotional bonds; this will enable spontaneous collectivism in creation to develop on an incomparably broader scale than hitherto, i.e., the direct collaboration of many people, even of the masses.

11. In the art of the past, as in science, there are many concealed collectivist elements. By disclosing them, the proletarian critics provide the opportunity for creatively assimilating the best works of the old culture in a new light, thereby adding immensely to their value.

12. The basic difference between the old and the new creation is that now, for the first time, creation understands itself and its role in life.

Declaration: Comrades, Organizers of Life, **1923 — LEF**

The journal *Lef* (Levyi front iskusstv—Left Front of the Arts) existed from 1923 until 1925 and then resumed as *Novyi lef* (Novyi levyi front iskusstv—New Left Front of the Arts) in 1927 and continued as such until the end of 1928. Among the founders of *Lef* were Boris Arvatov, Osip Brik, Nikolai Chuzhak, Boris Kushner, Vladimir Mayakovsky, and Sergei Tretyakov. Its editorial office was in Moscow. In 1929 the group changed its name to Ref [Revolyutsionnyi front—Revolutionary Front]. In 1930 the group disintegrated with Mayakovsky's entry into RAPP [Rossiiskaya assotsiatsiya proletarskikh pisatelei—Revolutionary Association of Proletarian Writers] and with the general change in the political and cultural atmosphere. LEF was especially active during its early years and had affiliates throughout the country including Yugolef [Yuzhnyi LEF—South LEF] in the Ukraine. As a revolutionary platform, *Lef* was particularly close to the constructivists and formalists; *Novyi lef* devoted much space to aspects of photography and cinematography, Aleksandr Rodchenko playing a leading part.

The text of this piece "Tovarischi, formovschiki zhizni!" appeared in *Lef* in 1923 in Russian, German, and English. This translation is based on the English version, pp. 7-8. This was the fourth declaration by *Lef*, the first three appearing in the first number of the journal: "Za chto boretsia LEF?" ("What Is LEF Getting Its Teeth into?"] and "Kogo predosteregaet LEF?" ["Whom Is LEF Warning?"]. However, they were concerned chiefly with literature and with history and had only limited relevance to the visual arts.

* * *

Today, the *First of May*, the workers of the world will demonstrate in their millions with song and festivity.

Five years of attainments, even increasing.

Five years of slogans renewed and realized daily.

Five years of victory.

And—

Five years of monotonous designs for celebrations.

Five years of languishing art.

So-called Stage Managers!

How much longer will you and other rats continue to gnaw at this theatrical sham?

Organize according to real life!

Plan the victorious procession of the Revolution!

So-called Poets!

When will you throw away your sickly lyrics?

Will you ever understand that to sing praises of a tempest according to newspaper information is not to sing praises about a tempest?

Give us a new Marseillaise and let the Internationale thunder the march of the victorious Revolution!

So-called Artists!

Stop making patches of color on moth-eaten canvases.

Stop decorating the easy life of the bourgeoisie.

Exercise your artistic strength to engirdle cities until you are able to take part in the whole of global construction!

Give the world new colors and outlines!

We know that the "priests of art" have neither strength nor desire to meet these tasks: they keep to the aesthetic confines of their studios.

On this day of demonstration, the First of May, when proletarians are gathered on a united front, we summon you, organizers of the world:

Break down the barriers of "beauty for beauty's sake"; break down the barriers of those nice little artistic schools!

Add your strength to the united energy of the collective!

We know that the aesthetics of the old artists, whom we have branded "rightists," revive monasticism and await the holy spirit of inspiration, but they will not respond to our call.

We summon the "leftists" the revolutionary *futurists*, who have given the streets and squares their art; the *productivists*, who have squared accounts with inspiration by relying on the inspiration of factory dynamos; the *constructivists*, who have substituted the processing of material for the mysticism of creation.

Leftists of the world!

We know few of your names, or the names of your schools, but this we do know—wherever revolution is beginning, there you are advancing.

We summon you to establish a single front of leftist art—the "Red Art International."

Comrades!

Split leftist art from rightist everywhere!

With leftist art prepare the European Revolution; in the U.S.S.R. strengthen it.

Keep in contact with your staff in Moscow (Journal LEF, 8 Nikitsky Boulevard, Moscow).

Not by accident did we choose the First of May as the day of our call.

Only in conjunction with the Workers' Revolution can we see the dawn of future art.

We, who have worked for five years in a land of revolution, know:

That only October has given us new, tremendous ideas that demand new artistic organization.

That the October Revolution, which liberated art from bourgeois enslavement, has given real freedom to art.

Down with the boundaries of countries and of studios!
Down with the monks of rightist art!
Long live the single front of the leftists!
Long live the art of the Proletarian Revolution!

Constructivism [Extracts], 1922 — ALEKSEI GAN

Born 1893; died 1942. 1918-20: attached to TEO Narkompros [Teatralnyi otdel Nar-komprosa—Theater Section of Narkompros] as head of the Section of Mass Presentations and Spectacles; end of 1920: dismissed from Narkompros by Anatolii Lunacharsky because of his extreme ideological position; close association with Inkhuk; cofounder of the First Working Group of Constructivists; early 1920s: turned to designing architectural and typographical projects, movie posters, bookplates; 1922-23 editor of the journal *Kino-fot* [Cine-Photo]; 1926-30: member of OSA [Obedinenie sovremennykh arkhitektorov—Association of Contemporary Architects] and artistic director of its journal, *Sovremennaya arkhitektura* (Contemporary Architecture); 1928: member of October group; during 1920s: wrote articles on art and architecture; died in a prison camp.

The translation is of extracts from Gan's book *Konstruktivizm* (Tver, October-December 1922). The book acted as a declaration of the industrial constructivists and marked the rapid transition from a purist conception of a constructive art to an applied, mechanical one; further, it has striking affinities with the enigmatic "Productivist" manifesto. It is logical to assume that the book's appearance was stimulated be the many debates on construction and production that occurred in Inkhuk during 1921 and in which Boris Arvatov, Osip Brik, El Lissitzky, Aleksandr Rodchenko, Varvara Stepanova, Nikolai Tarabukin, et al., took an active part, and also by the publication of the influential collection of articles *Iskusstvo v proizvodstve* [Art in Production] in the same year. Moreover, the First Working Group of Constructivists, of which Gan was a member, had been founded in 1920 (see p. 24iff). However, the book, like Gan himself, was disdained by many contemporary constructivists, and the significance of the book within the context of Russian constructivism has, perhaps, been overrated by modern observers.

In keeping with its tenets, the book's textual organization and imagery are highly "industrial": the elaborate typographical layout designed by Gan and the book's cover (designed allegedly by Gan but suggested probably by Rodchenko were intended, of course, to support the basic ideas of the text itself. Such terms as *tektonika* [tectonics], *faktura* [texture], and *konstruktsiya* [construction] were vogue words during the later avant-garde period, especially just after the Revolution, and implied rather more than their direct English translations. The concepts of texture and construction had been widely discussed as early as 1912-14, stimulating David Burliuk and Vladimir Markov, for example, to devote separate essays to the question of texture; and the concept of construction was, of course, fundamental to Markov's "The Principles of the New Art". The term "texture" was also used by futurist poets, and Aleksei Kruchenykh published a booklet entitled *Faktura slova* [Texture of the Word] in 1923. The term "tectonics" was, however, favored particularly by the constructivists and, as the so-called "Productivist" manifesto explained, "is derived from the structure of communism and the effective exploitation of industrial matter". But nonconstructivists also used the term; to Aleksandr Shevchenko, for example, a tectonic composition meant the "continual displacement and modification of tangible forms of objects until the attainment of total equilibrium on the picture's surface". To confuse matters further, Gan's own explanation of tectonics, texture, and construction was not at all clear: "Tectonics is synonymous with the organicness of thrust from the intrinsic substance... Texture is the organic state of the processed material. . . . Construction should be understood as the collective function of constructivism..." (*Konstruktivizm*). Nevertheless, despite Gan's rhetoric and obscurity, the value of his book lies in the fact that it crystallized, as it were, certain potential ideas in evidence since at least 1920 and presented them as what can be regarded as the first attempt to formulate the constructivist ideology.

* * *

From "Revolutionary Marxist Thought in Words and Podagrism in Practice"

Year in year out, like a soap bubble, Narkompros fills out and bursts after overloading its heart with the spirits of all ages and

peoples, with all systems and with all the "sinful" and "sinless" *values* (!) of the living and the dead.

And under the auspices of the quasi Marxists work the black thousands of votaries of art, and in our revolutionary age the "spiritual" culture of the past still stands firmly on the stilts of reactionary idealism.

Artistic culture—as one of the formal exponents of the "spiritual"—does not break with the values of Utopian and fanciful visions, and its fabricators do not reject **the priestly functions of formalized hysterics.**

The Communists of Narkompros in charge of art affairs are hardly distinguishable from the non-Communists outside Narkompros. They are just as fascinated by the beautiful as the latter are captivated by the divine.

Seduced by priestliness, **the transmitters and popularizers** reverently serve the past, while **promising the future by word of mouth.** This impels them toward the most reactionary, déclassé maniacal artists: of painting, sculpture, and architecture. On the one hand, they are Communists ready to fall in open battle with capitalism at the slightest attempt at restoration; on the other hand, like conservatives, they fall voluntarily, without striking a blow, and liturgically revere the art of those very cultures **that they regard so severely when mentioning the theory of historical materialism.**

Our responsible, very authoritative *leaders* are unfortunately dealing confusedly and unscrupulously with the art not only of yesterday, but also of today; and they are creating conditions in which there can be no possibility of putting the problems of intellectual-material production on the rails of practical activity in a collective and organized fashion.

And no wonder; they are of one flesh with those same putrid aesthetics against which the materialist innovators of leftist art rebelled.

That is why a campaign is being waged both in the open and in secret against the "nonideaists" and the "nonobjectivists." And the more thematic the latter, the more graphically reality supports them, the less stringently the priests of the old art carry on the struggle with them.

Now officially they are everything; they set the tone and, like clever actors, paint themselves up to resemble Marx.

It is only the proletariat with its sound Marxist materialism that does not follow them, but for all that, the vast masses do: the intellectuals, agnostics, spiritualists, mystics, empiriocrities, eclectics, and other podagrics and paralytics.

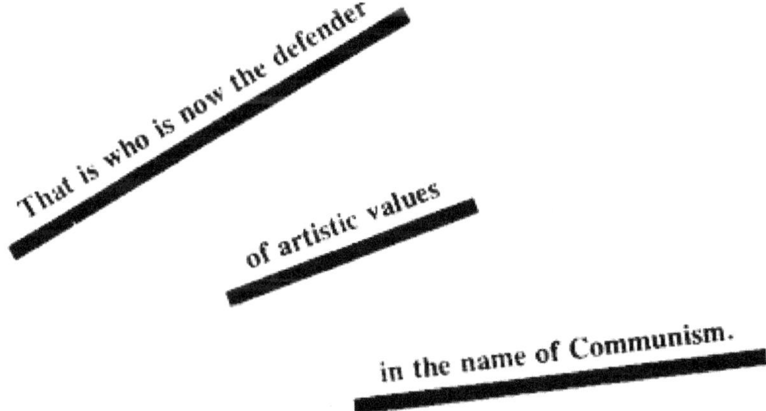

The priest-producers of these "artistic values" understand this situation and take it into account. It is they who are weaving the threads of falsehood and deception. Like the rotten heritage of the past, they continue to **parasitize and ventriloquize**, using the resources of that same proletariat that, writhing in agony, heroically, implements the slogans, **the promises of mankind's liberation from every supernatural force encroaching on his freedom.**

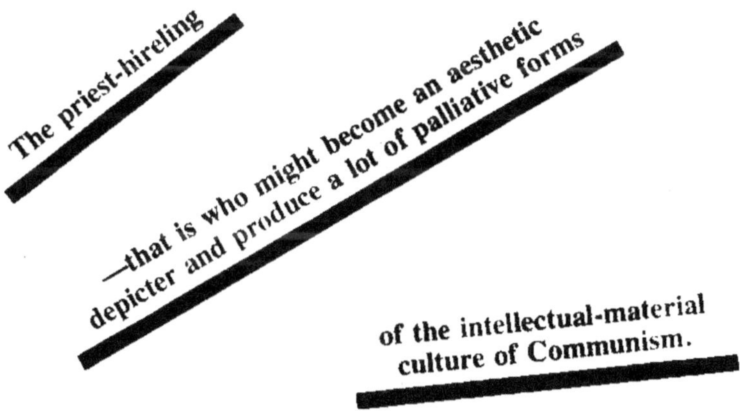

The proletariat and the proletarianized peasantry take absolutely no part in art.

The character and forms in which art was expressed and the "social" meaning that it possessed affected them in no way whatsoever.

The proletariat developed and cultivated itself independently as a class within the concrete conditions of the struggle. Its ideology was formulated precisely and clearly. It tightened the lower ranks of its class not by playacting, not by the artificial means of abstraction, not by abstruse fetishism, but by the concrete means of revolutionary action, by thematic propaganda and factual agitation.

Art did not consolidate the fighting qualities of the proletarian revolutionary class; rather it decomposed the individual members of its vanguard. On the whole it was alien and useless to a class that had its own and only its own cultural perspective.

The more vividly the artistic-reactionary wave of restoration manifests itself—the more distinctly will the sound, authentic elements of the proletariat dissociate themselves from this sphere of activity.

During the whole time of the proletarian revolution, neither the department in charge of art affairs, nor organizations, nor groups have justified their promises in practice.

From the broadcast of revolutionary calls to the future, they turned off into the reactionary bosom of the past and built their practice on the theory of "spiritual" continuity.

But practice showed that "spiritual" continuity is hostile to the tasks of a proletarian revolution by which we advance toward Communism.

THE CONTERREVOLUTIONISM OF THE BOURGEOIS VOTARIES OF ART WHO HAVE WONDERED CASUALLY FROM ART TO REVOLUTION HAS CREATED AN INCREDIBLE CONFUSION IN ITS VAIN ATTEMPT TO "REVOLUTIONIZE" THE FLABBY SPIRIT OF THE PAST BY AESTHETICS.

BUT THE SENTIMENTAL DEVOTION TO THE REVOLUTION OF THE IDEOLOGISTS OF THE PETIT-BOURGEOIS TENDANCY HAS PRODUCED A SHARP CRACK IN THE ATTEMPTS TO DECAPITATE THE

MATERIALISM OF REVOLUTIONARY REALITY BY THE OLD FORMS OF ART.

But the victory of materialism in the field of artistic labor is also on the eve of its triumph.

The proletarian revolution is not a word of flagellation but a real whip, which expels parasitism from man's practical reality in whatever guise it hides its repulsive being.

The present moment within the framework of objective conditions obliges us to declare that the current position of social development is advancing with the omen that the artistic culture of the past is unacceptable.

The fact that all so-called art is permeated with the most reactionary idealism is the product of extreme individualism; this individualism shoves it in the direction of new, unnecessary amusements with experiments in refining subjective beauty.

Art
is indissolubly linked:
with theology, metaphysics,
and mysticism.

It emerged during the epoch of primeval cultures, when technique existed in "the embryonic state of tools," and forms of economy floundered in utter primitiveness.

It passed through the forge of the guild craftsmen of the Middle Ages.

It was artificially reheated by the hypocrisy of bourgeois culture and, finally, crashed against the mechanical world of our age.

Death to art!
It arose naturally developed naturally
and disappeared naturally.

MARXISTS MUST WORK IN ORDER TO ELUCIDATE ITS DEATH SCIENTIFICALLY AND TO FORMULATE NEW PHENOMENA OF ARTISTIC LABOR WITHIN THE NEW HISTORIC ENVIRONMENT OF OUR TIME.

In the specific situation of our day, a gravitation toward the technical acme and social interpretation can be observed in the work of the masters of revolutionary art.

Constructivism is advancing—the slender child of an industrial culture.

For a long time capitalism has let it rot underground.

It has been liberated by—the Proletarian Revolution.

A new chronology begins
with October 25, 1917.

"From Speculative Activity of Art to Socially Meaningful Artistic Labor."

... When we talk about social technology, this should imply not just one kind of tool, and not a number of different tools, but a system of these tools, their sum total in the whole of society.

It is essential to picture that in this society, lathes and motors, instruments and apparatuses, simple and complex tools are scattered in various places, but in a definite order.

In some places they stand like huge sockets (e.g., in centers of large-scale industry), in other places other tools are scattered about. But at any given moment, if people are linked by the bond of labor, if we have a society, then all the tools of labor will also be interlocked: all, so to say, "technologies" of individual branches of production will form something whole, a united social technology, and not just in our minds, but objectively and concretely.

The technological system of society, the structure of its tools, creates the structure of human relationships, as well.

The economic structure of society is created from the aggregate of its productional relationships.

The sociopolitical structure of society is determined directly by its economic structure.

But in times of revolution peculiar contradictions arise.

We live in the world's first proletarian republic. The rule of the workers is realizing its objectives and is fighting not only for the retention of this rule, but also for absolute supremacy, for the assertion of new, historically necessary forms of social reality.

In the territory of labor and intellect, there is no room for speculative activity.

In the sphere of cultural construction, only that has concrete value which is indissolubly linked with the general tasks of revolutionary actuality.

Bourgeois encirclement can compel us to carry out a whole series of strategic retreats in the field of economic norms and relationships, but in no way must it distort the process of our intellectual work.

The proletarian revolution has bestirred human thought and has struck home at the holy relics and idols of bourgeois spirituality. *Not only the ecclesiastical priests have caught it in the neck, the priests of aesthetics have had it too.*

Art is finished! It has no place in the human labor apparatus.

Labor, technology, organization!

THE REVALUATION OF THE FUNCTIONS OF HUMAN ACTIVITY, THE LINKING OF EVERY EFFORT WITH THE GENERAL RANGE OF OBJECTIVES—

That is the ideology of our time.

And the more distinctly the motive forces of social reality confront our consciousness, the more saliently its sociopolitical forms take shape—the more the masters of artistic labor are confronted with the task of:

Breaking with their speculative activity (of art) and of finding the paths to concrete action by employing their knowledge and skill for the sake of true living and purposeful labor.

Intellectual-material production establishes labor interrelations and a productional link with science and technology by arising in the place of art—art, which by its very nature cannot break with religion and philosophy and which is powerless to leap from the exclusive circle of abstract, speculative activity.

From "Tectonics, Texture, Construction"

A productive series of successful and unsuccessful experiments, discoveries, and defeats followed in the wake of the leftist artists. By the second decade of the twentieth century, their innovational efforts were already known. Among these, precise analysis can establish vague, but nevertheless persistent tendencies toward the principles of industrial production: texture as a form of supply, as a form of pictorial display for visual perception, and the search for constructional laws as a form of surface resolution. Leftist painting revolved around these two principles of industrial production and persistently repulsed the old traditions of art. The suprematists, abstractionists, and "nonideaists" came nearer and nearer to the pure mastery of the artistic labor of intellectual-material production, but they did not manage to sever the umbilical cord that still held and joined them to the traditional art of the Old Believers.

Constructivism has played the role of midwife.

Apart from the material-formal principles of industrial production, i.e., of texture and of constructional laws, constructivism has given us a third principle and the first discipline, namely, tectonics.

We have already mentioned that the leftist artists, developing within the conditions of bourgeois culture, refused to serve the tastes and needs of the bourgeoisie. In this respect they were the first revolutionary nucleus in the sphere of cultural establishments and canons and violated their own sluggish well-being. Even then they had begun to approach the problems of production in the field of artistic labor. But those new social conditions had not yet arisen that would have allowed for their social interpretation and thematic expression in the products of their craft.

The Proletarian Revolution did this.

Over the four years of its triumphant advance the ideological and intellectual representatives of leftist art have been assimilating the ideology of the revolutionary proletariat. Their formal achievements have been joined by a new ally—the materialism of the working class. Laboratory work on texture and constructions—within the narrow framework of painting, sculpture, and senseless architecture unconnected with the reconstruction of the whole of the social organism—has, for them, the true specialists in artistic production, become insignificant and absurd.

AND WHILE THE PHILISTINES AND AESTHETES, TOGETHER WITH A CHOIR OF LIKE-MINDED INTELLECTUALS, DREAMED THAT THEY WOULD "HARMONICALLY DEAFEN" THE WHOLE WORLD WITH THEIR MUSICAL ART AND TUNE ITS MERCANTILE SOUL TO THE SOVIET PITCH, WOULD REVEAL WITH THEIR SYMBOLIC-

REALISTIC PICTURES OF ILLITERATE AND IGNORANT RUSSIA THE SIGNIFICANCE OF SOCIAL REVOLUTION, AND WOULD IMMEDIATELY DRAMATIZE COMMUNISM IN THEIR PROFESSIONAL THEATERS THROUGHOUT THE LAND—

The positive nucleus of the bearers of leftist art began to line up along the front of the revolution itself.

From laboratory work the constructivists have passed to practical activity.

TECTONICS

TEXTURE

and CONSTRUCTION

—these are the disciplines through whose help we can emerge from the dead end of traditional art's aestheticizing professionalism onto the path of purposeful realization of the new tasks of artistic activity in the field of the emergent Communist culture.

WITHOUT ART, BY MEANS OF INTELLECTUAL-MATERIAL PRODUCTION, THE CONSTRUCTIVIST JOINS THE PROLETARIAN ORDER FOR THE STRUGGLE WITH THE PAST, FOR THE CONQUEST OF THE FUTURE.

Abbreviations used:

AKhR (Association of Artists of the Revolution)
AKHRR (Association of Artists of Revolutionary Russia)
ASNOVA (Association of New Architects)
Inkhuk (Institute of Artistic Culture)
InternAKhR (International Association of Artists of the Revolution)
IKhK (Institute of Artistic Culture, Leningrad)
IZO Narkompros (Department of Visual Arts in the People's Commissariat for Enlightenment/Education)
FOSKh (Federation of the Association of Soviet workers in the spatial arts).
GAKhN (State Academy of Artistic Sciences)
LEF (Left Front of the Arts)
Narkompros (People's Commissariat for Enlightenment/Education)
NOZh (New Society of Painters)
Obmokhu (Society of Young Artists)
OKhRR (Society of Artists of Revolutionary Russia)

OMAKhR (Association of AKhR Youth)
Proletkult (Proletarian Culture)
RAKhN (Russian Academy of Artistic Sciences)
RAPKh (Russian Association of Proletarian Artists)
RAPP (Russian Association of Proletarian Writers)
REF (Revolutionary Front)
Svomas (Free State Art Studios)
TEO Narkompros (Department of Theatre in the People's Commissariat for Enlightenment/Education)
Tsit (Central Institute of Labour)
Vkhutemas (Higher State Art-Technical Studios)
Vkhutein (Higher State Art-Technical-Institute)

Endnotes

1 These selections were originally published in Bowlt (ed), *Russian Art of the Avant-Garde.*

IV

THE OBERIU CIRCLE
(DANIIL KHARMS AND HIS ASSOCIATES)

1. OBERIU: Daniil Kharms and Aleksandr Vvedensky on/in Time and History

Evgeny Pavlov

The literary group OBERIU is generally regarded as the last Russian avant-garde circle with whose demise the history of post-revolutionary experimentation in Russia comes to a halt.[1] A relatively recent explosion of scholarly interest in its two main figures, Aleksandr Vvedensky and Daniil Kharms (with the latter getting considerably more attention) has firmly established it among the most important experimental movements of twentieth century European literature.[2] In what follows, I would like to approach a topic that has not been particularly well-covered by OBERIU scholarship beyond some of its obvious implications for the group: history and the political in the work of Kharms and Vvedensky. Notwithstanding the fact that their most productive years coincided with the height of Stalinist terror in which they eventually perished, very little in their respective work is overtly concerned with either history or politics. Yet the obsessive thinking about time that marks the entire oeuvre of both men is not a mere exercise in abstract speculation, but inevitably represents an engagement with the political in ways that are no less radical than an open confrontation with the regime.

In his recent biography of Kharms, Aleksandr Kobrinskii cites in full Kharms's repentant "confession," forced out of him by Stalin's secret police at one of the interrogations of 1932, shortly before his conviction for anti-Soviet activities. Apart from confessing to having undermined Soviet power in his published works (especially for children), Kharms had to describe the philosophical basis of his convictions and to demonstrate their profoundly anti-Soviet and anti-Marxist tenor. The confession, in part, reads:

> The philosophy which I elaborated and sought, consciously removing myself from contemporary reality . . . is deeply hostile to contemporary life and will never be able to engage with it. . . . Immersing myself in trans-ra-

> tional work [zaumnoe tvorchestvo] and mystico-idealist philosophical quests, I consciously opposed myself to contemporary socio-political order. This forced me to look for a political order under which there would be no need for such opposition.[3]

Kobrinskii admits that although much of this was prompted by the interrogators, there is no reason to assume that there was no truth in Kharms' description on where he stands vis-à-vis the regime. His active opposition, however, was not some absurd conspiracy to restore monarchic rule or to adversely indoctrinate Soviet children (these were the charges), but rather in textual strategies that led to a very thorough deconstruction of every fundamental notion on which the regime based its legitimacy. Most of all, it was a deconstruction of the notion of time as a simple temporal progression and of the idea of history that went with it.

Much of the literary and artistic experimentation of the 1920s took place under the slogans of killing history as we know it (cf. Mayakovsky's "We'll ride the jade of history to death!"). Yet what in the first post-Revolutionary years seemed to many a utopian release from the empty time of linear history, by the early 1930s was firmly established as immutable cyclicity guaranteed by the supreme victory of absolute truth. As many recent studies point out, while the rhetoric of the revolutionary avant-garde is turned towards an open-ended future full of infinite possibilities, in Stalinist culture, the future has always already happened, and it is the past that gets constantly rewritten in order to legitimize the circular course of post-historical stability.[4] Stalin's present becomes a timeless continuum unproblematically embracing the entirety of the past and all of the future. A certain time machine is at work during the years of high Stalinism: it aims to conquer time by "petrifying the utopia" of the future and remaking history as it ought to have happened. As Evgeny Dobrenko argues, different competing strands of revolutionary culture eventually synthesized to create Socialist Realism, which in turn made them obsolete: "the attempt to 'leap out of history' proves to be history."[5] As a petrified utopia, the culture of Stalinism is no longer interested in the future because history has seen its completion in Stalinism's present moment. It is, in essence, a static and simultaneously backward-looking culture:

> Stalinism . . . does not simply 'use' history. History proves to be precisely the base of the legitimacy of Stalinism, and the adjustment of 'historical images' to fit their 'historical prototypes' becomes almost the main occupation of historicizing writing. The historicizing aspect of Stalinist art is found consequently to be the reverse side of socialist realism's lacquering practices . . .; just as the latter form the 'image' of Soviet reality, the historicizing texts (the historical novel, the biographical or historical-revolutionary film) form their 'prototype', undoubtedly fully conforming to the present of 'real socialism'.[6]

From the mid-1920s onwards, those literary avant-gardists who refused to adapt to the primitive temporality of the Stalinist age began to question and critique the very notion of history. This phenomenon was not unique to Soviet Russia; the Nazi regime sought to legitimize itself through history in a very similar fashion. As Mikhail Iampolsky comments in his fascinating study of Daniil Kharms,

> Artists, intellectuals get increasingly alienated from History (as a certain form of reality). As History becomes less and less humane (and humanistic), as the gap between history and the intelligentsia grows, the sense of history gets more and more clearly negated.[7]

Thus surviving Russian avant-gardists built literary machines of their own with which to critique and radically transform the commonly accepted notions of time and history. Kharms' and Vvedensky's machines were of the extreme variety, each in his own way questioning the very core of what constitutes our temporal perception and any philosophical and social systems we construct on its foundation.

Daniil Kharms (real name Iuvachev, 1905-1942) was the son of a revolutionary who in the 1880s belonged to a secret terrorist society planning the assassination of Alexander III, but later experienced a profound religious conversion. An exceptionally erudite and talented man, the writer's father was acquainted with many literary giants, including

Tolstoy, Chekhov, and Voloshin. In 1915, Daniil entered a German Realschule (St. Petrischule) which he was forced to abandon with the onset of the Revolution and the Civil War. He could only resume study in 1922, at another school outside Petrograd, and within two years was able to enter the Leningrad School of Electrical Engineering to which he applied under the name of Iuvachev-Kharms. The origin of the pseudonym is still debated, but a number of associations are possible—including the English words "harm" and "charm" (Kharms liked mystifications and magic), and Sherlock Holmes, whose pipe and Victorian-style jackets and hats Kharms adopted as trademarks of his artistic persona. From the early 1920s, Kharms already wrote poetry and began to perform it at various literary events. His first literary friendships began to take shape at around the same time.

Aleksandr Vvedensky (1904-1941) was born into a family of St. Petersburg professionals of noble descent. His father was an economist, his mother a well-known gynaecologist. Vvedensky attended a top private school in St. Petersburg popularly known as Lentovsky's school. It was there that he met two of his best life-long friends, Leonid Lipavsky and Iakov Druskin, who later formed the backbone of the circle Chinari out of which OBERIU emerged after Vvedensky met Kharms in 1925 and introduced him to Chinari. After graduation Vvedensky first entered the law faculty of Petrograd University and after a short time, the Chinese Department of the Oriental faculty where he wanted to study with T. A. Maier, with whom he was in love and would later marry. They both soon left the university, with Vvedensky taking up various jobs that were invariably just a means to an end, as his one and only interest in life was poetry.

Like the "petrified utopia" of Socialist Realism itself, the art of OBERIU came out of the living, trembling utopia of revolutionary culture, even though many of its principal members were schoolboys at the time of the 1917 revolution. Both Kharms and Vvedensky began their literary careers, following in the footsteps of Russian Futurists. In their 1925 application to the Leningrad Writers' Union, they clearly stated their literary orientation as "Futurist." The lineage they claimed went down to the founding fathers of the movement, Velimir Khlebnikov and Aleksei Kruchenykh. Their other major influences included, among others, futurist Igor Terent'ev, practitioner of trans-rational verse [zaum] Aleksandr Tufanov (Kharms and Vvedensky were one-time members of Tufanov's Order of *Zaumniki*) and the giants of Russian avant-garde art Kazimir Malevich and Pavel Filonov. This is not to say, of course, that either Kharms or Vvedensky, let alone other members of the group, such as Konstantin Vaginov or Nikolai Zabolotsky, had no other legacies. To various degrees and in various ways, a multitude of other early-twentieth-century literary and artistic schools and movements, from Symbolism to Acmeism, left an imprint on their work. What is important to note, however, is that at its inception, OBERIU's energies were fed by the same utopian currents that a decade before fed those of their predecessors in the revolutionary avant-garde.

The group out of which OBERIU eventually grew began as more or less just a circle of friends who from 1922 onwards met on a regular basis for conversation, readings, debate over endless cups of tea and bottles of wine. It originally comprised Aleksandr Vvedensky, philosopher Leonid Lipavsky, and philosopher and musicologist Iakov Druskin. Daniil Kharms joined the circle in 1925, after he met with Vvedensky at an evening of trans-rational poetry. The circle of friends who started calling themselves by the cryptic name Chinari which, according to Druskin, comes from the Russian word "chin" (rank), a reference to a spiritual hierarchy of sorts,[8] grew and in the same year already included two more prominent members, poets Nikolai Zabolotsky and Nikolai Oleinikov. In 1926, Kharms met Igor Bakhterev, who invited them to join his experimental theatre group Radiks. The performance group which aimed to practice "pure theatre" began to rehearse at Malevich's Institute of Artistic Culture with the latter's personal approval. Vvedensky, Kharms, and Radiks collaborated on a play made up of fragments from the two poets' work *My Mom is All Covered in Watches* (Moia mama vsia v chasakh). The project was never staged. It was after the collapse of Radiks that Kharms and Vvedensky suggested to Bakhterev and Zabolotsky that they continue working together as a group, which would shortly start calling itself OBERIU, Ob"edinenie real'nogo iskusstva (Union of Real Art). In the same year, the group was joined by the poet Konstantin Vaginov, who like Bakhterev was a graduate of the Leningrad Institute of Art History and had by then been a member of many literary and artistic circles, including Nikolai Gumilev's Second Guild of Poets, Nikolai Tikhonov's Islanders, and the intellectual circle around Mikhail Bakhtin.

The group gave a number of collective performances that included theatricalised poetry readings, sometimes accompanied by a ballerina and a magician. The most famous of these was "Three Left Hours" on 24 January 1928. The performance that actually took more like 4 or 5 hours and went into the early hours of the morning was split into three parts—poetry readings, performance of Kharms's play *Elizaveta Bam*, and a film screening; the evening concluded with a heated debate. Each poetry reading was a lively performance act. Vaginov recited his verse with ballerina Militsa Popova dancing around him; Vvedensky rode a tricycle around the stage before reading from his work, while Kharms recited while sitting on top of a cupboard. Overall, the evening was a success, even though the number of those critical of the OBERIU members in the audience was roughly equal to the number of those who liked their work.

Even better known than the actual performance that night was the OBERIU declaration with which the evening was announced. The declaration was produced mainly without Kharms and Vvedensky's participation, with the first two sections ("The Public Face of OBERIU," and "The Art and Poetry of the OBERIUts") composed by Zabolotsky and the other two by Aleksandr Razumovsky ("On the Road to a New Cinema") and Igor Bekhterev ("OBERIU Theatre"). It is in this document that the group's debt to, and difference from, their Futurist and Transrationalist colleagues is clearly stated. Not unlike their older Futurist colleagues, OBERIU members declare that they seek to unite all forms of art and to express a new feeling for life itself:

> Who are we? And why do we exist? We, the OBERIUts, are honest workers in art. We are poets of a new world view and of a new art. We are not only creators of a poetic language, but also founders of a new feeling for life and its objects. Our will to create is universal. It spans all genres of art and penetrates life, grasping it from all sides.[9]

At the same time, the very first section proceeds to defend the group from links with trans-rational poetry which by then had fallen under vicious attack by RAPP, the Russian Association of Proletarian Writers, in a prelude to what a few years later would result in the abolition of all artistic schools and movements, save for Socialist Realism. In its defence, the group declares itself to be more revolutionary and proletarian than any of its predecessors:

> We have not yet completely understood the undeniable truth that the proletariat cannot be satisfied in the area of art with the artistic method of old schools, that its artistic principles go much deeper and undermine old art at the roots. . . . We believe and know that only the left course in art will lead us to the highway to the new proletarian artistic culture.[10]

Notwithstanding the political expedience of this declaration, the authors of the manifesto sincerely believe themselves to be revolutionaries in the best possible sense of the word. The emphasis on *real* art, on the other hand, does not discard the semantic field; on the contrary, unlike *zaumniki*, OBERIU members aim to get to the "real object" by means of alogicality and collisions of meanings:

> No school is more hostile to us than *zaum*. We, people who are real and concrete to the marrow of our bones, are the first enemies of those who castrate the word and make it into a powerless and senseless mongrel. In our work, we broaden the meaning of the object and of the word, but we do not destroy it in any way. The concrete object, once its literary and everyday skin is peeled away, becomes a property of art. In poetry, the collisions of verbal meanings express that object with the exactness of mechanical technology.[11]

A point, fundamental to the work of the OBERIUts, is put forcefully here by Zabolotsky—and it certainly applies to the work of Kharms and Vvedensky even more than to his own: rather than liberating the word from meaning that the trans-rationalists, such as Tufanov proposed, the group proclaimed that the collision of meanings on which they base their poetics does not destroy the world but actually advances our knowledge of it. *Bessmyslitsa*, alogicality and senselessness is not an end in itself, but, paradoxically, a tool of cognition. This point will become even more important to the work of Kharms and Vvedensky as time goes on.

OBERIU itself only survived as a formal organisation for about two years. Vaginov and Zabolotsky both stopped collaborating with the group in 1928, the latter because of "irreconcilable aesthetic and personal differences between himself and the rest of the group."[12] In addition to these personal withdrawals, the political situation made the existence of such groups less and less possible. The group's performances began to receive denunciations in the press for excessive formalism, difficulty, and lack of apparent concern for proletarian cultural needs. From the late 1920s, the Russian Association of Proletarian writers began systematically to destroy any surviving avant-garde and "fellow-traveller" associations. The campaign began with an attack on the writers Boris Pil'nyak and Evgenii Zamyatin, then spread to the Formalists, with the critic Viktor Shklovsky renouncing his own method. Shklovsky's decision to adapt to the situation made it possible for him to stay afloat and continue getting published in this increasingly difficult environment. Those who chose to make no compromises began writing almost exclusively "for the drawer," with little hope of ever getting published. Kharms and Vvedensky chose this latter path. Most of their best writing, at least the writing that has come down to us, dates back to the years that followed the breakup of OBERIU.

The two friends' sole source of income from the late 1920s comes from children's literature: this route, along with literary translations was the only way to make a living for non-conforming writers. In fact, until Kharms', let alone Vvedensky's, return from oblivion in the last Soviet decade, they were known almost exclusively as children's writers. Kharms was the first to start writing for children after he struck up a friendship with Samuil Marshak, one of the pioneers of Soviet children's literature. Kharms and Vvedensky earned a living for several years writing for various children's magazines, primarily *Hedgehog* (Ezh) and *Siskin* (Chizh). Vvedensky's work for children, by most accounts, was simply a means to an end, while Kharms took this work seriously, often producing highly original, top-rate poetry with rhythmical repetitions and tautological rhymes. Vvedensky did not eschew the required political references in his children's work, while Kharms hardly had any at all in his. Notwithstanding this difference, when both friends got arrested in 1931, it was mostly their work for children that was used in charging them with anti-Soviet activities. The secret police had designs on the entire edifice of the Children's Publishing House; the interrogators tried to use Kharms and Vvedensky in order to obtain incriminating evidence against other children's writers, including Marshak. The two OBERIUts duly confessed their own anti-Soviet sentiments and the harmful influence of their work on children, but, unlike some other associates arrested in conjunction with the same case, said very little to incriminate others.[13] Their punishment was relatively mild (as Akhmatova famously put it, compared to the terror of the late 30s, those were still relatively "vegetarian" times, when instead of summary executions and decades in GULAGs, many were simply sent out to live in provincial towns). Kharms and Vvedensky were both sentenced to three years of internal exile, of which they only served out a few months in Kursk before they were allowed to leave and eventually return to Leningrad. The last ten years of their lives—the most miserable, horrific years, when all possible outlets for their creative work were systematically shut for them—were also the most productive. These were the years, when progressively destitute—and in Kharms' case, on the verge of starvation due to lack of income—they composed their most profound and philosophically intriguing works.

In 1933, the community of Chinari resumed their regular get-togethers at the home of Leonid Lipavsky where they held extraordinary conversations, some of which Lipavsky recorded for posterity. These transcripts tell us much about their literary work and about their aesthetic and philosophical convictions, particularly with regard to senselessness, *bessmyslitsa*, which becomes the key word in both men's poetics.

This is how Druskin describes the poetic *bessmyslitsa* of Kharms and Vvedensky in his essay "Chinari":

> Works of Vvedensky and Kharms are linked by "the star of senselessness":
>
> The star of senselessness is shining,
> It alone has no bottom,

writes Vvedensky in the epilogue to his large . . . dramatic poem "God is Perhaps All Around". I distinguish semantic senselessness which distorts rules of so-called "normal" speech from situational senselessness which follows from the alogical nature of human relationships and situations. Vvedensky has not only situational senselessness, but also semantic, while Kharms uses mostly that of the situational kind.[14]

In another essay on Chinari, "Stages of Understanding," Druskin says the following with regard to senselessness in the work of Vvedensky, whom, along with the philosopher Immanuel Kant and the composer Johann Sebastian Bach, he considered the greatest genius of humankind:[15]

> Vvedensky's star of nonsense always deepens, but its forms get clearer. Vvedensky's works in time become more profound and complicated—it is the star of senselessness that gets more profound, but at the same time it becomes clearer, the style and character of his work becomes so crisp and transparent that the absurd, the alogicality, and nonsense I feel as my, precisely my alogical, absurd existence; I already don't see the alogicality. On the contrary, the logicality, as Vvedensky demonstrates to me, is something absolutely alien to me, something external; the logicality itself, the very logic of Aristotle begins to appear to me the greatest absurdity. Vvedensky once said, 'I don't understand why my works are called transrational [zaumnye]. In my view, a newspaper editorial is zaumnaia.' It doesn't mean that senselessness and the absurd are relative. Senselessness is the absolute reality. It is Logos become flesh. The personal Logos itself is alogical, same as His embodiment. Absurd, nonsense is the absolute reality and same as the Good News isn't of this world. Vvedensky's works aren't of this world. Divine madness that put to shame human wisdom. But we all fell in Adam, we are all still reasonable, only in exceptional cases can we break through our reason—commune with Divine madness.[16]

Words thus do not mirror reality, and logic does not understand it. Language creates limits within which we are trapped. Death by contrast transcends limitation and is beyond language. For Vvedensky, alogicality and faith are our only hope, while true communication is only possible through a critique of language from within language, through what comes across as fragmentation and incoherence. By Vvedensky's own account, there were only three things in which he was interested: time, death, and God.[17] According to him, it is only at the moment of death that a true miracle can happen, and one could truly begin to understand time. But the least one can do until that moment is question all the logical connections that we as verbal beings take for granted. Consider his well-known pronouncement from Lipavsky's *Conversations*:

> Could one respond to this [the problem of time] with art? Alas, art is subjective. Poetry produces only a verbal miracle, not a real one. Besides, we don't know how to reconstruct the world. I infringed upon concepts, primary generalizations, which no one has done before me. By doing so I conducted a kind of poetic critique of reason—a more substantial one than that other, abstract critique. For example, I put in doubt that "house", "dacha", and "tower" must be connected and joined together by the concept "building". Maybe "shoulder" must be connected to "four". I did it in practice, in poetry, and thus proved it. And I saw for myself the falseness of previous connections, but I can't tell you what new ones should be. I don't even know whether there should be one system of connections or whether there are many of them. And I've got a general sense that the world is disjointed and time is fragmented. And since this contradicts reason, then reason doesn't understand the world. [18]

This passage sums up Vvedensky's poetics as practical critique of reason which certainly goes against the grain of the *Critique of Pure Reason*, the cornerstone of Immanuel Kant's critical philosophy which explains the mechanism of human rationality and circumscribes its limits. According to Kant, time is not a thing in and of itself. And yet, being the form of all forms, time also determines the reality of our appearance to ourselves; consequently, the subject inheres in time only to the same extent that time inheres in the subject. Vvedensky explores this thesis much more "thoroughly" in his poetry. As we read in his *Gray Notebook*, "Time is the only thing that doesn't exist outside us. It consumes all that exists outside us. Here the night of reason sets in. Time rises above us like a star."[19] That star is of course the star of senselessness.

To understand time is to step outside of it, which is impossible without dying—this is where we indeed enter the night of reason. If we want to move along in that darkness, only the star of non-sense can guide us because the question of death is particularly apt to disrupt all the conventional rules of thought, speech, and life. Vvedensky's art is after a verbal miracle that would allow him to live and die at the same time. To achieve this, one must shut down the faculty of understanding, which according to Kant dominates all other faculties through the synthesis of the imagination, and even reason submits to the role understanding assigns to it. In order to defeat understanding, imagination must stop its work of synthesis and instead do the work of fragmentation. How? For a start, one could try to stop schematizing time in terms of mathematical progression, in terms of the ticking clock and the linguistic attributes that go with it.

> If we were to erase the numbers from a clock, if we were to forget its false names, maybe then time would want to show its quiet torso, to appear to us in its full glory. Let the mouse run over the stone. Count only its every step. Only forget the word every, only forget the word step. Then each step will seem a new movement. Then, since your ability to perceive a series of movements as something whole has rightfully disappeared, that which you wrongly called a step (you had confused movement and time with space, you falsely transposed one over the other), that movement will begin to break apart, it will approach zero. The shimmering will begin. The mouse will start to shimmer. Look around you: the world is shimmering (like a mouse).[20]

Such a non-understanding of time would cancel not only the most basic connections of logic, but also of memory. The world and all its objects as we perceive them are consumed by time: "In actual fact, objects are a faint mirror image of time. There are no objects. Go on, get them."[21] What we can do instead is try some poison and see whether we could rid ourselves of our constant companion, the chain of time. Here is what we learn from Svidersky's story told in the *Gray Notebook*:

Once upon a time I walked poisoned down a road
And time walked in step by my side. . . .
I thought about why only verbs are
subjugated to the hour, minute, and year,
while house, forest and sky, like the Mongols
have suddenly been released from time.
I thought about it and I understood. We all know it,
that action became an insomniac China,
that actions are dead, they stretch out like dead men,
and now we decorate them with garlands.
Their mobility is a lie, their density a swindle,
and a dead fog devours them. . . .
I stopped. Here I thought,
my mind could not grasp the onslaught of new tribulations.
And I saw a house, like winter, diving.
And I saw a swallow signifying a garden
where the shadows of trees like branches make sound,
where the branches of trees are like shadows of the mind.
I heard music's monotonous gait,
I tried to catch the verbal boat.
I tested the word in cold and fire,
but the hours drew in tighter and tighter.
And the poison reigning inside me
reigned like an empty dream
Once upon a time.[22]

This scenario is more complex than the relatively simple mouse experiment. Here we deal with a narrative in which time is not merely the theme but also a force at work: of necessity, the story involves a temporal progression. "Walked," "thought," "understood"—all these are verbs that are points in a simple sequence of events. If, as Kant postulates, time is the immutable form of all that moves and changes, then one could try to dissociate it from movement and movement from its linguistic signifiers, verbs. Svidersky makes corpses of verbs denoting logical, sequential actions and stops his own movement only to unleash an attack of alogical actions, or "new tribulations," also of course sequential, that his mind can no longer grasp in their totality because his imagination has hit the limit of what it can synthesize. Once rules of logic and conventional signification have been declared dead, nothing stops the imagination from striving for a bad infinity of random connections between sign and referent. It cannot grasp the totality of it and falters, leaving us with a negative presentation of the effort. Unable to comprehend the bad infinity of alogical and useless actions his imagination now proliferates, he is left with mere verbal building blocks that time deprives of any referential meaning. The word "odnazhdy" [once upon a time] at the end of Svidersky's monologue is more than just a repetition of the "odnazhdy" at the beginning. It is the very word he has been testing "in cold and fire" only to see it snap under the pressure of "tightening hours." Now it is presented, exhibited as an empty shell that means everything and nothing. It can be interpreted as the point in the temporal series when time momentarily halts; in conjunction with the imperfective "vlastvoval" [reigned] it also indicates the open stretch of time in which the story ends. Finally, it can be taken to mean the very poison that reigns inside the speaker—or it could be the empty dream to which the poison is likened.

Chinari had another word to describe this kind of linguistic unit: hieroglyph. The hieroglyph, in its simplest sense, is a sign that contains several meanings, some of them mutually contradictory. By definition it is alogical. It seeks to make the individual sign itself an allegory whose signified is always elsewhere. For Vvedensky and for other Chinari such a sign is of supreme value because it is much closer to what this world is all about than what our rational understanding of it is able to deliver.

An example of Kharms's hieroglyph can be found in the following fragment from 1935.

> An interesting thing happened to me: I suddenly forgot what comes first—7 or 8.
>
> I went to the neighbours and asked them what they thought about it.
>
> How surprised we all were when they too discovered that they couldn't remember the order of numbers. They remembered 1, 2, 3, 4, 5 and 6, but forgot what comes next.
>
> We all went to the commercial shop "Gastronome" which is at the corner of Znamenskaya and Basseynaya and asked the cashier about our predicament. She smiled

> sadly, took a small hammer out of her mouth, moved her nose a bit and said,
>
> "I think seven comes after eight when eight comes after seven."
>
> We thanked the cashier and ran out of the shop feeling very happy. But then, thinking about her words, we again became sad as her words seemed to us completely lacking in meaning.
>
> What were we to do? We went to the Summer Garden and started counting trees there. But when we got to 6, we stopped and started arguing: some thought that 7 came next, while others thought 8.
>
> We would have argued a long time, but then fortunately some child fell off a bench and broke both his jaws. This distracted us from our argument.
>
> And then we went home.[23]

While in the case of Vvedensky's "odnazhdy," the "hieroglyph" is indeed semantic, the little hammer that comes out of the cashier's mouth in Kharms' story is situational. It is the only element that stands out in the narrative which, despite its absurdity, is otherwise situationally logical. Little hammers in mouths recur in Kharms' texts; these material signifiers usually take the place of words, signifying an aporia, an absence of language and memory.[24] The characters' amnesia that makes it impossible for them to synthesize one of the most basic abstractions, a simple numerical series, is a central motif of Kharms' works. Although formally quite different from Vvedensky's texts, they address the very same idea—the artificiality of our abstract ordering that, among other things, cuts up time into measurable units, thus obscuring our understanding of it.

Ultimately, Kharms' and Vvedensky's preoccupations in the 1930s demonstrate an emphatic departure from the earlier revolutionary avant-garde whose utopian dreams linked their art with a radical transformation of social reality. Everything Kharms and Vvedensky wrote at least since the creation of OBERIU implicitly critiques the notion of history as such. As Mikhail Iampolsky observes with regard to Kharms, the type of literature with which the latter experiments could be called "ideal" as it is constructed from an ontology of the extra-temporal, literary-abstract world that emerges as a result of the historical world's decay.[25] What defines Stalinist ideology and world view (including its understanding of time and history) is a reliance on single, stable meanings. The Stalinist delusion of having mastered time is an integral part of the same phenomenon. The "petrified utopia" of high Stalinism does not allow for any unknowns: it conceives of itself as eminently readable and stable, with no future developments able to change its immutable forms. In Iampolsky's terms, "attempts to order reality . . . have a paradoxical effect on it. Reality gets infused with abstraction and disappears."[26] Each in his own way, Kharms and Vvedensky confront Stalinism by killing the idea of a transparent, fully readable world.

Their tragic end, if anything, exemplifies the utter, horrific meaninglessness of the historical reality constructed by the totalitarian time machine which, by the mid-1930s, had come into its own with the advent of the Great Terror. Started as a campaign of repressions against saboteurs, later extended to Party dissenters accused of collaborating with foreign intelligence, then "wealthy" peasants (kulaks) who were unwilling to join collective farms, and soon to anyone at all who fell under the comprehensive brand of "enemies of the people." This was one of the twentieth-century's most tragic and surreal periods. It claimed the lives of millions, many of them shot without a trial, others executed after phantasmagorical court procedures in which they were found guilty on the basis of "confessions" obtained under torture and psychological pressure; countless others perished of inhuman treatment and slave labour in GULAGs scattered all across the vast expanse of the USSR. The Russian intelligentsia was forever transformed by these Purges. The period of Terror dealt a final blow to the remnants of pre-Revolutionary and early Revolutionary culture, breaking and destroying just about everyone who refused to play by the new rules (and even those who adapted to the rules were never immune). Osip Mandelstam, Boris Pilnyak, Isaak Babel, and Vsevolod Meyerkhold were just some of the cultural giants of the Silver Age and the 1920s who perished at the hands of Stalin's henchmen.

Following several years of living below the poverty line, and in Kharms' case, on the verge of starvation and madness, both Kharms and Vvedensky were arrested after Hitler's attack on the USSR in 1941. Although Kharms convincingly feigned schizophrenia and was found mentally incompetent, he was still deemed a threat to society and was committed to a Leningrad prison hospital where he soon died, most probably of starvation, during the worst period of the city's siege in 1942. Vvedensky perished a few months earlier, while being transported with other prisoners from the city of Kharkov where he had lived his last few years.

The survival of the OBERIU manuscripts is entirely due to the heroic effort of Iakov Druskin who rescued them from Kharms' apartment building, damaged in a Nazi bombing raid. Barely alive from hunger, he dragged the suitcase with precious papers halfway across the city on a sleigh in the dead of the Leningrad winter at the height of the siege. It is nothing short of a miracle that even the incomplete (and in Vvedensky's case, very incomplete) legacy of OBERIU has survived, but it is even more of a miracle that works of such originality, philosophical sophistication, and political courage were written during one of history's darkest moments.

Endnotes

1 An acronym for *Ob"edinenie Real'nogo Iskusstva*, Association of Real Art, the name describes a loose association of Leningrad writers founded by Daniil Kharms, Aleksandr Vvedensky, Nikolai Zabolotsky, Igor Bekhterev, and Konstantin Vaginov which lasted from 1927 to 1930.

2 For a thorough critical assessment of the movement in the context of the European avant-garde see Jakovljevic, *Daniil Kharms: Writing and the Event*.

3 Cited in Kobrinskii. *Daniil Kharms*, 215. Unless otherwise noted, all translations are mine.

4 See Dobrenko, *Stalinist Cinema and the Production of History: Museum of the Revolution*.

5 Ibid., 1.

6 Ibid., 19.

7 Iampolskii, *Bespamiatstvo kak istok*, 372.

8 Druskin, "Chinari," 103.

9 Gibian, *The Man in the Black Coat: Russian Literature of the Absurd*, 290.

10 Ibid.

11 Ibid., 237.

12 See Bakhterev, "Kogda my byli molodymi," 98-99.

13 See Kobrinskii, *Daniil Kharms*, 204-05.

14 Druskin, "Chinari," 105.

15 See Druskin, *Dnevniki*, 433-34.

16 Druskin, "Stadii ponimaniia," 644.

17 See Druskin, "Materialy k poetike Vvedenskogo," 167.

18 Lipavsky, "Razgovory," 186.

19 Vvedensky, *Polnoe sobranie proizvedenii v dvukh tomakh,* vol. 2, 78.
20 Vvedensky, *The Gray Notebook*, 11.
21 Vvedensky, *Polnoe sobranie proizvedenii v dvukh tomakh,* vol. 2, 80.
22 Vvedensky, *The Gray Notebook*, 9, translation modified.
23 Kharms. *Polet v nebesa*, 357.
24 For an interesting discussion of this, see Jakovljevic, *Daniil Kharms: Writing and the Event*, 36.
25 Iampolsky, *Bespamiatstvo kak istok,* 371.
26 Ibid.

2. Some Philosophical Positions in Some "OBERIU" Texts (Translator's preface)

Eugene Ostashevsky

Many of these translations come from a volume called *OBERIU: An Anthology of Russian Absurdism,* published a few years ago under my editorship.[1] The title I picked is inaccurate, since of the six figures represented in the collection, only three had been members of OBERIU, Russia's last and very short-lived avant-garde group (1927-1930). Even for these three—the poets Alexander Vvedensky, Daniil Kharms and Nikolai Zabolotsky—almost every text I included dates to a time after OBERIU folded, for the very simple reason that what they were writing in the 1930s, as part of their conversations with the poet Nikolai Oleinikov and the philosophers Leonid Lipavsky and Yakov Druskin, greatly surpasses the OBERIU-era material in depth and resonance. As for the term "absurdism" on the cover, the less said of it the better. It encourages undergraduates to speculate about the Absurd with a capital A, a Cold War concept whose fogginess allows for heroic overtones so dear to budding masculinities, and absolves them from trying to make sense of the texts. Why then did I pick such a misleading title? Because I wanted the manuscript to be published, reviewed, and read. "OBERIU" and "absurdism" at least had *some* precedent in English academic usage, and there was nothing much better available in Russian. Some Russian scholars have of late employed the term *chinari,* which may be preferable since it includes Lipavsky, Druskin and Oleinikov as well as Vvedensky and Kharms (and, I would argue, some of Zabolotsky)—but unfortunately these writers referred to themselves as *chinari* only in the 1920s, before the formation of OBERIU, while in the 1930s, when their collaboration was at its peak, they used no name at all. On the level of personal safety, given the authorities' passion for ferreting out conspiracies, being a member of an unsanctioned literary-philosophical association was simply a bad idea, and a name would make the existence of an association indisputable. On the philosophical level, the members of this nameless association no longer believed that words stand for the things they appear to stand for.

Vvedensky wrote a piece conventionally titled "Rug-Hydrangea" in late 1933 or early 1934. His reciting it to his friends is recorded in both the "Conversations" of Leonid Lipavsky and in Kharms' diaries. According to the "Conversations," Lipavsky remarked after the reading:

> Astonishing, how the exactly and correctly posed questions of your poem at the same time remain art. It's as gorgeous as light refraction. In your other pieces it sometime happens that indifference rules them to such an extent that they almost cease being art. But here there's an especial nobility or elegance. The piece is an elegy. In the beginning a facet of it recalls some of Khlebnikov's pieces, like "Animals, when they love..." But Khlebnikov would never have been able to say it so simply: "And then there's this grudge that I bear, / that I'm not a rug, nor a hydrangea."

Since grammatically "Rug-Hydrangea" has almost no questions, Lipavsky sees the questions posed by the work as existential ones. "What is it like to be temporal?" asks "Rug-Hydrangea." "What is it like to be temporary? What is it like to be alone among others?" Here is Vvedensky's response:

> This poem, unlike the others, I wrote over a long time, three days, weighing each word. Everything in it is meaningful for me, so one could even write a little treatise about it. It started when that thing about the eagle came into my head, that's what I wrote at your place the last time, do you remember? Then another variant appeared. I thought, why is always only one chosen, and included both. Writing about the hydrangea felt embarrassing; I even crossed it out initially. I wanted to end with the question: why am I not a seed. There are a lot of repetitions here, but I think they're all necessary, if you look at them closely, they repeat in another way, they explain. And the "candle that is grass" and the "grass that is candle," all of that is personally significant for me.[2]

Not only is the inclusion of both variants of the eagle lines a formally interesting device, reminiscent of folk ballads, but it also suggests that the discovery of contradiction in description of life does not invalidate the description, as it does logical or mathematical arguments. Elsewhere in the "Conversations" Vvedensky opines that "noncoincidence with our logical framework [is] present in life itself." His poem performs, on the level of composition, a philosophical position he shares with friends. Yakov Druskin, the only member of the group to survive to old age, wrote in his 1970s study of Vvedensky, *The Star of Meaninglessness* [or senselessness: *bessmyslitsa*], of the extent to which the poem realized the ideas of not just the poet but the whole group:

> Let us take... one of Vvedensky's poems: "Rug-Hydrangea" ("I regret that I am not a beast..."). There are some instances of meaninglessness here, occasionally ones you can make sense of. But this poem also forms an exception in Vvedensky's oeuvre: it is the most lyrical, in some way the most personal of all his pieces. And it is written almost without rhyme, in free verse, which Vvedensky never employs. Vvedensky called "Rug-Hydrangea" a philosophical treatise. This fact does not contradict its lyricism: "Rug-Hydrangea" is a lyrical philosophical treatise. But why philosophical? Vvedensky here is interested in what we were all interested in, in what Lipavsky and I called neighboring existences, neighboring worlds. "Rug-Hydrangea" intersects with Lipavsky's meditations on neighboring worlds (I simply call them L-worlds) and with my "Messengers." Perhaps this is why Vvedensky told me: "'Rug-Hydrangea' is a philosophical treatise, you should have written it." This does not mean that I could have written it. This means that "Rug-Hydrangea" has themes I touched on as well. In that sense, Lipavsky could have written it. And also Kharms, and Oleinikov.[3]

The second Vvedensky piece in this book, called "The Witness and the Rat," does not appear in my anthology.[4] The fact that it is both/neither poem and/nor play is only one of its many indeterminacies, with another being the utter randomness of the title (neither witnesses nor rats appear in the text). Its violations of the rules of logic, temporality, and narrative—and in general of the canons of realist literature—are so flagrant as to affect the self-identity of characters, whose names change for no apparent cause. At the same time, "The Witness and the Rat" displays rare lyricism in its treatment of incommunicability and solitude. The word I translated as "co-ed" stands for student of a women's college; it lacks an English equivalent. I chose "co-ed" because it sounds as archaic now as the Russian term did when the poem was written, over a decade after separate women's colleges had been abolished.

As far as "Frother" is concerned, Vvedensky composed it in 1936-1937 in Kharkiv, where he moved to be with his new wife. It is not a response to the death of Vvedensky's father, who passed away in 1939; but it may respond to Druskin's depiction of the death of his own father in 1934 (I included a translation in my *OBERIU* anthology). The Russian title of Vvedensky's poem-play-prose is *Potetz,* a portmanteau neologism combining the word *pot,* sweat, and *otetz,* father. Since the word "sweater" kept sabotaging attempts to render it literally, we opted for "frother," although this entailed the dubious substitution of "froth" for "sweat." Vvedensky's neologism sounds like *zaum'* but he treats it in a strikingly non-Futurist, philosophically significant manner. The piece is a meditation on semantics in the broad sense, as the relationships among linguistic forms, meanings and things. Its conceit is that the sons keep demanding from their dying father the meaning of the made-up and seemingly meaningless word "potetz." Their question is tantamount to asking "what is death?" but with the proviso that the "death" be understood not as a universal concept or fact, but a particular dying, my dying, dying as seen from the inside by the dying subject. The question thus becomes that of the relationship of private experience to public language: How can I convey what I am experiencing to somebody who has never experienced the same thing? Or, even more generally, since none of us ever experience quite the same thing as anyone else: How is it possible for me to be understood by anyone, anywhere? Such is Vvedensky's take on Lipavsky's concept of "neighboring worlds." The picture of the self as a particular temporally and linguistically bounded world in interaction with other "neighboring worlds" recalls Wittgenstein at the end of the *Tractatus Logico-Philosophicus*—for example, when he maintains that "The limits of my language mean the limits of my world" and "At death the world does not alter, but comes to an end" (5.6, 6.431)—although no one in the group had heard of Wittgenstein. Here is what Druskin wrote about "Frother":

> "Frother" is among his most perfect pieces; Lipavsky considered it the best thing Vvedensky ever wrote. Here the star of meaninglessness is given full reign. Perhaps nowhere else does Vvedensky achieve such a perfect and clear—both semantically or morphologically, and architectonically—construction of the star of meaninglessness; nowhere else does he reach such rigorously logical alogicality and completely uninterpretable meaninglessness... Many of Vvedensky's pieces could be called mystery plays. They are not imitations, not stylizations, but rather modern mystery plays, abstract drama, abstract theater that Vvedensky created twenty-thirty years prior to Beckett and Ionesco. Admittedly, in some few pieces Vvedensky is inspired by or parodies Russian seventeenth-century folk drama... But for the most part his mystery plays are altogether original, independent and modern. And perhaps this applies to "Frother" most of all. "Frother" is a mystery pantomime with short monologues and dialogues by the characters. I already said that Vvedensky's pieces are polyphonic. I'll add that they are also musical. Vvedensky himself thought his work could be set to music. Music could be written for "Frother": then it would be a pantomime ballet with a reader and singers.

Since Daniil Kharms is much better known to the English-language reader than Vvedensky, I will content myself with just a few comments; the excellent introduction by Matvei Yankelevich in his *Today I Wrote Nothing: The Selected Writings of Daniil Kharms* (New York: Overlook, 2007) should be consulted for further help. The selections here may be divided according to genre, with the poems operating with abstract philosophical concepts, while the more or less "realistic" stories show formal and conceptual similarity to the famous texts in the cycle "Sluchai," a word that has been translated as "events," "incidents," "accidents," and even "cases." (Three texts from "Sluchai" have been included for comparison.)[5]

First, the prose. Kharms' prose dates almost entirely from the thirties, marking his new aesthetic orientation towards what he saw as classical forms and away from the open alogism of Vvedensky's "meaninglessness." The unusual aspect of Kharms' classical forms, however, is that they overlay a distinctly anti-causal, alogical worldview. In other words, the rationalism of these stories is, basically, window-dressing: a close reading of them may show each event happening autonomously of those that precede or follow it. Kharms simply does not believe in sequences, and his view of causation resembles that of Hume, except it can also be read religiously: the fact that events (and therefore actions) are monadic constitutes an extreme affirmation of free will, as well as making each event, in the parlance of Kharms and Druskin, a "miracle," i.e. a violation of the sequence dictated by natural law.

Second, the poetry. The world "cisfinite" in "To Ring—To Fly" means something located *this* side of finitude, as opposed to *that* side of finitude, the latter represented by the transfinite numbers of Georg Cantor. The state of Cisfinitum for Kharms entails a breakdown of logic and of any other type of contingency; if you get sufficiently close to something, it ceases to be a whole, and the laws which seem from far away to govern its behavior no longer apply (he also describes this state as the "fifth meaning" of the object). To cite a parallel that Kharms was very dimly aware of: the laws of physics on the quantum scale differ greatly from the "standard-scale" laws of classical or relativity physics. Yet, in contrast to quantum behavior which can, for its seeming alogism, be mathematically expressed, Kharms, who believes that at extremely close range "standard-scale" relations among things dissolve, employs Cisfinitum as the location of free will and subjectivity. I am free because I am the degree zero of the constraints that exist with respect to me. It is in playful representation of cisfinite freedom that, for example, the laws of neither gravity nor grammar quite work in "To Ring—to Fly." (Kharms's agrammatical use of the infinite in this poem thus possesses philosophical meaning that such use of the infinitive lacks in Italian Futurism.)[6] In another poem, "Notnow," Kharms reinserts the free subject into seemingly objective logical operations by making all differences stem from the gesture distinguishing "this" from "that."

"This" and "that," as traces of subjective distinction that provides the pre-rational foundation of any rationality, also appear as key terms in the philosophical writings of Yakov Druskin.

The Texts

Alexander Vvedensky

Rug-Hydrangea

I regret that I'm not a beast,
running along a blue path,
telling myself to believe,
and my other self to wait a little,
I'll go out with myself to the forest
to examine the insignificant leaves.
I regret that I'm not a star,
running along the vaults of the sky,
in search of the perfect nest
it finds itself and earth's empty water,
no one has ever heard of a star giving out a squeak,
its purpose is to encourage the fish with its silence.
And then there's this grudge that I bear,
that I'm not a rug, nor a hydrangea.
I regret I'm not a roof,
falling apart little by little,
which the rain soaks and softens,
whose death is not sudden.
I don't like the fact that I'm mortal,
I regret that I am not perfect.
Much much better, believe me,
is a particle of day a unit of night.
I regret that I'm not an eagle,

flying over peak after peak,
to whom comes to mind
a man observing the acres.
I regret I am not an eagle,
flying over lengthy peaks,
to whom comes to mind
a man observing the acres.
You and I, wind, will sit down together
on this pebble of death.
It's a pity I'm not a grail,
I don't like that I am not pity.
I regret not being a grove,
which arms itself with leaves.
I find it hard to be with minutes,
they have completely confused me.
It really upsets me terribly
that I can be seen in reality.
And then there's this grudge that I bear,
that I'm not a rug, nor a hydrangea.
What scares me is that I move
not the way that do bugs that are beetles,
or butterflies and baby strollers
and not the way that do bugs that are spiders.
What scares me is that I move
very unlike a worm,
a worm burrows holes in the earth
making small talk with her.
Earth, where are things with you,
says the cold worm to the earth,
and the earth, governing those that have passed,
perhaps keeps silent in reply,
it knows that it's all wrong.
I find it hard to be with minutes,
they have completely confused me.
I'm frightened that I'm not the grass that is grass,
I'm frightened that I'm not a candle.
I'm frightened that I'm not the candle that is grass,
to this I have answered,

and the trees sway back and forth in an instant.
I'm frightened by the fact that when my glance
falls upon two of the same thing
I don't notice that they are different,
that each lives only once.
I'm frightened by the fact that when my glance
falls upon two of the same thing
I don't see how hard they are trying
to resemble each other.
I see the world askew
and hear the whispers of muffled lyres,
and having by their tips the letters grasped
I lift up the word wardrobe,
and now I put it in its place,
it is the thick dough of substance.
I don't like the fact that I'm mortal,
I regret that I am not perfect,
much much better, believe me,
is a particle of day a unit of night.
And then there's this grudge that I bear
that I'm not a rug, nor a hydrangea.
I'll go out with myself to the woods
for the examination of insignificant leaves,
I regret that upon these leaves
I will not see the imperceptible words,
which are called accident, which are called immortality,
which are called a kind of roots.
I regret that I'm not an eagle
flying over peak after peak,
to whom came to mind
a man observing the acres.
I'm frightened by the fact that everything becomes dilapidated,
and in comparison I'm not a rarity.
You and I, wind, will sit down together
on this pebble of death.
Like a candle the grass grows up all around,
and the trees sway back and forth in an instant.
I regret that I am not a seed,

I am frightened I'm not fertility.
The worm crawls along behind us all,
he carries monotony with him.
I'm scared to be an uncertainty,
I regret that I am not fire.

1934
Translated by Matvei Yankelevich

The Witness and the Rat

HE
Margarita open
the window for me quick.
Margarita speak
of fish and of beasts.
The shadow of the night descended,
light went out in the world.
Margarita the day is done,
the wind blows, the rooster sleeps.
Sleeps the eagle in the skies,
sleep the legumes in the woods,
the future coffins sleep,
the pine-trees, the firs, the oaks.
The warrior walks out towards disgrace,
the beaver walks out to rob and pillage,
and peering at tall stars
the hedgehog starts the count of nights.
Fish run up and down the river,
fish loiter in the seas,
and the starling softly holds
the dead temple in its hand.
And the blackbirds slightly sing
and the mournful lion roars.
God chases from afar
clouds onto our city

and the mournful lion roars.

HE
We don't believe that we're asleep.
We don't believe that we are here.
We don't believe that we are sad.
We don't believe that we exist.

HE
The cold illuminates the mountains,
the snowy pall of the great mountains,
and the horse beneath carpets
dives in the snow like a loon.
A co-ed rides on the carpets,
she is obscured by the moon.
A she-wolf glares at the horse,
saliva leaves her maw like drool.
The poor horseman, lazybones,
rides in the troika like a lackey,
enters a dark palisade
clutching a bone in his fist.
He hands his whip to the co-ed,
he hands his cane to the old lady.
Greeting each hour with a toast,
he caresses the bold bone.
And the co-ed stands all dusty
like a carriage.
She does not move her visage
from the unknown portrait. She glints.

HE
I was examining my thoughts.
I saw they had other forms.
I was measuring my emotions.
I found their close borders.
I was testing my body movements.
I determined their simple significance.
I was losing my benevolence.

I have no more concentration.
Those who guess will guess.
I have nothing left to guess.

HE
I will speak now.

As he speaks, a small room appears. Everything is cut apart into pieces. Where are you our world. You do not exist. And we do not exist. Upon the plates sit Petr Ivanovich Ivanovich Ivanovich, the co-ed, Grudetsky the steward, Stepanov-Peskov and four hundred thirty three Spaniards.

Enter Lisa or Margarita.

ONE OR THE OTHER
What do I see.
What is this, an infernal conclave.
It smells of fire and brimstone here.
Your necks are as if it were gunpowdery,
ears arms legs noses
and eyes. You're all so cataleptic.
For hours already it's been winter,
has murder happened here by any chance.

GRUDETSKY THE STEWARD
Margarita or Lisa
would you like some tea or a clock.

SHE (ONE OR THE OTHER)
You're a brownnose, Grudetsky.
From the days of Czar on
you're Simon.
I ask you: has a murder taken place.

And after this music sounded for three hours.
Various waltzes and chorales.
In the meanwhile Kirillov managed to get married. But still he just wasn't content.

STEPANOV-PESKOV
Murder. Don't speak so much of murder.
We still have not understood murder.
We still have not understood this word.
We still have not understood this deed.
We still have not understood this knife.

KOSTOMAROV, HISTORIAN
Thirteen years.
Twelve years.
Fifteen years.
Sixteen years.
Everything around us is shrubbery.

GRIBOEDOV, WRITER
What's there to talk about here,
he is a thief, that's clear.
Steep magic visions
visit my soul.
They promise me
unspoken sickly pleasures.
My head is spinning and I feel
as if I were a hamster in a wheel.
O otherworldly creatures get you hence,
I'm off to Georgia today like everyone else.

Four hundred thirty three SPANIARDS, *pale and seated upon a plate, cried out inimicably and unanimously:*

Let the murder begin.

And there the darkness of darkness happened. And Grudetsky murdered Stepanov-Peskov. But what's there to speak of, anyway.

They all ran into the civilian room and saw the following picture. Across the third table stood the following picture. Imagine a table and the following picture upon it.

Staring at the picture,
Grudetsky grasped
in his hand like a picture
the bloody cutlass.
Blood dripped in drops
and fell flat on the earth,
the earth revolved
and the planets rotated.
Stepanov-Peskov
lay flat on the floor
resembling an eagle
without socks or boots.
He lay barefoot
like wild rose confectionery.
This functionary
was stung by a bumblebee.

Thereupon LISA *enters again and screams:*

Aha, aha, didn't I say there was going to be a murder.

THEY *all cried hush at her and urged her to shut up.*

Quiet, Lisa. Lisa, quiet, quiet, you're one or the other.

Then HE *again started to speak.*

We saw the unfortunate body,
it lay without motion and force.
Life in it grew scanter and scanter
due to the wild blow of the cutlass.
Its eyes closed shut like nutshells.
What do we humans know of death.
We can be neither beasts nor mountains,
nor fish nor birds nor clouds.
Maybe the country or sofas,
maybe clocks and phenomena,
volcanoes, the deep of the sea

have some inkling of it.
Beetles and mournful birds
that spiral under the firmament
in their modest shirts,
for them death is a familiar event.

HE
What is the hour.
The hours run. They run.

HE
I noticed death.
I noticed time.

HE
They run. They run.

HE
Again the co-ed reappeared
like a noodle
and the student stooped over her
like a soul.
And the co-ed like a flower
achieved rest.
The swift troika sped away
to the east.

HE
What is the hour.

HE
The foliage stands in the forest like thunder.

HE
Now I will speak.
The tired taper now
is tired of burning like a shoulder.
And yet the co-ed still commanded

o kiss me stephan over and over,
why don't you kiss my thighs,
why don't you give my gut a kiss.
Stephan now felt bereft of force,
and terribly he clamored,
I cannot kiss you any longer,
I'm off to the university right now
to learn the discipline of science,
how to extract copper from metal,
how to fix electricity when broke,
how to spell bear,
and he declined then like a shoulder
without force upon the darling bed.

Then Kozlov came for his cure. He held loganberry in his hands and made faces. Future words rose before him which he pronounced right then and there. But none of this was important. There was nothing important in any of this. What could have been important in this. Nothing.

Then Stepanov-Terskoy came. He was entirely feral. But he was not Stepanov-Peskov. Stepanov-Peskov got murdered. Let us not forget that. We must not forget that. Why should we forget that anyway.

A SCENE ON THE SIXTH FLOOR

FONTANOV
For five years we've been together,
you and I, you and I,
like a barn owl and an owl,
like the river and the shore,
like the valley like the mountain.
You are co-ed as before,
your hair turns gray,
your female cheeks turn sallow,
in all this time you haven't,
why should I lie, filled out.
Your scalp is showing through,
your sweetness is decrepit.

I used to think about the world,
about the glimmer of the spheres,
about waves and clouds
and now I'm old and weak.
I now direct my thought
at radishes and pork,
Was it a co-ed that I married
or an independent clothing designer.

MARGARITA OR LISA, *now become* KATYA:
How do I live? My soul flies off
from a cloddy mouth. Fontanov,
you're pitiful and crude.
Your manhood, where is it?
I'll stand beside the open window.
Look at the massive undulation of the air.
Look we can see the neighbors' house.
Look, look, look, look all around us.
Look I clamber onto the windowsill,
Like a branch I stand on the windowsill.

FONTANOV
Co-ed, wait for me.

SHE
Like a cup I stand on the windowsill.

FONTANOV
Co-ed, what's with you.

SHE
Like a taper I stand on the windowsill.

FONTANOV
Co-ed, you've lost your mind.

SHE
I arrive.

It doesn't say anywhere here that she jumped out of the window, but she jumped out of the window. She fell down on rocks. And she died. Oh, it's so scary.

FONTANOV
I will not hesitate
but follow her,
smash all the plates,
rip up the calendar.
I'll light lamps everywhere,
call for the steward
and take a portrait of Grudetsky
with me forever for the road.

Then music sounded for three hours.

HE
Margarita quick
open the door,
the door to poetry is open,
Margarita speak
of sounds.
We hear the sounds of objects,
we chew music like fat.
Margarita for the sake of science
we don't believe that we're asleep,
we don't believe that we breathe,
we don't believe that we write,
we don't believe that we hear,
we don't believe that we are silent.

HE
Night was rising in the sky.
The dull crescent like a soul
soared above the earth,
rustling in the thick reeds
fish ran up and down in the river

and the mournful lion roared.
Towns stood upright,
the beaver raced after prey.

HE
I was losing my benevolence.

HE
The inevitable years
came at us like herds.
Around us green shrubbery
undulated sleepily.
It was not much to look at.

HE
We have nothing more to think with.

His head falls off.

1931-1934
Translated by Eugene Ostashevsky

Frother

3 PARTS

The sons stood by the wall, flashing their feet shod in spurs. They rejoiced and said:

> Promulgate to us dear father
> What is this thing called Frother.

The father, flashing his eyes, replied:

> Do not confuse, my sons
> The day of the end and the knight of spring.

Blue, terrible and grizzled is Frother.
I am your angel. I am your father.
I know its cruelty,
My death is close at hand.
Bald spots gape on my head,
Empty patches. I am bored.
And should my life drag on,
Neither a falcon nor a tuft of hair
Will remain anywhere.
This means death is at hand.
This means hello boredom.

The sons twinkled their bells and then rattled their tongues:

But that wasn't our question,
Our thoughts gestate like mansions.
Won't you tell us dear father
What is this thing called Frother.

And the father exclaimed, "The prologue!
In the prologue what matters is God.
Go to sleep, sons.
There are dreams: watch some."

The sons lay down to sleep. Having hid mushrooms in their pockets. Even the walls seemed obedient. Many things seemed, what of it. Actually not much seemed to us nor to them. But hark! What was that? Once more the father didn't give a direct answer. And to the sons who woke anew this is what he said, exclaiming and flashing his eyebrows:

Let the gray-haired people
Sing and dance.
Let them wave their arms
Like a man.

On a placid, beautiful day
You diminish in breath.
How soon I will apprehend

The perfection of death.

The horses rush like waves,
Hooves clop.
The steeds are dashing and ablaze,
Vanished they gallop.

But how to clasp their abatement,
And are all of us mortal?
What can you tell me, O moment,
Will I understand you?

The bed stands before me
I'll softly lie,
And under the wall I'll feign to be
A flag and gladioli.

Sons, sons. My hour approaches.
I'm dying. I'm dying.
Don't ride in coaches.
The end, it comes.

In rows, flashing their feet, the sons begin to dance a quadrille. The first son, or is it the first pair, says:

Please do tell us dear father,
What is this thing called Frother.

And the second son, or is it the second pair, says:

Maybe Frother is a tether,
A teether or a head in feathers.

Then the third son, or is it the third pair:

I can't understand O father
Where is Frother? What is Frother?

The father, flashing his eyes, moans menacingly:

O, I wallow in pillows!

The first son:

Father, I pallow in willows.
You must not die
Before you ply reply.

The second son, dancing like a loyal subject:

O Frother, Frother, Frother.
O father, father, father.

Finally the third son, dancing like a gunshot:

Dolls and dunce caps have burned out,
I'm a boat a boat a bout.

The sons stop dancing, because it can't all be fun and games, can it. They sit mutely and quietly by their father's expired bed. They look into his wilting eyes. They wish to repeat everything. The father is dying. He becomes fleshy like a bunch of grapes. We are terrified to look into his, so to speak, face. The sons say nothing as each of them enters his own superstitious wall.

Frother is the cold froth forming on the dead man's brow. It is the dew of death, that's what Frother is.

PART TWO

The father is flying over the writing desk. But don't think he's a spirit.

I saw, as you'd have it, a rose,
This tedious petal of earth.
The flower apparently was
Thinking its last thoughts.

It caressed the neighboring mountains
With the terminal breath of its soul.
Princesses floated and stars
Above in the heavenly pall.

As my sons went away
And my horse like a wave
Stood and clacked its hoof,
The moon yellowed nearby.

O flower convinced of delight,
The godly hour is at hand.
The world comes to like the dawn
And I have gone out like a light.

The father stops speaking in verse. He takes a puff on a candle, holding it in his teeth like a flute while sinking pillowlike into the armchair.

The first son enters and says: And he hasn't even answered our question. Therefore he now turns to the pillow with a question:

Pillow pillow
Tell us rather
What is this thing called Frother.

The pillow who is also the father:

I know. I know!

The second son asks in a hurry:

Then answer,
Wherefore speak you not.

The third son, utterly incensed:

In vain are you a widow,

O comfortable pillow.
Reply.

The first son:

So answer.

The second son:

Some fire here! Fire!

The third son:

I am going to hang somebody, I can just feel it.

The pillow, who is also the father:

A little patience,
Then maybe I'll answer all your questions.
I'd like to hear you sing.
Then maybe I'll grow loquacious.

I'm so exhausted.
Maybe art will give me a second wind.
Farewell, pedestal.
I wish to hear your voices set to music.

Then the sons could not deny their father's astounded request. They huddled together like cattle and broke into a universal song:

Big brat brother Brutus,
A marvelous Roman.
Everyone lies. Everyone dies.

That was the first stanza.
The second stanza:

Sang sank skittered stole

A lonely tightrope walker.
That acrobat. What gall.

Third stanza:

The stallion
In the netherworld
Is waiting for the clarion.

And as they sang, music resounded: wonderful, extraordinary, and all-conquering. And it seemed as if there were room left in the world for various feelings. Like a miracle the sons stood around the unsightly pillow, and awaited with meaningless hope the answer to their unenviable and savage, imposing question: What is Frother? And the pillow now fluttered, now soared into the heavens like a candle, now ran through the room like the Dnieper. Father sat over the cowwheatlike writing desk, and the sons stood against the wall like umbrellas. That's what Frother is.

PART THREE

The father sat atop a bronze steed while the sons stood at his sides. And the third son stood alternately by the horse's face and the horse's tail. As was apparent to him and to us, he felt out of place. And the horse was like a wave. No one spoke a word. They were speaking in thoughts.

Now the father sitting on the steed and stroking his darling duck exclaimed mentally, flashing his eyes:

You're waiting to hear what the father will blather.
Will he or won't he explain what is Frother.
O Lord I am a disconsolate widower,
A sinless singer.

The first son bending down picked up a five-kopeck piece from the floor. He moaned mentally and started flashing his feet:

Papa, the end is near.

I see a crown form above your ear.
Your breathing is tall and austere,
You're already a popsicle.

The second son was just as gloomy. He bent down on the other side and picked up a lady's purse. Then he cried thoughts and started flashing his feet:

If only I were a priest
Or a deceased released,
I would have visited your court,
Almighty Lord.

And the third son, standing at the horse's tail and plucking at his mustache with his thoughts, started flashing his feet:

Where is the key to my mind?
Where is that ray of light,
The sudden generosity of winter?

And as he relocated to the face of the horse that was like a wave, he smoothed his hair with his thoughts and started flashing his feet:

You see no eyebrows father,
How barren are the bloodlines of Frother.

Then the father took out of his pocket the barrel of a certain gun and, showing it to his children, exclaimed elated and loud, flashing his eyes:

Look: a gun barrel!
It's so big and unsterile!

First son:

Where? How? Teach us—

Second son:

Everywhere. Like finches.

Third son:

The last fear
After mass
Was past
Crumbled to dust.

And then the gates of heaven opened
And a nanny came out of the pen.
That nanny wore a bonnet hither.

And this again reminded everyone of their eternal question, namely:

What is this thing called Frother?

A horrible silence descended on everything. The sons lay strewn like candy across the night room, revolving their white grizzled occiputs and flashing their feet. Superstition overpowered them all.

The nanny wore a bonnet hither.
She hung in the room like a merchant, smothered.

The nanny began to put the father, who had turned small as a child's bone, to bed. She sang him a song:

Over your cradle
Drool swims on your lips
And the moon lives.
Over the grave, over the pine,
Sleep and repine.
Better not rise.
Better pulverize.
Hey there blacksmith jacksmith,
We'll sleep in your forge.
We're all prisoners.

And as they sang, music resounded: wonderful, extraordinary, and all-conquering. And it seemed as if there were room left in the world for various feelings. Like a miracle the sons stand around the father's softly expired bed. They wish to repeat everything. We are terrified to look into his, so to speak, face. And the pillow now fluttered, now soared into the heavens like a candle, now ran through the room like the Dnieper. Frother is the cold froth forming on the dead man's brow. It is the dew of death, that's what Frother is.

Dear God, the sons could have said if only they could. But we knew that already.

1936-37

Translated by Thomas Epstein, Eugene Ostashevsky, and Genya Turovskaya

Daniil Kharms

The Ewe

1.
The white ewe walked
the white ewe wandered
cried out in the fields above the river
called for its lambs and minor birds
waved its white hand
lay prostrate before me
invited me into the grass
and in the grass waving its hand
the white ewe walked
the white ewe wandered.

2.
Do you know the white ewe
do you believe the white ewe
stands in its crowns by the stove
the same identical as you
As if I were friends with you
as if it were bright crowns I held
you are above us and then I
and then a house on three pillars
and higher yet the white ewe
walks the white ewe.

3.
The white ewe walks
and after her the capricorn
with a big face among the saints
with a purse hirsute like the earth
stands in the pasture like a house
the earth below, thunder above
we to the side, earth all around
and God above among the saints
and higher yet the white ewe
walks the white ewe.

May 22, 1929
Translated by Eugene Ostashevsky

A Thing

Mama, Papa, and domestic help by the name of Natasha were sitting at the dinner table and drinking.

Papa was a total lush, no doubt about it. Even Mama looked down on him. But this did not prevent Papa from being a very nice person. He was laughing very genially and rocking in his chair. The maid Natasha, who wore a headpiece and an apron, was blushing in unbelievable embarrassment. Papa was making everyone laugh with his beard, but the maid Natasha bashfully lowered her eyes to convey her embarrassment thereby.

Mama, a tall woman with big hair, spoke with the voice of a horse. Mama's voice trumpeted in the dining room, reverberating throughout the apartment and into the yard.

After the first round, everyone fell silent for a moment and ate some cold cuts. A short while later they started talking again.

Then, out of nowhere, someone knocked at the door. Neither Papa, nor Mama, nor the maid Natasha had any idea who it could possibly be.

"How strange," said Papa. "Who could be knocking at the door?"

Mama expressed condolence with her face and poured an extra shot for herself, drank it and said: "Strange."

Papa refrained from comment, but he poured himself a shot as well. He drank it and rose from the table.

In height, Papa was nothing to look at. No comparison with Mama. Mama was a tall, full-bodied woman with a voice like a horse, whereas Papa was only her spouse. Moreover, Papa had freckles.

He got to the door in one step and asked: "Who's there?"

"It's me," said the voice behind the door.

Right then the door opened and the maid Natasha walked in, self-conscious and pink. Just like a flower. Just like a flower.

Papa sat down.

Mama drank some more.

The maid Natasha and the other one, the one just like a flower, turned red with shame. Papa looked at them and refrained from comment, except that he drank another shot, as did Mama.

To silence the unpleasant burning in his mouth, Papa opened a can of lobster pâté. Everyone was very happy and ate until dawn. But Mama sat in her seat saying nothing. This wasn't pleasant at all.

Just as Papa was about to sing something, there was a bang on the window. Mama jumped with fright and screamed that she clearly saw someone looking into the window from the street. The others tried to reassure her, saying this was impossible, insofar as the apartment was on the third floor. No one could have looked in from the street, you'd have to be a giant for that, or Goliath.

But the thought was firmly lodged inside Mama's head. Nothing in the world could have convinced her that nobody had looked through the window.

To calm her down, they poured her another shot. She drank it. Papa also poured one for himself and drank it.

Natasha and the maid who was just like a flower were sitting with their eyes lowered in embarrassment.

"I can't be in a good mood when we are being looked at through the window!" Mama was shouting.

Papa grew desperate. He had no idea how to reassure Mama. He ran down into the yard and tried to look from there into the windows of at least the second story. Of course, he was unable to reach even that high up. But Mama was not convinced by this at all. Mama never even saw that Papa failed to reach the windows of even the second story.

Papa blew into the dining room in great frustration and immediately gulped down two shots, pouring an extra one for Mama. Mama drank it but announced she was drinking only to display her conviction that someone had, in fact, looked in through the window.

Papa threw up his arms.

"Look," he said to Mama, and, approaching the window, pulled both frames ajar.

A man with a soiled shirt collar and a knife in his hands tried to climb in. Papa slammed the window shut and said: "There's no one there."

But the man with the soiled shirt collar was standing outside the window and staring into the room. He even opened the window and walked in.

Mama became awfully excited. She collapsed in a fit of hysterics, but, after drinking a bit of what Papa offered her and snacking on a marinated mushroom, she calmed down again.

Soon Papa too returned to his senses. Everyone sat back down at the table and went on drinking.

Papa picked up a newspaper and turned it around several times, trying to figure out which end is the top and which the bottom. But he didn't succeed no matter how hard he tried, and so set the paper aside for another drink.

"It's all good," said Papa, "but we're missing pickles."

Mama bellowed obscenely, which made the maids so embarrassed that they engrossed themselves in studying the patterns of the tablecloth.

Papa drank some more and then, snatching Mama, hoisted her up onto the wardrobe.

Mama's gray luxurious hairdo got knocked on its side, red splotches appeared on her face, and, all in all, she developed one excited mug.

Papa pulled up his pants and launched into a toast.

Just then a manhole in the floor opened, and a monk clambered out. The maids became so embarrassed that one of them even started to puke. Natasha propped her friend up by the forehead, trying to hide her disgraceful behavior.

The monk who clambered out from under the floorboards aimed at Papa's ear with his fist and then—wham!

Papa dropped back into his chair without finishing his toast.

Then the monk came up to Mama and hit her somehow from the bottom up—either with his hand, or with his foot, it was hard to tell.

Mama began to scream and call for help.

And the monk grabbed both maids by the collar, swung them in the air a bit, and let them go.

Then the monk hid back under the floorboards unnoticed and closed the manhole cover over his head.

For a long time Mama, Papa, and the maid Natasha could not come to their senses. But then, having caught their breath and straightened their clothes, they drank another round and sat back down at the table to eat pickled cabbage.

As they drank the next round, they sat around conversing peacefully.

But then Papa turned purple and started to yell.

"What! What!" Papa was shouting. "So you think I am petty! So I am a loser in your eyes! I'm no poor relative for you, I'm no mooch! You're scoundrels yourselves, that's what you are!"

Mama and the maid Natasha ran out of the dining room and locked themselves in the kitchen.

"He's going at it again, that boozehound! That old devil's hoof!" Mama was hissing in horror to Natasha who by now was as embarrassed as humanly possible.

And Papa sat shouting in the dining room until, in the morning, he picked up his folders, put on an official white cap, and went off modestly to work.

May 31, 1929

Translated by Eugene Ostashevsky

Notnow

This is This.
That is That.
This is not That.
That is not This.
What's left is either this, or not this.
It's all either that, or not that.
What's not that and not this, that is not this and not that.
What is this and also that, that is itself Itself.
What is itself Itself, that might be that but not this, or else this but not that.
This went into that, and that went into this. We say: God has puffed.
This went into this, and that went into that, and we have no place to leave and nowhere to come to.
This went into this. We asked: where? They sung in answer: Here.
This left That. What is this? It's That.
This is that.
That is this.
Here are this and that.
Here went into this, this went into that, and that went into here.
We watched, but did not see.
And there stood this and that.
There is not here.
That's there.
This is here.
But now both this and that are there.
But now this and that are here, too.
We long and mope and ponder.
But where is now?
Now is here, and now there, and now here, and now here and there.
This be that.
Here be there.
This, that, here, there, be, I, We, God.

May 29, 1930
Translated by Matvei Yankelevich

To Ring—To Fly (Third Cisfinite Logic)

And now the house flew.
And now the dog flew.
And now the dream flew.
And now the mother flew.
And now the garden flew.
The horse flew.
The bathhouse flew.
The balloon flew.
Now the rock starts to flying.
Now the stump starts to flying.
Now the moment starts to flying.
Now the circle starts to flying.
A house flies.
A mother flies.
A garden flies.
A clock to fly.
A hand to fly.
Eagles to fly.
A spear to fly.
And horse to fly.
And house to fly.
And period to fly.
A forehead flies.
A chest flies.
A stomach flies.
Oh-no, catch it—the ear is flying.
Oh-no, look—the nose is flying.
Oh-no, my monks—the mouth is flying.

2
The house rings.
The water rings.
The rock nearby is ringing.
The book nearby is ringing.
Mother, son and garden ring.

A rings.
B rings.
THAT flies and THAT rings.
The forehead rings and flies.
The chest rings and flies.
Hey, monks—mouth is ringing!
Hey, monks—forehead's flying!
What to fly, but not to ring?
The ring is flying and to ring.
THERE is flying and ringing.
Hey, monks! We're to fly!
Hey, monks! We're to flying!
We're to fly and THERE to fly.
Hey monks! We're to ringing!
We're to ringing and THERE to ring.

Spring 1930
Translated by Matvei Yankelevich

An Optical Illusion

Semyon Semyonovich, putting on his glasses, looks at the pine tree and sees a peasant sitting on the pine and threatening him with his fist.

Semyon Semyonovich, taking off his glasses, looks at the pine tree and sees that no one is sitting on it.

Semyon Semyonovich, putting on his glasses, looks at the pine tree and again sees that a peasant is sitting on the pine and threatening him with his fist.

Semyon Semyonovich, taking off his glasses, again sees that no one is sitting on the pine.

Semyon Semyonovich, again putting on his glasses, looks at the pine tree and again sees that a peasant is sitting on the pine and threatening him with his fist.

Semyon Semyonovich does not wish to believe in this phenomenon and considers the phenomenon an optical illusion.

1934
Translated by Eugene Ostashevsky

Andrey Semyonovich Spat into a Cup of Water...

Andrey Semyonovich spat into a cup of water. The water turned black immediately. Andrey Semyonovich squinted and stared critically into the cup. The water was very black. Andrey Semyonovich felt his heart racing.

Just then the dog of Andrey Semyonovich woke up. Andrey Semyonovich walked to the window and fell into deep thought.

Suddenly something large and dark whistled past the face of Andrey Semyonovich and flew out of the window. This was the dog of Andrey Semyonovich, flying like a crow onto the roof of the house across the street. Andrey Semyonovich sank into a squat and began to howl.

Into the room ran comrade Parrotsky.

"Is anything wrong? Are you ill?" asked comrade Parrotsky.

Andrey Ivanovich said nothing and just rubbed his hands across his face, over and over.

Comrade Parrotsky looked into the cup on the table.

"What is that in that cup?" he asked Andrey Ivanovich.

"I don't know," said Andrey Ivanovich.

Parrotsky vanished. The dog flew back into the window, lay where it lay before and fell asleep.

Andrey Ivanovich came up to the table and poured the blackened water out of the cup.

And the soul of Andrey Ivanovich distended with light.

August 30, 1934
Translated by Eugene Ostashevsky

Holiday

On the roof of a certain building two draftsmen sat eating buckwheat kasha.

Suddenly one of the draftsmen shrieked with joy and took a long handkerchief out of his pocket. He had a brilliant idea—he would tie a twenty-kopeck coin into one end of the handkerchief and toss the whole thing off the roof down into the street and see what would come of it.

The second draftsman quickly caught on to the first one's idea. He finished his buckwheat kasha, blew his nose, and, having licked his fingers, got ready to watch the first draftsman.

As it happened, both draftsmen were distracted from the experiment with the handkerchief and twenty-kopeck coin. On the roof where both draftsmen sat an event occurred which could not have gone unnoticed.

The janitor Ibrahim was hammering a long stick with a faded flag into a chimney.

The draftsmen asked Ibrahim what it meant, to which Ibrahim answered: "This means that there's a holiday in the city."

"And what holiday would that be, Ibrahim?" asked the draftsmen.

"It's a holiday because our favorite poet composed a new poem," said Ibrahim.

And the draftsmen, shamed by their ignorance, dissolved into the air.

January 9, 1935
Translated by Matvei Yankelevich

The Street Accident

One man once jumped off a tram, except he did it so awkwardly that a car hit him.

The traffic stopped and the policeman set about determining the cause of the accident.

The driver was explaining something for a long time and pointing to the front wheels of his car.

The policemen felt the wheels and wrote something down in his book.

A fairly numerous crowd gathered.

Some citizen with dull eyes kept falling off a traffic stone.

Some lady repeatedly glanced at another lady who, in turn, repeatedly glanced at the former lady.

Then the crowd dispersed and the traffic started moving.

But the citizen with dull eyes still kept falling off the traffic stone until finally he too put a stop to this occupation.

At this time some man carrying what appeared to be a freshly bought chair became lodged under a moving tram.

Again the policeman came, again the crowd gathered, and the citizen with dull eyes again started falling off the traffic stone.

Well and later everything was all right again, and Ivan Semyonovich Karpov even stopped by a self-service restaurant.

January 10, 1935
Translated by Eugene Ostashevsky

A Fable

One man of medium height said: "I would give anything if only I were even a little bit taller."

He barely said it when he sees a lady medegician standing in front of him.

"What do you want?" says the medegician.

But the man of medium height just stands there so frightened he can't even speak.

"Well?" says the medegician.

The man of medium height just stands there and says nothing. The medegician vanished.

And the man of medium height started crying and biting his nails. First he chewed off all the nails on his fingers, and then on his toes.

Reader! Think about this fable and it will make you very uncomfortable.

1935
Translated by Eugene Ostashevsky

A Sonnet

An astonishing incident happened to me: I suddenly forgot what comes earlier, 7 or 8.

I went over to my neighbors and asked them what they thought on the topic.

How great was their and my own astonishment, when they suddenly found they also couldn't remember the counting order. 1, 2, 3, 4, 5 and 6 they remember, but further on they forgot.

We all went to the commercial store called "Grocery," which is on the corner of Znamenskaya and Basseynaya streets, and asked the cashier about our perplexity. The cashier smiled sadly, took a tiny hammer out of her mouth and, after moving her nose a little, said: "I think 7 comes after 8 when 8 comes after 7."

We thanked the cashier and ran out of the store with joy. But then, thinking deeper the cashier's words, we again lost heart, because her words seemed to us to be lacking in any sense.

What were we to do? We went to the Summer Gardens and started counting the trees there. But when our count reached 6, we stopped and began arguing: according to some, 7 followed after, according to others, 8.

We would have argued for a very long time but then luckily some child fell off a bench and broke both his jaws. This distracted us from the argument.

After that we returned to our homes.

November 12, 1935
Translated by Eugene Ostashevsky

One Fat Man Invented a Way to Lose Weight...

One fat man invented a way to lose weight. And he lost it. The ladies began pestering him, trying to pry out his secret. But the thin man replied that it becomes men to lose weight, whereas it does not become ladies at all; that ladies, on the contrary, ought to be plump. And he was absolutely right.

Mid 1930s
Translated by Eugene Ostashevsky

Death of a Little Old Man

A little sphere sprang out of one little old man's nose and fell to the ground. The little old man bent over to lift up the little sphere and that's when a little stick sprang from his eye and also fell to the ground. The little old man was frightened and, not knowing what to do, moved his lips. At that moment, out of the little old man's mouth sprang a little square. The little old man grabbed his mouth, but then a little mouse sprang out of the little old man's sleeve. The little old man became ill with fear and, so as not to fall, he sat down into a squat. But then something snapped inside the little old man and, like a soft plush coat, he toppled to the ground. That's when a longish little reed sprang from the torn hole, and on its very end sat a thin little bird. The little old man wanted to scream out, but one of his jaws got stuck behind the other and he only hiccupped weakly and closed one eye. The little old man's other eye remained open. It ceased moving and glistening and became motionless and murky, like that of a dead person. In such a way, cunning death caught up to the little old man who had not expected it.

1935-36
Translated by Matvei Yankelevich

The Falling-Out Old Women

One old woman, because of her excessive curiosity, fell out of the window, dropped and got all smashed up.

Another old woman leaned out of the window and began looking down at the one who got smashed up, but, because of her excessive curiosity, also fell out of the window, dropped and got all smashed up.

Then a third old woman fell out of the window, then a fourth, then a fifth.

When the sixth old woman fell out, I got bored of looking at them, and I went to the Maltsevsky Market, where they say one blind man was presented with a knit shawl.

1936-37
Translated by Eugene Ostashevsky

The Lecture

Pushkov said:

"What is woman? An engine of love,"—and immediately got punched in the face.

"What for?" asked Pushkov but, receiving no answer, continued:

"This is what I think: you have to roll up to women from below. Women love that, they only pretend they don't."

Here Pushkov was again socked in the face.

"What's going on, comrades? Fine, if that's the case, I won't even talk!" said Pushkov but, after a quarter of a minute, continued:

"Women are arranged in such a way that they are all soft and moist."

Here Pushkov again got socked in the face. Pushkov tried to look as if he didn't notice anything and continued:

"If you sniff a woman..."

But here Pushkov got smashed in the face so hard that he grabbed his cheek and said:

"Comrades, it is absolutely impossible to lecture under such conditions. If this happens again, I won't talk!"

Pushkov waited a quarter of a minute and continued:

"Where were we? Oh—yes! So: Women love to look at themselves. They sit down in front of the mirror entirely naked..."

As he said that word he was punched in the face again.

"Naked," repeated Pushkov.

"Pow!" they whacked him in the face.

"Naked!" shouted Pushkov.

"Pow!" he got punched in the face.

"Naked! Naked everywhere! Tits and ass!" shouted Pushkov.

"Pow! Pow! Pow!" they kept punching him in the face.

"Tits and ass with a washtub!" Pushkov was shouting.

"Pow! Pow!" the punches rained down.

"Tits and ass with a tail!" shouted Pushkov, spinning to avoid the punches. "Naked nun!"

But then Pushkov was hit with such force that he lost consciousness and fell, as if mowed down, upon the floor.

12 August 1940

Translated by Eugene Ostashevsky

Endnotes

1 *OBERIU: An Anthology of Russian Absurdism.*

2 For the best Russian-language edition of the "Conversations," see Leonid Lipavsky's *Issledovanie uzhasa.* A shorter online version may be accessed at *http://anthropology.rinet.ru/old/4/lipavski1.htm.*

3 Druskin's studies of Vvedensky are published in *"Sborishche druzei, ostavlennykh sud'boiu": "Chinari" v tekstakh, dokumentakh i issledovaniakh.*

4 "The Witness and the Rat" came out in *Modern Poetry in Translation*, 21 (2003), 87-97.

5 Eugene Ostashevsky's translations of three "Sluchai"—"An Optical Illusion," "A Sonnet," and "The Falling-Out Old Women"—appear here for the first time, as do "Andrey Semyonovich Spat into a Cup of Water...," "A Fable," and "The Lecture." The rest have been reprinted from his *OBERIU,* op. cit.

6 See F. T. Marinetti's "Destruction of Syntax—Wireless Imagination—Words-in-Freedom".

V

RUSSIAN EXPERIMENTAL PERFORMANCE AND THEATER

1. Vsevolod Meyerhold

Alexander Burry

"We, too, will show you life that's real—very!
But life transformed by the theater into a spectacle most extraordinary."
—Vladimir Mayakovsky, *Mystery Bouffe*

"What we need are new forms!"
—Konstantin Treplev, in Anton Chekhov's *The Seagull*

"Meyerhold is to theater what Picasso is to painting. Their task is to search, to experiment, to chart new paths... Like Picasso, Meyerhold indicates possibilities. Without stopping at them, rushing to find strongholds that must be destroyed by the hand of the revolutionary warrior."
—Nikolai Foregger[1]

Perhaps more than any other early twentieth-century theater director, Vsevolod Meyerhold exemplified the avant-garde mission to destroy traditional artistic boundaries. His transformation of dramatic space, acting techniques, stage design, and all other elements of the theater was intended to shock spectators into viewing plays anew, and to increase their participation in the spectacle. By finding ways to remove or minimize the so-called fourth wall that separated spectators from the stage, and turned them—from Meyerhold's point of view—into passive observers, the director hoped literally to open up a new space in the theatrical structure itself, and to induce active, impassioned responses to his art.

Background and Theatrical Apprenticeship

Meyerhold's background distinguished him from other Russian avant-garde artists both because of his cultural heritage, and because he was considerably older than many of the figures, such as Vladimir

Mayakovsky and Nikolai Erdman, with whom he collaborated. Vsevolod Emilevich Meyerhold was born Karl Theodor Kasimir Meyergold on 10 February 1874 (28 January, old style), in Penza, a city near the Volga River in southeastern Russia. He was the eighth child of Russified German parents; his father Emil owned a vodka distillery. As the youngest child—and therefore unlikely to inherit the family business—he was able to explore his early love for theater in relative freedom. Despite its provincial location, Penza was a center of radical thought, and this politically charged environment strongly affected Meyerhold's development. The Penza Popular Theater, which he led in the mid-1890s, sought to bring culture to the masses. Thus began a lifelong quest by the director to produce theater that was politically relevant and, after the Bolshevik Revolution in particular, held mass appeal.

On his twenty-first birthday, Meyerhold converted from Lutheranism to Russian Orthodoxy, and chose Vsevolod (after the late nineteenth-century short story writer Vsevolod Garshin, whom he idolized) as his Orthodox Christian name. This conversion enabled him to become a Russian national, and thereby avoid conscription into the Prussian army. It also allowed him, as a member of the Orthodox Church, to marry his first wife, the Russian Olga Munt. After completing school in 1895, he studied law at Moscow University for two years, but left before completing his degree.[2] At the same time he was studying acting and violin, failing an audition for the Moscow University orchestra before successfully trying out for acting classes at Vladimir Nemirovich-Danchenko's Moscow Philharmonia School in 1896.[3] He studied there for two years, and then joined the company as an actor from 1898-1902.

Meyerhold's apprenticeship at the Moscow Art Theater revealed him to be an actor of exceptional abilities: along with Chekhov's wife-to-be, actress Olga Knipper, he earned a silver medal upon graduating in 1898. His first important role was Konstantin Treplev, a symbolist playwright and the hero of Chekhov's first major play, *The Seagull*. Treplev offered Meyerhold the first of many roles that he would act and direct of talented but alienated outsiders. Other major roles included the utopian *intelligent* Petr Trofimov in Chekhov's *The Cherry Orchard*, and Prince Shuisky and Ivan the Terrible in Aleksei Tolstoy's *Tsar Fyodor Ioannovich* and *The Death of Ivan the Terrible*, respectively. The intelligence and careful preparation Meyerhold brought to his roles, as well as his supple, flexible, precise movements, were qualities he would eventually look for and develop in other actors when he became a director. Already in the Moscow Art Theater, in part as a result of his interactions with Chekhov, his spare, economical acting contrasted with the expressive, passionately emotional style that director Konstantin Stanislavsky encouraged. Meyerhold's 1902 departure from the Moscow Art Theater, due to his dissatisfaction with its artistic principles and his increasingly difficult relationship with erstwhile mentor Nemirovich-Danchenko, coincided with the theater's own crisis. The 1901-02 season featured no successful productions, and the company had run into financial difficulties. Moreover, the dominant poetic movement of Symbolism, represented by poets such as Valery Briusov, Alexander Blok, Andrei Bely, and Viacheslav Ivanov, focused on lofty spiritual principles and images that clashed with the Art Theater's naturalist style. Stanislavsky himself realized that his theater was inadequate to convey this impulse, and that it needed to change.

Breaking from the Moscow Art Theater

Meyerhold's innovations as a director are commonly cast (by himself and others) in such direct opposition to those of Stanislavsky that it is well worth examining both the common ground and the crucial distinctions between their visions of theater. Although the two directors are generally viewed in terms of an innovator/traditionalist opposition, Meyerhold's theatrical revolution could not have taken place without the sweeping changes Nemirovich-Danchenko and Stanislavsky had made to Russian theatrical culture in the 1890s. Nineteenth-century theater before the Moscow Art Theater was essentially a star system in which the leading actors made all the decisions and the director was reduced to a mere functionary. Nemirovich-Danchenko and Stanislavsky's very emphasis on ultra-realist accuracy in staging, although it grated on Meyerhold, offered a much-needed corrective to the near absence of systematic staging technique earlier in the century, and paved the way for his own innovations in this area. In addition, the diffusion of focus among several actors in Chekhov's plays, which became a hallmark of the Moscow Art Theater, effectively replaced the star system and enabled Meyerhold to develop a method that required the director to attend to every detail of the actor's performance. Thus, not surprisingly, Meyerhold was shaped in many ways by his apprenticeship with Nemirovich-Danchenko and Stanislavsky. Although his differences with them became apparent very early on, a 1900 statement by Meyerhold could easily have come from one of his mentors: "Art should put before us a true picture of life. Let the individual himself find in it what he needs without pointers or tendentious emphasis."[4] A great deal of what Meyerhold absorbed at the Moscow Art Theater—a focus on the expressivity of the performer, emphasis on character analysis and the inner-outer dynamic of the actor, and the sense of a need for thorough training of the actor through constant experiment—became characteristic of his directorial style as well. Indeed, despite Meyerhold's continual polemics against the Theater throughout his career, he and Stanislavsky shared a mutual admiration that is documented in several sources.[5]

In formulating his own style, Meyerhold was not criticizing the Moscow Art Theater's naturalism in a vacuum. His arguments were to a great extent guided by and in agreement with Briusov's seminal article "An Unnecessary Truth," published in the journal *World of Art* in 1902. Briusov argued that Stanislavsky and Nemirovich-Danchenko's goal of destroying the illusion of theatricality in its drive to present "real life" undermined the basic nature of theater itself, and art in general: "Not only the art of the theatre, but art of any kind cannot avoid formal convention, cannot be transformed into a re-creation of reality."[6] Theatrical conventions such as the very act of buying a ticket, for him, precluded viewers from accepting what was taking place on the stage as reality and not art. In fact, the more the Moscow Art Theater tried to present a lifelike depiction of reality, the less convincing it was: Briusov cites Stanislavsky's use of crickets in his production of Chekhov's *Uncle Vanya*. Ultimately, he calls for theater directors to celebrate the conventionality (*uslovnost'*) of theater by highlighting its artifice through stylization: "Would it not then be better to abandon the fruitless battle against the invincible conventions of theatre, which only spring up with renewed strength, and rather than seeking to eradicate them, attempt to subjugate, to tame, to harness, to saddle them?"[7] Such a call inspired Meyerhold to find ways of effectively underscoring the theatricality of his productions.

Stylization

Meyerhold's approach to theater directing is commonly described as stylization. This method, which applies to everything from the actor's performances to setting to interpretation of the plays, directly opposes Stanislavsky and the Moscow Art Theater's mimetic approach of reproducing reality as closely as possible. It focuses instead on universal themes, character types, and situations, and on the overall rhythm, or musicality, of the production. Stylization seeks to reduce a play, scene, moment, action, or even historical period to its essence, to the main theme or conflict it contains.

One of Meyerhold's collaborators, theater historian Alexander Fevralsky, reported a detailed description by the director of his principles of stage acting. Meyerhold's comments here reveal a great deal about what differentiates his principles and techniques from Stanislavsky's:

> Each movement is a hieroglyph which has its own meaning. On the stage there must be only those movements which can be deciphered instantly, otherwise they are superfluous. I must point out that we, that is I, and all who are with me, are not concerned with the *psychic* world, but with the *physical* world. The work of the new actor on the stage will consist of the grouping of his movements and his technical achievements. That does not mean, of course, that the actor turns into an automaton without a psyche. No. In the actor-acrobat there is always a duality. In order to master a difficult piece of music, the pianist *divides it into segments*, and having mastered them, he stops making mistakes and gives a perfect rendering. The same thing applies to the work of the actor. Only after mastering the role *technically*, mathematically, can we *allow* ourselves *the ecstasy of inspiration*. Let us turn to Pushkin: "*inspiration is needed*, both in *geometry* and in *poetry*; *ecstasy is not required*." Ecstasy is that notorious emoting, that "emotional experiencing"; it is the system of my teacher, Konstantin Stanislavsky, which incidentally, he will probably soon reject. We don't need *ecstasy*, we need *arousal*, based on a firm physical foundation.[8]

This passage clarifies several of Meyerhold's essential artistic principles. Unlike Stanislavsky, who was most interested in the actor's psychological identification with his or her role, Meyerhold viewed the actor's craft more in terms of its physical dimensions. Rather than realistic movements, he called for the actor to perform precise, rhythmic, carefully prepared motions reflecting the inner spirit and dynamics of the play. In place of the individualized psychology typical of the Moscow Art Theater, Meyerhold sought universal representations of types drawn from diverse and seemingly incongruous theatrical traditions such as commedia dell'arte, Japanese Kabuki, ancient Greek tragedy, and cabaret. He used devices and figures such as masks, pantomime, and clowns that highlighted the meta-theatrical aspect of the performance. This did not, as detractors complained, involve a robotic, puppet-like elimination of emotions; psychological reactions simply proceeded from internalized, mechanized gestures rather than identification with an individual character.

Meyerhold's impatience with imitation of real life, along with his desire to underscore theater's "theatricality," also impelled him to create highly stylized sets. Echoing Briusov's points on the undesirability of maintaining an impossible illusion through close reproduction of nature, he notes: "Nobody believes that it is the wind and not a stagehand which causes the garland to sway in the first scene of *Julius Caesar*, because the characters' cloaks remain still."[9] Instead, Meyerhold aimed for sets that would use color, costumes, and designs to present a stylized environment that made the spectator think of other time periods and cultures, such as the France of Molière or Wagner's mythic world.

In Meyerhold's conception, theater became a place of worship and ritual, rather than an attempt to depict ordinary, everyday experiences.[10] This in turn completely changed the position of the spectator in relation to the events on stage. Throughout his career, Meyerhold sought to involve the audience in the given play by stirring up the spectators and forcing them into extreme, even violent reactions. Innovations such as removing footlights and extending the proscenium into the auditorium encouraged audience participation in the spectacle. In this manner, Meyerhold strove to make the viewers as well as the actors into co-creators of the play, along with the director and playwright. Moreover, he sought to shock the audience in every production. For him, a successful play divided the audience and inspired extreme emotional reactions:

a universally praised performance (not that this ever happened with Meyerhold's productions) would have seemed a failure. The director's deliberate attempts to astonish and at times even offend his audience with his stylized sets, acting, and reinterpretations of classic repertoire in many ways can be likened to the methods of literary Futurism. Poets such as Mayakovsky, Velemir Khlebnikov, and David Burliuk sought to provoke listeners both with flamboyant, outrageous dress and antics and with their poetry itself, which rejected nineteenth-century values of aesthetic beauty in favor of harsh images, consonantal rhymes, and jarring, violent verbal constructions.

A final distinction between the Moscow Art Theater and Meyerhold's goals as a director involves his insistence that his productions reflect urgent, contemporary circumstances. From his early upbringing in Penza, Meyerhold developed an interest in underground political writings, and participated in the 1901 Kazansky Sobor student demonstration during a visit to St. Petersburg. Objecting to Stanislavsky's non-partisan attitude, he strove to make theater a forum that always reflected current political concerns, even when it performed classics of Shakespeare, the Greek tragedians, and other non-contemporary playwrights.[11] Although one of the central critiques of his work by Soviet authorities was that he employed too few contemporary texts in his productions of the 1920s and 30s, he continually reinterpreted classics such as Mikhail Lermontov's *Masquerade*, Alexander Griboedov's *Woe from Wit*, and Nikolai Gogol's *The Government Inspector* in light of contemporary reality.

Symbolist Theater

Meyerhold's early experiences as a director in Kherson (1902-04) and Tiflis (Tbilisi, Georgia, 1904-05) were frustrating, but integral to the development of his innovative ideas. Audiences in Kherson preferred farce to the more serious fare Meyerhold offered; this, along with his insistence on developing new techniques "on the go," using the theater itself as a laboratory for experiments, tended to leave audiences bewildered. Nevertheless, in both cities he was able to expand their appreciation and knowledge of theater by introducing and re-conceptualizing playwrights such as Chekhov, Henrik Ibsen, Gerhart Hauptmann, and Artur Schnitzler.

Meanwhile, the Moscow Art Theater was undergoing its own crisis.

Its production of Maksim Gorky's *The Lower Depths* had revealed the limits of its naturalism, and Stanislavsky was searching for a way to respond to the changing literary aesthetics brought on by the Symbolist movement, while remaining politically relevant in light of the 1905 revolution. At great financial risk, he rented a Studio Theater on Povarskaya Street and invited Meyerhold to run it. This studio, since it was independently funded, provided Meyerhold with a laboratory for his experiments. His efforts culminated in a 1905 production of Maurice Maeterlinck's *The Death of Tintagiles*, an 1894 Symbolist play for marionettes that demonstrated the inability of humans to control their own fate. Meyerhold's production included non-realistic pictures drawn by designers Nikolai Sapunov and Sergei Sudeikin, rather than three-dimensional sets. It also featured stylized acting in which the actors' movements were carefully controlled and reduced to essential gestures, and Maeterlinck's words were declaimed in a monotone suggestive of a dream-state rather than spoken naturalistically. Although the performances were highly successful in capturing Maeterlinck's otherworldly atmosphere, Stanislavsky did not approve of the extent to which Meyerhold had departed from traditional theater. Later that year, the studio collapsed, Stanislavsky absorbed a great financial loss, and Meyerhold signed a contract to return to Tbilisi.

In May 1906, however, a new opportunity came from the well-known actress Vera Komissarzhevskaia, who had starred across from Meyerhold as Nina Zarechnaia in Chekhov's *The Seagull*, and was recognized as the leading actress of the turn of the century. Meyerhold accepted an invitation from Komissarzhevskaia to join her St. Petersburg theater as actor and artistic director.[12] Although this collaboration brought Meyerhold to the capital and gave Komissarzhevskaia the star director she was looking for, the pairing was less than ideal. As a lyric actress, Komissarzhevskaia embodied an emotionally demonstrative style that clashed sharply with Meyerhold's stylized techniques. The anti-naturalistic productions of such plays as Ibsen's *Hedda Gabler* and Maeterlinck's *Sister Beatrice* forced Komissarzhevskaia to make considerable adjustments in her acting. Creative differences eventually ended the collaboration, as Meyerhold left the company in 1907. However, the so-called "Theater on Ofitserskaia Street" provided an invaluable experience, and was the site of one of Meyerhold's most important and scandalous creative efforts: Blok's *Balaganchik*.[13]

Blok's lyric drama draws on diverse theatrical traditions ranging from ancient Greek tragedy to sixteenth-century commedia dell'arte, meanwhile parodying Symbolism and the poet's own earlier writings. The plot centers on a love triangle involving three commedia dell'arte figures: Pierrot, Columbine, and Harlequin.[14] After Columbine rejects Pierrot's love by going off with Harlequin instead, Pierrot attempts to reunite with her but discovers that she is actually the harbinger of Death. The play includes other stock figures such as a Clown and a set of Mystics, who represent parodies of the mysticism fashionable in St. Petersburg. Following the disappearance of these characters, Pierrot is left alone on the stage, and the play closes with him playing a mournful melody on the flute. Meanwhile, a Writer appears on stage several times, protesting that his authorial rights have been violated as Pierrot bemoans Columbine's infidelity, attempting to reunite the lovers, and apologizing for losing control of the plot.

Balaganchik inspired a variety of metatheatrical innovations on Meyerhold's part. He designed the Mystics as lifeless cardboard cutouts that came to life only when the actors put their arms and heads through the openings. At one climactic point of the play, the Clown is beaten with a wooden sword and collapses over the footlights with blood that is clearly cranberry juice streaming from his head. Stagehands were overtly visible throughout the production. Through these innovative strategies, Meyerhold "bared the device" of the theatrical conventions, exposing the illusions of theater and putting the actors in situations in which they were estranged from their stock roles.

The premiere of *Balaganchik*, which took place on 30 December 1906, caused an uproar, with many spectators shouting and even fighting with each other.[15] Overall, the audience was completely divided, as some spectators gave the play a standing ovation and others cursed and whistled; there was no middle ground. Most of the critical reviews were scathing, and not surprisingly, Blok and Meyerhold's satire alienated many Symbolists, notably Bely, and their followers. This outraged reaction became a pattern for Meyerhold's entire career, as his productions were routinely trashed by critics such as Alexander Kugel and Alexander Benois, who had ulterior motives, and critiqued more seriously by erstwhile supporters and collaborators such as Stanislavsky, Lunacharsky, and Mayakovsky (in the 1930s under Stalin, of course, negative criticism took on a much more ominous tone). Needless to say, such reviews did not faze Meyerhold in the least; in fact, he far preferred the type of scandal *Balaganchik* and most of his other productions provoked to universal acclaim. In fact, both negative reviews and the polarization of the audiences his productions usually caused—with half the viewers being thrilled and half disgusted—were integral to their success. Such reactions demonstrated that the performance had its effect of "estranging" the audience, forcing them to view theater anew.[16]

The production of *Balaganchik*, as Nicholas Rzhevsky points out, represents one of the many productive collaborations between Meyerhold and writers of literary texts: "In retrospect, the production suggests a particular, near ideal case of theater-literature contingencies based on the continued direct engagements of writer and director in the transformation from one form of representation to the other, on mutual respect, and on equality of talent. [...] In consequence, an unusually productive interaction was achieved between literature and theater that was quite unlike the familiar instances of adaptations in which the author is de-emphasized by the adaptor or by the director or both, or in which the author's and the director's reading of his/her text is subverted by the actors."[17] Meyerhold would collaborate in a similarly close, interdependent manner with other writers in the 1910s and 20s, most notably Vladimir Mayakovsky and Nikolai Erdman.

The Imperial Theaters

In April 1908, following his departure from Komissarzhevskaia's company, Meyerhold was made the director of the St. Petersburg Imperial Theaters. During this period, in which he took on the pseudonym Dr. Dappertutto,[18] he continued to develop the stylization he had begun while working for Komissarzhevskaia. His projects there included a striking 1910 production of Molière's *Don Juan*, in which he eliminated the footlights and curtain, created a proscenium that jutted into the auditorium, and directed the actors to walk with ballet rhythms rather than naturalistic movements. Meyerhold interpreted Don Juan as a puppet, used by Molière to settle personal accounts, and a wearer of masks. Typically for his productions of radically different time periods and cultures, Meyerhold attempted to convey the atmosphere of Molière's time rather than mechanically recreating the exact historical setting. Justifying his stylization of *Don Juan*, Meyerhold wrote the following remarks:

> The public comes to the theatre to see the art of man, but what art is there in walking about the stage as oneself? The public expects invention, play-acting, and skill. But what it gets is either life or a slavish imitation of life. Surely the art of man on the stage consists in shedding all traces of environment, carefully choosing a mask, donning a decorative costume, and showing off one's brilliant tricks to the public—now as a dancer, now as the intriguant at some masquerade, now as the fool of old Italian comedy, now as a juggler.[19]

Following this production, Meyerhold also directed Lev Tolstoy's *A Living Corpse*. Understandably, given Tolstoy's realist style, the play afforded Meyerhold far fewer opportunities than other plays for stylization, and the production was not successful. At the same time, however, he was working on his next major production: Mikhail Lermontov's *Masquerade*, which took seven years of work, and was not performed until 1917, just one day before the February revolution.

Lermontov's 1835 verse play, with its plot of jealousy and confusion of identity, was in many respects an ideal subject for Meyerhold. A young man named Arbenin mistakenly concludes that his wife Nina has cheated on him with another nobleman named Zvezdich, and as a result, he poisons her. Zvezdich, accompanied by an "Unknown," comes after Arbenin for revenge. When Arbenin reads a letter proving his wife's innocence, he goes insane. Konstantin Rudnitsky calls the leitmotif of the play "the theme of illusion, sham and ghostliness of that world which in these days was receding irretrievably into the past."[20] Meyerhold emphasized the role of Fate, vengeance, and prophecy of disaster inherent in Lermontov's play, employing masks to reflect the illusory nature of life and people's identity. He also stressed the hero Arbenin's autobiographical elements and highlighted the demonic role of the Unknown, making him into a representation of Nikolai Martynov, who had killed Lermontov in a duel. Finally, he used alternating curtains to open up or constrict the stage at various points, and to ensure rapid transitions between scenes.

Meyerhold and Opera

Vladimir Teliakov, the director of the imperial theaters, had hired Meyerhold to direct opera as well as drama at the Alexandrinsky Theater, and this became an equally important part of his career in the 1910s. Because music was so ingrained in Meyerhold's conception of theater art and played such a big role in his career, it is worth pausing to examine its influence on his career and theory. Meyerhold's notes and writings are deeply informed by his musical background, and saturated with musical references and techniques. He envisioned himself conducting a theatrical performance as though it were a musical one, and constantly used musical terms for tempo and dynamics.[21] Ernest Garin, one of Meyerhold's leading actors, recalls his director's musical abilities: "he possessed perfect pitch and an outstanding musical memory; he played the violin, was a marvellous conductor, read scores fluently, and had a musical sense of the word (poetry and prose) and of movement."[22] Perhaps most significantly, his system of biomechanics, which I will discuss below, is conceptualized in musical terms.

Meyerhold's 1909 production of Richard Wagner's *Tristan and Isolde*—his debut as an opera director—was an especially formative step in the development of his unique style. Meyerhold's profound attention to the interrelationship of arts on the stage stems in large part from his interest in Wagner's theory of a *Gesamtkunstwerk*, or total artwork. Given Meyerhold's consistent, lifelong aim of organizing the actors' movements according to a musical rhythm, Wagner's innovations were an important influence.[23] The composer's music dramas, including *Tristan* and the four operas of *The Ring of the Nibelung*, feature leitmotifs, or recurring themes heard in different variations in the orchestra. These leitmotifs, in addition to unifying the opera musically and supplementing what is going on onstage, express deeper psychological implications of the action; their plasticity allows them to change according to the given situation. Through such techniques, Wagner gives the orchestra a much greater role than previous operatic composers did, and allows the work's non-verbal material to supersede the text in its expression of the music drama's meaning.

Meyerhold, in directing *Tristan*, called for the actors to allow the orchestra to guide their rhythms, and to use gestures to supply what is unsaid in the music. However, he in no way followed Wagner's theory or indications verbatim. He considered the composer's stage directions unimaginative, and allowed the orchestra to dictate the action instead. Similarly, he constructed a relief stage based on Georg Fuchs's theory in his recent book *The Stage of the Future*, judging it superior to Wagner's Bayreuth theater.[24] For these reasons, *Tristan* is in many respects emblematic of Meyerhold's re-conceptualizing of classics in such a way as to breathe new life into them and bring out their full potential. As Edward Braun puts it, "Meyerhold's *Tristan and Isolde* must be acknowledged as probably the first attempt to free the composer's conception of the '*Gesamtkunstwerk*' from the banal conventions of the nineteenth-century and give it credible theatrical form."[25]

Following *Tristan*, Meyerhold directed many additional operas, including Christoph Willibald Gluck's *Orpheus and Euridyce*, Richard Strauss's *Elektra*, Petr Tchaikovsky's *The Queen of Spades*, and Alexander Dargomyzhsky's *The Stone Guest*, the latter two of which are based on works by Pushkin. *Queen of Spades* was one of Meyerhold's last productions. He was planning to direct Giuseppe Verdi's *Rigoletto* in Stanislavsky's Opera Studio-Theater—a position Stanislavsky had given him shortly before his death in 1939—when his work was interrupted by his arrest. Moreover, Meyerhold played an influential role in the composition of several major operas of the 1920s, including Sergei Prokofiev's 1921 *The Love for Three Oranges* and his 1927 revision of his youthful 1916 opera *The Gambler*, as well as Dmitry Shostakovich's 1928 *The Nose*.

Meyerhold and Revolutionary Theater

Meyerhold embraced the revolution immediately in 1917, becoming a member of the communist party right after the Bolsheviks came to power. Although it is difficult to extricate his enthusiasm for the Bolshevik cause from his aesthetic goals, there is no question that he professed a desire to create a theater that would reflect the ideals of the revolution from the beginning. His post-revolutionary theater began with a production of Mayakovsky's *Mystery-Bouffe*, which Rudnitsky calls "the *first* fully and thoroughly political play in the history of Russian theater."[26]

In many ways, the Futurist poet was the perfect artistic and ideological partner for Meyerhold. Mayakovsky's poetic style of the 1910s, with its harsh, provocative rhymes and urban, grandiose images in many ways parallels Meyerhold's style, with its attempts to shock the audience by exposing the theatricality of his productions. Like Meyerhold, who engaged in a harshly polemical relationship with critics and rivals, Mayakovsky, along with fellow poets Burliuk, Khlebnikov, and Vasily Kamensky, aimed to antagonize audiences and society at large both with the content of their art and their manner of performing it. These four poets were also co-signatories of several poetic manifestoes during the early 1910s, most notably *A Slap in the Face of Public Taste*, which famously proclaimed the Futurists' desire to "throw Pushkin, Dostoevsky, and Tolstoy overboard the steamship of modernity." In their early collaboration on Mayakovsky's play *Mystery-Bouffe*, the poet and director expressed a vision of the revolution that was both propagandistic and artistically innovative. Thus, the revolution provided an impetus toward greater ideological commitment and—especially for Meyerhold—a vehicle for long-desired artistic experiments.

Mayakovsky's play, which was written for the first anniversary of the October revolution, begins with instructions that insist on its contemporaneity: "In the future, all persons performing, presenting, reading, or publishing *Mystery-Bouffe* should change the content, making it contemporary, immediate, up-to-the minute."[27] In it, seven pairs of Western politicians and wealthy people (the "Clean") force seven pairs of proletarians ("the Unclean") into an ark, where they are oppressed by various leaders. The Unclean ultimately throw the Clean overboard and follow the Man of the Future (clearly representing Mayakovsky) into an earthly paradise. After additional cosmic struggles, the Unclean triumph and sing an ode to a future Soviet utopia. The play, which Mayakovsky co-directed, was highly episodic, and with its aim to educate the viewer ideologically, completely shunned the type of realist psychology that Meyerhold himself disliked. It contained elements of the circus and street theater, clowns and masks, and other devices that Meyerhold favored. Sergei Eisenstein, who was perhaps the most famous of Meyerhold's students, described it as a "circusization of the theater."

Mystery-Bouffe thus provided Meyerhold with ready-made solutions for the stylistic experiments he was trying to conduct. The director made the most of the political satire offered by the play, giving the "clean" forces clown-like costumes and dressing the "unclean" in identical gray costumes to demonstrate the solidarity of the masses. The sets and costumes were designed by the Suprematist painter Kasimir Malevich, who treated the theatrical space in a cubist manner, arranging the actors, as he put it, "in vertical compositions in the manner of the latest style of painting."[28] Anatoly Lunacharsky, the Soviet Commissar of Enlightenment, gave a positive review of *Mystery-Bouffe*, which was very successful overall. In 1921, Mayakovsky rewrote the play for Meyerhold, who put on a second production. This time, the director dispensed with the curtain, removed several rows of seats, and extended a long ramp into the audience; these measures allowed for the type of audience-actor interaction Meyerhold continually sought.

Following his first production of *Mystery-Bouffe*, Meyerhold underwent a period of creative inactivity during the Civil War that followed the October Revolution. After being arrested in Novorossisk and nearly executed by the Whites during a trip to Crimea, he returned to Moscow in 1920, and was appointed head of the Theatrical Department of the Commissariat by Lunacharsky. His new theater, the Russian Soviet Federal Socialist Republic (RSFSR) Theater no. 1, was an old space that was customarily used for political rallies. Meyerhold turned it into a revolutionary theater by removing the footlights and connecting the stage to the auditorium. He opened the theater with Belgian poet Emile Verhaeren's 1898 play *The Dawn*, which depicted a besieged people uniting with soldiers against a tyrannical oppressor. Meyerhold modernized the play to affirm the alliance between the Red Army and proletarian workers, directing the actors to speak as though they were at a rally. At one point, the audience joined in for a singing of the Internationale. Despite this example of spontaneous audience involvement, which Meyerhold always encouraged, he was already at this point critiqued for not portraying the revolution "correctly," as Nadezhda Krupskaia judged his portrayal of the proletariat to be inadequate.[29] As such, the mass theater episode was short-lived: with the onset of NEP policies following the victory of wartime communism, subsidies were withdrawn from the RSFSR Theater and it was forced to close down. Meyerhold was still searching for a physical space that would enable him to bring his vision to life, a search that continued for the rest of his career.

Biomechanics

Beyond Meyerhold's actual involvement in musical performances, his early interest in music, as mentioned previously, manifests itself most directly in biomechanics. This technique characterizes his theatrical work in the revolutionary period and the 1920s, following his Symbolist experiments of the 1900s and early 1910s. Although Meyerhold never developed a systematic approach to acting that could be seen as analogous to Stanislavsky's "method," his invention of biomechanics serves to codify some of his chief principles of theatrical art, and represents his most concrete legacy to disciples and subsequent theater directors.

As a theatrical technique, biomechanics draws from two major contemporaneous movements. Taylorism, invented by the American mechanical engineer Frederick Winslow Taylor, attempted to maximize factory worker efficiency through smooth, rhythmic, economical movements that would both make the worker's job easier and lead to greater productivity. Taylor proposed a system of work cycles with rhythmic, precise motions, which also included rest minutes. Despite this method's American, capitalist origins, it was approved by Lenin as a way of increasing production; he and Trotsky endorsed a version of Taylorism by poet, revolutionary, and factory worker Alexei Gastev. In 1920, Gastev had founded and directed the Central Institute of Labor in Moscow, where he developed a scientific study of worker efficiency in Soviet factories. Although Meyerhold never actually mentions Gastev as a source for biomechanics, he clearly applies Taylorist principles to dramatic productions starting in 1921, right at the time of Gastev's experiments.[30] The method suggested ways of making actors' movements more precise, and at the same time, allowed Meyerhold to reduce the total time of his productions, in some cases by an hour or more.[31]

In addition, Meyerhold drew upon the research of Russian physiologist Ivan Pavlov, famous for his experiments on saliva collected from dogs to measure their responses to food under different circumstances. Pavlov developed a theory of conditioned reflexes that investigated the relationship between stimuli and the involuntary movements they caused. This theory helped Meyerhold develop his ideas on the connection between physical movements and positions and the emotions that he felt reflexively proceeded from them.

The basic rhythm of biomechanics consists of three parts: the *otkaz*, or preparation of an action (such as crouching before jumping), the *posil'* (the action itself), and the *tochka*, or end point of the action, at which the actor is at rest and prepared to initiate further actions. Meyerhold used these techniques to establish a precise relationship between the actor's physical actions and the emotions they demonstrated. In keeping with the Pavlovian theory of reflexology that influenced him, Meyerhold wanted the actor to use mechanical movements to produce universal emotions; in this sense, again, his techniques directly contradicted Stanislavsky's method, which encouraged the actor to start with internal, individualized emotions, and use them to inspire gestures, expressions, and physical movements. Meyerhold's three-part rhythm was intended to structure all of the actor's movements, establish a common language between actors and the director, and create a quasi-musical effect of fluid, rhythmically-organized contrasts in shape, color, and gesture.

Meyerhold's biomechanics, which embodied his actor-training technique, were accompanied in the early 1920s by constructivist stage designs. This simultaneously developing movement, promulgated by Aleksei Gan in his 1922 book *Constructivism*, similarly emphasized industrial, mechanical aspects of art. Just as Meyerhold celebrated the actor's body as the key to performance, constructivist collaborators such as Liubov Popova and Varvara Stepanova produced machine-like sets comprised of various wheels, chutes, ramps, and other mechanical devices that complemented Meyerhold's principal productions of the time: Belgian playwright Fernand Crommelynck's 1920 farce, *The Magnificent Cuckold*, and nineteenth-century Russian playwright Alexander Sukhovo-Kobylin's 1869 *The Death of Tarelkin*, both produced in 1922.

The earlier of these productions, *The Magnificent Cuckold*, offered audiences an introduction to Meyerhold's biomechanics, as the director realized his ambition of creating a new theater with actors trained in his own style for the first time. Its comic plot of love and jealousy lent itself particularly well to the three-part motions underlying the technique. In one scene, the jealous Bruno, who has no grounds to suspect his wife Stella of infidelity, describes her virtues to her cousin Petri and orders her to undress in order to test them. Noticing Petri's lust for Stella, he slaps him, and the motion cues the wheels of Popova's constructivist sets; this slap is an oft-cited example of Meyerhold's biomechanical etudes. *The Magnificent Cuckold* contained a great deal of bawdy, erotic content, which outraged Lunacharsky and led to a series of written polemics between him and Meyerhold. However, Meyerhold actually deemphasized the play's sexual element in favor of tragicomedy, or what Braun refers to as "a universal parable on the theme of jealousy, with the style of performance furnishing a constant commentary on the dialogue and the situations."[32] Overall, the clown-like acrobatics of the production were pleasing to most audiences and critics, who praised it for its spirit of youthful freshness.

The Mandate *and* The Government Inspector

Following Meyerhold's early projects involving biomechanics, he achieved an unusual victory in his work on Nikolai Erdman's 1924 play, *The Mandate*: this was one of his few productions that received near unanimous acclaim. The play, which satirizes communal living and exposes the bourgeoisie, represents a twentieth-century continuation of Gogol's comic style; not surprisingly, many characteristics of Meyerhold's production of it anticipate similar qualities in his next important production, *The Government Inspector*. In this respect, *The Mandate* represents an important development in his career, as Meyerhold moved from a style featuring masks, contrasting social classes, and the playful humor and acrobatics of *The Magnificent Cuckold* and other earlier productions to a more realist style that focused on the daily life and psychology of ordinary people of identical class origin. Erdman's play, which premiered on April 20, 1925, drew a great deal of laughter from the audiences; however, the satire was more somber and even grotesque than in earlier productions, as it featured heavy use of mime and freezing during moments of shocking revelations. The grim satire was underscored by Meyerhold's use of moving walls and sidewalks on the stage, with the walls intended to symbolize the bourgeoisie's isolation from the world, and its inability to adjust to the Soviet regime. Erdman turned out to be the only major Soviet playwright besides Mayakovsky with whom Meyerhold experienced a creatively satisfying collaboration. However, their next project, Erdman's 1928 play *The Suicide*, was far less successful. In a sign of the changing times, it was halted in production, and Erdman was eventually arrested and exiled to Siberia for nine years.

Many elements of *The Mandate*, especially the grotesque, satirical focus on banal, everyday events and the use of frozen poses, paved the way for his production the following year of Nikolai Gogol's 1842 play. *The Government Inspector* represents the high point of Meyerhold's post-revolutionary experiments, and perhaps even of his entire career. It can be seen as a kind of a signature piece, a summation of many of his metatheatrical innovations, use of rhythm to organize a production, loose treatment of classic texts, and adaptation of them to reflect contemporary reality.

Gogol's *The Government Inspector* is widely considered the greatest play in Russian literature. Its plot revolves around a young, penniless civil servant named Khlestakov, who has stopped at a provincial inn on his way home from St. Petersburg, and is in danger of being thrown out for not paying his bill. Meanwhile, the Mayor of the town has just received a letter warning him of an upcoming visit from a government inspector. A comedy of errors ensues, as the townspeople are convinced that Khlestakov's behavior—not paying his bills but nevertheless demanding to be served good food—proves that he is the incognito inspector.[33] For his part, Khlestakov is briefly convinced early on that the Mayor is attempting to imprison him, until he brings him to his home, feeds him, and introduces him to his wife and daughter, who along with the townspeople fawn on him and are easily led to believe him when he boasts of exaggerated, fictitious wealth, connections, and accomplishments. After being extravagantly wined, dined, and bribed, Khlestakov leaves town, and the townspeople realize the truth about him only after the postmaster intercepts a letter to a friend in which Khlestakov ridicules them for mistaking him for an inspector, and suggests that his friend, a writer, should compose a literary work out of his experience. The play ends with the announcement of the actual inspector, at which the townspeople freeze in terror.

After its initial production in 1836, Gogol was dissatisfied with the play's reception, as most audiences—including Tsar Nicholas I—viewed it as a farce. He revised it in 1842, adding character sketches, and several other changes that clarified it as a tragicomedy. The changes include the epigraph "It's no use blaming the mirror if your face is crooked," which clarified the moral message of the Mayor's famous announcement—to the townspeople but facing the audience—"What are you laughing at? You're laughing at yourselves!" These revisions, and the generic ambivalence inherent in the play, which should really be considered a tragicomedy of "laughter through tears," gave Meyerhold special leeway in his adaptation of the play for his production.

Characteristically, Meyerhold altered the classic text in order to try to get closer to Gogol's central ideas, and in doing so, offered an interpretation of the play's relevance for contemporary Soviet reality.[34] He did so in part by using "surrounding" texts: these included both the 1835 and

1842 versions of *The Government Inspector*, drafts of the play, and other works by Gogol, including *Dead Souls*, *Marriage*, *The Gamblers*, and his Petersburg Tales. In addition to drawing from a variety of texts in this manner, Meyerhold also synthesized the entire history of interpretation of the play, rejecting the focus on realism and social critique favored by Vissarion Belinsky and other nineteenth-century critics, and absorbing the Symbolist critique of Dmitry Merezhkovsky and others at the turn of the century. Influenced as well by Ivan Yermakov's 1924 Freudian analysis of the play, he emphasized the sexual aspects of *The Government Inspector*, for instance by focusing on the mother-daughter rivalry between Anna Andreevna (the Mayor's wife) and Maria Antonovna, and underscoring Anna Andreevna's voluptuousness. Overall, the production was saturated with pantomime, eccentric gestures, and grotesque, demonic images. This begins with the performance of principal character Khlestakov by Garin, who underscored the character's chameleon-like nature by portraying him as a demonic, cynical con-man. The Mayor, driven insane by his foolishness in accepting Khlestakov as the inspector, is taken away in a strait-jacket. Meyerhold turns a character briefly referred to in the play, the Officer in Transit, into a shadowy double of Khlestakov, who follows him around and participates in his schemes. Perhaps most ingeniously, he ends the production by producing Gogol's famous frozen scene with life-size effigies of the townspeople (thus turning the "mute scene" designation into a literal description). In general, the production conceptualized Gogol's play—similarly to Meyerhold's interpretations of *Masquerade* and Griboedov's *Woe from Wit*—as depicting a sense of inevitable tragedy, of the emptiness and horror of life.

Meyerhold's innovative techniques in *The Government Inspector* involve so-called kinetic staging, which allowed him to achieve a variety of settings without lengthy scene changes: these include his use of double-doors and a truck-stage that could roll back and forth and supplement the full stage, as well as movable platforms, which allowed him to divide the stage into "frames." These devices also incorporated cinematic techniques into the production, as the moving equipment allowed him to use close-up shots. The musical score was one of Meyerhold's most complex, as it included selections from composers Mikhail Glinka, Alexander Dargomyzhsky, and Mikhail Gnesin, as well as Jewish bands reminiscent of those Meyerhold heard in weddings and balls growing up in Penza. In typical Meyerholdian fashion, the music was used to signal onstage action, to reflect psychological underpinnings of events, and to create a grotesque, horrifying atmosphere. In general, Meyerhold strove to avoid anything farcical in his staging, unlike in early productions that were saturated with clowns, buffoons, and other elements of commedia dell'arte, as he consistently interpreted *The Government Inspector* as grotesque tragicomedy.

The Government Inspector, like nearly all of Meyerhold's productions, inspired a great deal of harsh criticism. The production was violently criticized for the liberties Meyerhold took with Gogol's text, for its complexity and length (unlike most of Meyerhold's productions, which aimed for maximal concision, *The Government Inspector* was over four hours long), and for Zinaida Raikh's acting in the role of Anna Andreevna.[35] Anatoly Lunacharsky in particular criticized the "eroticism" of the production. Nevertheless, *The Government Inspector* proved to be one of Meyerhold's most enduring masterpieces: it was performed continuously until 1938.

Productions of the 1930s

The 1920s began as a period of great innovation for Meyerhold, in which he put his principles of biomechanics into effect in *The Magnificent Cuckold* and other productions, collaborated with Mayakovsky on three projects, and attempted to merge his interest in audience participation with Bolshevik principles by encouraging proletarian viewers to respond actively to his performances. It ended with growing frustration, as his production of Erdman's 1928 *The Suicide* was prevented by *Glavrepertkom*, the commission for approval of dramatic repertory, from reaching the stage. Similarly, following the success of *Mystery-Bouffe*, Meyerhold's productions of Mayakovsky's *The Bedbug* (1928) and *The Bathhouse* (1930), which satirize Soviet philistinism, were heavily critiqued by RAPP (the Russian Association of Proletariat Writers), who judged them to be "anti-Soviet." Thus, by the end of the decade, Meyerhold had gone beyond inspiring aesthetic controversy. Now, he was experiencing growing disfavor with the Soviet cultural authorities on ideological grounds. Moreover, with Mayakovsky's suicide in 1930, Meyerhold lost the writer-partner with whom he had experienced the most success.

The 1930s, then, were a period of stagnation for Meyerhold. This included not only a slowing down of his theatrical innovations, but also the frustration of his lifelong goal of creating his ideal theatrical space, a project which he pursued eagerly for years, but which never came to fruition. During this period, Meyerhold turned more to classics, putting on only eight new productions from 1932 to 1938. His best-known productions in this period include short plays of contemporary Soviet writers Yuri Olesha, Vsevolod Vishnevsky, Ilya Selvinsky, and Yuri German, his 1934 production of Alexandre Dumas's *Camille*, and Petr Tchaikovsky's *Queen of Spades*.

In a sense, Meyerhold's artistic and political downfall reflects the changing politics of the Soviet Union. The 1920s, especially before Stalin's rise to power in 1925, allowed for a great deal of experimentation. Various cultural trends, ranging from the avant-garde experiments of Meyerhold and others to the proletarian art promoted by groups such as RAPP and RAPM (Russian Association of Proletarian Musicians) to the work of so-called fellow travelers such as Stanislavsky and Mikhail Bulgakov were able to coexist.[36] With the codification of Socialist Realism as the official and only acceptable approach to literature and the arts in 1932, Meyerhold and many other avant-garde artists struggled to conform to the demands of the cultural establishment for greater artistic simplicity, narratives easily accessible to the general public, and clear ideological messages that embraced a teleological vision of the eventual triumph of Communism. An artistic system of this sort directly contradicted Meyerhold's vision in many ways, perhaps most notably in his view of the audience's role in his productions. Meyerhold's emphasis on encouraging spectators to draw their own conclusions about the events depicted on stage made for audiences who were frequently divided in their interpretations. Such division directly contradicted the unanimity Stalinism sought in artistic creation and reception. Meyerhold was branded a "formalist," an ominous term that presaged his tragic fate in the late 1930s.

In a sense, Meyerhold's biggest "production" of the 1930s did not take place onstage, but rather involved the creation of a stage. Since his earliest productions, he had been frustrated by the limitations of the traditional theater space, which not only separated the stage from the spectators, but also did not have the audience capacity that he wanted. Meyerhold worked on plans for a new theater throughout the decade, supervising designs of architects Sergei Vakhtangov and Mikhail Barkin. The new, unprecedented type of theater would have fulfilled Meyerhold's central ideas on how theater space should be constructed. It was to consist of an enormous amphitheater, with a floor level stage continuous with both the auditorium and the street. The planned structure removed all boundaries between the stage and the auditorium, and to an extent, even the public outside the theater. It did not have a curtain, footlights, or an orchestra pit, and the dressing rooms were not concealed from the audience. Meyerhold's plan therefore demonstrates the remarkable consistency of his theatrical vision, as he had argued for the need to highlight the theater's artifice and make the stage and audience constant since his first years as a director early in the twentieth century. The design changed continuously throughout the 1930s: for example, its capacity was eventually reduced from 3000 to a more modest 1600. Ultimately, Meyerhold's theater was liquidated in 1938, bringing the project to an unsuccessful conclusion.

Meyerhold's Fate

Meyerhold represents one of the major casualties of the notorious Stalinist purges of the late 1930s, along with writers Isaac Babel, Boris Pilniak, and Osip Mandelstam, and many other major cultural figures. The so-called "Great Purge" of 1936-1938, in which hundreds of thousands of political leaders, military officers, kulaks, and members of the intelligentsia were executed after a series of show trials, had actually passed its most intense point by the time Meyerhold was arrested in June, 1939. Realizing that the purges had gone too far, Stalin replaced the head of the NKVD, Nikolai Yezhov, with Lavrenty Beria, and the NKVD orders of systematic repression were cancelled. Nevertheless, arrests and executions continued, in somewhat diminished numbers, throughout the 1940s and early 50s, ending only with Stalin's death in 1953.

Meyerhold's death, and the subsequent legend of his courageous, defiant response to increasing repressive cultural and political authorities, has become a significant part of our understanding of both his life and career, and the purges themselves. For one thing, as Jonathan Pitches remarks, "any version of Meyerhold's life is somehow uncontrollably coloured by his death. The bitter irony of his demise hangs over his work, constantly reminding us of the volatile context within which he was practising his art."[37] In addition, his execution early in

1940 confirms the ongoing nature of the purges, which continued to affect millions of people long after their "high point" in 1937. Meyerhold actually felt he had some reason to hope for the restrictions against his artistic activities to be lifted shortly before his death, due to encouragement by Alexander Fadeev, Secretary of the Union of Soviet Writers, who called for greater freedom for artists. These hopes, of course, proved to be illusory.

The natural drive to find something redemptive in an atrocity of the scale of the purges, combined perhaps with the Russian predilection to create legends out of artists who die before their time, prompted a great deal of rewriting of history in the case of Meyerhold's relations with Soviet authorities in the last years of his life. The facts of Meyerhold's death and the surrounding circumstances were obscured by two principal factors: the Soviet reluctance to open up the archives even after his posthumous rehabilitation, and the émigré critic Yuri Elagin's misleading, fabricated account of Meyerhold's response to Soviet criticism in his 1951 biography of the director. Elagin inaccurately portrays Meyerhold as a defiant rebel and martyr by fabricating a more heroic version of his 15 June 1939 speech at the Union of Soviet Writers. Although the loud, repeated applause for Meyerhold, which clearly discomfited the establishment, may have indicated some *expectation* of a defiant speech, what Meyerhold actually delivered, as Braun points out, was "sadly deferential, rambling, and inconclusive."[38] Moreover, Meyerhold not only apologized for his past "mistakes" in a show of contrition that was typical of purged Soviet artists, but also named names of other directors supposedly guilty of "formalism." In reality, his speech received an unfavorable critical reception, as Isaac Kroll and Moissei Yanovsky wondered why Meyerhold compromised himself so much.[39] One may draw two conclusions from Meyerhold's behavior. First, it shows that he believed—like Fadeev and others—that he would be treated leniently and have opportunities for greater artistic freedom at this point in time when the Purges were (supposedly) coming to an end. In addition, it underscores his belief that, even at the age of sixty-five, he felt that he still had a great deal to offer the Soviet cultural world; his various planned projects, especially the still incomplete theater whose construction he was supervising, bear up that point.

Meyerhold's Legacy

Vsevolod Meyerhold's significance for the Russian avant-garde movement, in some respects, is easier to explain in relation to the work of his collaborators. Through his close work with Chekhov, Blok, Mayakovsky, Eisenstein, Shostakovich, Prokofiev, and many of the other major cultural figures in all areas during his life, Meyerhold played a major role in shaping the course of the other arts as well as theater. However, his directing is more difficult to illustrate in a concrete way than the contributions of these coworkers, in part simply because of the theatrical medium. Students of literature, film, and music can easily experience these artists' works through trips to libraries, video stores and online distributors, opera houses, and concert halls. By contrast, there is little extant film footage of Meyerhold's productions, and our knowledge of his direction derives largely from photographs, drawings, his own occasional notes, and reminiscences by students, colleagues, and critics. To some extent, of course, this is true of any director of theater, a medium whose impact hinges on unique, unrepeatable performances. Even in comparison to his erstwhile mentor and longstanding rival Stanislavsky, however, Meyerhold's oeuvre is difficult to experience directly. In contrast to Stanislavsky's legions of Russian and Western disciples, Meyerhold's techniques, writings, and productions were prohibited for decades. Moreover, photographs, which can never capture the dynamism of a play, are particularly inadequate for a director who made actors' motions and the overall rhythm of a production paramount.

Nevertheless, we still have a variety of ways to envision what Meyerhold did in his productions. Braun points out Meyerhold's extensive influence on a variety of major directors, including Peter Brooks, Yuri Liubimov, Anatoly Efros, Ariane Mnouchkine, Joan Littlewood, and Eugenio Barba.[40] Other critics have noted Meyerhold's more immediate influence on contemporary directors such as Bertolt Brecht and Edwin Piscator.[41] For the film director Grigory Kozintsev, Meyerhold's greatest influence was on cinema, as he lists himself, Leonid Trauberg, Nikolai Ekk, Avram Room, and of course, Eisenstein as products of Meyerhold's teaching.[42] As Law and Gordon point out, "Eisenstein, through his super-rational means, was the only avant-garde artist who fully explored the aesthetic and scientific principles of Biomechanics. Today, we owe much of our understanding of Meyerhold's ideas on acting and movement to Eisenstein's critical appraisal and elaborations."[43] The spirit of Meyerhold's dynamic experiments has lived on in these theater and film directors' works, and with the renewed possibilities for applying his biomechanics techniques not only in the West but also in Russia since the 1990s, the future of his method and influence is open and promising.

Endnotes

1 As quoted in Rudnitsky, *Meyerhold, the Director,* 320-321.

2 As Mel Gordon and Alma Law note, Meyerhold actually studied law less out of interest than to postpone his career while he searched for his niche in the artistic world (18).

3 For his audition, Meyerhold famously imitated Stanislavsky's performance of Othello.

4 As quoted in Rudnitsky, *Meyerhold, the Director,* 12.

5 Stanislavsky himself describes a reciprocal influence between Meyerhold and the Moscow Art Theater in *My Life in Art*.

6 Briusov, "Against Naturalism in the Theater," 27.

7 Ibid, 28.

8 Braun, *Meyerhold on Theatre*, 199-200 (Meyerhold's emphasis).

9 Ibid, 31.

10 In this, Meyerhold was greatly influenced by theater critic Georg Fuchs, author of *The Stage of the Future*. This work promoted the idea of drama as shared ritual, and such elements as its focus on the actor's rhythmic physical movements, and bringing the audience closer to the stage, helped shape Meyerhold's own theory.

11 As Edward Braun points out, Meyerhold's interest in Symbolist theater in the early 1900s created a clash between his political activism and artistic interests, since Symbolism was an artistic current whose concerns were generally more religious than political, and which often preached retreat from the physical world into the spiritual, the otherworldly. "Genuine as Meyerhold's populist sentiments remained," Braun remarks, "the more he embraced symbolism, the less his work remained in touch with the momentous events being enacted beyond the doors of the theater." Braun, *Meyerhold: A Revolution in Theatre*, 30.

12 Meyerhold had rejected a previous invitation from Komissarzhevskaia in 1904.

13 The Russian title presents considerable translation difficulties. "Balaganchik" has been translated variously as "The Puppetshow," "The Puppetshow Booth," and "The Fairground Booth," none of which quite get across its peculiar set of resonances. Rzhevsky, in a recent study of theater history, translates it as "A Little Tomfoolery" in an effort to convey those resonances.

14 *Balaganchik* is a "play à clef," as Pierrot, Harlequin, and Columbine represent Blok himself, Bely, and Blok's wife Liubov Mendeleeva, respectively; these three were involved in a love triangle at the time.

15 Rudnitsky, *Meyerhold, the Director,* 109-110.

16 Moreover, Meyerhold himself, of course, was a highly polemical writer. His antagonistic responses in his writings, to critics and opponents, was yet another quality that

was antithetical to the restraint practiced by Stanislavsky, himself a frequent target of Meyerhold's polemics.

17 Rzhevsky, *The Modern Russian Theater,* 13.

18 From E.T.A. Hoffmann's character. Meyerhold used it to express his sense of his dual, contradictory roles as director of an established state theater and experimenter who continued to teach and develop actors in cabaret theaters.

19 Meyerhold, *Meyerhold on Theatre*, 130.

20 Rudnitsky, *Meyerhold, the Director*, 234.

21 Law and Gordon, *Meyerhold, Eisenstein and Biomechanics*, 50.

22 Schmidt, *Meyerhold at Work*, 40.

23 See Braun, *Meyerhold: A Revolution in Theatre*, 86-95.

24 Meyerhold thought that Wagner's historical portrayals of the legends, complete with helmets and swords, were unrealistic. Characteristically, he preferred inspiring the audience to imagine the time period to recreating it precisely.

25 Braun, *Meyerhold: A Revolution in Theatre*, 95.

26 Rudnitsky, *Meyerhold, the Director*, 253 (his italics).

27 Mayakovsky, *Plays*, 39.

28 As quoted in Braun, *Meyerhold: A Revolution in Theatre*, 157.

29 As Braun remarks, Krupskaia, Lunacharsky, and other Bolsheviks were somewhat uncomfortable with the support avant-garde artists gave them, since they were concerned that it did not depict the proletariat accurately, or in a sufficiently compelling way (*Meyerhold: A Revolution in Theatre*, 156, 165).

30 Gastev, who was arrested and executed on false charges of counter-revolutionary terrorist activity, became one of the millions of victims of Stalin's Great Purge. He was shot to death on 14 April 1939, less than a year before Meyerhold experienced the same fate.

31 Moscow Art Theater productions, by contrast, did not establish strict time limits on the actors' emotional expressiveness, which often led to lengthy productions that Meyerhold felt lacked a guiding rhythm or pace.

32 Braun, *Meyerhold: A Revolution in Theatre*, 182. Most other critics, including Mayakovsky and People's Commissar of Public Health Nikolai Semashko, disagreed with Lunacharsky and praised the production. See Rudnitsky, 305-310, for a detailed discussion of the critical controversy surrounding *The Magnificent Cuckold*.

33 This premise is supposedly derived from Pushkin's account of being mistaken for a government inspector.

34 Meyerhold's production coincided with a revival of the Moscow Art Theater, who in addition to Mikhail Bulgakov's *White Guard*, produced classics such as *Hamlet*.

35 Meyerhold's bias toward former student Raikh, who became his second wife in 1924, is generally judged to be one of his most significant blind spots as a director. His insistence on using Raikh, not a first-rate talent, in roles that surpassed her range often led to discord with other actors. For instance, the actress Maria Babanova, whose performance as Stella in *The Magnificent Cuckold* first brought her prominence, left Meyerhold's theater in 1927, in large part because Raikh was receiving so many leading roles; another of his major actors, Igor Ilinsky, left the theater in 1925 for the same reason, although he returned three years later.

36 The term "fellow traveler" was first coined by Leon Trotsky in the second chapter of his 1924 *Literature and the Revolution*.

37 Pitches, *Vsevolod Meyerhold*, 3.

38 Braun, *Meyerhold: A Revolution in Theatre*, 149.
39 On this speech, see also Laurence Selenick, who calls Meyerhold "a talented opportunist, whose ideals were tailored to fit the occasion, in order to allow for his own work" (157). This description seems unfair: although Meyerhold did indeed embrace communism immediately in 1917, he did so at a time when most thought the Bolsheviks would not prevail. Moreover, despite his capitulation in this speech, he had earlier argued for the artist's right to experiment, and defended Dmitry Shostakovich against the notorious attacks on his opera, *Lady Macbeth of Mtsensk.*
40 Braun, *Meyerhold: A Revolution in Theatre*, 311.
41 See for instance Katherine Eaton and Peter Zazzali on his influence on Brecht.
42 Further, according to Leonid Kozlov, Meyerhold himself was the model for Eisenstein's Ivan the Terrible. Braun, *Meyerhold: A Revolution in Theatre*, 312.
43 Law and Gordon, *Meyerhold, Eisenstein and Biomechanics*, 75.

2. The Culture of Experiment in Russian Theatrical Modernism: the OBERIU Theater and the Biomechanics of Vsevolod Meyerhold

Michael Klebanov

It can be argued that the OBERIU Theater, whose agenda was proclaimed in 1929, sought to challenge the dominance of Meyerhold on the Russian experimental theatrical scene of the day, rather as Meyerhold in his early days departed from seeking more radical alternatives to Stanislavsky's system. However, whereas his "biomechanics" proceeded from the ambition to relieve actors from verbal speech, imparting particular intensity to their body language instead, its message hardly varied in its essence from that of the preceding theater schools. It is mostly the method of expression, the set of instruments that underwent substantial changes.

Although biomechanics, according to Meyerhold, strove to discover experimentally the laws of the actor's movement onstage, it still spoke of 'norms of human behavior' from which the rules of play-acting were to be derived. OBERIU devotees of the 'real (concrete) art', however, were quite ready to renounce all norms and use any available language for the sake of presenting, as their Manifesto states, 'the world of concrete objects onstage in their interaction and collision'. Furthermore, they asserted that the laws of 'reality' were inapplicable in the 'alternate' reality of theater. In what follows below, I aim to explore the relationship, if unilateral, between the two mindsets, with an emphasis on the novelty, though almost unmarked at its time, of the respective OBERIU ideas.

In a 1933 letter to the actress Klavdia Pugacheva,[1] Daniil Kharms (1905-1942), Russian poet, author and playwright, one of the founders and prominent members of the avant-garde union of artists OBERIU, made the following observation:

> I love theater dearly, but alas, there is no theater now. The age of theater, long poems and beautiful architecture was over a hundred years ago. Don't be tempted by

> the false hope that Khlebnikov wrote long poems, and Meyerhold's theater is still theater. Khlebnikov is better than all other poets of the second half of 19th and first quarter of 20th century, but his poems are only long verses, and Meyerhold has done nothing.[2]

Those even vaguely familiar with the theater director, actor, and producer Vsevolod Meyerhold (1874-1940) and the role he played in the development of Russian theatrical art, might find these words blunt, to the point of provocation. One might almost think that Kharms pretended to ignore Meyerhold's achievements for the sake of some purportedly radical gesture. However, this ostensibly nihilist rhetoric hides a deeper meaning. Nostalgia for the times when Neo-Classicists dominated European culture (eighteenth—early nineteenth century) is overt here, and it seems quite in line with the set of ideas that Kharms consistently pursued. As early as 1927, a group of prospective OBERIU members decided to call themselves *The Academy of Left Classicists*;[3] and almost a decade later Kharms publicly denounced both "impressionism" and "left art" in his speech at the Leningrad Writers' Union,[4] asserting that "the time has come when art can start developing again with a classical force."[5] One may question the sincerity of this speech, delivered in a politically charged and potentially dangerous atmosphere; it would be more questionable though to doubt the candour of the author's private correspondence. Referring to Klavdia Pugacheva's recently abandoned position at the Leningrad Young Spectator's Theater, Kharms wrote:

> If I were you, I would either try to create the new theater myself, if I felt grand enough for such an endeavour, or hold on to the theater of the most archaic forms. By the way, Children's Theater stands in a better position than theaters for adults. Even if it doesn't launch a new era of renaissance, even if it is contaminated by theatrical science, "constructions" and "leftism", due to the peculiar nature of the children's audience... it is still purer than other theaters.[6]

These lines seem to be in direct correspondence to the comprehensive revision that Kharms tried to apply in the 1930s to his early attempts to bond "left" (that is, avant-garde in terms of the early twentieth century) and "classic" art. In 1932, he returned to Leningrad from exile, to which he was sentenced as a consequence of the notorious "Three Left Hours" evening that turned out to be both the loudest and the very last public manifestation of OBERIU's artistic principles. He did resort in those years to the neo-classical mode in his poetry and prose,[7] which probably had little to do with repentance and even less so with conformism, since he hardly had a chance to publish them anyway. It must have been a considerable effort on his part to criticize Khlebnikov, who had been an enormous influence on him.[8] Was then Daniil Kharms really too harsh in his estimation of Meyerhold?

It is hard to ignore, of course, the almost polar differences in terms of social standing and formal success that existed between the two at the time. Within the theater that bore his own name,[9] Meyerhold enjoyed opportunities that Kharms could never realize for himself. The very first (and the last) production of the OBERIU theater, *Elizaveta Bam*, was arguably the most remarkable part of "Three Left Hours" that soon fomented the persecution and arrest of its organizers; while Meyerhold, in spite of the growing official criticism,[10] was able to exercise his directorial capacities until his own arrest in 1939. Apparently, Kharms could not help being irritated by Meyerhold's accord with the authorities and his celebrity status; a sardonic remark that he left in 1935 made witness to that:

> One lady, wringing her hands in dismay, said: "I need interest in life, not money. I'm looking for captivation, not wealth. I need a husband who isn't a rich man but a talent, a director, a Meyerhold."[11]

There are ways to prove nonetheless that Kharms' attitude towards the stalwart of the Russian theatrical avant-garde did not amount to pure envy, if his devotion to Neo-Classicism in tandem with the dismissal of "leftism" does not seem enough. One basic argument is unequivocally rooted in the dialectics of the avant-garde itself. Being more than thirty years younger than his famous counterpart, Kharms belonged to the generation that was naturally entitled to supersede the achievements of Meyerhold in order to establish themselves as the foremost artists of the day. Around the mid-twenties, when Kharms and his comrades were starting their first theatrical enterprise, *Radix*, Meyerhold already was a recognized authority as a theater director and theorist. Yet, submitting the request for rehearsal space for *Radix* to GINHUK[12] in 1926, Daniil Kharms wrote: "The theatrical group *Radix* . . . is setting itself a goal to create a *pure theater* production that would not be subject to literature [italics mine—MK]."[13] The declaration of intent seems to have been sufficiently clear that the theatre of Meyerhold was now passé (for OBERIU).

The name *Radix*, it should be noted, apart from its Latin etymology that is directly concerned with purification and looking back to the abiding origins, points quite ingenuously to the intention to be radical.[14] After a decade of Soviet power, Meyerhold's theater still thrived, along with Stanislavskii's,[15] and moreover, was still considered cutting-edge when compared to conservative academic theaters like the Maly. Unsurprisingly, this situation must have given OBERIU good reason to reflect upon the meaning of being truly radical rather than reputedly "progressive" or "avant-garde". It is worth remembering that in those same years, Dadaism and Surrealism gradually acquired the same kind of reputation. In his elucidating article *Dada, Surrealism and the Academy of the Avant-Garde*, Charles Millard argues that the cultural movements traditionally listed among the most vibrant and uncompromising had in fact eventually petrified into their own brands of academic conservatism.[16]

There is more than enough evidence that Meyerhold consistently did his best to create what would effectively become "his own academy." *The Theater of Meyerhold* as an institution is, perhaps, only the most superficial and obvious instance. The reports of his alleged "directorial tyranny"[17] evoke associations of a hardly less totalitarian nature than his constant attempts to devise doctrines like "biomechanics"[18] with which to rule his obedient team of actors. Even at the dawn of his career, Meyerhold seemed to arouse controversies with his stance on the actor's freedoms;[19] this trend only gained in strength over time. It can be argued, of course, that this strategy corresponded only too well to the overall tendency that Western theater of the Modernist period seemed to follow, causing Eugene Ionesco to complain as late as 1960: "when the theater could be the place of the greatest freedom, of the wildest imaginings, it has become that of the greatest constraint, of a rigid and set system of *conventions* [italic mine—MK]."[20] Three decades earlier, the academy of the avant-garde already was on its way to becoming a full-fledged reality, even as its over-dominant leaders, whether Vsevolod Meyerhold or André Breton,[21] were still able to strike the public imagination as purportedly revolutionary artists.

It is remarkable though that regardless of the increasingly aggressive attacks from the traditionalists, Meyerhold started receiving criticism from the "left artists" as early as the twenties. Daniil Kharms was probably one of the first[22] to reject him completely;[23] but it was the director Igor Terentiev, who was still under the influence of Meyerhold's ideas, who blasted him in 1926 for "the right deviation" in his production of Nikolai Gogol's "The Inspector General."[24] Terentiev's own production of the same play served as an extended polemical answer to Meyerhold's venture. The proponents of the emerging OBERIU theater, in their turn influenced by Terentiev,[25] were thus compelled to come forward with more than just an answer: nothing less than an entirely new ideological and conceptual approach was expected to emerge. *Radix*, according to the definition given by Kharms and cited above, intended "not to be subject to literature." It seems that being ever more radical, it obliged its participants at the time to step beyond literature in the full sense of the word: that is, beyond any possible interpretation of a literary text in general and a literary plot in particular for the purpose of creating a stage performance.

The idea of a theater that would be independent of literature, as emphasized in the *Radix* declaration, appeared to be very appropriately positioned at the edge of the evolution that theatrical art, particularly in Russia, came to experience in its relationship with literature since the nineteenth century.[26] Any possible reaction or protest against Meyerhold's methods from the more radical standpoint was bound to echo his own protest against the method of Konstantin Stanislavskii that he launched from the experimental studio within the Moscow Art Theater (MAT).[27] However, Stanislavskii himself gained his fame first and foremost for the revolt against his predecessors and their tackling of the dramatic text. "The process-oriented approach he developed was a reaction against the artificiality and grandiloquence of 19th century theatricality."[28] Stanislavskii sought to replace the pretence of the contemporary theatrical academy with the "truth" of action: the issue that still revolved around the determining role of the literary basis provided by the playwright. The main concern dealt with the fictitious nature of a play's internal reality and the ways of converting it into an actual reality of representation onstage. The tradition of transposing this literary reality as it were onto stage resulted in the affectation of performance; the desire to substitute it completely with the imitation of ordinary life led to the naturalism that was also much in vogue in Stanislavskii's early days. The third way that he eventually established followed another fashion of the day, the growing interest in psychoanalysis and the human psyche in general. There was another, yet untapped reality, the hitherto unexplored world of the actor's psyche which one could translate into a new kind of scenic image projected through the prism of the dramatic character. This approach inevitably emphasized the actor's significance, substantiating Stanislavskii's reputation as "the first Western director to explicitly set criteria by which the work of the actor might be appraised, and the function of theater evaluated."[29] Indeed, theater could consequently exceed its function as a mere galvanizing (in terms of the nineteenth century, rather than of modern technology) machine to enliven the corpse of a literary text. Nevertheless, preoccupation with reality even in this mode remained inseparable from a preoccupation with literature, so that the outcome in fact amounted to a new variety of realism, but was obviously far from what OBERIU would call "real art" (as per their Manifesto, to be discussed below).

For Stanislavskii, "realistic" was quite synonymous with "real," as evidenced in his words of blessing for Meyerhold when entrusting him with the experimental Theater Studio workshop in 1905: "Realism is outlived. The time has come to stage the unreal."[30] Little though the MAT maitre appreciated that experiment,[31] his prejudice against Symbolism, by then the main opposing artistic movement to Realism in Russia, apparently blinded him as to whether Meyerhold really intended to stage the "unreal." Meyerhold's own words may suggest that his objectives were not so unlike those of Stanislavskii, but in order to reach them, very different means were to be employed:

> In my opinion the concept of "stylization" is indivisibly tied up with the idea of convention, generalization and symbol. To "stylize" a given period or phenomenon means to employ every possible means of expression in order to reveal the inner synthesis of that period or phenomenon, to bring out those hidden features which are to be found

deeply embedded in the style of any work of art.[32]

These words with all of their explicitly Symbolist message contain two terms that Meyerhold used intensively at the start of his directorial career: "stylization" and "convention." It cannot be missed, however, that he cares to interpret them in his own way instead of adopting unconditionally the jargon of the Symbolist movement. In fact, as a director Meyerhold soon started to veer away from the movement rather than towards it; his association with the "renegade Symbolist" Aleksandr Blok[33] for the sake of producing the latter's *The Fairground Booth* made it quite apparent. While Stanislavskii, in his pursuit of "authenticity", labored to extract the emotional "truth" through the actor's identification with the character, Meyerhold and Blok, argues Edward Braun, "were able to articulate this same fundamental truth" by their own means, "and in so doing give their art a crucial new direction away from the resigned immobility of Symbolism."[34] In this way, the clear-cut choice between Symbolism and Stanislavskian Realism was avoided, and a new alternative was devised in order to proceed. Meyerhold, in whose eyes Stanislavskii's "identification" certainly did not exhaust "every possible means of expression," opposed it with its reversal, distanciation[35] that was bound to evoke polemics around the notion of theatricality. "For Stanislavsky, theatricality appears as a kind of distancing from reality—an effect of exaggeration, an intensification of behavior that rings false when juxtaposed with what should be the realistic truth of the stage."[36] For Meyerhold, however, and for those to follow him, adherence to theatricality signified, in one way or another, the beginning of a return to what Kharms called "pure theatre."

Meanwhile, it must have been clear to any protagonist of this new "theatrical" theater, that if it was to withdraw from the guardianship of literature, it had to abandon literary language as well. "The stage must speak its own language and impose its own laws."[37] It can be argued that Meyerhold's definition of "stylization" already hinted at the new language to come; and even his early productions (notably *The Fairground Booth*) employed a kind of symbolic language where gestures and movements, or all things that could be used as symbols, were most heavily relied upon.[38] This tendency developed further with the introduction of what Silvija Jestrovic calls the "defamiliarization devices."[39] Those included predominantly elements of such theatrical forms as *commedia dell' arte*, circus, or marionette theater, all characterized by both the dominance of theatricality and artificiality over illusionist elements and the dominance of performance over the written text to be referred to onstage. Later, similar ideas were adopted to some extent by Alexander Tairov[40] and became incorporated in the theoretical writings of Nicolai Evreinov.[41] With Meyerhold himself, they climaxed in his arguably most famous invention, "biomechanics."

There is, however, another thing worth mentioning that concerns Meyerhold's attempts to redefine the language of theatre—his notion of the grotesque. In 1912, he formulated the following definition:

> The grotesque mixes opposites, consciously creating the harsh incongruity, playing entirely on its own originality . . . The grotesque deepens life's outward appearance to the point where it ceases to appear merely natural . . . The basis of the grotesque is the artist's constant desire to switch the spectator from the plane he has just reached to another that is totally unforeseen.[42]

While this quote betrays its author's somewhat straightforward urge to appear "original," it seems more important that it touches, in its own way, upon the same problem of representing reality. Perhaps, the word "incongruity" attracts the most attention here. When Josette Feral says that for Meyerhold, there is no equivalence between representation and reality, it is noteworthy that she refers to his theatrical philosophy as "a kind of grotesque realism."[43] Should we accept the suggestion that Meyerhold's art was, for all its innovations and eccentricities, realistic rather than "real"? In his treatise "On Theater," the director himself made a remark that may prove interesting in this regard: "the grotesque, devoted to making decorative what is monstrous, does not allow beauty to become sentimental."[44] Did he then believe that the function of the grotesque was to be pacifying rather than disturbing? It would be hard to deny that "grotesque realism" in theater may turn out to be as much influenced by grotesque-oriented literature, as traditional realism was and is influenced by the traditional Realist literature. Similarly, the language of grotesque performance may reveal itself as an expansion of the same literary language brought to a certain extreme and, at its best, translated into a different system of signs (alternative to that of verbal language). Still, there is an affinity between the words "incongruity" and "absurd" that cannot be easily ignored.

In spite of his criticism of Meyerhold, Igor Terentiev seemed to remain the latter's ardent supporter, and even progeny. Jean Philippe Jaccard maintains that both directors, after all, shared the same aspiration for the kind of performance that would follow its own rules and acquire its own autonomous reality, "with the aid of the new system of designations preset by conventions".[45] We remember that Meyerhold spoke about conventions in connection with the idea of stylization; moreover, he came to define his idea of theater in general as the "theater of conventions": "Theater is *uslovnyi* [that of conventions] when the audience never for a moment forgets that these are actors acting, nor the actors, that they have before them an audience."[46] Here is then yet another question: is it the same theater equipped with a new semiosis that Jaccard has in mind? Meyerhold seems to prefer the term "uslovnyi" so as to avoid any mention of "formalism," a word scarcely used in the Soviet Union of the thirties out of the political context.[47] Kharms, we should remember as well, used the "discussion" on formalism in 1936 as a formal occasion to denounce the "left art"; and again, it would be misleading to attribute it entirely to his good sense of self-preservation. Apparently, Kharms' attitude to formalism was quite as ambiguous as he admitted in his speech at the Writers Union[48]. In his jeeringly comic poem "The Bath of Archimedes" he complains jokingly (or half-jokingly?) through Archimedes' mouth about being "befouled by the names of the most famous persons, particularly formalists."[49] At the same time, contrary to his hero Terentiev, he definitely did not like Meyerhold. It is difficult to imagine that he would praise him for the same cause for which he praised Terentiev. This is where the opposition of realism and classicism transpires most vividly: Kharms could hardly appreciate *realistic* art, however, "left" or grotesque. On the other hand, if the semiosis that Jean Philippe Jaccard hints at was so powerfully productive as to facilitate the new reality, then this is precisely what the Association for Real Art (OBERIU) would long for.

The "OBERIU Theater" section of the OBERIU Manifesto says the following:

> Until now, all the [theatrical] elements have been subject to the dramatic plot, the drama. Drama is an account of a

> certain event. All that happens onstage aims at explaining the meaning and the course of that event: as clear, comprehensibly and lifelike as possible.[50]

It is easy to see that the Manifesto, first published in 1928, utterly dismisses all of the possible attempts of the OBERIU predecessors to prevent the theatrical performance from being driven by the "dramatic plot": including, naturally, those of Meyerhold. Plain ignorance of the latter's work must be excluded here; rather, these sentences sound very much in keeping with the remark that Kharms made five years later: "Meyerhold has done nothing."[51] Moreover, albeit Igor Terentiev is mentioned in the introductory part of the Manifesto, here Meyerhold is passed over in silence, along with leading figures of the Russian avant-garde: Alexey Kruchenykh, Kazimir Malevich[52], Vassily Kandinsky[53] and Pavel Filonov[54]. OBERIU did leave the impression of being radical to the furthest possible extreme.

One may wonder whether this radicalism proceeded from anything but a sheer excess of youthful self-confidence;[55] it might be advisable though to have another look at the text of the Manifesto before finalizing the conclusion. "It will be theater", it says, "even if it [whatever occurs onstage—MK] happens with no relation to the dramatic plot."[56] At this point, it seems necessary to clarify what is meant here by "dramatic plot." Does "dramatic plot" equal "dramatic text" in this particular context? What we know about Meyerhold may suggest that he would consistently resist the influence of the dramatic text, at least with reference to its "literary" side, since the word "literary" kept being used on the corresponding occasions. "Very early in his writings on theater he is opposed to the idea of performance as a mere embodiment of the dramatic text, stating that theater is not in the service of literature."[57] The simple thing is that the dramatic text can be either abandoned completely or kept in one way or another; and if it is to be kept, it has to be reckoned with. In the latter case, it can be either deviated from or translated into a different medium, or at least these are two possible options. The most trivial method to deviate from the dramatic text is to allow actors to improvise, failing which the director takes the risk of becoming an involuntary (or vice versa) co-author of the dramatist. We know, however, that this is exactly what Meyerhold, throughout his directorial career, had been reluctant to do, unless it was within the rigid directional frame he would set for the occasion.[58] It may be true that he "shifted the emphasis from the dramatic text to the actor's body;"[59] but if "the actor is the key and minimal unit that enables a theatrical event to take place, even when the performance is stripped of all other components and properties,"[60] then the pressure upon him/her must exceed anything possible in the psychological theater of Stanislavsky.

In the case of Meyerhold, an apparently authoritative director, following the principles of well-elaborated systems like "biomechanics" would inevitably turn an actor as a "minimal unit" into a unit of the special code, that is, a new language, a medium to supplant the "literary" language of the dramatic text. The actor's personality, submitted to the system's laws, was not supposed to hinder its discourse.[61] To all appearances, Meyerhold was little troubled by accusations that he converted actors into puppets, dating as far back as to the days of his break-up with Vera Komissarzhevskaya.[62] Much more than that, his agenda for the actor: "no pauses, no psychology, no 'authentic emotions' either on the stage or whilst building a role"[63] was manifestly aimed at converting an actor into a kind of sign intended to convey a message as a modular part of the overall systemic message of the performance. Surely, it falls very neatly in line with Meyerhold's idea of the "uslovnyi" theater, since terminologically there is not much difference between a "system of conventions" and a "system of preset designations (or signs)"; in fact, this also goes along with the above-cited words of Jean Philippe Jaccard. As if to maintain that by "uslovniy" Meyerhold actually meant "formalistic", his own assistants accentuated in 1926 that "the basis of Meyerhold's system is *the formal display of the emotional.*"[64] Silvija Jestrovic joins this suggestion, asserting that Meyerhold strove to achieve anti-Stanislavskian "retheatricalization" through practising distanciation from the "familiar" (that is, traditional) theatrical devices in a way most reminiscent of "*ostranenie*" (estrangement) as elaborated by Russian Formalists.[65] It is curious that the whole idea of the "theater of conventions" seems to proceed directly from the principles of the original Symbolist drama where, according to Jenny Stelleman, "the dramatis persona was not seen as a 'character' but as a personification of abstract idea and was part of total scenery."[66] No matter how much the Russian Constructivism[67] might oppose itself to the Russian (and any other) Symbolism, there is a clear path from the "abstract idea" (personified by an actor) as part of "total scenery" to the "minimal unit" (represented by an actor) as part of a "system of preset designations", hardly less total in the way it was organized. Anyway, it can be concluded that Meyerhold admittedly managed to devise his own systemic language[68] with which to trans-code the message of the dramatic text and thus free himself of its literary fetters, if only for the sake of "displaying the emotional." The question still is how successfully he managed to free himself of the dependence on the *dramatic plot*.

It must be noted, meanwhile, that notwithstanding his efforts to increase the autonomy of theatrical language, Meyerhold apparently never considered renouncing the dramatic text as such. Marjory Hoover points out that even in the "acrobatically constructivist" "Death of Tarelkin" (staged after the nineteenth century Russian playwright Sukhovo-Kobylin's comedy) the actors spoke their lines unexceptionably.[69] Being unwilling to depend on literature, this eminent progenitor of the modern-day "physical theater"[70] was unable to let it go. "At his best, he interpreted literature in a highly sophisticated, often controversial, always interesting manner."[71] Still, with all due respect to that, he seemed to be in constant need and pursuit of literary patterns to interpret. It became most evident in the early thirties, when the atmosphere in the country was steadily worsening and Meyerhold, bereft of the contemporary playwrights to work with, gave himself up almost entirely to "reinterpreting" classical drama (and did so until the end of his professional career)[72]. His last productions show basically the same approach as the early ones: the text was indeed reinterpreted and recoded, but the plot was followed, or modified to become just another literary plot. Let us turn again to the OBERIU manifesto:

> A succession of events, organized by a director, will produce a theatrical performance with its own plotline and its own scenic meaning. That will be the kind of plot that only theater can offer. The plot of theatrical performance is theatrical, just as the plot of the musical piece is musical. They all depict the world of phenomena as it is, but relay it differently with respect to their medium... The object and the phenomenon, transposed from life to the stage, lose their life-related consistency and acquire a new, theatrical logic.[73]

There are several points that can be inferred from this passage. Firstly, the OBERIU theater suggests forming the plot of a theatrical performance *onstage*. It does not exclude the pre-existence of the dramatic plot, yet vows no exclusive obedience to it, either. The counterbalance of "events" and the plot unfolding onstage is to be orchestrated by a director, yet the element of improvisation is not shunned, and maybe even encouraged: for instance, if the actor impersonating a minister, as the Manifesto suggests, is expected at some moment to combine this mission with impersonating a wolf. If Meyerhold used the literary basis so as to create a theater where "the word is employed as only one among several elements" (see above), the OBERIU clearly aimed at creating a kind of theater where the *plot* would be employed in the same non-oppressive way. Secondly, comparing theater to music in this context, they point to the possibility for theater to become as unique and independent a medium as music can be: both non-figurative and non-literary. Thirdly, the performance at the OBERIU theater is supposed to be *free of interpretation*: that is, free of interpreting the external sources of the performance, notably, the dramatic text. Instead, it chooses to *present*, rather than represent, those sources "as they are," relieved of their extra-theatrical interrelations, while producing its own authentic meaning in situ to be interpreted by the audience. "Our task is to present the world of concrete objects onstage in their interactions and collisions."[74] If for Meyerhold "there is no equivalence between representation and reality" (see above), for the OBERIU there is no equivalence between the scenic reality of representation and the reality presented onstage. Fourthly, therefore, since this theater aspires to present reality rather than interpret or even represent it, it must speak its own language, that of "real", rather than realistic art.

All of this, of course, has nothing to do with the question whether these principles are feasible for realisation at all. Their most basic and irreducible importance exists at the level of manifestation. In 1932, Antonin Artaud[75] raised the same problem of autonomous and authentic theatrical language in the First Manifesto of the Theater of Cruelty. It is obvious that he, too, did so quite regardless of Meyerhold, and that for him blending the realistic "verbal" theater of the nineteenth century with elements of pantomime, ballet and circus was not enough to constitute this specific language. After all, as far as French culture is concerned, Jean Cocteau[76] had already pioneered by then this method in his debut production, *Parade*.[77] Artaud was undoubtedly aware of this, even if he did not follow the experiments of Meyerhold. Still, he insisted: "theater will not be given its specific powers of action until it is given its language."[78] Jean Philippe Jaccard did not miss the parallel between the Theater of Cruelty and the *Radix*/OBERIU theater in his treatise on Kharms,[79] but there is one important thing that he does not mention. According to Artaud, "this language cannot be defined except by its possibilities for dynamic expression in space as opposed to the expressive possibilities of spoken dialogue."[80] Does it apply to OBERIU as well? Their own Manifesto is silent on this.

Vladimir Maximov, Russian scholar and practitioner of the Theater of Cruelty, contends that "for Artaud, there is no art, text or theater but reality".[81] He says further that the same is true of OBERIU, but in the latter case the same is achieved through a reverse practice, the "theatricalization of life." Maximov's observation on the similarity of what these two opposing methods envisioned seems most important here. The evolution of the very notion of theatricality reaches its extreme in the cases of OBERIU and Artaud alike. For Stanislavskii, it meant artificiality and pretence, for Meyerhold, evidence of theatrical representation (explicit for actors and audience alike), for OBERIU and Artaud it came to mean the inseparable unity of theater and life.

As regards Meyerhold, the mode of theatricality that he pursued appears to rely heavily on the backbone concept of carnival. It "arises in the relationship between the world of carnival and the world of everyday life."[82] It aims, as a consequence, to provide members of the audience with something that would distract them from their everyday lives. For this purpose, the audience must be constantly reminded that it *is in a theater*. Edward Braun notes that ever since the days of *The Fairground Booth*, Meyerhold's productions were structured to stimulate and exploit audience reaction, "confounding its expectations as often as they confirmed them".[83] In his essay "On the History and Technique of the Theater", written at about the time of his collaboration with Blok, Meyerhold states very clearly that his method of "stylization" presupposes an active role of the spectator as a "fourth creator" of the performance along with the author, the director and the actor. The spectator, he says, is compelled "to employ his imagination creatively."[84] However, he did set limitations to the spectator's supposed creativity and freedom of interpretation. He would not give up reference to the literary source, thus allowing allusions to textual prototypes of his productions. Furthermore, he would not renounce the verbal element completely: although his "biomechanical" figures are strongly reminiscent of Artaud's "hieroglyphs,"[85] his actor's "unexceptionably spoken" remarks are a far cry from the "language of sounds" that Artaud speaks about.[86] His spectators were expected, and even so only partially, to interpret and appreciate the deviations from the dramatic text and its pre-existent stereotype of actions, but still had to follow the line of the dramatic plot and, most crucially, the consistency of its inherent logic.

The founders of the ruefully short-lived OBERIU theater defied their future audience with the words: "[In our performance], you look forward to the usual logical conformity of the kind that you think you deal with in life. But you won't find it here!"[87] They obviously expected their audience to get not partially confounded, but totally flabbergasted. The logic that Meyerhold's productions followed was the logic of the dramatic text at their foundation, however boldly and masterfully recoded into alternative semiotic systems. "Carnivalistic theatricality takes as a starting point . . . an ordered universe where hierarchies are intact."[88] There can be no doubt that Meyerhold managed to stir these hierarchies, and perhaps to a considerable extent: but did he overturn them completely, and did he mean to? The apparent fact is that he simply was not radical enough. He became one of the most prominent avant-garde artists of the Modernist movement, but the academy he created with his own hands inadvertently imposed limitations on his art, as is shown by the course of his career, aggravated by the regrettable circumstances of his biography. Daniil Kharms who, in his more mature years, came to shun Modernism, must have intuited in his earlier years that true radicalism would oblige him to meet this "left" academism with the new, ultimately "real" mode of Neo-Classical art. About the same time, Antonin Artaud committed a fairly similar act with respect to André Breton and Surrealism.

> Traditional academicism trades on and tries to preserve past styles, as do both Dada and Surrealism. It emphasizes the importance of literary content and "expression," as do the two more recent movements, sharing with them thereby a quasi-theatrical character.[89]

One must admit, nevertheless, that it is precisely due to his limited radicalism that Meyerhold became one of the most seminal and original theater directors of the twentieth century. Correspondingly, it was precisely due to their *excess* of radicalism that Kharms and Artaud largely failed their own theatrical endeavours, never reaching the extremes they dreamt of. The difference between the (grotesque) "incongruity" of Meyerhold and the "absurdity" of Kharms[90] seems to have overridden the factor of minimal accessibility, thus causing the latter's theatrical work to be rejected by his contemporaries, just as Artaud's was by his. The language of reality unobstructed by interpretation and representation proved to be most incomprehensible for the general public: be it the language of concrete objects in their interaction and collision, or of cruelty that, as Jerzy Grotowski remarked, is cruel because it is real,[91] and not the other way around. Many of the dramatic or supposedly dramatic pieces written by Daniil Kharms are sufficiently cruel and grim in their content, and it is not without reason that Jean Philippe Jaccard speaks of the "tragedy of language" in *Elizaveta Bam*[92]. Regardless of other possible meanings, that was the tragedy of the theatrical ideology unable to convey its message to the audience as adequately as it would supposedly aspire to. Today, however, it is certain at least that time has diminished the distance between Kharms and Meyerhold in terms of public appreciation, if not in terms of comprehension.

Endnotes

1 Klavdia (Kapitolina) Pugacheva (1906-1996), Soviet actress of stage and screen, particularly known for her work in the Leningrad Young Spectator's Theater; at the time of the cited correspondence with Kharms, engaged in the Moscow Theater of Satire.

2 Kharms, *Polnoe sobranie sochineniy*, Vol. 4, 76. Translations from Russian are mine, unless noted otherwise.

3 Kharms, *Polnoe sobranie sochineniy*, Vol. 5, 147.

4 In this speech, Kharms was supposed to reply to those who accused him of "formalism", but he preferred to evade this task, speaking of formalism with ambivalence and condemning in fact the whole of Modernist art (addressing, in particular, pejorative remarks to "Joyce, Schoenberg, Braque, etc."). The critical school of formalism had a considerable influence in Russia since World War I, but came under sharp criticism from Soviet authorities in the 1930's as allegedly incompatible with the principles of Socialist Realism.

5 Kobrinsky, *Daniil Kharms*, 342. Alexander Kobrinsky cites these words in his biographical essay on Kharms without referring to the source, presumably archival records.

6 Kharms, *Polnoe sobranie sochineniy*, Vol. 4, 76.
7 Adrian Wanner draws a curious parallel in this respect between Kharms and Ivan Bunin in his "Russian Minimalism: from the Prose-poem to the Anti-story" (Wanner, "Russian Minimalist Prose: Generic Antecedents to Daniil Kharms's 'Sluchai'," 142).
8 Velimir (Viktor) Khlebnikov (1885-1922), an influential Russian poet, primarily associated with the Russian Futurist movement. "Kharms numbered Khlebnikov among his mentors, and a number of his poetic and dramatic works contain allusions to Khlebnikov and his works" (Cornwell, *The Absurd in Literature*, 434). An early account of this influence can be found in: Jaccard, *Daniil Kharms i Konetz Russkogo Avangarda*, 26-33.
9 The Meyerhold Theater existed in Moscow from 1923 until its closure in 1938.
10 See Braun, *Meyerhold: a Revolution in Theater*, 272.
11 Kharms, *Polnoe sobranie sochineniy*, Vol. 2, 88.
12 The State Institute of Art Culture existed in Leningrad as an autonomous institution between 1923 and 1926.
13 See: Jaccard, *Daniil Kharms i Konetz Russkogo Avangarda*, 66.
14 Jean Philippe Jaccard points at the startling instance of Antonin Artaud using the same word ('radix') to denote a return to the sources of theater on his own terms (Jaccard, *Daniil Kharms i Konetz Russkogo Avangarda*, 435). On the affinity between Artaud and Kharms, see below.
15 Konstantin Stanislavskii (1863-1938), the influential Russian theater director, actor and theorist, famous for creating the so-called "Stanislavskii method." For an introduction, see, for instance: Benedetti, *Stanislavski, His Life and Art: A Biography*.
16 Millard, "Dada, Surrealism, and the Academy of the Avant-Garde," 113-116.
17 See, for instance: Sullivan, "Nikita Baliev's Le Theater de la Chauve-Souris: An Avant -Garde Theater," 20.
18 For an extensive and detailed account of "biomechanics" see the chapter "Biomechanics and Constructivism" in: Braun, *Meyerhold: a Revolution in Theater*, 171-187.
19 "Meyerhold explained that . . . in future he would pursue the 'sculptural style' of production already initiated in 'The Fairground Booth' and 'The Life of Man'. With some justification, Komissarzhevskaya doubted that this signified any greater creative freedom for the actor, whereupon Meyerhold 'declared categorically that whatever method of production in the future, he would continue to exert pressure on any actors who failed to grasp his conception in order to realize that conception'" (Braun, *Meyerhold: a Revolution in Theater*, 75-76).
20 Ionesco, "The Avant-Garde Theater", 48.
21 As a founder and a long-standing leader of the French Surrealist movement, the French author and poet Andre Breton (1896-1966) was often accused of authoritarian and intolerant treatment of his followers.
22 In 1933, when the cited letter to Klavdia Pugacheva was written, Kharms had already reconsidered his position with regard to the "left" art, but back in the twenties he still apparently was part to it, at least judging by the names of the artistic unions that he co-founded, like "The Academy of Left Classicists" or "The Left Flank."
23 Kharms, *Polnoe sobranie sochineniy*, Vol. 4, 76, see above.
24 Nikolai Gogol (1809-1852), Russian author and playwright, one of the progenitors of Russian literary Realism. "The Inspector General" is one of his best-known works. See the article "Odin protiv vsekh" (Terentiev, *Sobranie sochineniy*, 333-335).
25 It may suffice to mention that Terentiev is the only theater director mentioned in the OBERIU Manifesto as an exponent of the "true" revolutionary art.

26 Although it was definitely a common tendency, at least as far as the Western theater is concerned. "During the 20th century . . . stage practice began to distance itself from the text, assigning it a new place in the theatrical enterprise. Once under siege, the text was no longer able to guarantee the theatricality of the stage (Feral, "Theatricality: The Specificity of Theatrical Language", 94).

27 The Moscow Art Theater was founded in 1898 by Stanislavskii and Vladimir Nemirovich-Danchenko as a principal venue for the brand of theatrical Realism they intended to promote.

28 Magnat, "Theatricality from the Performative Perspective," 149.

29 Ibid. The author obviously considers Stanislavskii part of the European theatrical tradition.

30 See: Hoover, "V. E. Meyerhold: A Russian Predecessor of Avant-Garde Theater," 239.

31 See: Stanislavskii, *Sobranie sochinenii,* Vol. 7, 413 (Letter No. 302).

32 With this definition of "stylization" Meyerhold repudiated the "decorative stylization" of the "traditional" Symbolist drama, also characteristic of his earliest productions. Meyerhold, *Meyerhold on Theater*, 43.

33 Aleksandr Blok (1880-1921), Russian poet and playwright, originally was reckoned as one of the younger Symbolists, but gradually abandoned the movement in favor of more realistic tendencies.

34 Braun, *Meyerhold: a Revolution in Theater*, 66-67.

35 "One may view the process of identification as being linked to the 'window onto real life' aesthetics, whose inception Jan Kott ascribes to Konstantin Stanislavski's implementation of the 'fourth "transparent" wall.' Kott also identifies a second type of aesthetics that he considers a 'return to theatrical forms . . . as a persistent destruction of the "window" aesthetics of theater'... The latter can be perceived as being linked to the process of distanciation, which was Meyerhold's and Vakhtangov's response to Stanislavski, well before Brecht's." (Magnat, "Theatricality from the Performative Perspective", 152).

36 Feral, "Theatricality: The Specificity of Theatrical Language," 103.

37 Ibid.

38 "Everything about him is sharply angular... In Meyerhold's skill as an actor there was a plasticity, a suppleness verging on the acrobatic, that was quite unique at the time... Waves of his sleeves conveyed various emotions. These stylized gestures were inspired by the musical conception of the characterization; they were eloquent because... they were prompted by the inner rhythm of the role" (Braun, *Meyerhold: a Revolution in Theater*, 64).

39 Jestrovic, "Theatricality as Estrangement of Art and Life in the Russian Avant-Garde," 44.

40 "Tairov's actor had to possess abilities generally identified with the ballet: mime and gesture to enhance the intoned dialogue, a sense of rhythm to perform with a musical score especially composed for the production, and a physical ability to execute the choreographic movement developed by the director" (Sullivan, "Nikita Baliev's Le Theater de la Chauve-Souris: An Avant-Garde Theater," 20).

41 "It could be asserted that performativity, having its distant roots in both *literariness* and theatricality, works in two directions... There are at least two kinds of theatricality—the one that retheatricalizes theater, foregrounding its self-referential aspects; the other that theatricalizes life, awakening in Evreinov's terms our "will to play" (Jestrovic, "Theatricality as Estrangement of Art and Life in the Russian Avant-Garde",

44).

42 Braun, *Meyerhold: a Revolution in Theater*, 68.

43 Feral, "Theatricality: The Specificity of Theatrical Language", 103.

44 Meyerhold, *Meyerhold on Theater*, 159.

45 Jaccard, *Daniil Kharms i Konetz Russkogo Avangarda*, 207.

46 Meyerhold, *Meyerhold on Theater*, 86.

47 "Meyerhold himself, reserving "formalist" and "formalism" to counter a reproach uses uslovnyi and uslovnost' to designate the kind of theater which he espoused" (Hoover, "V. E. Meyerhold: A Russian Predecessor of Avant-Garde Theater," 237).

48 "I find it hard to use the terms "formalism" and "naturalism" in the sense they are being used in literary discussions... The meaning of the term "formalism" is so diverse and is being interpreted so differently by each and every speaker that I see no possibility to impart to it any definite meaning" (Kobrinsky, *Daniil Kharms*, 340).

49 Kharms, *Polnoe sobranie sochineniy*, Vol. 1, 104.

50 Kharms, *Polet v nebesa*, 327.

51 The theatrical section of "The OBERIU Manifesto" was written by Doivber Levin and Igor Bakhterev; there is no doubt, however, that they acted in full accord with Kharms who took special care of the projected OBERIU theater.

52 For a detailed reference to the theatrical production of Russian Futurism, "Victory Over the Sun" by the poet Aleksei Kruchenykh (1886-1968) and painter Kazimir Malevich (1879-1935), see Douglas, "Victory Over the Sun". See also: Goryacheva, "Teatral'naya konzepziya Unovisa na fone sovremennoy szenografii; Shatskikh, Postyanovki i proekty Unovisskogo 'novogo teatra'"; Gubanova, "Motivy balagana v 'Pobede nad solnzem'".

53 Vassily Kandinsky (1866-1944), the seminal Russian Abstractionist painter and art theorist. For his ideas on theater, see Turchin, "Teatral'naya konzepziya V.V.Kandinskogo".

54 Pavel Filonov (1883-1941), Russian Futurist artist and poet. On his concept of "magical theater", see Tarasenko, "Magicheskiy teatr Pavla Filonova".

55 At the time, Doivber Levin, Kharms, and Igor Bakhterev were about 24, 23 and 20 years old respectively.

56 Kharms, *Polet v nebesa*, 327.

57 Jestrovic, "Theatricality as Estrangement of Art and Life in the Russian Avant-Garde", 45.

58 In his speech at the opening of the "RSFSR No.1" theatrical company, Meyerhold mentions "the principle of improvisation . . . that promises to be most valuable," showing that he seriously intended to outline such principles in advance. It is remarkable though that in the mid-thirties, when Meyerhold was feverishly looking to diversify his method so as to escape the nets that the state was already preparing for him, he eventually relinquished this habit during the 1935 production of the musical drama "The Queen of Spades" (see: Braun, *Meyerhold: a Revolution in Theater*, 281).

59 Jestrovic, "Theatricality as Estrangement of Art and Life in the Russian Avant-Garde", 45.

60 Ibid.

61 As regards Alexander Tairov's disagreement with Meyerhold: "An early disciple of Meyerhold, Tairov soon rejected Meyerhold's manipulation of the actor as a puppet on the stage... It was Tairov's purpose to restore to the actor a central place in the drama, which Meyerhold denied him" (Sullivan, *Nikita Baliev's Le Theater de la Chauve-Souris: An Avant-Garde Theater*, 20). Another note by the same author on Nikita Baliev's "Chauve-Souris" theater: "It does not suggest that he, like Meyerhold, obscured his art-

ists from view, cloaking them in a maze of directorial effects achieved at their expense" (Ibid., 21).

62 Vera Komissarzhevskaya (1864-1910), Russian actress; since 1904, the owner of the theater that bore her own name and was directed by Meyerhold in 1906-1907. "The path we have been following the whole time is the path that leads to the puppet theater" (from Komissarzhevskaya's letter of dismissal to Meyerhold, see: Braun, *Meyerhold: a Revolution in Theater*, 77).

63 Braun, *Meyerhold: a Revolution in Theater*, 162.

64 Ibid, 176.

65 Jestrovic, "Theatricality as Estrangement of Art and Life in the Russian Avant-Garde," 42. For the basic notion about the concept of "ostranenie," see: Shklovsky, "Art as Technique."

66 Stelleman, *Aspects of dramatic communication: action, non-action, interaction*, 108.

67 Russian constructivism is the avant-garde artistic movement and ideology that originated in Soviet Russia soon after the October Revolution and exercised major influence on art and architecture in Russia and elsewhere until as late as the mid-30's. After the revolution, Meyerhold's theatrical theory and practice became the essential part of the Constructivist movement.

68 "It can be said with certainty that Meyerhold stood at the origins of a semiotic model of the new kinetic theatrical behavior where new sign forms played the key role in the performance: such as gestures, facial expression, poses, body movements and manners of the actor" (Sakhno, "'Stratografiya tela' v futuristicheskom teatre", 655).

69 Hoover, "V. E. Meyerhold: A Russian Predecessor of Avant-Garde Theater," 248.

70 "Physical theater" has been among the most influential varieties of the avant-garde theater throughout the second half of the 20th century. As a basic principle, physical theater presumes the prevalence of gesture and body movement over spoken word. For an overview, see: Callery, *Through the Body: A Practical Guide to Physical Theater*.

71 Hoover, "V. E. Meyerhold: A Russian Predecessor of Avant-Garde Theater", 248.

72 See Braun, *Meyerhold: a Revolution in Theater*, 272 in particular, and the whole chapter "An Alien Theater" on the last years of Meyerhold's life and career.

73 Kharms, *Polet v nebesa*, 327.

74 Ibid.

75 Antonin Artaud (1896-1948), the French author, playwright, theater director and art theorist. Originally listed among the Surrealists, he abandoned the movement in the 30's in order to pursue his own, highly radical aesthetical agenda.

76 Jean Cocteau (1889-1963), the influential French Modernist poet, artist, playwright and film director.

77 "Cocteau's *Parade*, which for the first time blends theater and such related media as circus, music-hall, and the ballet" (Bishop, "Changing Concepts of Avant-Garde in XXth Century Literature," 37).

78 Artaud, *The Theater and Its Double*, 89.

79 Jaccard, *Daniil Kharms i Konetz Russkogo Avangarda*, 208.

80 Artaud, *The Theater and Its Double*, 89.

81 Maximov, *Esteticheskiy fenomen Antonena Arto*, 195.

82 Gran, "The Fall of Theatricality in the Age of Modernity," 255. The dichotomy between carnival and everyday life lies at the foundation of Mikhail Bakhtin's seminal work, *Rabelais and His World*.

83 Braun, *Meyerhold: a Revolution in Theater*, 292.

84 Ibid, 71.
85 Artaud, *The Theater and Its Double*, 90.
86 Ibid.
87 *Afishi Doma Pechati*, 13.
88 Gran, "The Fall of Theatricality in the Age of Modernity," 255.
89 Millard, "Dada, Surrealism, and the Academy of the Avant-Garde," 113.
90 Jean Philippe Jaccard asserts in his book on Kharms that the "real art" of OBERIU opened a doorway to the theater of the absurd, on the grounds that "the real art can only be chaotic, in the likeness of disorder reigning in the world" (Jaccard, *Daniil Kharms i Konetz Russkogo Avangarda*, 214). A Russian scholar Dmitry Tokarev dedicated to this issue a detailed and inspired work, *Kurs na khudshee* [Heading for the Worst], where Kharms as one of the founders of the theater of the absurd is juxtaposed with Samuel Beckett. Other essential works that should be mentioned in this regard include: *Daniil Kharms and the Poetics of the Absurd* in *The Absurd in Literature* by Neil Cornwell, and *Allegoriya pis'ma: 'Sluchai' D. Kharmsa (1933-1939)* by Mark Lipovetsky that concentrates in particular on the "Sluchai" (*Incidents*) cycle.
91 Jerzy Grotowski (1933-1999), the Polish theater director and theorist, one of the prominent practitioners of the "physical theater." See: Magnat, "Theatricality from the Performative Perspective," 155.
92 See Jaccard, *Daniil Kharms i Konetz Russkogo Avangarda,* 213-217.

VI

AVANT-GARDE CINEMATOGRAPHY: SERGEI EISENSTEIN AND DZIGA VERTOV

1. Eisenstein: A Short Biography

Frederick H. White

Sergei Mikhailovich Eisenstein is acknowledged as one of the founding fathers of cinema, best known for his montage style and one of the greatest films ever made—*The Battleship Potemkin*. Eisenstein, however, was a complex man who may also be considered a talented film theorist, teacher, essayist, set-designer and much more. For the many facets of his character, there are just as many interpretations for understanding his life. Was he an apologist for political tyranny, Iosif Stalin's lackey, or a victim of that tyranny? Did he actively keep alive the ideals of the Russian intelligentsia during the dark times of Soviet repression or simply play the system against itself? These are difficult questions that are still being debated. What can be said is that Eisenstein has had a profound influence on world cinema as well as generations of experimental filmmakers. What follows is a short biography of his life.

Eisenstein was born on 3 January 1898 in Riga. His father was a civil engineer and his mother was the daughter of a wealthy St. Petersburg merchant. Unfortunately, it was not a successful marriage. Eisenstein's mother considered her husband vulgar and thought that her son should grow up to become a man of culture. With this aim in mind she not only supplied him generously with books of all kinds, but even took him at the age of eight to Paris where he saw many things, but remembered most of all an early film of George Méliès, *Four Hundred Jokes of the Devil*. Even so, Eisenstein mainly lived with his father in Riga, after his parents divorced, and was raised in the style typical of the upper classes—a private governess, tutors and instructors for music, dance and horseback riding.

As a child in Riga, Eisenstein was an avid reader in three foreign languages—German, French and English. He was greatly impressed by the circus and the theater, the later being his first true passion while cinema was still in its infancy.[1] Although Eisenstein's international fame would eventually rest on his reputation as a film director, he was actually accomplished in many other artistic areas. He became an author of film scripts, essays, memoirs; his first published work was as a caricaturist at the age of 19, he designed sets and costumes for many plays and films he directed; and he returned to the stage in 1939 to direct Richard Wagner's opera *Die Walküre* at the Bolshoi Theater in Moscow. Eisenstein's path from a childhood of privilege in Riga to a leading Soviet film director was not a simple one, especially given the political upheaval of the times.

Still under his father's influence, Eisenstein registered as a student at the Institute of Civil Engineering in 1915. The urge to become an artist, and especially work in the theater, became ever more persistent while a student in Petrograd, where the opportunities were much greater than they had ever been in Riga. Yet, it was the 1917 Revolution, according to Eisenstein himself, which changed his mind about becoming an engineer. With most of his fellow students he volunteered in 1918 to fight for the Red Army in the Civil War, although his mother was able to secure a post for him far from the military action. In the fall of 1920 Eisenstein was demobilized. By then, he had decided to make his career in Moscow rather than Petrograd, for it was clear that in the new Russia, Moscow would be the artistic as well as the political center of the country. That November, he ran into a childhood friend, Maxim Strauch, at the Kamerny Theater. After the performance they realized that they were equally enthralled by the theater and the Revolution. In response to this revelation they both joined Moscow's Proletkult Theater (Worker's Culture), where Eisenstein accepted a job as a set designer.

One of the first productions made Eisenstein famous among the theater community. The play was based on Jack London's *The Mexican*. In the play, Mexican anarchists need to send one of their own into the boxing ring in order to win money for the weapons they need to buy. The first episode is among the anarchists, the second in the office of the boxing manager and the third is the boxing match. Eisenstein, showing the influence of both Cubism and the circus, made the office of one of the managers circular and the other square. This stylization applied to the actors' costumes as well as to the theater lay-out. On stage left the cast had square heads and wore square, checkered costumes, and on stage right they were all circular. The central moment of the play was a boxing match which was to take place off-stage while the visible cast merely reacted to it. Eisenstein, however, transformed the boxing match into the focal point of the scene, placing the boxing ring downstage and as close to the audience as possible. He made the sporting as real as possible by hiring a boxer to fight one of the actors. The stage production completely captured the imagination of the theater-going public.

Realizing that he still lacked practical experience, Eisenstein applied to study at The Technical Theater College. In the fall of 1921 he was accepted into Vsevelod Meyerhold's "Higher Workshops in Directing." Meyerhold was now interested in developing his system of biomechanics within the context of an experimental theater of Constructivism. As part of his course work, Eisenstein was asked to produce a play at the end of the first term. For this, he exchanged the auditorium with the stage so that the audience was facing out into the original auditorium and, therefore, actually watched the play preformed in the "wings" of the theater. Liubov Popova, the Constructivist visual artist who taught the stage design course, was not impressed with what she considered Eisenstein's traditional design. A short time later, Eisenstein left the workshop after Meyerhold accused him of sharing the school's secrets with another director.

After this great disappointment, Eisenstein returned to Proletkult as a director and was given his own pupils. It was at this time that he met Lev Kuleshov, who was in charge of the first Soviet State School of Cinematography. Kuleshov needed space for his own students, so he struck a bargain with Eisenstein. Kuleshov's students could use the large floor space of Proletkult for their "films without film" and in return Kuleshov gave lectures on cinema to Eisenstein's actors.[2] Eisenstein was himself interested and learned from Kuleshov all that there was to know about filmmaking. Kuleshov had worked as a set designer for the silent film director Evgenii Bauer, but his own films reflected the vitality of the new society. He called this cinema style "American," representing the excitement of technology, tempo and energy. Kuleshov's films were dynamic whereby movement was condensed with long static focus shots which would transition into a montage of short, rhythmic fragments.

Eisenstein's first experience with film occurred when he incorporated a short sequence film as part of his stage production of *A Wise Man*. The play opens with the character Glumov explaining that his diary has been stolen and that he is afraid that the secrets of his life will be exposed. At the back of the stage a film is then projected onto a screen which shows Glumov's thoughts and actions over a period of a week. It begins with the theft of his diary by a man in a black mask. Glumov then encounters many people, transforming himself into what they want him to be. Using dissolves, Glumov is transformed into a machine gun, a donkey, a baby, etc. Ronald Bergan explains: "Glumov then wanders over rooftops, climbs a steeple, waves at an aeroplane flying above, hangs his top-hat on the steeple, loses his footing and falls into a motorcar that takes him to the very theatre (the Proletkult) where the show is taking place." As the film ends, Glumov burst through the screen and onto the stage holding a reel of film.[3] In this production, we might see Eisenstein's transition from the stage to the screen. Although his passion had always been for the theater, there were exciting opportunities for the young director offered by the new technology of cinema.

Eisenstein's last production in the theater was a play entitled *Gas Masks*, which was staged in a real gas works. The audience sat on rows of wooden benches placed around the factory floor. It was not a success, but its importance lies in the fact that Eisenstein had moved from the unreal circus-like atmosphere of his previous plays to a more naturalistic style. Following the failure of this play, Eisenstein turned his full attention to film. At this time the Soviet cinema industry was divided into two camps. One was the school of Dziga Vertov and the Cine-Eyes (*kinoki*) who rejected all forms of drama within cinema as it reflected, so they believed, pre-Revolutionary bourgeois culture. Vertov wished to capture the dynamism of life for the new Soviet citizen so as to inspire the masses and effect change in their political consciousness. The other camp was concerned with more conventional film dramas. Influenced by the large influx of Western films, there were Soviet feature films that addressed Revolutionary subject matter, such as *Brigade Commander Ivanov* and *The Little Red Devils*, while embracing the Hollywood genres of adventure, comedy and romantic melodrama.

In 1924 Eisenstein was given the opportunity to make his first full-length feature, *Strike*. The film was about a labor strike at a factory in reaction to the exploitation of workers by the factory bosses. Although there were doubts originally about Eisenstein and his methods, the film was a success as the film seemed to capture the spirit of the Revolution. In fact, it was Eisenstein's radical use of montage that was innovative. The audience was shocked and exhausted by Eisenstein's rapid combination of stimuli, connected arbitrarily, which played upon their human reflexes. In the film, as an example, demonstrators are fired upon and then an ox is brutally slaughtered. The juxtaposition of the demonstrators and the dying ox conveyed the feeling of a human slaughter. *Strike* was typical of Eisenstein's early work as there were no significant individual heroes, but rather a big event and vast crowd scenes.

Olga Bulgakowa writes, "The new medium fascinated Eisenstein for a number of reasons. The radical avant-garde approach to art—deformation, fragmentation, dynamism, discontinuity, simultaneity, penetration of space and time—now became technically grounded. The camera could deform and segment reality, then reassemble it in every possible way. It could speed up or slow down the passage of time. Film was the modern Futurist art form *par excellence*."[4]

The following year, Eisenstein started work on his next project. The original intention had been to make a film called *The Year 1905*, showing many of the important events of that early revolutionary year. However, there was limited time as the film was meant to be shown before the end of the anniversary year—so, in effect, there were only nine months to write the script, shoot the film, edit it and have it ready for showing. When filming started, the weather in Leningrad was awful so the film crew was eventually sent to Odessa to work on another sequence. While there, Eisenstein wrote/edited the script for what would become *The Battleship Potemkin*.

Potemkin is shorter than *Strike* and has a more consistent style. None of the echoes of the circus are found in this second film as it is essentially a dramatized documentary—even though many of the finest scenes have no historical basis and were conceived by inspiration. In this film, the unbearable conditions on the *Potemkin* come to a head when the ship's doctor declares rotten meat in the sailors' soup safe to eat. The sailors who refuse to eat the meat are to be shot as mutineers. Just before the execution, the mood of the ship changes and both officers and sailors are killed in a skirmish. The whole city gathers at the funeral of Vakulinchik, the sailor who led the uprising and seeing the dead sailor as a unifying symbol of sacrifice, the citizens of Odessa join the *Potemkin* in revolt. Cossacks soon arrive in their summer tunics to restore order. The most famous scene in this film is the massacre that occurs on the port steps of Odessa. Here the common people are confronted with the unstoppable force of the state. The Cossacks march down the steps firing into the innocent crowd. A woman is shot and a baby carriage rolls down the steps along with the fleeing crowd. In response, the *Potemkin* fires on military headquarters in Odessa in support of the revolt. Warships are then sent to destroy the *Potemkin* and the tension builds as the sailors prepare for battle. Rather than a final bloodbath, however, the film ends with a sense of catharsis as the squadron refuses to fire on the *Potemkin*—ultimate defeat has been avoided. The film has been generally regarded as a masterpiece of the filmmaker's art, though spontaneously created in many of its details, it was also loyal to Eisenstein's consistent beliefs that film-editing should be a montage of collisions, bristling with a few focal points and a good punch in the audience's nose.

The public premiere of *Potemkin* was on 18 January 1926. The theater was decorated like a ship with the ushers dressed in naval uniforms. The film received a lukewarm response from audiences who preferred Hollywood fare. Attendance figures were exaggerated by Soviet officials, however, to demonstrate to the rest of the world that there were large audiences for Soviet films. It was only after the enthusiastic reaction of the foreign press that the film was shown in the best theaters in the Soviet Union. Mike O'Mahony writes: "Critical responses were largely positive, perhaps the most euphoric being N. Volkhov's declaration in *Trud* that *Potemkin* signified 'the true victory of Soviet cinematography' and that the film constituted 'an authentic work of cinematographic art, deeply thrilling in its perfection.' Alexei Gvozdev added that the film was 'the pride of Soviet cinema' and that even Hollywood had not managed to produce a film 'that is so captivating in its execution and at the same time so significant in its content.'" Eisenstein's contemporaries, such as Kuleshov and Vsevolod Pudovkin, were less enthusiastic.[5]

Significant in our present context, O'Mahony argues that the visual vocabulary of Russian Constructivism can be found in both *Strike* and *Potemkin*. One must remember that Eisenstein had studied with Meyerhold, Popova and others who had helped to define this movement's artistic vocabulary. Eisenstein emphasizes industrial machinery in both films and frames individual shots to highlight geometrical and quasi-abstract forms. Eisenstein also exposes the filmmaking process, his cinematic techniques, thus making apparent the structural principals of his art. In both films he engages the dynamism, technology and tempo of Russian Constructivism, its central ideological tenets, as well as the theatrical pageants and parades that dominated the early Soviet period.[6]

Consequently, it was Eisenstein's next project which brought him into direct contact with Soviet ideology and those who made political policy. The suicide of Sergei Esenin, the famous village poet, in December 1925 had seemingly caused a mysterious wave of copy-cat suicides, which called into question the Russian national character. Was it embodied in anarchism, alcoholism and a lack of personal discipline? Eisenstein was to combat this notion with the *Americanization* of the Russian village in *The General Line*, which was to be, in essence, a topical movie about Stalinist collectivization. Eisenstein's ideas for the film, however, were quite radical. He refused to use a professional actress for the lead part and instead hired a bony and haggard peasant with a syphilitic nose. The old village was to be depicted as crude, but able to be transformed into a Constructivist utopia. In the film, machines would meet Russian paganism and a milk separator would produce an orgasm to epitomize the ecstasy of the farm's transformation. To add good measure, the montage would be augmented with the rhythms of American jazz.

Production on *The General Line* was halted, however, when Eisenstein was ordered to begin a film on the October Revolution. This new project was meant for the up-coming anniversary celebration, but also to counter Western films that were glorifying the last days of the Romanov dynasty. Eisenstein began shooting *October* in April 1927 and the film was released to the general public in March 1928. It is best known for its mass storming of the Winter Palace with over 5,000 extras, for the 90 arc lights that turned night into day and for Eisenstein riding on a motorcycle, directing a horde of extras through a megaphone. *October* is much less disciplined than *Potemkin* and suffers from the defects of *Strike*, mixing satire with realism and naturalism with fantasy.

Bulgakowa writes that the film did not strengthen the myth of the October Revolution as intended, but became a game of intellectual montage that dismantled the myth of history itself. "[Eisenstein] felt like a genius, for in this film he had not only grasped history, but had mastered the film medium itself: he had gone beyond the basic phenomenon of film, namely the illusion of movement. He no longer needed that illusion, since he could create movement in a different manner. To this end he used montage of extremely short, static shots of statues and things. Montage made these static objects dynamic and triggered the movement of *thought*. This discovery gave him a sense of total freedom. He now could control not only reflexes and emotions, but even dialectical thinking. He had invented a new language that visualized thought—this was his world mission. He called his new theory—largely developed in a psychedelic delirium—'intellectual film'."[7] The film was not considered a success in the Soviet Union at the time of its showing.

Even so, Eisenstein was respected the world over as the most prominent representative of "Russian montage" and international visitors began to come to Moscow seeking his advice.

While Eisenstein was editing *October,* he continued to work on *The General Line*. The first Five-Year-Plan was passed in April 1929, however, marking a sharp change in Soviet policy on agriculture. After screening a version of the film, Stalin asked for significant changes to reflect the new political realities. If these were completed, Stalin would allow Eisenstein and his colleagues to go abroad to learn new cinema techniques. *The General Line* was renamed and reworked to become *The Old and the New*. This was Eisenstein's last Soviet "silent" film and also his last work to be completed for nearly ten years. As promised, it was a political film about the rural revolution, which brought collectivization and modern farming methods to Russia. In it the peasant Marfa Lapkina protests against the general ignorance of her own district and, with the help of official representatives of the new policy, she inspires her neighbors to form a co-operative. The Moscow premiere took place on the twelfth anniversary of the Revolution—7 November 1929. Eisenstein was not present because, as promised, he had been allowed to leave for Berlin—a journey that would eventually take him to the United States and Mexico. The main reason for the trip was to study the use of synchronized sound, which at that time had not yet been developed in Soviet cinema.

The stock crash of 1929 wreaked unexpected havoc on Eisenstein's initial plans to go to Hollywood. United Artists studio no longer was able to offer the director a contract and Eisenstein was forced to look for work while stranded in Europe. Just as the situation had become dire due to a lack of money and an expired French visa, Paramount studios offered Eisenstein a contract to make a film in the United States. After eight months in Europe, Eisenstein arrived in New York on 12 May 1930. Eisenstein's experience in Hollywood, however, was disappointing. After working unsuccessfully on two scripts, Paramount decided to distance themselves from the director. Anti-Semitism and anti-Bolshevism most certainly played into this decision. It was then decided, with the financial help of the literary figure Upton Sinclair and others, that Eisenstein should shoot an independent film in Mexico where the costs would supposedly be significantly less. A four month shooting schedule, however, stretched into fourteen months. By the end of that time, filming still was not complete, Sinclair was out of money, as well as patience, and Moscow had long ago requested that Eisenstein return home.

On 9 May 1932 Eisenstein returned to a very different Soviet Union, one in which his radical montage and creative independence were no longer highly valued. Cinema was now controlled by a central organ involved in every aspect of production and distribution. Stalin personally supervised filmmaking and indicated the direction that each film should take. This would soon result in an era of *Socialist Realism*, an imposed romantic realism meant to depict a not too distant Soviet utopia, as the only acceptable type of artistic expression.

Unable to adapt to this new political reality, Eisenstein wrote several unsuccessful film scripts, but mainly taught at the State Institute of Cinema (GIK—VGIK after 1934). It was here with his students that he examined topics that could never be explored in Soviet films of the 1930s. Like Meyerhold's earlier workshops, Eisenstein asked his students to develop equally their minds, bodies and spirits, engaging them in Socratic dialogue in order to find the solutions to staging a scene. Each exercise helped Eisenstein to further develop his own theoretical language. The problem was that many believed that Eisenstein needed to direct a new film, not continue to develop complex film theory. Eisenstein eventually got the message and agreed to film a *politically relevant* film, *Bezhin Meadow*, based on the life-story of Pavel Morozov, the young boy who exposed his own father as an "enemy of the people" and then was killed by his grandfather.

As with many of his other projects, Eisenstein's artistic vision did not coincide with those producing the film. In this case, when Stalin saw some of the first cuts of the film, he was furious, unable to comprehend many of Eisenstein's artistic allusions. Eisenstein was condemned for wasting state resources and a three-day conference was held to discuss what had gone wrong. Eisenstein was forced to publish an article, *The Mistakes of Bezhin Meadow*, as well as attend endless meetings in which he accepted full responsibility for these mistakes. These attacks were part of a larger campaign against Formalism in the arts. As such, Eisenstein had to admit that his entire life had been a *political mistake*. Although there were some who wanted to ensure that Eisenstein did not work again, a powerful minority thought that the director should be given a new project with very strict oversight in place.

After several proposals were rejected, Eisenstein began work on a film about Alexander Nevsky, the medieval warrior who defended

Russia in the thirteenth century from the Teutonic Knights. The film, *Alexander Nevsky*, was made with extraordinary speed amidst incredible political pressure. Many of the director's friends had been arrested and were charged with espionage while Eisenstein himself continued to face heavy scrutiny. He began work in the late summer of 1937 and completed it in November 1938. A year later, he received the Order of Lenin for this film—the highest award in the Soviet Union.

Alexander Nevsky is a historical film with contemporary overtones. The defeat of the Teutonic Knights by the forces of Alexander Nevsky became, by implication, a comment on Nazi aggression and proved to be a prophecy of what was to happen in the Soviet Union three years later. O'Mahony argues that the main theme of the film is the defense of national borders. Eisenstein uses visual devices, from the opening shots of the boundless ancient Rus to the final battle on the ice, to depict national unification and the affirmation of border integrity. The film also concentrates on Nevksy as the only hero able to unify and defend Rus with clear allusions to Stalin as the only individual who can defend the Soviet Union from National Socialist Germany.[8]

The film is undoubtedly one of Eisenstein's more disciplined works, featuring his first collaboration with the composer Sergei Prokofiev for an original score. Bulgakowa writes: "*Alexander Nevsky* was Eisenstein's first completed sound film. He knew that two separate stimuli—visual and acoustic—could either suppress or intensify each other. In this film, he explored a synaesthetic correspondence where the visual image acted as a sort of seeing-eye dog for the music and vice versa. The movement of the music made the movement within the image perceptible—it highlighted not only the obvious physical motion, but also the hidden emotional dynamism. The music enabled the viewer to grasp the visual structure of the image. Eisenstein did not want the music to increase the representative qualities of the image; instead, he wanted the music to intensify the reception of the image's *shape*. In this simple, narrative film, Eisenstein explored the theoretical and practical foundations for an abstract musical film. He described the counterpoint in the Lake Peipus battle scene as 'the simplest abstract case' that only hinted at the possibilities of true counterpoint. However, he managed to make the visual and acoustic levels so interchangeable that British Radio played the sound track as a radio drama in 1943. The sound alone carried the entire content of the image."[9]

The success of *Alexander Nevsky* returned Eisenstein to Stalin's favor and he was eventually requested to make a film about Ivan the Terrible. The historical figure was undergoing a reinterpretation at the time. No longer was Ivan IV a sadistic and perverse ruler, he was now a strong-willed individual who established a Russian absolute monarchy and united a country, transforming it into a centralized state. His personal army (*oprichnina*) was his purposeful instrument in this consolidation of power. This reinterpretation of the tsar was meant to also provide commentary for Stalin's own actions during the Great Terror. Eisenstein was immediately fascinated by the project and everything was left at his disposal as he began to research and then to formulate the project. Even as the war forced Eisenstein to relocate to Alma-Ata with most of the rest of the Soviet movie industry, he continued revising and editing his script. Although it had been passed in principal, Eisenstein could not begin shooting until Stalin himself had read and accepted the final version.

Filming finally began in April 1943 in Alma-Ata without official permission. Eisenstein had abandoned his "Russian montage" style in favor of the dark lighting effects of German Expressionism, which had been made famous by his contemporaries Fritz Lang, Paul Leni and F.W. Murnau. This meant that Eisenstein had to replace his long-time friend and cameraman Eduard Tisse with Andrei Moskvin, who had vast experience with Expressionist lighting and the manipulation of shadows. Such a visual effect would work well within the Kremlin halls and cathedrals which would seem to have no exits, creating a menacing and claustrophobic feel for most scenes. When Stalin finally granted his official approval, everything was placed at the director's disposal, even at a time of war.

Although there were to be three separate parts to the movie, Eisenstein attempted to shoot them simultaneously. In actuality, part one was shot in Central Asia at the end of the war, part two was completed after the war and part three was never made. The first part was to deal with Ivan's youth and ascent to the throne as well as his conquest of Kazan. The second part would depict Ivan's formation of a personal army (*oprichnina*) and the conspiracies of the Boyars who poisoned the tsar's wife and planned to replace him with the simpleton Vladimir Staritsky. The third part was to show the conquest of Novgorod and the war against Livonia. Eisenstein was not limited by historical facts in his creative choices. For example, the democratic cities of Novgorod and Pskov became hotbeds of reactionary Boyars. It was Eisenstein's idea that Ivan the Terrible would be shown as he really was with all the bloodshed and cruelty that accompanied his consolidation of power in Russia, but it would be done in such a way as to prove that there could have been no other way to unify all of Russia around Moscow.

Nearly a year after the first day of shooting part one, the film was being edited, as were sections of part two. In December 1944, part one officially passed the censor. Stalin himself had watched the film and had given his positive recommendation, viewing it as an educational film which interpreted correctly the complex role that Ivan IV played in Russian history. The premiere took place in mid-January at a movie theater across from the Kremlin and the reviewers were ecstatic. The film was also a success when shown in Europe and the United States. All of these accolades, however, only placed more pressure on Eisenstein to produce an equally successful part two.

On 2 February 1946 Eisenstein completed the editing of part two and that same evening attended a dinner party to celebrate receiving the Stalin Prize for part one a week earlier. At two o'clock in the morning he collapsed on the dance floor of a heart attack and was taken by ambulance to the Kremlin hospital. Towards the end of May he was moved to a sanatorium outside the city, and a month later was allowed to convalesce in his house in the country. There, he read the first published criticism of *Ivan the Terrible*. On 4 September the Central Committee of the Communist Party issued a statement attacking Soviet filmmakers in general and Eisenstein in particular. Stalin personally disliked the second part of the film. Soviet critics, as well as Stalin, believed that Eisenstein had not depicted the *oprichnina* as a royal army, but a vigilante militia. Ivan IV himself is indecisive and afraid to make a decision. Rather than a wise ruler, the tsar is constantly told what he ought to do. Although Ivan IV states in the film that he has acted to secure a stable and unified Russian state, other scenes seem to intimate that the tsar's cruelty has not been driven by political necessity, but by childhood traumas. The film's camera work and shadow-effects were also criticized, as well as the tsar's physical appearance. Eisenstein agreed that he would re-cut the film and address all of these problems, although he never did. Part two was shown in public only ten years after Eisenstein's death

On 23 January 1948, Eisenstein celebrated his fiftieth birthday and just over two weeks later, he collapsed in his study and died. Eisenstein is a household name today for students of cinema. In twenty years he completed only seven films, but they are fundamental in the history of film, especially in the area of film editing. In 1958, at the World's Fair in Brussels, an international jury of over a hundred film critics and historians voted *The Battleship Potemkin* as the best film ever made. Eisenstein's fame is connected with the montage, the rapid juxtaposition of frames to create a meaning or message. Eisenstein believed that film is synthetic—the idea that the filmmaker can put together material in such a way that the sum of the various units produces an entirely new quality. Bergan argues, "Eisenstein's theory of montage is one of collision, conflict and contrast, with the emphasis on a dynamic juxtaposition of individual shots that forces the audience consciously to come to conclusions about the interplay of images while they are emotionally and psychologically affected."[10]

Endnotes

1 As Mike O'Mahony describes: "In May 1896, the first film screening took place in Russia, presented as a novelty at a summer amusement park in St. Petersburg. Within two decades, the Empire boasted over 4,000 movie theaters with 229 in Petrograd alone. Although dominated in the early days by foreign imports, the first native film studio was established in 1907, also in St. Petersburg, and it was then that the history of filmmaking in Russia began in earnest." See O'Mahony, *Sergei Eisenstein*, 14.

2 At the time, film stock was scarce so Kuleshov was forced to simulate with his students cinema on stage. This "films without film" imitated the frame of each shot and practiced the expressions and body language of cinema (as opposed to stage).

3 Bergan, *Eisenstein: A Life in Conflict*, 85.

4 Bulgakowa, *Sergei Eisenstein: A Biography*, 50-51.

5 O'Mahony, *Sergei Eisenstein,* 59-60.

6 Ibid., 77.

7 Bulgakowa, *Sergei Eisenstein: A Biography*, 77.

8 O'Mahony, *Sergei Eisenstein*, 163-169.

9 Bulgakowa, *Sergei Eisenstein: A Biography*, 198.

10 Bergan, *Eisenstein: A Life in Conflict*, 112.

2. Allegory and Accommodation: Vertov's *Three Songs of Lenin* (1934) as a Stalinist Film[1]

John MacKay

Until at least the late 1980s, most film historians in the USSR (if not elsewhere) would doubtless have identified *Three Songs of Lenin* (1934; silent version 1935; re-edited in 1938 and 1970) as Dziga Vertov's greatest and most important contribution to Soviet and world cinema.[2] Although its reputation has now been definitively eclipsed by that of *Man with a Movie Camera* (1929), *Three Songs* was certainly more widely exhibited and unambiguously honored than any of Vertov's other films during his lifetime.[3] After being briefly shelved during the first half of 1934,[4] the film was shown to great acclaim at the Venice Film Festival in August 1934.[5] Prior to its general Soviet release in November 1934,[6] starting in July 1934, the film was exhibited in Moscow at private but publicized screenings to both Soviet (Karl Radek, Nikolai Bukharin, Stanislav Kossior) and foreign (H.G. Wells, André Malraux, M.A. Nexoe, Paul Nizan, William Bullitt, Sidney Webb) cultural and political luminaries; tributes to *Three Songs* by all of these figures were widely disseminated in the Soviet press.[7]

For unknown reasons, the original sound version of *Three Songs* was withdrawn somewhere around 13 November from the major Moscow theaters where it had been playing, although it continued to be exhibited, apparently in substandard or fragmentary copies, for some time after that in Moscow and elsewhere.[8] A silent version prepared especially for cinemas without sound projection capability was completed in 1935 and distributed widely in the USSR; both this version and the original sound *Three Songs* were re-edited by Vertov and re-released in 1938.[9] Vertov never ceased speaking of *Three Songs* with pride, even (or especially) when he was compelled to apologize for his earlier "formalist" works;[10] and it was the one Vertov film singled out for attention by Ippolit Sokolov in his 1946 collection of reviews of Soviet sound films.[11] During the Vertov revival of the post-Stalin years, *Three Songs* was apparently the first of his (in 1960) to receive publicized re-release in the

USSR.[12] A few years later, the film was subjected to a most problematic "restoration," carried out in 1969 by Vertov's wife and co-creator Elizaveta Svilova, together with Ilya Kopalin and Serafima Pumpyanskaya, and released (along with a very informative book)[13] as part of the 1970 Lenin centenary. It is this 1970 version, distributed by Kino Video on VHS and DVD, which most of us know as *Three Songs of Lenin*.

Despite all of this, and notwithstanding its ready availability on VHS/DVD in the US and Europe, *Three Songs* has attracted remarkably little scholarly attention, at least until recently. Surely this neglect has something to do with the political-ethical embarrassment now attendant upon both the film's ardent rhetorical participation in the Lenin cult and its unabashed celebration of the "modernization" of the Muslim regions of the USSR and hymning of Soviet industrial and agricultural achievement more generally. It would seem that, for many critics, *Three Songs* stands in the same relation to Vertov's earlier films as *Alexander Nevsky* (1938) does to Sergei Eisenstein's experimental work of the 1920s: a clear sign of that regression into authoritarianism and myth that came to compromise both filmmakers as creative artists and Soviet culture as a whole over the course of the 1930s.[14] Meanwhile, the film's fraught history, involving three major reedits and the consequent disappearance of the original sound and silent versions, has no doubt made scholars rightly wary of investing too much interpretive energy in such a dubious text. The three versions coincide with three quite different political movements—specifically, the full-scale inauguration of Stalin's "personality cult" (and the waning of Lenin's)[15] during the Second Five-Year Plan (1933-37); the complete establishment of the Stalin cult by the purge years of 1937-1938; and the ongoing anti-Stalinist revisionism of the early "stagnation" period (1969-1970). Given that the transition into (and out of) "Stalinist culture" is the real issue here, it is inevitable that the presence or absence of "Stalin" and "Stalinism" in *Three Songs* will figure centrally in any interpretation of the film.

Although many questions remain unanswered about the original 1934 *Three Songs*, archival evidence demonstrates rather clearly that Stalin's image was far more prominent in that original film than in the familiar Svilova-Kopalin-Pumpyanskaya reedit, which can be described, with only the slightest qualification, as a "de-Stalinization" of the versions of the 1930s. Contemporary reviews, for instance, make it plain that Stalin and references to Stalin were conspicuous in the third of the three "songs." A critic who went by the Gogolian pseudonym "Vij," writing about H.G. Wells' viewing of the film (in Moscow on 26 July 1934), indicated that "the writer saw Lenin at the beginning and middle of the film, and Stalin in the middle and the end."[16] Timofei Rokotov, who later became well-known as the editor of the journal *International Literature*, praised the film's conclusion in the following terms in his review of 4 November 1934:

> It's difficult to imagine a better ending to the film than that image of the super-powered train "Joseph Stalin," rushing irrepressibly forward, above which shine the words of our leader: "The idea of storming [capitalism] is maturing in the consciousness of the masses."[17]

The earliest extant versions of *Three Songs* (sound and silent) both contain the image of this well-known train, with "Joseph Stalin" inscribed on the front, near the film's conclusion, and Rokotov's comment strongly suggests that it was in the 1934 original as well.

Certainly, the fact that Stalin's then-famous comment—"the idea of storming [capitalism] is maturing in the consciousness of the masses," from his report to the 17th Party Congress (24 January 1934)—served as the film's concluding slogan is directly confirmed by Vertov's script for *Three Songs*.[18] Rokotov makes an even more intriguing reference in his review to the film's famous prologue, with its image of the "bench" on which Lenin sat:

> . . . a little detail [that] says so much . . . here is the same bench, well-known because of the photograph, where the great Lenin and his great student and comrade-in-arms Stalin sat and conversed—not so long ago, it would seem.[19]

Similarly, one V. Ivanov, in a review for *Rabochaia Penza* of 31 December 1934, describes the same section of the prologue as follows:

> The bench. The memorable bench. You remember the picture: Lenin and Stalin in Gorki, 1922.[20]

In contrast to the 1970 reedit, which offers a photograph of Lenin sitting alone on a bench during the prologue, the 1938 versions present a very famous and widely distributed image of Lenin sitting together with Stalin (Image 1). Clearly enough, the comments by Rokotov and Ivanov strongly suggest that the portrait of Lenin with Stalin was the one displayed in the original *Three Songs.* [21]

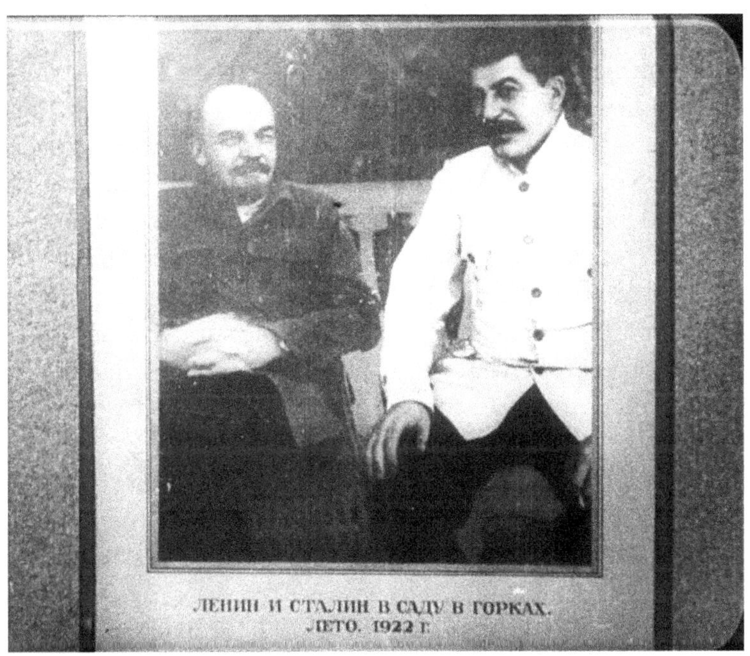

Image 1: The photo of the "seated Lenin" in the 1938 (and probably the 1934) versions of the prologue to *Three Songs*

Finally, some of the most telling evidence of Stalin's presence in the 1934 film comes from Vertov's own notes and plans. In a letter of complaint dated 9 November 1934 to Mezhrabpomfil'm administrator Mogilevskii about the bad quality of the print of *Three Songs* being shown in Moscow's *Taganka* theater, Vertov notes that the shot of "Stalin walking about the Kremlin" is missing, among other absent footage; again, this shot is present in the extant (1938) versions in the third song, though not in the 1970 reedit.[22] Most strikingly, perhaps, a remarkable set of instructions from 1934 compiled by Vertov for the film's sound projectionist indicate not only that Stalin appeared throughout the film, but that Vertov generally intended the volume of the soundtrack to take on "maximum loudness" when the dictator appeared, as (for example) during the funeral sequence.[23] By contrast, the 1970 version mutes the sound almost completely when Stalin appears at the funeral of Lenin —the only appearance he makes in the film.[24]

In truth, one needs to acknowledge that even a cursory examination of the Soviet press in 1934 should have alerted film historians to the improbability of Stalin's absence from the original *Three Songs of Lenin*; Stalin's image was already ubiquitous by this time, and the notion of "the Party of Lenin and Stalin" quite firmly established.[25] Yet the question remains: what effect should this knowledge have on our *reading* of the film, in contrast to our necessary efforts to establish a correct original text? That is, what precise difference does the presence or absence of Stalin make to our considerations of Vertov's artistic evolution and of the structure and ideology of *Three Songs*, apart from what is already apparent from the 1970 version? To be sure, the idea of "Stalin" had become far more central to Soviet culture by 1934 than it had been in 1930, for instance, when Vertov made the film that preceded *Three Songs*, *Enthusiasm: Symphony of the Donbass*. And even the lack of an authoritative version of *Three Songs* has not prevented those scholars who have ventured to write on the film (invariably, the 1970 reedit) over the last 20 years or so to identify it, quite rightly in my view, as marking a crucial turning point in Vertov's artistic career—specifically, the turning point between the "avant-garde" 1920s and the "Stalinist" 1930s—though the evaluations of this watershed moment differ significantly.

The critical consensus on the film—established perhaps first by Annette Michelson, and developed further by Klaus Kanzog and Oksana Bulgakowa—holds that *Three Songs* involves a rhetorical turn to "religious" or quasi "sacred" cinematic discourse (grounded, according to Kanzog's analysis of the film's "internalized religiosity," in deep cultural memories of religious practice),[26] whether conceived as a passage from the "epistemological" to the "iconic" and "monumental" (Michelson),[27] or from the "documentary" to the "allegorical" (Bulgakowa).[28] In an essay that dissents from this "discontinuity thesis" while offering a newly positive evaluation of the film, Mariano Prunes stresses the continuities between *Three Songs* and the 1920s visual practice of both Vertov and his contemporaries in photography and film, arguing that the film incorporates and summarizes all the main streams of photographic visual practice of the preceding decade (constructivist *faktura*, documentary factography, and emergent Stalinist mythography), and in so doing "seriously brings into question the traditional view of Soviet art in the 1930s as absolutely intolerant of previous experimental practices."[29] Accordingly, Prunes does not regard the presence or absence of Stalin in the 1970 version as especially important, suggesting at most that the 1934 film was perceived as paying insufficient homage to Lenin's "Successor" (thus necessitating the 1938 reedit with its "supplementary material on Stalin").[30] For their part, Michelson and Bulgakowa regard the "Stalin" of *Three Songs* as a kind of structuring absence, as prying open "[a] space in which the Beckoning Substitute is now installed" (Michelson),[31] or even as an omnipresent but invisible quasi-divinity, "present only in metonymic indicators" (Bulgakowa).[32] But once again, Stalin was neither a structuring absence in *Three Songs* nor actually absent: he was simply, explicitly part of the film's message and visual rhetoric.

To determine what that "part" actually consists in will first necessitate a reconsideration of the rhetoric of *Three Songs of Lenin*, both in terms of changes within the trajectory of Soviet culture and in relation to Vertov's artistic response to those changes. In what follows, I hope to show that both the "continuity" and "discontinuity" theses have important merits, but that they need to be thought of in terms of the concrete strategies through which the "avant-gardist" Vertov reacted artistically to the new authoritarian-populist imperatives of early Stalinism. *Three Songs of Lenin* demonstrates that, as far as Vertov was concerned, the most important feature of Stalin-era aesthetic doctrine as it evolved between 1932 and 1936 was its sharp rejection of avant-gardist complexity, anti-humanism and anti-psychologism, and its concomitant turn toward "character," simplicity, and supposedly popular "folk" sentiment. In this essay, I hope to show how Vertov adapted two related features of the new discourse of the 1930s—attention to individual experience, and textual appeals to "folk sensibility" (or *narodnoe tvorchestvo*: "folk creativity")—in ways that, in *Three Songs of Lenin*, enabled him to fit into the new discursive order while continuing to pursue his old avant-garde concern with the representation of sheer change and dynamism, with material process, and with cinema as a means of reconfiguring perception and spatial-temporal relations. At the same time, I will suggest that "folk" poetic materials incorporated in *Three Songs* functioned for Vertov both as publicly verifiable texts that could satisfy the growing institutional need for some pre-verbalizing of the films, and as "sources" to which he could appeal in order to legitimate his own directorial decisions. It was in *Three Songs of Lenin*, I will argue, that Vertov found a way of accommodating the "populist" and centralizing imperatives of the new 1930s cultural order within his already fully formed, fundamentally constructivist artistic worldview and style.[33]

* * *

Some of the rhetorical specificity of *Three Songs of Lenin* can be pinpointed through a comparative examination of the stylistic use made by that film of Vertov's own master-trope, namely, the great revolutionary passage from the Old to the New—cinematically conceived in his case not primarily as narrative, but rather as sheer movement and sense of movement, the making-visible of (as Deleuze put it in his superb discussion of Vertov in *Cinema I*) "all the (communist) transitions from an order [that] is being undone to an order [that] is being constructed . . . between two systems or two orders, between two movements."[34] Vertov was fascinated by the cinematic representation of process, especially processes of long duration, whether natural or historical. While working on *One Sixth of the World* (1926), his film about (among other things) methods of organizing the exploitation of natural resources, he jotted out plans for exceedingly brief film-sketches, unfortunately never produced, on themes of process, such as "death-putrefaction-renewal-death." He planned one film that would begin by showing a woman burying her husband, followed by the corpse's consumption by bacteria and worms, the full conversion of the body into soil, and the emergence of grass out of the soil; a cow would eat the grass, only to be devoured in its turn by a human being, who dies, is buried, and then is absorbed into the whole process again, although the eventual addition of manure into the cycle is shown to generate a kind of productive upward spiral. Another Beckett-like[35] four-shot film would show a fresh-faced peasant girl—then one wrinkle on her face—then a bunch of wrinkles—and finally a thoroughly wrinkled old woman. Another featured a man going bald, over the course of three shots.[36]

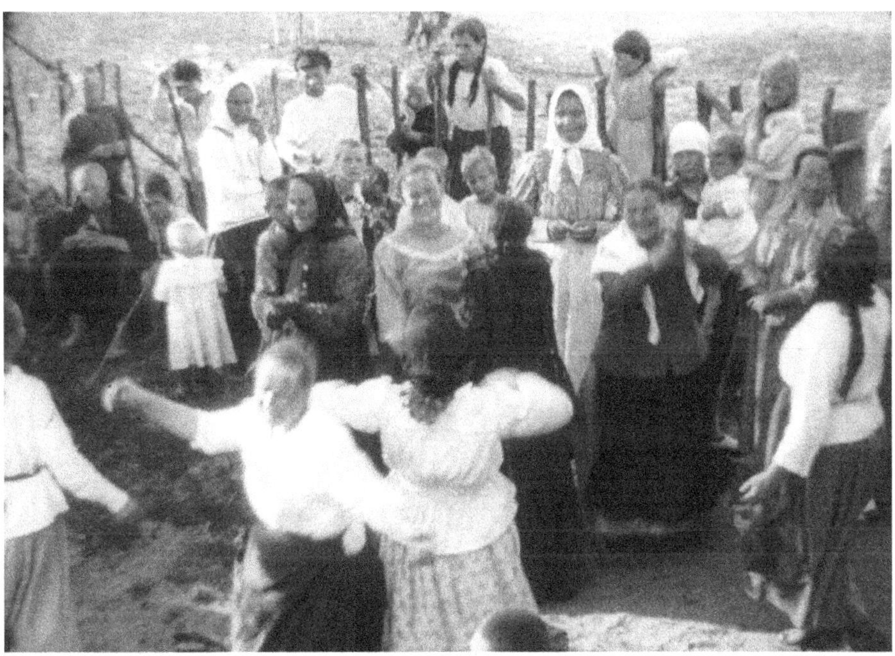

Image 2: Peasant women dancing "in the round" (from *Kino-Eye* (1924))

The fine internal mechanism of any change is, of course, notoriously hard to explain in any non-regressive way. But transition in Vertov's cinema is usually something to be *sensed* rather than articulated or explained; and Vertov tries to generate the required perceptual jolts or shifts by making transition as visually and aurally tangible as possible, as in the opening of his first major feature, *Kino-Eye* (1924). The film is about members of the Young Pioneers organization from both the village of Pavlovskaia and from the proletarian Krasnopresnenskaia area of Moscow, and shows the youngsters engaged in philanthropic and leisure activities in various urban and rural settings. *Kino-Eye* begins, as so often in Vertov, with a sequence representative of the Old: here, the jubilant, besotted dancing of (mainly) women who've had a bit too much to drink during a church holiday. Visually, a dominant circular motif is established gradually but very assertively: circularity links the spinning movements of the women, the circle of the "round dance" itself (Image 2), and objects like the pot, tambourine, and even the faces of the women themselves (Image 3). The ecstatic twirling is both exhilarating and enervating, and, after a while, it starts to suggest that the women are trapped within what Russians would call a "*zamknutyi krug*" (closed circle), although Vertov would resist such aggressive translation of his visual formulae into words. Clearly enough, however, the enormous energy of the women is compelled to inscribe one circle after another, repetition within repetition, creating an image of encompassed and squandered vitality.

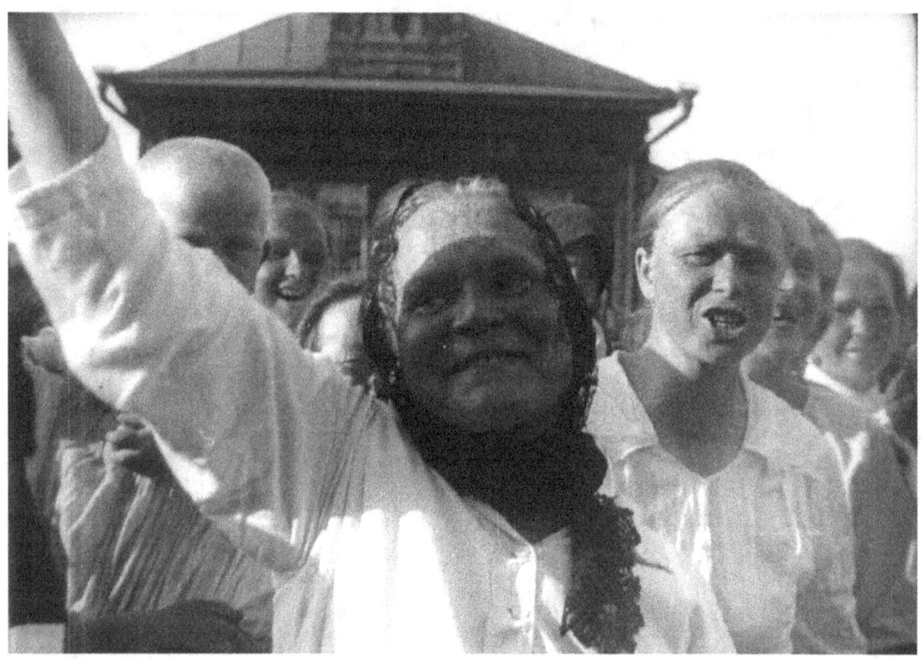

Image 3: The round faces of jubilant peasant women (*Kino-Eye*)

The transition to the New—though we are still very much in the village—occurs across a gap, without any "pivot point" whatsoever. Only an intertitle ("with the village pioneers") signals any change. However, the material sense of transition is stressed in classic constructivist fashion by a sudden preponderance of rectilinear shapes and movements: beginning with the siding on the building, then the poster pasted on by the Pioneers (Image 4), the picket fence, the waterfall (falling, rolling streaks of water is one of Vertov's favorite images of revolution), and the straightforward movement of the marching pioneers (Image 5).

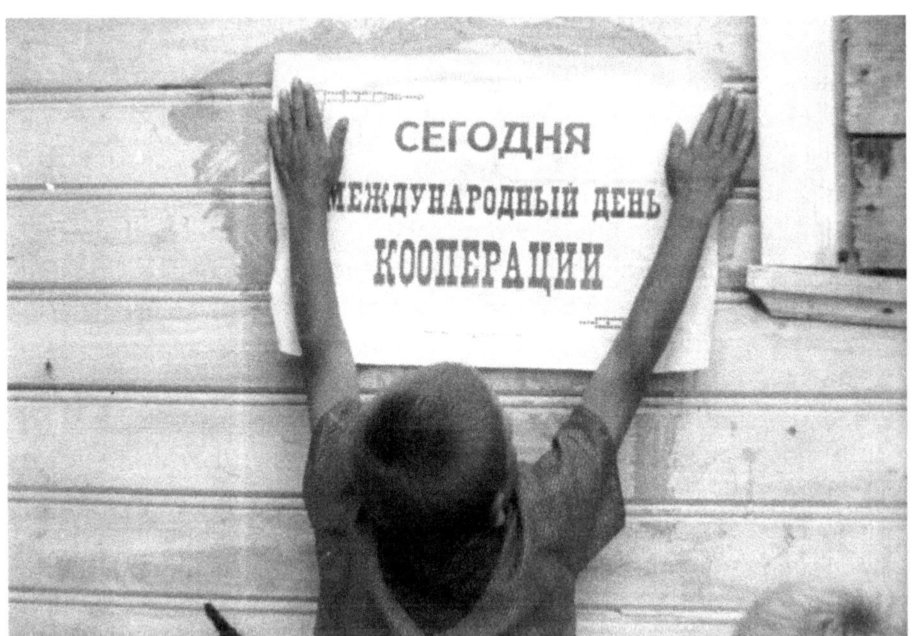

Image 4: The Pioneers arrive with rectilinearity (the sign reads, "Today is the International Day of Cooperation") (*Kino-Eye*)

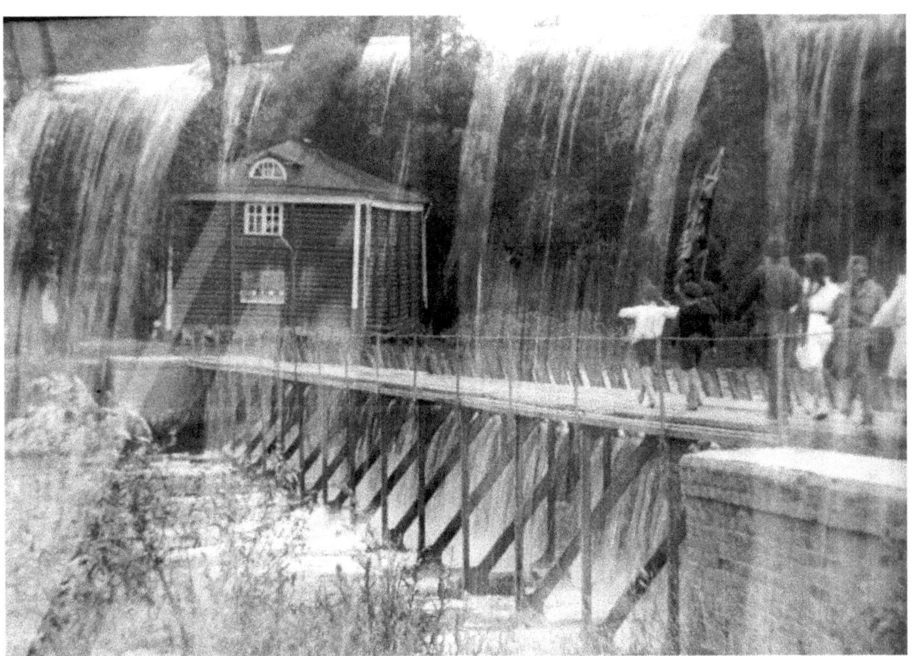

Image 5: Streaks of water, geometrical form and forward movement (*Kino-Eye)*

The series culminates with a nearly abstract sequence linking striking overlaps of surging water with the orderly, forward-directed advance of the children, concluding with a demonstration on the main street of the village. Translating again, the message would seem to be: force previously wasted on the inscription of drunken circles is re-channeled (cinematically) into a progressive and architectural rectilinearity; and Vertov hopes to make this "point" by provoking the spectator's perceptual entry into these two differently patterned spaces.

The same topos is found, in a dizzying variety of permutations, in nearly all of Vertov's films.[37] Thus at the end of the prologue to *Man with a Movie Camera* (which contains several such transitions) we see the sudden passage from the stasis of an orchestra—a traditional kind of artistic collective—thrust into a new kind of motion by the activation of the film projector, inaugurating the film (for the audience *in* the film) that we have already started watching. We find a very striking Vertovian transition in the first reel of *Enthusiasm: Symphony of the Donbass* (1930), a film that can be seen as a grandiose rewriting of *Kino-Eye* in a number of respects. *Enthusiasm* begins with a polemical alternation between scenes of drunken behavior and religious devotion—religion as "opiate of the masses" is the intended message—with the camera mimicking both the repetitive motions of prayer and the aimless stumbling of brawling alcoholics (Image 6). The sense of thudding stagnation intended here is underscored by repeated shots of church bells, shots themselves saturated with repetitive movement and sound.

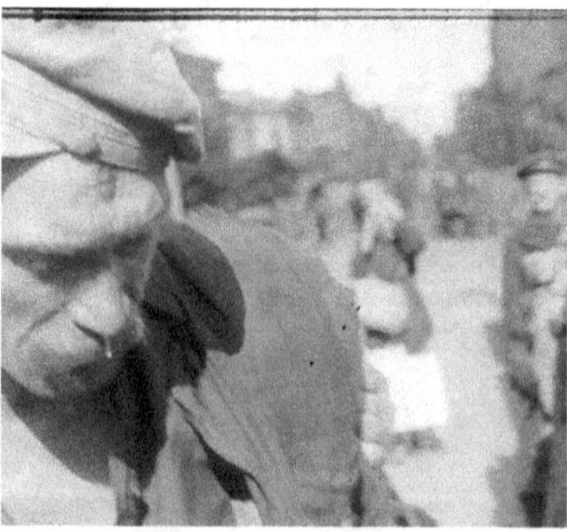

Image 6: A drunken man staggers to his feet in *Enthusiasm* (1930)

Suddenly, an industrial siren blares, its nearly vertical plume of smoke transected by parallel power lines and garnished by a splash of spontaneous, natural growth (Image 7).[38]

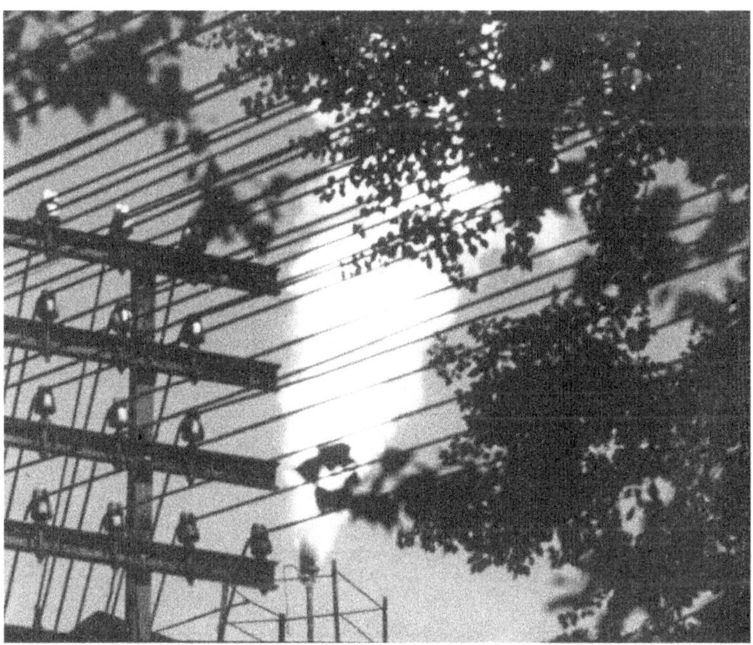

Image 7: The siren of industrial modernity (*Enthusiasm*)

This siren was apparently shot and recorded using documentary sync sound; thus, the shot serves as a pivot point between old and new, announcing at once the arrival of socialist construction and (on the cinema front) documentary sound film. And once again, this siren blast, seemingly a purely arbitrary cut into the mobile but unprogressive texture of everyday life, is succeeded by the geometrically inflected patterns of a Pioneer parade, now accompanied by documentary sound, with the orderly lines and sharp angles formed by the youngsters matched graphically by the trolley-car tracks across which they march (Image 8). Four years after *Enthusiasm*, and ten years after *Kino-Eye*, with the opening of the first of the *Three Songs of Lenin*, we see something new emerging in Vertov's art of transition.[39] The first song opens with what are probably shots taken in a city in Uzbekistan, possibly Tashkent or Bukhara, showing women wearing the *paranji* and *chachvon* veils (Image 9).

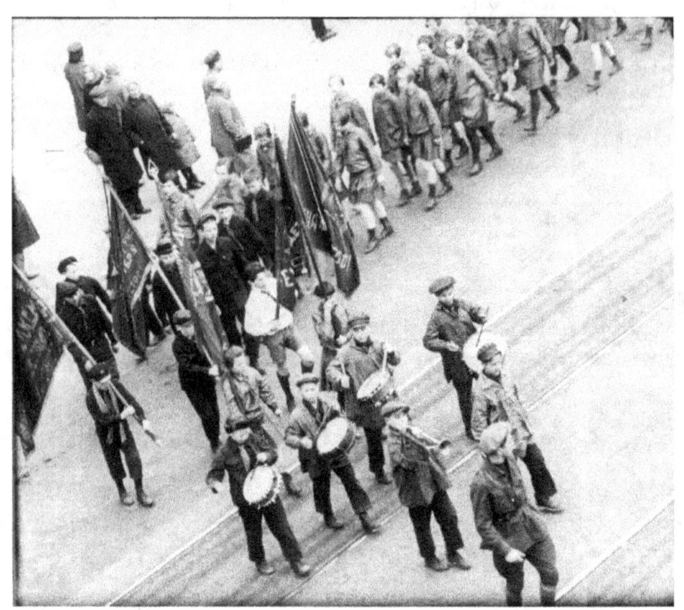

Image 8: The Pioneers bringing (visual) order to chaos (*Enthusiasm*)

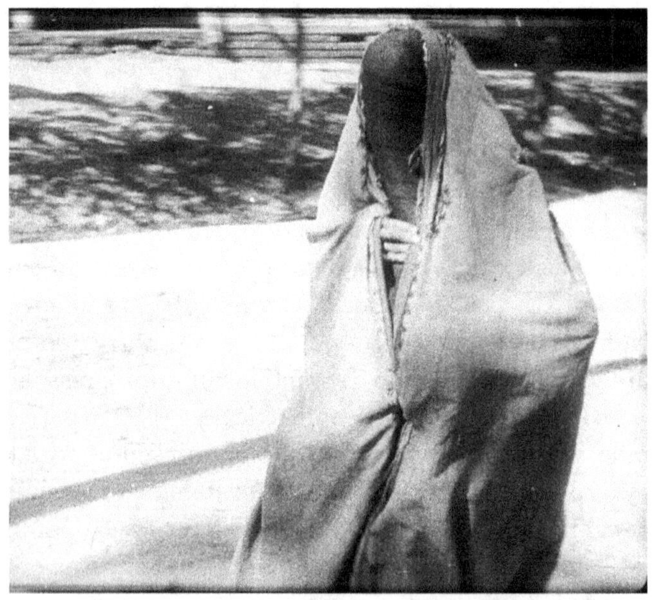

Image 9: The veil (*Three Songs of Lenin* (1934))

It is not unimportant here that it is impossible to tell if the women are looking at the camera or not, and that their gazes are withdrawn. For Vertov, the ability to see is virtually tantamount to the ability to understand and to confront one's oppressor: tantamount to possession of power, in short. It suffices to recall how, in the famous satire on European colonialism in the first reel of *One Sixth of the World*, we get an unforgettable depiction of an African woman "confronting" (through false continuity) her class enemy; or the great sequence in Vertov's next film, *The Eleventh Year* (1928), where at one moment the female "comrade from India" becomes the exemplary witness of the revolutionary collective as a whole. In shaping the rhetoric of *Three Songs*, Vertov could also rely on existing Soviet discourse on the veil—discourse well established even before the *hujum* ("assault" on traditional Central Asian customs and taboos) of 1927—which represented the veil as a kind of imposed blindness. For Soviet agitators (as Gregory Massell puts it),

> the implications of freeing a Moslem woman from her veil were far more dramatic than the mere reversal of a physically undesirable condition. It would mean, in effect: to liberate her eyes—"to enable [her] to look at the world with clear eyes," and not just with unobstructed vision; to liberate her voice, a voice "deadened" by a heavy, shroud-like cover . . . to free her from [being] a symbol of perpetual "degradation," a "symbol of . . . silence, timidity . . . submissiveness . . . humiliation."[40]

Thus, although (of course) the veil does not blind its wearer in fact, the sequence clearly links veil wearing to blindness, and therefore (in Vertovian logic) powerlessness.

The second shot seems to be a camera-simulation of the motions of prayer, reminiscent of the "drunken camera" in the last reel of *Man with a Movie Camera*, the "praying camera" in *Enthusiasm*, and other moments of camera mimicry in Vertov (Image 10).

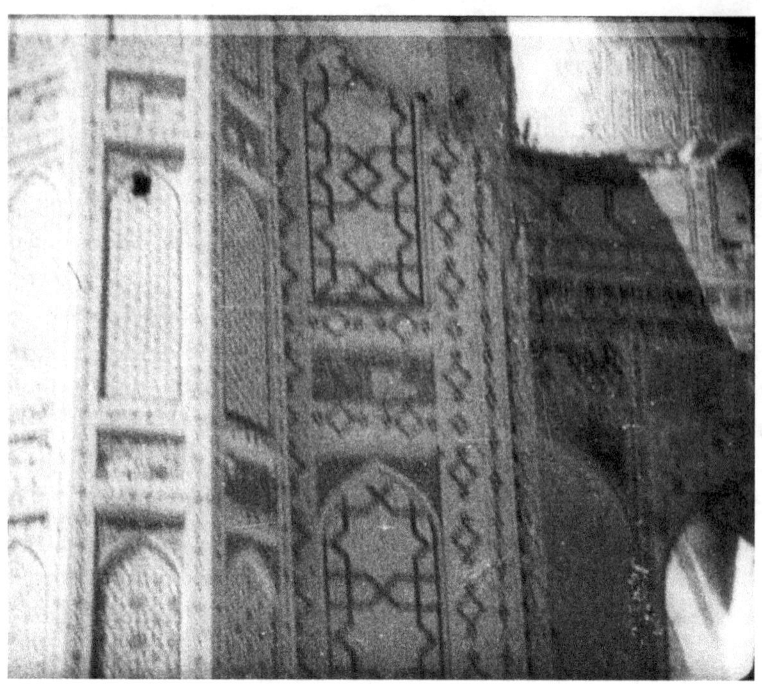

Image 10: The "praying camera" in motion (*Three songs of Lenin*)

The lens inscribes a circular movement of rising and prostration that is intended to elicit the idea and the feeling of dull repetition, entrapment, and mindlessness, an impression retroactively confirmed a few shots later when we get an overhead view of men praying.[41] In some of the succeeding shots, one might read the essentially illegible gestures of the veiled women passing laterally across the screen as evasive, hostile, or indicative of possible interest in the camera. (Historian Sheila Fitzpatrick has shown how important the rhetoric of "tearing off the masks" was during the first 20 years or so of Soviet power; to be sure, Vertovian *kino-pravda* ("film-truth") participates in its own way in this unmasking project.[42] Yet these particular veils, of course, were masks thought to have been clamped onto the women against their will by a male-dominated Islamic society.) A shot of men apparently leaving some kind of domicile, perhaps taken from an implied female point of view, stuck back in the house, is followed by some classic "associative" montage rhetoric incorporating shots of male prayer and of a blind, half-paralyzed woman stumbling down a road. Taken together, the sequence definitively links the veil with blindness, with ignorance and non-enlightenment, with empty ritual, and with misery.

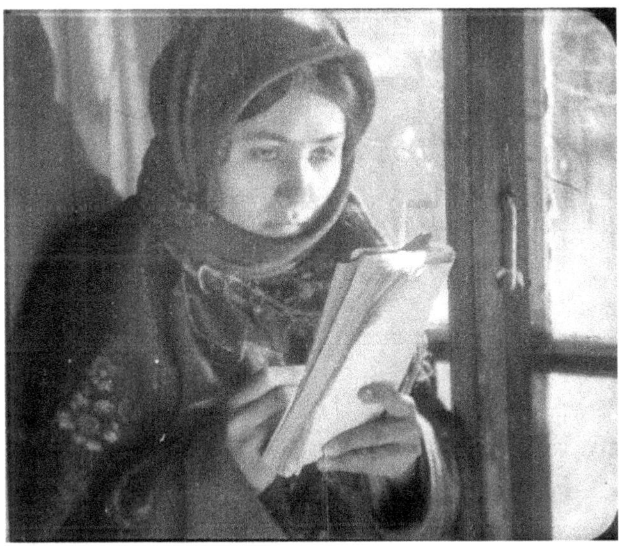

Image 11: The activist making her notes, linking old and new (*Three Songs of Lenin*)

What happens next is truly remarkable within Vertov's corpus, though it may not appear so at first. The cut to the next shot, accompanied on the soundtrack by a shift from Uzbek music to a proletarian fanfare, yields the hooded face of a young woman jotting something down by a window; she needs the sunlight, for apparently her home has not yet been "electrified" (Image 11). We are now in Baku, not Uzbekistan, and the woman (not named in the film) is almost certainly one Aishat Gasanova, a Party activist who worked among women in her native Azerbaidzhan and later in Daghestan.[43] Perhaps not immediately, we realize that the "documents" we have just seen are flashbacks or meditations, "interior" to Gasanova's consciousness, and in the process of being converted into text by the writing hand of Gasanova herself. That we are within the realm of subjectivity is soon confirmed, when the classic Vertovian device of false match-shots—through a window in this case (Image 12)—opens onto a utopian image of young Pioneers marching through a lush forest next to a stream (Image 13).[44]

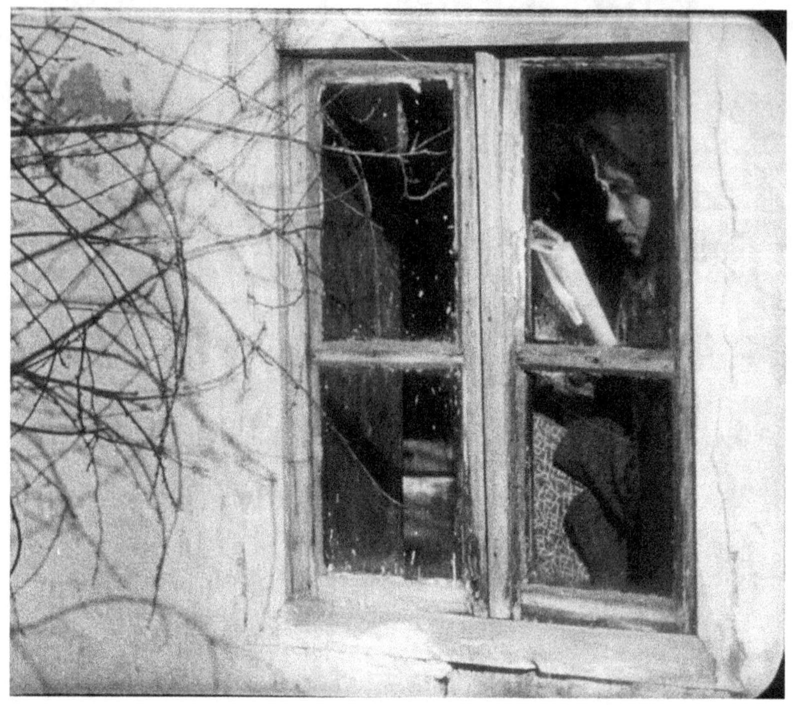

Image 12: The activist looks into the future (*Three Songs of Lenin*)

From imagining the Old in Uzbekistan, Gasanova turns to the New, still figured by marching young people but (importantly) in a pastoral rather than industrial setting. As in *Kino-Eye* and *Enthusiasm*, though less assertively, Vertov orchestrates a geometrical contrast with the preceding section. The upright bodies rhyme with the birch trees, even as the panning camera stresses lateral dynamism as well as forward movement: all is linear, lucid and forward-directed, as opposed to the clutter and repetition of the previous sequence.

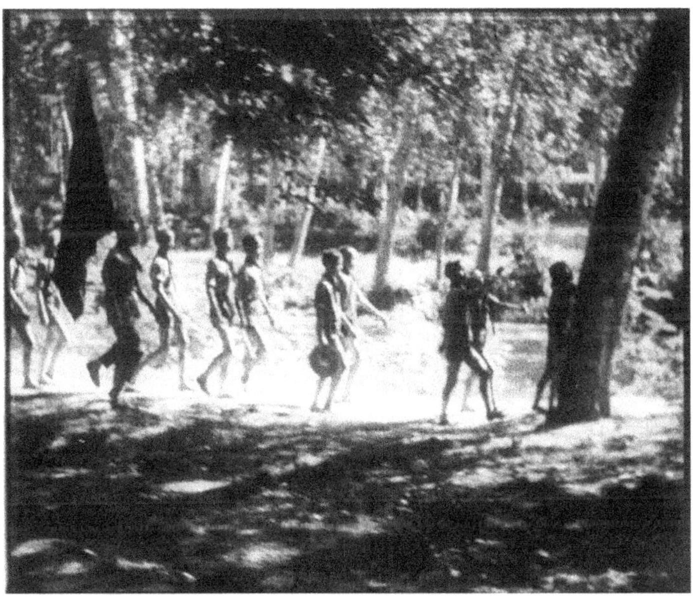

Image 13: Pioneers marching on the riverbank (*Three Songs of Lenin*)

What is new here for Vertov is the unobtrusive inclusion of a subjective, psychological pivot linking the two movements of the passage from the Old to the New, as opposed to the raw leaps characteristic of his earlier films. Within the rhetoric of the sequence, that is, Gasanova occupies the same place that the impersonal, mechanical siren did at the beginning of *Enthusiasm*—but not without inflecting the sense of the "Old-New" topos in a new, subjectivizing direction. The activist becomes arguably the closest thing to a "character" to be found in any major Vertov film, inasmuch as we are offered a representation, briefly but powerfully sketched, of her daily and emotional life:[45] we later see her on her way to the Ali Bairamov club for women, still later her intense participation in a Lenin memorial at the club. This new psychologism was noted, not without smugness, by critics at the time of the release of *Three Songs*, who recalled the director's early-1920s comments on the "absurdity" of the "psychological Russo-German film-drama—weighed down with apparitions and childhood memories."[46] At a preview on 27 October 1934, critic V. Bartenev noted how Vertov's old "LEF-type 'thing-ism' [*veshchizm*] was overturned by this film," and that in *Three Songs* "we even see—horror of horrors!—human psychological experience": "from empiricism [Vertov] has moved to a subjective sensation of the world."[47]

To be sure, neither Vertov nor his critics were working within a discursive void; as Sheila Fitzpatrick has shown, the celebration of ordinary "working-class heroes," involving the dissemination of many photographic portraits and interviews, became a major feature of Stalinist culture from the early 1930s onwards.[48] And it is no accident that the majority of Vertov's later films (whether produced or not) focus on the life stories of exemplary Soviet citizens (women, mostly), thereby contributing to this large-scale proliferation of biographical celebrations of the "little man and woman."[49] In neither *Kino-Eye* nor *Enthusiasm* is anyone included in the diegesis as a subjective guarantor of the transition from Old to New; the implication is that, by the time of *Three Songs*, there are such guarantors around, people like Gasanova who have "made" or can imaginatively articulate the passage across the developmental gap.[50] Yet it is clear enough that, on the level of style, the insertion of this new psychological "pivot" enabled Vertov to continue his exploration of dynamics—the purely visual materialization of process—in sublimated form.[51]

* * *

Much the same can be said about the mediating function performed by the "folk" material utilized in *Three Songs*, although I would argue that this material performed an important institutional function for Vertov as well, inasmuch as it involved the use of written texts. *Three Songs* was apparently the last film on which Vertov was able to work at least part of the time in his notoriously loose, improvisational, "unscripted" manner. As is well known, Vertov throughout the 1920s took a principled stand against the pre-scripting of films, usually on the grounds that scripts inhibit some more authentically cinematic approach to the organization of visual and sonic material. This stand arguably led him into even more trouble than his notorious taste for quarrel and polemic: he was famously fired from the Central State Cinema Studio in Moscow (Sovkino) in January 1927 in large part because he refused to present studio chief Ilya Trainin with a script for the "scriptless" film he was then working on—a project that eventually became *Man with a Movie Camera*.[52]

With the ascension of the pragmatic anti-avant-gardist Boris Shum-yatsky to the top of the cinema ministry in 1929, and the liquidation of semi-independent artistic groupings in 1932-33 (and the attendant bureaucratization and centralization), it became impossible for Vertov to maintain this principled anti-script position.[53] It was with *Three Songs of Lenin* that Vertov made his last real attempt to produce a "scriptless" documentary or, as he preferred to put it, unplayed or non-acted film. He complained loudly to studio administrators about demands for a script even after finally turning in a scenario at an advanced stage in the production (on 23 August 1933—the film was essentially finished by mid-January 1934):

> This is the first time I've had to explain a montage construction in words. And when it comes to a film like this one, this is a truly thankless task. . . . I have tried to overcome my own objections today, in light of your persistent requests. And so I renounced visuals, sound, the mutual interaction of montage phrases with one another, tonal and rhythmic combinations, expressions of faces and gestures . . . that all develop visually and aurally, organically linking together into an idea without the help of intertitles and words. . . . To write out each shot in detail, one after the other, link after link, montage phrase after phrase, would make sense, except that it's far more time-consuming and complex than actually putting the film together. It's a pity I had to do this.[54]

In truth, Vertov had drafted a variety of plans, if not exactly "scripts," for the film; the early ones had a biographical character and would have brought Vertov to many of Lenin's European haunts (Zürich, Paris, London and so on) while emphasizing Lenin's role as leader of the international proletariat.[55] As it turned out, improvements in sync sound recording enabled Vertov to incorporate some directly recorded testimonial material by workers, peasants and engineers, thereby partially circumventing the need for script. At the same time, the core of the scenario that Vertov finally did produce became three so-called "folksongs" about Lenin, selected from among a large number of mostly anonymous Lenin-dedicated verses produced in the Central Asian republics (Tadzhikistan,

Turkmenistan, Kirghizstan and Uzbekistan) in and around 1924.

It is well known that a great deal of "folk" (or "pseudo-folk") culture was generated as the result of official sponsorship in the various national republics, with an intense burst occurring after 1933-1934, after *narodnost'* ("national content," or "folk sensibility") had become a valued dimension of the socialist-realist template.[56] The incorporation of "folk material," along with the sync sound interviews, were precisely the aspects of *Three Songs* that made the greatest impression on early audiences. In fact, Vertov began to make recourse to "folk" materials only at the very end of 1932, nearly midway through the production;[57] and there was no small irony in this "experimental" filmmaker, previously associated (if only informally) with the Left Front of the Arts (LEF), attempting to make his art more accessible by making it "folksier."[58] In later years, Vertov repeatedly spoke of folk material as opening up his personal path to socialist realism, with *Three Songs* as his inaugural success in this area. In an unpublished talk "On Formalism" that he gave on 2 March 1936, he identified "folk creation" as the central weapon in the struggle for "the unity of form and content" against "formalism and naturalism." Theoretician P.M. Kerzhentsev was right, Vertov opined, to suggest that "the composer Shostakovich"—recently pilloried in *Pravda* for his *Lady Macbeth of the Mtsensk District*—ought to "travel around the Soviet Union collecting the songs of the people," to discover that "foundation, on the basis of which [he] might grow creatively."[59]

It has been claimed that much of the "folk" writing produced in the Soviet period was more-or-less pure fabrication, done by professional writers working in Moscow and the republican capitals. Vertov's "songs," however, seem to have a more banal origin: most likely, they were penned in the mid-1920s by young people associated with worker's or women's clubs or the Komsomol (Young Communist Youth League) organization—that is, in settings where Lenin was frequently commemorated, and the production of memorial verses and songs was encouraged (one might look to our own "essay contests" linked to various national or state holidays for an analogue). These poems were collected, and sometimes appeared on the pages of major central newspapers like *Pravda*.[60]

Thus we needn't spend much time worrying about the authenticity of these "folk" productions *as* folk productions; clearly, the important thing is that they were examples of anonymous, "naïve" poetry, and could thus at once be presented as documents of popular sentiment while cohering (inasmuch as they were *documents*) with Vertov's own kino-eye "life-as-it-is" precepts.[61] As scripts or components of scripts, they were texts bearing "folk" legitimacy that could be presented to studio administrators to give them a sense of his direction; they were also collections of images, often (at least in the examples selected by Vertov) images of very physical, elemental, seasonal character, and thus adaptable to his established *faktura* practices.

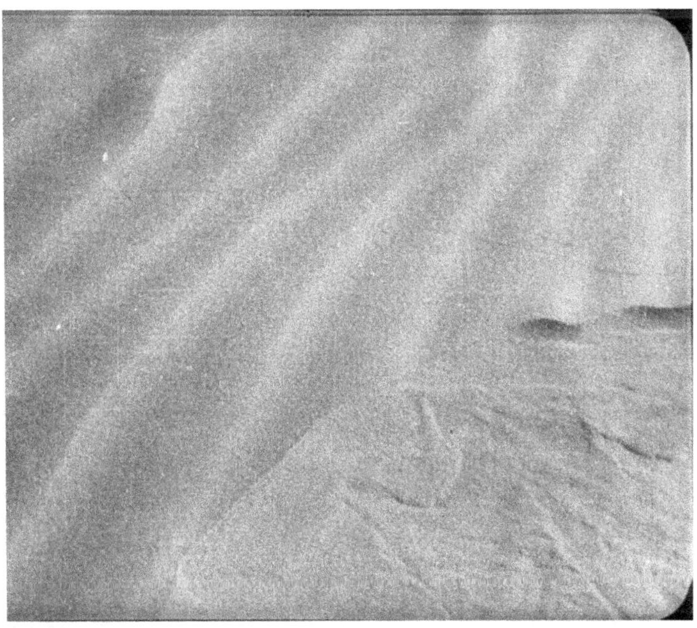

Image 14: The immobile Kara-Kum desert, near the beginning of the third song (*Three Songs of Lenin*)

An example is this anonymous "Kirghiz Song," the main text in the third of the three songs:

> In Moscow, in a big stone city,
> Where those chosen by the people gathered,
> There is a nomad's tent on a square,
> And in it Lenin lies.
> If you have great sadness,

And nothing comforts you,
Go up to this tent,
And look upon Lenin,
And your woe will disperse like water

And your sadness float away like leaves in an *aryk* [stream or canal].[62]

In *Three Songs* itself, this movement from sadness to "flow" and dispersal occurs in the best Vertov style, as the vast, nearly unmoving expanse of the Kara-Kum desert, rippling with suppressed energy (Image 14), gives way to motion and flow (catalyzed by Lenin's mausoleum (the "tent")); what was frozen and locked-in suddenly becomes a multi-branched stream linking marchers (Image 15), mass produced texts (specifically, copies of Lenin's works rolling off the assembly line), and eventually irrigative water as such (Image 16). Now, however, the formal representation of change is motivated, perhaps even justified, by the "people's" own words.

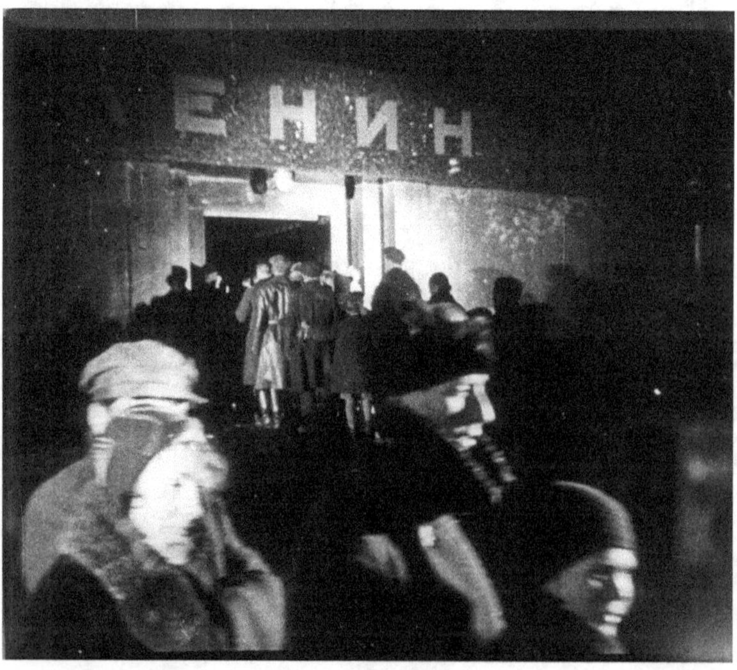

Image 15: The double-flow of marchers into the mausoleum (*Three Songs of Lenin*)

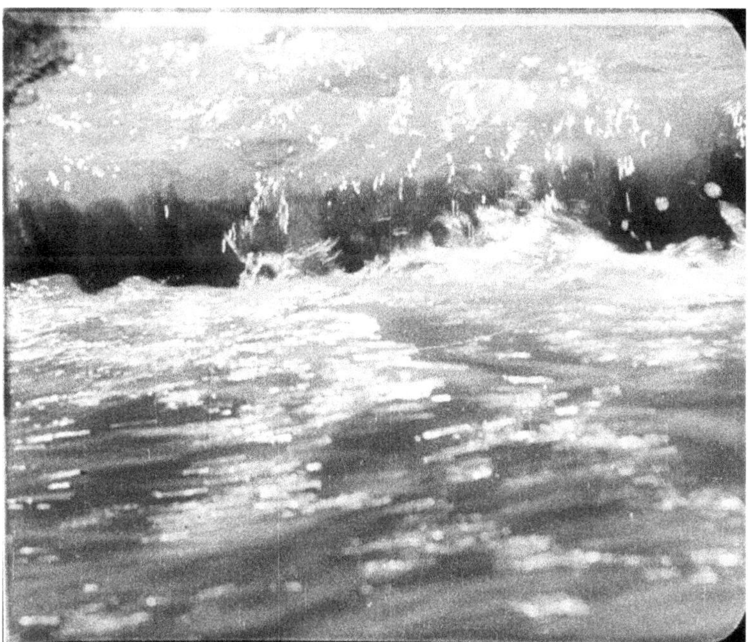

Image 16: The core image of the sequence: water (*Three Songs of Lenin*)

* * *

We have already suggested historical reasons for Vertov's adoption of character and folklore in *Three Songs*. Two final and related questions concern the respective places of Lenin and Stalin in the film, and how we might account for the film's actual appeal (repeatedly attested by early viewers) to its contemporary audiences. Noël Burch was correct, I think, when he wrote that, "among the Soviet masters, Dziga Vertov alone advocated an uncompromising tabula rasa."[63] I interpret this phrase to mean not only that Vertov was (as Malevich saw) drawn to a cinema of near-abstract dynamism in contrast to more theatrically-based contemporaries like Eisenstein, but was committed to a translation of politically revolutionary radicalism into cinema, a translation that would require not only a purgation from literary and theatrical dross but a rebuilding of cinema from some presumed ground-level of perception. (Perhaps the destruction of the Civil War, leading to very palpable "levelings" of all sorts, helped condition this attitude as well.)

In part, this is what accounts for critics at the time decried as Vertov's "infantilism," his frequent reinventings of the wheel, carried out as though all the established resources of cinema had to be accumulated again and reconfigured.[64] And Vertov seemed truly to believe that these sorts of renovations of vision would have a virtually immediate political effect:

> Gradually, through comparison of various parts of the globe, various bits of life, the visible world is being explored. . . . Millions of workers, having recovered their sight, are beginning to doubt the necessity of supporting the bourgeois structure of the world.[65]

But with the move to full-scale "socialist construction" in 1929 and the massive production of "Soviet" subjectivities, more efficacious, less implacably corporeal mechanisms for configuring the "revolutionary passage" for Soviet citizens was required. For Vertov, these new mechanisms were precisely the subjective trajectories of biographical individuals and the lure of folk authenticity, into whose vocabularies the raw material-perceptual transitions and leaps of earlier avant-garde *faktura* could be translated. Now, passages between old and new that had previously been represented in a non-"humanist" (or even "non-human") manner were recoded in terms that invited sympathy and subjective investment; the material relationship between the static and the active slowly mutated into a narrative-figural one, like the relationship between promise and fulfillment.

If Vertov's work of the 1920s had mobilized material dynamics as both a figure for and a way of effecting (on a perceptual level) revolution, the films of the 1930s, typified by *Three Songs*, insert two additional mediating levels: revolution as a personal, biographical trajectory (or what medieval Christian hermeneutics would call the "moral" level of interpretation), and a new base-stratum of presentiment of revolution, as expressed in folksong (or what those same medieval allegorists would call the "literal" level). This new "machinery for ideological investment," to use Fredric Jameson's phrase, is thus arguably more complex as an *ideological* structure than what we find in Vertov's work of the 1920s; a diagram of its significant layers, in accord with the four medieval exegetical levels, would look like this:[66]

Anagogical (collective, historical destiny; communism)
Moral (the individual process of becoming "new," "Soviet": psychology)
Allegorical (the perceptual-somatic revolution; modernizing of the senses)
Literal (here, folk poetry and music, with its utopian imagery: narodnoe tvorchestvo)

In other words, the desires for change expressed in folk poetry ("your woe will disperse like water": the historically prior or "literal" level) can also *mean* a desire for world-historical socialist transformation (the anagogical level), a desire which can also *be expressed* in terms of individual progress toward revolutionary consciousness (the moral level); and all of these levels can find *representation*, if properly articulated, in the "pure dynamics" of cinema (the allegorical level).

Unsurprisingly, such figurative reading was indeed characteristic of the discourse of the '30s. We find a rather painful example of Vertov's own allegorizing in an article he wrote about *Three Songs* in 1935, where after noting that he structured one section of the "second song" in accord with the cadences of folk poetry ("through fire/yet they go/they fall/yet they go/they die/yet they go/the masses who won the Civil War/that is Ilich-Lenin"), he goes on to argue that precisely the same passage from defeat to victory characterizes "the revolution in the consciousnesses of the workers on the White Sea Canal."[67] This canal project, in fact a brutal Gulag-style forced labor enterprise built between 1931 and 1933, was widely publicized as (and indeed, thought by many to *be*) as a grand reform-through-work venture, a disciplinary mechanism for the creation of Soviet citizens.[68]

These grim motifs bring us back, at long last, to the role of Stalin in the film, and, by extension, that of Lenin. It seems best to assert that the Lenin of *Three Songs* functions as a kind of guarantor of the ultimate mutual inter-translatability of the four levels indicated above. Lenin is at once the exemplary revolutionary person (moral), the great theorist of communism and founder of the USSR (anagogical), and a folk hero to the "people" (literal);[69] as the great "electrifier" or modernizer of the country, he can be assimilated to the more properly Vertovian "allegorical" level as well. But what of Stalin, who, as we know, was prominently on view throughout the film? Paradoxically enough, my analysis suggests, I think, that "Stalin" was not especially essential to the overall structure and rhetoric of *Three Songs of Lenin*. Judging from the contemporary reviews (whether Soviet or otherwise), he seems in fact to have made very little impression; few mentioned him at all, and very few seemed to regard his role as an essential part of the "meaning" of the film. In truth, this is unsurprising, for Stalin in *Three Songs* neither "replaces" Lenin nor comes to occupy the pole of the "New" (as opposed to Lenin's "Old"). Inasmuch as Stalin is shown "continuing the work" of Lenin, he is like everyone else in the film; inasmuch as he "fulfills" Lenin's directives, he remains decidedly secondary to the primary model (and the original film, I should add, apparently contained no folksong references to Stalin, though it certainly could have included them). Most importantly, the very allegorical structure of the film, fusing folk collective, individuals, historical destiny and cinematic *faktura* explorations into a single "Leninist" revolutionary paradigm, absolutely precludes a central tenet of the (in 1934, already dominant) Stalin cult: namely, that Stalin was "the intermediary between Lenin and the people," that through "Stalin's works, writings, and person Lenin's spirit was accessible to all."[70] Whether in 1934 or 1970, *Three Songs of Lenin* argues, on the contrary, that "Lenin" is in some sense omnipresent and immanent in discourse, historical action, and artistic practice alike. (Was this the feature that made the 1938 reedit of the film—which includes a speech by Stalin about Lenin—necessary?)[71]

We should not be tempted to think that this rhetorical sidelining of Stalin occurred because of some conscious "dissident" impulse on Vertov's part (of which there is no evidence in any case).[72] Rather, it emerged out of Vertov's effort to preserve a space for his established artistic practice, even while creating an "accessible" and politically useful work. Thus we might see his work on *Three Songs* as a form of preservative figuration or *allegoresis*, a way of saving the old forms, as the Neoplatonist Porphyry did with his philosophical allegory of the Homeric "cave of the nymphs," for example, by rereading them as versions of some newly legitimated brand of knowledge.[73] That an avant-gardist would need to preserve his beloved forms not through appeal to new science or philosophy but to "the folk" and "subjectivities" may be one feature that makes the story of Vertov's own creative passage from the Old of the 20s to the New of the 30s a peculiarly Soviet one.

Endnotes

1 This article was originally published in *Film History: An International Journal* 18.4 (2006): 376-391.

2 A note on the English translation of the original title (*Tri Pesni o Lenine*): strictly speaking, the most obvious translation of the pronoun "o" in the title is "about" rather than "of," and indeed the title *Three Songs about Lenin* has been offered both in articles and in exhibition contexts (as the title of the Kino Video DVD of the film, for instance). English-language writers have been inconsistent about the title from the beginning, however; in his review for the *Guardian* (24 November (1934): 11), Huntly Carter calls the film *Three Songs on Lenin*! For my part, I would endorse the title *Three Songs of Lenin* on generic grounds. The film is a "film-poem," after all, and the translated title should render that hint of "epic" archaism, on an analogy with titles like *The Song of Roland*, *The Lay of Igor's Campaign*, and so on; the flat literalism of "*Three Songs about Lenin*" misses this important nuance.

3 *Three Songs of Lenin* was commissioned in late 1931, about two years in advance of the projected 10th anniversary commemoration of the Soviet leader's death in 1924. The film's extraordinarily troubled production history had a happy ending for Vertov; he received the Order of the Red Star for his achievements in cinema (and for his work on *Three Songs* in particular) in January 1935 (see Roshal', *Dziga Vertov*, 237). Interestingly, the Red Star was a military award; Vertov was apparently a reservist during this period (he was called before a military commissariat while making *Three Songs* (on 10 February 1934), but got a deferment), which perhaps explains why he received a military rather than civilian honor (RGALI (Russian State Archive of Literature and Art) f. 2091, op. 2, d. 423, l. 14). In the numbered references that follow to materials in the Vertov archive, I use the following standard abbreviation system, utilized at RGALI itself: f. (archive, "fond"); op. (list or inventory, "opis"); d. (file, "delo"); l. (page, "list").

4 Vertov was already showing rushes of the film by ca. 15 January 1934 (RGALI f. 2091, op. 2, d. 423, ll. 93-94), and was soon complaining bitterly (through May 1934) about the refusal of Mezhrabpomfil'm administrator who was later associated with the Lenin Museum, to release it (RGALI f. 2091, op. 2, d. 423, ll. 94ob, 119). However, it appears likely that the original film's "third song" contained the shots—present in the 1970 reedit as well—of the triumphal arrival of the rescued members of the abortive "Cheliuskin" polar exhibition; see RGALI f. 2091, op. 2, d. 274, l. 22. This material could not have been incorporated earlier than April 1934.

5 This festival marked one of the first great exhibitions of "new Soviet cinema" in the West; among the films shown (sometimes only as excerpts) were Dovzhenko's *Ivan*, Boris Barnet's *Outskirts*, Aleksandr Ptushko's *New Gulliver*, and Grigori Alexandrov's *Happy Guys* (see "Vostorzhennye otzyvy"). Vertov fought desperately to attend the festival, but was unable to get permission to go (RGALI f. 2091, op. 2, d. 423, ll. 26-30).

6 Apparently, *Three Songs* was pre-screened in the Donbass city of Kramatorsk on the occasion of the opening of the enormous machine-building plant there on 28 September 1934; see Gurevich, "Segodnia " and RGALI f. 2091, op. 2, d. 274, l. 63. The film was shown as far away as Ufa, Semipalatinsk and Tashkent, and received a New York release as well (after a shot of a woman breastfeeding her child was removed: see letter of New York State Department of Education to Amkino Corp., 3 November 1934 (housed in Anthology Film Archives)) in November; it was reviewed favorably in both the *New York Times* and the *Herald Tribune* (RGALI f. 2091, op. 1, d. 93, l. 100).

7 See in particular Vij, "Pisatel' i fil'ma" [on Wells' reaction to the film]; Roger, "Un beau film de Dziga Vertoff". *Pravda* published numerous articles that either discussed or mentioned the film, always positively—including a major piece by D. Osipov on 23 July 1934, with stills from the film ("Kinopoema o Lenine," 4), but also on 16 September and 10, 20, and 24 November 1934, and 11 January, 6, 21 and 27 February, and 2 March 1935—contrary to what has recently been claimed (see Bulgakowa, "Spatial Figures in Soviet Cinema of the 1930s," 75). The group photo of the winners of the cinema prizes (including Vertov, who won his prize for *Three Songs*) was actually the cover photo of *Pravda* on 28 February 1935.

8 RGALI f. 2091, op. 2, d. 423, ll. 52-53. Certainly, the film was shown, in some form or other, in cities all over the Soviet Union through at least to 1 May 1935 (RGALI f. 2091, op. 2, d. 274, l. 361).

9 See Deriabin, "*Three Songs of Lenin*," 75. On the differences between the 1938 version and the (now lost) 1934 and 1935 original versions, see below.

10 See, for example, his use of *Three Songs* as a defense against charges of "cosmopolitanism" during the notorious anti-Semitic campaign of the late '40s-early '50s (RGALI f. 2091, op. 2, d. 222, ll. 3-4).

11 Fevral'skii, "Tri Pesni o Lenine," 67-70.

12 See *Komsomsol'skaia Pravda* 22 March (1960), and RGALI f. 2091, op. 2, d. 274, l. 1037.

13 Vertova-Svilova and Furtichev, *Tri Pesni o Lenine.*

14 See, for example, Denise J. Youngblood's evaluation of the film's third section as "almost fascistic in its treatment of the People and the Leader and in its emphasis on the human body. This abysmal film marked the bitter end of the career of a great and original director whose artistic politics helped shape the cinema debates of a decade. *Three Songs of Lenin* is typical of what the Soviet 'documentary' would become" (*Soviet Cinema in the Silent Era,* 230).

15 On this, see Tumarkin, *Lenin Lives!,* 252-54.

16 Vij, "Pisatel' i fil'ma,"; RGALI f. 2091, op. 1, d. 93, l. 24. The prominence of Stalin in the film's last section is confirmed by other reviewers; e.g., "The third song is the song of today—the swelling, triumphant song of socialist construction, of the continuation of the work started by Lenin and now carried ever further by the Leninist party under the leadership of Stalin" (Moen, "*Three Songs About Lenin*: A New Kind of Film Portraying Great Achievement"; RGALI f. 2091, op. 1, d. 93, l. 31).

17 Rokotov, "Tri Pesni o Lenine"; RGALI f. 2091, op. 1, d. 93, l. 89.

18 Although it was clearly added at a fairly late date in the production: RGALI f. 2091, op. 1, d. 48, l. 17.

19 Rokotov, "Tri Pesni o Lenine."

20 Ivanov, "Tri Pesni o Lenine"; RGALI f. 2091, op. 2, d. 274, l. 22.

21 One of the most widely distributed publications on which this photo appeared as a cover image, Stalin's booklet *About Lenin*, was likely on Vertov's desk as he was preparing *Three Songs*, inasmuch as direct quotations from it appear with some frequency in his notes for the film: e.g., "departing from us, comrade Lenin bequeathed to us the duty of holding high and preserving the purity of the great calling of Party member; we swear to you, comrade Lenin, that we will carry out your commandment with honor," a well-known refrain from Stalin's funeral speech for Lenin of 26 January 1924 (*O Lenine*, 1-2) and jotted down by Vertov on 3 December 1933 (RGALI f. 2091, op. 2, d. 246, l. 41).

22 RGALI f. 2091, op. 2, d. 423, l. 47.

23 RGALI f. 2091, op. 2, d. 423, ll. 65-68, here 66. It seems that Vertov prepared this "sound passport" in part for the film's exhibition in Venice, to ensure that the sound was projected properly (RGALI f. 2091, op. 2, d. 423, l. 28).

24 Much more could be said about the relationships between the various versions, though this is not the place to engage in a full-scale comparison. The notorious 1938 "Stalinized" sound version was essentially augmented by a long, dull speech by Stalin (about Lenin) in the final reel, more footage of various luminaries in the Stalinist hierarchy (e.g., Voroshilov, Ezhov), and by shots relating to the Spanish Civil War (e.g., of Dolores Ibárurri ("La Passionaria") delivering a speech); much of the same Spanish material appeared in Vertov's *Lullaby* (1937), and at least some was retained in the 1970 reedit. The 1938 *Three Songs* was also abbreviated by the exclusion of now-repressed "enemies of the people" who had appeared in the original (such as Marshal Tukhachevskii (RGALI f. 2091, op. 1, d. 48, ll. 9, 16)).

25 See, for example, the cover of *Pravda* for 7 November (1934) (the 17th anniversary of the October Revolution), with its side-by-side portraits of Lenin and Stalin, among scores of other examples.

26 Kanzog, "Internalisierte Religiosität," 218.

27 Michelson, "The Kinetic Icon and the Work of Mourning," 119, 129.

28 Bulgakowa, "Spatial Figures in Soviet Cinema of the 1930s," 59.

29 Mariano Prunes, "Dziga Vertov's *Three Songs about Lenin* (1934)," 274. Prunes focuses primarily on the co-presence of differing approaches to still photography in *Three Songs*, but much of what he says holds true for the relationship between *Three Songs* and earlier Vertov works. The 1925 *Lenin Kino-Pravda*, for instance, provides the clear template for important features of the "mourning" sequence in the second of the three songs (entitled "We Loved Him").

30 Prunes, "Dziga Vertov's *Three Songs about Lenin* (1934)," 272.

31 Michelson, "The Kinetic Icon and the Work of Mourning," 129.

32 Bulgakowa, "Spatial Figures in Soviet Cinema of the 1930s," 59.

33 The perceptive Aleksandr Fevral'skii, reviewing *Three Songs* prior to its release in November 1934, concluded by noting how the film "affirms the art of socialist realism, thereby showing that even within a story-less cinema (which is not to say without theme or topic), socialist realism can find sufficiently vivid expression" ("Tri pesni o Lenine,"; cited in Sokolov *Istoriia Sovetskogo Kinoiskusstva Zvukovogo Perioda*, 70).

34 Deleuze, *Cinema 1*, 39. All of Deleuze's comments on Vertov here (especially 39-40 and 82) are of the greatest interest.

35 I am thinking here of a play like *Breath* (1969).

36 RGALI f. 2091, op. 2, d. 235, ll. 3-6.

37 The intriguing, vitally important exception seems to be *One Sixth of the World* (1926).

38 The idea of revolution as a "socialist springtime" was an important one, especially during the years of the first Five Year Plan (1928-32); the trope partially informs Mikhail Kaufman's great *In Spring* (1929).

39 In the analysis of *Three Songs* that follows, I will be relying on sections of the 1970 reedit—the only version readily available outside of Russia—that correspond, to the best of my knowledge, to the original 1934 sound version in all essentials.

40 Massell, *The Surrogate Proletariat*, 138. The Soviets themselves were borrowing, of course, from a long Euro-American tradition of incorporating, in Leila Ahmed's words, "the peculiar practices of Islam with respect to women" into "the Western narrative of the quintessential otherness and inferiority of Islam" (*Women and Gender in Islam*, 149).

41 These rapid re-focalizations are a striking feature of *Three Songs*. Apparently simple in its structure as compared with the late silent features, in fact one often finds the whole relation between spectator, camera and observed object changing from one shot to the next, without intermediate steps. Vertov himself said that it was the most complexly edited of his films.

42 "Tear off each and every mask from reality" had been the slogan of the proletarian writers' group RAPP, a group toward which Vertov was in fact profoundly hostile (the feeling was mutual). Interestingly, "the RAPP leader, Leopold Averbakh, took the slogan from Lenin's comment that the 'realism of [Lev] Tolstoy was the tearing off of each and every mask'" (Fitzpatrick, *Tear off the Masks!*, 65).

43 Vertov writes of Gasanova and of filming her at her home in his working notes for the film: RGALI f. 2091, op. 1, d. 48, 5, and op. 2, d. 66, ll. 41-46. See Gasanova, *Raskreposhchenie zhenshchiny-gorianki v Dagestane*; and *Podgotovka zhenskikh kadrov v Dagestane i ikh rol' v khoziastvennom i kul'turnom razvitii respubliki*. The script for the film refers to her as "Mel'kiu"; see Deriabin, *Iz naslediia. tom pervyj*, 170-171.

44 The setting would seem to be central-Russian, although a closer look at the marching Pioneers suggests that they are of Central Asian ethnicity; Vertov described their musical theme as the "eastern Pioneer march."

45 Gasanova's strongest competitor in this respect is Maria Belik, whose sync sound interview appears in the third of the three songs. The female radio-listener who eventually appears sculpting a Lenin bust in the first section of *Enthusiasm*—a woman referred to as "Tasia" in Vertov's notes for the film (RGALI f. 2091, op. 2, d. 239, l. 75ob)—is a minor precursor; the "man with a movie camera" incarnated by Mikhail Kaufman in the film of that name is another obvious "protagonist," although he does not, to my mind, emerge as a subjectivized character in any significant sense. To be sure, full-fledged characters do appear in Vertov's later work, realized and unrealized; the married couple at the center of *To You, Front!* (1942) is probably the apotheosis here.

46 *Kino-Eye*, 5.

47 RGALI f. 2091, op. 2, d. 423, l. 37. The turn to "humanism" was a characteristic of cultural discourse at the time; see the self-critical speech by former LEF-ist Viktor Shklovsky at the first Congress of Soviet Writers, "In the Name of the New Humanism," 3.

48 "The newspapers ran many stories on the extraordinary achievements of ordinary people, whose photographs, serious or smiling, looked out from the front page" (Fitzpatrick, *Everyday Stalinism*, 74). This trend intensified with the "Stakhanovite" movement that began in 1935: "Stakhanovites' photographs were published in the newspapers; journalists interviewed them about their achievements and opinions . . . [they] were also celebrated for their *individual* achievements and encouraged to show their individuality and leadership potential" (ibid.; Fitzpatrick's emphasis).

49 The culmination of this tendency is certainly Vertov's *Lullaby* (1937), which continually links celebratory footage of Soviet "reality" (parades, speeches and so on) with various implied subjectivities—in many cases, those of children and even infants. Much of Vertov's later work offers similar focus on "personalities"; see, for instance, *Three Heroines* (1938), about the famous women aviators Valentina Grizodubova, Polina Osipenko, and Marina Raskova. As a qualification, it is worthwhile adding that "testimonial" writing, whether in prose or poetry, had a major role to play in the gradual development of the cult of Lenin from the very beginning (1924). Nina Tumarkin singles out Grigori Zinoviev's citation of workers' writings about Lenin as imparting to Zinoviev's tributes a demonstrably more galvanizing effect on his audiences than that exerted by other

Party leaders. One of the writings was a letter, "written by a miner, [and began] in a traditional folk idiom—'the sun has grown dim; the star has disappeared'—and reads like a folk tale. . . . In reading this story Zinoviev was [saying] that Lenin had become, for the narod [common people] a leader of enormous stature, a prophet, and a savior" (*Lenin Lives!*, 155).

50 Critics have been right to notice that the autoreferential Vertov likes to represent ideal viewers and exemplary subjects in his films; it is less often recognized that the majority of these viewers and subjects are women. Without getting into the very large topic of Vertov's feminism in general (about which I can say almost nothing of substance here), it should be mentioned that, in *Three Songs*, the images and voices of women are given a crucial historically "connective" role differentiating them from what we find in the earlier films. Even after the veil is tossed away and modernity has been embraced, women in *Three Songs* continue to be shown in "native dress," participating in "folk celebrations"—one female bard is shown competing against a man in a *dutar*-playing contest—thus making visible that ideal link between national and Soviet identity promoted by the official ideology.

51 What I am claiming here needs to be augmented by Annette Michelson's brilliant observation that, in *Three Songs*, Vertov's exploration of cinematic time and space becomes psychologized as the "working-through" of Lenin's death: "Vertov's deployment of the cinematic anomalies, the optical panoply of slow motion, of stretch printing, looping, the freeze-frame, reverse motion, originally constituted as an arsenal in the assault upon the conditions and ideology of cinematic representation . . . are now deployed as an admittedly powerful instrument in that labor of repetition, deceleration, distension, arrest, release and fixation which characterize the work of mourning" (Michelson, "The Kinetic Icon and the Work of Mourning ,"129).

52 He later made the film at the VUFKU (Ukrainian) studio (released 1929).

53 To give the devil his due, it is not hard to imagine why, given the limited resources for film and all the political pressures of the day, the bureaucrats in charge of the film industry were sceptical of Vertov's preferred approach. They feared that it would lead to inefficiency on the production level and to a "lack of ideological orientation" within the film itself; for both these inadequacies, needless to say, the bureaucrats themselves would have borne ultimate responsibility.

54 RGALI f. 2091, op. 2, d. 423, l. 4. Mezhrabpomfil'm was the studio that produced *Three Songs*. The note was addressed to Mezhrabpomfil'm administrator Babitskii.

55 RGALI f. 2091, op. 1, d. 50, ll. 1-12.

56 See Gunther, "Totalitarnaia narodnost' i ee istoki," 377-389; and Miller, *Folklore for* Stalin, 7-13.

57 Vertova-Svilova and Furtichev *Tri Pesni o Lenine*, 107. An itinerary plan for the film under the working title "About Lenin" from August 1932 contains no hint of any structuring "folk" content (RGALI f. 2091, op. 1, d. 50, ll. 1-12).

58 LEF had been deeply hostile to folk art, seeing in it (in Frank Miller's words) "a worthless remnant of a patriarchal society, a cart that should be replaced by a truck" (*Folklore for Stalin*, 6).

59 RGALI f. 2091, op. 2, d. 212, l. 8. The famous article "Muddle Instead of Music" appeared in *Pravda* on 28 January 1936.

60 One section of text from the "first song," beginning with the line "We never saw him," is actually an excerpt that appeared in *Pravda* ("Vostochnyi epos," 22 April (1927): 3) from a longer verse called "The Death of Lenin" by the "Komsomol member Atabaev";

the poem had been written down in Kanibadam, Tadzhikistan in March 1925 (RGALI f. 2091, op. 2, d. 422, l. 14). Although Vertov did collect poetic texts and record folk musical performances *in situ* in Central Asia and Azerbaidzhan, it seems likely that much of the poetic material out of which he culled the "three songs" came from sources in Moscow such as possibly the *Pravda* offices, where his friend Mikhail Kol'tsov worked.

61 Vertov wrote as much in a diary note from 1936: "The same impulse that had once prompted me to collect doggerel verse awoke again within me [during the production of *Three Songs*]. In the first place, these were song-documents; as is well known, I have always had great interest in the arsenal of documentary" (Vertova-Svilova and Furtichev *Tri Pesni o Lenine* , 107).

62 "Written down in Kirghiz-Kishlak, Fergana region, in February 1926" (RGALI f. 2091, op. 2, d. 422, l. 26).

63 Burch, "Film's Institutional Mode of Representation and the Soviet Response," 93.

64 At a meeting of the kinocs in 1923, Vertov spoke of the need for the "abrogation of literary trash" in the following terms: "The productive resources of cinema need to be purged, in a manner analogous to a purge of the Communist Party [of which Vertov was never a member], to renounce all of its harmful and enervating components in the name of its full recovery and victorious growth" (RGALI f. 2091, op. 2, d. 390, l. 6).

65 *Kino-Eye*, 39.

66 My reading here is based on Jameson's comments on medieval exegesis in *The Political Unconscious*, although the anagogical level occupies a somewhat different place in my analysis: "[I]t is precisely in [the generation of the moral and anagogical levels] that the individual believer is able to 'insert' himself or herself (to use the Althusserian formula), it is precisely by way of the *moral* and *anagogical* interpretations that the textual apparatus is transformed into a 'libidinal apparatus,' a machinery for ideological investment" (*The Political Unconscious*, 30). For medieval exegetes, the literal level is the Old Testament (especially the story of the Exodus); the allegorical is the New Testament (especially the life of Christ); the moral, the tale of the "redemption" of the individual believer; and the anagogical, the eventual historical destiny of all mankind in the Second Coming and Last Judgment. It needs to be stressed (to avoid all misunderstanding) that Jameson's analysis is an attempt to understand the ideological effectiveness of certain textual constructs, not an advocacy of medieval Christian hermeneutics as an interpretive method. By the same token, my use of Jameson's interpretation is meant to indicate the kind of *ideological* work *Three Songs* is performing, not that Vertov is adopting a "religious" framework in any explicit way.

67 "Poslednii opyt." A well-known "History of the Construction of White Sea-Baltic Canal" was edited by Maksim Gor'kii (1934), and contained contributions by Shklovsky and Zoshchenko among others.

68 See Morukov, "The White Sea-Baltic Canal," 151-162. Vertov actually received permission to film a documentary about the project on 25 February 1934, but this film apparently never got off the ground (RGALI f. 2091, op. 2, d. 247, l. 103ob).

69 In his working notes for the film, Vertov included the following quotation from *Pravda*, 22 April 1927: "In the stories, songs and tales of the peoples of the East, Lenin is characterized as a *bogatyr'* [folkloric prince] who has expanded into a hero for all humanity and raised a holy war against the rich, the violent, the insulters, and defeats them in his role as 'scourge of the land.' No one can stand up to his power. On the other hand, he is a simple and good father."

70 Nina Tumarkin's words in *Lenin Lives*!, 253.

71 Perhaps—though the main reasons for the revision were almost certainly 1) to "update" the film for the Lenin memorials in January 1938, when it was released; and 2) to "Stalinize" the film as part of the lead-up to the large-scale tributes to the despot on his 60th birthday (December 1939).

72 What I am suggesting raises the very interesting question of just how difficult it was for Svilova and her collaborators to "restore" *Three Songs* in 1969—that is, how easy it was to excise Stalin from the film, while retaining its rhetorical coherence. At this point, I have no evidence on this score; clearly enough, my interpretation here suggests that the restoration was not (in this respect) difficult to realize.

73 "The Greeks wished to renounce neither Homer nor science. They sought for a compromise, and found it in the allegorical interpretation of Homer. [. . .] Homeric allegoresis had come into existence as a defense of Homer against philosophy. It was then taken over by the philosophical schools, and also by history and natural science. [Later], all schools of philosophy find that their doctrines are in Homer" (Curtius, *European Literature and the Latin Middle Ages*, 204-205).

Concluding Addendum:
The Tradition of Experimentation in Russian Culture and the Russian Avant-Garde

Dennis Ioffe

We believe that radical modernism and the avant-garde in Russia developed as the result of a tradition of profound experimentation. In order to discuss the legacy of this experimental "testing"[1] culture in Russia of the last three centuries, it is necessary to start by determining the capacity of experimentation as a phenomenon, along with reviewing the complex of ideas and historical factors relevant for this purpose. It appears important to try to comprehend, in the first place, what the word "experiment"[2] means, especially with regard to various Russian cultural practices. Experiment is always invoked by a certain measure of dissatisfaction with the existing state of affairs in this or another sphere of human existence.

Experiment proceeds from the necessity to alter the state of things by the means of testing an experience, which has been obtained in accordance with a certain scientific or cultural agenda. This experience is expected to establish a sequence of major changes addressing a certain phenomenon or object, with the intention of creating a "new reality" based on this experiment. First and foremost, experiment is a method of research, scrutinizing a phenomenon in terms of particular conditions. Consequently, it always takes place within the limits of a certain laboratory (or semi-laboratory) test. The *laboratory* ad hoc can be represented by almost any set of circumstances actually playing this role, that of a field of inquiry. Thus, for Russian Symbolists, such conditions of inquiry emerged during the revolution of 1905; and for Russian Futurists, during the period of the two revolutions of 1917. The degree of involvement with the phenomenon in question is pivotal for the backbone of the experiment, ever aiding to expand the limits of the relevant area of expertise.

Changing paradigms of knowledge, along with various revolutions occurring in science, are also closely tied to experiment. The validity of any hypothetical component of practical knowledge, as well as stability of any given social condition (the so called "social experiment" is an example), has to be assessed by the means of special testing procedures, which put every theory through a practical and empirical trial, as noted by Karl Popper.[3] The issues related to the psychological constituent of experiment were seminally examined in the mid-1950's by Robert M. Gottsdanker[4]. The species of *psychological experiment* was intended to analyze the mental experience of a person or a group of people in their interaction with either scientists conducting scholarly inquiry or cultural actors in search of new ideas.

One of the most essential things in order to understand experimentation is that in almost every case its concrete results may not (and should not) be fully predictable. Moreover, an experiment cannot always proceed in full compliance with the way in which it was conceived, planned and designed. The *Stochastic nature* of experimentation (the term originates from the Greek στοχαστικός, "able to guess") becomes apparent in the intuitive perception of the fortuity of a given phenomenon. The *stochastic* intuitivism largely forms the conceptual basis of phenomenology and the prognostics of experiment. The contemporary methodology of experiment owes a lot to William Gilbert and Galileo Galilei; and also to Francis Bacon who was one of the first to come up with the initial theoretical description of an experiment as a phenomenon.[5] The tradition of the "visionary" creative experiment enlists such names as Jacob Boehme, Emmanuel Swedenborg and William Blake; and later, about the same time as the early stages of Russian modernism, Rudolph Steiner. It is also worth mentioning that the entire history of alchemy, that is, the realm of (esoteric) communion between the spheres of spiritual and physical matter has also directly involved permanent experimentation with chemical, alchemistic and other substances.

The possibility to delimitate between the "theoretical" and the "empirical" was disputed in the following years. In the context of contemporary science, in the aspect of its fundamental methods and principles, experiment is usually intended to determine theoretical validity and, ideally, some universal significance for the hypothesis. In this regard, the importance of "mental" experimentation cannot be overstated with reference to the issues associated with culture and society, particularly the creations of the human spirit that often cannot be fully implemented in an empirical sense. Here the experiment conducted in the imagination is perceived as part of a transcendental function of conscience where implementation of an experiment is modelled in the mental sphere. Experiment is staged in order to test a theory and, if possible, to find something serendipitously. The question of value with respect to theory is rather controversial, since experiment can confirm theory as like as not, even though some of the routine conventions of such fundamental academic disciplines as mathematics may oppose that. By confirming the theory, the experiment determines its significance and validity. A theory, as a rule, possesses no particular universal value per se until some experiment empirically confirms it or contributes to its affirmation in some other way. One can argue whether theoretical applicability can exist apart from the "practical." The further contemplation of these matters will require a demarcation between such terms as "theory" and "hypothesis."

The purely "creative" constituent of a "mental experiment," it seems, cannot be overestimated. It can prove especially relevant for Russian modernism with its tendency to articulate the utopian life-creation program which manifests itself through cultural activity. The typical instance is the "insane" episode with "centaurs and unicorns" of the younger generation of Russian Symbolists (especially where Andrei Bely is concerned). They were experimenting with reality, distorting its basic positions, looking at its immediate perception by uninvolved witnesses. This type of behaviour can be viewed through the lens of the imaginarium of the Romantic mythopoetics with the cultivation of "deviation," "sickness," and extravagant perversion. The experimental basis (invoking Goethe's treatise on the importance of experimentation and his "color theory")[6] is no less obvious in the case of the older Symbolists, with Vyacheslav Ivanov's (1908) call for *a realibus ad realiora* (from real to most real)[7] appearing particularly significant. The visionary experimentation of Vyacheslav Ivanov was aimed at achieving an ideal existential environment that would harmoniously implement the principles of his aesthetic theory and literary practice. The machinery of experimentation appropriated by Russian modernism was directly concerned with the life-creational attitude intent upon rearranging the established state of affairs in society, culture, science and philosophy.

The issue of imaginary "ideal models" employed by certain cultural practices deserves special attention in terms of the so-called "elusive experiment." Endowed with a function of "testing" the theory, experimentation can either "reinforce" the original theory or demonstrate its painful fiasco. The model basis of any experiment involves establishing relatively strict conditions for its implementation, having a clear understanding of its goals, and looking for means that would aid reaching them. The heuristic basis of experimentation is established in all spheres of the human experience including, apart from the natural sciences, social life and culture. Contemplating the structure of society, the way it works and is being managed, may not be possible without conducting a kind of "social experiment"—as mentioned above.[8] This sphere of action was, among other things, of particular interest for the modernist Utopia that was evolving in the West and in Russia.[9]

The experimenting modernists can be likened in this sense to real scientific researchers whereas their minds and bodies were fully involved in the range of activities they chose to analyze. It can be concluded that a typical experiment is invariably directed at studying the very nature of a phenomenon by the means of an appropriate testing device. In this perspective, the banality of affirmation that every theory must be *tested* by an applied experiment becomes less obvious, since a *banal* fact does not cease being a *fact* because of its banality. In this way, the experiment turns into a crucial and, maybe, dominant ingredient of any serious scientific effort. If there is no experiment, there can be no active science at all. An experiment, in principle, evolves into a metaphor—a "problem" intended to promote a possible (re)solution. If there is no "problem," there can be no research. The scientific work that is not directed at a particular "problem" cannot be actually considered *scientific*. In this sense, *experiment* and *problem* become parts of the integral approach that is indispensable for any scholarly inquest in any discipline of the contemporary academy. Accordingly, active experimentation is essential for every national culture in general and each one of its segments in particular. If any of these segments will fail—then the cultural development will become ultimately ineffectual, falling into stagnation. As a heuristic phenomenon, this experiment is invariably *futuristic* by its nature and, therefore, is set to determine the future productivity of the tested substances.

Speaking of cultural practices, it can be said that the modern humanities, from the Russian Formalists to the Structuralists and Post-Structuralists, have persistently employed various "probing" literary texts for the sake of substantiating their innovative ideas. This can be true not only for such well-known theorists of Russian Futurism and Formalism as Victor Shklovsky and Roman Jakobson, Grigory Vinokur and Boris Eichenbaum, but also for the world-famous French Post-Structuralists such as Gilles Deleuze and Jacques Derrida. The critical constituent of any experiment always lives up to the criteria of verity, substantially clear for grasping its essence and applicable to the examined hypotheses and theories. Here a question can arise: what are these criteria of verity? The main problem is whether the hypothesis is correct. In the process of studying the given phenomenon, hypotheses and theories should be formulated before proceeding to affirm the relevance of the object under scrutiny. Moreover, ideally, any experiment should be expected to produce a certain result, yet unattained through the means of existing doctrines, hypotheses and theories.

The scope and popularity of experimentation in life, science and culture is immense. Every experiment is always preceded by a phase of observation, since no experiment is possible without a carefully planned schedule of monitoring changes that occur to the given phenomenon. It is important to note that these changes surrounding the term "experiment" act like a halo of synonyms related to its many functional and creative implications. As a consequence, it is hardly surprising that the topic of this comprehensive modification of reality became the focal point for that part of the Russian cultural tradition that I suggest to associate, ad hoc, with the legacy of *total experimentation*.

It appears that experimentation has been immanent for almost the whole of Russian culture and, speaking broadly, Russian history since the earliest phases of its genesis. The "Russian experiment" should, in my opinion, be particularly closely affiliated with the *language issue*. Means of expression occupy no less, and often even more place in the history of Russian culture than thematic content: it is equally true for the entire range of historic events related to the cultural aspects of the "Russian experiment," from Cyril and Methodius to the Russian Formalists. It can be noted that the brothers from Thessaloniki, as well as the members of the main Russian Formalist/Futurist organizations *OPOIAZ* and the *Moscow linguistic circle*, were largely preoccupied with "how" rather than with "what." I believe that the "invention" of the Slavic written system (Slavic alphabet and Church Slavonic language script) by Cyril and Methodius can be rightfully considered the first event of the *experiment* with "Russia in the making." Having laboriously trained in the best religious schools of Constantinople, they studied both the open and secret wisdom of the most important disciplines of the day (philosophy, rhetoric, arithmetic, astronomy, geometry, but also *many languages*). St Cyril eventually became the "learned keeper" (*chartophylax*) of the library of the St Sophia Cathedral. He, admittedly, was a perfect candidate for the "experiment" within the culture of the Eastern Slavs. The Byzantine "politico-lingual" experiment of inventing and propagating the Slavic written language proved mostly successful and in many ways predetermined the further course of Russian history.

The next distinct milestone of this *legacy of experiment* in Russian culture is the famous "episode" with the selection of a religion that we owe to the grand prince Vladimir I of Kiev. As far as we can judge, Vladimir experimented a lot with the "spiritual" sphere and religious life of his fellow compatriots; having begun with an interesting reform of the pantheon of pagan gods, he eventually came to favour the religious belief of his grandmother, grand princess Olga, who was baptized in Constantinople, according to the Primary Chronicle. Prior to making a decision of such importance, Vladimir carefully listened to the delegates of the three religions that were most influential in the view of his geopolitical interests. This "experimental study" of the various religions undoubtedly relates to the very essence of experimentation or, otherwise, *testing the truth*. According to the Chronicle, referring to this experimental event in Russian history as "The choice of religions," the grand prince Vladimir had to make his decision while relying on the general description of religious systems provided by the exponents of Islam (who came assumedly from Volga Bulgaria); Judaism (most likely, from the Judaic Khazars); Orthodox Christianity (represented by influential Byzantium); and the *Latin faith* (international, but especially prominent was German Catholicism). As is well-known now, for certain "experiment-inspired" reasons, some of them quite peculiar (e.g. "the joy of Rus' is drinking"), the grand prince made his eventual political and spiritual choice in favour of Constantinople.

All of the subsequent development of Russian civilization can also be broadly interpreted as a sequence of rather risky experiments with crucial issues, such as the combined Mongol-Slavic, that is, Eurasian cultural heritage; the gradual evolvement of the Moscow Grand Duchy; the emergence of the first self-sufficient Russian tsars, never too scrupulous about brutal experimentation with the lives of their subjects

(Ivan the Terrible); and so on. This tradition of *total experimentation* with the fate of the country was maintained and carried forward by the forthcoming heads of Russian state, whether Peter the Great, Alexander II, Bloody Nicholas, Vladimir Lenin, Joseph Stalin, Nikita Khrushchev, Mikhail Gorbachev, or Boris Yeltsin. It seems, however, to have ultimately stopped in the days of Vladimir Putin, although there is a chance it will spring to life again with the ideas of the (just one more) "modernization" of Russia, instilled by the fledgling president Dmitry Medvedev. The only question is how far will he be able to advance, given the pernicious limitations of the notoriously branded "tandem of power" that he is subject to, due to the very fact of the very *experimental* way in which he was elected President.

Speaking of all of the multifarious contingencies of Russian culture, it is hard to ignore this trait of manifold experimentation, continuous throughout virtually all of the stages of its history. It extends to book printing, invented in Russia by Ivan Fedorov in the sixteenth century; to the summoning of the "cultural Varangians" personified by the Western (Italian) architects, artists and musicians. Eventually, Russian culture gained its fully-fledged *experimental independence* that subsequently gave birth to the purely Russian, singular brand of arts and sciences (*The Academy of Sciences*, *Moscow University* etc.). Russia therefore represents a truly unique field of experimentation, quite unthinkable in any other part of the world. It is remarkable in that some of the more receptive contemporary Russian poets have registered this fact in their unmistakably experimental legacy.[10] The most essential means by which to comprehend the Russian experiment is, as it seems, language. It is hardly by chance that the Russian experiment starts with the problem of language (Cyril and Methodius). The issue of verbal culture, of forming the initial means of expression, codifying the communicative reality, seems to have been of crucial importance all throughout Russian cultural history. The comprehensive experimentation with language started by Cyril and Methodius unquestionably reached its culmination in the twentieth century. What is the moving force and fundamental principle of the "Russian experiment"? It is based on searching for new ways of description, creating a new style that would change the whole structure of the preeminent language employed for this purpose. All of Russian history can be presented as a sequence of experimental reforms woven around the dominance of a certain established style. "Style" and "language" have proven important devices to control reality, from the type of calendar (Gregorian, not Julian) to the radical political reform of orthography instilled by Lenin and his comrades. The calendar symbolically controls *time*; the new established language style governs human thought. The new mentality of Soviet language renounces the obsolete segments and superfluous entities like "yer" and "yat," optimizes the functionality of the entire grand narrative of administration: not unlike the reforms of the Great French Revolution that eliminated the bureaucratic inadequacies of the *ancien regime* in favour of Maximilien Robespierre's "new pragmatics" during the same eighteenth century France.

This scenario of experimental reformation is quite well-known: experimenting action intended to instigate revolutionizing change almost always dialectically results in some "aggravating regress". In the context of the political-social total experiment, the Emperor Napoleon (much more a tyrant than Louis XVI) takes Danton's place; Stalin (a dictator evidently more monstrous than Nicholas II) comes to reign after a milder Kerensky and gravely ill Lenin; similarly, the "pragmatic" Fidel Castro, onetime revolutionary romantic and yet worse dictator than Batista, governs his country steadfastly, having parted ways with Che Guevara and his juvenile utopian dreams. The dialectical spiral of experimentation reduces essences to their actual antitheses.

It has already been mentioned above that the experiment in Russian culture and civilization per se started with the mission of Cyril and Methodius. The testing of a new alphabet and Church Slavonic language that later became the language of the liturgy proved so successful that all of the subsequent "experiments" with Russian culture appeared to conform to the same Byzantine cultural paradigm, with Third Rome coming in place of the Second. Language and an *emblematic* representation of phenomena determined the outcome of the most important historic events in Russia, from the confrontation between Ivan IV and Metropolitan Philipp to Count Uvarov's desire to control and regulate the whole of Russian culture for the sake of the principles he proclaimed: *Autocracy, Orthodoxy and National Character*. "Language," that is, the instrument of narrative, has always been and still is being perceived in Russia as a primary tool of manipulating reality and serving political goals.

In this respect, it is hardly by any chance that all of the power of Russian radical innovation, all of the *raison d'être* of the Russian "heroic" experiment, was very much concerned with language, style and the concrete means of *embodying the culture* in every single aspect of art. Experimenting with verbal expression has always been commonplace in Russian literature. The idea of dissociating the Russian language from Church Slavonic was masterfully accomplished by Mikhailo Lomonosov in the eighteenth century. Furthermore, experimenting with language is visibly present in the texts of many prominent Russian authors of the nineteenth century, such as Gogol, Pushkin, Lermontov, Saltykov-Shchedrin, Leskov, Dostoevsky, Karamzin, and Tolstoy. However, cultural experiment reaches its true climax only with Russian historic modernism (in its "early" incarnation as well as in the more "advanced" mode of the avant-garde).

Aesthetical experimentation sets the principal milestones of the international modernist movement. The influx of French (and international) Symbolism welcomed by the "elder" Russian "Modernist Symbolists" and carried on by the proceeding generation was comprehensively utilized to probe the aesthetical ideologies that seemed most appealing at any given moment. The legacy of "experimentation" with life and culture left by the early Russian modernists of the Symbolist current was further championed by Russian Futurism as personified by Velimir Khlebnikov, David Burlyuk, Vladimir Mayakovski, Ilya Zdanevich, Alexey Kruchenykh, and many of their sundry companions. The language experimentation of Russian modernists is at the center of the recently published monograph by Vladimir Feshchenko.[11]

As has already been noted above, one of the major challenges for Russian cultural history was the matter of political experimentation. Avant-garde ideology turned out to be an integral issue for its *pragmatics of action* focused on deliberate èpatage and cultural shock. It should be no surprise that the early Russian avant-garde took an obvious left turn politically, which effectively coincided with the Bolshevik Revolution. The idea of a *total experiment* was something held in common by both the avant-garde and the Revolution.

The presence of the leftist/Marxist "radicalizing" experimental element in the avant-garde was noted in the 1960's by the Italian-American theorist Renato Poggioli.[12] He was keen to underline the aggressive, militant character of the avant-garde, its preoccupation with the ideas of social revolution and its rhetoric of radical political action.[13] Speaking about the peculiar gentility of avant-garde art, Poggioli nonetheless found it necessary to admit that the political sympathies of the avant-garde movement lay, in his terms, with "leftist ideologies." In particular, he observed: "We recognize that the avant-garde more often consciously adheres to, and superficially sympathizes with, leftist ideologies; we affirm that the anarchistic ideal is congenial to avant-garde psychology."[14] Poggioli expanded his vision, elaborating on the crucial influence of the "communist experiment" in the European avant-garde in its entirety, noting that it de-facto continued to exercise a particular fascination for the avant-garde mind, even though this experiment was "totalitarian and anti-libertarian, hostile to any individual exception or idiosyncrasy."[15] Peter Bürger, the author of one of the most influential treatises on the theory of avant-garde art, followed the course parallel in many ways to that of Poggioli, even though in his own fashion.[16]

I suggest, on the one hand, to separate avant-garde "ideology" from the Napoleonic[17] negative taint, by proceeding to perceive it in a neutral way; and on the other, to regard it as an issue inseparable from critical and functional politics. In my opinion, ideology inevitably means politics; otherwise it must be something else: theory, mythology, philosophy, philology, etc. Thus, ideology, unlike any of those disciplines, invariably appeals to the stratum of *political pragmatics*, at the obvious expense of all the other multifarious human activities.[18] We may or may not share the opinion that the term "ideology" should be interpreted in an overly wide sense, so as to allow it to mingle with philosophy, general thought and cultural theory.

Along with that, ideology should not, strictly speaking, be mixed with political philosophy since the latter tends to remain theoretical in the first place, avoiding the pragmatics of *realpolitik* to which ideology applies itself. Consequently, ideology is part of the real and tangible world of politically and socially conditioned phenomena open to empirical comprehension. Ideology must always be concerned with the pragmatics of *the real*, and ideally, must never be reduced to abstraction.

We may proceed and establish a plausible relation between the layers of politics and art in the Russian avant-garde and particularly Futurism. We may argue that Russian Futurists were deliberately orchestrating their left-wing political rhetoric in just the same fashion of èpatage as in their numerous artistic activities. The motion of politics and ideology, therefore, coincides with the matters of pragmatics and creative actionism, which is directed, among other things, at the strategic promotion of their art, thereby gaining the public's attention.

We might conclude that the leading members of Radical Modernism in Russia shared a strong belief in the necessity to destroy the existing empirical world in order to establish a new one upon its ruins. The Grand-utopian attitude of Futurism (mixed with ambivalent eschatology) was quite characteristic of their poetical mind. One of the notable examples of this can be Aleksei Kruchenykh's "The world is going to die" (*Mir gibnet*), where Kruchenykh expressed his profound delectation with the ongoing demise of the tangible universe:

> the world is dying
> and who are we to stop this
> the beautiful world is dying
> we won't mourn its extinguishment
> with even one single word.

The main ideological presuppositions of Russian Futurism are its obvious over-identification with all things *Left*, which were generally shared by the main protagonists of Russian Futurism, even if in a more low-key mode. The leftist inclination of Russian Futurists might be compared to the similar bias of the French Surrealists (especially in poetry).

A critic quite close to Russian Futurism, Nikolai Punin, published shortly after the Revolution (early 1918) a paper with a very telling title "Futurism is the art of the State" (Futurism—gosudarstvennoe iskusstvo). In that paper he preached using the power of the all-mighty state to implement the artistic ideas of Futurism. It was hardly by coincidence, since the dominant line of the Futurist public strategy endorsed generating various proclamations, manifestoes, and political appeals intended to assist Futurism in its intent to become the newly affirmed, powerful art, which would be entrusted to create a post-revolutionary state-culture.

Nearly all of the prominent Futurist artists and writers tried to gain a certain preferential status within the freshly established Soviet institutions affiliated with the field of culture. Their "art," therefore, was meant not only to serve life, but actually to become part of *real* life. Transforming art into life, and vice versa, comprised the existential legacy of modernism that was inherited from its predecessors, the Russian Symbolists. The intention was to erase the boundaries between the two realms, that of art and that of life, which became increasingly obvious in the early years after the Russian Revolution. Not surprisingly, such a typical Soviet cultural institution as the "Theatrical Division of the Soviet Ministry of Education" (*TheO Narkomprosa)* brought together the most outstanding figures of the two dominant Russian modernist currents: Symbolism and the avant-garde (Viacheslav Ivanov and Vsevolod Meyerhold).

It was this strategic trend that led to establishing the famous *Communists/Futurists* (*ComFuty*) association created by a lesser known Futurist poet Boris A. Kushner, assisted by Osip Brik and Vladimir Mayakovsky in 1919. Velimir Khlebnikov, Vasily Kamensky, and Nikolai Aseev were among the prominent members of this group. The main concern of this association amounted to coming as close as possible to the new political government, enrolling in the main cultural projects of the reigning Revolutionary mandate. Ideological propaganda and semi-campaigning verses were published not only by Mayakovsky, but also by Khlebnikov and Kruchenykh.

The main publication of this group was the revolutionary newspaper "The Art of the Commune" (*Iskusstvo Communny*). The manifesto of *ComFuty* that was published there stated that all forms of everyday life, philosophy, morality, and art must be re-created using the new, Communist criteria. The Communist revolution would not be able to develop without the New Art of the *ComFuty*, claimed the manifesto. The Revolution championed by the Futurists also had a notable Utopian scent, alluding in a way to the mystical Symbolist "Revolution of the Spirit" (*Revolutsia Dukha*). Yet again it was hardly by coincidence that one of the founders of Mystical Anarchism (a Symbolist current), Viacheslav Ivanov cooperated energetically with the revolutionaries during the early years of the Bolshevik regime. The quasi-Symbolist "Spirit of the Revolution" was actually mentioned in the "Manifesto of the Flying Federation of the Futurists" published in 1918 by David Burliuk, Vasily Kamensky, and Vladimir Mayakovsky. All of the major Futurist "political" ideas were further developed within the "The Left Front of Arts" (*Levyi Front Iskusstv*) (since 1922 onwards). This journal was headed by the Futurists and proceeded to put the New Art, as it were, in the service of the October Revolution.

The important fact to be stressed in summary is that the ideology of the avant-garde, in a broad sense, as well as its politics (the politics of avant-garde action in the first place) seems to function as the direct result of avant-garde pragmatics. Therefore, all of the publicly delivered political/ideological gestures of avant-garde artists must be interpreted in accordance with the rules of the avant-garde's "shocking" popular practice. A radical political gesture by an experimenting artist immediately gets caught in the cultural fabric that bars it from the *realpolitik* familiar to everyday usage. I believe that this ideology should be attentively examined with respect to *experimental èpatage* perceived as a strategic goal of performance, in agreement with the more penetrating tendencies of analyzing this type of art.[19]

Endnotes

1 This playful term is used here with reference to the tradition of Soviet "newspeak": e.g. "testing pilot" (a Soviet cultural icon V. P. Chkalov).

2 "*Esperment* (Old French, mid-14th c.): practical knowledge, cunning, enchantment; trial, proof, example, lesson, from Latin *experimentum*: a trial, test, proof, noun of action from *experiri*—to test, try."

3 See: Oberheim, "Karl Popper. Using and abusing critical rationalism."

4 See, for instance: Gottsdanker and Edwards, "The Prediction of Collision," 110-114.

5 Apart from other things, his prospective works included such titles as "The Phenomena of the Universe or a Natural and Experimental History for the foundation of Philosophy" and "Parasceve ad Historiam Naturalem et Experimentalem."

6 See "The experiment as mediator between subject and object" (1772), "Der Versuch als Vermittler von Objekt und Subjekt," 10-20.

7 Ivanov's text clearly indicates his original interest in life-creation, poised at the peculiar variety of metaphysical *experimentation* with the reality of being and its perception: "... In my explorations of the aesthetics of symbol, myth, choral drama, realiorism (let me use this neologism with its reference to the maxim I'm offering to artists: *a realibus ad realiora*, that is, from the visible reality and through it, to the more real reality of the same things, inner and innermost), I am like the one who carves a chalice out of crystal, expecting a noble liquid to be poured into it, maybe the sacred wine" (see: Ivanov, "Dve stikhii v simvolisme," 143–169). Speaking of Leo Tolstoy, Vyacheslav Ivanov also emphasizes a kind of life-creational, experimental basis of his doings: "...Leo Tolstoy is *memento mori* of the contemporary culture, and *memento vivere* to the Symbolism that dares artists to ascend from the real to the most real (*a realibus ad realiora*) while possessing the strength of faith to face the mundane reality and, dispatching towards it a builder and creator of life, bringing him down to the real after wanderings in the realm of exalted realities (*ad realia per realiora*), bids him farewell with the words: let the meanest be like the most exalted, and the real like the most real (realia sicut realiora)" (see his "Lev Tolstoy i literatura", op. cit., 273–281).

8 On this issue, see: Webster, Sell, *Laboratory Experiments in the Social Science*.
9 On the Modernist Utopia see, in particular: Paperno, Grossman *Creating Life: The Aesthetic Utopia of Russian Modernism*.
10 See the album of songs, titled accordingly ("The Russian Field of Experiments") by the neo-avant-garde poet Egor Letov (1964-2008): http://www.gr-oborona.ru/pub/ruspole/
11 See: his *Laboratoria logosa. Yazykovoy eksperiment v avangardnom tvorchestve*.
12 See: Poggioli, "The Theory of the Avant-Garde."
13 Ibid., 27.
14 Ibid., 99.
15 Ibid.
16 See: Bürger, "Theory of the Avant-Garde."
17 Rumors have it that it was Napoleon who pioneered the use of the term "ideology" and its derivatives in the derogatory sense, calling "ideologues" those politicians and authors that he found unworthy.
18 The most illustrious instance showing how defective and limited ideology (an "ideologist" as a "political animal") may seem in comparison with, say, a "philosophical" or "theorizing animal," is presented by Vladimir Lenin. As an ideologist par excellence, he is no philosopher, no critic, and even no culturologist. See the timely written works by Berdyaev ("The Origin of Russian Communism") and Vysheslavtsev ("The Philosophical Poverty of Marxism").
19 See, for instance, Maxim Shapir's approach.

List of Contributors

Basner, Elena has a PhD in Art History from the St. Petersburg State Academic Institute of Painting, Sculpture and Architecture. She is one of the leading experts in the visual art of the Russian avant-garde and has authored hundreds of publications in her field of research. Dr Basner works in the Department of Modern Art at the State Russian Museum in St. Petersburg. She teaches at the European University of St. Petersburg and consults for the Bukowskis auction house (Sweden & Finland). She has been a curator for a number of major exhibitions concerning the Russian avant-garde, both in Russia and abroad, including the first Malevich International exhibition (1988-91, Leningrad, Moscow, Amsterdam, Washington, Los-Angeles, New-York), "New Art for the New Era" (Barbican Art Centre, London), "Russian Futurism" (2000), "Kazimir Malevich" (2000) and many others.

Bowlt, John E. is a professor of Slavic Languages and Literatures at the University of Southern California, Los Angeles, where he is also director of the Institute of Modern Russian Culture. He has written extensively on Russian visual culture, especially on the art of Symbolism and the avant-garde, his latest book being *Moscow, St. Petersburg. Art and Culture during the Russian Silver Age*. Dr Bowlt has also curated or co-curated exhibitions of Russian art, including "A Feast of Wonders. Sergei Diaghilev and the Ballets Russes" at the Nouveau Musée de Monte Carlo, Monaco, and the State Tretiakov Gallery, Moscow (2009-10); and "El Cosmos de la vanguardia rusa" at the Fundacion Marcelino Botin, Santander, and the State Museum of Contemporary Art, Thessaloniki. He is now preparing an exhibition entitled "Di fuoco e di ghiaccio: Siberia, Asia e l'avanguardia russa" for the Palazzo Strozzi, Florence, for 2013. In September, 2010, he received the Order of Friendship from the Russian Federation for his promotion of Russian culture in the USA.

Burry, Alexander holds a PhD from Northwestern University. Currently, he is an Associate Professor of Slavic and East European Languages and Cultures at The Ohio State University. He recently published a book entitled *Multi-Mediated Dostoevsky: Transposing Novels into Opera, Film, and Drama*, and has also written articles on Dostoevsky, Chekhov, Prokofiev, Venedikt Erofeev, and other writers and cultural figures.

Groys, Boris received a PhD in Philosophy from the University of Münster. He is the Global Distinguished Professor of Russian and Slavic Studies at New York University and a Senior Research Fellow at the Karlsruhe University of Arts and Design in Karlsruhe, Germany. He is best known as the author of *The Total Art of Stalin*. This work is credited for introducing Western readers to Russian postmodernist writers. Dr Groys has authored many books on Russian art and philosophy, and has also edited several collections of articles in Russian and German as well as published over a hundred scholarly articles.

Ioffe, Dennis (PhD University of Amsterdam) is an Assistant Professor ("Doctor-Assistent"), at The Faculty of Arts and Philosophy, Ghent University, Belgium. He is also a research fellow at the UvA Slavic Seminarium and the Amsterdam School for Cultural Analysis (ASCA). In the previous years he served as Visiting Assistant Professor in Russian and German Studies at Memorial University (Canada) and as Teaching & Research Fellow, managing the Russian Centre at the University of Edinburgh, (Scotland, the UK). Dr Ioffe has authored more than 50 scholarly articles, and edited and co-edited several academic collections.

Klebanov, Michael holds a Bachelor's Degree of Architecture from Technion, Israeli State Institute of Technology, and presently continues his research at the Royal Architectural Institute of Canada. He is an architectural & design professional and an independent scholar based in Toronto, Canada. Aside from architecture, his academic interests include the history of the Russian avant-garde, experimental performance and creative philosophy. He has published widely on the history of Russian literature, music, and art.

Kovtun, Evgeny Fedorovich (1928-1996) was one of the leading researchers of the Russian avant-garde. After defending his PhD in Art History at the State University of St Petersburg, he worked at the State Russian Museum of Art until his death. During his scholarly career Dr

Kovtun published many dozens of pioneering studies on the Russian art of the avant-garde.

Lodder, Christina is a Professor of Art History at St. Andrews University, Scotland, UK. She is an Honorary Fellow of the History of Art at the University of Edinburgh and Vice-President of the Malevich Society. Her research focuses on Russian painting, sculpture and architecture of the first few decades of the twentieth century and its relationships with Western art (notably German and French) of the 1910s and 1920s. Dr Lodder is the author of numerous fundamental scholarly studies devoted to various aspects of Russian and European art and design.

MacKay, John is the Chair of the Film Studies Program at Yale University. He has a PhD from Yale University (Comparative Literature) and a BA in English from The University of British Columbia. Aside from Russian cinema, Dr. MacKay's scholarly interests embrace nineteenth and twentieth century Russian literature, Russian/Soviet culture, comparative literature, literary and cultural theory, and comparative film studies (esp. film theory and documentary cinema). Dr MacKay has published extensively on avant-garde cinema.

Markov, Vladimir is Professor Emeritus in the Department of Slavic Languages and Literatures at the University of California, Los Angeles, where he taught for thirty years. His first book, *The Longer Poems of Velimir Xlebnikov*, established him as a major specialist on the Russian avant-garde. His publications include *Russian Imagism, 1919-1924*, and the two-volume *Kommentar zu den Dichtungen von Konstantin Balmont*. Professor Markov edited major poetic anthologies and works by Russian modernists, while also publishing scores of articles on Russian lyric poetry from the eighteenth to the twentieth centuries.

Ostashevsky, Eugene holds a PhD from Stanford University. He is currently teaching Humanities courses in the Liberal Studies Program at New York University. He is a productive translator of Russian avant-garde literature. His main achievement in this field is *OBERIU: An Anthology of Russian Absurdism*—a selection of 1930s "underground writings" by Alexander Vvedensky, Daniil Kharms and others in their circle. He has also authored two books of poetry published by the Ugly Duckling Presse (NY).

Pavlov, Evgeny holds a PhD from Princeton University. He is a Senior Lecturer in Russian and German within the School of Languages, Cultures and Linguistics at the University of Canterbury. His voluminous research agenda includes Russian and European Modernism, Postmodernism, literary theory, comparative literature, translation studies and film. Dr Pavlov is the author of many studies devoted to Russian Modernism, European philosophy and theory, Osip Mandelshtam, Walter Benjamin, and Russian contemporary poetry.

Sharp, Jane A. holds a PhD from Yale University. She is an Associate Professor in the Department of Art History at Rutgers University and is the Research Curator of the Dodge Collection at the Zimmerli Art Museum. Her fields of expertise include Twentieth Century Art, Russian and Soviet Art and Soviet Nonconformist Art. Dr Sharp has published widely on many topics related to Russian avant-garde art, including Russian Conceptualism.

Weststeijn, Willem G. is a Professor Emeritus in the Department of Slavic Languages and Literatures at the University of Amsterdam, the Netherlands. He has published hundreds of scholarly articles and dozens of book collections on a great variety of topics in Russian literary Modernism, Dutch-Russian cultural links and the art of the Russian avant-garde. His main areas of research focus on Velimir Khlebnikov, the languages of poetry, Russian conceptualism and contemporary art.

White, Frederick H. holds a PhD from the University of Southern California. Presently, he is the Associate Dean of the College of Humanities and Social Sciences at Utah Valley University. He is one of the leading specialists on the Russian writer Leonid Andreev and has published in the areas of Russian Modernism, psychology and literature, pseudoscience in the Russian *fin de siècle* and the economics of culture.

Bibliography

Various transliteration systems exist and are employed in academic publications. Because of this, there are often two or more spellings for the same person, for the same publication, or for the same work. Maksim Gor'kii may also be Maxim Gorky. Vladimir Mayakovsky may also be Vladimir Maiakovskii. One of our editorial choices was to re-publish many of these seminal texts in their original form, which means that within this *Reader*, you will find several conflicting methods of transliteration from article to article. If we were to regularize the transliteration system for the bibliography, then the endnotes of the articles themselves would not correspond with the bibliographic entries. Therefore, we have chosen to provide a bibliography using the transliteration systems employed in the articles themselves. As a result, one may find an entry for the same person in two different places—Khlebnikov and Xlebnikov, for example. We have chosen to reflect this condition in the compiled bibliography included in this *Reader*.

Ahmed, Leila. *Women and Gender in Islam: Historical Roots of a Modern Debate.* New Haven: Yale University Press, 1992.

Andersen, Troels. *Moderne Russisk Kunst 1920-1925.* Copenhagen: Borgen, 1967.

-------. *K.S. Malevich. The world as Non-Objectivity.* Essays Vol. III. Copenhagen: 1976.

Andrews, Richard and Milena Kalinovska, intro. *Art into Life: Russian Constructivism 1914—1932.* Seattle: The Henry Art Gallery, University of Washington and New York, Rizzoli, 1990.

Anonymous. "Beseda s N. S. Goncharovoi." *Stolichnaia molva*, no. 115 (5 April 1910): 3.

Anonymous [V. Giliarovskii?]. "Brattsy-estety." *Golos Moskvy*, no. 69 (25 March 1910): 4.

Anonymous. "Bubnovaia dama pod sudom." *Protiv techeniia* (4 January 1911): 4.

Anonymous. "Moskovskaia khronika: Delo Obshchestva svobodnoi estetiki." *Rech'* (23 December 1910): 3.

Anonymous. "O. Kh." *Golos Moskvy*, no. 45 (24 February 1912).

Artaud, Antonin. *The Theater and Its Double.* Translated by Mary Caroline Richards. New York: Grove Press, 1958.

Arvatov, Boris. "Proletariat i levoe iskusstvo." *Vestnik Iskusstvo*, no. 1 (1922): 10.

------. "Oveshchestvelennaya utopiya." *Lef*, no. 1 (1923): 61-64.

Arvatov, B. "Über die Reorganisation der Kunstfakultaten an den VChUTEMAS." In *Zwischen Revolutionskunst.* Edited by Gassner and Gillen. 154-55.

Avtonomova, N., et. al. eds. *N. Goncharova, M. Larionov: Issledovaniia i publikatsii.* Moscow: Nauka, 2003.

Bakhterev, Igor. "Kogda my byli molodymi." In *Vospominaniia o N. Zabolotskom*. A. Zabolotskaya et al. Moscow: Sovetskii pisatel', 1987.
Bakhtin, Mikhail. *Rabelais und His World.* Translated by Helene Iswolsky. Bloomington: Indiana University Press, 1984.
Barskaia, A. *French Painting in the Hermitage from the mid-18th to the 20th Century.* Leningrad: Hermitage, 1975.
Basner, E. V. "Metamorfy 'chuzhogo siuzheta' v zhivopisi M. F. Larionova i N. S. Goncharovoi." *Stranitsy istorii otechestvennogo iskusstva, XVIII-XX vek*, vypusk IX. St. Petersburg: Palace Editions, 2003.
Begicheva, Anna. "Vospominaniya o Tatline. Do kontsa ne razgadai." MS, private archive, Moscow.
Benedetti, Jean. *Stanislavski, His Life and Art: A Biography.* London: Methuen, 1999.
Benois, A. "Posledniaia futuristskaia vystavka." *Rech'*, Petrograd, (9 January 1916).
Berdiaev, Nikolai. "Picasso." *Sofiia*, 1, no. 3 (1914): 57-8; 161-2.
Berezark, I. "Veshch' na stene." *Novyi zritel'*, no. 32-3 (1929): 10.
Bergan, Ronald. *Eisenstein: A Life in Conflict*. New York: The Overlook Press, 1999.
Bilibin, Ivan Iakovlevich. *Stati, pis'ma, vospominania o khudozhnike*. Leningrad: Khudozhnik RSFSR, 1970.
Bishop, Thomas. "Changing Concepts of Avant-Garde in XXth Century Literature". *The French Review* 1 Vol.38 (1964): 34-41.
Bogdanov, Alexander. "The Proletarian and the Art." In *Russian Art of the Avant-Garde*. Edited by J. Bowlt. 177.
Bowlt, J. ed. *Russian Art of the Avant-Garde: Theory and Criticism 1902-1934*. New York: Viking, 1976.
Bowlt, John and Olga Matich, eds. *Laboratory of Dreams: The Russian Avant-Garde and Cultural Experiment*. Stanford: Stanford University Press, 1999.
Bowlt, John E. and Matthew Drutt, eds. *Amazons of the Avant-Garde*, exhibition catalogue. London: Royal Academy of Arts, 1999.
Braun, Edward. *Meyerhold: A Revolution in Theatre*. Iowa City: University of Iowa Press, 1995.
-------. "Vsevolod Meyerhold: The Final Act." In *Enemies of the People: The Destruction of Soviet Literary, Theater, and Film Arts in the 1930s*. Edited by Katherine Bliss Eaton. Evanston: Northwestern University Press, 2002, 145-62.
-------. tr. and ed. *Meyerhold on Theatre*. London: Methuen; Hill & Wang, 1969.
Brik, Osip. "Drenazh iskusstvu." *Iskusstvo kommuny*, no. 1, 7 December (1918): 1.
-------. "Primechanie redaktsii." *Iskusstvo kommuny*, no. 8 (1919): 2.
-------. "V poryadke dnya." *Iskusstvo v proizvodstve*, Moscow: IZO Narkompros, 1921, 6-7.
-------. "Ot kartiny k sittsu." *Lef*, no. 2 (6) (1924): 27-34.
Briusov, V., *Dnevniki 1891-1910. Zapisi proshlogo*. Moscow: Sabashnikov, 1927.

-------. "Against Naturalism in the Theater" (from "An Unnecessary Truth"). In *The Russian Symbolist Theatre: An Anthology of Plays and Critical Texts*. Edited by Michael Green. Ann Arbor: Ardis Publishers, 1986, 25-30.

Brooks, Jeffrey. *When Russia Learned to Read: Literacy and Popular Culture, 1861-1917*. Princeton: Princeton University Press, 1985.

Brown, Edward J. *Mayakovsky: A Poet in the Revolution*. Princeton: Princeton University Press, 1973

Bulgakowa, Oksana. *Sergei Eisenstein: A Biography*. Translated by Anne Dwyer. Berlin: Potemkin Press, [1998] 2001.

-------. "Spatial Figures in Soviet Cinema of the 1930s." In *The Landscape of Stalinism: The Art and Ideology of Soviet Space*. Edited by Evgeny Dobrenko and Eric Naiman. Seattle: University of Washington Press, 2003, 51-76.

Burch, Noël. "Film's Institutional Mode of Representation and the Soviet Response." *October*, 11, Winter (1979): 77-96.

Bürger, P. *Theory of the Avant-Garde*. Translated by Michael Shaw. Foreword by Jochen Schulte-Sasse. Minneapolis: University of Minnesota Press, 1984.

Burliuk, D., Aleksandr Kruchenykh, V. Maiakovskii, and Victor Khlebnikov. *Poshchechina Obshchestvennomu Vkusu*. Moscow: G. Kuzmin & S. Dolinskii, 1912.

Burliuk, Dav. Dav. and N. D. Burliuk. *Galdiashchie "benua" i novoe russkoe national'noe isskustvo*. St. Petersburg: Shmidt Publishers, 1913.

Burliuk, David. *Biografiia i stikhi. 1924. K 25-tiletiiu khudozhestvenno-literaturnoi deiatel'nosti (stikhi 1898-1923)*. New York: M. N. Burliuk Publishers, 1924.

-------. *Fragmenty iz vospominanii futurista. Pis'ma. Stikhotvoreniia*. St. Petersburg: Pushkinskii Dom, 1994.

Burliuk, N. "Vladimir Davidovich Burliuk. Ego tvorchestvo." In *"Soiuz molodezhi" pri uchastii poetov "Gileia,"* no. 3. St. Petersburg: Soiuz molodezhi, 1913, 35.

Callery, Dympha. *Through the Body: A Practical Guide to Physical Theater*. London: Nick Hern Books, 2001.

Chamot, Mary. *Gontcharova*. Paris: La Bibliotheque Des Arts, 1972.

Chekhov, Anton. *The Plays of Anton Chekhov*. Translated by Paul Schmidt. NY: Harper, 1998.

Cherri. "Ssora 'Khvostov' s 'Valetami'." *Golos Moskvy*, no. 285 (11 December 1911): 5.

Chulkov, Georgii. "Demony sovremennosti: mysli o frantsuzskoi zhivopisi." *Apollon*, 1-2 (Jan.-Feb. 1914): 64-75.

Chuzhak, Nikolai. "Pod znakom zhiznestroeniya." *Lef*, no. 1 (1923): 12-39.

Chuzhoi, "Moskovskie otkliki, Oslinyi khvost." *Rech'* (13 March 1912): 2.

Clark, T. J. *Farewell to an Idea: Episodes from a History of Modernism*. New Haven: Yale University Press, 1999.

Cooke, Ray. *Velimir Khlebnikov. A Critical Study*. Cambridge: Cambridge University Press, 1987.

Cornwell, Neil. *Reference guide to Russian literature*. Chicago: Fitzroy Dearborn, 1998.

-------. *The Absurd in Literature*. Manchester: Manchester University Press, 2006.

Curtius, Ernst Robert. *European Literature and the Latin Middle Ages*. Translated by Willard R. Trask. Introduction by Peter Godman. Princeton: Princeton University Press, 1990.

Deleuze, Gilles. *Cinema 1: The Movement-Image*. Translated by Hugh Tomlinson and Barbara Habberjam. Minneapolis: University of Minnesota Press, 1986.

Depaule, Judith. *Igor Terentiev: metteur en scène futuriste*. DEA de theater en arts du spectacle, sous la direction de B. Picon-Vallin. Paris III: Sorbonne Nouvelle, 1993.

Deriabin, Aleksandr. "*Three Songs of Lenin*," *23rd Pordenone Silent Film Festival Catalogue*. Sacile: Giornate del Cinema Muto, 2004.

-------, ed. *Iz naslediia. tom pervyj: Dramaturgicheskie opyty*. Moscow: Eizenshtein-Tsentr, 2004.

Dmitrieva, N. "Esteticheskaia kategoriia prekrasnogo." *Iskusstvo* (Jan.-Feb. 1952): 78-89.

Dobrenko, Evgeny. *Stalinist Cinema and the Production of History: Museum of the Revolution*. New Haven: Yale University Press, 2008.

Dobrenko, Evgeny and Eric Naiman. *The Landscape of Stalinism: The Art and Ideology of Soviet Space*. Seattle: University of Washington Press, 2003.

Doronchenkov, Ilya. "Picasso in Russia at the Turn of the 1920s: On the History of Perception." *The Petersburg Journal of Cultural Studies*, 1, no. 3 (1993): 69-80.

Douglas, Charlotte. "Victory Over the Sun." *Russian History/Histoire Russe* 8 (1981): 69-89.

Drubek-Meyer, Natascha and Jurij Murashov, eds. *Apparatur und Rhapsodie: Zu den Filmen des Dziga Vertov*. Frankfurt am Main: Peter Lang, 2000.

Druskin, Iakov. "Chinari." *Avrora*, 6 (1989).

-------. *Dnevniki*. St. Petersburg: Akademicheskii proekt, 1999.

-------. "Materialy k poetike Vvedenskogo." In *Polnoe sobranie proizvedenii v dvukh tomakh*. A. Vvedenskii. Moscow: Gileia, 1993.

-------. "Stadii ponimaniia." In *Sborishche druzei, ostavlennykh sud'boiu... Chinari v tekstakh, dokumentakh i issledovaniiakh*. Moscow: Ladomir, 1998.

Eaton, Katherine Bliss. *The Theater of Meyerhold and Brecht*. Westport, CT: Greenwood Press, 1985.

Eganbiuri, Eli (Il'ia Zdanevich). *Natalia Goncharova. Mikhail Larionov*. Moscow: Miunster, 1913.

Eght, A. "Khudozhnik G. Klutsis." *Dekorativnoe iskusstvo*, no. 11 (1966): 8.

Engelstein, Laura. *The Keys to Happiness: Sex and the Search for Modernity in Fin de Siècle Russia*. Ithaca: Cornell University Press, 1992.

Evseeva, S.B. *David Burliuk. Faktura i tsvet*. Ufa: Bashkortostan, 1994.

Ezhegodnik Rukopisnogo otdela Pushkinskogo doma na 1974 god. Leningrad: Nauka, 1976.

Farwell, Beatrice. *Manet and the Nude: A Study in Iconography in the 2nd Empire*. New York: Garland Publishing, 1981.

Fedorov-Davydov, A. "Vopros o novom realizme v sviazi s zapadno-evropeiskimi techeniiami v iskusstve," *Russkoe i sovetskoe iskusstvo*. Moscow: Iskusstvo, 1975.

Fer, Briony. "Metaphor and Modernity: Russian Constructivism." *Oxford Art Journal*, no. 1 (1989): 14.

Feral, Josette. "Theatricality: The Specificity of Theatrical Language". *SubStance* 98-99, Vol. 31 (2002): 94-108.

Feschenko, V. V. *Laboratoria logosa. Yazykovoy eksperiment v avangardnom tvorchestve* Moscow: Yazyki slavyanskikh kultur, 2009.

Fevral'skii, Aleksandr. "Tri Pesni o Lenine" [reprinted from *Literaturnaia Gazeta* (89) 16 July 1934]. In *Istoriia Sovetskogo Kinoisskustva Zvukovogo Perioda*. Edited by Ippolit Sokolov. 67-70.

Filonov, P. *Intimnaia masterskaia zhivopistsev i risovalshchikov "Sdelannie kartiny."* Petrograd: 1914.

Fitzpatrick, Sheila. *Everyday Stalinism: Ordinary Life in Extraordinary Times: Soviet Russia in the 1930s*. Oxford: Oxford University Press, 1999.

-------. *Tear off the Masks! Identity and Imposture in Twentieth-Century Russia*. Princeton: Princeton University Press, 2005.

Gan, Aleksei. *Konstruktivism*. Tver': 1922.

-------. "Chto takoe konstruktivism?" *Sovremennaya arkhitektura*, no. 3 (1928): 79-81.

Gasanova, A. I. *Raskreposhchenie zhenshchiny-gorianki v Dagestane (1920-1940 gg.)* Makhachkala: Institut imeni G. Tsadasy, 1963.

-------. *Podgotovka zhenskikh kadrov v Dagestane i ikh rol' v khoziastvennom i kul'turnom razvitii respubliki (1945-1965 gg.)*. Makhachkala: Institut imeni G. Tsadasy, 1969.

Gassner H. and E. Gillen, eds. "K. Malevich on AkhRR." In *Zwischen Revolutionskunst und Sozialistischem Realismus*. Cologne: DuMont, 1979, 270-271.

Gassner, H. *Alexander Rodschenko: Konstruktion 1920*. Frankfurt a.M: Fischer, 1984.

Gerasimov, A. M. "Zadachi khudozhestvennogo obrazovaniia." In *Akademiia khudozhestv SSSR: Pervaia i vtoraia sessii*. Moscow: Izd-vo Akad. khudozhestv SSSR, 1949, 127-149.

Gethmann-Siefert, Annemarie. "Das klassiche als das Utopische. Über-legungen zu einer Kulturphilosophie der Kunst." In *Über das Klassische*. Edited by Rudolf Bockholdt. Frankfurt a.M.: Suhrkamp, 1987.

Gibian, George, trans. *The Man in the Black Coat: Russian Literature of the Absurd.* Evanston: Northwestern University Press, 1987.

Glagol', S. "Bubnovyi valet." *Stolichnaia molva*, no. 156 (13 December 1911): 5.

Glebov, A. *Inga*. Moscow: Teakinopechat', 1929.

Goethe, J. W. "The experiment as mediator between subject and object" (1772; Der Versuch als Vermittler von Objekt und Subjekt). In *Goethe's Werke*. Hamburger Ausgabe, Bd. 13. Munich: Verlag C. H. Beck, 2002, 10-20.

Goryacheva, T. V. "Teatral'naya konzepziya Unovisa na fone sovremennoy szenografii". In *Russkiy avangard 1910-h–1920-h godov i teatr*. Edited by G. F. Kovalenko, 106-115. St. Petersburg: Dmitry Bulanin, 2000.

Gottsdanker, Robert M. and Ralph V. Edwards. "The Prediction of Collision." *The American Journal of Psychology*, vol. 70, no. 1 (March 1957): 110-114.

Grabar', Igor'. "Soiuz" and "Venok" [Vesy, no. 1 (1908): 142]. In Burliuk, D. *Fragmenty iz vospominanii futurista*, 355-56.

Gran, Anne-Britt. "The Fall of Theatricality in the Age of Modernity." *SubStance* 98-99 Vol. 31 (2002): 251-264.

Gray, Camilla. *The Great Experiment: Russian Art, 1863-1922*. London: Thames and Hudson, 1962.

Green, Michael. *The Russian Symbolist Theatre: An Anthology of Plays and Critical Texts*. Ann Arbor: Ardis, 1986.

Glagol', S. "Bubnovyi valet." *Stolichnaia molva*, no. 156 (13 December 1911): 5.

Greenberg, Clement. "Towards a Newer Laocoön." *Partisan Review*, VII, 4 (July-August, 1940): 296-310.

Gregory, Paul R. and Valery Lazarev. *The Economics of Forced Labor: The Soviet Gulag*. Stanford: Hoover Institution Press, 2003.

Groys, B. *The Total Art of Stalinism: Avant-Garde, Aesthetic Dictatorship, and Beyond.* Translated by C. Rougle. Princeton, N.J.: Princeton University Press, 1992.

Gubanova, G. I. "Motivy balagana v 'Pobede nad solnzem'". In *Russkiy avangard 1910-h–1920-h godov i teatr*. Edited by G. F. Kovalenko. St. Petersburg: Dmitry Bulanin, 2000: 156-165.

Guchkov. "Inostranets o Moskovskoi pornografii." *Russkoe slovo* (24 November 1910): 5.

Gunther, Hans and Evgeny Dobrenko, eds. *Sotsrealisticheskii Kanon*. St. Petersburg: Akademicheskii Proekt, 2000.

Günther, Hans. "Verordneter oder gewachsener Kanon?" *Wiener Slawistischer Almanach*, vol. 17, Vienna, (1986): 305-28.

-------. "Totalitarnaia narodnost' i ee istoki." In *Sotsrealisticheskii Kanon*. Edited by Hans Gunther and Evgeny Dobrenko. 377-389.

Gurevich. "Segodnia—Torzhestvennyi Pusk Kramatorskogo Zavoda: Nakanune Puska." *Izvestiia* 228, 28 September (1934). Newspaper clipping in RGALI f. 2091, op. 2, d. 274, l. 63.

Holmgren, Beth. "Gendering the Icon: Marketing Women Writers in Fin-de-Siècle Russia." In *Russia, Women, Culture,* Helena Goscilo and Beth Holmgren, eds. Bloomington: Indiana University Press, 1996: 321-46.

Hoover, Marjorie. "V. E. Meyerhold: A Russian Predecessor of Avant-Garde Theater." *Comparative Literature* 3, Vol.17 (1965): 234-250.

Howard, Jeremy. *The Union of Youth: An Artist's Society of The Russian Avant-Garde.* Manchester: Manchester University Press, 1992.

Iakhot, Iegoshua. *Podavlenie filosofii v SSSR (20-30 gody).* New York: Chalidze Publications, 1981.

Iampolskii, Mikhail. *Bespamiatstvo kak istok.* Moscow: Novoe literaturnoe obozrenie, 1998.

Ionesco, Eugene. "The Avant-Garde Theater." *The Tulane Drama Review* 2 Vol. 5 (1960): 44-53.

Iskusstvo kommuny, No. 3, Petrograd (1918).

Ivanov, V. "Tri Pesni o Lenine." *Rabochaia Penza,* 286, 31 December (1934). Newspaper clipping in RGALI f. 2091, op. 2, d. 274, l. 22.

Ivanov V. I. "Dve stikhii v sovremennom simvolisme." In *Rodnoe i vselenskoe.* Edited by V.M. Tolmachev. Moscow: Respublika, 1994, 143–169.

Jaccard, Jean Philippe. *Daniil Kharms i Konetz Russkogo Avangarda.* St. Petersburg: Akademicheskii Proekt, 1995.

Jakobson, Roman. *Smert' Vladimira Mayakovskogo.* Berlin: Petropolis, 1930.

Jakovljevic, Branislav. *Daniil Kharms: Writing and the Event.* Evanston, IL: Northwestern University Press, 2009.

Jameson, Fredric. *The Political Unconscious: Narrative as a Socially Symbolic Act.* Ithaca: Cornell University Press, 1981.

Jestrovic, Silvija. "Theatricality as Estrangement of Art and Life in the Russian Avant-Garde." *SubStance* 98-99 Vol.31 (2002): 42-56.

Kamensky, Vasily. *Put' entuziasta.* Moscow: Federatsia, 1931.

-------. *Zhizn s Mayakovskym.* Moscow: Goslitizdat, 1940.

Kanzog, Klaus. "Internalisierte Religiosität: Elementarstrukturen der visuellen Rhetorik in Dziga Vertovs *Drei Lieder über Lenin.*" In *Apparatur und Rhapsodie: Zu den Filmen des Dziga Vertov.* Edited by Natascha Drubek-Meyer and Jurij Murashov, 201-220.

Katalog vystavki kartin Davida Burliuka. Neskol'ko slov ot khudozhnika. Samara: 1917.

Katalog vystavki proizvedenii Gustava Klutsisa. Riga: Gosudarstvennyi khudozhestvennyi Muzei, Nos. 13-26.

Khan-Magomedov, Selim O. *Rodchenko: The Complete Work.* London: Thames and Hudson, 1986.

Khardzhiev, N. *K istorii russkogo avangarda. K. Malevich. M. Matiushin.* Stockholm: Gileia, 1976.

Khardzhiev, N. and V. Trenin, *Poeticheskaya kultura Mayakovskogo.* Moscow: Iskusstvo. 1970.

Kharms, Daniil. *Polet v nebesa.* Leningrad: Sovetskii pisatel', 1988.

-------. *Polnoe sobranie sochineniy,* Vols. 1-5. Edited by Valery Sazhin. St. Petersburg: Akademicheskii Proekt, 1997-2004.

Khlebnikov, Velimir. *Neizdannye proizvedeniia.* Edited and with commentaries by N. Khardzhiev and T. Grits. Moscow: 1940.

-------. *Collected Works of Velimir Khlebnikov.* Vol. I. *Letters and Theoretical Writings.* Translated by Paul Schmidt. Cambridge: Harvard University Press, 1987.

-------. *Collected Works of Velimir Khlebnikov.* Vol. II. *Prose, Plays, and Supersagas.* Translated by Paul Schmidt. Cambridge: Harvard University Press, 1989.

-------. *Collected Works of Velimir Khlebnikov.* Vol. III. *Selected Poems.* Translated by Paul Schmidt. Cambridge: Harvard University Press, 1997.

Kobrinskii, Alexander. *Daniil Kharms.* Moscow: Molodaya Gvardiya, 2008.

Kollontai, Aleksandra. "Novaia zhenshchina." *Sovremennyi mir,* 9 (1913): 153-4.

Konstruktivisty. K. K. Medunetskii, V. A. Stenberg, G. A. Stenberg. Exhibition catalogue, Moscow: Kafe Poetov, January (1922).

Kopp, Anatole. *Constructivist Architecture in the USSR.* London, Academy Editions; New York: St. Martin's Press, 1985.

Kozhinov, Vadim. "Mayakovsky and Russian Classical Literature." In *Vladimir Mayakovsky: Innovator.* Moscow: Progress Publisher, 1976, 74-93.

Kručenyx, A. *Sdvigologija Russkogo stixa.* Moscow: Moskovskaia Assotsiatsia Futuristov (MAF), 1923.

-------. *15 let russkogo futurizma.* Moscow: VSP, 1928.

Krusanov, A. *Russkii avantgard: 1907-1932 (Istoricheskii obzor),* 1. St. Petersburg: Novoe literaturnoe obozrenie, 1996.

Kudriavtsev, Sergei, ed. "*Terentyevskiy sbornik*" Nos. 1-2. Moscow: Gileya, 1996-1998.

Kul'bin, N. I. *Studija impressionistov.* St. Petersburg: Izdatel'stvo N.I. Butkovskoj, 1910.

Kushner, Boris. "Kommunisty-futuristy." *Iskusstvo kommuny,* no. 9 (1919): 3.

Larionov, M. F. "Gazetnye kritiki v roli politsii nravov." *Zolotoe runo,* 11/12, 1909 (1910): 97-8.

Lavrentiev, Alexander. "Experimental Furniture Design in the 1920s." *The Journal of Decorative and Propaganda Arts* (Florida), no. 11, Winter (1989): 142-167.

Law, Alma H. and Mel Gordon. *Meyerhold, Eisenstein and Biomechanics: Actor Training in Revolutionary Russia.* Jefferson, NC: McFarland & Company, 1996.

Lawton, Anna, ed. *Russian Futurism through its Manifestoes, 1912-1928.* Texts translated and edited by Anna Lawton and Herbert Eagle. Ithaca: Cornell University Press, 1988.

-------, ed. *The Red Screen: Politics, Society, Art in Soviet Cinema*. New York: Routledge, 1992.

Lazarevskii, Iv. "I tut zhe neistovyi Burliuk... napisal i vystavil samyi realisticheskii peizazh." *Verchernee vremia*, no. 595, 26 (October 1913).

LeDant'iu, Mikhail. "Zhivopis' Veskov." Edited and introduced by John E. Bowlt. *Minuvshee*, 5 (1988): 183-202.

Lifshits, Benedikt. *The One and a Half-Eyed Archer.* (Translation of *Polutoraglazy strelets*, 1933). Newtonville, MA: Oriental Research Partners, 1977.

Lipavsky, Leonid. "Razgovory." In *"...Sborishche druzei, ostavlennykh sud'boiu...": Chinari v tekstakh, dokumentakh i issledovaniiakh*. Moscow: Ladomir, 2000.

-------. *Issledovanie uzhasa*. Moscow: Gileia, 2005.

Lipovetsky, Mark. "Allegoriya pis'ma: 'Sluchai' D. Kharmsa (1933-1939)." *Novoe Literaturnoe Obozrenie* 63 (2003): 123-152.

Livshits, Benedikt. *Polutoraglazyi strelets*. Leningrad: Izdatel'stvo pisatelei v Leningrade, 1933.

-------. *The One and a Half-Eyed Archer*. Edited, annotated, and translated with an introduction by John E. Bowlt. Newtonville: Oriental Research Partners, 1977.

-------. *Polutoraslazyi strelets: Stikhotvoreniia, perevody, vospominaniia*. Leningrad: Sovetskii pisatel', 1989.

Livšic, Benedict. *Gileja*. New York: Izdatel'stvo M. Burliuk, 1931.

-------. *Polutoraglazyi strelec*. Leningrad: Izdatel'stvo pisatelei, 1933.

Lodder, Christina. *Russian Constructivism*. New Haven: Yale University Press, 1985.

Lombroso, C., *G. Ferrero, La donna delinquente: la prostituta e la donna normale*. Turin : Fratelli Bocca, 1893.

Lonnqvist, Barbara. *Xlebnikov and Carnival. An Analysis of the Poem 'Poet'*. Stockholm: Almqvist & Wiksell International, 1979.

Lopatin-Shuiskii, B. P. "Vystavka 'Sojuz Molodezhi'." *Protiv techeniia*, no. 20 (28 January 1912): 2.

-------. "Moskva: Khudozhestvennyi disput." *Protiv techeniia*, no. 22 (18 February 1912): 3.

Luchishkin, S. A. *Ia ochen' liubliu zhizn'. Stranitsy vospominanii.* Moscow: Sovetskii khudozhnik, 1988.

Lukanova, A. G., ed. *Mikhail Larionov—Natalia Goncharova: Shedevry iz Parizhskogo naslediia*. Collection catalogue, State Tretiakov Gallery, Moscow: RA, 1999.

Lukhmanov, N. "Bez slov." *Zhizn' iskusstva*, no. 22 (1929): 4.

Lunacharsky, A. "Russkie khoduzhniki v Berline." *Ogonek*, Moscow, No. 30 (1927).

MacKay, John. "Allegory and Accommodation: Vertov's Three Songs of Lenin (1934) as a Stalinist Film." *Film History: An International Journal* 18.4 (2006): 376-391.

Magnat, Virginie. "Theatricality from the Performative Perspective". *SubStance* 98-99 Vol. 31 (2002): 147-166.

Makovskii, Sergei. "Khudozhestvennye itogi." *Apollon*, no. 7 (1910): 29-30.

Malevich, K. *Ot Kubizma k suprematizmu. Novyi zhivopisnyi realism*. Petrograd: 1916.

-------. *Suprematism*. 34 risunka. Vitebsk: 1920.

-------. *Diegegenstandlose Welt*. Munich: 1927.

-------. *Suprematismus—diegegenstandslose Welt*. Cologne: DuMont, 1962.

-------. "God Is Not Cast Down." In K. Malevich. *Essays on Art*. Edited by Troels Anderson. Translated by Xenia Glowacki Prus and Arnold McMillin. Copenhagen: Borgen, 1968, 188-223.

-------. "Glavy iz avtobiografii khudozhnika." In *K istorii russkogo avangarda*. Edited by N. Khardzhiev, K. Malevich and M. Matiushin. Stockholm: Hylaea, 1976.

Marinetti, F. T. "Destruction of Syntax—Wireless Imagination—Words-in-Freedom." In *Futurist Manifestos*. Edited by Umbro Apollonio. Boston: MFA Publications, 2001.

Markov, Vladimir. *The Longer Poems of Velimir Khlebnikov*. Berkeley: The University of California Press, 1962.

-------. *Russian Futurism: A History*. London: MacGibbon and Kee, 1968; 1969.

Massell, Gregory J. *The Surrogate Proletariat: Moslem Women and Revolutionary Strategies in Soviet Central Asia, 1919-1929*. Princeton: Princeton University Press, 1974.

Matiushin, M. "O vystavke poslednikn futuristov." *Ocharovannyi strannik*. Almanakh vesennii, Petrograd: 1916.

Matsa, Ivan. *Sovetskoe iskusstvo za 15 let. Materialy i dokumentatsiya*. Moscow; Leningrad: Gosizdat, 1929.

Maximov, Vladimir. *Esteticheskiy fenomen Antonena Arto*. St. Peterburg: Giperion, 2008.

Maiakovskii, Vladimir. "Ia Sam." In *Vladimir Maiakovskii: Polnoe sobranie sochinenii*, v. I. Moscow: Institut mirovoi Literarury im. A.M. Gor'kogo, 1955, 16-18: 423-4.

Mayakovskii, Vladimir. "Prikaz po armii iskusstva." *Iskusstvo kommuny*, no. 1 (7 December 1918): 1.

Mayakovsky, Vladimir. *Polnoe sobranie sochinenii I-XIII*. Moscow: Khudozhestvennaia Literatura, 1955-61.

-------. *How are Verses Made*? Translated by G. M. Hyde. London: J. Cape, 1970; 1974.

-------. *Selected Works in Three Volumes*. Vol. 3: Plays. Articles. Essays. Moscow: Raduga, 1987.

-------. *Plays*. Translated by Guy Daniels. Evanston: Northwestern University Press, 1995.

McCauley, Elizabeth. *A. A. E. Disderi and the Carte de Visite Portrait Photograph*. New Haven: Yale University Press, 1985.

Meyerhold, Vsevolod. *Meyerhold on Theatre*. Translated by Edward Braun. New York: Hill and Wang, 1969.

Michelson, Annette. "The Kinetic Icon and the Work of Mourning: Prolegomena to the Analysis of a Textual System." In *The Red Screen: Politics, Society, Art in Soviet Cinema*. Edited by Anna Lawton, 113-130.

Millard, Charles. "Dada, Surrealism, and the Academy of the Avant-Garde." *The Hudson Review* 1, Vol. 22 (1969): 111-117.

Miller, Frank J. *Folklore for Stalin: Russian Folklore and Pseudofolklore of the Stalin Era*. Armonk, NY: M. E. Sharpe, 1990.

Mitter, Shomit, and Maria Shevtsova, eds. *Fifty Key Theater Directors*. New York: Routledge, 2005.

Moen, Lars. "*Three Songs About Lenin*: A New Kind of Film Portraying Great Achievement," *Moscow Daily News*, 181, 6 August (1934). Newspaper clipping in RGALI f. 2091, op. 1, d. 93, l. 31.

Mokul'skii, S. S. ed. *Teatral'naia entsiklopediia*, v. II. Moscow: Sovetskaia entsiklopeida, 1961-62.

Morukov, Mikhail. "The White Sea-Baltic Canal." In *The Economics of Forced Labor: The Soviet Gulag*. Edited by Paul R. Gregory and Valery Lazarev. Stanford: Hoover Press, 2003, 151-162.

Mukhortov, F. "Progressivnyi paralich (Vystavka kartin M. F. Larionova)." *Golos Moskvy* (9 December 1911): 5.

Nedoshivin, G. "Otnoshenie iskusstva i deistviternosti." *Iskusstvo* (July-August 1950): 80-90.

Needham, Gerald. "Manet, 'Olympia,' and Pornographic Photography." *Art News Annual*, 38 (1972): 80-9.

Neprintsev, Iu. "Kak ia rabotal nad kartinoi 'Otdykh posle boia'." *Iskusstvo* (July-August 1952): 17-20.

Neznamov, P. "Proz-raboty A. Lavinskogo." *Lef*, No. 3 (7) (1925): 76-77.

Oberheim, E. "Karl Popper. Using and abusing critical rationalism." In his *Feyerabend's philosophy*. Berlin: Walter de Gruyter, 2006.

Oginskaya, L. *Gustav Klutsis*. Moscow: Sovetskii khudozhnik, 1981.

O'Mahony, Mike. *Sergei Eisenstein*. London: Reaktion Books, 2008.

Oslinyj khvost i Mishen'. Moscow: S. A. Miunster, 1913.

Ostashevsky, E., ed. *OBERIU: An Anthology of Russian Absurdism*. Evanston: Northwestern University Press, 2006.

Parkin, V. "Oslinyi khvost i Mishen'." *Oslinyi khvost i Mishen"*. Moscow: S. A. Miunster, 1913.

Paperno, Irina A. and Joan D. Grossman, eds. *Creating Life: The Aesthetic Utopia of Russian Modernism*. Stanford: Stanford University Press, 1994.

Pertsov, Viktor. *Za novoe iskusstvo*. Moscow: Vserossiiskii proletkul't, 1925.

Petrova, Evgeniia, ed. Catalogue of Works. *Natalia Goncharova: the Russian Years*.

St. Petersburg: Palace Editions, 2002.
Pitches, Jonathan. *Vsevolod Meyerhold*. London: Routledge, 2003.
Pjast, V. *Vstreči*. Leningrad: Federatsia, 1929.
Poggioli, R. *The Theory of the Avant-Garde*. Translated by G. Fitzgerald. Cambridge, MA: Belknap Press of Harvard University Press, 1968.
Popova, Lyubov'. "Vstuplenie k diskussii Inkhuka o 'Velikodushnom rogonostse'." MS, private archive, Moscow: 1922.
Pospelov, G. G. "O 'valetakh' bubnovykh i valetakh chernykh." *Panorama iskusstv*, 1977, Moscow (1978): 127-42.
-------. *Bubnovyi valet*. Moscow: Sovetskii khudozhnik, 1990.
"Programma uchebnoi pod-gruppy konstruktivistov Inkhuka." Typescript, private archive, Moscow: 1921.
Prunes, Mariano. "Dziga Vertov's *Three Songs about Lenin* (1934): A Visual Tour through the History of the Soviet Avant-Garde in the Interwar Years." *Criticism*, 45: 2 (2003): 251-78.
Pskovitinov, E. "Oslinyi khvost." *Protiv techeniia*, nos. 27-8 (21 April 1912): 4-5.

"Razval Vkhutemasa. Dokladnaya zapiska o polozhenii vysshikh khudozhestvenno-tekhicheskikh masterskikh." *Lef*,4 (1923): 28.
Referent. "Bubnovyi valet—khudozhestvennyi disput." *Protiv techeniia*, no. 24 (10 March 1912): 4.
"Rodchenko v Parizhe. Iz pisem domoi." *Novyi Lef*, 2 (1927): 9-21.
Roger, S. "Un beau film de Dziga Vertoff: *Trois Chants Sur Lenine*." *Le Journal de Moscou*, 15, 18 August (1934). Newspaper clipping in RGALI f. 2091, op. 1, d. 93, l. 40.
Rokotov, T. "Tri Pesni o Lenine." *Vechernaia Moskva*, 255, 4 November (1934). Newspaper clipping in RGALI f. 2091, op. 1, d. 93, l. 89.
Roshal', Lev. *Dziga Vertov*. Moscow: Iskusstvo, 1982.
Rostislavov, A. "Vystavka Soiuza molodezhi." *Rech'* (24 January 1912): 3.
Rudnitsky, Konstantin. *Meyerhold, the Director*. Translated by George Petrov. Ann Arbor: Ardis, 1981.
Rzhevsky, Nicholas. *The Modern Russian Theater: A Literary and Cultural History*. Armonk: M. E. Sharpe, 2009.

Sakhno, I.M. "'Stratografiya tela' v futuristicheskom teatre". In *Avangard i teatr 1910-h–1920-h Godov*. Edited by G. F. Kovalenko, et al. Moscow: Nauka, 2008: 651-661.
Sazhin, V., ed. *Sborishche druzei, ostavlennykh sud'boiu: "Chinari" v tekstakh, dokumentakh i issledovaniakh*, 2 vols. Moscow: Ladomir, 2001.
Schmidt, Paul, ed. *Meyerhold at Work*. Austin: University of Texas Press, 1980.
Selenick, Laurence. "The Making of a Martyr: The Legend of Meyerhold's Last Public Appearance." *Theatre Research International* 28: 2 (July 2003): 157-68.

Sevost'ianov, E.I. *Esteticheskaia priroda sovetskogo izobrazitel'nogo iskusstva*. Moscow: Sovetskii khudozhnik, 1983.

Shapir, M. I. "Aestheticheskii opyt XX veka: avangard i postmodernism." *Philologica*, vol. 2, nos. 3-4 (1995): 135-143.

Sharp, Jane A. "Review Essay." *Art Bulletin*, LXXVII, no. 3 (September 1995): 502-506.

Shatskih, A.S. "Postyanovki i proekty Unovisskogo 'novogo teatra'." In *Russkiy avangard 1910-h–1920-h godov i teatr*. Edited by G. F. Kovalenko. St. Petersburg: Dmitry Bulanin, 2000, 129-143.

Shevchenko, Aleksandr. *Neo-primitivizm. Ego teoriia. Ego voz-mozhnosti. Ego dostizheniia*. Moscow: 1aia Moskovskaia trudovaia artel', 1913.

-------. *Printsipy kubizma i drugikh sovremennykh techenii v zhivopisi vsekh vremen i narodov.* Moscow: A. Shevchenko, 1913.

Shklovsky, Viktor. "Prostranstvo v iskusstve i suprematisty." *Zhizn iskusstva*, Petrograd, No. 196-97 (1919).

-------. "In the Name of the New Humanism." *Izvestia*, 24 August (1934): 3.

-------. "Art as Technique". In *Literary Theory: An Anthology*. Edited by Julie Rivkin and Michael Ryan. Malden: Blackwell Publishing, 1998.

Shterenberg, David. "Pora ponyat'." *Iskusstvo v proizvodstve*. Moscow: IZO Narkompros, 1921, 5-6.

Sjeklocha, Paul and Igor Mead. *Unofficial Art in the Soviet Union*. Berkeley: University of California Press, 1967.

Skanskii, B. [Viktor Petrovich Iving]. "Anri Matiss." *Zhivoe slovo*, no. 35 (31 October 1911).

Sokolov, Ippolit, ed. *Istoriia Sovetskogo Kinoisskustva Zvukovogo Perioda*. Vol. 1. Moscow: Goskinoizdat, 1946.

Solov'ev, Vladimir. *Sobranie sochtnenii*. Brussels: Foyer Oriental Chretien, 1966.

Songaillo, V. N. *O Vystavke kartin Natalii Goncharovoi*. Moscow: V. M. Sablin, 1913.

Stalin, Iosef. *O Lenine*. Moscow: Molodaia Gvardiia, 1932.

Stambok, A. "O nekotorykh metodologicheskikh voprosakh iskusstvoznaniia." *Iskusstvo* (Sept.-Oct. 1952): 42-46.

Stanislavsky, Konstantin. *Sobranie sochineniy*. Vol.7. Moscow: Iskusstvo, 1960.

Stelleman, Jenny. *Aspects of dramatic communication: action, non-action, interaction.* Amsterdam: Rodopi, 1992.

Stites, Richard. *The Women's Liberation Movement in Russia: Feminism, Nihilism, and Bolshevism 1860-1930*. Princeton: Princeton University Press, 1978.

Sullivan, Lawrence. "Nikita Baliev's Le Theater de la Chauve-Souris: An Avant-Garde Theater." *Dance Research Journal* 2, Vol.18 (1986): 17-29.

Tarasenko, O. A. "Magicheskiy teatr Pavla Filonova". In *Russkiy avangard 1910-h – 1920-h godov i teatr*. Edited by G. F. Kovalenko. St. Petersburg: Dmitry Bulanin, 2000, 176-188.

Tatlin, Vladimir, Tevel Shapiro, Iosif Meerzon and Pavel Vinogradov. "Nasha predstoy-i Rabota." *VIII sezd sovetov. Ezhednevnyi byulleten s'ezda*, no. 13 (1 January 1921): 11.

Terentiev, Igor. *Sobranie sochineniy*, edited by Massimo Mazarduri and Tatyana Nikolskaya. Bologna: S. Francesco, 1988.

Tokarev, Dmitry. *Kurs na hudshee*. Moscow: Novoe literaturnoe obozrenie, 2002.

Tret'jakov, S. *Buka russkoj literatury*. Moscow: 41 Gradus, 1923.

Trudy 10go s'ezda pri zhenskom obshchestve v S-Peterburge, 10-16 dekabria, 1908ogo goda, St. Petersburg, 1909.

Tsvetaeva, Marina. "Natal'ia Goncharova: Zhizn' i tvorchestvo." *Volia Rossii*, V-VI, VII, VIII-IX, Prague, 1929.

-------. "Natal'ia Goncharova." Ed. D.V. Sarabianov, *Al'manakh Prometei*, 7, Moscow: Molodaia Gavardia Publishers, 1967, 161-162.

Tugendkhol'd, Iakov. "Vystavka kartin Natalii Goncharovoi: Pis'mo iz Moskvy." *Apollon*, 8 (November 1913): 71-72.

-------. "Sovremennoe iskusstvo i narodnost'." *Severnye zapiski*, 11 (November 1913): 153-60.

-------. "SSSR na parizhskoi vystavke." *Krasnaia Niva*, no. 39 (1925): 932-33.

-------. "Zhivopis' revoliutsionnogo desiatiletiia." *Iskusstvo oktiabr'skoi epokhi*. Leningrad: Academia, 1930.

Tumarkin, Nina. *Lenin Lives! The Lenin Cult in Soviet Russia*, revised edition. Cambridge: Harvard University Press, 1997.

Tupitsyn, Margarita, ed. *Sots-art*. New York: The New Museum of Contemprary Art, 1986.

Turchin, V. S. "Teatral'naya konzepziya V. V. Kandinskogo". In *Russkiy avangard 1910-h–1920-h godov i teatr*. Edited by G. F. Kovalenko. St. Petersburg: Dmitry Bulanin, 2000, 73-105.

Valkenier, Elizabeth. *Ilya Repin and the World of Russian Art*. New York: Columbia University Press, 1990.

Varst [Varvara Stepanova]. "Rabochii klyub. Konstruktivist A. M. Rodchenko." *Sovremennaya arkhitektura*, no. 1 (1926): 36.

[Various authors]. *Futuristy: Pervyi žurnal russkix futuristov*. No. 1-2, Moscow: Pervyi zhurnal russkikh futuristov, 1914.

Verbitskaia, Anastasiia. "Zhenshchina o zhenshchine." *Golos Moskvy*, no. 63 (18 March 1910): 5.

Vertov, Dziga. "Poslednii opyt." *Literaturnaia Gazeta*, 18 January (1935): n.p.

Vertova-Svilova, E. I. and V. I. Furtichev, eds. *Tri Pesni o Lenine*. Moscow: Iskusstvo, 1971.

Vij. "Pisatel' i fil'ma." *Kino Gazeta*, 35, 4 August (1934).

Vinokur, G. O. *Mayakovsky novator jazyka*. Moscow: Sovetskii Pisatel', 1943.

Voloshin, M. "Oslinyi khvost." *Apollon: Russkaia khudozhestvennaia letopis'*, 7 (April 1912): 105-109.

-------. "Bubnovyi valet." *Apollon: Russkaia khudozhestvennaia letopis'*, 1 (January 1911): 9-15.

-------. *Liki tvorchestva*. Leningrad: Nauka, 1988.

"Vostorzhennye otzyvy: Ogromnyi uspekh sovetskikh fil'mov v Venetsii." *Komsomol'skaia Pravda*, 196, 23 August (1934). Newspaper clipping in RGALI f. 2091, op. 1, d. 93, l. 45.

Vroon, Ronald. *Velimir Khlebnikov's Shorter Poems: A Key to the Coinages*. Ann Arbor: The University of Michigan, 1983.

Vvedensky, Aleksandr. *The Gray Notebook*. Translated by Matvey Yankelevich. New York: Ugly Duckling Presse, 2002.

Vvedensky, Irinarkh. "Trediakovsky." In *Russkie pisateli o perevode: XVIII-XX vv*. Edited by Y. D. Levin and A. F. Fedorov. Leningrad: Sovetskii pisatel', 1960.

Wanner, Adrian. "Russian Minimalist Prose: Generic Antecedents to Daniil Kharms's 'Sluchai'." *The Slavic and East European Journal*, 3 Vol. 45 (2002): 451-472.

Webster, Murray and Jane Sell, eds. *Laboratory Experiments in the Social Sciences*. Amsterdam, Boston: Academic Press/Elsevier Science, 2009.

"Weg." "Nashi estety" *Golos Moskvy*, no. 70 (27 March 1910): 2.

Weststeijn, Willem G. *Velimir Chlebnikov and the Development of Poetical Language in Russian Symbolism and Futurism*. Amsterdam: Rodopi, 1983.

Wollen, Peter. "Fashion/Orientalism/the Body." *New Formations*, 1 (Spring 1987): 5-33.

Xlebnikov, Velimir. *Neizdannye proizvedenija*. Moscow: Xudozhestvennaia literatura, 1940.

-------. *Zverinec*. Ed. A. Kručenyx. Moscow: Izdatel'stvo gruppy druzei Xlebnikova, 1930.

Yablonskaya, M. N. "Natalya Goncharova." *Women Artists of Russia's New Age, 1910-1935*. New York, Rizzoli, 1990, 52-81.

Youngblood, Denise J. *Soviet Cinema in the Silent Era, 1918-1935*. Ann Arbor: UMI Research Press, 1985.

Zazzali, Peter. "Did Meyerhold Influence Brecht? A Comparison of Their Antirealistic Theatrical Aesthetics." *The European Legacy* 13:3 (June 2008): 293-305.

Zdanevich, Ilia, ed. *Oslinyi khvost i mishen'*. Moscow: C.A. Munster, 1913.

www.ingramcontent.com/pod-product-compliance
Lightning Source LLC
LaVergne TN
LVHW020053110826
845155LV00022B/75
9781936235452